THE CAMBRIDGE COMPANION

SCHOPENHAUER

Each volume of this series of companions to major philosophers contains specially commissioned essays by an international team of scholars, together with a substantial bibliography, and will serve as a reference work for students and nonspecialists. One aim of the series is to dispel the intimidation such readers often feel when faced with the work of a difficult and challenging thinker.

Arthur Schopenhauer (1788–1860) is something of a maverick figure in the history of philosophy. He produced a unique theory of the world and human existence based upon his notion of will. This collection analyzes the related but distinct components of will from the point of view of epistemology, metaphysics, philosophy of mind, aesthetics, ethics, and the philosophy of psychoanalysis. This volume explores Schopenhauer's philosophy of death, his relationship to the philosophy of Kant, his use of ideas drawn from both Buddhism and Hinduism, and the important influence he exerted on Nietzsche, Freud, and Wittgenstein.

New readers will find this the most convenient and accessible guide to Schopenhauer currently available. Advanced students and specialists will find a conspectus of recent developments in the interpretation of Schopenhauer.

Christopher Janaway is Reader in Philosophy at Birkbeck College, University of London.

The Cambridge Companion to

SCHOPENHAUER

Edited by Christopher Janaway
Birbeck College, University of London

CAMBRIDGE
UNIVERSITY PRESS

CAMBRIDGE UNIVERSITY PRESS
Cambridge, New York, Melbourne, Madrid, Cape Town, Singapore, São Paulo

Cambridge University Press
40 West 20th Street, New York, NY 10011-4211, USA

www.cambridge.org
Information on this title: www.cambridge.org/9780521621069

© Cambridge University Press 1999

First published 1999
Reprinted 2000, 2005

Printed in the United States of America

A catalog record for this publication is available from the British Library.

ISBN-13   978-0-521-62106-9   hardback
ISBN-10   0-521-62106-2   hardback

ISBN-13   978-0-521-62924-9   paperback
ISBN-10   0-521-62924-1   paperback

CONTENTS

ACKNOWLEDGEMENTS

Chapter 11 appeared in an earlier version as Martha C. Nussbaum, 'The Transfiguration of Intoxication: Nietzsche, Schopenhauer, and Dionysus', in *Arion*, Third Series, vol. 1, no. 2 (1991), 75–111.

I would like to acknowledge with gratitude the excellent editorial assistance of Christine Lopes. – C. J.

CONTRIBUTORS

DAVID E. CARTWRIGHT is Director of the North American Division of the Schopenhauer Society and a member of the *wissenschaftliche Leitung* of the *Schopenhauer-Gesellschaft*. In addition to editing Schopenhauer's *On the Will in Nature* and *On Vision and Colors*, he has published a number of articles on Kant, Nietzsche, Schopenhauer, and ethics. He is currently Professor of Philosophy at the University of Wisconsin–Whitewater.

CHERYL FOSTER is Associate Professor of Philosophy at the University of Rhode Island, where she teaches and writes on topics in aesthetics, ethics, the environment, and existentialism. She currently sits on the board of directors of the North American Nature Photography Association and is at work on a book about nature photography.

SEBASTIAN GARDNER was for several years a member of the Department of Philosophy at Birkbeck College, London, and is presently Lecturer in Philosophy at University College, London. He is the author of *Irrationality and the Philosophy of Psychoanalysis* (1993), *Kant and the 'Critique of Pure Reason'* (1999), and articles on the philosophy of mind and psychoanalysis.

HANS-JOHANN GLOCK is Reader in Philosophy at the University of Reading. He has been Visiting Professor at Queen's University, Ontario, and is currently a Research Fellow of the Alexander von Humboldt Foundation. He is the author of *A Wittgenstein Dictionary* (1996) and of several articles on Wittgenstein, philosophy of language, philosophy of mind, and the history of analytic philosophy. He has edited *The Rise of Analytic Philosophy* (1997) and co-edited (together with Robert Arrington) *Wittgenstein's Philosophical*

Investigations (1991) and *Wittgenstein and Quine* (1996). He is currently working on a book on Quine and Davidson and is editing *Wittgenstein: A Critical Reader* (forthcoming).

PAUL GUYER is the Florence R. C. Murray Professor in the Humanities at the University of Pennsylvania, where he has been a member of the Philosophy Department since 1982. His books include *Kant and the Claims of Taste* (1979, second edition 1997), *Kant and the Claims of Knowledge* (1987), and *Kant and the Experience of Freedom* (1993). He has edited *The Cambridge Companion to Kant* (1992) and other anthologies. He is general co-editor of *The Cambridge Edition of the Works of Immanuel Kant*, in which he has translated the *Critique of Pure Reason* (1998) with Allen Wood, and is currently translating the *Critique of the Power of Judgment*.

DAVID HAMLYN is Emeritus Professor of Philosophy at Birkbeck College, University of London, where he was Head of Department for many years, and latterly Vice-Master, until his retirement in 1988. He is the author of twelve books, including one on Schopenhauer in Routledge's Arguments of the Philosophers series (1980). He has also written many articles and contributions to books, of which six are explicitly on Schopenhauer, while many others allude to aspects of Schopenhauer's philosophy, especially its emphasis on will, which he sees as important for the philosophy of mind.

DALE JACQUETTE is Professor of Philosophy at The Pennsylvania State University. He has received research fellowships from the Alexander von Humboldt-Stiftung and the National Endowment for the Humanities, and in 1996 held the J. William Fulbright Distinguished Lecture Chair in Contemporary Philosophy of Language at the University of Venice. He has recently published *Philosophy of Mind* (1994), *Meinongian Logic: The Semantics of Existence and Nonexistence* (1996), and *Wittgenstein's Thought in Transition* (1998). He has also edited a collection of essays on *Schopenhauer, Philosophy, and the Arts* (1996). His articles, primarily on philosophical logic and metaphysics, have appeared in numerous philosophical journals.

CHRISTOPHER JANAWAY is Reader in Philosophy at Birkbeck College, University of London. He is the author of *Self and World in Schopenhauer's Philosophy* (1989), *Schopenhauer* (1994), and *Images of Excellence: Plato's Critique of the Arts* (1995), and editor of *Willing and Nothingness: Schopenhauer as Nietzsche's Educator* (1998). He has published numerous articles on aesthetics and the history of philosophy.

MOIRA NICHOLLS is a former lecturer in philosophy at the University of Tasmania. Her Ph.D. is on Schopenhauer's metaphysics, and she has published papers in *Schopenhauer-Jahrbuch* (1991, 1995) and *Kant-Studien* (1994).

MARTHA C. NUSSBAUM is Ernst Freund Professor of Law and Ethics at the University of Chicago, where she holds appointments in the Philosophy Department, the Law School, and the Divinity School and is an Associate Member of the Classics Department. Her most recent book is *Sex and Social Justice* (1998).

F. C. WHITE is Emeritus Professor of Philosophy at the University of Tasmania. His works include *Plato's Theory of Particulars* (1981), *Knowledge and Relativism* (1982), *On Schopenhauer's Fourfold Root of the Principle of Sufficient Reason* (1991), *Kant's First Critique and the Transcendental Deduction* (1996), and *Schopenhauer's Early Fourfold Root* (1997). He is soon to publish *A Defence of Plato's Platonism*.

GÜNTER ZÖLLER is Professor of Philosophy at the University of Munich. He is the author of *Theoretische Gegenstandsbeziehung bei Kant* (Objective Reference in Kant) (1984) and *Fichte's Transcendental Philosophy* (1998), editor of Schopenhauer's *Prize Essay on the Freedom of the Will* (forthcoming), Kant's *Prolegomena to Any Future Metaphysics* (forthcoming), and *The Cambridge Companion to Fichte* (forthcoming), and co-editor of *Minds, Ideas, and Objects: Essays on the Theory of Representation in Modern Philosophy* (1993) and *Figuring the Self: Subject, Individual, and Others in Classical German Philosophy* (1997).

REFERENCES TO SCHOPENHAUER'S WORKS

The following abbreviations are used for Schopenhauer's writings:

BM	*On the Basis of Morality*, trans. E. F. J. Payne (Providence and Oxford: Berghahn Books, 1995).
FR	*On the Fourfold Root of the Principle of Sufficient Reason*, trans. E. F. J. Payne (La Salle, Ill.: Open Court Press, 1974).
FR¹	*Schopenhauer's Early Fourfold Root* [1813 edition], trans. F. C. White (Aldershot: Avebury, 1997).
FW	*On the Freedom of the Will*, trans. Konstantin Kolenda (Oxford: Blackwell, 1985).
MR	*Manuscript Remains*, trans. E. F. J. Payne (Oxford: Berg, 1988), 4 vols.
P1,P2	*Parerga and Paralipomena*, trans. E. F. J. Payne (Oxford: Clarendon Press, 1974), vols. 1 and 2.
W1,W2	*The World as Will and Representation*, trans. E. F. J. Payne (New York: Dover, 1969), vols. 1 and 2.
W1¹	*Die Welt als Wille und Vorstellung. Faksimiledruck der ersten Auflage 1819 1818* (Frankfurt: Insel Verlag, 1987).
WN	*On the Will in Nature*, trans. E. F. J. Payne (New York and Oxford: Berg, 1992).

Unless otherwise specified, the number immediately following the work's abbreviation gives a page reference to the translation or edition listed here. After an oblique stroke, corresponding passages from the standard German editions are cited.

H.	*Sämtliche Werke*, ed. Arthur Hübscher (3rd edn., Wiesbaden: Brockhaus, 1972; 4th edn., 1988), 7 vols.

Hn.   *Der handschriftliche Nachlass*, ed. Arthur Hübscher
           (Frankfurt: Waldemar Kramer, 1966–75; repr. Munich:
           Deutscher Taschenbuch Verlag, 1985), 5 vols.
Z.   *Werke in zehn Bänden*, ed. Arthur Hübscher (Zurich:
           Diogenes Verlag, 1977), 10 vols.

For example, *W1* 272/H. 2, 320 refers to page 272 of Payne's translation of *The World as Will and Representation*, vol. 1, and to the
corresponding passage on page 320 of Hübscher's *Sämtliche Werke*,
vol. 2. Note that in volumes of H. which contain more than one of
Schopenhauer's works, each work has its own pagination.

Introduction

Arthur Schopenhauer lived from 1788 to 1860. His thought took shape early in his life, in the decade from 1810 to 1820, yet until the 1850s he was virtually unknown, and the period in which he became a powerful influence began only in the second half of the nineteenth century. He admired Rossini and Bellini but inspired Wagner, knew Goethe, and met Hegel, but was an influence after his death on Thomas Mann, Nietzsche, and the young Wittgenstein. His vision of the world is in some respects more bleak and cynical than we might expect for its period, more akin to that of existentialism or even of Samuel Beckett. Schopenhauer's world is neither rational nor good, but rather is an absurd, polymorphous, hungry thing that lacerates itself without end and suffers in each of its parts. None of us is in control even of our own nature; instead, we are at the mercy of the blind urge to exist and propagate that stupefies us into accepting the illusion that to be a human individual is worthwhile. In truth it would have been better had nothing existed. Although this philosophy originated in a pre-Darwinian and pre-Freudian age, it has a prescient cutting edge that can make the later time of evolutionary theory, psychoanalysis, and the 'Great' War seem the more truly Schopenhauerian era. 'By what mere blind propulsion did all these thousands of human creatures keep on mechanically living?' wrote Edith Wharton in a war novel of 1923,[1] sounding, perhaps unknowingly, a Schopenhauerian note.

Yet Adorno's irresistible description of Schopenhauer as 'peevish ancestor of existential philosophy and malicious heir of the great speculators'[2] has some justice to it. If Schopenhauer can appear antiquated, it is at least in part because his philosophy aspires to give a unitary metaphysics of the whole world, in something of the old spirit of Spinoza or Leibniz, albeit with reversed value polarity. In his day and ours he has always had the air of an outsider among philosophers, and it is safe to say that little twentieth-century philosophy has arisen from close engagement with his work. It is hard for analytical philosophy to claim him as a forerunner. One reason for this, conventionally, is that he is too literary and rhetorical a writer, too much prone to metaphorical effusion and dogmatism, too little exercised by rigour and argument. In fact Schopenhauer argues constantly, debates with all the major and some minor figures in philosophy's past, and is as committed as any thinker has been to the goal of truth. A more profound reason for his appearing alien to analytical philosophers may lie in his assumption about the role and prime subject matter of philosophy. Analytical philosophy has tended to claim as its own those who give some priority to questions about scientific enquiry and the philosophy of logic. If a thinker places art and aesthetic experience at the pinnacle of human achievement, assigning them a higher cognitive value than the sciences, and has as his driving pre-occupation the struggle for significance in a life riven by suffering, he is less amenable to co-option. And the grand metaphysical aspiration makes him an unsympathetic figure to the likes of scientific naturalists and logical positivists.

The German philosophical tradition in which Hegel has a central place is also unlikely to look favourably on Schopenhauer. This is not just because of his contempt for the career academics, Hegel and Fichte, whose tedious vocabulary and, as he thought, wrongheadedness and intellectual dishonesty prevented him from serious argumentative engagement with the idealist mainstream of his early years. The rift is deeper than that: to anyone brought up in a more or less Hegelian way, the brazenly ahistorical and apolitical cast of Schopenhauer's thought must also place him beyond the pale. Schopenhauer's deepest concerns are with what it is to be a human individual anywhere at any time, how one relates to one's body, what suffering is, what happiness is and is not, whether one is free, how life can become bearable, how to regard one's own death, what in the individual is unconscious and uncontrollable, and what it is for the individual to make and experience art. History is quite literally an irrelevance for him. This made him, as Nietzsche said, 'un-German to the point of genius'.[3] And for the so-called continental philosophy of the second half of the twentieth century Schopenhauer's place at or beyond the margins of sight is probably over-determined by his metaphysical conservatism and commitment to timeless truths, his anti-Hegelianism, his neglect by formative figures such as Heidegger or Levinas, and the apparent readiness of today's readers to take at face value (wrongly, I would argue)[4] the rude and dismissive remarks made about him by the later Nietzsche.

Yet there are reasons to think that twentieth-century philosophy has more in common with Schopenhauer than it realizes. As the history of modern philosophy becomes more intensively and more responsibly studied by philosophers, the fact that Schopenhauer – widely read, scholarly, and fiercely argumentative – locates himself in continuity with Hume, claims to solve problems initiated by Descartes, debates the relation of Kant to Berkeley, criticizes the Leibnizian tradition, and appropriates some ideas from Spinoza should alert us to the extent of the common inheritance we share with him. He belongs in any narrative of how modern philosophy developed from the seventeenth to the twentieth century. One feature uniting many kinds of recent philosophy is an increasing recognition that we are working within the legacy of Kant, and interest in retrieving what happened in the intellectual world immediately after Kant is steadily growing. Schopenhauer is a comparatively early and unique inhabitant of this post-Kantian landscape, relating to his admired predecessor both as critic and as revisionary follower. Then again, looking forward, if Schopenhauer was an influence on Wittgenstein, Freud, and Nietzsche, he may have played a significant, if concealed, part in the development of twentieth-century philosophy itself.

Sometimes Schopenhauer is treated piecemeal by contemporary philosophy. In aesthetics we might recognize him as the prototypical 'aesthetic attitude' theorist (one who believes that aesthetic value attaches to objects when we experience them in detachment from desire and conceptualization) and as a proponent of one of the most striking theories of musical expression. In ethics we find him claimed as an early anti-Kantian virtue ethicist. In feminist studies he is the arch-misogynist. In the philosophy of psychoanalysis he is an adumbrator of the conception of the unconscious, in Nietzsche studies the old enemy to be exorcised and castigated, and in studies of Kant's epistemology the sharp critic who takes Kant to task over his conception of causality and much besides.

All these angles reveal genuine facets of Schopenhauer, but in summing up his own philosophy, as presented in his major work, *The World as Will and Representation*, he himself attributes to it a peculiar and extreme unity. It is, he says, the expression of a 'single thought' and should be approached as such:

A *single thought*, however comprehensive, must preserve the most perfect unity. If, all the same, it can be split up into parts for the purpose of being communicated, then the connexion of these parts must ... be organic, i.e. of such a kind that every part supports the whole just as much as it is supported by the whole; a connexion in which no part is first and no part last, in which the whole gains in clearness from every part, and even the smallest part cannot be fully understood until the whole has first been understood. But a book must have a first and a last line, and to this extent will always remain very unlike an organism.... Consequently, form and matter will here be in contradiction. (*W 1* xii–xiii/H. 2, viii)

So the best advice to the reader is to read his book through twice so that the beginning can be illuminated by the middle and the end. This organic conception should warn us not to make too premature a judgement about the nature of Schopenhauer's philosophy. The would-be Kantian line presented in the first quarter of the book, a transcendental idealist account of the world of objective experience, will gain its proper (and quite un-Kantian) significance only when we have learned how limited this objective experience is for Schopenhauer, how he hopes it may be supplemented by philosophical reflection and finally revoked in favour of certain superior modes of consciousness.

But what is *der einzige Gedanke*, the single thought? Schopenhauer does not explicitly tell us. But unless literally the whole book is needed for any expression of the thought, we should be able to state it in abbreviated, provisional form. Rudolf Malter has proposed that the thought is 'the world is the self-knowledge of the will',[5] and Schopenhauer himself says in the *Manuscript Remains* that this expression summarizes his whole philosophy.[6] The world is what is represented in experience by the subject – it is the world as representation – but the subject itself is in and of the world it represents, and the 'inner essence' of this subject is will. The self that knows is given to itself in self-consciousness as identical with the self that wills, and this allows the will, via its manifestation in a representing intellect, to become conscious of itself as will, and from there conscious of the whole world of representation as will.[7] Such a summary is correct as far as it goes, though its drawback for the purposes of exposition is that before one has read Schopenhauer, it is fairly opaque. A further problem is that, while the First Book of *The World as Will and Representation* presents the world as representation and the Second Book the world as will, there remain two substantial books concerning aesthetics, ethics, and salvation, books which Schopenhauer labels respectively the 'Second Aspect' of the world as representation and the 'Second Aspect' of the world as will. If we are to take the talk of a 'single thought' seriously, we must be able to incorporate the Third and Fourth Books in it – indeed, they should supply its culmination.

A more sophisticated answer is offered by John Atwell, who finds for the single thought a formulation that does justice to more of the components of Schopenhauer's unfolding presentation and gives the first-time reader a slightly better sense of what to expect. For Atwell, the single thought of *The World as Will and Representation* is as follows:

The double-sided world [i.e., the world as will and as representation] is the striving of the will to become conscious of itself so that, recoiling in horror at its inner, self-divisive nature, it may annul itself and thereby its self-affirmation, and then reach salvation.[8]

This single, if complex, thought stands in need of much interrogation. But its most important and most authentically Schopenhauerian feature is its idea that knowledge culminates in a kind of abnegation. Cognitive self-realization leads to conative self-cancellation. Let us approach this distinctive and difficult idea by rehearsing the stages of Schopenhauer's presentation more slowly.

First, then, the world as representation. This is the world as present to ordinary perceptual experience, a world of individual material objects which can also be investigated scientifically. Schopenhauer follows Kant's general line that in order to make a priori discoveries about the nature of this world of objects, we must renounce the attempt to know what they are in themselves. Objects are representations for the subject. We can have knowledge of empirical objects and we can know the a priori forms – space, time, and causality – contributed by the subject to the experiencing of objects. The intellect or understanding of the subject shapes experience to the extent that there can be no objects without a subject whose representations they are. In addition to this representation of individual objects, or intuitive (*anschaulich*) representation, there is a more indirect and derivative kind of representation which distinguishes human minds from others, and that is the concept. Schopenhauer calls concepts 'representations of representations'. They are what enable human beings to reason and to have language, but it is part of Schopenhauer's aim to show that these capacities are by no means the most basic features of the human mind.

The demotion of concepts and conceptual thinking from pride of place in the description of humanity is a theme running through the whole of Schopenhauer's philosophy. He takes the capacity for reasoning to be instrumental, concerned with working out means to ends that are antecedently desired rather then being provided by reason itself. He argues that rationality confers on us no higher moral status than that of other sentient beings, that conceptual thought never makes anyone morally better, and that the concept is likewise 'unfruitful in art'; it is only from an immediate vision of the universal in the particular object of perception that genuine art can spring. Some philosophy too, according to Schopenhauer (and he has his immediate contemporaries in mind), is worthless because it wanders around in mere concepts – 'the absolute' and such like – without ever being grounded in firsthand experience of the world.[9]

The world as representation is an orderly world because the subject of experience must always connect any representation with other representations, according to a fixed set of principles. This idea provided the topic of Schopenhauer's first work, his doctoral thesis entitled *On the Fourfold Root of the Principle of Sufficient Reason* (1813). The principle of sufficient reason, a mainstay of the Leibnizian philosophy on which the academic tradition of the German Enlightenment had been founded, says, in its simplest form, that nothing is without a reason or ground (*Grund*) for its being rather than not being. The young Schopenhauer observed quite rightly that there were different species of 'grounding' which were not always properly distinguished by the tradition. For example, a cause is the ground of its effect, but this is distinct from the way in which a conclusion has its ground in a premise or a geometrical truth has its ground in the nature of space. He claims that there are four basic modes in which the principle can be interpreted (the fourth is the grounding of an action in its motive, which is, however, a variant of the grounding of an effect in its cause). When he published *The World as Will and Representation* in 1818,[10] Schopenhauer stated that *The Fourfold Root* was an essential prelude to it. Nor did he change his mind on that score: in 1847, following publication of the revised and greatly extended edition of *The World as Will and Representation* three years earlier, he undertook a considerable re-write of *The Fourfold Root*. This shows that he had not left it behind as a juvenile work, but saw it as integral to his mature philosophy – though it may be said that he lost much of the lightness and incisiveness of the 1813 version in making his revisions. Since he refers to the principle of sufficient reason frequently in *The World as Will and Representation* without repeating the detailed exposition of *The Fourfold Root*, it is sensible to study the latter as if it were a component of the larger work, where it belongs naturally with the First Book on the world as representation.

The Second Book announces that the world is will. This is not supposed to be a negation of the claim that the world is representation, but rather a presentation of another aspect of the same world. Schopenhauer is not satisfied with comprehending the orderly manner in which the world of objects of experience must present itself to the experiencing subject. He asks what the essence of this world is: or, as he puts it in Kantian vocabulary, what the world is in itself. His answer, patently, is that the world in itself is will. But it is not immediately obvious what this means or even what kind of claim Schopenhauer intends to make when he says it. Will is a general principle of striving or being directed towards ends, but it does not presuppose the rationality associated traditionally with the human (and the divine) will. For Schopenhauer, creatures do not will something because they believe it to be good; rather, something is called good because it is something that some creature wills. Willing is thus more basic than rationality. Nor is will necessarily accompanied by consciousness or even by a mind. Everything in the world – humans, animals, plants, water, and stones – manifests will in Schopenhauer's new sense: no individual thing remains perpetually in a state of self-sufficiency, but everything is always – as it were – trying to be somewhere and in some state. Perhaps we should regard talk of 'willing', 'wanting', or 'trying' as ineliminable metaphors in this global picture. Schopenhauer says that 'everything presses and pushes towards *existence*, if possible towards *organic existence*, i.e. *life*, and then to the highest possible degree thereof' (W2 350/H. 3, 399). His fundamental belief is that we can make sense of our own existence and behaviour by understanding our own inner essence as will, and that there is an imperative to understand or 'decipher' the world in the same way. This reveals an underlying assumption that my inner essence must be the same as that of the world at large, a thought he sometimes expresses as the identity of the microcosm and the macrocosm (see W1 162/H. 2, 193).

This goal of incorporating the self in the world – not only making it something bodily, but finding for it an essence shared by every part of the world – cuts across the Kantian programme that was initiated with the account of the world as representation. It does so because of the role of the subject in the latter account. In the account of the world of representation there is, necessarily, a subject that represents objects. But this subject is 'an eye that cannot see itself'. It never occurs as its own object, and so it cannot be located anywhere in space, time, and the causal order. It is (though Schopenhauer does not use this term) the transcendental self – the self required purely as an a priori condition of the possibility of experience. The pivotal section in the whole of *The World as Will and Representation* is §18, where Schopenhauer confronts this transcendental self, the pure subject of cognition, with the fact that each individual human subject is rooted in material reality via intimate knowledge of his or her body in action. I know myself immediately as embodied will, and were I not to do so, I would remain a detached and ghostly pure subject that comprehended the inner significance of nothing at all in the world of its experience.

From this notion of the will as the individual's inner essence cognized in bodily action, Schopenhauer travels a great distance, stretching the concept of will as he goes. The whole body is will in that it manifests the means of securing ends for the organism. The body, and each part and function within it, is an expression of the 'will to life', *Wille zum Leben*. Often this term is translated as 'will to live' (or 'will-to-live', as E. F. J. Payne has it). But that translation is misleading (a) because it implicitly excludes the drive to reproduce life, and hence towards sexual behaviour, to which Schopenhauer gives great prominence and (b) because it lets in the wrong assumption that Schopenhauer is talking about a conscious *desire* to live, whereas *Wille zum Leben* primarily operates to originate and shape the organism prior to any question of its having desires. (Sometimes contributors to this volume use 'will to life', even to the extent of altering the wording when quoting from Payne's translation.)

Schopenhauer finally suggests that the whole world in itself is will. There are serious questions concerning the status of this theory. If the thing in itself is supposed to be unknowable, how can Schopenhauer claim to know what it is? If 'will' need not connote rationality, consciousness, or even mentality, what does it connote? What does it mean to say that every object is the phenomenal manifestation (or 'objectification') of will? However, the chief importance of the theory of will as essence is its impact upon the human self-image. We have to regard ourselves as driven by something at our core which presses us to prolong our lives and to have sexual intercourse, and to pursue myriad goals that arise from our nature as living creatures, often for purposes that are hidden from our conscious view. The individual's idealization of a singular object of sexual desire, for instance, masks the fact that he or she is being 'used' by the will to life in order to perpetuate itself. And in general, the individual's willed actions are not free. His or her willing is fixed not only by the general human character, will to life, but also by an individual unchangeable character which Schopenhauer calls the individual's essence or individual will.

Schopenhauer's pessimism is closely linked with his account of the will. There is no absolute good because good exists only relative to some particular strand of willing manifest somewhere in the world of phenomena. Willing can never cease in the universe and can never be satiated. It has no ultimate point or purpose. And it opens each individual to suffering which is not redeemed by any positive benefit. Schopenhauer appears to believe that the sheer existence of suffering shows everything to be invalid: because of it 'we have not to be pleased but rather sorry about the existence of the world' (W2 576/H. 3, 661). By the end of the Second Book, following the initial clue that we cannot be merely the transcendental self which represents objects, and that our essence is will, we have descended into a disturbing picture of a world that is will, manifesting itself in millions of individuals, and through them inflicting on itself pointless and unredeemed suffering, a 'world of constantly needy creatures who continue for a time merely by devouring one another, pass their existence in anxiety and want, and often endure terrible afflictions, until they fall at last into the arms of death' (W2 349/H. 3, 398). The notions of a benevolent creator and a world of perfection so prevalent in the Judaeo-Christian tradition and in philosophical rationalism would never have occurred, claims Schopenhauer, to anyone who had looked at the evidence.

The tide turns with the Third Book of *The World as Will and Representation*, where Schopenhauer presents a theory of art and aesthetic experience that gives them an almost unparalleled positive value. In aesthetic experience, willing temporarily ceases and the subject is blissfully free from striving and the suffering associated with it. If ordinary existence is restless torment, aesthetic experience is repose and release. But in addition to this palliative dimension, it has high value as a species of cognition. Throwing off the a priori subjective forms of experience the intellect uses when it is an 'instrument' of the will and abandoning the principle of sufficient reason, the subject of aesthetic experience can perceive more objectively 'what really is' – a series of Ideas (*Ideen*) or Forms that constitute a timeless aspect of reality. The producer of genuine art is a genius, whose defining characteristic is the propensity to let the intellect work at perceiving objects independently of the underlying will. This vision of a timeless objectivity achieved in art by leaving behind ordinary consciousness was one of the earliest parts of Schopenhauer's philosophy to develop, as his early *Manuscript Remains* testify. Having begun philosophy by reading Plato as well as Kant, he conceived the notion of a 'higher consciousness'[11] that elevated the subject above the mundane, ephemeral, and painful reality presented in ordinary empirical consciousness. He retained ever after the thought that the subject in intense aesthetic contemplation loses its sense of bodily individuation and attains the status of a 'pure subject of knowing', while its object is transformed from the spatio-temporally individuated empirical thing into an Idea or, as he often says, a '(Platonic) Idea'. Art gains its unusually high value as temporary escape into timeless purity, away from an ordinary existence to which Schopenhauer has assigned an exceptional lack of worth.

Schopenhauer's final Fourth Book contains some of his most moving and profound writing. It concerns ethics, in both a broad and a narrow sense. The latter comprises issues such as right and wrong, moral motivation, egoism and justice, the virtues and moral judgement, the former issues such as the significance of human sexuality, our attitudes towards death, the philosophy of religion, the meaning (if any) of life, and the possibility of what Schopenhauer calls 'salvation' from it. Although *The World as Will and Representation* deals to some extent with ethics in the narrower sense, Schopenhauer's best treatment of these issues occurs in two self-contained essays, *On the Basis of Morality* and *On the Freedom of the Will*, which he published together in 1841 under the title *The Two Fundamental Problems of Ethics*. The former essay contrasts Schopenhauer's account of ethics with Kant's, of which he is mercilessly critical. Kant's ethics is founded upon the notion of an autonomous rational agent and an absolute imperative – issued by whom, asks Schopenhauer, unless by a presupposed absolute being? Schopenhauer opposes to this an ethics founded upon the incentive of compassion, a basic feature of human beings which gives rise to acts of justice and philanthropy (or love of humankind, *Menschenliebe*). His moral psychology of the virtues claims to be an empirical theory that accounts for the virtues and vices which motivate human action in practice. In *On the Freedom of the Will* he argues that the individual's actions are determined by a combination of his or her unalterable character and the motives, contingently occurring mental states, that cause his or her actions. It is a strong defence of determinism – yet Schopenhauer is aware that the argument will not disperse the sense we have of being responsible for our deeds. He proposes to solve this problem by invoking the idea of our intelligible character, the will which is our kernel, our essence.

The broader ethical concerns of life and death show Schopenhauer at his most challenging. Life is dominated by the fact that it ends in death, yet this is strangely at odds, he comments, with the way people normally live – as if they will never die. But what value does life really have for the living anyway? Schopenhauer deepens his pessimistic vision, arguing that the only real hope for a human being is to reach the insight that existing as an individual is worthless. Although in his metaphysics Schopenhauer is an uncompromising atheist, he finds in three of the major world religions – Christianity, Hinduism, and Buddhism – the correct degree of disdain for ordinary human existence. The ascetic practices associated with these religions point in the right direction: towards a denial of one's will, a stilling of desires and needs which can be a step towards complete self-renunciation, a cessation of willing which Schopenhauer conceives to resemble a prolongation of the blissful will-lessness of aesthetic experience. Salvation ultimately consists in the will within oneself turning and denying itself. One can then abandon one's allegiance to the desires one has as an individual and attain a viewpoint on the world which does not fundamentally differentiate oneself as subject from the whole.

Hinduism played an important role in shaping these culminating thoughts. Schopenhauer's favourite book was said to be a translation of the *Upanishads* which he acquired as a young man while writing *The World as Will and Representation*. He was one of the first Western thinkers to make extensive efforts to align his thought with that of India, and we should not underestimate this distinctive influence upon him. He repeatedly ranks Hinduism with Plato and Kant, saying of his philosophy that it could not have occurred until all three shone their rays into one mind[12] and saying of the prospective reader of his main work that 'if . . . [he] has also already received and assimilated the divine inspiration of ancient Indian wisdom, then he is best of all prepared to hear what I have to say to him' (*W1* xv/H. 2, xii). Later on he became a serious and engaged student of Buddhism, finding a deep affinity with some of its central doctrines, which influenced at least the presentation of his broader ethical insights, if not also some of the content.

Now let us return to the 'single thought' and Atwell's formulation of it: 'The double-sided world is the striving of the will to become conscious of itself so that, recoiling in horror at its inner, self-divisive nature, it may annul itself and thereby its self-affirmation, and then reach salvation.' If the will is to become self-conscious, it must first objectify itself as a being that has consciousness at all. It does this in the human being, whose body, with its advanced nervous system capable of consciousness, exists as an instrument of the will to life. But in some individuals, cognition of the world reaches a point where its subject can see through the veil of empirical objects in space and time, and realize that the subject itself has its nature in common with the whole world, that all the objective individuals that compete against one another belong equally to the whole. This essentially mystical vision that sees beyond individuality is what 'quiets' the will, or annuls its expression within the individual who has the mystical vision. Thus far Atwell's formulation makes considerable sense. Possibly more contentious is his implication that for Schopenhauer the world is working towards a single *purpose* that consists in such self-annulment. Schopenhauer does say that 'nothing else can be stated as the aim of our existence except the knowledge that it would be better for us not to exist' (W2 605/H. 3, 695), but does the world as a whole strive in order to reach its own non-existence? It seems rather that there is no determinate content to will as such, and that the question of *what* is willed can be asked only in respect of its particular phenomenal manifestations. As Schopenhauer says, 'absence of all aim, of all limits, belongs to the essential nature of the will in itself, which is an endless striving' (W1 164/H. 2, 195). Also, the will as such could not literally annul itself since it is indestructible (see W2 486/H. 3, 556). It seems that ultimate reality endlessly strives simply to be, to which end it must appear in individual empirical manifestations of itself, and that when it reaches its highest manifestation in an individual who is self-conscious and can reflect on his or her own nature as a manifestation of will, it can cancel itself out in that particular individual.

Although Schopenhauer's relationship to Kant is clearly of the first importance, it should be apparent even from the quick summary given here how un-Kantian a philosopher he is. He uses Kant's vocabulary pervasively, but the shape and motivation of his philosophy are very different. The influences of Plato and Hinduism should immediately alert us to this fact. Schopenhauer sets out from the start to show that the existence of every human individual is worthless, and that it must be set aside in favour of the higher consciousness of timeless entities not subordinate to the forms of space, time, and causality. He also sets out to demote rationality from its centrality in the description of humanity, to show that the concept is unfruitful in ethics, to argue that the will of the individual cannot be free, and to decry the use of the idea of God in legitimating morality.

In aesthetics, where commentators customarily find continuity between Schopenhauer's 'pure will-less subject' and Kant's notion of 'disinterestedness', the motivations of the two theories are also quite different. Schopenhauer's vision of art pits it against the remainder of life in a way that would be alien to Kant, and his idea that art is cognitively superior to (or more objective than) both empirical perception and the sciences is something Kant could never support. Even the 'will-lessness' of aesthetic experience is arguably at odds with what Kant's theory of aesthetic judgement requires. Kant is concerned with a pleasure whose basis is not in one's desire for the existence of the object one contemplates, but he does not posit a higher state of consciousness cleansed of all desire and conceptualization. It is Schopenhauer rather than Kant who pre-figures the 'aesthetic attitude'.[13]

Finally, there is room for debate about the relationship between Schopenhauer's conception of transcendental idealism and Kant's. Schopenhauer begins his presentation with a theory of knowledge which appears to owe a great deal to Kant, but he finishes *The World as Will and Representation* with a substantial Appendix entitled 'Critique of the Kantian Philosophy'. This should prepare us for both continuity and opposition. But it is not clear how much continuity there really is if one looks at the basic motivations of Schopenhauer's theoretical philosophy. Schopenhauer not only contradicts Kant's own views in interpreting Kant's idealism as akin to Berkeley's, but also seems never to accept the implication that transcendental idealism must systematically reject the question of ontology. In finding Kant's philosophy incomplete for not giving an account of what the self 'really is' or what the objects of experience 'really are', and in saying that the world as representation amounts to an insubstantial dream, Schopenhauer arguably reveals a fundamental commitment to metaphysical realism that is alien to the transcendental project.

After writing *The World as Will and Representation*, Schopenhauer never renounced the philosophy that it contained. His subsequent writings are predominantly explorations of new areas of application for his thought and elaborations of it in the light of copious readings in philosophy, science, literature, and comparative religion. In 1836 he published *On the Will in Nature*, which took stock of a large body of scientific writings, arguing that they confirmed his central claims concerning the will. Around 1840, as we have mentioned, he wrote his two essays on ethical subjects, entering them in competitions set by the Norwegian and Danish Scientific Societies, respectively. Having amassed a wealth of further observations and having arrived at some adjustments to his theory, Schopenhauer then undertook a major revision of *The World as Will and Representation*, which was published in 1844. He wrote a long second volume consisting of essays paralleling, book by book, the presentation of the original work. Some of these essays are scholarly ruminations that add little to the force of the original work. But in some cases, Schopenhauer achieves his most powerful writing, augmenting the energy of his youthful style with a gravity few philosophical writers can match. One might mention here especially the passages on the relation of the will to the intellect (chapter 19), the metaphysics of sexual love (chapter 44), and the 'vanity and suffering of life' (chapter 45).

With the added essays, the original *World as Will and Representation* now became Volume 1 of a two-volume set. But Schopenhauer did not leave it untouched. The text of Volume 1 that we commonly read, whether in German or in translation, incorporates many changes made in 1844, including interpolations of literary and philosophical parallels to his ideas and bitter diatribes against Fichte and Hegel, whose success, though now well in the past, he still could not stomach. The 'Critique of the Kantian Philosophy' was heavily altered, principally to accommodate Schopenhauer's recent discovery of Kant's *Critique of Pure Reason* in its first edition of 1781, which we nowadays call the A edition and are used to reading alongside the 1787 B version. Schopenhauer also revised *The Fourfold Root* in 1847. In 1851 a large new work appeared in two volumes, entitled *Parerga and Paralipomena*. It ranges widely over Schopenhauer's many intellectual interests, containing popular essays, re-presentations of his central philosophical views, and reflections on the history of philosophy. *Parerga* also contains a piece for which Schopenhauer is notorious, his essay 'On Women' (*P2* ch. 27), a nasty, gratuitous piece of misogyny, whose only conceivable merit is that it is written with his characteristic vigour. His generalized view of women appears to be drawn solely from jaundiced personal experience and has, I believe, no very interesting connection with his philosophy. (There is little evidence of Schopenhauer's having been a nice person to know, but anyone who has any doubts should perhaps read this essay.) The publication of these 'works on the side and left-overs' (as we might translate *Parerga and Paralipomena*) first made their author well known to a wider audience. By the end of his life Schopenhauer received visits and correspondence from many who had read his work, he began to be studied in the universities, and in the last decade of his life there were new editions of *On the Will in Nature*, *The Two Fundamental Problems of Ethics*, and a third edition of *The World as Will and Representation*, incorporating more changes into the text.

Schopenhauer's philosophical thought is both idiosyncratic and very tightly organized around his central conceptions of will, representation, subject, object, intellect, individuation, and the principle of sufficient reason. Hence it can be difficult to consider his views in one philosophical area without re-stating much of what he thinks overall, and the reader of the present volume should be prepared for some overlap between its different essays. Two of the essays range across all four books of *The World as Will and Representation*, Günter Zöller's piece looking at the self, and in particular the relation of will and intellect, and David Hamlyn's at the different conceptions of knowledge Schopenhauer appears to presuppose at different stages of his argument.

The essay by F. C. White concentrates on the important doctrines of *The Fourfold Root*, looking at both the first and second editions of that work. *On the Basis of the Morality* forms the chief material for David Cartwright's essay on Schopenhauer's ethics, though he also discusses a number of other works. *On the Freedom of the Will* is summarized in the first of two pieces by Christopher Janaway, which concerns Schopenhauer's conception of the will in human action and in nature as a whole, drawing chiefly on the Second Book of *The World as Will and Representation*. The Third Book's aesthetic theory and philosophy of art and genius are discussed fully in the essay by Cheryl Foster and play a part also in Martha C. Nussbaum's essay, which explores Schopenhauer's influence on Nietzsche with particular reference to the theme of tragedy.

Two other contributions are specifically concerned with aspects of Schopenhauer's influence on later thinkers. Sebastian Gardner examines Schopenhauer as a precursor of the Freudian theory of the unconscious against the background of the history of philosophy since Kant. Hans-Johann Glock makes an assessment of the different spheres – such as logic, metaphysics, ethics, and the philosophy of action – in which an influence on Wittgenstein has been claimed for Schopenhauer. As regards influences on Schopenhauer, Paul Guyer looks at his relationship to Kant's epistemology, emphasizing both his differences from Kant and his criticisms of his predecessor. Schopenhauer's criticism of Kant's ethics is examined in the piece by Cartwright mentioned earlier. Moira Nicholls contributes an account of Schopenhauer's knowledge of Indian thought, and of the role that Hinduism and Buddhism played in the development of his metaphysics, especially his conception of the thing in itself.

The culminating Fourth Book of *The World as Will and Representation*, though reflected in a number of the other pieces, is given most attention by Dale Jacquette in his piece on the central Schopenhauerian theme of death and our attitudes to it, and by Christopher Janaway in his essay on Schopenhauer's pessimism, which also contains some material on religion and Schopenhauer's influence on Nietzsche.

NOTES

1 Edith Wharton, *A Son at the Front* (1923, repr. DeKalb: Northern Illinois University Press, 1995), 216.
2 Theodor Adorno, *Minima Moralia*, trans. E. F. N. Jephcott (London: Verso, 1978), 153.
3 *Beyond Good and Evil*, sect. 204.
4 See Christopher Janaway (ed.), *Willing and Nothingness: Schopenhauer as Nietzsche's Educator* (Oxford: Clarendon Press, 1998).
5 See Rudolf Malter, *Der Eine Gedanke. Hinführung zur Philosophie Arthur Schopenhauers* (Darmstadt: Wissenschaftliche Buchgesellschaft, 1988).
6 *MR* 1 512/Hn. 1, 462.
7 As John Atwell puts it, 'the will–intellect union knows, in virtue of the intellect component, what it as will wills, that is, what its nature is, only by knowing the world of appearance. Or ... the world of appearance reveals to the will–intellect union, or specifically to the intellect component, the nature of the will.' (*Schopenhauer on the Character of the World: The Metaphysics of Will* [Berkeley: University of California Press, 1995], 28).
8 Ibid., 31.
9 See *W2* 82–3, 643–4; *W1* 273, 483–4, 521/H. 3, 90, 739–41; H. 2, 321, 574, 618.
10 The work came out in December 1818 but had 1819 on its title page.
11 See *MR* 1, 44, 48–57, 86, 113–14, 120, 132, 162–4, 191/Hn. 1, 41–4, 45–53, 79, 104–5, 110–11, 122–3, 149–51, 175 – all notes written by Schopenhauer in 1813–14.
12 *MR* 1, 467/Hn. 1, 421–2.
13 See Christopher Janaway, 'Kant's Aesthetics and the "Empty Cognitive Stock"', *Philosophical Quarterly* 47 (1997), 459–63.

1　Schopenhauer on the Self[1]

I THE SELF AS WILL AND INTELLECT

In the German language, as in English, the pronoun or pronominal adjective *selbst*, or 'self,' lends emphasis to something or someone previously named. In its nominalized form, *das Selbst*, or 'the self,' the pronoun serves chiefly to identify a human being or person. A specifically philosophical usage of the nominalized form came into currency in England, chiefly through the work of John Locke, in the late seventeenth and early eighteenth centuries, from where it seems to have made its way into German philosophical terminology a few decades later. A main function of the philosophical term has been to identify the core or essence of a human being, as opposed to what might be accidental or contingent about him or her. In particular, the self has been identified with a human being's soul or mind as opposed to his or her body. In a secondary usage, the term has been employed to distinguish between constituent parts or aspects of one and the same being, in particular to articulate the special status of someone's or one's own 'better self.'

In German philosophy the term and concept of the self plays a systematically foundational role in the works of Kant and several of his idealist successors. In Kantian and post-Kantian thinking, the self is no longer a being alongside other beings but rather is that due to which all beings and the world that encompasses them first come into view.[2]

The development of the term and concept of the self in Schopenhauer occurs against the background of the general discourse on the self in modern philosophy and the particular significance accorded to the self in the recent German tradition. Schopenhauer continues the usage of the term 'self' to designate the core or essence of the human being; he employs the term to distinguish between different, and differently valued, levels of human existence; and he partakes in the post-Kantian elevation of the self to the rank of the nonworldly necessary correlate of the world.

Yet, while Schopenhauer takes over the key functions of the term 'self' from the philosophical tradition, he has a radically different understanding of what is the core of the human being designated by the word self, of what constitutes the form of human existence referred to as the better self, and of what it means for the self to underlie the world and everything in it. The basic disagreement between Schopenhauer and the philosophical tradition on the self concerns the standard identification of the self, as the core of the human being, with the intellect (understanding, reason) or the faculty of cognition. On Schopenhauer's account, the intellect is neither the sole nor necessarily the main factor of the self. In addition to the rational side or aspect of the self, Schopenhauer countenances an altogether different essential feature of the self, which he designates as *will*.

Unlike earlier accounts of the self, which subordinate the human will to reason by construing the will as applied or practical reason, Schopenhauer insists on the will's original independence from reason and understanding. The will in the human self is seen as arational, 'blind' striving. Moreover, the will for Schopenhauer not only supplements the intellect in the constitution of the human self. The will underlies that self, including its intellectual side, as the source of the self's very being. Finally, in stressing the centrality of the will in the self, Schopenhauer radically revises the status of the human body by rethinking the traditional mind–body relation as a will–body identity.

Yet, rather than simply replacing the earlier primacy and monopoly of the intellect with that of the will, Schopenhauer provides a subtle and detailed account of the complex relations between the intellectual and volitional sides or aspects of the human self. Moreover, Schopenhauer stresses the dynamic interaction between intellect and will in the self. He distinguishes two alternative but complementary conceptions of selfhood: one in which the will forms the core of the human being and one in which the human being achieves selfhood through the cultivation of the intellect.

The two contrasting conceptions of selfhood in Schopenhauer are linked through the notion of the self's possible or ideal development from a will-centered to an intellect-centered self. According to Schopenhauer, the agency behind the development of the self away from the will is none other than the will itself. The self-realization of the will may take the form of the will's radical self-negation. The psycho-machia of the self in Schopenhauer is rendered more dramatic yet through the role that the self plays in relation to the world. More specifically, the cosmo-machia involving self and world turns on the twofold role of the self as intelligence and as will. As intelligence, the self is the ineliminable and indispensable formal condition of objects of all kinds. As will, the self is the most articulate manifestation of the blindly striving drive that underlies all reality.

Thus the account of the self is not a clearly demarcated, specialized topic in Schopenhauer's overall philosophy but, in essence, is coextensive with his portrayal of 'the world as will and representation'. Accordingly, an account of Schopenhauer on the self best orients itself after the overall organization of *The World as Will and Representation* (1818; second edition 1844; third edition 1859) – more specifically that of the first, one-volume edition and of the corresponding first volume of the subsequent two-volume editions – by moving from the role of the intellect in the epistemology of Book One, through the function of the self in the manifestations of the will in the philosophy of nature of Book Two, to the role of the pure intellect in the contemplation of the Ideas in the aesthetics of Book Three and the self-recognition and self-denial of the will in the ethics of Book Four. This order of presentation also captures the developmental nature of Schopenhauer's thinking, which he himself portrays as the successive unfolding of a 'single thought' (*der eine Gedanke*), which, however, can only be stated through the system in its entirety.[3]

The selective reading of the main work will be preceded by a discussion of pertinent aspects of Schopenhauer's relation to Kant and a more detailed consideration of the systematic basis of *The World as Will and Representation* in general and its theory of the self in particular in Schopenhauer's doctoral dissertation *On the Fourfold Root of the Principle of Sufficient Reason* (1813; second edition 1847). Further writings of Schopenhauer that supplement the account of selfhood in the main work and the dissertation include *On the Will in Nature* (1836; second edition 1854) and the *Prize Essay on the Freedom of the Will* (1841; second edition 1860).[4]

II FROM KANT TO SCHOPENHAUER

The starting point for the post-Kantian discussion in general and post-Kantian theories of the self in particular is Kant's 'critical distinction'[5] between things as they appear (appearances [*Erscheinungen*]) and things as they are in themselves (things in themselves [*Dinge an sich*, also *Sachen an sich*]). On Kant's view, the basic formal features of experience and of its objects, such as space, time, and causality, do not pertain to the things themselves but only to our human ways of cognitively encountering things. On Kant's view, it is exactly the restriction of all humanly possible cognition of objects to appearances that guarantees the latter's reference to actual or possible empirical objects.[6] Kant's doctrinal term for the inapplicability of the human cognitive forms to the things in themselves is 'transcendental idealism'; his term for the correlated doctrine of the applicability, indeed the necessary application, of the cognitive forms to appearances is 'empirical realism'. For Kant transcendental idealism ensures empirical realism, while any doctrine ignoring the distinction between the things in themselves and the appearances ('transcendental realism') results in skepticism about the knowability of objects ('empirical idealism').[7]

Kant's doctrinal dualism poses some difficulties when it comes to determining the status of the self. The role of the self as the bearer and contributor of the a priori forms of cognition seems to elude the distinction between the self as empirically known appearance and the self as unknowable thing in itself. In addition to the empirical self, whose study Kant assigns to empirical psychology and anthropology, and the non-empirical self traditionally entertained by the metaphysical study of the soul (rational psychology), there is a third self, or third sense of self, that is neither empirical nor metaphysical but transcendental or 'pertaining to the conditions of the possibility of experience.'[8]

Schopenhauer takes over the Kantian distinction between things in themselves and appearances with two modifications, one of them more a matter of emphasis, the other one quite substantial. More consistently and explicitly than Kant,[9] Schopenhauer argues that the appearances are nothing but 'representations' (*Vorstellungen*) in the human mind with no independent extramental existence. In a radical departure from Kant's agnosticism regarding the things in themselves, he identifies the latter with the will as revealed to the human mind in conative and affective self-experience and subsequently recognized as the essence of all reality, human as well as non-human.

Such purported intimate knowledge of the ultimate reality behind or beneath the appearances seems to transgress the critical interdiction against seeking knowledge of the unknowable things in themselves and therefore to constitute a relapse into pre-Kantian dogmatism or transcendental realism, thus turning Schopenhauer's work into a puzzling conjunction of transcendental philosophy and transcendent metaphysics of the will.[10] But what might appear as the uncritical reestablishment of a previously destroyed metaphysics is actually yet another step in the direction taken by Kant himself – that of limiting all our knowledge in general and philosophical knowledge in particular to the realm of experience and the sum total of the latter's pure forms or conditions. With his restriction of reason to the faculty of cognition (theoretical reason) and his vehement rejection of a rational metaphysics of morals and its associated practico-dogmatic postulates of an immortal soul and a personal God,[11] Schopenhauer is even less of a metaphysician than Kant himself, who had sought to compensate for the metaphysical poverty of pure theoretical ('speculative') reason with the otherworldly riches of pure practical ('moral') reason.

Accordingly, Schopenhauer's immanent metaphysics of the will should be seen as part and parcel of his transcendental philosophy rather than as a heterogeneous and oversized appendix.[12] Schopenhauer expands the scope of the transcendental project by including non-theoretical, conative self-consciousness and its affects and emotions in the evidential basis for the reflection on experience in general that is philosophy.[13] The subjectivism and idealism that inform the view of the world of cognition as one of representation ('world as representation') are matched by the view of the world of feeling as one of will ('world as will'). Both cases involve the world *as experienced*. Schopenhauer's work is as much about the self that experiences the world in either of those two forms as it is about the world or worlds so experienced.

Schopenhauer's radical reworking of crucial Kantian positions is also evident in his reconceptualization of the two key ingredients of the self, viz., the intellect and the will.[14] The will in Schopenhauer is radically dissociated from reason and a power sui generis, thus marking Schopenhauer's radical departure from the Kantian conception of will as practical reason.[15] In his account of the faculty of cognition, Schopenhauer emphasizes the difference between understanding (*Verstand*) and reason (*Vernunft*), which he explains as the difference between the capacity for preconceptual, intuitive knowledge and the capacity to form and employ concepts based on the prior intuitive grasp of things.[16] Unlike Kant, who had severed the tie between intuition and intellection by declaring all humanly possible intuition to be sensible, Schopenhauer argues that our intuition of objects (including the intuition of ourselves taken as object) is informed not only by the forms of intuition (space and time) but also by the prereflective employment of the category of causality, which conditions a priori the mind's spontaneous transition from sensible affection to the positing of a corresponding affecting object in space. [17] Schopenhauer holds that the causally informed intuition of spatial objects pertains in principle to all animal life. Only the formation and use of concepts in rational knowledge, and its associated capabilities of deliberative thought, language, and science, set human mentation apart from the mental life of our prerational fellow creatures.[18]

In addition to the intellect, Schopenhauer countenances the will as the second of the two key ingredients in the constitution of the human self. 'Will' is here used as a covering term for the entire affective and volitional side of the self, effectively grouping together what Kant had distinguished as the faculty of desire and the feeling of pleasure and displeasure.[19] Schopenhauer provides a negative characterization of the acts of the will by stressing the non-representational nature of all such 'feelings'.[20] Unlike the intellect, which generates images and thoughts of things (representations), the will is not about anything else and outside of itself but is the domain of our affective self-experience – something that is felt or lived rather than being by nature something representing or something represented.

III THE SUBJECT OF COGNITION AND THE SUBJECT OF WILLING

As the two structuring forms underlying the self's cognitive and conative life, the intellect and the will in Schopenhauer have the status of the 'subject of cognition' (*Subjekt des Erkennens*) and the 'subject of willing' (*Subjekt des Wollens*), respectively.[21] Every cognition is had by the intellect qua subject, and every conation is had by the will qua subject. Moreover, neither the subject of cognition nor the subject of willing is given *as such*.[22] The subject of cognition is the knower in everything known and is never itself known, except in the attenuated sense that the states of the subject of cognition may be known through reflection. Analogously, the subject of willing is that which feels in all feeling (wills in all willing) but is never itself felt, except in the attenuated sense that the states of the subject of willing may be felt internally. The cognitive and conative subject functions of the self have the status of non-empirical conditions of all experience, inner as well as outer, cognitive as well as affective.

In addressing the unity of the self amidst its composition out of two radically different constituent subjects, Schopenhauer maintains that the subject of willing functions as the internal, 'immediate' object of the subject of cognition.[23] In the original, internal, subjective subject–object relation there are united a subject of cognition, which is itself empty and without any object to be known, and a subject of willing, which is itself blind and without any awareness of itself. Only the conjunction of the will's content and the intellect's vision permits the proper functioning of each of the two constituent parts of the self. Citing a fable by the eighteenth-century Swiss writer J. F. Gellert, Schopenhauer likens the compensatory co-operation between will and intellect to the strong, blind one carrying the lame, seeing one on his shoulders.[24]

The particulars of the subject–object relation between intellect and will in the self belong to the wider context of Schopenhauer's account of the overall structure of consciousness and its objects under the 'principle of sufficient reason' (*Satz vom zureichenden Grund*).[25] In its four manifestations as the principle of becoming, of being, of knowing, and of acting, this supreme transcendental principle governs the relations of ground and consequent (of *ratio* and *rationatum*) between objects of all kinds (physical, mathematical, logical, and psychological objects), always in correlation to the subject of cognition in one of its capacities as understanding, pure intuition, reason, and inner sense or empirical self-consciousness, respectively. Accordingly, the principle specifies the real, mathematical, logical, or psychological connections among objects as so many instances of the principle's general point that nothing is without a reason or ground.

The principle of sufficient reason, which governs the relations among objects, is borne and applied by the subject, more specifically the subject of cognition. Accordingly, the subject itself, from which issues this basic law, does not stand under the principle in question. For Schopenhauer the relation between the subject and any and all of the objects which are subject to the principle is not a relationship of one-sided dependence but a *correlation* in which none of the members can be what it is without the other ones. This also holds for the special case of the self's internal subject–object relation between the subject of cognition and the subject of willing.[26]

In the case of the principle of sufficient reason of acting, also called the 'law of motivation,' the subject–object correlation obtains between the subject of cognition under the form of empirical self-consciousness or inner sense, on the one hand, and the will or faculty of volition in its manifestations as particular acts of willing, on the other hand. According to Schopenhauer, the cause of an act of willing is in each case a cognition which necessarily moves the will to the respective act of willing – hence the very term 'motive' (*Motiv*). The causal connection between a given cognition that functions as motive and the resultant act of volition is experienced internally, through empirical self-consciousness or inner sense.

In locating the intellect–will relation of the self in the context of Schopenhauer's theory of motivational causation, it is imperative to realize that the relation of ground and consequent holds only among the different kinds of objects correlated to the subject of cognition in any one of its capacities (as understanding, pure intuition, reason, and inner sense) – and not between the relata of the basic subject–object correlation itself, which underlies all objects and their sufficiently grounded relations among each other. Specifically, the intellect qua subject of cognition does not ground the will qua subject of willing. Rather, the two subjects are the inseparable poles of an original complex unity on the basis of which all intellection and volition comes to pass. In motivation the relation of grounding obtains between some cognition and the particular act of the will which that cognition motivates. Hence it is not the will as such but the particular act of willing that is grounded or psychologically caused. The will itself, as well as the intellect, are not subject to the principle of sufficient reason.

For Schopenhauer the non-causal structural correlativity that holds between the subject of cognition and the subject of willing ultimately amounts to their identity.[27] This claim can be taken to convey the thought that in the original subject–object relation between the subject of cognition and the subject of willing, the knower (subject of cognition) and the known (subject of willing) are one and the same being. It is not some being other than the one exercising the function of the subject of cognition that is being known as the subject of willing but that very same being, only in a different though correlated function.[28] Hence the ultimate identity of the subject of cognition and the subject of willing in the basic subject–object relation is constitutive of the very unity of the self, which is not the unity of a whole encompassing constituent parts but a unity established by the identical bearer of mutually supplementary basic functions.

Schopenhauer does not claim any further insight into the identity underlying the self. He contents himself with declaring this identity to be the 'miracle "par excellence"'[29] and to represent nothing less than the 'knot of the world,'[30] suggesting that in it, self and world are deeply intertwined and inseparable. The metaphor of the world knot further indicates the wider significance that the miraculous identity underlying the human self takes on in Schopenhauer's transcendental theory of the world in its relation to the self.

IV   THE IDENTITY OF BODY AND WILL

The wider cosmological perspective of Schopenhauer's theory of the self is further informed by a second identity claim involving intellect and will, this one specifically directed at the twofold nature of the self as intelligence and will. Schopenhauer maintains that in the case of the human self, the double perspective on the world as will and representation takes the form of a twofold experience of ourselves, one as object given to the intellect operating under the principle of sufficient reason, the other as will and its affective life, and hence largely independent of the forms and functions of the intellect.[31] The self as object of our own and others' cognitive relation to ourselves is the 'living body' (*Leib*).

Schopenhauer holds that for each of us our own body is the intellect's 'immediate object'.[32] Any knowledge of other objects is mediated by our bodily self-experience and is a result of the (typically unconscious) inference from given bodily sensations to their causal origin in some object or objects other than ourselves or our own body. In Schopenhauer, one's own body taken as object of one's own cognition thus occupies a peculiar position. It is the original object of all our knowledge and is known in a most immediate manner, but it is still an object and as such is subject to the formative rules of the intellect. In principle, the knowledge that we each have of our own body is not different from the knowledge that we have of other bodies or the knowledge that others have of our own body.

Yet according to Schopenhauer, our own body is not only an object of knowledge for our and others' intellect but also something that we each *are*, and that moreover belongs to the very core of our existence. The account of our body's relation to our intellect is to be supplemented by the account of our body's relation to our will and the latter's acts or volitions. We each relate to our own body not only cognitively and intellectually but also practically and affectively. A given movement of our body is not only an object of knowledge to us (and others) but also an act of ours which we experience *from within* as relating to our own act of volition. Schopenhauer rejects a causal account of the relation between volitional act and bodily act. Instead he considers the two acts to be the different sides of one and the same underlying reality that precedes the overt distinction between the mental and the physical.[33]

It should be stressed that, on Schopenhauer's understanding, the aspect duality of the self, as innerly felt will and outerly observed body, is not the product of some artificial, specifically philosophical reflection but occurs naturally in each and every one of us. For Schopenhauer the self is not just *regarded* or *considered* in alternative ways but *shows itself*, prereflectively, in this twofold manner and with these two sides. The 'lived' character of the self's two aspects in Schopenhauer marks a crucial difference from the philosophical reflection that goes into drawing the 'critical distinction' between things in themselves and appearances in Kant. While Kant's is a distinction between two ways of philosophically considering the same things,[34] Schopenhauer's is a distinction between two ways of experiencing oneself and, by extension, the world. In standard philosophical terminology, Schopenhauer's dual-aspect account of the self is concerned with the relation between the mental and the physical, and provides an identity theory for their relation: the body is the mind (will) experienced externally, and the mind (will) is the body experienced internally.[35]

V THE PRIMACY OF THE WILL OVER THE INTELLECT

Yet the philosopher's distinction between things in themselves and appearances is not altogether lost in Schopenhauer's dual account of the self as will and body or volition and action. For in addition to the twofold experiential perspective on the self, there is the level of philosophical reflection on this self-experience, which results in the recognition that the two kinds of experience, while phenomenologically distinct, are about one and the same human being. More important, there is the further recognition on the part of the self reflecting upon itself that the two sides or aspects of the self are not of equal rank. The phenomenological dualism of the self as will and body is supplemented by a monistic doctrine regarding the deep structure of the self that underlies the latter's overt division into will and body.

According to Schopenhauer, the reality underlying the dual appearance of the self is not some indeterminate and indeterminable generic stratum; it is none other than the root of one of the two phenomenological constituents of the self, viz., the will. In a move that follows the idealist privileging of the inner or mental over the outer and physical, Schopenhauer traces the duality of will and body to its origin in the will, thereby granting the will primacy over the body. Ultimately, the self is will – will that manifests itself internally as particular acts of will (*Willensakt*) and externally as particular bodily acts (*Aktion des Leibes*). The duality of will and body in the self forms part of a three-tiered structure of will, act of will, and bodily action.

When Schopenhauer sums up the complex relation between our will and our body by maintaining that the two are the same or identical,[36] this points further to the 'ultimate identity' of that which appears (our acts of willing) and that as which it appears (our voluntary bodily acts), with the will as the self's kernel out of which everything else grows and develops. More specifically, Schopenhauer maintains that what underlies our mental and physical existence is the immutable nature of our *individual* will or our *character*, which

informs all of our activity as the underlying force. Schopenhauer here
builds on Kant's notion of the intelligible character of a human being
as the thing in itself underlying all the person's deeds.[37] For Schopenhauer the core of the self or its character constitutes our individuality, as well as our personal identity over time. Moreover, he considers
an individual's character to be established from the beginning ('innate') and unchanging ('constant') and to be known by ourselves as
well as by others only over the course of time ('empirical').[38]

The plural manifestations of the will's unitary character are not
to be regarded as so many effects of an underlying unitary cause or
so many consequents of a given ground. The absolute, non–representational nature of the will's intelligible character eludes the
principle of sufficient reason and any of its ground–consequent relations. Schopenhauer seeks to ban any notion of grounding from
the relation between the thing in itself (the will qua intelligible
character) and its temporal appearances (acts of will available to the
subject's immediate experience) or its spatio-temporal appearances
(overt bodily acts). In his alternative conception of the relation between the will and its manifestations, the latter is the objectivity
(*Objektität*) in general or the specific objectification (*Objektivation*)
of the will.[39] The appearances (acts of will, voluntary bodily motions)
are the thing in itself (will qua intelligible character) *as objectified*,
as rendered object for a subject through the a priori cognitive functions of the intellect. Thus Schopenhauer affirms the constitutive
role of the intellect in the spatiotemporal realization of the will.
Even our own will is not known to us as it is 'in itself' but only as
it appears to us under the intuitional form of the multiple successive states that we undergo internally and observe in their outward
manifestations.[40]

Yet while the necessary correlation between intellect and will in
inner as well as outer experience suggests a radical *equiprimordiality*
between the constitutive poles of the self, Schopenhauer also insists
on the *primacy* of the will over the intellect. The intellect is supposed
to be secondary or derivative, and derived from the will at that. The
details of the subordination of the intellect to the will are part of
Schopenhauer's more comprehensive account of the subordination
of the world of the intellect (world as representation) to the metaphysically conceived will. In that account the ultimate nature of the
human self as will serves Schopenhauer as the key to unlocking the

secret nature of the world as a whole, viz., that – in addition to being of the nature of representation – it is will through and through.[41] The world is here understood on the model of the human self: the role of the intellect in the illumination of the human will is likened to the role of intelligent and rational life forms in providing self-knowledge to the otherwise blind cosmic will.[42] As in the case of the human self, the dual nature of the world–self in Schopenhauer goes together with the primacy of the will over the intellect. The will can be said to bring forth the intellect, initially to better guide the will's blind striving[43] – but with the eventual result that the intellect breaks loose from its origin in the will, first supplanting the tyranny of the will with the free realm of disinterested cognition through artistic production and enjoyment[44] and ultimately attempting the very negation of the will – a self-negation in which the very distinction between self and world collapses.[45]

VI   THE SELF IN THE WORLD

The internal, radically immediate perspective on the essence of the self afforded by the latter's self-experience as will serves a crucial function that further extends the scope of selfhood in Schopenhauer. In turning to the consideration of the external, physical world, as it appears under the causal version of the principle of sufficient reason, Schopenhauer notes the limits of an externalist understanding of the causal relations among empirical objects, including the causal interactions involving one's own body. In particular, he stresses that the externally observed lawful relations between causes and effects disclose nothing about the actual causal nexus involved. No matter how accurate and predictive of the future course of events the knowledge of external causal relations may be, such knowledge remains forever at the surface of things and cannot explain how some cause brings about an effect.[46]

There is only one case, according to Schopenhauer, in which we have deeper insight into the causal connections involved. This is the case of the causation involved in human volition. To be sure, the causality of the will is not a matter of some willing causing some acting. For in the self the willing does not cause the acting but the two are identical, the acting being nothing but the will as viewed externally, mediated through the operations of the understanding or intellect. The causality peculiar to the will concerns not the relation between a given act of willing or volition and the respective acting but the very coming about of the particular volition (along with its bodily manifestation) in the first place. In the case of willing, the causal relation obtains between some cognition functioning as motive or motivational cause and some act of willing together with the corresponding bodily activity as its effect.

Considered from the outside, motivational causation between cognition and willing qua acting is not different from a causal relation that does not involve human volition. In each case, the merely external lawful sequence of causing and effected events leaves the actual generation of the effect entirely unexplained. But, as Schopenhauer points out, one's internal experience of volitional causation is entirely different and outright revelatory about the dynamics of causation. In the process of willing we *feel* the cause qua motive solicit the respective manifestation of our will. We experience internally and immediately the interaction of motive and will: the will is all ability and potential waiting to be called forth and realized through the approach of the motive. What remains a 'secret' or 'mystery'[47] from the external perspective – how the effect comes out of the cause – is disclosed in the inner experience of the self's willing: the causes (motives) do not actually generate the effect but call it forth, bring it out, produce it from the underlying will qua character. The motive as cause merely provides the occasion for the specific manifestation of the will.

In his philosophy of nature Schopenhauer generalizes the occasionalist account of motivational causation by introducing the notion of *force* as the generic term corresponding to the specific role of the will qua character in the willing self. According to Schopenhauer, force is that in nature which manifests itself in predetermined and lawfully governed ways when subject to the influence of corresponding 'occasional causes'.[48] More specifically, Schopenhauer distinguishes three main kinds of forces and associated types of causes: the physicochemical forces of inorganic nature that operate through cause in the narrow sense; the forces of plant life that operate through stimulus; and the forces of animal life, including human life, that function through motivating cognition (motives).[49]

But the self's self-experience as willing provides not only the decisive 'clue'[50] about the generic structure of causation involving occasioning causes and underlying forces. Schopenhauer goes on to claim that the otherwise unknown forces in nature are essentially akin to the human will *as such*, that is, the human will considered in separation from the intellect which always accompanies the will in the dual unity of the human self. The notion of will that is thereby attributed to each and every force in nature is that of sheer drive or striving, without any consciousness and a fortiori without the cognition of some end to strive for.

The radical use of the inner experience of one's own willing to capture the inside or inner essence of the world outside the self may seem to further extend the foundational role that the self plays in the constitution of the world. Previously Schopenhauer had worked out the function of the self qua subject of cognition as the necessary condition for the consciousness of objects of all kinds. Now he might be seen as supplementing or consolidating the centrality of the self in epistemological matters with the self's centrality *in ontologicis*. But the apparent parallelism of cognitive and volitional idealism does not quite hold. Rather than promoting the subject qua will to the status of the world's inner being or essence, Schopenhauer's conception of the 'world as will' in effect demotes the self from the epistemic centrality occupied by the subject of cognition to the complete integration of the subject of willing into the dynamic totality of nature. After all, the specific notion of the will supposedly shared by the human will and the 'will in nature' is that of a force that is essentially 'blind' or operating without consciousness either of itself or of any other object. The cosmic expansion of the self's will leads to the conception of a will without self.

The integration of the self qua will into the world as will also affects the self qua intellect. Schopenhauer shows in great detail how the human intellect, which on his own previous view functioned as the necessary correlate of the world as representation, is entirely part of the world as will as one of the many and varied manifestations of the will in nature. Adopting an explicitly evolutionary perspective, he places the emergence of intelligence in animals at the top of a scale of increasingly complex organization of natural life. More specifically, he notes the appearance of cognition as the medium of causal efficacy in animals; animals are motivated, and their bodies are moved accordingly, under the causal influence of perceiving relevant objects in their environment.[51]

In human animals, cognition and its ensuing volition-cum-motion are no longer limited to the *perception* of actually present objects but can also operate through the mere *conception* of things, by means of thought and its recording in speech and writing, and without those objects being sensorily given. Still, the human perceptual and conceptual abilities have an entirely natural origin and serve the biological purpose of providing a highly complex organism with the detailed grasp of the environment required for the maintenance of its life. Accordingly, the human cognitive abilities, including the exclusively human ability of conceptual thought, are best suited to practical, that is, biological tasks and ill-equipped for the merely theoretical usage, including the philosophical one, to which those abilities have eventually and occasionally been put in the history of the human animal.[52]

Schopenhauer's naturalization of the human self, especially the unprecedented frankness with which he discusses the sexual manifestations of the will,[53] have been compared to other major displacements of the human being from the central position in the universe that it was thought to occupy, such as its astronomical decentralization through the work of Copernicus.[54] But within the overall account of the self in Schopenhauer, the integration of the human will into the cosmic will and the subordination of the self to the world as will is neither the starting point nor the end point of the inquiry.

Still, even limiting the scope of the naturalized self in Schopenhauer to that of a phase or moment in a more comprehensive account leaves open the question of how the self qua intellect can be both the a priori condition of the world and part of the world as one of its evolutionary products. There seems to be a vicious circle here: the world rests on the self qua intellect, and the intellect in turn rests on the world. The circle seems especially problematic for the relation between the self's intellect and the self's own worldly part or aspect, viz., the body: the intellect conditions the body and the body conditions the intellect. Pointing out that the world is regarded differently in each case – once as world of representation, once as world of will – will not suffice. Either of those worlds is supposed to involve the intellect, in one case as the world's ultimate condition, in the other case as one of its entities. It is not the duality of worlds that creates the circle but the dual occurrence of the same intellect in regard to both worlds.

The apparent circularity between self and world in Schopenhauer has long been noted and has typically been attributed to Schopenhauer's oscillating between a post-Kantian transcendental idealism and a materialist realism.[55] Yet the alleged materialism in Schopenhauer's account of the world and the self as will does not hold up to closer scrutiny. Schopenhauer clearly distances himself from a materialist explanation of world and self and traces apparently independently existing physical objects to the will, which he considers 'something spirit-like' or 'mind-like' (ein Geistiges).[56] There is a close structural similarity between the cognitivist reduction of the world as representation to the intellect and the conative reduction of the world as will to some originally arational mind or spirit. In both cases, what appears to exist on its own (world) is shown to exist only in relation to something that is first and foremost given as or in some subject (intellect and will, respectively). Moreover, both basic forms of subjectivity and the corresponding worlds have a common origin in the absolute reality of the will itself.

The apparent problem of the circle between the intellect conditioning the world, including the body, and the world, including the body, conditioning the intellect can be solved by recognizing that the body and the intellect each are to be taken in two senses and can therefore pertain differently to each of the two worlds: the body that conditions the intellect pertains to the world as will, which as such is not subject to representation and its forms, while the body that is conditioned by the intellect belongs to the world as representation. Analogously, the intellect as manifestation of the will belongs to a reality outside and independent of the order of representation, while the intellect objectively considered, as brain, belongs to the world as representation.[57] To be sure, the identity of the self amidst the twofold occurrence of its intellect as well as body remains unexplained in Schopenhauer. It is considered an inexplicable basic fact.

VII   THE SELF BY ITSELF

The dual membership of the intellect in the world as representation (as physical object) and the world as will (as metaphysical force) is rendered more complex yet by the role that the intellect plays in the possible gradual emancipation of the self from the world, from the will, and from itself. In addition to arguing for the dependence

of the world as representation on the self qua intellect and the em-
beddedness of the self qua will in the world as will, Schopenhauer
seeks to demonstrate the potential for an altogether different form
of selfhood, one that would disengage the self qua intellect from the
subservience to the will, including the self's own will. The portrayal
of the emancipation of the self from the primacy of the will does
not take back Schopenhauer's own earlier account of the self but
enlarges the picture of the self to include forms of consciousness
and self-consciousness that have been neglected in the focus maintained so far on the cognition of nature and the nature of cognition.
Moreover, the extension of Schopenhauer's thinking about the self
does not simply add further features to an already established body
of knowledge but significantly alters the overall assessment of the
self by providing a unifying perspective on the relation of intellect
and will in the self.

Schopenhauer distinguishes two basic ways in which the self can
undergo – and to some extent even actively bring about – a radical
alteration both in its internal composition and in its external relation to the world. The first kind of alteration concerns the role of the
self as intellect in the world as representation; the second kind involves the relation of the self as will to the world as will. According
to Schopenhauer, the altered intellect comes into play in the self's
aesthetic attitude to the world, while the altered will comes to the
fore in the *ethical* outlook of the self.

In addition to the intellect's ordinary relation to individual objects, which are distinguished from each other and related to each
other according to the principle of sufficient reason, Schopenhauer
countenances an extraordinary relation or correlation between subject and object independent of the principle of sufficient reason.[58]
The relation in question is extraordinary in that, with the falling
away of individuality and hence the lack of ground–consequent relations between individual objects, both the subject and the object
become disengaged from the will-dominated interconnectedness of
the world. Schopenhauer likens the preindividual, isolated, 'eternal'
object or objects to the 'Forms' (*Ideen*) in Plato. The Forms or Ideas
are the unchanging forces, laws, and structures that govern the myriad individual manifestations of the will. Like the will itself (the
thing in itself), the Ideas are beyond the scope of the principle of sufficient reason and hence outside of time, space, and causality. Yet

unlike the will itself and as such, the Ideas are plural and possible objects of cognition. The Ideas are the preindividual 'immediate objectivity of the will,'[59] to be distinguished from all other objects as the will's mediated and individualized objectivity.

In Schopenhauer, though, unlike in Plato, the Ideas are not independently existing beings. They emanate, in a manner reminiscent of the neo-Platonic adaptation of Plato, from the ultimate reality. Moreover – and this makes them comparable to 'ideas' (with a small 'i') or representations in the modern sense – they are possible or actual objects of cognition for a human intellect. More precisely, the necessary correlate of the pre- or *praeter*-individual objects (Ideas) is an equally non-individual subject, the 'pure subject of cognition'. On Schopenhauer's account, the required purity of the self qua intellect is achieved and maintained by the subject of cognition temporarily disengaging itself from the subject of willing and its outward manifestation, the body. In the contemplation of Ideas, for Schopenhauer, the exclusive focus on those special objects eclipses anything else: with respect to the world, it eclipses any other object; with regard to the self, it eclipses the latter's existence as individuated will.

Schopenhauer locates the exclusive presence of Ideas to the intellect and the associated out-of-world experience of the self in the blissful states of ultimate concentration on one thing – and utter forgetfulness about anything else – that mark the production and reception of art.[60] The focus here is not on the work of art as a material object but on art as the vehicle of Ideas. In aesthetic activity, be it of the contemplative or the productive sort, the self as subject of cognition loses track of everything else, the world as much as its own other self, which is inwardly its own will and outwardly its own body. Further, it could be said that the aesthetic self is lost in the contemplation of the Ideas to the point of forgetting itself entirely, of forgetting that it is a self and vanishing in the object contemplated – like the legendary Chinese artist who completed his painting by stepping into it and vanishing.

Schopenhauer acknowledges that any such aesthetic transport is only temporary and in fact short-lived. Yet the experience, more precisely its very possibility, reveals the radical heterogeneity of intellect and will in the self. The aesthetic dissociation of the intellect from the will, of the self from the world, and of the self from itself points to a conception of selfhood independent of the will. For Schopenhauer a more complete and possibly lasting emancipation from the will inside the self and outside of it is to be sought in the ethical sphere. In the latter, the will is not just temporarily bracketed, disregarded, or 'forgotten' by the intellect, as it is *in aestheticis*, but 'negated' (*verneint*). As the choice of a term from logic suggests, the suspension of the will is a result of some cognition or intellectual realization. In fact, Schopenhauer groups the *negation* of the will together with the latter's *affirmation* as the two basic responses of the will attaining self-knowledge.[61]

In a colossal anthropo-cosmic analogy, Schopenhauer interprets the evolutionary occurrence of consciousness in animals as a process in which the will, that originally blind drive, gradually adds awareness and cognition to its myriad other manifestations. The process culminates in the advent of conceptual cognition and self-consciousness in the human animal, specifically in the latter's eventual or occasional realization that the world is in essence will.[62] The subject or bearer of the will's self-knowledge *as will* is in each case a human individual. But the very point of the individual self's recognition of the world as will and representation is the insight that any individual, including oneself, is only a fleeting appearance of the eternal will. Technically put, the individual self recognizes that individuation pertains only to the manifestations of the will and not to the latter itself and as such.

One possible response to the 'philosophical cognition of the essence of the world'[63] is the self's *affirmation* of the will: the human individual accepts, even embraces, the ultimate reality of the will and rests assured in the realization 'that he himself is that will of which the whole world is the objectification or copy'.[64] But further insight reached either through continued reflection or through personal experience reveals to the self that the will is never satisfied, remains forever striving, and is therefore essentially bound up with the feeling of lack, that is, suffering.[65] In particular, the self, recognizing its ultimate identity – as will – with everyone and everything else, overcomes the egoistic fixation on its own individuality. The recognition 'that our true self exists not only in our own person ... but in everything that lives'[66] may lead first to the pursuit of justice and eventually to the altruistic ethics of Christian love (*caritas*, *agape*) or pity (*Mitleid*),[67] in which the suffering of others is regarded as one's own.

The possible end result of this process of the self's recognition of itself in all others is the *negation* of the will, initially of the self's own will and by extension of the will altogether, as evidenced in the religious practices of asceticism (*Askese*) and resignation (*Entsagung*).[68] Schopenhauer argues for the – admittedly paradoxical, if not outright contradictory – possibility that the will in one of its manifestations, as cognition, turns against itself. In addition to providing the motives that engage the will, cognition may, in rare cases, provide disincentives of a radical sort, which do not merely steer the will of the self away from this or that course of action but render it altogether unmoved, immobile, or quiet. The philosophical cognition or personal experience of the will's and its world's essential suffering can be such a 'quietive' (*Quietiv*),[69] through which the will indirectly suspends itself.

At the level of the individual self, the 'mortification of the will'[70] is said to result in a state of bliss in which 'only cognition remains, the will has disappeared.'[71] But nothing further can be ascertained about the consciousness and cognition had by the will-less self, which 'no longer has the form of subject and object.'[72] Analogously, the repercussions that the pacifying revolt of the intellect has on the will at large remain hard to grasp. Schopenhauer maintains that the self-negation upon self-recognition of the will includes the negation of representation and its world as well: 'no will: no representation, no world'.[73] That still leaves open the possibility of the will's continued existence outside and independent of its manifestation as world or to us. But then again, such a will without world would also be a will without self.

With its culmination in a worldless and selfless self and a will that wills its own ending, Schopenhauer's sustained reflection on the self offers a dramatic counterpart to the 'history of self-consciousness' and the 'phenomenology of mind' developed by his immediate predecessors, Fichte, Schelling, and Hegel. In a manner reminiscent of the musical practice of parody, in which an earlier composition is fitted with an entirely different text, often switching from the secular to the religious or vice versa, Schopenhauer has taken the key ingredients of the idealist accounts of self-realization through insight and action and fitted them with a reverse story line – of self-absorption, even self-loss, of the horrors of self-recognition and of the bliss of self-dissolution. But to a trained ear, it still sounds like German idealism – turned world-weary and unselfish.

NOTES

1 References to Schopenhauer's works are standard, except that *FW* refers to the following edition: *Prize Essay on the Freedom of the Will*, ed. Günter Zöller and trans. Eric F. J. Payne (Cambridge: Cambridge University Press, 1999). References to Kant's *Critique of Pure Reason* are to the original pagination of the work's first and second editions (A and B, respectively), which is indicated in most editions of the *Critique*, including the English translations by Norman Kemp Smith (New York: St. Martin's Press, 1965), Werner Pluhar (Indianapolis and Cambridge, Mass.: Hackett, 1996), and Paul Guyer and Allen Wood (Cambridge: Cambridge University Press, 1998). All other references to Kant's works employ the pagination of the Academy edition, *Kant's gesammelte Schriften*, ed. Royal Prussian Academy of Sciences and its successors (Berlin, later Berlin and New York: Reimer, later de Gruyter, 1900ff.), which is indicated in the recent translations of Kant's works.
2 For a recent survey of thinking about the self in German philosophy around 1800, see *Figuring the Self: Subject, Individual, and Others in Classical German Philosophy*, ed. David Klemm and Günter Zöller (Albany: State University of New York Press, 1997).
3 See W1 xii, 257, 272, 286, 408/H. 2, vii, 303, 320, 337, 483. Payne is not consistent in his rendering of the German phrase employed by Schopenhauer in these passages, which involves the attribute use of the indefinite article (*ein*) as numeral for a singular. Rudolf Malter has identified Schopenhauer's 'single thought' as the thought that the world is the self-knowledge of the will (*Der Eine Gedanke. Hinführung zur Philosophie Arthur Schopenhauers* [Darmstadt: Wissenschaftliche Buchgesellschaft, 1988]).
4 Two earlier detailed discussions of the self in Schopenhauer are Christopher Janaway, *Self and World in Schopenhauer's Philosophy* (Oxford: Clarendon Press, 1989), and Peter Welsen, *Schopenhauers Theorie des Subjekts: Ihre transzendentalphilosophischen, anthropologischen und naturmetaphysischen Grundlagen* (Würzburg: Königshausen und Neumann, 1995). Janaway's sympathetic reading demonstrates the relevance of Schopenhauer for today's English-speaking philosopher. Welsen argues for the inconsistency of Schopenhauer's account of the self, which

he assesses solely on the basis of Schopenhauer's epistemology and philosophy of nature.

5 *Critique of Pure Reason*, B XXVIII.

6 On Kant's theory of objective reference, see my *Theoretische Gegenstandsbeziehung bei Kant. Zur systematischen Bedeutung der Termini 'objective Realität' und 'objective Gültigkeit' in der 'Kritik der reinen Vernunft'* (Berlin and New York: de Gruyter, 1984).

7 See *Critique of Pure Reason*, A 369ff.

8 See Kant's definition of 'transcendental' in *Critique of Pure Reason*, A 12/B 25; Prolegomena, *Academy edition*, IV, 373 note. For a critical overview of recent work on Kant's 'third self,' see my 'Main Developments in Recent Scholarship on the *Critique of Pure Reason,' Philosophy and Phenomenological Research*, 52 (1993), 445–66.

9 For support of such a phenomenalist reading in Kant, see *Critique of Pure Reason*, A 370–1 and B 518–19/A 490–1.

10 For a classic metaphysical interpretation of Schopenhauer, see Johannes Volkelt, *Arthur Schopenhauer. Seine Persönlichkeit, seine Lehre, sein Glaube* (Stuttgart: Fr. Frommann, 1900).

11 For Kant's post-Critical project of a practical-dogmatic metaphysics of postulates, see *Preisschrift über die Fortschritte der Metaphysik*, in Academy edition, vol. 20; English translation as *What Real Progress Has Metaphysics Made in Germany since the Times of Leibniz and Wolff?* tr. T. Humphrey (New York: Abaris Books, 1983). On Kant as a metaphysician, see Max Wundt, *Kant als Metaphysiker. Ein Beitrag zur Geschichte der deutschen Philosophie im 18. Jahrhundert* (Stuttgart: Ferdinand Enke, 1924).

12 For a sustained reading of Schopenhauer as a post-Kantian transcendental philosopher, see Rudolf Malter, *Arthur Schopenhauer. Transzendentalphilosophie und Metaphysik des Willens. Quaestiones. Themen und Gestalten 2* (Stuttgart-Bad Canstatt: Frommann-Holzboog, 1991). See also my discussion of Malter's interpretation of Schopenhauer in 'Schopenhauer and the Problem of Metaphysics. Critical Reflections on Rudolf Malter's Interpretation,' *Man and Word* 28 (1995), 1–10.

13 On Schopenhauer's conception of philosophy as immanent metaphysics or non-empirical theory of experience, see *W2* 182–3, 640/H. 3, 202–3, 736.

14 On the distinction between intellect and will, see *FR* 207–20/H. 1, 140–9.

15 Schopenhauer concedes the role of reason in deliberative action but rejects the motivational role of reason as such. See *W1* 84/H. 2, 100.

16 See *W1* 6ff./H. 2, 7ff.

17 On the role of the understanding in intuition, see *W1* 19–20/H. 2, 22–3. A possible source of Schopenhauer's theory of the intellectuality

of intuition is Fichte's account of cognition in the Second Book of *The Vocation of Man* (1800).

18 See *W1* 20–1/H. 2, 24–5.

19 See *Critique of Judgment*, Academy edition, V, 167–70.

20 See *FR* 211/H. 1, 143.

21 See *FR* 207/H. 1, 140. Payne renders *Subjekt des Erkennens* as 'subject of knowledge'. Schopenhauer also calls the subject of cognition 'the representing I' (*das vorstellende Ich*); Payne translates this phrase as 'the ego that represents' (*FR* 208/H. 1, 141), marking a contrast to the represented I or the I as object. In general, Schopenhauer restricts the use of the term 'I' to the intellectualist function of self.

22 See *W1* 5/H. 2, 5.

23 *FR* 207/H.1, 140.

24 See *W2* 209/H. 3, 233.

25 On the main results of Schopenhauer's treatment of the principle of sufficient reason, see *FR* 221–36/H.1, 150–60.

26 See *FR* 42–3, 208–9/H. 1, 27, 141–2.

27 See *FR* 211–12/H. 1, 143.

28 The thought that the subject and the object of the self-relation are identical goes back to Kant and Fichte. See Kant, *Critique of Pure Reason*, B 155–6, and J. G. Fichte, *The System of Ethics*, Introduction.

29 *FR* 211–12; *W1* 102,251; *W2* 203/H. 1,143; H. 2, 121, 296; H. 3, 226.

30 *FR* 211/H. 1, 143.

31 The human will is not totally independent of the intellect and its forms in that the affections of the will occur successively and are ordered in time.

32 See *W1* 5/H.2, 5–6.

33 See *W1* 100; *W2* 247–8/H. 2, 119; H. 3, 280. Schopenhauer's identity thesis regarding the mind–body relation bears a striking resemblance to the account provided by Fichte in the second chapter of *The System of Ethics*. For the main features of Fichte's theory, see my *Fichte's Transcendental Philosophy: The Original Duplicity of Intelligence and Will* (Cambridge: Cambridge University Press, 1998), 63–7.

34 See *Critique of Pure Reason*, B XVIIIf. note. For a sustained reading of Kant's distinction between things in themselves and appearances as involving different ways of considering the same things, see Gerold Prauss, *Kant und das Problem der Dinge an sich* (Bonn: Bouvier, 1974), and Henry E. Allison, *Kant's Transcendental Idealism: A Defense* (New Haven, Conn., and London: Yale University Press, 1983).

35 For a closer examination of Schopenhauer's relation to the philosophy of mind and action theory, see Janaway, *Self and World in Schopenhauer's Philosophy*, 208–29.

36 See *W1* 101/H. 2, 121.

37 See *Critique of Pure Reason*, A 538/B 566–A 557/B 585.

38 On the four essential traits of the human character, See *W1* 155–9; *FW* 42–6/H. 2, 185–9; H. 4, 48–53. See also John Atwell, *Schopenhauer: The Human Character* (Philadelphia: Temple University Press, 1990), and my editor's introduction to Schopenhauer, *Prize Essay on the Freedom of the Will*, xx–xxiii.

39 See *W1* 108; *W2* 245/H. 2, 128; H. 3, 277. On the difference between *Objektität* and *Objektivität* in Schopenhauer, see Gustav Friedrich Wagner, *Schopenhauer-Register*, ed. Arthur Hübscher, 2nd enlarged ed. (Stuttgart-Bad Cannstatt: Frommann-Holzboog, 1982), 465 note.

40 See *FW* 43–4/H. 4, 49–50.

41 See *W1* 109/H. 2, 130.

42 See *W1* 410; *W2* 259/H. 2, 485; H. 3, 294. For a detailed treatment of the analogy between the character of the world and the character of the self, see John Atwell, *Schopenhauer on the Character of the World: The Metaphysics of Will* (Berkeley: University of California Press, 1995).

43 See *W1* 149–50/H. 2, 178–9.

44 This is the main contribution of the Third Book of Volume One of the main work (*W1* 167ff./H. 2, 197ff.).

45 This is the main point of the Fourth Book of Volume One of the main work (*W1* 269ff./H. 2, 317ff.).

46 See *W1* 120–2/H. 2, 144–5.

47 *FR* 213; *W1* 125/H. 1, 144; H. 2, 149.

48 See *W1* 137–8/H. 2, 163–5, where Schopenhauer refers explicitly to Malebranche's doctrine of *causes occasionelles*.

49 See *W1* 114–17; *FW* 25–32/H. 2, 135–40; H. 4, 29–36.

50 *W2* 274/H. 3, 309.

51 See *W1* 150–2; *WN* 59–61, 75–84/H. 2, 178–82; H. 4, 48–51, 69–79.

52 See *W2* 272–92/H. 3, 307–31.

53 See *W2* 531–67/H. 3, 607–51.

54 See Volker Spierling, 'Die Drehwende der Moderne. Schopenhauer zwischen Skeptizismus und Dogmatismus,' in *Materialien zu Schopenhauers 'Die Welt als Wille und Vorstellung,'* ed. Volker Spierling (Frankfurt/Main: Suhrkamp, 1984), 14–83, esp. 14–30.

55 For a representative selection of essays on the 'problem of materialism' (*Materialismusproblem*) in Schopenhauer, see Spierling (ed.), *Materialien zu Schopenhauers 'Die Welt als Wille und Vorstellung,'* 341–92.

56 *WN* 35–6/H. 4, 20 (translation modified). See also *WN* 21/H. 4, 4.

57 See *W2* 259, 276/H. 3, 294, 312. This solution strongly resembles Kant's solution to the problem of the circle between freedom and morality by means of the dual citizenship of the moral subject in the world of

appearances and the world of things in themselves in section three of *Foundations of the Metaphysics of Morals*, Academy edition, IV, 450, 453.

58 See the title of Book Three of the first volume of *The World as Will and Representation*: 'The Representation Independent of the Principle of Sufficient Reason ...' (*W1* 167/H. 2, 197).

59 *W1* 170/H. 2, 201.

60 On the systematic status of the aesthetic in Schopenhauer, see Barbara Neymeyr, *Ästhetische Autonomie als Abnormität: Kritische Analysen zu Schopenhauers Ästhetik im Horizont seiner Willensmetaphysik* (Berlin: de Gruyter, 1996); see also my review of the work in *Journal of the History of Philosophy* 36 (1998), 458–9.

61 See the title of Book Four of the first volume of *The World as Will and Representation*: 'With the Attainment of Self-Knowledge, Affirmation and Denial of the Will-to-Live' (*W1* 269/H. 2, 317).

62 See *W1* 287–8/H. 2, 339.

63 *W1* 283/H. 2, 334 (translation modified).

64 *W1* 284/H. 2, 335.

65 See *W1* 310/H. 2, 366.

66 *W1* 373/H. 2, 441.

67 See *W1* 374/H. 2, 443.

68 See *W1* 327–8/H. 2, 386. Payne translates *Entsagung* as 'renunciation'.

69 *W1* 379/H. 2, 448. Payne translates *Quietiv* as 'quieter'.

70 *W1* 388/H. 2, 459.

71 *W1* 411/H. 2, 486 (translation modified).

72 *W1* 410/H. 2, 485.

73 *W1* 411/H. 2, 486.

2   Schopenhauer and Knowledge

It is one of the paradoxes of Schopenhauer's philosophy, but one which is perhaps not sufficiently remarked on, that while the idea of knowledge seems central to that philosophy and crucial at various points for its interpretation, Schopenhauer himself says very little about it. Yet his starting point in *On the Fourfold Root of the Principle of Sufficient Reason* is the idea of a knowing consciousness, and the conclusion of his main work, *The World as Will and Representation*, brings in the conception of a form of salvation, a freedom from the ravages of the will, which is mediated by knowledge. It is not that Schopenhauer says nothing about knowledge. He claims, for example, that perception provides the basic form of direct knowledge of objects, and as the philosophical system develops, other forms of direct knowledge are introduced. By contrast, abstract knowledge, the only real form of knowledge proper (*Wissen*, as opposed to *Erkenntnis*, which is the general term for knowledge, including knowledge of objects), requires, as Aristotle also demanded, seeing why whatever is known is so, so that there is reference to a ground or reason for the truth in question. The notion of a ground or reason has a crucial role to play in Schopenhauer's conception of things. Indeed, the *Fourfold Root* is based on that idea, maintaining that all representations, as objects for a knowing consciousness, must stand in a lawlike relation which is determinable a priori, the only additional question being what that relation is for different (indeed four and only four different) kinds of object. As far as representations are concerned (and I shall leave that notion unexamined for the time being), knowledge of such objects is thus conditional upon their standing in such a relation. But that is not to say that knowledge of such objects entails *seeing* what their ground is. The direct knowledge of representations as objects is certainly conditional upon those objects standing in law-like relations, but it is not the same as abstract knowledge and does not depend upon seeing what the lawlike relations are.

In effect, this distinction between direct and abstract knowledge is the only contribution that Schopenhauer makes to the discussion of the issue which has so dominated recent epistemological concerns – the nature of knowledge. He is content in general to see knowledge as involving simply a relationship between a so-called knowing con-sciousness and an object, a relationship between subject and object, without much concern for the question of exactly what that relation-ship is. It may be that Schopenhauer is, in this respect, not out of line with the other philosophers of his time, but given all the discussions of the nature of knowledge that have taken place since that time, the fact has to be noted. It has two consequences. First, Schopen-hauer seems to assume that knowledge entails consciousness, so that, whether or not he recognises the fact, the idea of any form of unconscious knowledge seems thereby ruled out (though it has to be admitted that the fact that something is a knowing consciousness does not by itself entail that all of its forms of knowledge are con-scious). Second, apart from the question of whether the knowledge is direct or abstract, the only differences recognised between kinds of knowledge arise from differences between the kinds of object of knowledge involved.

There are, as I shall indicate in more detail later, four kinds of object of knowledge. These are (1) ordinary representations (ordinary deliverances of consciousness), (2) will, (3) Ideas (which have the na-ture of Platonic Forms), and (4) whatever is the object of the knowl-edge which can provide salvation from the will by seeing through what Schopenhauer calls the principle of individuation to an accep-tance of that will as the one underlying reality. Schopenhauer deals with these four kinds of object in successive sections of *The World as Will and Representation*. The form of knowledge adduced in the final section, discussion of which stems from his account of ethics, is, as we shall see, dubiously to be described as knowledge of an object, although it does depend upon knowledge of an object – the underly-ing will. On the other hand, the first two objects of knowledge, ordi-nary representations and will (initially in the ordinary human sense), have to be sharply distinguished by Schopenhauer if there is to be any hope of showing that the will is the thing-in-itself and beyond

representation. That is why it is important for him that knowledge
of perceptual representations is conditional, while knowledge of will
is unconditional.

However, given what I said earlier, the distinction between conditional and unconditional knowledge of objects, which is, in the way
indicated, central to an adequate interpretation of Schopenhauer's
philosophy, cannot be a distinction between forms of knowledge
with different natures; it is, rather, a distinction between the circumstances in which something can be an object of knowledge, and
that in turn depends solely on the kind of object involved. Some objects amount to objects of knowledge only when they are subject to
conditions, when, for example, as must be the case with representations, they occur in lawlike structures. Other objects can be objects
of knowledge without the satisfaction of such conditions, and in the
case of certain objects – for example, the will – this not only can be
so, it must be so, and it is this fact that makes the knowledge in question unconditional. (In the following discussion, I shall continue to
speak of conditional and unconditional knowledge, but it must be
remembered that the sense in which knowledge can be one or the
other is a function of the objects involved, and not, as one might put
it, one which turns on features of knowledge as a state. I shall return a little later to the fact which in the context of Schopenhauer's
philosophy explains, if not justifies, this.)

In the *Fourfold Root* (*FR* 41–2/H. 1, 27) Schopenhauer asserts that
'to be object for the subject, and to be our representation ... are the
same thing' and adds that 'All our representations are objects of the
subject, and all objects of the subject are our representations.' But
as the system develops, this does not seem to be strictly true. There
seem to be objects of knowledge which are not representations. Indeed, since all knowledge of representations is conditional in that
representations as objects of knowledge must stand to each other
in one of four different relations, it follows that any unconditional
knowledge must have as its object something other than representations. Indeed, that point has a cardinal importance for the argument
that identifies the will with the thing-in-itself, given that we have
unconditional knowledge of our intentional (and so willed) action.
It does not, of course, follow from this that there is not conditional
knowledge of other objects apart from representations. The claim in
the statement of the fourfold root that the only objects of knowledge

are representations does, of course, rule out that possibility, but if, as I have said, it does turn out as the system develops that there *are* other objects of knowledge, it may be thought that there may be other examples of conditional knowledge. If there are, they do not figure in Schopenhauer's philosophy.

On the other hand, what I have quoted Schopenhauer as saying about representations turns out not to be strictly true either. The term which is now conventionally, though perhaps misleadingly, translated as 'representation' is *Vorstellung*. Schopenhauer inherited the notion that the term expresses from Kant, and it was generally accepted in German philosophy of the period, just as ideas and impressions were the accepted building blocks of British Empiricism, in accordance with the so-called way of ideas introduced by Descartes. *Vorstellungen* are simply presentations to consciousness, and that is why they constitute objects of direct knowledge. How could knowledge of such things be other than direct? But when Schopenhauer asserts in the *Fourfold Root* that all representations must stand in lawlike relations and thus be subject to one or another version of the principle of sufficient reason, he has in mind as representations fairly straightforward objects of consciousness – perceptions, concepts, mathematical entities, and our own actions. Yet when at the end of the second book of his main work he introduces, more problematically, the Ideas, construed as Platonic Forms, and when in the third book he brings these to bear on the nature of art, he is quite clear, first that these too are representations, and second that they are independent of the principle of sufficient reason. So we have here a form of knowledge of objects which is both concerned with representations and thus direct and, unlike the knowledge of perceptual representations, unconditional in that the objects stand by themselves at least to the extent that they do not demand an application of the principle of sufficient reason. This requires further comment, and I shall return to the issue later.

A further consideration that must be remarked upon here is the one that to some extent explains, if not justifies, the point, already noted, that the conditionality of knowledge depends on that of its objects. This is that there is an implicit idealism in the suggestion (made clear in the statement of the fourfold root) that all objects of the subject are representations. It is clear that Schopenhauer thought that idealism was an obviously correct view and one that hardly needed argument. He asserts this at the beginning of the second volume of his main work under the headings of 'No object without a subject' and 'No subject without an object' (though the latter is less obviously relevant to idealism than the former). If the commitment to idealism is not seen, it will be less obvious why Schopenhauer thinks that knowledge of ordinary representations is conditional. For if objects were other than representations, it would not be clear why the fact, if it is one, that all objects must stand in lawlike relations entails that knowledge of them is conditional. For is not the claim about the necessary application of the principle of sufficient reason to representations a claim about *objects* and not one about knowledge of them? But if there is no object without a subject and if objects are necessarily presented to consciousness as objects of direct knowledge, the status of objects cannot be independent of the status of knowledge of them. In the heading to the third book, Schopenhauer makes it clear that Ideas are representations, so that if they are independent of the principle of sufficient reason, and if to that extent at least they stand by themselves, so to speak, it is understandable that knowledge of them can be said to be unconditional; for the objects of that knowledge are not subject to conditions.

On the other hand, it is also clear that to say that knowledge of an object is direct does not imply anything about the conditional or unconditional status of that knowledge. Direct knowledge of perceptual representations, for example, is conditional, but direct knowledge of the representations which constitute Ideas is unconditional. Nevertheless, and finally, if there is direct knowledge of anything which is not a representation, nothing really follows, as I have already said, from anything that Schopenhauer says about the unconditionality of such knowledge, though it is clear that he does in fact think that such knowledge must be unconditional. I have argued elsewhere[1] that Schopenhauer's argument for the identification of the thing-in-itself with the will is weak to the extent that he shows only that the unconditional nature of knowledge of will in action implies that our consciousness of will in action cannot amount to consciousness of a representation. It does not show what the status of the object is in fact. I would now add as well that the fact that the direct knowledge of will in action is not knowledge of a representation does not by itself show that the knowledge is unconditional, only that it is not conditional in the way that knowledge of ordinary representations is in their being subject to the principle of sufficient reason.

So far, I have been concerned with the distinctions between direct and abstract knowledge and between conditional and unconditional knowledge of objects. Schopenhauer also makes play with a distinction between immediate and non-immediate knowledge, a distinction which on the face of it has more to do with the character of the knowledge itself than with that of the object. He relies upon the idea that knowledge of willing is immediate to show that the will is unlike ordinary representations in being unconditional. I shall discuss that crucial move later in connection with the will as an object of knowledge. At present it may be useful to note one or two points about the relation between this distinction and those already discussed, although I shall leave until later a more adequate attempt to make clear what immediacy involves.

Schopenhauer is clear that it does not follow from the fact that knowledge of an object is direct that it is also immediate. Does it follow from the fact that an object of knowledge is conditional, as ordinary representations are, that the knowledge is not immediate? Perhaps it does in that the object is not presented to the mind by itself but only in a nexus of relations. Moreover, Schopenhauer thinks that it is the work of the understanding to make those relations clear. As opposed to Kant, who saw the function of the understanding as that of bringing intuitions under concepts in judgment, Schopenhauer sees all that as the work of reason. Indeed, he says in one place (W1 38–9/H. 2, 46) that the one function of the understanding is to provide immediate knowledge of the relation of cause and effect. To speak of that knowledge as immediate is perhaps confusing in that it suggests another candidate for immediate knowledge apart from the knowledge of willing, which he elsewhere (W2 196/H. 3, 219) says is the one case of immediate knowledge. But presumably knowledge of the relation between cause and effect is not knowledge of an *object*, as knowledge of representations and knowledge of the will are, respectively. What sort of knowledge it is is not clear, but since knowledge of the cause of something is knowledge of the reason why that something occurs, it is tempting and perhaps right to view this knowledge as a form of abstract knowledge. However that may be, it seems clear that for Schopenhauer the fact that an object cannot exist by itself, as is the case with ordinary representations, is enough to make knowledge of it non-immediate. (I leave out of account here the problems which arise over sensations, which Schopenhauer distinguishes from perception, but which he sometimes characterizes as representations, and equally sometimes speaks of as having an immediate presence to the mind, as the representations of perception do not. Schopenhauer is to be praised for recognizing a distinction between sensation and perception, but he is less good than Thomas Reid, whom he approved of in this connection, in working out the consequences of it.)

As I indicated earlier, there are in his system four kinds of objects of direct knowledge. I shall discuss them in turn and consider how they stand in relation to immediacy and unconditionality. Whether the knowledge in question is different for each kind of object is a matter which I shall also consider in the course of things; but since the knowledge is in each case direct, it appears that it always amounts to a kind of intuition, a seeing of something as so. (*Anschauung*, the word which is translated as intuition in Kant's case, sometimes tends to be translated as 'perception' in the case of Schopenhauer; this is fair enough to the extent that it brings out what is involved in perceptual representations, though it can introduce oddities in other contexts. It remains true that where knowledge is direct in Schopenhauer's philosophy, that knowledge does amount to a form of intuition, whatever other differences obtain.) The four cases are as follows:

(1) There are ordinary representations (representations which are either perceptual or derived from those in some way), and it is of perceptual representations which, given Schopenhauer's idealism, the world of appearance is made up. While knowledge of all such representations is direct, it is also conditional in that its objects must, as the *Fourfold Root* makes clear, stand in one or another lawlike connection; those objects cannot stand by themselves. Hence, in having a given representation, we have knowledge of it as such only if it does stand in the requisite relation, and in the case of perceptual representations in particular only if it stands in a relation of cause and effect. Schopenhauer regards the understanding, as we have seen, as that which takes one from effect to cause in this way; unlike what was the case with Kant, for whom the job of the understanding is to make judgment possible, Schopenhauer thinks of it merely as a

means for taking one from one intuition to another, and it is less than clear how this is supposed to work. Nevertheless, unless there are the means and possibility of this happening, there could not be the form of direct, but non-immediate, knowledge that perceptual intuition is said to involve. So the knowledge in question is conditional, not in the sense that there are conditions, such as things about the person in question or in his brain, which have to be satisfied, but only in the sense that the object of knowledge cannot stand by itself. This might be thought a somewhat odd sense in which to speak of conditions of knowledge, as I have remarked before, but it must be understood that for Schopenhauer there are no objects without a subject, so that what holds good for representations as objects equally affects that subject's knowledge of them. The effect of the idealism is to link the ontology closely (too closely, one might think) to the epistemology. Nevertheless, Schopenhauer does not think, as we shall see he does think with respect to the Ideas, that in having a perceptual representation, for example, the subject is simply a knower or in any way identical with the object. Our having perceptual representations is subject to the causal processes which take place in the body and brain and to the processes in the world (all, in turn, a matter of representation, of course).

(2) There is the will, which manifests itself primarily in intentional bodily action – what Schopenhauer calls its 'objectification' or 'objectivity'. Because, as far as we human beings are concerned, exercises of will are evident in this way only in bodily action, there are problems, to which Schopenhauer is to a large extent sensitive, about the form which consciousness of agency has. For bodily movement, and thus bodily action, by the very fact that it involves the body, brings in representations which are subject to the conditions noted in the previous section. For this reason Schopenhauer does say that an act of will 'is only the nearest and clearest *phenomenon* of the thing-in-itself' (*W*2 197/H. 3, 221), the thing-in-itself being identified in the course of his argument with the will. A further and connected point is that intentional actions of this kind are by reason of their bodily objectification subject to motives as conditions, motives being, he says, causes seen from within, so that when a bodily movement is a case of action, what the agent sees as motives others may see as causes. Despite this complication, the will itself is not subject to conditions and is the only thing that is not. The

question arises, however, how Schopenhauer knows this to be the case. Given that our awareness of our agency is not like that of anything else (it is not a matter of any kind of observation), and that it is direct, though not as knowledge of representations is because it is immediate, does it follow that the knowledge in question is unconditional? (Earlier I raised the question of whether it followed from the fact that an object was conditional that knowledge of it was not immediate. The question now is whether the entailment holds good in the opposite direction – whether it follows from the fact that knowledge of an object is immediate that that object is unconditional. For it must be remembered that conditionality/unconditionality is a function of the object of knowledge, not of the state of knowledge.) What we can infer from the considerations which Schopenhauer adduces about knowledge of action or agency is that the knowledge is of a different kind from knowledge of representations in being immediate; moreover, we cannot know of agency simply by way of representations, even if representations are involved in some way, through the body, in what we are conscious of in action. It is not clear, however, that it follows from that that knowledge of agency is unconditional, only that it is not subject to the same conditions as knowledge of ordinary representations.

It might be objected that in what I have said I have not treated the idea of immediacy seriously enough. It is not simply that knowledge of agency is not like other kinds of knowledge; it is different in being *immediate*. Unfortunately, the notion of immediate knowledge, to the extent that it goes beyond direct knowledge, is not clear, despite the numerous occasions on which it has been invoked in philosophy. Presumably, to say that knowledge is immediate is to say that it is not mediated by anything. In Schopenhauer's view, knowledge of a perceptual representation, for example, has to bring in its connection with other representations and is in that sense mediated by them. Hence one can see why it might be thought that the conditionality of such a representation might be taken to imply its non-immediacy, as I said earlier. But if all I know is that a certain form of knowledge is immediate, it is far from clear what, if anything, I can infer about the character of its object, and that is a point which has often been made about, for example, attempts to refute materialism by reference to the direct and immediate access which we may be taken to have to our own states of mind. Is our knowledge of agency mediated by anything? Not obviously, but it remains unclear what follows about the ontological status of agency and the will.

For some part of Schopenhauer's purposes, it is enough to have shown that the will is not a matter of representation. The argument for the identification of the will with the thing-in-itself requires rather more than that,[2] in particular the thesis that anything which is not representation must be a thing-in-itself. But the importance of his insights into agency and the will remains. On the other hand, I emphasised in connection with representations that their ideality explains, if it does not justify, the running together of their conditionality, as objects of knowledge, with the conditionality of knowledge of them. None of that can, strictly speaking, apply to the will and knowledge of it, especially when it is concluded that the will is the thing-in-itself. For in that case the will falls outside the area to which idealism applies (even if the existence of a thing-in-itself is a component feature of an idealism which, like Kant's, is transcendental). It does look as if Schopenhauer believes that the peculiar directness and immediacy of knowledge of the will in agency is enough to show its unconditionality, but whether or not that holds good, it remains true that that peculiar directness – its uniqueness, one might say – is of fundamental importance for our assessment of the place of human beings in the world. For it is at least arguable that it applies to nothing else.

But while this is enough for some part of Schopenhauer's purposes, it is by no means enough for all of them. While his belief in the place of will in nature depends upon the key provided by our insight into our own wills, it also requires the idea that what lies behind our representations, the thing-in-itself, is to be identified with that will. The same applies to all those other fundamental parts of Schopenhauer's philosophy, including the pessimism and the role of sympathy, which turn on a belief in an underlying reality distinct from representations. Hence, while the considerations about knowledge of the will are important in general, as well as important for Schopenhauer's metaphysical views, their validity is, perhaps unfortunately for Schopenhauer, more obvious in the former connection than in the latter.

(3) There are the Ideas, which have often been seen as one of the more difficult elements in Schopenhauer's philosophy. This is not the place to attempt to provide a thorough exegesis of the notion of Ideas.[3] Schopenhauer says that they constitute grades of the

objectification of the will, but that scarcely helps us to understand what they are. Suffice it to say here that they have the status of ideal prototypes – something that is both token and type. (That does something to explain why Schopenhauer invokes the Platonic Ideas in this connection since Platonic Ideas or Forms, in being both universals and exemplars or ideals, if anything of that kind were possible, have just that status.) For Schopenhauer such things are as much representations as other objects of knowledge, apart from the will, but it would be difficult to see how they could be subject to the same conditions as perceptual representations, and it is clear that he does not think that knowledge of them is conditional in that sense. On the other hand, he does say (W2 364/H. 3, 416) that Ideas as apprehended spring from knowledge of mere relations, and that this is the crucial respect in which they differ from the will. This implies that their status is in a sense secondary, as indeed is also implicit in the suggestion that they are grades of the objectification of the will. Knowledge of them must also be in some sense secondary or derivative, if only in that we should have no knowledge of them if we did not have knowledge of representations in perception. Whether it also implies that our knowledge of Ideas depends on a kind of abstraction from perceptual phenomena is another matter. There are suggestions that he does not think this is the case, for example, the suggestion (at W1 175/H. 2, 207) that on the 'impossible presupposition' that were we not individuals with bodies we should apprehend only Ideas and our world would be a *nunc stans*, without events, change or plurality (sic). But since this depends on an 'impossible presupposition', it is not clear what has to be considered as possible. Nevertheless, it does seem to be his view that, as things are, our knowledge of Ideas is in one way or another dependent on knowledge of perceptual representations, and this holds true in the case of art, the main source of knowledge of Ideas on his view.

For Schopenhauer thinks that the main role of art is to provide us with knowledge of Ideas, though some forms of art do this more obviously than others do. Moreover, Schopenhauer thinks that in artistic contemplation the absorption in question brings about the result that we become pure subjects of knowledge, and that this offers a respite, if only temporarily, from the will. At the same time, since both the individual and the objects are in their underlying nature will, the absorption in artistic contemplation constitutes the first of the two examples in Schopenhauer's philosophy of the will denying itself. These two examples, of which the second is the supposedly permanent one (as contrasted with the more temporary one achievable through art) which is said at the conclusion of the system to provide a form of salvation as the result of asceticism, are the two great paradoxes in Schopenhauer's philosophy in which the will, the underlying reality, somehow denies itself. For present purposes, when considering knowledge of the Ideas in artistic contemplation, the crucial question is what that knowledge consists of. It is presumably direct, and one might think that it must also be immediate, since the identity of knower and known which the absorption entails would not be possible otherwise. Moreover, the objects in question are not, in being known, necessarily such as to stand in the sort of relations which the principle of sufficient reason demands. An Idea stands, in this respect at least, by itself. That holds good even if it is also the case that we should not have such knowledge if we were not individuals with knowledge of perceptual objects. So there is a sense in which the knowledge of the Ideas is a form of unconditional knowledge. Indeed, in the sense in which knowledge of perceptual representations is conditional, that is, that such representations must stand in lawlike relations to other representations, knowledge of the Ideas is certainly unconditional. The fact, if it is one, that such knowledge is dependent on another form of knowledge, that involved in perception, is irrelevant to that point.

The question remains what all this shows about the nature of the knowledge involved in this context. I have suggested that it must be direct, and one might think that it must also be immediate, but it is scarcely immediate in the way that knowledge of willing is. Moreover, Schopenhauer has already said that knowledge of willing is the only case of immediate knowledge. What therefore is one to make of the idea that in contemplation of the Ideas the knower and the known are identical? Does not that suggest, as I have already said, that the knowledge in question must be direct and immediate? Knowledge of willing in one's own case is immediate in that there is no way in which the knowledge could be mediated (and it is important that this is restricted to knowledge in one's own case, as knowledge of other people's willing is far from being immediate in this sense). Is there any way in which knowledge of an Idea could be mediated? I think that the answer to this question must be 'Yes', since if Ideas are grades of the objectivity of the will, the very notion of a grade surely implies the possibility of inference from one grade to another. So knowledge of an Idea is on that count not necessarily immediate. Once again, here one is up against the consideration that when concerned with the immediacy or conditionality of knowledge of X, Schopenhauer has in mind the nature of X rather than the nature of the state of the knower involved. Knowledge of an Idea can certainly be direct, and indeed must be so when one is involved in contemplation of it; but that is not to say that knowledge of it must be immediate in the way that knowledge of one's own willing must be. What then *is* implied about knowledge of an Idea by the identity of knower and known which is involved in the contemplation of it?

What is involved in contemplation of an Idea is very similar to what Aristotle seems to have had in mind in speaking of *theoria* (a term which is usually translated as 'contemplation' or perhaps 'philosophical contemplation'). Aristotle sometimes represents this as the intellectual or scientific ideal and as what divine thought consists in. It is the actualization of a form of knowledge which is dispositional (a *hexis*), as indeed knowledge might generally be supposed to be. In interpreting Aristotle, it has always been difficult to make clear what he had in mind. In what sense, for example, can it be said to be an activity, and one that the gods might pass their time engaged in? I have suggested elsewhere[4] that it ought to be construed as a form of intellectual savouring. What Schopenhauer seems to have in mind in speaking of knowledge of the Ideas is something like that. Aristotle too would have maintained the identity of the knower and the known in some sense of those words. The point is at least that in the contemplation one is caught up, so to speak, in the object in question, so that nothing else matters. It is in that sense that, according to Schopenhauer, the will is stilled. One might say, however, that that makes the contemplation more than mere knowledge, and that it might be positively misleading to suggest that it is *simply* knowledge that brings salvation, if only temporarily, on such occasions. We shall find that such considerations become even more telling when one comes to the more permanent form of salvation which Schopenhauer adduces at the end of his philosophical inquiry. Nevertheless, as far as knowledge itself is concerned, the conclusion to be drawn from all this is that knowledge of an Idea, at least as manifested in artistic contemplation, is no different from any other form of knowledge *of* something, including perceptual representations, except that an Idea is not tied to the kinds of lawlike connection to which perceptual representations are tied. Moreover, it might be argued that it is the necessity for that lawlike connection in the case of perceptual representations that rules out the possibility of our being caught up in them in the way in which one is said to be with the Ideas. Even if the Ideas as *grades* of the objectivity of the will can be related to each other, this does not prevent our being caught up in them, considered individually.

There is a further question which may as well be addressed at this stage. This is the question of how these forms of 'knowledge of' are related to 'knowledge that'; it is a question which once again Schopenhauer does not address directly, and it is one the answer to which is complicated by other things that he does say. The knowledge by acquaintance which Russell and others have invoked has always been supposed to be quite distinct from any form of knowledge that, but in the ordinary sense of the words, knowledge of something does not have that implication. To the extent that we have knowledge of something, there may be various things that we know about it, and it would be very strange to say that we had knowledge of something if we knew nothing at all about it. That is not to say that we can make explicit what we know in terms of some proposition to the effect that such and such is the case. What has sometimes been called 'tacit knowledge' is by no means unusual; in a multitude of cases it is the normal rule. Nevertheless, knowledge of something does generally imply knowledge about it to the effect that such and such is the case with regard to it. If that applies to Schopenhauer's scheme of things, then knowledge of a representation of whatever kind would entail knowledge that something was the case with regard to it. In the case of knowledge of willing, the situation might at first seem to be different. Indeed, the knowledge involved in intention has sometimes been said to be nonpropositional.[5] Nothing, however, prevents the knowledge involved in willing or acting intentionally from having propositional content, even if that content is different from what it is when the knowledge in question is the knowledge of what one is willing or doing. Knowing that one is doing is different from knowing what one is doing, and elsewhere[6] I have made that distinction, one which is cardinal in interpreting what Schopenhauer has to say about the immediacy of knowledge of the will by contrast with knowledge

of the motives for one's action. But concerning knowledge of willing
simpliciter, it can still be construed as knowledge *that* one is willing,
and that knowledge has a propositional content, even if minimal.

The complication about this in Schopenhauer's case, as I have mentioned, is that it is far from clear whether he could put things in
these terms. That is because knowledge that, as I have represented
it, is arguably concept dependent, and so has a propositional content through concepts being brought to bear upon the thing in question. If that is the case, knowledge of an object – a representation in
Schopenhauer's case, whether a perception or an Idea – and indeed
knowledge of willing itself is something that one could not have unless one were already equipped with concepts to some extent (something that has considerable implications for genetic epistemology,
the philosophical understanding of how the development of knowledge in the individual is possible, though I shall not elaborate on
that here). But Schopenhauer thinks that concepts are the product of
reason, whereas much of the knowledge with which we have been
concerned, and certainly the knowledge involved in having perceptual representations, is a function of the understanding, which does
not presuppose reason. In holding this view about the relations between understanding and reason, Schopenhauer unfortunately de-
serted the insights which Kant had. For the latter, understanding
and judgment go together, whereas for Schopenhauer judgment is
a function of something separate, namely, reason. Whether or not
one wishes to express knowledge that in terms of judgment, there
is an obvious affinity between the two, and it is an affinity which
Schopenhauer cannot consistently acknowledge. However that may
be, it is something which we must acknowledge on his behalf.

There is one further point which deserves to be made in connection
with knowledge of the Ideas. I noted earlier that in Schopenhauer's
view Ideas are representations, though not perceptual representations, whether or not knowledge of them is independent of knowledge of perceptual representations. While a *Vorstellung* need not be
a representation in the literal sense, it is clear from Schopenhauer's
treatment of the individual arts that he sees forms of art as somehow
representing Ideas even when they also represent concrete objects or
states of affairs. Indeed, he argues (*W1* 212/H. 2, 250–1), paradoxically it might at first seem, that the actual grade of the will's objectivity that the Idea constitutes affects the nature of the aesthetic

experience, so that where a low grade is involved 'the enjoyment of pure will-less knowing will predominate', while in the case of Ideas of a high grade, the aesthetic enjoyment 'will consist rather in the objective apprehension of these Ideas that are the most distinct revelations of the will'. That may seem paradoxical because one might have expected objects which are a reflection of a high-grade Idea to be more likely to bring about a more detached state of knowing. On reflection, however, it seems evident that a higher grade of Idea is more likely to bring about an involvement in *it*, though it is less than clear what moral this might have for one who wants to emphasise the point, as Schopenhauer does, that aesthetic experience is a way of escaping the demands of the will by the will denying itself. However that may be, it *is* clear that in apprehending a perceptual representation in an aesthetic context one *ei ipso* apprehends a representation of an Idea, whether or not that second apprehension brings about the predominance of a state of pure will-less knowing. Hence the relationship between knowledge of an Idea in an aesthetic context and knowledge of some perceptual representation is even more direct than I suggested earlier when considering how, if at all, knowledge of Ideas in general is dependent on perceptual knowledge. But in that case it must be the aesthetic attitude which somehow makes the difference. Why it should do so I shall not discuss here; that would involve a discussion of Schopenhauer's aesthetics, which is not my immediate concern. (It might be as well, however, to remark that Schopenhauer's belief that music is a copy of the will itself and not, like the other arts, a copy of the Ideas does not affect the general point that the apprehension of the will which is involved is dependent on a form of perceptual apprehension, in this case hearing. But how that is supposed to work has to be even more complicated than what holds good for other forms of aesthetic apprehension.)

(4) I must turn, finally, to the knowledge which is involved when Schopenhauer puts forward his account of salvation, the only way in which freedom from the tyranny of the will can finally and permanently be attained. What Schopenhauer says about this follows from the central point of his ethics, the suggestion that the key to this is sympathy and that the metaphysical basis of this is that underneath we are all one, since the underlying reality is the single will. Schopenhauer describes this as involving a 'seeing-through' of the *principium individuationis* (the principle of the individuation of

things), and this is a form of knowledge. It is this same knowledge which brings about the will's denial of itself, though it is a knowledge which is combined with asceticism (or perhaps, as a second possibility, suffering itself). In the case of ordinary virtue the person concerned sees others as himself, but by what Schopenhauer says is analogous to an effect of grace, he may then go on to acquire a strong aversion to his inner nature. Asceticism is thus, he says (*W1* 392/H. 2, 463), a '*deliberate* breaking of the will by refusing the agreeable and looking for the disagreeable, the voluntarily chosen way of life of penance and self-chastisement, for the constant mortification of the will'. Yet he says that the will cannot be abolished by anything else except knowledge (*W1* 400/H. 2, 473). So asceticism by itself cannot bring about the denial of the will. If one chooses to say that knowledge can do this, it has to be recognised that this is no ordinary knowledge; otherwise, the knowledge presupposed in virtue alone would have the same effect. If the key to it all lies in seeing through the *principium individuationis*, the knowledge involved has to have the consequence that the person himself enters into the process of asceticism as so described, and that does not appear to be a necessity.

Moreover, it does not appear that the knowledge in question can be described as simply the knowledge that the underlying nature of things is the single will. Nor has this knowledge anything to do with representations except to the extent that it involves the insight that reality is something beyond all representations. But insight it nevertheless is, and an insight which has, in a sense, practical implications. So much also was true of the knowledge of what was said to be the metaphysical basis for sympathy, except that a supposed insight to the effect that there is no real difference between oneself and others, combined with a simple account of human motivation, leads more directly to sympathy as a practical consequence than does the more general seeing through of the *principium individuationis* to the denial of the will. In fact, Schopenhauer's claim that the will cannot be abolished by anything else except knowledge is of a piece with the point that nothing that one can do via representations alone can affect the thing-in-itself. For knowledge is a state of the subject, and although in Schopenhauer's view there can be no subject without an object, the subject itself does not consist of anything at the level of representations. Nevertheless, that alone does not justify the claims for the practical consequences of the knowledge in question.

For that reason, if for no other, the view that the will can deny itself remains a paradox.

While the concept of knowledge which is presupposed in all this – the concept of a form of insight – is in itself an intelligible one, it is difficult to see how it fits in with what Schopenhauer says about knowledge in general. It is not knowledge of an object, as the other forms of knowledge which I have considered have been, though much that he says seems to suggest that it is direct. But for this last point, one might conceivably classify it as a form of abstract knowledge, involving an insight into the reason why things are so, but it is in any case rather more than that because of its practical consequences. However that may be, Schopenhauer shows no sensitivity to the question of how it fits in with such views as he has about the nature of knowledge. Despite all this, he does emphasise very definitely that it is knowledge which in the end provides the solution to the problems entailed by our involvement in the kind of metaphysical system which he describes. In particular, it is knowledge which in the end provides a way out of suffering, though it is equally clear that that way is not available to most people, to say the least. As I have said, the concept of knowledge in question is not an unintelligible one. People do sometimes have forms of insight which have practical consequences. Moreover, Schopenhauer emphasises the extent to which his conception of things at this point is similar to certain religious conceptions, even if he thinks that they are inferior to what he has in mind. The problem is simply that if one expects a philosopher to be clear about his or her terms of reference, Schopenhauer falls short when it comes to a consideration of the nature of knowledge.

It might well be argued that none of this matters. If he had wished and had thought it necessary, Schopenhauer could simply have added something to show how what he says about knowledge in relation to salvation is to be understood. In that case there would simply be a lacuna in Schopenhauer's system, not an incoherence. It is not quite as simple as that, however. Knowledge does play a very important role in Schopenhauer's thinking, and given the importance of that role, one has the right to demand that he be clear about it. Unfortunately, he is not. Moreover, at the start of his thinking, the only form of knowledge contemplated, apart from abstract knowledge, is one that requires a direct relation to an object. The knowledge which is

supposed to make salvation possible does not really meet the specification of abstract knowledge in involving the apprehension of a
ground, and it is difficult to see it as involving a direct relation to an
object, even if it depends upon the direct and immediate knowledge
of an object, the will. While much that he has to say is unaffected
by such facts, and while he often uses the notion of knowledge in
a quite uncontroversial way, he does not offer an account of knowledge into which it all fits. There are also problems, as I have tried to
indicate, about the details of the knowledge of the various kinds of
object the specification of which *are* essential to his philosophy. In
all this Schopenhauer undoubtedly falls short, but so do, I suspect,
most philosophers of his time, however that is to be explained. The
most important thing to recognise in this area for an understanding
of Schopenhauer's philosophy, however, is how much depends on
the nature and status of the objects of knowledge, as he sees them,
rather than on the nature of knowledge itself.

NOTES

1 David Hamlyn, *Schopenhauer* (London: Routledge and Kegan Paul,
  1980), 92–4.
2 As I have indicated (ibid.).
3 Though I have tried to provide that in Hamlyn (1980), ch. 6.
4 David Hamlyn, 'Aristotle's God', in *The Philosophical Assessment of
  Theology: Essays in Honour of Frederick C. Copleston* (Tunbridge Wells,
  U.K.: Search Press 'in association with' Washington D.C.: Georgetown
  University Press, 1987), 15–33 (see esp. 26–8).
5 For example, in S. N. Hampshire, *Thought and Action* (London: Chatto
  and Windus, 1959), esp. 103ff.
6 Hamlyn (1980), 85.

3   The Fourfold Root

On the Fourfold Root of the Principle of Sufficient Reason was written as an academic dissertation in 1813 when Schopenhauer was twenty-five. He presented it to the University of Jena, was awarded the degree of doctor of philosophy on the strength of it, and in the same year paid to have it published. Almost immediately afterwards he set himself to writing what was to be his major work, *The World as Will and Representation*, and this he completed in 1818. Many years later, he substantially revised and added to the *Fourfold Root*, publishing a second edition of it in 1847.[1]

In his preface to this second edition, Schopenhauer refers to the *Fourfold Root* as 'a treatise on elementary philosophy,' and within limits that is precisely what it is. Consequently, it can profitably be read, especially in its first edition, as a self-contained treatise on the nature and structure of the world of common sense and science, and on the principles of knowledge, explanation, and necessity governing that world. But Schopenhauer also says in his second-edition preface that the *Fourfold Root* became the foundation of his 'entire system,' and almost from the start that is how he regarded it. In the first edition of his *World as Will and Representation* he asserts that without an acquaintance with the *Fourfold Root* 'it is quite impossible to understand the present work properly, and the subject matter of that essay is always presupposed here as if it were included in the book' (*W1* xiv/H. 2, x). Again, the First Book of *The World as Will and Representation* is subtitled *The Representation Subject to the Principle of Sufficient Reason* . . . , and readers soon discover the impossibility of understanding it without a grasp of the principle of sufficient reason, as expounded in the *Fourfold Root*; in any event, Schopenhauer repeatedly refers them back there.

Given these facts, and given the widespread interest in Schopenhauer as a philosopher articulating an 'entire system,' this chapter will consider the *Fourfold Root* principally as a foundation to his system.

The following are the doctrines of that system having immediate bearing here. The everyday world of commonsense and scientific inquiry does not exist independently, but only within the consciousness of those experiencing it; that is, it exists merely as a set of representations.[2] However, there is more to reality than representations:[3] there is also the thing in itself, which is Will. Representations constitute the outer side of reality, the thing in itself the inner, and there is no inferential path from one to the other. Knowledge of the thing in itself is unique and direct.

Given this selective summary, it is possible to say at once where the importance of the *Fourfold Root* lies with respect to Schopenhauer's system. It lies in its attempt to establish that the everyday world is representational, to establish that the principles of reasoning governing that world license no inference to a reality beyond it, and to refute the many claims of those who hold otherwise.

I   THE FOURFOLD ROOT IN OUTLINE

The basic assertion of the *Fourfold Root* is that the everyday world is made up of objects of four classes, all of which are representations. The first class consists of 'real objects,'[4] such things as tables and chairs; the second of concepts and such combinations of concepts as true judgments; the third of time and space; the fourth of particular human wills.

These objects are uniformly interconnected in a variety of ways, so that questions specific to the several classes can be asked and in principle always answered. To begin with, real objects are subject to change, and of any change the question 'Why does it occur?' can be asked and in principle answered. There is always a reason. Second, concepts combined in appropriate ways constitute true judgments, and of any true judgment the question 'Why is it true?' can be asked and in principle answered. Third, time and space are made up of parts, and of any part the question 'Why does it possess its characterising mathematical properties?' can be asked and in principle answered. Again, there is always a reason. Finally, human agents perform actions, and of any action the question 'Why is it performed?' can be asked and in principle answered. Yet again, there is a reason.

The reasons in question are sufficient reasons, and since they divide into four kinds, providing specific answers to questions concerning the four classes of objects, each class may be said to be ruled by a special form of the principle of sufficient reason, the principle asserting in its most general form that nothing is without a reason or an explanation of why it is rather than not.[5] The four forms of the principle thus arising are these: every change in a real object has a cause; the truth of every true judgment rests upon something other than itself; all mathematical properties are grounded in other mathematical properties; every action has a motive.

The scheme of things then comes to this. The everyday world comprises objects of four classes, those in the first class being subject to change, those in the second bearing truth, those in the third possessing mathematical properties, and those in the fourth giving rise to actions under the influence of motives. But these objects and their properties do not coexist in bare juxtaposition; rather, they are interconnected by bonds of a double necessity in the following systematic ways. *Necessarily* all changes, all instances of truth, all mathematical properties, all actions, have reasons, and these reasons are *sufficient* for their consequents – that is, they *necessitate* them.[6] For example: *necessarily*, if a change E occurs, there is a reason for E, namely, a cause C. Pari passu, C is sufficient for E; that is, C *necessitates* E.[7] It follows that in the everyday world there are twin necessary connections of four kinds – between changes and causes, between truth and grounds, between mathematical properties and other mathematical properties, between actions and motives – and each kind supports a specific form of the principle of sufficient reason. At the same time, each constitutes a root of that principle in its general form. More briefly, there are four kinds of necessary connectedness in the everyday world, each constituting a root of the general principle of sufficient reason. Because of this, that general principle is said to possess a fourfold root.[8]

Side by side with its fundamental assertion that the everyday world consists of representations, the *Fourfold Root* contains a materialist theory of mind, asserting that the mind is identical with the brain. As will be seen, this combination of doctrines gives rise to problems within the foundations of Schopenhauer's system that are perhaps insoluble.

II THE FIRST CLASS OF OBJECTS AND THE FORM OF THE PRINCIPLE OF SUFFICIENT REASON GOVERNING IT

Schopenhauer begins by describing objects of the first class as *intuitive, complete, empirical representations,* and while they are more simply referred to as *real objects,* their lengthier and Kantian description is a concise statement of what Schopenhauer holds concerning them. As was said earlier, in calling them *representations* he means that, unlike the thing in itself, they do not exist independently. In calling them *intuitive* he means that, by contrast with concepts, they are particular.[9] To illustrate his meaning, Bucephalus is an intuitive representation; the concept of *horse* applied to him is not. In calling them *complete* he means that they have both formal and material properties, and the distinction referred to in these terms is important in pointing to an underlying reason for Schopenhauer's following Kant in believing real objects to be representations. The formal properties of real objects are those that are necessary to their being real objects as such; that is, necessary to their being real objects rather than to their belonging, say, to this or that specific kind of real object. All other properties are material. To illustrate the distinction, existing in time and existing in space are formal properties of real objects; being red, round, and shiny are material. Schopenhauer follows Kant in explaining the necessity of the formal properties of real objects by considering them to be imposed by the intellect upon sensory data: its faculty of inner sensibility imposes the form of time, its faculty of outer sensibility imposes the form of space, and its faculty of understanding imposes the form or category of causality. The result is real objects, which, in being dependent upon the intellect for their formal properties, are representations.[10]

Schopenhauer argues in some detail that time, space, and causality are conjointly necessary for the existence of real objects. Real objects, he points out, are things that *perdure,* and perdurance demands both time and space. This is because for objects to perdure is for them to retain identity coexistently with change around them. But the idea of a thing's thus retaining identity is not intelligible in terms of time alone, since in time as such there is no coexistence, only succession. Consequently, an added dimension is needed, and this is provided by space: given time and space together, a thing can retain its identity through change. For analogous reasons, the idea of a thing's retaining identity coexistently with change is not intelligible in terms of space alone, since in space as such there is no succession and therefore neither change nor perdurance.

While for these reasons time and space are necessary for the existence of real objects, they are not sufficient. They need to be joined by a third component, and it is the faculty of understanding that provides this component by imposing its unique category upon what is given to it.[11] This category, says Schopenhauer, is causality or matter, and what he has in mind is this. Time and space are not sufficient to account for real objects, since plainly there would be no real objects if there were but empty time and space. The two, then, need to be 'filled,' and it is matter that fills them. It is able to do this, thinks Schopenhauer, because matter is identical with causality, and by this in turn he means that something is material, by contrast with being an empty region of time and space, if and only if it has causal powers. In short, for a thing to be a real object is, on the one hand, for it to be located in time and space, and, on the other hand, for it to affect and be affected by other objects. Its specific properties, such as being red, round, or long-lasting, are specific instantiations of its causal powers or specific realisations of its location in time and space.[12]

In addition to describing real objects as intuitive and complete, Schopenhauer describes them as empirical, and by this he means two things: first, that awareness of real objects is sensuous awareness – that is, real objects are apprehended through the senses; second, that they belong to a 'totality of experience,' an interconnected whole in which all objects are temporally, spatially, and causally interrelated. This whole he calls *empirical reality*.

The causal interconnectedness of real objects brought about by the imposition of the category of causality gives rise to a specific form of the principle of sufficient reason named the principle of sufficient reason of *becoming*. This principle, identical with the law of causality, asserts two things. One, if a change occurs in a real object, it is necessarily preceded by another change, the first being the sufficient reason or cause, the second the effect. Two, causes similar in kind are followed by effects similar in kind, and effects similar in kind are preceded by causes similar in kind.

Schopenhauer repeatedly claims that causes and effects are changes in real objects, and a simplified model will serve to illustrate his thought here. Let us suppose that I swing a hammer and hit a nail, driving it into a piece of wood. The hammer's movement, a relational change of state in the hammer, is the cause, and the nail's movement, a relational change of state in the nail, is the effect. In this simplified model, then, cause and effect are changes in real objects, and Schopenhauer holds this to be true of all causes and effects: all and only changes are causes and effects, and consequently real objects themselves are neither. His reasoning here is that real objects are substances – that is, they are constituted by matter – and, since matter is eternal and unalterable, he believes, substances have no beginning and no end. It follows that they are not changes, and therefore neither causes nor effects. There is nonetheless a temptation to think that real objects are causes: there is a temptation to think, say, that the hammer is the cause of the nail's movement through the wood. But a moment's reflection shows this to be false. If the hammer qua object were the cause of the nail's movement, there would be no explanation of the movement's occurring now rather than five minutes ago, the hammer having been as much an object then as it is now. It is obvious, therefore, that it is changes in the hammer that constitute the cause of the nail's movement – the hammer's swinging through the air, its transference of kinetic energy, and so on.

There is a corresponding temptation to think that real objects are effects – that hammers are the effects of smiths, and so on – but plainly they are not, since substances, being eternal and unalterable, are not produced by anyone or by anything.

It is precisely because Schopenhauer believes changes and only changes to be causes and effects that he refers to the law of causality as the principle of sufficient reason of *becoming*. According to this principle, every change of state E in a real object is an effect, following upon the occurrence of a preceding change which is a sufficient reason for E and constitutes its cause. This cause is a complex state, comprising events severally necessary and jointly sufficient for E, and, being itself a change, it too has a cause, and this cause has a cause, and so on ad infinitum.

Schopenhauer's assertion, on the one hand, that the law of causality concerns only changes of state in real objects and, on the other
hand, that every change has a cause, is of fundamental importance
to his system. For, if true, it refutes all traditional arguments for the
existence of God as a *first cause uncaused*. God cannot be a cause,
since God is not a change, and only changes can be causes; nor can
changes in God be causes, since there are no changes in God. Apart
from that, the world of real objects cannot be an effect of God as
its cause, since real objects are substances and therefore, unlike effects, have no beginning. In any event, the very notion of a cause
uncaused is incoherent, since every cause is a change, and therefore
itself requires a cause. Incoherent too is the notion of God as self-
causing or *causa sui*;[13] such a notion is contradictory and indeed,
thinks Schopenhauer, laughable.

These points about arguments attempting to reach God as a first
cause apply equally to arguments attempting to reach Absolutes,
Egos, or Kantian noumena. They also apply to arguments attempting to reach objects from subjects or subjects from objects, since the
principle of sufficient reason of becoming concerns only changes in
objects and so cannot be applied to a relationship between objects
and subjects. All arguments of these kinds, then, are worthless. Inferences based upon the principle of sufficient reason of becoming
cannot lead beyond empirical reality: they can do no more than lead
from one empirical change to another.

This last point in more general form applies to all classes of representations. 'The principle of sufficient reason explains connexions
and combinations of phenomena, not the phenomena themselves'
(*W1* 82/H. 2, 98).

III PERCEPTION OF THE OUTER WORLD

So far, Schopenhauer has proposed an analysis of causality and has
argued that the principle of sufficient reason governing real objects
cannot take us beyond them; he has also proposed an analysis of
real objects themselves, according to which their essential properties are temporality, spatiality, and causal power. But these analyses
and arguments, even if persuasive, do nothing to show that real objects are representations. What is needed is a proof that their essential properties, and ideally their non-essential properties too, are

dependent for their existence upon the minds of those who perceive them.

It is true that, in speaking of time, space, and causality as forms of the faculties of sensibility and understanding, Schopenhauer has assumed that the essential properties of real objects are contributed by the mind and are consequently dependent upon it, and he may even fairly be thought to have referred his readers implicitly and in general terms to arguments from Kant's Aesthetic and Analytic.[14] It is true, too, that he has assumed real objects to be things that are dependent in virtue of the fact that, precisely qua objects, they depend upon a subject.[15] But assumptions and references are not proof, and it is proof that is now needed if Schopenhauer is to convince his readers that real objects – such plain things as tables and chairs – have an ontological status as dependent as that of illusions and dreams.

Proof is in fact attempted in great detail, but almost by accident. What happens is that, having completed his analysis of real objects in terms of time, space, and causality, and of causality itself in terms of necessary and sufficient conditions, Schopenhauer presents an argument to show that the principle of causality is known to us a priori,[16] and it is the core of this argument that constitutes his 'proof' of the representational nature of real objects. It is a proof that the world of perceptible objects as such is a creation in toto of the minds of its perceivers, a creation that is impossible without the principle of causality.

To use Schopenhauer's own phrase, the aim of this proof is to show that 'perception is intellectual,' that is, to show that the world of real, perceptible objects is created by the intellect. But it is important to note that the word *intellect* in this context has a restricted range of application. Elsewhere it is synonymous with *mind* and so covers all mental faculties: inner sensibility, outer sensibility, understanding, and reason. Here, however, it excludes the faculty of reason, which to us might seem to constitute the very essence of the intellect, and Schopenhauer's proof therefore is that the world of real, perceptible objects is the creation of the faculties of sensibility and understanding alone. The importance of this will soon become clear.

The proof itself may now be summarised as follows. Everything that goes to make up perception is subjective; consequently, when we perceive we do not apprehend objects existing independently of

us. On the contrary, what we apprehend are constructions of our
own intellects. Our intellects are presented with sets of sensations
or sensory data,[17] and by imposing the forms of time, space, and
causality upon these, they create real objects. The data of perception,
then, are subjective, the forms imposed upon them are subjective,
and consequently the objects fashioned out of both are subjective
too. The data are subjective because they are nothing but sensations
occurring within particular bodies, and the forms are subjective because they are nothing but structures of particular intellects. Given
this, perception is intellectual in the sense that it is a creation of
objects by the intellect; it is not a matter of having bare sensations.
As Schopenhauer forcefully remarks, there is no possibility of the
world's finding its way into our heads through bare sensations; these
are too meager in content for that.

Sensibility plays an important part in the creation of real objects
by imposing time and space upon the data given to the intellect, but
it is the faculty of understanding that plays the leading role, both
'summoning space' to its aid and imposing its own form of causality upon the data. What happens is that sensory data are presented
to the intellect and 'conceived of' by the understanding as *effects*;
or, to put the point another way, the understanding infers that objects cause the data. Since inner sensibility imposes its form of time
upon the data, and since outer sensibility at the bidding of the understanding imposes its form of space, the outcome is an inferred,
spatiotemporal, and causally active object.[18] To illustrate the process, what happens when we perceive a red billiard ball is this. We
receive a set of sensory data, 'red,' 'shiny,' 'smooth,' and so on. But
these data are sensations inside us, whereas the red billiard ball is
perceived as outside us, in public time and space. The explanation is
that the faculties of inner and outer sensibility add time and space
to the sensory data, as a result of which these present themselves
as existing 'out there' in public time and space. But this is still not
enough, since in perceiving the red billiard ball we do not apprehend 'red,' 'smooth,' and 'shiny' as purely temporal and spatial. We
apprehend them as jointly belonging to an object, and to an object
that we apprehend as existing independently of our perception and
as causing our states of consciousness. The explanation this time is
that the faculty of understanding infers that the temporal and spatial data present to our consciousness are the complex effect of an

object existing independently of them, an object perduring in time and located in space.

The faculty of understanding does not employ concepts in carrying out this creative work, concepts being the exclusive domain of the faculty of reason. In other words, the understanding does not conceptually, reflectively, discursively, or linguistically apprehend sensory data as effects. It apprehends them intuitively. A fortiori, it does not go through a process of learning in order to apprehend sensory data as effects; in apprehending them, it subsumes them immediately under the law of causality known to it a priori.

This completes the outline of Schopenhauer's proof that perception is intellectual. Its importance needs no emphasising, since, if successful, it shows that even the most obtrusive objects of common sense are representational, and Schopenhauer himself emphasises the proof's importance by devoting more than a fifth of the second edition of the *Fourfold Root* to it. The proof is also important because, at any rate within Schopenhauer's own scheme of things, the existence of the other classes of objects is contingent upon that of real objects, so that, if successful, the proof shows all four to be representational.[19] For these reasons the proof merits more attention than other topics in this essay.

By contrast with its importance, the cogency of the proof is not easy to assess, largely because it becomes entangled, as will be seen, in a thicket of irrelevant examples. The best way to make a start in assessing it, then, is to focus on the central point that it needs to establish if it is to be successful, namely, that the intellect creates real objects out of sensory data that are *formless* – that is, data that are neither temporal, spatial, nor causally active. This is the principal point that needs to be established because the whole purpose of the proof is to show that time, space, and causality are not present from the start but only 'subsequently' imposed upon data lacking them.

In the course of deploying his proof, Schopenhauer cites many examples of data worked on by the understanding, and some of these are exactly what he requires – formless visual data, such as colour, light, and shade, and formless tactile data, such as feelings of resistance and pressure. Contrary to what is sometimes asserted, there is nothing incoherent in considering data of these kinds to be formless, and Kant himself in the *Critique of Pure Reason* suggests a way in which they can intelligibly be distinguished from the forms accompanying them. If we think of a body, Kant argues, and then one by one remove those of its properties that are given to us in experience – properties such as colour, hardness or softness, weight, and impenetrability – we find that, although the body ceases to exist, the space it occupies remains; more important, it cannot be removed. It follows that occupancy of space is a necessary property of bodies and that the concept of space is a priori (B 4–6). If we reverse Kant's procedure, if we think of a body and then one by one remove those of its properties that are necessary to it as such, namely, time, space, and causality, we arrive at those that are material or formless, namely, colour, light, shade, hardness, softness, and so on.

So Schopenhauer could have articulated his proof coherently, arguing that the intellect is presented with formless data to which it subsequently gives form. But almost at the outset he loses sight of what he is after, turning to examples of the intellect's activity upon data that are not formless at all. He speaks, for example, of the understanding as judging two coins to be one, as judging the moon to be of a certain relative size, as judging distances by noticing visual and optic angles, as setting retinal images the right way up, as interpreting what is seen on the vertical plane in one way and what is seen on the horizontal plane in another, and so on. But clearly the data here are temporal, spatial, and causal: coins and the moon are real objects, while visual angles and retinal images presuppose them.

What makes Schopenhauer's proof even more difficult to assess is that in the course of it he advances a materialist theory of mind and perception that patently undermines any claim that the intellect is presented with formless sensory data.[20] It soon becomes clear that even the most basic data are material; even sensations of light, dark, and resistance are material, being bodily and located in the retinae, in the hands, just beneath the skin, and so on (FR 77/H. 1, 52). At the same time, the intellect itself is bodily, identical with the brain (FR 77/H. 1, 53), and the world of real objects is a 'cerebral phenomenon' (FR 103/H. 1, 71). More specifically, the faculty of understanding is the brain (FR 121/H. 1, 84), and the three forms of time, space, and causality are located there (FR 77, 118/H. 1, 53, 82).

Two prima facie disastrous consequences follow from this materialist account of the intellect and perception. One, already made plain, is that when Schopenhauer asserts all elements of perception to be subjective, he must now be taken to mean that, being bodily, they are located within the perceiver's body. But this entails that all sensory data presented to the intellect are bodily and therefore cannot play the role of formless data required of them. The other consequence, more embarrassing in the light of Schopenhauer's strictures on traditional metaphysicians, is that the intellect, because it is identical with the brain, is a real object. It follows from this that, like other real objects, the intellect is created by the intellect. It is *causa sui*.

It is sometimes concluded from these consequences that Schopenhauer's proof is in ruins from the start, and that the foundations of his system are left with nothing to recommend them beyond Kantian arguments in the background. But such a conclusion is unjustified, since what he says concerning the physiology of perception contains the seeds of a proof that cannot easily be brushed aside.

Schopenhauer's fundamental point on perception is expressed in his remark that one would have to be forsaken by all the gods to imagine that the world of real objects could have found its way into our heads through mere sensation and so have a second existence like the one outside them (*FR* 76/H. 1, 52). This point, however oddly expressed, is important, as may be seen if it is recast and extended in the following way. When a person, Mary, visually perceives a billiard ball, the ball clearly does not enter Mary's head as it enters her hand when she catches it. What happens is that light is reflected from the ball, producing images in Mary's retinae and inducing neuronal firings there. As a result of these, together with related chemical activities, electrons travel along Mary's neural pathways, in turn affecting her visual cortex and forming a 'representation' of the billiard ball there. All of this we know. What we do not know is how from these events Mary comes to perceive the red, round, shiny billiard ball supposedly before her.[21]

The assertion is sometimes made that Mary 'just does perceive' the billiard ball; moreover, that she perceives it directly, her neuronal processes being no more than necessary conditions of her doing so. But this is unhelpful. To mention but one problem,[22] it offers no account of the disparity between the billiard ball as described by Mary on the basis of her perceptions and the same billiard ball as described by theoretical physicists on the basis of their hypotheses and observations. If Mary perceived the billiard ball directly, one would expect her to apprehend it as it exists independently of her.

Indeed, what else could be meant in the context by her perceiving it directly? But this, if what physicists say about the make-up of billiard balls is correct, is not what happens. Mary does not perceive the billiard ball as physicists describe it, that is, as consisting of leptons, quarks, and fields of force, but as a red, round, hard, shiny object possessing a continuous surface.

The disparity needs an explanation, and from many points of view the simplest explanation to hand is that the billiard ball as Mary perceives it is a construction of her brain and therefore a 'cerebral phenomenon'. And if this is true, Schopenhauer is right in holding that 'perception is intellectual' and that no real or perceptible objects exist independently of the intellect.

There is not enough space here to develop this construal of Schopenhauer's proof in detail, but at least two objections to it call for mention. The first is that the proof as now construed turns out to be straightforwardly self-refuting, premising that such things as bodies with organs of sense and brains exist and concluding that they do not.

It is not difficult to meet this objection. Schopenhauer's conclusion does not contradict his premises, any more than the conclusion of physicists about the nature of physical reality contradicts theirs. Physicists begin by considering photographic plates, cloud chambers, Geiger counters, and so on, and conclude that what really exists is a world of fundamental particles without determinate position and momentum. In other words, reflection and argument lead them to conclude that real objects are not as they appear but are in large measure representational. Much the same is the case with Schopenhauer. Reflection and argument lead him to conclude that real objects are not as they appear, but are in toto representational.[23]

The second objection, already adverted to, is this. Real objects, according to Schopenhauer, are created by the intellect. But since, given the thesis of materialism, the intellect is itself a real object, it follows that the intellect is created by itself. It is *causa sui*.

This objection may be met as follows. It is true that Schopenhauer's thesis of materialism entails that the intellect creates itself, but this is only a description of appearances, not of how the world is in itself: the world as it is in itself contains no intellects, whether creating or not creating themselves. It is therefore ill founded to accuse Schopenhauer of affirming the intellect to be *causa sui* absolutely, and consequently his doctrine does not resemble the metaphysician's doctrine of God.

Schopenhauer himself implicitly makes this point by asserting that the doctrine of materialism is absurd if taken as a doctrine concerning what exists *absolutely*. It is absurd, he says, because it leaves the subject out of account (*W2* 13/H. 3, 15; see *FR* 52/H. 1, 33); it 'regards matter, and with it time and space, as existing absolutely, and passes over the relation to the subject in which alone all this exists.' So absurd is this, thinks Schopenhauer, that when we dwell on the final implication of the doctrine of materialism, namely, that knowledge is a mere modification of matter, with the subject left out of account, we are seized by 'a sudden fit of the inextinguishable laughter of the Olympians' (*W1* 27/H. 2, 32).

Materialists will no doubt retort that they do not leave the subject out of account, asserting that in knowing itself, the brain is both subject and object at once. But it is not clear that this identity of subject and object is possible, even if Schopenhauer's quick rejection of it is unsatisfactory.[24]

To conclude on perception. Whatever the merits of his proof, it is clear that Schopenhauer thinks of the world of real objects as being a pure creation of the intellect and therefore as providing no knowledge of reality beyond it. To quote his own words, 'we find residing within ourselves all the elements of empirical intuitive perception and nothing in them that would reliably point to something absolutely different from us, to a thing in itself' (*FR* 118/H. 1, 82). It is equally clear that in saying this, Schopenhauer is not declaring himself to be a subjective idealist, holding that representations make up the sum of reality. Indeed, only a few sentences later he makes plain that he does not. 'In my chief work,' he says, 'I have shown that we cannot reach the thing in itself – that is, whatever it is that exists independently of our representations – by following along the path of representations themselves. In order to reach it we need to follow a quite different path, one leading through the inside of things and letting us enter the citadel as if by treachery' (*FR* 119–20/ H. 1, 83). In short, Schopenhauer holds that there is a thing in itself and that our knowledge of it is *toto coelo* different from our knowledge of the everyday world. He even holds, disconcertingly in the light of the principal thesis of the *Fourfold Root*, that the world of representations has 'a metaphysical explanation' (*eine metaphysische*

Erklärung), different in kind from those provided by the principle of sufficient reason and transcending appearances.[25] The task of metaphysics, he is later to assert, 'is the correct explanation of experience as a whole' (*W2* 181/H. 3, 201).

IV THE SECOND CLASS OF OBJECTS AND THE FORM OF THE PRINCIPLE OF SUFFICIENT REASON GOVERNING IT

The objects that make up the second class of representations are concepts. These are abstract, unlike either real objects, images, or words, all of which are concrete (*FR* 145, 152/H. 1, 97, 102); and they are general, subsuming innumerable particulars under them (*FR* 147/H. 1, 98–9).[26]

Although at times Schopenhauer speaks as if concepts might be real universals, existing beyond time and space (*FR* 152/H. 1, 102; cf. *W2* 66/H. 3, 70), his fundamental view is that they are totally dependent upon the everyday world and partly constitutive of it. They are abstracted from perceptible particulars (*FR* 146/H. 1, 98),[27] the faculty of reason that abstracts them is the brain or a function of the brain,[28] and they themselves are lodged in the brain (*FR* 146/ H. 1, 98). They are therefore as much a part of the everyday world as perceptible objects, to which indeed they owe their origin and existence.

Concepts are representations, not things in themselves, in being created by the faculty of reason and in existing solely within the intellect. Moreover, since the objects from which they are abstracted are themselves representations, concepts are 'representations of representations,' doubly phenomenal.

Concepts and the faculty of reason are important because they enable us to make judgments, plan the future, construct scientific theories, act purposively, and cooperate with others. But they provide us with no knowledge of reality. 'All that is material in our knowledge – that is to say, all that cannot be reduced to subjective form – comes from without, and thus ultimately from the objective perception of the corporeal world, a perception that has its origin in sensation' (*FR* 170–1/H. 1, 115). All direct knowledge of reality – that is, all 'primary knowledge' (*FR* 113/H. 1, 78) – is attained by the understanding alone (*FR* 104/H. 1, 72); all grasp of causal connections and all great discoveries are the province of the understanding without the employment of concepts (*FR* 103, 113/H. 1, 71, 78 cf. *W1* 21/H. 2, 24–5). And so on. The faculty of reason, then, is distinctly unimportant compared with the faculty of understanding: it provides only '*secondary* knowledge' – that is, knowledge not of reality, but of truths, by means of concepts and words (*FR* 103/H. 1, 71). 'Every simpleton has the faculty of reason; give him the premises and he will draw the conclusion. But the understanding supplies *primary* and therefore intuitive knowledge' (*FR* 113/H. 1, 78). Because of this, Schopenhauer is contemptuous of those who hold that reason transcends experience and, 'as a faculty of the supersensuous,' intuits things in themselves (*FR* 166/H. 1, 112).

Concepts are not useful in isolation but only when combined to form true judgments and express knowledge. But, while judgments are useful in expressing knowledge, none can provide it out of its own resources; that is, none is intrinsically true. Truth, Schopenhauer accordingly asserts, is a relational property: if a judgment is true, it is based upon something other than itself, upon an external ground or reason. In summary, Schopenhauer holds that necessarily every true judgment has a reason external to it and constituting its ground.[29] He also holds that the reason in question is a sufficient reason, so that necessarily the truth of its judgment follows.

This relation between the truth of judgments and reasons constitutes what Schopenhauer considers to be the root of the second form of the principle of sufficient reason, named not altogether happily the principle of sufficient reason of *knowing*.[30] It states simply that every true judgment has a sufficient reason for its truth.

Schopenhauer classifies reasons forming grounds of truth under four kinds, and accordingly he holds that there are four kinds of truth: logical, empirical, transcendental, and metalogical.[31] A judgment possessing logical truth is one based upon the truth of another judgment or other judgments; the conclusion of a syllogism, for example, possesses logical truth, being based upon the truth of its premises. A judgment possessing empirical truth is one based upon the world of empirically real objects. *The cat is on the mat*, for example, possesses empirical truth, based upon the fact that one empirically real object, a cat, is positioned upon another, a mat. A judgment possessing transcendental truth is one based upon the existence or nature of time, space, or causality, the forms of the faculties of sensibility and understanding. *Two straight lines do not enclose a space*, for example, possesses transcendental truth, based upon the nature of space, and so does the judgment *Nothing can happen without a cause*, based upon the nature of causality. Finally, a judgment possessing metalogical truth is one based upon the formal conditions of all thought. *No predicate can be asserted and simultaneously denied of a subject* possesses metalogical truth, based upon the impossibility of our thinking in ways contrary to it.

The part played in Schopenhauer's system of thought by this account of concepts, judgments, reason, and truth is at once obvious. Concepts are representations, being creations of the intellect and derived from other creations of the intellect or from its formal conditions. Judgments too are representations, being combinations of concepts that have as their subject matter creations of the intellect or its formal conditions. It follows that neither concepts nor judgments provide knowledge of absolute reality; in fact, as has been noted, they do not even provide primary knowledge of representational reality. Further, given that all reasons constituting grounds of true judgments are themselves representations, consisting of judgments, real objects, or forms of the intellect, all inferences from judgments to reasons, or from reasons to judgments, lead merely from representations to representations. In particular, deductive reasoning, the rationalist's would-be ladder of ontological ascent, remains within the domain of judgments and therefore of representations.[32]

If Schopenhauer is right, all metaphysicians assigning an intuitive role to reason are mistaken; that is, all metaphysicians are mistaken who assert that reason is capable of an immediate grasp of reality. Mistaken too are those who assert that reason is capable through inference of reaching reality as it is in itself. From this it follows that the ontological argument is fallacious, moving as supposedly it does from concept to concept, along with all other arguments seeking to reach reality through the inferences of reason. But at the same time, Schopenhauer's assertions threaten his own metaphysics. For if all concepts and all words are derived from representations,[33] if all that is material in our knowledge comes from perception of the corporeal world and has its origin in sensation, and if reason cannot take us beyond representations, then we cannot reason to the Will, nor can we meaningfully talk or think about it. Still less can we acquire conceptual knowledge of it.

The position reached so far in the *Fourfold Root*, then, is this. The faculty of understanding, with the assistance of sensibility, creates real objects and has experiential knowledge of them. But the only *inferences* it can make concerning them are inferences from changes in one to changes in another. Similarly, the faculty of reason creates concepts and has knowledge through them. But the only *inferences* it can make are from one judgment to another. Consequently, if knowledge of the thing in itself is to be attained, this will not be through the understanding or through reason.

V   THE THIRD CLASS OF OBJECTS AND THE FORM OF THE PRINCIPLE OF SUFFICIENT REASON GOVERNING IT

The objects that make up the third class of representations are time and space. These, like real objects and concepts, are representations, given that they are dependent for their existence upon the intellect. They are the forms of inner and outer sensibility (*FR* 193/H. 1, 130), existing within the brain (*FR* 77/H. 1, 53), and imposed upon sensory data to bring about the perception of real objects. From another point of view, however, as outward projections, so to speak, of the faculty of sensibility, time and space are themselves perceived, constituting the objects of pure, a priori, and immediate perception (*Anschauung*) (*FR* 193/H. 1, 130); and as such they are particulars, not concepts.

As particulars, time and space are made up of parts, and the systematic interrelatedness of these parts constitutes the root of the third form of the principle of sufficient reason, named the principle of sufficient reason of *being*. Time is made up of an infinite number of ordered moments, rather like points on a line, and each moment has a determinate position in relation to and dependent upon the others, these together constituting its sufficient reason. Space is correspondingly made up of an infinite number of ordered points, forming lines, angles, areas, and volumes, and any one of these is where it is and as it is because the others are where they are and as they are. In other words, the geometric properties of any given part of space have as their sufficient reason the geometric properties of some other part or parts of space. Further, the sufficient reason in question is neither causal nor conceptual, but ontological. That is, if we ask of any part of space why it *is* as it *is*, in principle we find an answer in terms of how other parts of space *are* as they *are*. If we ask, for example, why the angles of a given triangle are as they are, we find that they are as they are because the sides of the triangle are as *they* are.

The existence of numbers, thinks Schopenhauer, and therefore the existence of arithmetic, rests upon the possibility of counting in time, and from this he concludes that arithmetic is a systematic and intuitive grasp of temporal relations, corresponding to the grasp of spatial relations attained in geometry – at any rate, in geometry as this ought to be. The qualification here is important. Geometry as it ought to be, thinks Schopenhauer, is a direct non-empirical perception of the parts of space and their relations, and he criticises the proofs of Euclid on the grounds that these are not what geometry ought to be, but instead mere conceptual exercises relating judgments to judgments. In other words, Euclid's proofs, thinks Schopenhauer, are mere exercises of reason – indeed, 'a brilliant piece of perversity' (*W1* 70/H. 2, 84) – affording no insight into the reality of space and its properties. On the other hand, it does not follow that the judgments constituting Euclid's conclusions are not true. They are true. But the truth that they have as conclusions is logical, depending upon the truth of their premisses, and it is because of this that the proofs themselves are concerned with concepts, not space.[34]

This criticism of Euclid provides confirmation of Schopenhauer's low estimation of reason as incapable of apprehending reality. He is convinced that perception alone, non-empirical in the case of time and space, is capable of that.

It is at once obvious how Schopenhauer's views on time, space, and mathematics fit into his system. Time and space are representations, creations of the intellect, and genuine mathematics provides insight into their nature. But it does no more. It provides no intuition of the thing in itself, and the only inferences it draws are from parts of time or space to other parts of time or space.

If true, this is a blow to the rationalist tradition in philosophy. For that tradition in the main regards mathematics as the exemplar of knowledge reaching to absolute reality through thought alone.

VI THE FOURTH CLASS OF OBJECTS AND
THE FORM OF THE PRINCIPLE OF
SUFFICIENT REASON GOVERNING IT

The objects that make up the fourth class of representations are our individual selves, and these we know directly in the experience of self-consciousness. But although we thus know ourselves directly, we do not know ourselves as subjects of knowing, but rather as subjects of willing or wills. In other words, in self-consciousness we do not confront ourselves as things that know, but instead as things that will. The reason for this, argues Schopenhauer, is that knowing subjects cannot know themselves as such, that is, cannot know themselves as knowing subjects, because if something is known it is known as an object (FR 208/H. 1, 141). To put the point differently, objects and only objects are known; consequently, when we know ourselves, the selves that we know are not our knowing selves as such, but something else. They are, says Schopenhauer, wills.

Although our selves as wills are assigned to a class of objects different from our bodies, this does not mean that according to Schopenhauer each of us comprises two different beings, a body and a will. On the contrary, each of us is one and undivided. However, while we are one, we know ourselves in two independent ways. We know ourselves from the outside, and from this vantage point know ourselves as bodies, and we know ourselves from the inside, and from this vantage point know ourselves as wills. The difference, then, between ourselves as bodies and ourselves as wills is one of knowledge, not being.

Schopenhauer later adds that the subject knowing itself as will is identical with that will, both being the selfsame 'I.' But this identity, which he describes as the ultimate point of unity in the universe (der Weltknoten), cannot, he says, be explained; it is given in immediate knowledge (unmittelbar gegeben). It cannot be explained because explanations are of objects and relations between objects, and what is at issue here is the identity between an object and something necessarily not an object. Consequently, this identity is radically beyond explanation and can only be described as the most outstanding of miracles (das Wunder κατ᾽ ἐξοχήν).

This account of ourselves as twofold in respect of knowledge is completed and confirmed by Schopenhauer's account of action, which goes as follows. We know with certainty that every action is preceded by an occurrence called its motive. Indeed, we find it as inconceivable that an action should be without a motive as that the movement of a lifeless body should be without a cause. The reason for this is that motives are causes: they are causes seen from within, as wills are bodies seen from within.

In most instances of causation, namely, mechanical, chemical, and the like, we know that causation is present and even discern its necessity; but, remaining on the outside, we know nothing of its inner nature. But in the case of our own actions, things are different. We do indeed have knowledge of these from the outside, just as we have knowledge of ourselves as bodies from the outside; but we also have knowledge of them from the inside. 'Here we stand behind the scenes, so to speak, and discover the inmost nature of the process by which a cause produces its effect' (FR 213/H. 1, 145).

The relationship between motives and actions, then, is identical with that between causes and effects in real objects; but, because it is known in a different way, Schopenhauer considers it to constitute the root of a separate form of the principle of sufficient reason, which this time he names the principle of sufficient reason of *acting*. It states simply that every action has a motive.

What Schopenhauer says concerning individual wills is important in relation to his system for an obvious reason. If wills are identical with bodies, it follows that, like other real objects, they are creations of the intellect and so provide no immediate knowledge of the thing in itself. At the same time, if motives and actions, being causes and effects, are changes in real objects, inferences concerning them lead from changes in objects to changes in other objects, never beyond.

There is also a reason that is not so obvious for the importance to his system of what Schopenhauer says. The fact that our bodies seen from within are our wills, he tells us, constitutes the foundation stone of his 'whole metaphysics' (FR 214/H. 1, 145). What he means by this is that immediate knowledge of our selves as wills gives us a grasp of the inner nature not only of our bodies, but of all representational reality; each of us serves as a microcosmic part to reveal the whole. Simultaneously, he believes, this knowledge leads us to a grasp of the thing in itself; for 'this *thing in itself*, this substratum of all appearances, and consequently of the whole of nature, is nothing but what we know immediately and very intimately, and find within ourselves as *will*.'[35] This transition from knowledge of wills to knowledge of the Will is possible because wills are objectifications and in some sort revelations of the Will.

It must be added that it is only from other works that we know this to be what Schopenhauer means. The *Fourfold Root* gives us no more than hints.

VII NECESSITY

In his concluding chapter, Schopenhauer briefly discusses the nature and scope of necessity, and his chief contention here is that what necessity means is nothing other than the inevitability with which a consequent follows upon its reason, so that only conditional relations have necessity – relations of the form *if x, then y*. Given this, it makes no sense to attribute necessity to a thing, as opposed to a relation, and it follows besides that the notion of a thing's being *absolutely* necessary is contradictory. What Schopenhauer seems to have in mind here is that to say of a thing that it is absolutely necessary is to say that it is simultaneously absolute and necessary, and that this entails its being simultaneously not dependent and dependent. It entails its being not dependent because to say of a thing that it is absolute is to say that it is not dependent, and it entails its being dependent because to say of a thing that it is necessary means, insofar as it means anything,[36] that it follows from something else.

Schopenhauer concludes by saying that the only necessary relations are those embodied in the four forms of the principle of sufficient reason, and that consequently there are four kinds of necessity: logical necessity, in virtue of which a conclusion has to follow from its premises; empirical necessity, in virtue of which an effect has to follow from its cause; mathematical necessity, in virtue of which a set of mathematical properties has to follow from some other set constituting its reason; and moral necessity, in virtue of which an action has to follow from its motive.[37]

If what Schopenhauer says is right, this makes the entire tradition of rationalist metaphysics wrong; since, to characterise it in a word or two, that tradition attempts to infer the existence and nature of an absolutely necessary reality from absolutely necessary premises. But absolutely necessary realities and premises, declares Schopenhauer, are absurdities. It is worth adding that the necessities that Schopenhauer does allow are of no interest to the rationalist metaphysician, since they arise from the brain and reflect the brain's limitations. When speaking of the necessity with which we think in accordance with the laws of thought, Schopenhauer says that 'it is just as impossible to think in opposition to them as it is to move our limbs in a direction contrary to their joints' (FR 162/H. 1, 109). He might have added that this is for closely analogous reasons.

If metaphysics is to survive in Schopenhauer's scheme of thought, then, it cannot be based upon reasoning from necessities to necessities. It must appeal to immediate knowledge.[38]

VIII TWO IMPLICIT ARGUMENTS

Given the pervasive importance of the issue, it will be useful to conclude by saying something about Schopenhauer's arguments for the representational nature of the everyday world that he implies rather than plainly expresses in the *Fourfold Root*.

Before he discusses the objects making up the everyday world, he says that the knowing consciousness is divided into subject and object, and that to be an object for a subject is one and the same as to be a representation (FR 41–2/H. 1, 27). If by this he means to argue, as probably he does,[39] that tables, chairs, concepts, and so on exist in consciousness as objects dependent upon a subject, and that therefore they exist *only* as objects dependent upon a subject, what he says is unimpressive.[40] For, considered as objects in the sense of being *present to a subject*,[41] tables, chairs, and the rest are undoubtedly dependent upon a subject. But it does not follow that, considered as objects in the sense of being *things* thus present, tables, chairs, and the rest are dependent upon a subject. To think that it does is like thinking that, because Mrs. Smith considered as a wife is dependent upon her husband, she is therefore dependent upon him *sans phrase*.[42]

A better argument, Kantian in origin and alluded to clearly though tersely in the *Fourfold Root* (FR 28–9, 232/H. 1, 20–1, 158), goes as follows. Given that the principle of sufficient reason is a necessary truth, known a priori, it is dependent for its origin and existence upon the intellect, and from this it follows that all objects whose nature is constituted by the relationships expressed in that principle are likewise dependent upon the intellect. The world made up of such objects, therefore, is a world of representations, not things in themselves; such a world, 'presenting itself by virtue of a priori forms, is precisely on that account a mere phenomenon' (FR 232/ H. 1, 158).[43]

The argument when applied to real objects comes to this. The principle of sufficient reason of *becoming* is a necessary truth, known a priori, and is therefore dependent for its origin and existence upon the intellect. But it is a truth expressing relationships that are constitutive of the nature of real objects. It tells us that necessarily all changes in real objects have causes and are themselves causes, and that this is a property of real objects constitutive of their nature. It follows that real objects, like the relationships expressed by the a priori principle of sufficient reason of becoming itself, are dependent upon the intellect; they are therefore representations. The understanding 'first of all makes perception possible, for the law of causality, the possibility of effect and cause, springs only from the understanding, and is valid also for it alone; hence the world of perception exists only for it and through it' (W1 20/H. 2, 23).

This argument can succeed only if the principle of sufficient reason of becoming is known a priori; but, as the following considerations will serve to bring out, there are no serious grounds for believing that it is. The principle states that necessarily all changes in real objects are caused, that necessarily every cause belongs to a series having neither beginning nor end, and, by way of corollary, that necessarily matter is eternal (FR 64–5/H. 1, 42–3). But there are no good grounds for holding any of this to be true, let alone a priori. On the contrary, there are good grounds for holding that atoms can decay without cause, that matter came into existence some fifteen billion years ago, and that all causal series, like time and space themselves, had a beginning. Future thought and experiment may well show these beliefs to be false; but, true or false, they cannot be dismissed as contradictory or otherwise inconceivable.

The argument applied to time and space is, even more briefly, as follows. The principle of sufficient reason of *being* is a necessary truth, known a priori, and is therefore dependent for its origin and existence upon the intellect. But it is a truth expressing relationships that are constitutive of the nature of time and space. It tells us that the parts of time are interconnected by the relationships expressed in the truths of arithmetic, an interconnectedness that is constitutive of time, and it tells us that the parts of space are interconnected by the relationships expressed in the theorems of Euclidean geometry,[44] an interconnectedness that is constitutive of space. It follows that time and space, like the relationships expressed in the a priori truths of arithmetic and Euclidean geometry, are dependent upon the intellect.

This argument is unconvincing for the following reasons. While the relationships expressed in the truths of arithmetic are known a priori, there is no plausibility to the claim that they are constitutive of time, since what constitutes time is transitory succession, arithmetical relations holding good of it being no more than supervenient properties. Similarly, the relationships expressed in the theorems of Euclidean geometry are a priori,[45] but there is no plausibility to the claim that they are constitutive of space, since they are not even true of space. At any rate, given that the theorems of other geometries have as much claim to be accepted as those of Euclidean geometry,[46] it is more plausible to suppose that all alike are true in virtue of the axioms they stem from, and that these are matters of choice and convention.

It is clear from these brief remarks that Schopenhauer cannot establish the representational nature of time, space, real objects, and individual wills by appealing to the principle of sufficient reason,[47] any more than he can by appealing to the truth that an object needs a subject. But it will be recalled that the story does not end there. There is the argument based upon considerations of the physiology of perception, and the supposedly important point that Schopenhauer infers from these may well be justified. 'The important point is that any experience that arises in consciousness is a subjective experience, and is not part of an independent external world. This independent external world is a fiction generated for us by the brain, which we have mistakenly taken as real.'[48]

If Schopenhauer is right in holding that the everyday world is mere representation, he is probably right too in holding that we cannot draw inferences from it concerning the nature of the thing in itself. For, to put the point in a nutshell, such inferences would be from properties characterising the everyday world to analogous properties characterising the thing in itself. But reflection on the properties of the everyday world provides no grounds for believing that the thing in itself is characterised by analogous properties, because it provides no grounds for believing it to be characterised by properties at all.

If we are to have knowledge of the thing in itself, then, our knowledge will have to be non-inferential.

NOTES

1 The edition of 1847 is so different from that of 1813 that it is almost another book. The edition of 1813 is superior in style, coherence, and even content to that of 1847, and it displays none of the bitterness and grotesque rudeness of the latter. However, I base this chapter on the edition of 1847 because that is the edition most English readers are familiar with and because it contains the discussion on perception that is central to the theme of this chapter. The translation that I refer to as *FR* is by E. F. J. Payne (La Salle, Illinois: Open Court, 1974), though I occasionally alter the wording where I think it can be made clearer. The 1813 edition (*FR*[1]) has recently been translated into English by F. C. White under the title *Schopenhauer's Early Fourfold Root* (Aldershot: Avebury, 1997).

2 Representations, *Vorstellungen*, are the immediate contents of consciousness, whether or not they are produced by or point to something beyond them.

3 To forestall confusion, it should be added that Schopenhauer's 'Platonic Ideas' are representations too, though *toto coelo* different from the representations of the everyday world. The Third Book of *The World as Will and Representation* is subtitled *The Representation Independent of the Principle of Sufficient Reason*.

4 Schopenhauer's *reale Objekte* are what we would call *material* or *physical* objects.

5 In most contexts, *reason* and *explanation* are synonymous. 'Denn der Satz vom Grunde ist das *Princip aller Erklärung*' (*FR* 229 /H. 1, 156).

6 If, to put the point crudely, the consequent does not *have* to follow, then the reason is simply not sufficient in the first place.

7 Schopenhauer also holds that necessarily every event is a cause. This is a third necessity.

8 Ultimately, each kind of connectedness depends upon one form of the principle of sufficient reason, which is synthetic a priori and therefore has its origin or root in the intellect. Consequently, the fourfold root is *ultimately* in the intellect. (See, e.g., *FR* 232/H. 1 , 158.)

9 The adjective *anschaulich* is translated here as *intuitive*; it could be translated, and in some contexts is better translated, as *perceptible*. The same remark applies, mutatis mutandis, to *Anschauung* and to the verb *anschauen*.

10 This point will be taken up further in the concluding section of this essay.

11 In the 1813 edition Schopenhauer speaks of the understanding as having many categories, but here he assumes that their number is reducible to one.

12 More accurately, when we see something red, what happens is that we receive a sensation which, through an application of the category of cause, we attribute to a causal power in an object. When an event lasts for five minutes, the event is seen as occupying a specific period of time, as well as being attributed to an object in which it occurs.

13 Schopenhauer is quite unfair to traditional metaphysicians who refer to God as *causa sui*. They mean that, given God's nature, God has and needs no explanation. They do not mean anything so absurd as that the divine being first exists and then causes itself to come into existence, or that somehow it is different from itself and so is able to cause itself.

14 See, for example, *FR* 29, 65–6/H. 1, 21, 43–5 and see the concluding section of this essay.

15 This point will be returned to.

16 This does not really need arguing for, since we know a priori that no change can take place without a cause. Nonetheless, in the 1813 edition Schopenhauer gives as a first 'proof' of it the unshakeable certainty with which we expect experience to conform to it (*FR*[1] 26/H. 7, 36), though in the 1847 edition he treats this 'proof' as simply confirmation of the proof from perception. Elsewhere he speaks of proof as not being necessary and as being useful merely for the disputatious (*W1* 67–8/H. 2, 80–1).

17 *Empfindungen* are *sensations*, but it is possible to distinguish between *Empfindungen* as subjective occurrences of awareness, calling these *sensations*, and the objects of those subjective occurrences of awareness, calling these *sensory data*. The distinction is that made from time to time between *sensations*, on the one hand, and *sensata* or *sensa*, on the other.

18 Schopenhauer is careless in talking of real objects as causes of sensations. Given that on his view objects cannot be causes, he must be taken to mean that the understanding infers there to be objects in which the relevant causal changes occur.

19 Schopenhauer holds that concepts, time, and space are all functions of (or in some sense identical with) the brain, and that individual wills are identical with individual bodies. Since, therefore, bodies and brains are real objects, a proof that real objects are representational is eo ipso a proof that concepts, time, space, and wills are representational. This will become clearer in later sections of this essay.

20 I use the word *materialist* because that is the word used by Schopenhauer. The word *physicalist* would be more accurate.

21 It is sometimes asserted that neuroscience is making progress in explaining these things, but that is surely false. Neuroscience tells us more and more about neurones and their interrelations, and about their correlations with conscious states, but that is all.

22 Other well-canvassed problems concern the relativity of perception, hallucinations and illusions, dreams, and the seemingly inevitable effects of interaction between perceiver and perceived.

23 In fact the position of theoretical physicists concerning the world of perceptible objects is at bottom identical with Schopenhauer's. There are two reasons for my saying this. One is that the properties attributed to things by present-day physicists are embedded in theories that will almost certainly be replaced. The other is that the properties attributed to things by physicists are relational properties, and we have no idea what the intrinsic properties of things are. The upshot is that in the end our account of perception has to be something like this: x, bearing unknown intrinsic properties F, causally affects y, bearing unknown intrinsic properties G, as a result of which x appears to y as a billiard ball or something else of the sort, and y appears to y as a brain.

24 This is looked at later on in the discussion of the fourth class of objects.

25 '...über die Erscheinung hinausgehenden' (FR 69/H. 1, 46). Once the thing in itself is allowed an explanatory role, it is possible for Schopenhauer to escape the charge of making the intellect its own cause in any ultimate sense. That is why earlier on I limited myself to saying that the intellect's being its own cause was a prima facie disaster for Schopenhauer.

26 But see W1 41–2/H. 2, 49–50.

27 They are derived either from individuals of the first class, which are objects of empirical perception, or from individuals of the third class, which are objects of pure perception.

28 As was made clear earlier, the intellect is the brain, and the faculty of reason is part of the intellect.

29 A true judgment can have more than one reason for its truth. For example, the judgment *Some men are mortal* has the judgment *All men are mortal* as a reason, but it also has empirical facts.

30 There is an irony in its being called the principle of sufficient reason of *knowing*, given that primary knowledge can only be acquired by the understanding; Schopenhauer would perhaps have done better to call it the principle of sufficient reason of *truth*. Even so, it is clear what he means: he means that the sufficient reason in question is sufficient for the judgment to *express* knowledge, not to acquire it.

31 In FR[1] and W1 Schopenhauer uses the word *metaphysical* where later he uses *transcendental*.

32 Schopenhauer usually speaks as if the sole inferential activity of reason is deduction, and he does not investigate the nature of inductive reasoning.

33 According to Schopenhauer, concepts and words are inseparable (*FR* 148/H. 1, 99), and what is properly called *thinking* is always 'carried out with the aid of words' (*FR* 153/H. 1, 103).

34 While as conclusions they have logical truth, as resting on the form of outer sensibility they have transcendental truth.

35 *WN* 20/H. 4, 2. Compare: 'It is just this double knowledge of our own body which gives us information about that body itself, about its action and movement following on motives, as well as about its suffering through outside impressions, in a word, about what it is, not as representation, but as something over and above this, and hence what it is *in itself*' (*W1* 103/H. 2, 123).

36 Schopenhauer seems to have in mind that from the proposition *If x, then y* you can conclude that y itself is necessary in the sense that necessarily it follows from x.

37 Schopenhauer is particularly careless in his formulations here, making them neither uniform nor complete, and he pays no attention to the double necessity involved in each form of the principle of sufficient reason.

38 This is what Schopenhauer himself believes. 'The core and the main point' of his doctrine, its 'proper and essential metaphysics,' is 'that this *thing in itself*, this substratum of all phenomena, and therefore of the whole of Nature, is nothing but what we know DIRECTLY and INTIMATELY, and what we find within ourselves as the *Will*.' (Small caps mine.) *WN* 19–20/H. 4, 2.

39 See *FR* 51–2/H. 1, 32–3, where there is also an allusion to the argument that non-representational objects are a superfluous duplication (cf. *W2* 9/H. 3, 11). See also *FR* 209–10; *FR*[1] 18, 51, 53; *W1* 3–5, 14, 30–4; *W2* 4–15/H. 1, 141–2; H. 7, 24, 69–70, 72–3; H. 2, 3–6, 16, 35–41; H. 3, 4–18.

40 Schopenhauer's argument is difficult to interpret because he wants a representation to be subject as well as object and yet to be opposed as a whole to the thing in itself. This suggests that subject and object combined are dependent upon some further subject.

41 Literally, *thrown against*. The word is from the verb *obiicere*, meaning to *throw against* or *oppose* to.

42 Elsewhere Schopenhauer attempts to strengthen his argument by appealing to our inability to know or even imagine what an object would be like separated from its subject; but he still unjustifiably asserts that the existence of objects without a subject is *inconceivable* and *contradictory*. See, e.g., the whole first chapter of *W2* 3–18/H. 3, 3–22.

43 'The form under which the principle of sufficient reason rules in a class of representations also always constitutes and exhausts the whole nature of this class' (*W1* 40/H. 2, 48).

44 It is important to note that when he talks about the principle of sufficient reason of being as applied to space, Schopenhauer has in mind that space is Euclidean and that 'reasons of being' are Euclidean properties. His criticism of Euclid, it will be recalled, concerns Euclid's method, not the substance of his theorems. What Schopenhauer wants is to intuit Euclidean relations, not just entertain propositions concerning them. In keeping with this, when he gives examples of reasons of being, they are simply Euclidean properties. The properties of a right-angled triangle, for example, constitute a reason of being for the fact that the square on its hypotenuse equals the sum of the squares on the other two sides.

45 That its theorems follow from its axioms is not a matter of empirical discovery or confirmation.

46 In a Euclidean plane $s^2 = a^2 + b^2$; in an elliptic plane (taking the radius as the unit) $\cos s = \cos a \cos b$; in a hyperbolic plane (taking the constant k as the unit) $\cosh s = \cosh a \cosh b$. All are equally acceptable.

47 Individual wills are real objects, albeit seen from within. I leave out mention of concepts here, the remaining class of Schopenhauer's objects, because the representational nature of these, understood as states of the intellect (as Schopenhauer understands them), poses no threat to realism.

48 This quotation, which could easily have come from the *Fourfold Root*, is from an article in the *New Scientist*, 'Can brains be conscious?' by P. Fenwick and D. Lorimer, 5 August 1989.

4 Schopenhauer, Kant, and the Methods of Philosophy

I TRANSCENDENTAL PHILOSOPHY WITHOUT TRANSCENDENTAL ARGUMENTS

As the title of his magnum opus, *The World as Will and Representation*, suggests, Schopenhauer held that we know the world in two different ways, through our representations of objects in space and time and through our experience of our ability to move our own bodies by willing to do so. In his account of our knowledge of the world through representation, he accepted the core of Kant's transcendental idealism, the view that the spatial and temporal forms in which experience presents objects to us, as well as the basic structure of the concepts by means of which we think about and judge these objects, above all the category of causality, are impositions of our own minds on our experience, that is, they reflect the structure of our own perception and conception of reality but not any structure that reality has in itself independently of our representation of it. In his account of our knowledge of the nature of reality through our own will, however, Schopenhauer rejected Kant's inference that transcendental idealism, while it allows us to *conceive* of certain features of how things may be in themselves by means of our categories, and even to adopt certain *postulates* about them for the sake of our practical reason, that is, morality,[1] completely precludes us from having any actual *knowledge* of them. Instead, Schopenhauer argued that in our own experience of willing we have a mode of access to the nature of reality that is a genuine complement to our usual spatial, temporal, and causal framework for the representation of objects, and on this basis he created a picture of the real nature of existence as endless strife and striving that Kant could hardly have imagined,

93

let alone accepted, and which in fact leads to a moral philosophy, based on compassion rather than reason, that is antipodal to Kant's.

At least part of the reason why Schopenhauer could develop a philosophy that is so close to and yet so far from Kant's is a fundamental difference in their *methodologies*. Schopenhauer adopted Kant's idea that we have *transcendental knowledge* of the fundamental conditions of the possibility of experience, but he did not accept Kant's idea that such transcendental knowledge is based on what Kant called *transcendental proofs* or what we now call *transcendental arguments*; and thus he also did not think himself bound by the conclusions about the *limits* of our knowledge that Kant drew from his transcendental arguments as he understood them. Instead, Schopenhauer thought that he could employ a more straightforward method of the scrutiny of experience itself, a method much more akin to the empiricism of Hume before him and of phenomenologists such as Edmund Husserl after him, and thought that such a direct scrutiny of our experience shows that we have in fact not one but two ways of comprehending it: through our representation of the spatial, temporal, and causal relations of objects, on the one hand, and through our own capacity for willing, on the other. Given his own conception of philosophical method and his rejection of Kant's method of transcendental argument, Schopenhauer saw no need to reject one of these two modes of comprehension. This chapter, however, will not attempt to tell the whole story of how Schopenhauer exploited his methodological difference with Kant in the construction of his own philosophy. Instead, it will only take the preliminary step of examining Schopenhauer's critique of Kant's general method of transcendental argument and several of its applications, including Schopenhauer's famous critique of Kant's treatment of causation.

Kant offered various characterizations of the transcendental method for philosophy that he took himself to have invented. None of these is clear and complete enough to make the interpretation of his intended method an easy matter. But the following statement, from the opening of the 'System of All Principles of Pure Understanding', the all-important section of the *Critique of Pure Reason* in which Kant attempts to draw from his previous demonstrations of the spatio-temporal form of all our experience (in the 'Transcendental Aesthetic') and the judgmental form of all conscious thought about this experience (in the 'Transcendental Deduction') the proofs

of the most fundamental principles of empirical knowledge, above
all the principles of the permanence of substance, the universality
of causation for all events in time, and the reality of interaction between all objects in space, brings out features of Kant's method that
will be crucial for the contrast with Schopenhauer. Here Kant says:

A priori principles bear this name not merely because they contain in themselves the grounds of other judgments, but also because they are not themselves grounded in higher and more general cognitions. Yet this property
does not elevate them beyond all proof. For although this could not be carried further objectively, but rather grounds all cognition of its object, yet this
does not prevent a proof from the subjective sources of the possibility of a
cognition of an object in general from being possible, indeed even necessary,
since otherwise the proposition would raise the greatest supposition of being
a merely surreptitious assertion. (A 148–9/B 188)

Kant is suggesting that the most fundamental principles of knowledge – he refers to them as 'a priori principles', although the context
makes clear that he means 'synthetic a priori principles', that is, universal and necessary but also substantive principles, which cannot
be known to be true through the analysis of concepts alone, which
yields only analytic a priori principles[2] – provide the ultimate justification for all more particular claims to knowledge, but are nevertheless themselves capable of being proved by philosophical reflection
on 'the subjective sources of the possibility of a cognition of an object in general', or what he usually calls reflection on the 'conditions
of the possibility of experience in general', which 'are at the same
time conditions of the possibility of the objects of experience, and
on this account have objective validity in a synthetic judgment a
priori' (A 158/B 197). His basic idea is that although our assurance
that any object that we can encounter can be assigned a determinate
size or duration, for example, is grounded on our certainty that space
and time are the form of all our empirical intuition of particular objects, and our assurance that there is some particular cause for any
event we can experience is grounded on the universal validity of the
principle that every event has a cause, these general principles themselves – the universal validity of space, time, and causation for all our
experience – can be derived from an even more fundamental form of
reflection on the possibility of experience as such. In Kant's view, we
can derive the universal validity of space and time from reflection on

how it is possible for us to individuate objects as numerically distinct at all (A 23/B 38); we can derive the universal validity of categories in general by reflection on the fact that any consciousness of an experience as our own at all takes the form of a judgment linking that experience to others that we recognize as our own (e.g., B 133–5); and we can derive the universal validity of a specific principle like that of causation from the combination of these two reflections, that is, from reflection on the fact that we must make our judgments about an array of data – in Kant's terms, a manifold of intuition – that is always presented to us as spatial and temporal (see especially A 155/B 194). This form of reflection is what Kant means by transcendental proof, or at least a major part of what he means (we will see in Section II that the story is a little more complicated than has thus far been suggested).

Schopenhauer accepts much of Kant's results. In fact, by using as my examples space, time, and causality, I have mentioned only those among Kant's conditions of the possibility of experience which Schopenhauer also believes to be the basis for our experience of objects through representation. And he agrees with Kant in characterizing his knowledge of the indispensability of these forms of experience as 'transcendental'. But Schopenhauer does not accept Kant's characterization of his method for discovering these fundamental principles of knowledge as a special kind of reflection on the conditions of the possibility of experience. Instead, Schopenhauer thinks that we discover the ubiquity of space, time, and causality in our representation of objects by means of a direct and immediate scrutiny of our experience. In his words:

An essential difference between Kant's method and that which I follow is to be found in the fact that he starts from indirect, reflected knowledge, whereas I start from direct and intuitive knowledge. He is comparable to a person who measures the height of a tower from its shadow; but I am like one who applies the measuring-rod directly to the tower itself. (W1 452–3/H. 2, 537)

As we will see in Section III, Schopenhauer defends his use of a 'direct' rather than a 'reflected' method for philosophy, a method for discovering transcendental knowledge without transcendental arguments, by arguing that the idea of a transcendental argument is actually incoherent – in his view, a fundamental principle of knowledge is by definition one that cannot be derived from anything more fundamental. The chief issue for a full study of the relationship between the theoretical philosophies of Kant and Schopenhauer would be how this methodological difference leads to the substantive differences between them, above all Schopenhauer's claim that we have access to the real nature of existence through our own will. But this chapter will focus on the genuine question about the possibility of transcendental arguments that Schopenhauer succeeds in raising – a question that has been extensively debated in recent years, though without explicit reference to Schopenhauer[3] – and on his critique of several of Kant's particular transcendental arguments. Before we can begin even this limited project, however, we will have to undertake a brief review of some of Kant's most important transcendental arguments as he understood them.

II KANT'S TRANSCENDENTAL ARGUMENTS

It is not surprising that Schopenhauer should have found Kant's transcendental method suspect. Not only did Kant himself never provide a detailed account of his method; worse, the several comments about the character of transcendental arguments that he did make suggest two different models of how such arguments are supposed to work. On the one hand, several of Kant's characterizations of his transcendental method, above all his characterizations of what he means by a transcendental deduction of the categories of thought, suggest that a transcendental argument is one that establishes the universal and necessary validity of certain concepts and/or principles that are given and known a priori as the necessary condition of the possibility of any knowledge of objects at all, even if that knowledge is itself considered to be empirical. On such a conception, a transcendental deduction may justify and explain a priori knowledge of objects, but it does not presuppose any such knowledge. Kant provides characterizations of this sort when he says:

The transcendental deduction of all *a priori* concepts therefore has a principle toward which the entire investigation must be directed, namely this: that they must be recognized as *a priori* conditions of the possibility of experiences (whether of the intuition that is encountered in them, or of the thinking). (A 94/B 126)

In the comparison of philosophical with mathematical method that is a centerpiece of the concluding 'Doctrine of Method' of the *Critique of Pure Reason*, Kant makes even more explicit a characterization of transcendental arguments on which they are supposed to discover a priori conditions for even merely empirical cognitions: 'through concepts of the understanding, however, [reason] certainly erects secure principles, but not directly from concepts, but rather always only indirectly through the relation of these concepts to something entirely contingent, namely **possible experience**' (A 736–7/B 764–5). By referring to 'possible experience' as 'contingent', Kant implies that possible experience consists of or at least includes merely empirical knowledge, and thus implies that transcendental arguments discover a priori conditions of empirical knowledge. In other places, however, Kant suggests that a transcendental argument assumes the existence of some particular body of synthetic a priori knowledge, and provides an explanation of the possibility of such knowledge which may in turn imply the existence of other synthetic a priori knowledge, not previously assumed. Characterizations like this may be found in the 'Transcendental Aesthetic', where Kant says 'I understand by a **transcendental exposition** the explanation of a concept as a principle from which the possibility of other synthetic *a priori* cognitions can be gained' (B 40),[4] and in the *Prolegomena to Any Future Metaphysics*, the brief work that Kant published in 1783 to try to popularize the *Critique of Pure Reason*, where he wrote:

We have therefore some at least *uncontested* synthetic cognition *a priori*, and we do not need to ask whether it is possible (for it is actual), but only: *how it is possible*, in order to be able to derive, from the principle of the possibility of the given cognition, the possibility of all other synthetic cognition *a priori*.[5]

To be sure, Kant offers this as a characterization of what he calls the 'analytic' method of the *Prolegomena*, which he contrasts to the 'synthetic' method of the *Critique*, which is supposed to proceed 'by inquiring within pure reason itself, and seeking to determine within this source both the elements and the laws of its pure use, according to principles'.[6] In fact, however, the transcendental arguments of the *Critique* and the *Prolegomena* do not differ in logical form, but only – sometimes – in the strength of their premises, that is, in just what or how much is assumed to be synthetic a priori cognition at the outset.[7] Thus what we find in the *Critique* is this: some of Kant's transcendental arguments attempt to prove that there are a priori forms of sensibility and understanding in the human mind that are the conditions of the possibility of any knowledge at all, even strictly empirical knowledge, while others assume that we have some specific synthetic a priori cognition, and attempt to show that the existence of a priori forms of sensibility and understanding in our minds are the conditions of the possibility of that synthetic a priori cognition.

Arguments of the latter form might seem to be patently circular: while supposed to prove the existence of a priori knowledge, they apparently simply assume the existence of synthetic a priori knowledge. In fact, Kant's transcendental arguments in this form are not guilty of such a glaring error; rather, what they attempt to do is to show that the a priori conditions of the possibility of some supposedly noncontroversial synthetic a priori cognition turn out to entail the existence of some other, more controversial or possibly even previously unsuspected synthetic a priori cognition.[8] For example, Kant argues that the existence of an a priori intuition of the form of space, which is necessary to explain our (supposedly) synthetic a priori cognition of the axioms of geometry, also entails the necessary spatiality of anything we experience as an external object at all, and the (supposedly) synthetic a priori cognition that we have of the necessary numerical identity of our selves in all of our possible representations – what Kant calls the 'transcendental unity of apperception' (A 107–8, A 113) – is supposed to entail synthetic a priori cognition of the applicability of logical forms of judgment and associated categories of the understanding to anything we can experience at all. If there is a problem with Kant's arguments of this form, then, it is not circularity or vacuity, but simply plausibility: although they do not assume what they are supposed to prove, they may still assume too much, that is, assume to be noncontroversial knowledge claims that are in fact highly controversial. Even if they do not assume the same synthetic a priori cognition the existence of which they are supposed to prove, the claim to synthetic a priori knowledge from which they do begin may still be questioned.

Schopenhauer does offer a blanket objection to Kant's transcendental arguments, but it does not depend on the details of Kant's arguments or have much to do with Kant's ambivalence about what sort of premises such arguments actually assume. In fact, Schopenhauer helps himself to some of Kant's particular conclusions while objecting to his style of argument. Before we can turn to Schopenhauer's critique of Kant's style of argument, however, we must catalogue some of Kant's most important instances of transcendental arguments.

In the 'Transcendental Aesthetic' of the *Critique of Pure Reason*, Kant made both of the two kinds of argument previously described about space and time. In the second edition of the *Critique*, Kant would distinguish these two types of argument under the titles 'Metaphysical' and 'Transcendental Exposition', but since we find the same two styles of arguments recurring without such a distinction elsewhere in Kant, even within the text of the 'Transcendental Deduction' of the categories itself, we can take both to fall within the scope of Kant's conception of transcendental argument. The two types of argument are as follows. On the one hand, Kant argues that we could not acquire our representations of space and time as such from an experience of individual objects in space and time because we need to represent objects as existing at different positions in space or moments in time, and thus already have a priori representations of space and time, in order to individuate distinct objects in the first place (A 23–4/B 37–8; A 30–1/B 46–7). Moreover, Kant continues, since we can only represent distinct regions in space or periods in time by regarding them as regions or periods bounded in all dimensions by more space and time, we can realize that we must have a priori intuitions of space and time as unitary but infinite wholes (A 24–5/B 39–40; A 31–2/B 47–8). Thus Kant argues that we must have a priori representations of space and time which are the conditions of all of our empirical intuitions – immediate and singular representations of empirical objects – and which are themselves pure intuitions, or immediate and singular representations in their own right. These arguments are supposed to be ones that do not presuppose any synthetic a priori cognition, but instead start off with the minimal assumption that we can experience distinct objects in distinct regions of space and time, yet can prove thereby that we must have a priori representations of space and time that can yield synthetic a priori cognition of the structure of space and time themselves. But Kant also argues that propositions of mathematics – geometry and arithmetic – are synthetic a priori, that is, known to be universally and necessarily true yet not derivable from any mere analysis of concepts, and that this can be explained only by supposing that we have a priori representations of space and time in which we can construct mathematical objects that will verify the synthetic a priori propositions of mathematics (A 24/B 40–1; A 31/B 47).[9] Thus, whether we start merely from the assumption that we have empirical knowledge of numerically distinct objects or from the assumption that mathematics is a body of synthetic a priori cognition, Kant argues, we must reach the conclusion that we have a priori representation of the nature and structure of space and time themselves.

This conclusion, in turn, supplies the premise for Kant's first argument for transcendental idealism, which Schopenhauer was to accept without demur. Before we turn to this further stage of Kant's reasoning, however, we need to consider more of the particular transcendental arguments that Kant constructed. Kant follows his 'Transcendental Aesthetic' with a 'Transcendental Logic', the first section of which is a 'Transcendental Analytic' which is, in turn, divided into an 'Analytic of Concepts' and an 'Analytic of Principles'. Kant's arguments throughout these sections of the *Critique* are numerous, obscure, and both interlocking and overlapping, so any brief description of them will have to simplify them greatly. But Kant's early readers did not go in for close textual analysis either, so a brief account of these arguments can still present them in a way that Schopenhauer and other readers of his time would have recognized. Kant's first argument – what the second edition dubs the 'metaphysical deduction' (B 159) – is that all cognition, even the most ordinary empirical knowledge, is expressed in the form of a judgment, that all judgments are constructed in accordance with a variety of logical functions – they must have a quantity, that is, be universal or particular; have a quality, that is, be affirmative or negative; and so on – and that our concepts of objects must be constructed in accordance with certain categories, as correlatives of these logical functions of judgment, if we are to be able to make judgments about objects by means of our concepts of them. For example, we must conceive of objects as substances with accidents if we are to be able to have cognition of them through judgments with a subject–predicate form (see A 68–70/B 92–5; A 77–81/B 102–6). Next, in the 'transcendental deduction' properly so called, Kant argues that if I am in fact conscious of a representation at all, I am conscious of it as belonging to the numerically identical self that has all of my other representations, and such a consciousness, as a kind of combination, must be expressed through a judgment; thus he infers that the functions of judgment, with their correlative categories, must in fact apply to all my representations. By this means Kant tries to argue not merely that we each must use the categories whenever we make judgments about objects, but also that we must in fact be able to make judgments, ultimately judgments about objects, about all of our experience. Sometimes Kant presents this as if it were an argument that depends only on an empirical assumption that we have any experience at all, thus a transcendental argument of the first form we identified (B 132–5); but often he writes as if the premise that I am conscious of a manifold of representations as my own is itself a synthetic a priori cognition that entails an *a priori* synthesis of my representations antecedent to any empirical knowledge (e.g., A 107, A 111–12, A 116–19, B 135–6). Finally, in the 'Analytic of Principles' Kant explores the consequences of the fact that the manifold of representations which we are each conscious of as our own is a manifold of spatial and temporal representations, and argues that there are principles of judgment that are the necessary conditions for having knowledge of the determinate positions in space and time of both our representations and the objects they represent. It is at this stage of his argument that Kant attempts to show not just that the manifold of our intuitions 'is **determined** in regard to one of the logical functions for judgment' (B 143), and thus *some category or other*, but also that *each* of the categories, above all each of the relational categories of substance, causation, and interaction, must be applicable to *all* of our experience: the categories of substance and causation to all of our experiences in time, whether spatial or not, and the category of interaction to all of our experience of objects in space as well as time.

The most important of Kant's transcendental arguments in the 'Analytic of Principles' – all of which take the first form of Kant's transcendental arguments, that is, demonstrate that there are synthetic a priori principles even for merely empirical knowledge claims – are these. In the 'First Analogy of Experience', Kant argues that we can have determinate knowledge of the occurrence of an event in time, that is, a change of states of affairs, only insofar as we represent that change as an alteration in the state of a continuing substance; otherwise, we should have no way of knowing whether the change was located in anything outside us at all or was only a change in our own representations of an otherwise unchanging reality (A 188–9/B 231–2). But the existence of an enduring substance is only one condition of the possibility of determinate knowledge of objective change; in the 'Second Analogy', Kant argues that since the actual order of our representations merely as such could just as readily be a product of our own imagination as of any change in objects, we can determine that an objective change has occurred only if we can subsume the represented states of affairs under a rule according to which one state has to follow another because of the action of a cause of the latter state (B 233–4). Our knowledge of the existence of causation is thus another necessary condition of the possibility of our determinate knowledge of objective change. In the 'Third Analogy', Kant then argues that we can have determinate knowledge of the existence of different objects at different locations in space only if we conceive of those objects as interacting with each other in such a way that neither could be just as and where it is unless the other were also as and where it is; thus two objects can be determined to exist simultaneously only if each is both cause and effect of the current state of the other (A 211–14/B 257–61). Finally, in the 'Refutation of Idealism' that he added to the second edition of the *Critique*, Kant argues that determinate consciousness of the order of our own experiences as such is not in fact to be taken for granted, but is itself dependent upon interpreting our experiences as representations of enduring objects changing in time in accordance with causal laws, which objects, precisely because they must be thought to endure in ways that mere representations do not, cannot themselves be conceived of as mere representations (B 275–6). Thus, although Kant generally takes transcendental arguments to entail transcendental idealism – the point to which we will turn next – in this case he provides a transcendental argument that leads to a realist conclusion, that is, a conclusion that we must know something about objects beyond our own representations after all. This may seem like a complete contradiction – it did seem so to many of the contemporary critics of Kant with whose work Schopenhauer was familiar and to Schopenhauer himself[10] – but in fact it is not.

We can now turn to Kant's inference from the conclusion of a transcendental argument to his doctrine of transcendental idealism. As we have now seen, a transcendental argument, whether it attempts to discover the condition of the possibility of an empirical knowledge claim or of some cognition that is itself synthetic a priori, leads to the conclusion that we possess a certain representation, whether it be the pure intuition of space or time, for example, or a category like the concept of substance or causation, a priori. Kant then infers that what is represented by such an a priori representation, for example, space, 'is not any property at all of any things in themselves nor any relation of them to each other, i.e., no determination of them that attaches to objects themselves and that would remain even if one were to abstract from all subjective conditions of intuition.' The reason that he gives for this conclusion is that 'neither absolute nor relative determinations can be intuited prior to the existence of the things to which they pertain, thus be intuited a priori' (A 26/B 42). This might seem an obvious conclusion: after all, if we can know something prior to our encounter with an object, it might seem natural to think we do not really know anything about that object at all, but about something else, and if we know something prior to our encounter with any objects, it might seem as if that something else could only be ourselves. And Schopenhauer, for one, took this conclusion to be obvious. But it is not obvious, for we often know things about objects prior to our experience of at least those particular objects. For example, we can know before we hear it that the next sound we hear will have a frequency somewhere between about twenty hertz and twenty megahertz, because we can know what the limits of the human auditory apparatus are, without this in any way implying that this sound does not actually have the frequency we take it to have. In other words, when we know that there are certain constraints on our experience, constraints that allow us to experience only certain kinds of objects, we have no reason to doubt that whatever objects we experience do, in and of themselves, satisfy those constraints. Instead, the best explanation of why we do perceive them seems to be precisely that they do have the properties that the constraints on our perceptual abilities require them to have. Why should it be any different with constraints on our experience that we discover by some a priori rather than empirical means? To be sure, the discovery that humans can hear only those frequencies between about twenty hertz and twenty megahertz was empirical, so our knowledge that the next sound we hear, whatever it is, will indeed fall within that range of frequencies is also in an important sense empirical; but even if the knowledge that any object we can perceive must be located at a determinate position in space is a priori rather than empirical, why should it not be the case that any object we do succeed in perceiving, given this constraint, is really in space? Indeed why should we not conclude that it is nothing less than the fact that the object really is in space that explains why we do perceive it, given that we know a priori that we can only perceive objects in space?

Though Kant often wrote as if the mere fact of apriority is enough to imply the transcendental ideality of that which we do know a priori, he did not in fact think that this conclusion is self-evident. In several key passages he attempted to provide an argument for it. His thought is not merely that whatever we can know a priori must be a fact about ourselves rather than about anything else. Rather, what he assumes is that whatever we know a priori is also something that we know to be *necessarily* true, but that we have no reason to believe that anything that is true of an object independently of our representing it as such is more than *contingently* true. That is, the problem is not that objects could not themselves be spatial independently of our representing them as spatial, but rather that if they were, they would be so, as far as we could possibly know, only contingently, not necessarily; yet, Kant assumes, whatever we know a priori we know to be necessarily so. Kant reveals that this is what he is thinking at least twice in the *Critique of Pure Reason*. First, in the conclusion of the 'Transcendental Aesthetic', he writes:

You must therefore give your object *a priori* in intuition, and ground your synthetic proposition on this. If there did not lie in you a faculty for intuiting *a priori*; if this subjective condition regarding form were not at the same time the universal *a priori* condition under which alone the object of this (outer) intuition were possible; if the object (the triangle) were something in itself without relation to your subject: then how could you say that what necessarily lies in your subjective conditions for constructing a triangle must also necessarily pertain to the triangle in itself? (A 48/B 65)

But in fact what Kant is assuming is that whatever we know of the triangle a priori must be necessarily true, so if we could not know anything to be necessarily true of a triangle if it existed independently of us, then such a thing had better be a product of our representations alone and not anything that exists independently of us after all.

Likewise, Kant makes a similar argument in the conclusion of the 'Transcendental Deduction'. Here Kant rejects what he calls a 'preformation system' of the categories, that is, a proposal on which it would be true of us that we can only know objects that conform to the categories, and true of whatever objects that we do know that they conform to the categories quite independently of being known by us, on the ground that such a proposal would not show why it is *necessarily* true that such objects satisfy the categories. As he writes:

> In such a case the categories would lack the *necessity* that is essential to their concept. For, e.g., the concept of cause, which asserts the necessity of a consequent under a presupposed condition, would be false if it rested only on a subjective necessity, arbitrarily implanted in us, of combining certain empirical representations according to such a rule of relation. I would not be able to say that the effect is combined with the cause in the object (i.e., necessarily), but only that I am so constituted that I cannot think of this representation otherwise than as so connected. ... (B 168)

Again, what Kant is supposing is that when we know something a priori we know it to be necessarily true, and indeed necessarily true of any object of which it is true at all; so since whatever is true of objects independently of how we represent them is, as far as we can know, only contingently true of them, whatever we know a priori cannot be true of objects that exist independently of us at all, but can only be true of our representations of objects.

Kant's transcendental idealism thus rests on two premises, not just one. It depends on his proof(s) that we have a priori knowledge of various of the properties of our objects of representation, to be sure, but also on the further and certainly questionable claim that whatever we know a priori must be necessarily true of any object of which it is true at all. None of Kant's immediate contemporaries or successors, including Schopenhauer, seems to have recognized the role of this second premise in Kant's inference from a priori knowledge to transcendental idealism. Schopenhauer in fact rejected Kant's method of transcendental argumentation while taking Kant's inference from our a priori knowledge of a feature of objects to its merely subjective validity completely for granted. This seems to me a serious error; but in what follows, I will focus on the criticisms of Kant's method that Schopenhauer did make rather than on the one he failed to make.

III   SCHOPENHAUER'S REJECTION OF
TRANSCENDENTAL ARGUMENTS

Schopenhauer never objected to Kant's inference from the necessity
of conditions of the possibility of experience to their transcendental
ideality; like Kant, he assumed that anything identified as an a priori condition of experience is also only subjectively valid. Thus, in
The Fourfold Root Schopenhauer writes that 'a world that presents
itself by virtue of a priori forms is precisely on that account a mere
phenomenon' (*FR* 232/ H.1, 158), and in *The World as Will and Representation* Schopenhauer praises Kant's idea of 'transcendental philosophy', which holds 'that the objective world as we know it does
not belong to the true being of things-in-themselves, but is its mere
phenomenon, conditioned by those very forms that lie *a priori* in the
human intellect (i.e., the brain); hence the world cannot contain anything but phenomena' (*W1* 421/H.2, 499). Schopenhauer does recognize that placing the a priori forms of experience not in the mind but
in the brain is a departure from Kant (see *W1* 418/H.2, 495), though
he does not consider whether assuming the reality of the brain is
already assuming enough about a real physical world to undermine
transcendental idealism. Nor does he ask whether the assumption
about necessity on which Kant bases his move from transcendental
arguments to transcendental idealism is itself necessary, and thus he
misses a chance to criticize what one who would now be friendly to
Kant's transcendental arguments without adopting his transcendental idealism would regard as Kant's cardinal error. Nevertheless, he
does raise a fundamental issue about the character of transcendental arguments themselves that any defender of such arguments must
confront, as well as important questions about some of Kant's most
important examples of such argumentation, especially his argument
about causation. I will consider Schopenhauer's general objection to
transcendental arguments in this section and his objections to Kant's
particular arguments in the next two.

As Schopenhauer always insisted, much of *The World as Will and
Representation* depends on arguments expounded in his first published work, *On The Fourfold Root of the Principle of Sufficient
Reason* (first edition 1813). From one point of view, this work is
profoundly Kantian in inspiration. Kant's distinction between analytic and synthetic judgment, and his use of this distinction as
the foundation of his critique of the rationalist fantasy of deriving

all knowledge from the analysis of concepts alone, had its origin in his recognition of the distinction between logical and real relations, for example, the difference between the logical relation of contradiction and a real relation of opposed motions. Such relations should not be confused with each other, Kant argued in his short but seminal essay *Attempt to Introduce the concept of negative magnitudes into philosophy* (1763), because while the conjoint assertion of a proposition and its contradictory results in no assertion at all, a logical nullity, the existence of equal but opposed motions or forces does not result in a logical impossibility, but rather in a state of equilibrium, a physical state just as real as any other.[11] This insight was the basis for Kant's argument in the *Critique of Pure Reason* that real relations such as those of causation and interaction cannot be derived from logical relations among concepts alone, but rather arise only when we use the forms of judgment afforded by logic to make our spatial and temporal experience determinate. In *The Fourfold Root*, Schopenhauer extends Kant's distinction by arguing that all of our thought takes the form of seeing one thing as determined by another, but that there are four distinct kinds of determination, which should not be confused with each other: spatial and temporal determination, where any position in space or time is rendered determinate by reference to other positions; causal explanation, where an event is determined by prior events; logical determination, where the truth value of one proposition is determined by the truth value of others; and the determination of actions, where the occurrence of an action is determined by the occurrence of a motive serving as a reason for it.[12] But Schopenhauer's acceptance and refinement of Kant's distinction between logical and real relations is not accompanied by an acceptance of the method of transcendental argument that Kant eventually developed in order to explain the possibility of our insight into those relations that could not be seen to be true on the basis of logic alone. Instead, Schopenhauer insists that we simply can and must see the validity and necessity of each of the basic forms of determination, that is, that each of these basic forms of thought is simply self-evident. To try to argue for them, he holds, would be self-contradictory, precisely because they are the basis of all knowledge and thus of all argument. He expresses this in no uncertain terms. First he states the point in terms of proof:

As ... the principle of sufficient reason is the common expression [of the different laws of our cognitive faculty], it will follow as a matter of course that the principle in general cannot be proved. On the contrary, Aristotle's remark applies to all those proofs (with the exception of the Kantian which is directed not to the validity but to the *a priori* nature of the law of causality), namely where he says: 'They seek a reason for that which has no reason; for the principle of demonstration is not demonstration.' For every proof is a reduction of something doubtful to something acknowledged and established, and if we continue to demand a proof of this something, whatever it may be, we shall ultimately arrive at certain propositions which express the forms and laws and thus the conditions of all thinking and knowing. Consequently all thinking and knowing consist of the application of these; so that certainty is nothing but an agreement with those conditions, forms, and laws, and therefore their own certainty cannot again become evident from other propositions. (*FR* 32/H. 1, 23)

In this passage, the young Schopenhauer, not yet ready to move as far from Kant as he was to do later, actually tries to salvage something in Kant's method of argument by separating the proof of the apriority of the principle of causality from the proof of its validity, a separation that Kant, who poses the problem about the categories of the understanding precisely as the problem of their objective validity (see A 88–92/B 120–4), surely would not have understood. Later in the book, Schopenhauer puts his point in terms of the explanation rather than the proof of the certainty of the principle of sufficient reason, and here he does not seem to make any exception for Kant:

If a chain of judgements rests ultimately on a proposition of transcendental or metalogical truth and we still go on asking why, then to this there is no answer, because the question has no meaning and thus does not know what kind of a ground it demands. To explain a thing means to reduce its given existence or connexion to some form of the principle of sufficient reason. According to this form, that existence or connexion must be as it is. The result of this is that the principle of sufficient reason itself, in other words, the connexion expressed by it in any of its forms, cannot be further explained, since there is no principle for explaining the principle of all explanation; just as the eye sees everything except itself. (*FR* 229/H. 1, 156)

Neither the general principle of sufficient reason nor any of its four determinate forms can be explained, according to Schopenhauer,

simply because they are the fundamental principles of all explanation. In other words, there can be no transcendental arguments for
transcendental knowledge because all explanation must come to an
end somewhere,[13] and transcendental knowledge is precisely where
explanation does come to an end. This general objection seems intended to apply to Kant's attempt to prove the principle of sufficient
reason as a condition of the possibility of experience, as well as to
all previous attempts to prove it.

In *The Fourfold Root*, Schopenhauer does not accompany these
blunt rejections of the very idea of transcendental arguments with
an equally explicit characterization of his own alternative methodology. He does attempt to do this in *The World as Will and Representation*. Here he does not exempt Kant from his objection to previous
philosophical methodology but makes him the focus of his objection,
and states that the alternative to the hopelessly circular method of
proving or explaining the fundamental is simply perceiving the fundamental. He makes this plain in the passage the opening lines of
which were quoted earlier:

An essential difference between Kant's method and that which I follow is
to be found in the fact that he starts from indirect, reflected knowledge,
whereas I start from direct and intuitive knowledge. He is comparable to a
person who measures the height of a tower from its shadow; but I am like
one who applies the measuring-rod directly to the tower itself. Philosophy,
therefore, is for him a science *of* concepts, but for me a science *in* concepts,
drawn from knowledge of perception, the only source of all evidence, and
set down and fixed in universal concepts. He skips over this whole world
of perception which surrounds us, and which is so multifarious and rich
in significance, and he sticks to the forms of abstract thinking. Although
he never states the fact, this procedure is founded on the assumption that
reflection is the ectype of all perception, and that everything essential to
perception must therefore be expressed in reflection, and indeed in very
contracted, and therefore easily comprehensible, forms and outlines. (*W1*
452-3/H. 2, 537)

For Schopenhauer, philosophy begins in perception, and essentially
consists in giving abstract and 'contracted' expression to the most
salient features of perception. He thinks that when Kant argues for
the indispensability of space and time in all our representation of
objects, he is himself relying on what is simply the most salient fact
about our perception, and it is only when he departs from this secure

ground that he goes astray. As we will see, Schopenhauer thinks that
Kant does go astray when he insists that all the abstract categories
of logical theory must also be present in our knowledge of objects.
For Schopenhauer, the method of philosophy must always be to base
its abstractions on what is evident in perception, and even the different forms of the principle of sufficient reason that he catalogues
in *The Fourfold Root* must, at least retrospectively, be understood
as abstract and contracted expressions of what is evident in our perception itself. This will lead to the view of *The World as Will and
Representation* that our comprehension of objects in terms of space,
time, and causality and our comprehension of the ultimate nature
of reality as will are *both* based on our own perception, our perception of objects outside of us, on the one hand, and our perception
of our own action in willing, on the other. Though we cannot fully
explore this claim here, the 'primacy of perception'[14] is the basis for
Schopenhauer's positive philosophy as well as his critique of Kant.

What should we make of Schopenhauer's critique of the very idea
of transcendental arguments? One thing we might say is that while
the charge that there simply cannot be either a demonstration or
an explanation of a truly fundamental principle of knowledge has a
certain kind of plausibility,[15] it is not clear that this abstract objection really does justice to the complex structure of some of Kant's
most important transcendental arguments. In particular, it could be
argued, this objection does not do justice to the structure of Kant's
arguments in the 'Analytic of Principles', above all the three 'Analogies' and the 'Refutation of Idealism', which one can see as proving
the validity of the permanence of substance, causation, and interaction and the necessity of applying these principles to objects genuinely distinct from our own representations by *combining* the forms
of intuition and thought previously discovered, that is, by determining what are the conditions under which the forms of thought and
judgment that we have can be applied to the spatio-temporal kind of
intuition that we have. Indeed, here one might be able go along with
Schopenhauer's account of his own methodology and that which he
thinks Kant ought to have used, and concede that Kant might have
discovered the spatio-temporal form of intuition, on the one hand,
and the judgmental character of thought, on the other, by some kind
of intense scrutiny of perception, but then interpret Kant as having
demonstrated the validity of the principles of empirical thought by

combining these results to yield new principles rather than by fruit-lessly attempting to prove what was already obvious. Then one might even argue that Schopenhauer failed to exploit the resources which his own division of the species of the principle of sufficient reason in *The Fourfold Root* should have afforded him – he failed to see, that is, that the concept of causality and the principle of universal validity could be seen as arising from the inevitable combination of the ideas of space and time, on the one hand, and logical entailment, on the other.

Yet it must also be conceded that there is a certain justice in Schopenhauer's objection to Kant's transcendental arguments. Kant himself may be taken to have conceded that while we may be able to show by analysis of our complex cognitions *that* we must have a priori representations of space and time, on the one hand, and categories for thinking in judgments, on the other, we certainly could not explain why we have just the forms of intuition and the categories that we do. The latter concession is explicit in the second edition of the *Critique* (which Schopenhauer read first but subsequently declared to be inferior to the first[16]):

But for the peculiarity of our understanding, that it is able to bring about the unity of apperception *a priori* only by means of the categories and only through precisely this kind and number of them, a further ground may be offered just as little as one can be offered for why we have precisely these and no other functions for judgment or for why space and time are the sole forms of our possible intuition. (B 145–6)

In other words, at least when it comes to the explanation of the essential forms of our experience, Kant too recognized that explanation must come to an end somewhere.

Further, it could also be argued that even in Kant's most complex transcendental arguments, which do not appear to fall immediately before Schopenhauer's blanket objection to trying to prove or explain what is supposed to be fundamental, there still comes a point at which Kant must be characterized as ultimately relying on a brute fact about the nature of human perception. The arguments of the three 'Analogies' and the 'Refutation of Idealism' are arguments about time determination, about what is necessary to achieve '**synthetic unity** in the temporal relation of all perceptions' (A 177/B 220). In the most general terms, Kant's argument in these proofs is that 'since time itself cannot be perceived', that is, the determinate order of events in objective time is not immediately given, 'the determination of the existence of objects in time can only come about through ... *a priori* connecting concepts' (A 176/B 219). But what is the epistemic status of Kant's premise that 'time itself cannot be perceived'? Does he have an *argument* from some more fundamental premise that our experience could not be like the telecast of a sporting event with a digital clock ticking away in the corner, allowing us to see immediately when in the game any event occurs and how long it lasts? Kant certainly does not make any such argument; instead, the claim that the determinate temporal position and duration of events are not immediately perceived seems to be a brute fact about our experience – a deep fact, in the sense that it may take subtle philosophical reflection to bring us to see it and in the sense that it may underlie many of our more obvious cognitive practices, but a brute fact nonetheless. To the extent that Kant's successful transcendental arguments rely on a premise like this, Schopenhauer may be right in objecting to any suggestion that transcendental arguments can actually prove the very most fundamental premises of our knowledge and in insisting that the ultimate bedrock of philosophical concepts must lie 'in perception'.

At the deepest level, then, Schopenhauer may be absolutely right about the prospects for transcendental arguments. At the same time, his insistence on the ultimate limits of such arguments and on the foundation of all philosophical concepts and principles in perception may make him unduly impatient with some of the more interesting or even most significant features of Kant's analysis of the conditions of our cognition. This is evident in his critique of Kant's account of causation, but also in several of his more general objections to Kant, particularly his objection to Kant's contrast between intuitions and concepts and his scorn for Kant's analysis of the forms of judgment. I will turn to these next.

IV SCHOPENHAUER'S CRITIQUE OF KANT ON INTUITION, CONCEPT, AND JUDGMENT

In the lengthy and detailed 'Criticism of the Kantian Philosophy' that Schopenhauer appended to *The World as Will and Representation*, he claims that 'again and again in the *Critique of Pure Reason* we come across that principal and fundamental error of Kant's ... namely the complete absence of any distinction between abstract, discursive knowledge and intuitive knowledge' (*W1* 473/H. 2, 562). This is a startling claim, since Kant himself clearly thought that his discovery of the distinction between intuitions and concepts was one of his most fundamental accomplishments (A 50/B 74), the basis for his critique of all prior philosophy (see A 42–6/B 59–63) and the key to the solution of the problem of synthetic a priori knowledge, the most important cases of which, as we saw earlier, Kant holds to be grounded on the combination of the pure forms of intuition and the pure concepts of the understanding. It is also puzzling, since a few lines later Schopenhauer blames Kant for 'the monstrous assertion that without thought, and hence without abstract concepts, there is absolutely no knowledge of an object, and that, because perception is not thought, it is also not knowledge at all' (*W1* 474/H. 2, 562; see also 439/H. 2, 520). This is confusing because Schopenhauer seems to be blaming Kant for having failed to make any distinction between intuitions and concepts and then blaming him for having made precisely that distinction. He cannot be doing both, so one can only assume that he is blaming Kant not for having failed to make any distinction between intuition and concept at all, but for somehow having made a false or inadequate distinction between them. But what could be wrong with Kant's distinction? Perhaps Schopenhauer's next claim will give us a clue:

Concepts obtain all meaning, all content, only from their reference to representations of perception, from which they have been abstracted, drawn off, in other words, formed by the dropping of everything inessential. If, therefore, the foundation of perception is taken away from them, they are empty and void. Perceptions, on the other hand, have immediate and very great significance in themselves ... they represent themselves, express themselves, and have not merely borrowed content as concepts have. For the principle of sufficient reason rules over them only as the law of causality, and as such determines only their position in space and time. (*W1* 474/H. 2, 562–3)

Now Kant too says, indeed famously, that 'thoughts without content are empty' (A 51/B 75), or that concepts depend upon information from intuition, ultimately empirical intuition (see B 147), to give us any knowledge of actual objects. Schopenhauer cannot mean to deny that. Instead, his objection seems to be that Kant makes the distinction between intuitions and concepts *too soon*: for Kant, the understanding and its machinery, the categories, have to be added to intuition before we have any representation of an object at all, whereas in Schopenhauer's view perception as such already presents us with representations of objects, and the understanding is necessary only in order to perform further acts, such as referring the objects with which perception itself presents us to determinate locations in space and time, by linking them to causes active at those locations, and forming pared-down, abstract concepts of the objects that perception presents us with in order to make generalizations about them. Even after this is said, however, Schopenhauer's position remains puzzling because Kant seems to hold that our conscious recognition of any object already involves a synthesis of intuitions in accordance with concepts: 'we say that we cognize the object if we have effected synthetic unity in the manifold of intuition' (A 105). For example, if I am conscious that what I am holding is a lump of ore, I am not merely aware of a sensation of red color and a feeling of weight, but I am also rather conscious that what I have in my hand is a single thing that is the subject of both the predicates *red* and *heavy*. Why isn't this exactly what Schopenhauer has in mind, that is, a case of having a perception that is already a presentation of an object?

The answer would seem to be this. For Kant, the thesis that our recognition of an object requires both intuition and concept cannot be based on any direct scrutiny of our consciousness of an object, certainly not any direct scrutiny of a temporal process of coming to know an object, precisely because his theory is that all consciousness of objects already involves a synthetic unity of intuitions under concepts. For Kant, such a thesis can only be extracted from our cognition of objects by some kind of philosophical reflection, for instance, reflection on the nature of judgments as asserting a combination of predicates of some single entity. The separate roles of intuitions and concepts, in other words, must be inferred from the different roles of the reference to a particular and references to common properties in judgments. But Schopenhauer does not place much stock in any such reflective method of philosophy, and instead treats Kant's distinction between intuition and concept as if it were intended to be the kind of phenomenologically self-evident distinction that Schopenhauer himself favors. That is, when Kant distinguishes intuitions and concepts and says that we have no cognition of objects unless we combine the two, Schopenhauer takes him to be saying that we are separately *conscious* of both intuitions and concepts and are then *conscious* of combining them into a cognition of objects that in turn represents a further state of consciousness, clearly distinct from the prior states and especially from the initial state of intuition. Thus, he concludes, Kant does not recognize that the initial state of consciousness, which Schopenhauer identifies with perception, is already cognition of objects. But in distinguishing between intuitions and concepts, Kant clearly does not intend to be distinguishing between sequential conscious states; instead, Kant's argument is that our consciousness of objects is *already* a cognition of them precisely because it already represents the synthesis of intuition and concepts – something much closer to what Schopenhauer himself believes. Because Schopenhauer proceeds as if Kant's method is phenomenological, like his own, when it is not, he thinks there is a greater difference between their views than there really is.

Notice that in Schopenhauer's charge against Kant he allows that although other features of the thought of an object must already be included in our perception of it, the concept of causation can be regarded as an addition of the faculty of understanding to what is immediately given in intuition. This brings us to Schopenhauer's critique of Kant's theory of categories. Schopenhauer holds that Kant's table of categories is a sham, and that the only genuine concept of the understanding is the category of causality. While Kant himself recognized that some aspects of his table of categories would seem problematic – the addition of the quantitative category of singularity to that of generality and particularity, for example, or of the qualitative category of limitation to those of reality and negation (A 71–2/B 96–7) – and while many critics have rejected Kant's justification of the inclusion of those problematic categories or found other problems in Kant's list,[17] no one other than Schopenhauer seems to have thought that we could get by with the category of causality alone. After all, what could we think is caused other than a state of some substance? And how can we think of causality except by thinking of all substances in some class as behaving in the same way in the same circumstances? In other words, how can we even think about causality without also using categories of quantity, the concept of substance, and so on?

Once again, Schopenhauer's preference for his 'direct' method rather than Kant's 'indirect' or 'reflective' method seems to be the basis for his criticism. Here is one of his chief statements of it:

Generally, according to Kant, there are only concepts of *objects*, no perceptions. On the other hand, I say that objects exist primarily only for perception
[*Anschauung*], and that concepts are always abstractions from this perception. Therefore abstract thinking must be conducted exactly according to
the world present in perception, for only the relation to this world gives
content to the concepts, and we cannot assume for the concepts any other
a priori determined form than the faculty for reflection in general. The essential nature of this faculty is the formation of concepts, i.e., of abstract
non-perceptible representations, and this constitutes the sole function of
our faculty of *reason*. ... Accordingly, I demand that we throw away eleven
of the categories, and retain only that of causality, but that we see that its
activity is indeed the condition of empirical perception, this being therefore
not merely sensuous but intellectual. ... (W1 448/H. 2, 531)

Like the pre-Kantian empiricists, Schopenhauer seems to base his
analysis of the nature of thought on a phenomenology in which perceptions are always already regarded as consciousness of objects, and
to think of the category of causation as the only essential addition to
perception because a judgment that assigns an object or its state to
another as its cause can be thought of as an act of thought that is
phenomenologically distinguishable from the independent and antecedent perception of the object itself. Because of his phenomenological approach, Schopenhauer is not receptive to Kant's view that
all cognition is already judgment, although that might not be its phenomenologically most salient feature, and that since all judgments
are formed out of the logical functions of judgment such as quantity,
quality, and relation, all cognition of objects must already involve
the categories of quantity, quality, and at least the relational category of substance and accident because these are the fundamental
forms for our conception of objects that are necessary if we are to be
able to make judgments about them. Since the concept of causation
can be seen as being used in order to connect separate perceptions
of distinct objects, Schopenhauer is prepared to see it, but it alone,
as a concept that is *added* to our perception of objects by an act of
the understanding that is distinct from perception. On Kant's view,
however, a merely phenomenological difference such as that we can
actually have some consciousness of objects – that is, in his view,
make some judgments about them – using the other categories before we are aware of applying the category of causation to them – that
is, in his view, make a further, causal judgment about them – is of no

significance when it comes to the fundamental issue of the source of the various aspects of our thought about objects. For Kant, those aspects of the conceptual structure of our thought about objects that may be present in what seems to be our immediate awareness of them are just as surely supplied by the understanding as is the concept of causation, even if we might be aware of the application of that concept to our perceptions of objects only subsequently, because the understanding is the faculty of judgment, and all of the categories must be added to the raw material of perception, even though we are hardly conscious of any such addition, because the categories are the conditions of the possibility of making judgments about objects at all.

Of course, Schopenhauer cannot reject the categories altogether, and subsequent to this blast against Kant, he does nothing less than reintroduce them as the conditions of the possibility of making judgments about objects. This is, of course, just how Kant introduces them; the key difference is that Schopenhauer clearly regards making judgments as an activity of secondary importance to perception itself. He indicates this by treating the activity of judgment not as an activity of the understanding, as Kant does, but as an activity of reason, which he regards as a faculty for abstract thinking that is entirely parasitical on the far more important cognitive activity of perception. 'The whole of reflective knowledge, or reason,' Schopenhauer writes, 'has only one main form, and that is the abstract concept. It is peculiar to our faculty of reason itself, and has no direct necessary connexion with the world of perception' (W1 454/H. 2, 539). The cognitive significance of perception is not dependent upon judgment, Schopenhauer holds, and thus animals, which do not make judgments, can have knowledge of objects by means of perception; but the forms of our judgments are either due to the structure of reflection itself, a cognitive activity of secondary importance in the sense that we already have knowledge of objects prior to it, or else are derived by reflection from the primordial knowledge of objects already present in perception. 'For the most part, these forms can be derived from the nature of reflective knowledge itself, and hence directly from the faculty of reason, especially in so far as they spring from the four laws of thought. ... Others of these forms, however, have their ground in the nature of knowledge of perception' (W1 454/H. 2, 539).

Thus, Schopenhauer argues, the category of the 'quantity of judgment springs from the essential nature of concepts as such' (W1

455/H. 2, 539), for it is essential to concepts to have a range, or as we now say, an extension, from which more or fewer instances can be picked out for the purposes of some particular abstraction. For example, asking about acorns, we can judge that 'Some trees bear acorns' but 'All oaks bear acorns' (W1 455/H. 2, 540). But, of course, on Schopenhauer's view, trees, oak trees, and acorns are already given to us as objects in perception alone, and our perception of them as objects does not await our making such abstract judgments. Similarly, Schopenhauer argues, 'the *quality* of judgements lies entirely within the province of our faculty of reason, and is not an adumbration of any law of the understanding that makes perception possible' (W1 455–6/H. 2, 540); that is, the fact that we can affirm or deny conjunctions of concepts ('This seed is not an acorn') depends upon our perception of objects, while our perception of objects does not depend on our making such judgments. Finally, Schopenhauer argues, the 'form of the *categorical judgment* is nothing but the form of the judgement in general, in the strictest sense' (W1 457/H. 2, 542), the form we use whenever we give abstract expression to our knowledge of objects, which is itself, of course, grounded in perception, and *'disjunctive judgments* spring from the law of thought of the excluded middle ... they are therefore entirely the property of pure reason' (W1 459/H. 2, 544). That is, they express the basic form of the act of making abstract comparisons among objects, but are not necessary for perceptual knowledge of objects as such. The hypothetical form of judgment, however, Schopenhauer argues to be 'the abstract expression of that most universal form of all our knowledge, the principle of sufficient reason' (W1 456/H. 2, 541), but it gets its specific force as the expression of causality only when it is applied to our perceptions of objects, with their distinctive spatial and temporal form: 'in order to distinguish' the different applications of the principle of sufficient reason, Schopenhauer argues, 'we must go back to knowledge of perception' (W1 457/H. 2, 542). So, he concludes, all the forms of judgments, and the categories that Kant correlated with them, are the inherent structures of the activity of abstract thinking in general or are dependent upon the application of the former to perception, but in no case does the knowledge of objects inherent in perception depend upon these forms of abstract thinking.

Kant would have been unmoved by this argument. He could have admitted that the activity of expressing abstract judgments can seem phenomenologically subsequent to the perception of objects, but still have insisted that we can make such judgments only because our conscious perception of objects is itself already the product of a synthesis that informs our sensations not only with spatio-temporal form but also with the basic conceptual structure – as quanta, realities, substances, causes, and so on – that will allow us to make judgments about them. From Kant's point of view, it is nothing like a direct scrutiny of our experience that determines what factors are contributed by the various powers of the mind, but rather reflection on the structure of our thoughts themselves: fundamental differences in structure, such as the difference between the singularity of intuitions and the generality of concepts, demand different sources in the mind, even if we do not experience these sources as separate. The very complexity of the judgments we can make about our perceptions is, on Kant's 'indirect' method, the evidence for the multiplicity of factors that have already entered into the constitution of our conscious perception of objects.

V   SCHOPENHAUER'S CRITIQUE OF KANT'S TREATMENT OF CAUSATION

The best-known of all of Schopenhauer's criticisms of Kant's theoretical philosophy is undoubtedly his critique of Kant's treatment of causation. Once again, much of the difference between Schopenhauer and Kant turns out to rest on the difference between the phenomenological method of the former and the transcendental method of the latter: Kant argues that our knowledge of the determinate temporal order of objective states of affairs depends upon our knowledge of causal laws, while Schopenhauer takes knowledge of temporal succession to be independent of any such condition because it seems to be immediately given. A closer look at Schopenhauer's view, however, will show that apart from his insistence upon phenomenological facts to which Kant pays little attention, there is less difference between their positions than first appears. Nevertheless, we will also see that, as in the case of his general critique of transcendental arguments, Schopenhauer does raise a fundamental issue about Kant's treatment of causation that would need to be resolved successfully by any defense of Kant's theory.

Schopenhauer presents his main critique of Kant's proof of the validity of the universal law of causality in §23 of *The Fourfold Root*.

In the second 'Analogy of Experience' in the *Critique of Pure Reason*, Kant had argued that the existence of causal laws, and thus the validity of the universal law of causality itself (the law that every event has a cause), is a condition of the possibility of cognition of a determinate succession of states of affairs. Kant's argument, as already mentioned, turns on the assumption that we cannot perceive the objective position of states of affairs in time immediately because we do not perceive time itself as a framework in which objective positions are marked. It also depends on the further claim that we cannot immediately infer the objective order of represented states of affairs that are supposed to constitute a change from what we take to be the succession of our own representations, not only because *all* of our successions of representations, whether we take them to be representations of objective change or not, are successive, but also because we can always imagine reversing or otherwise varying the order of any subjective succession of representations. Thus, since the existence of an objective change or succession of states of affairs cannot be known either from an immediate perception of the position in absolute time of the several states of affairs involved or from an inference directly from the sequence of our several representations of those states of affairs, Kant concludes that the existence of an objective succession of states of affairs must be inferred from causal laws dictating that one of those states of affairs can only occur after the other, and that a determinate sequence of representations as such must be inferred from the determinate sequence of the states they represent rather than vice versa – in Kant's words, 'I must therefore derive the **subjective sequence** of apprehension from the **objective sequence** of appearances, for otherwise the former would be entirely undetermined' (A 193/B 238). Kant illustrates this argument with his famous contrast between the perception of a moving ship and of an unchanging house. In the perception of a ship sailing downstream, 'The order in the sequence of the perceptions in apprehension is therefore here determined, and the apprehension is bound to it', and thus because the ship is sailing downstream I can only perceive it at a location downstream after I have perceived it upstream; but in perceiving an unchanging house, while I might have perceived its foundation first and its roof only subsequently, 'my perception could have begun at its rooftop and ended at the ground' (A 192/B 237). Kant's point is this: while in the case of the changing position of the ship – an event – I take the order of my perceptions to be irreversible, and in the case of the unchanging house – a non-event – I take the order of my perceptions to be reversible, still I cannot infer the irreversibility of my perceptions in the former case directly from their succession, since my perceptions in the latter case are successive too, nor can I infer it directly from the successive positions of the ship, for I am only given those by my perceptions; instead, I must infer the successive positions of the ship from causal laws dictating that in the given circumstances it must be sailing downstream, and then infer the irreversibility of the sequence of my perceptions from that.

Schopenhauer's first objection to this argument is that the sequence of my perceptions in the case of the unchanging house is just as determinate as the sequence of my perceptions in the case of the moving ship and is just as much to be explained by an event governed by causal laws: the only difference between the two cases, he insists, concerns *which* object it is that is appealed to in order to explain the sequence of perceptions. In the case of the moving ship, I explain the sequence of my perceptions by the motion of the ship, taking it for granted that my own position as an observer remains fixed, while in the case of the sequence of perceptions of the house I do not explain this sequence by appealing to any change or motion in the house, but rather by invoking bodily changes in my own position as an observer, as I raise my head while looking at the building and thus change the position of my eyes relative to it. 'Both are events,' Schopenhauer maintains;

the only difference is that in the [house] case the change starts from the observer's own body whose sensations are naturally the starting-point of all his perceptions. Yet this body is nevertheless an object among objects, consequently is liable to the laws of this objective corporeal world. . . . From the fact that the succession in the perceptions of the parts of the house depends on his own arbitrary choice, Kant tries to infer that this succession is not objective and not an event. But moving his eye from the roof to the basement is one event, and the opposite movement from basement to roof is another, just as is the sailing of the ship. (*FR* 124–5/H. 1, 86–7)

Moreover, Schopenhauer holds, since we can know the determinate order of our perceptions whether they are due to a change in an external object or not, we must know about succession directly, and be able to recognize it 'quite easily without there being any causal connexion between the objects successively acting on' our bodies (*FR* 125/H. 1, 87).

Schopenhauer's next objection is also meant to show that we have direct cognition of the objective succession of states of affairs without inferring it from causal laws. Schopenhauer argues that if we had to know that one thing is the cause of another in order to know that the latter necessarily follows the former – that is, that 'The objectivity of a change can be known only through the law of causality' (*FR* 126/H. 1, 87) – we could know that one state of affairs follows another only when the former is the cause of the latter. But this is clearly not so: if I'm struck by a falling roof tile after I leave my house, I will certainly know that its fall followed my departure from the house, though the departure from the house was presumably not the cause of the fall of the tile; if I hear a succession of notes in a melody, I can know that the later notes follow the earlier ones without thinking of the earlier notes as the cause of the later notes; and I can certainly know that day invariably follows night without having to believe that night is the cause of day (*FR* 126–7/H. 1, 88). In all these cases, Schopenhauer assumes, we know an objective sequence of states of affairs without assuming that the earlier is the cause of the later, although this is not meant to imply that there are not causes of the various events we know to take place. As Schopenhauer says, 'Nor is the law of causality prejudiced thereby; for it is still certain that every change is the effect of another change, since this truth is firmly established *a priori*; only that every change follows not merely on the single one that is its cause, but on all which exist simultaneously with that cause, and with which it stands in no causal relation, (*FR* 126/H. 1, 87–8). But his assumption is nevertheless that since I do not and indeed could not use the causal connections that do exist between an event such as the falling of a tile and its cause to determine the moment that it strikes me, my knowledge of temporal sequence in a case such as that must be independent of my knowledge of causality altogether.

Finally, Schopenhauer objects that on Kant's view we would have to assume that each one of us possesses an impossibly extensive knowledge of particular causal laws. We are constantly aware of objective temporal successions, and if we had to base our knowledge of each and every one of these on knowledge of the causal laws determining the occurrence of the events that we know to take place, we would have to know a vast number of causal laws. In Schopenhauer's words:

> If Kant's assertion were correct, which I challenge, our only way of know-
> ing the *reality* of succession would be from its *necessity*; but this would
> presuppose an understanding embracing all the series of causes and effects
> simultaneously, and thus an omniscient understanding. Kant has burdened
> the understanding with an impossibility merely in order to have less need
> of sensibility. (*FR* 131/H. 1, 91)

With this last remark, Schopenhauer clearly means to connect his criticism of Kant's argument for our knowledge of causal laws with his general insistence that Kant undervalues immediate perceptual knowledge while exaggerating the importance of the conceptual contributions of the understanding.

Schopenhauer's three objections, then, are these: (1) all of our sequences of perceptions are events, whether they represent changes in any object other than our own bodies or not, and our knowledge of the sequence of our own perceptions, as well as of the states of what we perceive, cannot therefore depend on causal laws entailing changes in the represented objects alone; (2) we know many objective successions of states of affairs in which the earlier members of such successions are not the causes of the later ones, so again, our knowledge of succession cannot depend upon our knowledge of causality; and (3) finally, given how many objective successions we can recognize, our knowledge of causal laws would have to be impossibly vast if all of our knowledge of succession really did depend on knowledge of causal laws. Schopenhauer's first two objections depend upon misunderstandings of Kant's argument, and again misunderstandings connected to the contrast between Schopenhauer's phenomenological method and Kant's own 'reflective' or transcendental method. By contrast, Schopenhauer's third objection by no means depends on a misunderstanding of Kant, but it raises a genuine issue that would have to be resolved in any successful reconstruction of Kant's position.

(1) First, Schopenhauer's objection that even what seem to be merely subjective changes in our perceptions are to be explained by causal laws just as much as objective changes are misconstrues Kant's use of examples in his transcendental argument. We should

conceive Kant's argument to proceed in the following manner. Let us suppose, we can take him to begin, that we can recognize the difference between a change in our own representations that represents a change in an object other than ourselves and a change in our representations which does not represent any such external change. *For example*, we can recognize the difference between a change in our perceptions of the position of a ship which represents a change in the position of the ship, and a change in our perceptions of a house which does not represent any change in the house itself. How do we make this distinction? We cannot make it merely by observing a change in the sequence of perceptions because that is present in both of the cases. Nor can we make it by inferring the irreversibility of the sequence of perceptions in the case of the ship from our knowledge of the positions of the ship itself, for that is what we are supposed to be discovering. Instead, we can only make it by inferring the positions of the ship, and thus the irreversibility of the perceptions of the positions of the ship, from causal laws dictating what the positions of the ship and thus the sequence of perceptions of it must be. Now, in this argument Kant assumes for the sake of discussion that we know what the sequence of perceptions is in the case of both the ship and the house; what he is trying to show is that even if we knew that, we could not know from that alone that there has been a change in the position of the ship, for that could be inferred only from the modal fact of the irreversibility of the sequence of the perceptions of the ship, and that is not given immediately any more than the positions of the ship itself are: both the positions of the ship and the irreversibility of the perceptions of the ship have to be inferred from causal laws. This argument, however, does not in fact assume that we really know the actual sequence of any of our perceptions without any objective conditions. On the contrary, it is compatible with the realization that since at any given time we can always imagine varying any sequence of representations we take ourselves to have had – as Kant puts it, the imagination can always 'combine the two states in question in two different ways' (B 233) – we can never know the sequence of our representations immediately, but can always know their determinate sequence only by correlating them with the rule-governed changes of some enduring object. Indeed, this is precisely what Kant ultimately argues in his refutation of idealism, completed not even in the second edition of the *Critique of Pure Reason* but in a series of notes written three years after that edition was published. Here Kant writes:

Since the imagination . . . is itself only an object of inner sense, the empirical consciousness (*apprehensio*) of this condition can contain only succession. But this itself cannot be represented except by means of something which endures, with which that which is successive is simultaneous. This enduring thing, with which that which is successive is simultaneous . . . cannot in turn be a representation of the mere imagination but must be a representation of sense, for otherwise that which lasts would not be in the sensibility at all.[18]

This passage suggests the following picture. If I take it for granted that I know the sequence of my representations as such, and only want to know if a given sequence represents a change in an external object, I cannot infer that from knowledge of the irreversibility of my sequence of representations, because in any case I don't know *that*, and must instead infer both the occurrence of the event and the irreversibility of my sequence of representations from causal laws about the behavior of the object. But if I reflect further, I will realize that I never know the determinate sequence of my representations at all without objective conditions, and so even in a case in which I take myself to know that I have had a determinate sequence of perceptions of an object that has not undergone any change, I must still infer the determinate sequence of my representations from *some* object undergoing change; for instance, I could determine the sequence of changes in my perception of an unchanging house by correlating them with successive positions of my own body by means of psychophysical laws. In this case, my own body would be the enduring object with successive states of which my successive representations are simultaneous – just as Schopenhauer argues.

Why did Schopenhauer fail to see that he was expounding what is essentially the continuation of Kant's argument rather than an objection to it? Schopenhauer may never have understood Kant's refutation of idealism, having notoriously disliked the second edition of the *Critique* precisely because of its inclusion,[19] and in any case could not have known of the unpublished notes in which Kant finally came close to making explicit the argument the refutation actually needed. But in addition to that, the difference between the methods of the two philosophers seems to be at work again. In the

'Analogies of Experience', indeed in the larger section on the 'Systematic Representation of all Synthetic Principles' in which the analogies are included, Kant took himself to be expounding the conditions on which the possibility of our making determinate judgments about our spatio-temporal experience rests. He did not take himself to be describing the actual course of our experience. Further, and reasonably enough, he did not think he could expound all of the conditions of the possibility of our judgment of experience at once, or on the basis of any single example. Rather, he had to expound all the presuppositions of our capacity for empirical judgment sequentially, and whenever he introduced an example he meant it to illustrate only the single condition at issue, not the whole character of our lived experience. Schopenhauer, however, hostile as he is to transcendental arguments, thinks the task of philosophy is to characterize something like the process of our experience itself, so when he reads Kant's contrast between the perception of a moving ship and the perception of an unchanging house, he thinks Kant is characterizing two phenomenologically different kinds of experience, and then thinks that Kant's supposed distinction is belied by the fact that even in the case of our perception of an unchanging house we can still experience the changing position of our own bodies and sense organs. Kant might not have cared about this one way or the other – his concern was not to describe what our experience is like but to ferret out the presuppositions on which our judgments about our experience rest. And in any case, he simply had not yet arrived at the stage of his argument at which he would argue that even our empirical consciousness of the temporal order of our own experience as such rests, contrary to all previous suppositions, on the assumption that we are perceiving an external world of changing but enduring bodies by means of our own body, which is a changing and enduring object among others. Kant himself was to imply the necessity of acknowledging our own embodiment in order to judge our experience when he wrote, 'We are first *object of outer sense* to ourselves, for otherwise we could not perceive our *place* in the world and thus intuit ourselves in relation to other things.'[20] Schopenhauer was never able to read this remark of Kant's, but even if he had, he would not have been receptive to the kind of transcendental argument of which it was a conclusion.

(2) Schopenhauer's second objection to Kant, which is in essence that Kant commits the fallacy of believing post hoc, ergo propter

hoc, that is, thinking that whatever follows something else must be the effect of the former, seems to rest on a more superficial misunderstanding of Kant's argument. Schopenhauer thinks that Kant believes that we can judge that one state of affairs follows another in time only if it follows *from* it, that is, only if the earlier state is itself the cause of the latter. But Kant does not generally say exactly that; rather, what Kant says is just that the later state must follow the earlier in accordance with a rule dictating that sequence. In Kant's words, 'This connection must therefore consist in the order of the manifold of appearance in accordance with which the apprehension of one thing (that which happens) follows that of the other (which precedes) **in accordance with a rule**' (A 193/B 238). It might be natural to think that such a rule must be the rule that the earlier state of affairs is the cause of the latter, and that the latter can only follow the earlier because it is its effect. But Kant's statement does not actually imply that: what it implies is that the later state must follow the earlier because of the causal law in accordance with which the later state occurs, whatever that law might determine to be the cause of the later state, not that the earlier state must itself be the cause. Thus, for example, Kant is not committed to the view that day must follow night because night is the cause of day, but because of that which is the cause of day, namely, the change in the position of a place on earth relative to the sun over the course of its daily rotation; and he is not committed to the view that the falling of a roof tile must follow my exit from my house because the latter is the cause of the former, but because of the time of the occurrence of that which is its cause, for example, the failure of the roofing nail. Another way that Kant puts his point is by saying that there must be a rule according to which what we are thinking of as the later state of affairs in a temporal sequence follows from *something* in the preceding state, but not necessarily the particular element of the preceding state to which we are contrasting it:

Thus if I perceive that something happens, then the first thing contained in this representation is that something precedes, for it is just in relation to this that the appearance acquires its temporal relation, that, namely, of existing after a preceding time in which it did not. But it can only acquire its determinate temporal position in this relation through something being presupposed in the preceding state on which it always follows, i.e., follows in accordance with a rule: from which it results, first, that I cannot reverse the series and place that which happens prior to that which it follows. . . . (A 198/B 243)

When we judge that the tile falls after the door is opened, this is not necessarily because we judge the opening of the door to be the cause of the fall of the tile, but because we judge that there is something that determines that the tile could not have fallen before the door was opened.

In fact, once again Schopenhauer's objection to Kant seems to be close to Kant's own considered position. Schopenhauer claims:

Phenomena can quite easily *follow on one another* without following *from one another*. Nor is the law of causality prejudiced thereby; for it is still certain that every change is the effect of another change, since this truth is firmly established *a priori*; only that every change follows not merely on the single one that is its cause, but on all which exists simultaneously with that cause, and with which it stands in no causal relation. (FR 126/H. 1, 87–8)

This could describe Kant's position as well: what follows need not be the effect of the particular thing that it is judged to succeed, but it must be the effect of something in the total state of affairs obtaining before it occurs, which determines that it can occur only after that which it is judged to follow. Thus temporal judgments need causal laws, but we are not confined to judging only that effects follow their own causes in time. Why does Schopenhauer fail to see that he and Kant essentially agree? Perhaps it is just a superficial misreading. Or perhaps once again it is their methodological difference at work: failing to appreciate the transcendental character of Kant's position as an analysis of the conditions under which we can make certain kinds of judgments, Schopenhauer instead interprets Kant as if he were doing a kind of phenomenology, in which he associates the causal connections our judgments of temporal order depend upon with what is most salient in our experience, namely, the observation that one thing follows another in time. But Kant does not mean to suggest that the causal connections upon which our judgments depend are themselves what is salient in our experience; quite the contrary, they are more often something like an unstated framework within which our conscious experience is conceived. In Kant's view, judgments of temporal order depend upon causal connections but are not themselves immediate or direct expressions of those connections.

(3) The last of Schopenhauer's objections, however, raises a deep and enduring issue for Kant's treatment of causation. Schopenhauer objects that if our knowledge of temporal succession is not immediate but really depends upon our knowledge of the causal laws dictating the occurrence of the successions that we know, then our knowledge of causal laws would have to be impossibly vast. As formulated, the objection assumes that our knowledge of temporal succession is itself very extensive, and one might think to block Schopenhauer's objection by questioning that premise. But the same objection could be made without reference to quantity: one could simply adduce as a counterexample to Kant's theory any case in which one seems to know the temporal succession of the states of some event, although one does not yet know the explanation or perhaps even believes a false explanation of it. For example, to modify an example from Schopenhauer's second objection to fit the present one, it might be insisted that people in many primitive cultures certainly knew or know that day follows night without understanding the laws of the planetary motions that explain this sequence. In other words, it seems implausible not only that all of our knowledge of temporal succession depends upon knowledge of causal laws; it seems equally implausible that many of our particular judgments about temporal succession depend upon knowledge of the particular causal mechanisms and laws that explain those successions.

Without reference to Schopenhauer, many commentators on Kant's treatment of causation have nevertheless argued for a position that could be a reply to this last objection: namely, that all that Kant means to establish is that we have a priori knowledge of the general principle of causality, that every event has some cause, and not that we have a priori knowledge or even any knowledge at all of the particular causal laws that explain the temporal successions of which we are very well aware.[21] But this defense does not reflect the way Kant's argument in the Second Analogy actually works, for Kant derives his certainty about the validity of the general law of causality precisely from his analysis of how our judgments of temporal succession depend upon the particular causal laws determining the occurrence of the sequences that we judge. That I 'cannot reverse the series of perceptions' that I have when I perceive a ship sailing downstream, for instance, is not entailed by the general law that every event has some cause, but is entailed only by the particular causal laws about winds, currents, and so on that entail that in those particular circumstances that particular ship must indeed be sailing downstream instead of remaining stationary or sailing upstream. If my knowledge of the sequence of my perceptions and of the positions of the ship itself depends upon knowledge of causal laws at all, it depends upon knowledge of particular causal laws and not the general law of causality. But if this is right, then it does indeed seem that on Kant's account we must all know a great number of causal laws, explaining all sorts of occurrences that we might have thought we could not presently explain, for we certainly do seem to be able to make a vast number of reliable judgments about the temporal succession both of our own perceptions and of the objects they represent.

Among the few commentators who have recently recognized that Kant's argument does indeed seem to make our capacity for determinate temporal judgments depend upon knowledge of particular causal laws, two strategies for dealing with the problem that Schopenhauer's objection raises have been suggested. One suggestion, which I have made elsewhere,[22] anticipated the thesis of the present chapter by arguing precisely that we cannot see Kant's argument as an essay in the phenomenology or psychology of time determination but rather must see it as an essay in the epistemology – or, as Kant himself would call it, the transcendental logic – of time determination. That is, we should not see Kant as arguing that our ordinary *consciousness* of or mere *belief* in judgments about temporal succession depends upon knowledge of the particular causal laws that actually explain the successions of which we are aware, because that would indeed require knowledge and perhaps even a priori knowledge of an impossibly large body of particular causal laws; instead, we should see Kant as analyzing the conditions for the *justification* of our particular judgments of temporal succession. That we might not be able to justify many of the judgments we make everyday unless we possess adequate knowledge of the relevant causal laws, or even that we might have to revise some of the judgments about temporal succession that we take for granted once we learn the causal mechanisms and laws actually involved, would be no objection to Kant's argument – after all, the whole history of science has constantly required us to modify everyday judgments that have previously seemed sufficiently self-evident to be considered as if they were immediately given. Thus, the scientific acceptance of Copernican astronomy has ultimately required any well-informed person to revise what seemed to any pre-modern person the phenomenologically self-evident truth that the heavenly bodies rotate around our own fixed position, and the subsequent discovery of the finitude of the speed of light and the great distance of many of the stars that we can see has required us to give up what might seem like the phenomenologically obvious belief that when we see something we see it pretty much as it is now – for what our scientific theory now tells us is that we do not see many of the stars as they are now, but as they were millions or billions of years ago, when the light that we now detect first left those distant stars, some of which might no longer even exist. Once again, the force of Schopenhauer's objection to Kant appears to depend upon a phenomenological interpretation of Kant's claims that may not be what Kant himself intended.

An even bolder suggestion would be that Kant really does suppose that our a priori knowledge of particular causal mechanisms and laws is much greater than most of us initially suppose, and thus that what Schopenhauer finds so implausible is not implausible after all – in fact, we can and do have extensive knowledge of particular causal laws. This suggestion comes from an approach to Kant's philosophy of physical science on which it is argued that Kant understood as synthetic a priori not only the most general principles of judgment that he derived in the *Critique of Pure Reason* but also the more particular laws of Newtonian physics, the laws of terrestrial and celestial kinematics, dynamics, and mechanics that he derived in the *Metaphysical Foundations of Natural Science*.[23] To be sure, Kant thought that we could derive these more particular causal laws from the purely synthetic a priori principles of the *Critique* only by adding an empirical concept of matter in motion to the abstract concept of substance used in the derivation of the principles of judgment, so that the principles of natural science would not be *pure* synthetic a priori cognitions,[24] but he nevertheless held that this addition did not undermine the apriority of our knowledge of the laws of Newtonian physics. On this view, then, Kant really would be prepared to maintain that we do have knowledge and indeed synthetic a priori knowledge of at least the most important causal laws on which the truth of our judgments of the temporal order of the events that we observe actually depends.

This solution to Schopenhauer's objection also requires that we be prepared to distinguish Kant's transcendental methodology from what I have been calling the phenomenological method of Schopenhauer. When we classify the laws of Newtonian physics as a priori, we are surely not describing any knowledge that is immediate and self-evident in the daily experience of every human being; human beings lived for millennia before these laws were formulated a little over three centuries ago, most human beings in the last three centuries have continued to live in ignorance of them, and even many who have learned them may not have learned how more recent science restricts their application. So from what is supposed to be the standpoint of 'direct' and 'immediate' consciousness adopted by Schopenhauer, this defense of the argument of Kant's Second Analogy might not seem very promising. By contrast, the committed Kantian might think that Schopenhauer's approach, what I have been calling a phenomenological method *avant la lettre*, can never do justice to the transcendental character of Kant's proof. However this may be, it seems clear that Schopenhauer has put his finger on an issue of fundamental importance in Kant's philosophy. If Kant really does mean to argue that our empirical consciousness of temporal order depends upon particular causal laws, then he does owe us an account of the possibility of our knowledge of such laws. Further, even if Kant's theory is not meant to be a description of the salient or most immediate features of our experience, but a transcendental account of the conditions of the possibility of such experience, it would still seem reasonable to expect him to have provided some account of the relation between such transcendental conditions and the everyday experience the possibility of which they are supposed to ground, an issue about which he was largely silent. In his general critique of transcendental arguments, as we saw, Schopenhauer may have been hasty in his suggestion that such arguments cannot get off the ground at all, but he was quite right to suggest that there is a deep issue about the status of the most basic premises of such arguments. Likewise, in his critique of one of Kant's most important particular transcendental arguments, he may have been hasty to reject Kant's analysis outright on the basis of the phenomenology

of our experience of temporal order, but he was nevertheless right
to raise a fundamental issue about the relation between this phenomenology and the transcendental conditions of our experience,
an issue that Kant barely touched. The profound difference between
Kant's philosophical method and his own may have left Schopenhauer blind to some of Kant's intentions and presuppositions, but
at the same time, it allowed him to raise issues of enduring importance and difficulty about some of Kant's most basic assumptions
and conclusions.

NOTES

1 It is this aspect of his doctrine to which Kant refers in his famous statement 'I had to deny **knowledge** in order to make room for **faith**,' in the
Critique of Pure Reason, Preface to the second edition, B xxx. Quotations from the *Critique of Pure Reason* will be from the translation by
Paul Guyer and Allen W. Wood (Cambridge: Cambridge University Press,
1998); citations will be located by the traditional method using the pagination of the first (A) and/or second (B) edition. I will follow this edition's
use of boldface type to represent Kant's use of *Fettdruck* (bigger and
bolder type than the surrounding text) for emphasis. References to other
works by Kant will be located by the customary method of citing the volume and page of the *Akademie* edition, *Kant's gesammelte Schriften*,
edited by the Royal Prussian Academy of Sciences (Berlin: Georg Reimer,
later Walter de Gruyter, 1900–).
2 For this distinction, see *Critique of Pure Reason* B 3–6, A 6–19/B 10–14,
and A 150–8/B 189–97. Among the many discussions of this distinction,
the most useful is found in two papers by Lewis White Beck, 'Kant's
Theory of Definition' (1956) and 'Can Kant's Synthetic Judgments Be
Made Analytic?' (1955), both reprinted in his *Studies in the Philosophy
of Kant* (Indianapolis: Bobbs-Merrill, 1965), 61–91.
3 Kant's method of transcendental arguments was given renewed prominence in recent philosophy by the British philosopher Peter Strawson,
first in his original work *Individuals: An Essay in Descriptive Metaphysics* (London: Methuen, 1959) and then in his widely influential
book *The Bounds of Sense: An Essay on Kant's Critique of Pure Reason*
(London: Methuen, 1966). Transcendental arguments were then subjected to a barrage of criticisms; three of the seminal critiques were Barry
Stroud, 'Transcendental Arguments', *Journal of Philosophy* 65 (1968),
241–56; Stefan Körner, 'The Impossibility of Transcendental Arguments',
in Lewis White Beck (ed.), *Kant Studies Today* (LaSalle, Ill.: Open Court,

1969), 230–44; and Richard Rorty, 'Strawson's Objectivity Argument', *The Review of Metaphysics* 24 (1970), 207–44, and 'Verificationism and Transcendental Arguments', *Noûs* 5 (1971), 3–14. Useful surveys of the debate that ensued can be found in Peter Bieri, Rolf-Peter Horstmann, and Lorenz Krüger (eds.), *Transcendental Arguments and Science: Essays in Epistemology* (Dordrecht: Reidel, 1979); Anthony L. Brueckner, 'Transcendental Arguments I', *Noûs* 17 (1983), 551–75, and 'Transcendental Arguments II', *Noûs* 18 (1984), 197–225; and Paul Guyer, *Kant and the Claims of Knowledge* (Cambridge: Cambridge University Press, 1987), 'Afterword', 417–28.

4 As the citation indicates, this statement occurs in a passage added in the second edition of the *Critique of Pure Reason*, which Schopenhauer disliked (see note 16). It is part of a contrast between 'metaphysical' and 'transcendental expositions' that Kant did not make in the first edition of the *Critique*. For these reasons, it might be thought that it is not an apt characterization of Kant's method of transcendental argument in general as Schopenhauer might have understood it. But although Kant added this characterization of a 'transcendental exposition' only in the second edition, it does aptly characterize the epistemic status of the assumptions of some of his central transcendental arguments in the first edition, and it does seem reasonable to use it as one general characterization of how Kant understood his method.

5 *Prolegomena*, 4:275; in the translation by Gary Hatfield (Cambridge: Cambridge University Press, 1997), 26.

6 *Prolegomena*, 4:274; Hatfield, 26.

7 Indeed, Kant's discussion of the a priori sources of our knowledge of objects in space and time in the second edition of the *Critique*, from which the definition of a 'transcendental exposition' just cited is drawn, takes over much material from the *Prolegomena* (compare *Prolegomena* §2, 4:268–9 with *Critique of Pure Reason*, B 14–17) and undercuts Kant's claim that the two works have an essentially different method.

8 For this characterization, see Dieter Henrich's famous article 'The Deduction of the Moral Law' (1975), translated in Paul Guyer (ed.), *Kant's Groundwork of the Metaphysics of Morals: Critical Essays* (Lanham, Md.: Rowman and Littlefield, 1998), 303–41.

9 For the way I have put things in this sentence, see D. P. Dryer, *Kant's Solution for Verification in Metaphysics* (London: George Allen & Unwin, 1966).

10 See *W1* 434–7/H. 2, 514–18; note Schopenhauer's reference there to the anonymous 1792 work *Aenesidemus* of his teacher G. E. Schulze, a critique of Kant cast in the form of a critique of Kant's one time disciple Karl Leonhard Reinhold.

11 See, e.g., *Attempt to introduce the concept of negative magnitudes into philosophy*, 2:171–2; in Immanuel Kant, *Theoretical Philosophy, 1755–1770*, ed. David Walford (Cambridge: Cambridge University Press, 1992), 211. Kant could have supported this argument, although he did not, by appealing to Galilean relativity: what counts as a state of rest produced by equal and opposite forces in one inertial framework might in fact appear as motion in another.

12 The seeds of Schopenhauer's subsequent contrast between representation and willing can be seen in his contrast between the first two forms of determination and the fourth in this early work.

13 A passage like the present one could well be adduced as evidence of Schopenhauer's influence on Ludwig Wittgenstein – an influence present not only in Wittgenstein's early *Tractatus Logico-Philosophicus*, where Wittgenstein famously uses the example of the eye that is not itself part of its visual field to support the more general idea that the subject is not part of its world, which in turn introduces the idea that the logical forms of propositions are not like mere contents or things in the world (see propositions 5.632–5.641, immediately preceding proposition 6), but also in the later *Philosophical Investigations*, where it is expressed in such statements as 'If I have exhausted the justifications I have reached bedrock, and my spade is turned. Then I am inclined to say: "This is simply what I do."'

14 I borrow this expression from Maurice Merleau-Ponty; see *The Primacy of Perception*, ed. James M. Edie (Evanston, Ill.: Northwestern University Press, 1964).

15 Indeed, Kant himself may be seen to have anticipated this point in his early critique of rationalism; see his prize-winning essay of 1762, *Inquiry concerning the distinctness of the principles of natural theology and morality* (published in 1764), 2:293–6; in Walford (ed.), *Theoretical Philosophy, 1755–1770*, 267–9.

16 See *W1* 434–7/H. 2, 514–18. Schopenhauer's fundamental objection to the second edition was that its 'Refutation of Idealism' marred the purity of the idealism of the first edition and suppressed the best expression of the pure idealism, the first-edition version of the fourth 'Paralogism of Pure Reason'. This charge is entirely correct, although for many recent readers it is the basis for preferring the second to the first edition.

17 See, e.g., Jonathan Bennett, *Kant's Analytic* (Cambridge: Cambridge University Press, 1966), §22.

18 Reflection 6313, *Akademie* 18:614; translation from Paul Guyer, *Kant and the Claims of Knowledge* (Cambridge: Cambridge University Press, 1987), 305.

19 See note 16.

20 Reflection 6314, 18:619; quoted from *Kant and the Claims of Knowledge*, 314.

21 For a long list of those who take such a view, including noted commentators such as H. J. Paton, Lewis White Beck, and many others, see Michael Friedman, 'Causal Laws and the Foundations of Natural Science', in Paul Guyer (ed.), *The Cambridge Companion to Kant* (Cambridge: Cambridge University Press, 1992), 193, n. 6. For a recent addition to this list, see Béatrice Longuenesse, *Kant and the Capacity to Judge* (Princeton, N.J.: Princeton University Press, 1998), 269–70.

22 See *Kant and the Claims of Knowledge*, 258–9. As a matter of fact, I did bring Schopenhauer into my discussion of Kant's treatment of causation in that work, but I mentioned only Schopenhauer's second objection to Kant, not the third one that I am presently discussing.

23 This approach has been most extensively and persuasively developed by Michael Friedman in his article 'Causal Laws and the Foundations of Natural Science' in Guyer (ed.), *The Cambridge Companion to Kant*, 161–99, and in his book *Kant and the Exact Sciences* (Cambridge, Mass.: Harvard University Press, 1992), especially chapters 3 and 4.

24 For the distinction between 'pure' and 'impure' synthetic a priori cognitions, see Konrad Cramer, *Nichtreine synthetische Urteile a priori: Ein Problem der Transzendentalphilosophie Kants* (Heidelberg: Carl Winter Verlag, 1985).

5   Will and Nature

A recent short entry on 'will' in *The Oxford Companion to Philosophy* uses one-tenth of its word length to inform us that 'the will reached its philosophical apotheosis in Schopenhauer's *The World as Will and Idea* (1818, 1844)'.[1] This is correct insofar as the central term of that work's account of human nature, and of the nature of the whole world, is *Wille*, a word we can translate only as will. But it is apt to mislead. For in the history of the concept of will, Schopenhauer's intervention is idiosyncratic and perturbing. He does not simply take a pre-existing conception and give it an unwonted importance; he takes the word *Wille* and proposes for it a use that is revolutionary and far from straightforward.

I   WILL AND 'THE RIDDLE'

Will makes its dramatic debut in Schopenhauer's main work in §18 after a well-orchestrated build-up that allows it to be presented as 'the answer' to a tantalizing and vital riddle. The First Book of *The World as Will and Representation* has given a systematic account of the world of objects. Objects are objects of experience for a representing subject: there can be no object without subject, no subject without object. Objects are organized by space, time, and causality, the a priori forms of all representation. The subject perceives or has 'intuitive representations'[2] and, using concepts, it thinks, reasons, and judges. Throughout all this its representations are ordered, each representation being grounded in others in accordance with the principle of sufficient reason in one of its four versions. But something is missing from this orderly scenario. The problem is brought into the open as the curtain rises on the Second Book: it is that we as investigators cannot be content to have cognition of the relations pertaining among our representations, but must enquire into their 'inner nature', a term that is to recur throughout the Second Book.[3] The riddle is, then: What is the inner nature of things, which the orderly relations among representations themselves do not reveal? Will's role is to provide the answer, to be that inner nature.

But what precisely is the problem? Here is part of Schopenhauer's build-up, before the explicit entrance of will:

We are not satisfied with knowing that we have representations, that they are such and such, and that they are connected according to this or that law, whose general expression is always the principle of sufficient reason. We want to know the significance [*Bedeutung*] of those representations; we ask whether this world is nothing more than representation. In that case it would inevitably pass by us like an empty [*wesenloser*] dream, or a ghostly vision not worth our consideration. Or we ask whether it is something else, something in addition, and if so what that something is.... Here we see already that we can never get at the inner nature [*Wesen*] of things *from without*. However much we may investigate, we obtain nothing but images and names. We are like a man who goes round a castle, looking in vain for an entrance, and sometimes sketching the façades. (*W1* 98–9/H. 2, 117–18)

Most commentators have taken Schopenhauer to be exercised by the thought that the Kantian (or more or less Kantian) thing in itself is an unknowable something lying hidden behind, or shrouded deep inside, the world of our experience, unable to be an object of our acquaintance. Elsewhere Schopenhauer uses metaphors of penetration which suggest that this thing in itself can be known to the subject in a unique way, most notably the following: 'a way *from within* stands open to us to that real inner nature of things [*selbst-eigenen und inneren Wesen der Dinge*] to which we cannot penetrate *from without* ... so to speak a subterranean passage ... which, as if by treachery, places us all at once in the fortress that could not be taken from without' (*W2* 195/H. 3, 218–19). Here it looks as if the initial problem is the subject's having no avenue of acquaintance with a thing in itself that is unknowable because it lies in a realm beyond all experience. But if that is his starting point, Schopenhauer seems set to perpetrate a muddle, saying that we can know an unknowable.

However, there is an alternative reading, put forward recently by John Atwell.[4] Atwell's prime thesis is that Schopenhauer is concerned with the world's being understandable or 'readable' to the philosophical enquirer. In the passage from *W1* 98–9/H. 2, 117–18 just quoted, Schopenhauer says that we want to know the meaning (*Bedeutung*) of the world of representations. Here and elsewhere he talks of the world's threatening to be strange or alien (*fremd*), or uninformative or insignificant to us (*nichtssagend*, literally, 'having nothing to say') (*W1* 95/H. 2, 113). When the world is displayed to us in its scientifically discoverable causal connections, it consists of representations that 'stand before us like hieroglyphics that are not understood' (*W1* 97/H. 2, 115); experience is a 'cryptograph' we must decipher (see *W2* 182–4/H. 3, 202–4). Schopenhauer's talk of 'essence' or 'inner nature', Atwell suggests, concerns equally the 'meaning' or 'content' of things.[5] The riddle or puzzle is to do with our interpreting the world we experience or making it appear less alien to ourselves.

Atwell's view makes very good sense of Schopenhauer's initial discussion in §18, where he imagines how *I myself* might fail to be intelligible to myself. Were I to regard myself as nothing but the subject that experiences an objective world of spatio-temporal, causally interacting things, then I would not be able to locate myself at any particular point within the world I experience. I would float around in detachment from the world like 'a winged angel's head without a body'.[6] What I call my body would be for me on a par with any material thing I experience: 'its movements and actions ... would be equally strange and incomprehensible'.[7] This would make me the individual who acts and moves in the objective world, some kind of riddle to myself.

Atwell is right about the nature of the riddle here. Schopenhauer is not saying that if I were merely the subject of representations, I would lack all knowledge of or be unacquainted with my body and its movements. The point is that the body to which I owe my status as one objective individual among others would indeed be *experienced* by me, but *experienced as* alien and incomprehensible – I would not make sense to myself. However, none of this is the case, as Schopenhauer rightly says. There is an important way in which I do make sense to myself. This body's movements are, when I am acting, intelligible to me directly because I am moving my body, because the actions involving these movements are mine. So Schopenhauer's project is to use the absence of riddle regarding the part of the objective world that I am, to address a genuine riddle concerning the rest of the objective world apart from me: 'From yourself shall you understand nature, not yourself from nature.'[8]

It is less clear on this interpretation (1) what kind of understanding or deciphering of *the world's* meaning Schopenhauer hopes for; and (2) how it deals with his prominent claims to be discovering the nature of the thing in itself left unknowable by Kant. I shall return to these questions at the end of the chapter.

II HUMAN WILLING AND ACTION

Schopenhauer's account of the will begins innocently enough by giving an analysis of what we might term 'human willing'. I mean by that what I take to be more or less traditionally conceived as willing: a conscious mental state of a human agent, which is directed at, and typically brings about, an action that the agent regards as 'up to her' in virtue of its being brought about by her state of willing. In this traditional conception the subject of human willing is an agent, someone who does something; what she does is 'up to her' because of its relation to this mental state of hers; and this mental state is already something she (or her mind) does: it is an act of will.

Schopenhauer's first step is to insist on the bodily nature of human willing.

Every true act of his [the subject's] will is also at once and inevitably a movement of his body [*Bewegung des Leibes*]; he cannot actually will the act without at the same time being aware that it appears as a movement of the body. The act of will and the action of the body [*Aktion des Leibes*] ... do not stand in the relation of cause and effect, but are one and the same thing, though given in two entirely different ways, first quite immediately and then in perception for the understanding.... Resolutions of the will relating to the future are mere deliberations of reason about what will be willed at some time, not genuine acts of will. Only the carrying out stamps the resolve; till then, it is always a mere alterable intention, and exists only in reason, *in abstracto*.[9]

Schopenhauer's theory of willing is anti-volitionalist and anti-dualist.[10] For him there are no volitions, where those are understood as would-be occurrences of willing in the category 'mental and not physical' (or 'mental and not bodily'). There is an act of will (*Willensakt*), but it is not an occurrence falling into that category. An act of will is a 'movement of the body' or – seemingly for him an interchangeable term – an 'action of the body'.[11] Going by what Schopenhauer says about 'resolutions', certain antecedents of this action which could prima facie fall in the category 'mental and not bodily' are not properly acts of will at all. So presumably someone's merely intending to act in a certain manner but not acting, or deciding to act but not doing so, fall short of the description 'genuine act of will'. Yet elsewhere Schopenhauer makes it clear that the category 'willing' (if not that of 'act of will') does include resolves or decisions. In his prize-winning essay *On the Freedom of the Will* of 1839 (which I discuss more fully in Section V) he talks of 'decisions [*Entschlüsse*] or decided acts of will' which 'though they originate in the dark recesses of our inwardness, will always enter the perceptible world at once' as bodily movements.[12] One conception of willing suggested by Schopenhauer's remarks is that it is a conscious mental state of setting oneself to act, which *is* a willed bodily movement in that it naturally becomes or develops into such a movement. According to his essay, self-consciousness contains 'decided acts of will that immediately become deeds [*entschiedenen, sofort zur That werdenden Willensakten*]' and 'formal resolves together with the actions that issue from them [*förmliche Entschlüsse, nebst den aus ihnen hervorgehenden Handlungen*]'.[13] An even more clearly developmental picture is found in these remarks: 'as long as [an act of will] is in a state of becoming, it is called a *wish* [*Wunsch*], when it is complete, a *resolve* [*Entschluss*]; but that this is what it is is shown to self-consciousness only in the deed [*That*]: for until the deed it can be altered'.[14] Willing then is progressive: a wish or a state of wanting to do something is (becomes) a resolve of the will, which is (becomes) an act of will, which is (becomes) a deed or bodily action.

Schopenhauer's reason for holding that genuine acts of will are identical with movements of the body lies in the nature of our cognitive access to the body:

To the subject of knowledge ... this body is given in two entirely different ways. It is given as representation in intellectual intuition as an object among objects, and subordinate to the laws of objects. But it is also given at the same time in a completely different way, namely as that which is known immediately to everyone and is denoted by the word *will*.[15]

What situates me in the world of objects is my having immediately given to me, as subject, the actions of the bodily individual I am identical with. Schopenhauer thus puts forward – with, it must be said, very little detailed analysis – what can be called a dual aspect view of action.[16] Actions of the body, as he calls them, are movements in space and time of a particular material object. The agent is aware of the body's movement in space and time and its causal relations to other objects, but is aware of those same movements as his or her own will in operation. In action, something of which we are 'inwardly' conscious enters the world of objective phenomena, providing 'a bridge between the inner and the outer worlds which otherwise remained separated by a bottomless abyss'.[17]

III   WILL AS 'INNER NATURE'

With this anti-dualist thesis concerning the bodily nature of human willing, we catch merely the tip of a long strand in Schopenhauer's thinking, which could be described as a kind of naturalization of human willing, in the sense that it aims to subsume willing as merely one instance of organic process at work in nature. At any given time, an organism – human or non-human – tends towards some localized telos. Whatever localized telos it tends towards, its functioning is governed by enduring ends that must be secured repeatedly – nutrition, for example – and the single overarching telos which explains them all (to which they are all instrumental) is that of being alive and perpetuating life. This pattern of tending towards ends which provide the explanation for behaviour is common throughout the natural world. And human willing is one among a multitude of ways in which organisms tend towards a telos. An episode of human willing, identical with an action of the body, is distinguished from other organic processes by the kinds of causal antecedents which deflect the organism's course. There are three basic kinds of causal relation: *cause* pure and simple, *stimulus*, and *motive*.[18] While other processes in nature are either instances of bare cause and effect, or of the relation of stimulus to response, human willing (or an act of will) occurs when the body's movements are caused by motives, these being mental states in which an objective world is presented to consciousness, among them conceptual judgements which may have been arrived at by reasoning.

Once we have said something about these distinctive antecedents (the capacity for which can itself, Schopenhauer believes, be given a naturalistic explanation in terms of the functioning of the human organism, in particular its brain[19]), human willing is nothing special. The boundary between human willing and other processes of organic end-directedness is not one between metaphysical kinds. I as agent have an 'inner nature' in virtue of which I tend towards local ends and the overarching end of life – being alive and reproducing life. The very organized structure and normal functioning of my body, its growth, and all the processes of it which presuppose neither consciousness nor even mindedness, are manifestations of the same tendency. The inner nature of the human being is that it tends towards maintaining and propagating life, and this same inner nature is common to every inhabitant of the organic world. A tiger, a sunflower, or a single-celled organism have the same inner nature or essence. Schopenhauer even argues that at the most fundamental level the same inner nature must be that of the whole phenomenal world, not only in the organic but also in the inorganic realm, where it underlies the processes of gravitation, magnetism, and crystal formation: 'That which in us pursues its ends by the light of knowledge ...here, in the feeblest of its phenomena, only strives blindly in a dull, one-sided, and unalterable manner'.[20] Of course, it is not the case that the material world in every one of its formations pursues life. But Schopenhauer wants to say that at the broadest level of generality every part of the world possesses the same essence as I do; like me it – as it were – pursues, strives, or tends somewhere. 'It will not cost us a great effort of the imagination' to recognize this, he comments.[21]

Schopenhauer has reasons for his view. We have seen that he believes there is a 'puzzle' or 'riddle' about the world's inner nature that needs a solution. We should note three further fundamental premises: (1) that in my own case my bodily acts of willing give me a knowledge or understanding of myself that has a unique immediacy and transparency not shared by any other experience I have; (2) that scientific explanation of phenomena is essentially incomplete and requires a metaphysical foundation in an account of the inner nature underlying the world of phenomena; (3) that, on pain of the world's being unintelligible to me, I cannot regard my own inner nature as different from that of reality as whole. Schopenhauer seems to assume that if I am to understand the world from my own nature, then, what it really is to be me cannot be different from what it really is to be anything in nature.

The following passage shows Schopenhauer's strategy with tolerable clarity:

In everything in nature there is something to which no ground can ever be assigned, for which no explanation is possible, and no further cause can be sought. This something is the specific mode of the thing's action, in other words, the very manner of its existence, its essence [*Wesen*]. . . . [I]t was supposed that, starting from the most universal forces of nature (e.g. gravitation, cohesion, impenetrability), we could explain from them those forces which operate more rarely and only under a combination of circumstances (e.g., chemical quality, electricity, magnetism), and finally from these could understand the organism and life of animals, and even the knowing and willing of man. . . . [But] do we understand more about the inner nature of these natural forces than about the inner nature of an animal? Is not the one just as hidden and unexplored as the other? Unfathomable, because it is groundless, because it is the content, the *what* of the phenomenon, which can never be referred to the form of the phenomenon, to the *how*, to the principle of sufficient reason. . . . [M]y body is the only object of which I know not merely the one side, that of the representation, but also the other, that is called *will*. Thus instead of believing that I would better understand my own organization, and therefore my own knowing and willing, and my movement on motives, if only I could refer them to movement from causes through electricity, chemistry, and mechanism, I must, in so far as I am looking for philosophy and not for etiology, first of all learn to understand from my own movement on motives the inner nature of the simplest and commonest movements of an inorganic body which I see ensuing on causes. I must recognize the inscrutable forces that manifest themselves in all the bodies of nature as identical in kind with what in me is the will, and as differing from it only in degree.[22]

If, as Schopenhauer claims, my self-consciousness as bodily agent gives me a uniquely unmediated knowledge of myself, this may well suggest that it is an accurate pointer towards the inner nature of the portion of the world that is me. If the world and my place in it can be intelligible to me only if I interpret the world as having the same inner nature as myself, and if a unifying metaphysical account is what the necessary limitation of scientific explanation leaves us crying out for, then it would be irresponsible not to apply the knowledge of my own nature to the metaphysical unriddling of all of the world. 'Obviously,' says Schopenhauer, 'it is more correct to teach understanding of the world from the human being than understanding of the human being from the world, for it is from what is immediately given, that is self-consciousness, that we have to explain what is mediately given and belongs to outer perception; not the other way round.'[23] Not everyone nowadays will identify strongly with Schopenhauer's task of revealing the supra-scientific essence and significance of reality in itself, or his idea that a subject's self-consciousness must play the primary role in achieving it (though at the time he was writing, broadly analogous conceptions could be found in the mainstream philosophy of the German Idealists). His monistic assumption that my fundamental nature cannot be different from that of the whole of reality is not obviously disreputable, though it may well seem too big (or too vague) a thought to handle comfortably.

Nevertheless, by something like this argument, Schopenhauer arrives at his alleged common inner nature of all things, and it is this inner nature that he calls *the will* (*der Wille*), or better simply *will* – an adventurous exercise in nomenclature which enables him to say that human willing is merely one instance of will, one manifestation of will in the world of empirical nature. For example, he says:

What appears... as plant, as mere vegetation, as blindly driving force [*blind treibende Kraft*], will be taken by us, according to its inner nature, to be will, and it will be recognized by us as the very thing which constitutes the basis of our own appearance, as it expresses itself in our actions.[24]

It is peculiar to human willing that it is caused by motives, which are representations of the objective world, perceptions and conceptual representations occurring in consciousness and causing episodes in which the bodily human being approaches some *telos*. Human willing, then, is that form of natural end-directedness whose local goals are fixed by conscious empirical knowledge of objects. But having this aetiology does not belong to the essence of the will as such:

we have ... to get to know more intimately this inner nature of the will, so that we may know how to distinguish from it what belongs not to it itself, but to its appearance.... Such, for example, is the circumstance of its being accompanied by knowledge, and the determination by motives which is conditioned by this knowledge.... [T]his belongs not to the inner nature of the will, but merely to its most distinct phenomenon as animal and human being.[25]

Just how we are to understand this inner nature, and just why it is appropriate to call it will, are problems Schopenhauer never fully resolves. But we can, I believe, sympathize with his general predicament. He seeks a continuity between the mind and nature which he thinks can be secured neither by dualism nor by materialism. Dualism is unavailable because there is no immaterial substance: the only substance is matter.[26] But materialism starts by removing conscious subjectivity from its picture and can never work its way back to including it. We could never explain our being conscious of ourselves as subject of our own mental states in materialist terms; materialism is 'the philosophy of the subject who forgets to take account of himself'.[27] Looking for another alternative, we might be tempted to classify Schopenhauer's strategy as a species of panpsychism, understood as 'the view that the basic physical constituents of the universe have mental properties'.[28] We might see him as trying to ensure that the phenomena of human willing are part of physical reality by claiming that a truly mental willing is found everywhere, each tiniest portion of nature containing a degree of mentality in virtue of which it primitively wants or tries to achieve some end. But I think this is not accurate. Mind, for Schopenhauer, is what the single principle of nature can manifest itself *as*, at one end of the scale. But when at other points on the scale this principle manifests itself 'dully and blindly', as gravitational force or as light-seeking movement in plants, it is not manifesting itself as mind at all. Some parts of phenomenal reality are minds, but most are not, for Schopenhauer. The challenge is to explain how one and the same fundamental reality can manifest itself as me – acting with mind and consciousness – and as a falling stone or a growing crystal.

Perhaps by retaining a mentalistic *word*, 'will', Schopenhauer hopes to make it plausible that the underlying reality could manifest itself phenomenally as a human agent. But tension shows in his strategy when he warns that his use of the word is radically revisionary and effectively tells the reader to think away its mentalistic connotations:

if I say that the force which attracts a stone to the earth is of its nature, in itself . . . will, then no one will attach to this proposition the absurd meaning that the stone moves itself according to a known motive, because it is thus that the will appears in man.[29]

We must heed this warning throughout if Schopenhauer is not to be plain laughable. But then why call the inner nature will rather than something else? He addresses this objection and replies that

the word *will*, which ... is to reveal to us the innermost essence of everything in nature, by no means expresses an unknown quantity ... but something cognized absolutely immediately, with which we are so well acquainted that we know and understand what will is much better than anything else.[30]

This is an effective reply only if it means that we know better than anything else what it is *in general* to seek, to strive, or tend towards an end, whether blindly and dully or with consciousness and rational motivation. Or: we know, by what is immediately given to us in experiencing the directedness of bodily action, what it is to be any part of nature. Not the least strange feature of this account is the thought that the deliverance of my *consciousness* of myself doing something uncovers the nature of being or activity as such, whether conscious or not, throughout the whole of reality. The term 'inner nature' is perhaps being stretched too far here. Many philosophers would acknowledge with Schopenhauer that there is something that it is like 'from the inside' to be myself engaged in bodily action, and that were it not for this, I would be unintelligible to myself. They might, perhaps, acquiesce in his assumption that every part of reality must in itself be something – or have an essence – that exceeds its manifestation in the world of appearances. But it would be quite another matter to suppose that for every part of reality there is something that it is like to be it. Although Schopenhauer does not make this supposition, it is hard in its absence to see how the alleged common 'inner nature' of all things could be that which I cognize immediately through 'inner awareness' of myself as agent. How could a thing that never acts, or experiences, or has any self-consciousness – a stone, say – be in its own nature just what I discover myself to be in the self-conscious experience of being an agent?[31]

Leaving aside these admittedly severe difficulties, a salient feature of Schopenhauer's account is the continuity of kind it claims between human willing and all other processes in organic nature. His task of 'unriddling' nature gives primacy to the deliverances of self-consciousness over the experience of external phenomena. But the upshot is that, in understanding what I most fundamentally am, I am brought to acknowledge my kinship with and incorporation in nature at large. It is as though I must admit that when I act, it is one specialized case of nature doing what it does everywhere and one specialized case of living organisms doing as they do everywhere. When I described Schopenhauer's account in terms of life as the overarching telos of all organic behaviour and morphology, I was describing what Schopenhauer characterizes as 'will to life' (*Wille zum Leben*). The end-seeking movements of all living things, and their very formation and functioning, answer to no purpose consciously entertained in a mind, but do all subserve the end of life. Hence, according to Schopenhauer, 'the fundamental theme of all the many different acts of will is the satisfaction of the needs inseparable from the body's existence in health; they have their expression in it, and can be reduced to the maintenance of the individual and the propagation of the race.'[32] If my inner nature is 'will', it can also be more narrowly described as 'will to life'. Indeed, he says that 'the real self is the will to life':[33] in other words, the real self is the principle of blind striving for existence and reproduction that manifests itself as organic body, as me, the bodily individual, while not pertaining to me alone.

Schopenhauer also believes there is a unique character peculiar to me, which he calls my will, and which he tends to describe using the Kantian expression 'intelligible character' (saying that Kant's distinguishing of empirical and intelligible characters is one of his greatest achievements[34]). My intelligible character is my trans-empirical character: what I am in myself. In *On the Basis of Morality* Schopenhauer writes:

With his unalterable inborn character that is strictly determined in all its manifestations by the law of causality... the individual is only the *phenomenon*. The *thing in itself* underlying the phenomenon is outside space and time and free from all succession and plurality of acts; it is one and unchangeable. Its constitution *in itself* is the *intelligible character*, which is equally present in all the actions of the individual and is stamped on every one of them, like the signet on a thousand seals. The *empirical character* of this phenomenon, manifesting itself in time and in the succession of acts, is determined by the intelligible.... *Operari sequitur esse* [doing follows from being]. This means that everything in the world operates in accordance with what it is, with its character and quality, in which all its manifestations are therefore already contained potentially. These appear actually when external causes bring them about, for in this manner that very quality or character itself is revealed. Such quality is the *empirical character*; on the other hand, its inner ultimate ground, one that is not accessible to experience, is the *intelligible character*, in other words, the essence *in itself* of this thing. Here man forms no exception to the rest of nature; he too has his fixed disposition and unalterable character, which, however, is entirely individual and different in each case.[35]

But this account of the intelligible character is troubling because it seems to fly in the face of Schopenhauer's repeated assertion that the world at the level of the thing in itself is beyond individuation. Kant does not appear to realize this so clearly. But, for Schopenhauer, if space and time are the principle of individuation, that is, that which makes it possible for there to be distinct individuals at all, and if the world in itself is expressly not in space and time, because space and time are the a priori forms of intuition that have their seat only within the subject's cognitive apparatus, then it follows that there are no spatio-temporal individuals in the world as it is in itself: at that level we can speak only of 'what there is' or 'the world' in a quite undifferentiated sense. That the world in itself does not split up into separate individuals, that individuality is phenomenal only, is a fundamental and consistent tenet of Schopenhauer's philosophy. It is for this reason that in his ethics Schopenhauer can rely on the thought that ultimately individuality is an illusion.

However, at the same time, he wants my will or intelligible character to be an individual essence which determines that I behave in certain ways in certain environments, that makes me always, if you like, tend to 'gravitate' a certain way. If only the world as a whole can have an intelligible character, then clearly 'my' intelligible character ought not to pertain to me as an individual. What I am in myself ought to be no different from what you are in yourself, or indeed from what any phenomenal object is in itself. But then if the intelligible character of a thing determines its empirical character – the way it observably behaves under various causal influences – why is it that every object does not behave in the same way? Not only does Schopenhauer wish to avoid that absurdity, he wants it to be precisely my intelligible character that marks my actions as having a quality unique to me, 'like the signet on a thousand seals'. A little-noticed late passage in *Parerga and Paralipomena* shows an openness to the problem, if not a solution:

individuality does not rest solely on the *principium individuationis* and so is not through and through mere *phenomenon*, but ... it is rooted in the thing-in-itself, the will of the individual; for the character itself is individual. But how far its roots here go, is one of those questions which I do not undertake to answer. (*P2* 227/H. 6, 242)

The best we can say is that there is considerable elasticity in Schopenhauer's account of what I am in myself. His short answer is that what I am in myself, that is, my essence or inner nature, is will. But in practice, this answer contains at least three different thoughts about my essence. It is either (1) will (an essence I share with everything in the world), (2) will to life (an essence I share with organic nature as a whole), or (3) my individual will or underlying character (which is peculiar to me). Schopenhauer often relies on answers (2) and (3) when he seeks to corroborate his metaphysics of the will by means of empirical evidence.

IV   WILL AND OUR SEXUAL NATURE

One of Schopenhauer's themes is that the will in nature is greater than the individual living thing and has the individual at its mercy. A prime illustration of this occurs in his discussion of human sexuality.[36] A human individual is the objecthood of the will to life, his or her body one of its empirical manifestations. Many aspects of the human organism function to keep the individual alive; but others are directed towards life beyond the individual, and they are the will to life in its most blatant expression; as Schopenhauer puts it, 'the genitals are the focus of the will', as opposed to the brain, which is the focus of the intellect. Even though the brain too is an instrument of the will to life, the sexual functioning of the body is the latter's primary expression. The sex-drive[37] is the 'kernel of the will to life ... the concentration of all willing' (*W2* 513–14/H. 3, 588): hence it is the kernel of the kernel of human beings.

it may be said that the human being is concrete sexual impulse, for his origin is an act of copulation, and the desire of his desires is an act of copulation, and this impulse alone perpetuates and holds together the whole of his phenomenal appearance. It is true that the will to life manifests itself primarily as an effort to maintain the individual; yet this is only a stage towards the effort to maintain the species.... The sex-drive is therefore the most complete manifestation of the will to life. (*W2* 514/H. 3, 588)

It is not surprising, then, if sexual love (*Geschlechtsliebe*) directed towards another individual is a powerful force in human life:

> It is the ultimate goal of almost all human effort; it has an unfavourable influence on the most important affairs, interrupts every hour the most serious occupations, and sometimes perplexes for a while even the greatest minds. It does not hesitate to intrude with its trash, and to interfere with negotiations of statesmen and the investigations of the learned. It knows how to slip its love-notes and ringlets even into ministerial portfolios and philosophical manuscripts ... it appears on the whole as a malevolent demon, striving to pervert, to confuse, and to overthrow everything. (W2 533–4/H. 3, 610–11)

'It' is clearly being conceived here as some agency or purpose which is not subject to the individual's control, and Schopenhauer appears to wish it were. Sexuality is not only ubiquitous for him but tormenting.[38]

His account of sexual love operates on two levels: at the level of individual consciousness, the other is singled out as the object of desire and idealized. He or she is apparently beloved for qualities of value he or she uniquely possesses; and satisfaction of the desire by another interchangeable object is ruled out. Thus it seems to the individual lover. But all this is an illusion, according to Schopenhauer. The individual is merely being used. For at the deeper explanatory level, all (heterosexual[39]) sexual desire can be explained functionally as enabling reproduction:

> The sex-drive ... knows how to assume very skilfully the mask of an objective admiration, and thus to deceive consciousness; for nature requires this stratagem in order to attain her ends. But in every case of being in love, however objective and touched with the sublime that admiration may appear to be, what alone is aimed at is the generation of an individual of a definite disposition. (W2 535/H. 3, 612)

Schopenhauer has a eugenic conception of sexual attraction and human beauty. We are instinctively drawn to those in whom we detect features that will enhance the species when we produce offspring with them. 'The passion of being in love really turns on what is to be produced and on its qualities';[40] 'A slight downward or upward curvature of the nose has decided the happiness in life of innumerable girls, and rightly, for the type of the species is at stake.'[41] Schopenhauer would doubtless have spoken of the 'selfish gene' if he had known about genes. As it is, he talks of the 'will of the species' as directing the behaviour of individuals while deluding them that they pursue by choice their own individual preferences and purposes, such as seeking their own pleasure. Since the will as thing in itself is beyond individuation, it lives on in future generations: thus 'the kernel of our true nature' is indestructible and shared with our whole species.[42] He even says it is the will to life of the as yet unconceived child that draws a man and a woman to love one another.[43] In general, the unique intensity of the passions which attend sexual behaviour and the (sometimes absurd and ruinous) seriousness with which it is pursued confirm Schopenhauer in his view that it expresses the very core of human inner nature which is the will to life.

V   UNFREEDOM OF THE INDIVIDUAL'S WILL

Whether we give emphasis to the global will, the will to life, the will of the species, or the inborn will of the individual, once we attain the Schopenhauerian vision of the individual subject as *a phenomenon whose inner essence is will*, it must have an effect upon our conception of human action and thought. The self-conscious thinking self that I usually take myself to be is not the true origin of my bodily actions. Given my character and the course my experiences actually take, I could not have willed otherwise than I did on any particular occasion. Motives channel me but are not the driving force within me:

From without, the will can be affected only by motives; but these can never change the will itself.... All that the motives can do ... is to alter the direction of the will's effort, in other words to make it possible for it to seek what it invariably seeks by a path different from the one it previously followed.... But such an influence can never bring it about that the will wills something actually different from what it has willed hitherto. This remains unalterable, for the will is precisely this willing itself, which would otherwise have to be abolished.[44]

On Schopenhauer's conception, in simply being a living and hence a striving thing, I am – to adapt a related simile he sometimes uses himself[45] – like a stream of water rushing ahead, its course shaped both by contingencies in its path and by tendencies towards movement inherent in its own nature. The stream has no control over its own inner nature or the direction it actually takes given what it meets – and no more do I. The ways in which I differ from a stream of water, in having a mind, having conscious states, and being caused to will by rational motives, do not alter the case. Georg Simmel, writing in 1907, provides the following excellent summation of Schopenhauer's view: 'I do not will by virtue of values and goals that are posited by reason, but I have goals because I will continuously and ceaselessly from the depth of my essence.'[46] Whatever coherence Schopenhauer's general theory of the will may have or lack, this displacement of the rational, thinking self from explanatory and ontological primacy is one of the most influential aspects of his thought.

Although Schopenhauer deals with the question of free will in *The World as Will and Representation*,[47] his most accessible discussion of it occurs in the essay *On the Freedom of the Will* of 1839.[48] The essay responded to a specific question set by the Royal Norwegian Scientific Society: 'Is it possible to prove the freedom of the human will from the evidence of self-consciousness?' Schopenhauer's answer to that question is 'No'.[49] But the essay has a great deal to say about the conception of freedom. It is a self-contained piece of writing that starts not from Schopenhauer's metaphysics of the will, which the occasion did not allow him either to assume or to expound, but from an analysis of the fundamental concepts used to pose the problem.

The main outline of the extended argument of *On the Freedom of the Will* can be summarized as follows:

1. Freedom of the individual human will must be distinguished from freedom of action (the ability to do X if one wills to do X).
2. There is freedom of will only if occurrences of the individual's willing enjoy absence of all determination or necessity.
3. An agent's self-consciousness can provide no answer to the question of whether the agent's acts of will are necessitated by a ground that determines them.
4. But an objective account of the occurrence of acts of will shows that they must be grounded in causes that necessitate their occurrence.
5. Hence there is no freedom of the individual agent's will in this sense: no acts of will can be without a ground that necessitates them.

6. This conclusion does not remove the sense one has of being responsible for one's deeds, which must be accounted for from a different standpoint.

Schopenhauer's thesis that self-consciousness cannot decide whether the will is free is given extra poignancy by his initial claim in the essay that self-consciousness embraces *only* the will. I am conscious of myself not as a knower, he says, but 'altogether as one who *wills* [*durchaus als eines* Wollenden]' (*FW* 11/H. 4, 11). It is only as having states of my own willing (*das eigene Wollen*)[50] that I can know myself. But 'willing' now emerges as a very broad classification. Anything pertaining to positive or negative attitude or affect is called a 'movement of the will'. Desiring is a movement of the will, so are a great many emotions: 'longing, hoping, loving, rejoicing, jubilation, . . . abhorring, fleeing, fearing, being angry, hating, mourning, suffering pain', and 'even that which goes under the name of feelings of pleasure and displeasure [*Gefühle der Lust und Unlust*]' and 'bodily sensations [*Empfindungen*]'.[51] In this context Schopenhauer does not concede, as he does in *The World as Will and Representation*, that some affections of the body in sight, hearing, and touch may not move the will at all and are 'mere representations'.[52] But details are not so important: we may regard Schopenhauer's widening of the concept of will as something of a digression here. The central thesis that self-consciousness tells us nothing about the freedom of willing can still be upheld, regardless of the claim that self-consciousness embraces only willing in a wide sense. The question need only concern whatever portion of self-consciousness is taken up with willing.

When I am aware of a state of wanting to do something, and of the action that this state 'immediately becomes', as Schopenhauer puts it,[53] I may describe myself as being able to do what I will. Self-consciousness gives evidence of what it is that I will, and of my ability to act in accordance with what I will. That can be taken as self-consciousness confirming my freedom. But what freedom? Schopenhauer makes an acute distinction between freedom to do what I will (the 'empirical, original, and popular concept of freedom', *FW* 16/H. 4, 16) and freedom of *willing*. Ordinary people, and some philosophers, think that the question of free will is exhausted by attending to the first conception. But the real question left unanswered is whether I could have *willed* to do otherwise than I willed in fact. This is the difficult metaphysical question of free will. Schopenhauer is surely right to say that an agent's self-consciousness is powerless to discover whether she could have *willed* to do other than she did on some particular occasion.

For the will to be free in the required sense would be for it to be subject to no necessity. With self-consciousness unable to ascertain whether willing is necessitated, we must turn to consciousness of things other than self. But this consciousness is that of the world as representation, and Schopenhauer's firm view is that every representation in that world is subordinate to the principle of sufficient reason and hence to necessity. In particular, we must consider any event in the spatio-temporal realm of empirical things subject to the necessity with which an effect follows on from a cause. That the cause of a human willed action is a motive, not a cause pure and simple, makes no difference. Considered as events in the world as representation, human actions are subject to causal necessity. They are jointly determined by motives, the experiences and thoughts that occur in the mind (equated by Schopenhauer with states of the brain[54]), and by the character of the agent. Hence the will of every individual human being, as manifested in his or her wants, decisions, and actions, is not free.

Schopenhauer's defence of determinism and its incompatibility with freedom of the individual will is clinically argued, and he never wavers from it. Yet he realizes that this is not the end of the philosophical problem. We still feel responsible for our actions; we regard ourselves as the doers of our deeds. In some sense, then, a 'higher sense', we must be free, as Schopenhauer says at the end of his essay:

my exposition does not eliminate freedom. It merely moves it out, namely, out of the area of simple actions, where it demonstrably cannot be found, up to a region which lies higher, but is not so easily accessible to our knowledge. In other words, freedom is transcendental. (FW 99/H. 4, 98)

In an acute commentary on Schopenhauer's conception of freedom ('The fable of intelligible freedom'), Nietzsche suggested that Schopenhauer's argument has shown the *feeling* of responsibility to be wholly without foundation, a consequence Schopenhauer could not see because of his deep attachment to the morality of Christianity,[55] hence his resort to the 'higher region'. That is a diagnosis with some plausibility. But a prior problem is to understand what positive conception of freedom Schopenhauer is putting forward.

First, we must shift our understanding of responsibility away from actions to character. Schopenhauer has argued that, given who someone is, what his or her character is, his or her action upon given experiences or motives is necessitated. But it is necessitated not absolutely, only relative to the agent. Hence 'under the influence of the motives which determined him, a quite different action . . . was quite possible and could have happened, *if only he had been another* – this alone kept him from doing something else'.[56] Conclusion: he feels responsibility for his character or for his being – *Seyn und Wesen*.[57] The idea is that if everything I do proceeds inevitably from the unchanging source within me that makes me genuinely what I am, that is, my will, then my feeling of being the doer is wholly justified. What else should the target of praise or blame be but my own innermost self?

Schopenhauer admires Kant's distinction between the empirical and intelligible characters, as we have seen; he also mentions as one of Kant's great achievements the assignment of freedom to the realm of the thing in itself as opposed to that of phenomena.[58] By exploiting this dichotomy, Schopenhauer hopes to save a sense of freedom which can give foundation to the human feeling of responsibility:

the condition and the basis of [a human being's] whole appearance . . . is his intelligible character, i.e. his will as thing in itself. It is to the will in this capacity that freedom, and to be sure even absolute freedom, that is, independence of the law of causality (as a mere form of appearances) properly belongs. . . .

As can easily be seen, this road leads to the view that we must no longer seek the work of our freedom in our individual actions . . . but in the whole being and essence (*existentia et essentia*) of the man himself. This must be thought of as his free act, which only presents itself to the cognitive faculty as linked to time, space, and causality in a multiplicity and variety of actions. . . . Everything acts according to its nature, and its acts as they respond to causes make this nature known. Every man acts according to what he is, and the action, which is accordingly necessary in each case, is determined solely by the motives in the individual case. . . .

The consciousness of self-determination [*Eigenmächtigkeit*] and originality [*Ursprünglichkeit*] which undeniably accompanies all our acts, and by virtue of which they are *our* acts, is therefore not deceptive. . . . But its true content reaches further than the acts and begins higher up. In truth it includes our being and essence itself. . . .[59]

To make it more plausible that my feeling responsible for particular actions indicates a genuine reponsibility for my being, Schopenhauer calls my being a 'free act' occurring in the realm of the 'in itself'. It is desperately unclear, however, what kind of act *of mine* this could be. If everything acts according to its nature, and my acting according to mine is merely an instance of this, then I am only as responsible for my behaviour as any other part of the world is for its. The difference between me and a shark or a tidal wave is that they merely act according to their nature, while I have additional feelings of being the responsible doer. But if this is the only difference, it seems Nietzsche was right: nothing justifies those feelings. Schopenhauer's very notion of the will's being my underlying, non-rational, unchosen essence, in virtue of which I have the goals I have and behave as I do, seems to rob me, the self-conscious individual, of autonomy. Trying to restore my individual autonomy by appeal to the same notion of will as thing in itself seems an unpromising strategy.

Sometimes Schopenhauer intimates that while the will of each phenomenal individual is determined, the will in itself, beyond individuation, is free.[60] The concealed significance of this emerges later in his grand plan. Freedom of the will as thing in itself from any necessitation or grounding by anything outside it (and there is nothing outside it) facilitates Schopenhauer's culminating idea that the will to life might of its own accord give up its attachment to life, or annul itself within a human being, while there survives a pure consciousness detached from all striving and evacuated of all affect. The central thought of Schopenhauer's philosophy is really that this self-abolition of the will is the only hope of our re-claiming value from a life that is otherwise worse than non-existence. To keep that hope alive, he has to leave the will free from any constraint that would prevent it from spontaneously denying itself.

VI   WILL AND THING IN ITSELF

It can be argued[61] that Schopenhauer commits a gross fallacy by holding both that

(a) we can have no knowledge of the thing in itself

and that

(b) we can know that the thing in itself is will.

The second claim seems to be the single crucial point of the arguments we have so far pursued. The first seems to follow from
Schopenhauer's insistence that 'being-known of itself contradicts
being-in-itself' (W2 198/H. 3, 221), that knowledge is limited to our
representations (*Vorstellungen*), and that thing in itself and representation are utterly divorced from one another. However, in
stating such a stark contradiction we may be over-simplifying
Schopenhauer's views; there are other alternatives worth exploring.
One might suggest that Schopenhauer holds merely the following:

> (a′) by way of representation, we can have no knowledge of the
> thing in itself,

but

> (b′) we can have direct acquaintance, not by way of representa-
> tion, with our own will, which is what we are in ourselves.

From this direct acquaintance – the present reading continues – we
can achieve knowledge *that* the world in itself is will, but such
knowledge *that* the world is will is not a direct acquaintance with
anything. We experience the rest of the world, apart from ourselves,
as a multitude of spatio-temporal phenomena, and comprehend
the world's inner nature as will by inference and analogy from the
one thing (our own will) with which we are directly acquainted. The
combination of (a′) and (b′) avoids contradiction. And it allows (b)
also to be true: we can know *that* the thing in itself is will. Immediate acquaintance with our own will allows us to infer the nature of
the thing in itself in everything else of which we have only mediated
knowledge. The following often-quoted passage from the chapter 'On
the Possibility of Knowing the Thing-in-Itself' is evidence for this interpretation:

on the path of *objective knowledge*, thus starting from the *representation*,
we shall never get beyond the representation, i.e. the phenomenon. We
shall therefore remain at the outside of things; we shall never be able to
penetrate into their inner nature [*ihr Inneres*], and investigate what they are
in themselves.... But now, as the counterpoise to this truth, I have stressed
that other truth that we are not merely the *knowing subject*, but that *we
ourselves* are also among those beings [*Wesen*] we require to know, that *we
ourselves are the thing in itself*. Consequently, a way *from within* stands

open to us to that real inner nature of things to which we cannot penetrate *from without*. It is, so to speak, a subterranean passage, a secret relationship [*Verbindung*] which, as if by treachery, places us all at once in the fortress that could not be taken by attack from without. Precisely as such, the *thing in itself* can come into consciousness only quite directly, namely by *it itself being conscious of itself*; to try to know it objectively is to desire something contradictory.... In fact, our *willing* is the only opportunity we have of understanding simultaneously from within any event that outwardly manifests itself; consequently, it is the one thing known to us *immediately*, and not given to us merely in the representation, as all else is. Here, therefore, lies the datum alone capable of becoming the key to everything else ... we must learn to understand nature from ourselves, not ourselves from nature. (W2 195–6/H. 3, 218–19)

This seems to assert (a'), (b'), and (b) quite clearly in order. Both (b') and (b) entail the falsity of (a), which said that there can be *no* knowledge of the thing in itself.

Now this resolution of the problem requires Schopenhauer to believe – as he indeed asserts in the passage quoted – that our 'direct acquaintance' with our own will is not a matter of representation at all, but rather something *toto genere* distinct from representation. If it is true that whenever we experience through representation we do not attain knowledge of the thing in itself, and that yet our awareness of our own will does provide knowledge of the thing in itself, then our awareness of our own will could not be a matter of experiencing representations at all. But this is not a happy position because the willing we are immediately aware of is, at the very least, a case of something's being an object for a subject of experience – and this feature is definitive of a representation: 'To be object for the subject and to be our representation ... are the same thing' (*FR* 41/H. 1, 27). Furthermore, the willing we are aware of as agents is, minimally, something that occurs in time, a form which applies not to the thing in itself, but only to the world as representation. So my own willing is at least a temporal object for myself as experiencing subject, and so cannot fail to be a representation, as Schopenhauer acknowledges in the very next paragraph of 'On the Possibility of Knowing the Thing-in-Itself':

even the inward perception we have of our will still does not by any means furnish an exhaustive and adequate knowledge of the thing in itself. It would do so if it were a wholly immediate observation. But ... [i]n the first place, such knowledge is tied to the form of the representation . . . and as such falls apart into subject and object. . . . Hence even in inner knowledge there still occurs a difference between the being-in-itself of its object and the perception of this object in the knowing subject. But the inner knowledge is free from two forms belonging to outer knowledge, the form of *space* and the form of *causality* which mediates all sense-perception. On the other hand, there still remains the form of *time*, as well as that of being known and of knowing in general. Accordingly, in this inner knowledge the thing in itself has indeed to a great extent cast off its veils, but still does not appear quite naked. In consequence of the form of time which still adheres to it, everyone knows his own *will* only in its successive *acts*, not as a whole, in and for itself [*an und für sich*]. (W2 196–7/H. 3, 220)

This modification will yield another revision to Schopenhauer's claims. Now he will be committed to:

(a′) by way of representation, we can have no knowledge of the thing in itself,

but

(b″) in *inner* representation, we can have immediate knowledge of our own will,

and finally

(b) we can know that the thing in itself is will.

By such qualifications, drawn from Schopenhauer's own discussion, we reach a position that avoids contradiction. But it is unclear whether this is always Schopenhauer's position. The 'secret passage' image is surely a metaphor for the thing in itself becoming *directly conscious of itself*. There inner acquaintance was supposed to reveal my inner nature, essence, or thing in itself *sans phrase*. But that bold claim is not consistent with Schopenhauer's other views about knowledge.

Thus on the present reading Schopenhauer is caught between two stances, one bold, one circumspect. According to the 'bold' stance, my awareness of my own willing is all at once a penetration straight to the level of the thing in itself: I experience directly my trans-phenomenal inner nature, my own 'in itself', and can then use that as the key from which to infer the inner nature of the world, the nature of the world in itself. According to the circumspect stance, I only ever experience phenomena: the phenomenon of my own willing allows me to judge that my inner nature or essence is will because it is mediated by fewer forms of representation than the phenomena of outer experience, and from this judgement about my own inner nature I can move to a judgement about the inner nature underlying all the other phenomena of which I have only outer experience. For the 'circumspect' stance, *knowing the thing in itself* is a project always rooted in the knowledge of phenomena and is always a matter of surmising what lies beneath a veil. It is just that where the veil is thinnest – in my inner awareness of willing – the surmising is easiest.[62]

Recent commentators have responded to such difficulties by suggesting that Schopenhauer never really means to claim that the thing in itself is will, or that we can have knowledge of the thing in itself – or that we have not yet understood what he means by that. Thus Julian Young suggests that Schopenhauer would have been committing a 'crime' of some 'enormity' had he seriously maintained (as he appears to in the 'secret passage' discussion, for example) that we have experiential access to the thing in itself. He would have misunderstood Kant's idealism, in which neither outer *nor inner* sense provides access to anything but phenomena. And he would have been guilty of an outrage not unlike that with which he charges Hegelianism, that of positing 'a "faculty of the supersensuous" . . . in short, an oracular ability within us designed directly for *metaphysics* . . . an immediate rational intuition of the absolute'.[63] Not a happy situation for one who praises Kant's idealism highly and in some detail, and regards Hegel and his Absolute as nothing but charlatanry. Hence Young suggests that Schopenhauer's position must be understood as really eschewing metaphysical knowledge of the thing in itself:

Such an understanding would be possible if we were to abandon the simple Kantian dichotomy between appearance and ultimate, noumenal reality and adopt instead a trichotomy, interposing . . . a third world distinct from either. This third world, non-noumenal and hence situated within the Kantian boundaries, yet esoteric and so distinct from the ordinary world, could then constitute the topic of metaphysical investigation.[64]

This is fairly openly intended as a rational reconstruction (what Schopenhauer would have to have said if he were doing philosophy at his best, according to our assessment). Aside from the fact that 'noumenal' and 'non-noumenal' are not terms Schopenhauer uses, there is little evidence of his thinking in terms of such a trichotomy. The impression that the world has just *two* important aspects is pervasive in Schopenhauer's main work: 'this much is certain, that . . . nothing can be found except representation and thing in itself';[65] 'If . . . the material world is to be something more than our mere representation, we must say that, besides being the representation, and hence in itself and of its inmost nature, it is what we find immediately in ourselves as will.'[66] Assuming that Schopenhauer wants to make some qualification to save himself from contradiction, he is more likely to say that will is the aspect of the phenomenal world closest to the absolute thing in itself, or that it is the aspect of the thing in itself closest to knowability. He is very unlikely to say that will at the level of metaphysical investigation is neither thing in itself nor representation. Finally, we should not forget that Schopenhauer says over and over again that the thing in itself is will. Anyone who begins reading at §19 of *The World as Will and Representation* will gain the impression, before reaching the end of §29, of being told outright some thirty times that will is the thing in itself. If this was not what Schopenhauer really wanted to say, he had ample opportunity to expunge at least some of these passages from the later editions of the work, in which he made many other changes. But he retained all of them. It is thus not credible that he does not mean the will is the thing in itself, at least in some sense.

For a similar but more convincing 'saving' interpretation we may return to Atwell, who observes that the propositions 'the will is the thing in itself' and 'the will is not the thing in itself' are not contradictory if there are two senses of 'thing in itself' at play.[67] Consider the following passage in Volume 2 of *The World as Will and Representation*:

the question may still be raised what that will, which manifests itself in the world and as the world, is ultimately and absolutely in itself; in other words, what it is, quite apart from the fact that it manifests itself as *will*, or in general *appears*, that is to say, *is known* in general. This question can *never* be answered, because, as I have said, being-known of itself contradicts

being-in-itself, and everything that is known is as such only phenomenon.
(*W2* 198/H. 3, 221)

Schopenhauer uses this idea in order to explain that the world *entirely* in itself, prescinding *absolutely* from anything we can know of it, cannot be said to be will. For will is the world as we can know it in metaphysics, by philosophical reflection. The questions 'What is the world, quite apart from the fact that it manifests itself as will?' or 'What is it ultimately and absolutely in itself?' can in principle never be answered. To reconcile this with Schopenhauer's constant talk of the will's being known as the thing in itself, Atwell proposes the notion of 'will as *the thing in itself in appearance*'. When Schopenhauer is seeking the inner nature of the world as representation, it is another aspect of the knowable world that he seeks, not something lying implacably detached from the knowable world. Will is the essence of me, the human individual, and of each individual, objectively experienceable thing, the essence common to all the objectively experienceable things that compose the world as representation. It is the side *of the world as representation* revealed not to experience, but to philosophical reflection. Hence we might display Atwell's tri-partite picture thus:

Aspects of the world	What the world consists of	Possibility of knowledge	How known
1. World as representation	Individual objects: spatio-temporal, causally connected	Knowable	(i) Empirically (ii) According to its a priori forms
2. World as will, the thing in itself in appearance	Undifferentiated inner nature of all objects	Knowable	(i) In one's own case, immediately (ii) In the case of other objects, by philosophical reflection
3. World as absolute and ultimate thing in itself		Unknowable in principle	

This absolves Schopenhauer of gross contradiction while explaining (more comfortably than Young's view) the sense in which he argues the thing in itself to be will.

If, as seems likely, Schopenhauer does not always observe this ambiguity in the expression 'thing in itself', his train of thought becomes more explicable. He might well confuse the unknowability in principle of the 'absolute' thing in itself with the 'hiddenness' or 'undecipherability' of the inner nature of the world of appearance, the latter but not the former being susceptible of discovery or decoding by philosophy. He might sometimes be tempted to present himself as paradoxically pursuing knowledge of that which is in principle unknowable. He might say both that there is an 'in itself' character peculiar to the individual and that the 'in itself' is wholly prior to individuation. If Atwell's reading makes us aware that Schopenhauer's programme can avoid gross inconsistency, the best we can say for Schopenhauer is that he does not uniformly demonstrate the same awareness.

VII CONCLUSION

Schopenhauer has often been read as if he is simply competing with Kant on the same territory: Kant treats the thing in itself (or things in themselves) as unknown and unknowable; Schopenhauer tries to show that the very same thing in itself is knowable and known after all. Even Schopenhauer seems to be reading himself this way: his claim that Kant's greatest merit is the distinction of appearance from thing in itself[68] is followed by the qualification that Kant 'did not arrive at the knowledge that the appearance is the world as representation and that the thing in itself is will'.[69] Yet in truth, Schopenhauer's notion of his task is quite distinctive and is not a direct competitor of Kant's.

Without entering into questions about the interpretation of Kant, we can isolate two features of what Schopenhauer believed Kant's position to be: (1) he assumed that the Kantian division between appearance and thing in itself was an ontological one; (2) he assumed that for Kant the thing in itself was the causal ground of phenomena.[70] Now it would be wrong to see Schopenhauer as claiming knowledge of the thing in itself *so conceived*. He competes with Kant rather by offering a rival conception of the thing in itself which rejects both of these features. The Schopenhauerian thing in itself, inasmuch as it is knowable in philosophical reflection, is the *essence*[71] of the world of appearance, not in any way its cause. And it is the essential *aspect* of that same world of appearance, not any thing of a distinct ontological kind. Schopenhauer's project is to render 'meaningful' what is otherwise a cryptograph: to decipher our *experience* and the world it reveals to us. His chapter on 'Man's Need for Metaphysics' (W2 160–87/H. 3, 175–209) makes clear that this means searching for a unified description of the multiplicity of phenomena, for 'connexion' and 'agreement'[72] where ordinary experience and even science cannot detect them. This metaphysics is to be immanent, not transcendent (W2 183/H. 3, 204): it is not really about peeking behind the veil of appearance, for though it speaks of the 'thing in itself', it does not mean to do so 'otherwise than in reference to appearance'. Metaphysics 'discloses only the true understanding of the world lying before it in experience'.

But it is Schopenhauer's protracted execution of his metaphysical task that best elucidates how he conceives it: first, he must show that each individual thing, each event, each process encountered discretely in experience and explained in science has an essence that unifies it with every other thing, event, and process; that nature, in its basic character, makes up one whole, with each individual expressing the same character over and over again. The single essential character of the world is that everything in it is alike in continually 'striving' to be, yet for no point or purpose beyond its merely being. At the same time, his task is to reveal humanity as having the same character as the rest of reality and to show how human self-consciousness bears this out, thereby bringing our representation of empirical reality and our cognition of ourselves into agreement.

Kant had disenchanted the world of appearance by subjecting earlier rationalistic and theistic metaphysics to a critique from which it could not recover. He finally put an end to 'scholastic philosophy', as Schopenhauer says.[73] What Schopenhauer misleadingly calls 'knowing that the thing in itself is will' is an attempt to fill a vacuum he considers was left by Kant, to rescue a single overall 'meaning' for the world as experienced and investigated in science, and to show the subject what place it has in the world of nature. But Schopenhauer's metaphysics does not re-enchant the world. The 'meaning' he uncovers is bereft of comfort: the essence of things contains no rationality, no higher purpose, no final vindication of the world or of the self. The world, and humanity within it, merely strives to be, in multiple instantiations, in perpetuity. Our inner nature, and that of the world-whole, pushes each of us hither and thither, overwhelms our efforts with its own larger striving, and leads us only into suffering. Having deciphered this part of the 'meaning' by the mid-point of *The World as Will and Representation*, it remains to grasp the more profoundly significant sequel that teaches abandonment of our attachment to our inner nature, and discovers genuine value, salvation, in the will's turning against itself.

NOTES

1 Roy C. Weatherford, 'Will', in Ted Honderich (ed.), *The Oxford Companion to Philosophy* (Oxford: Oxford University Press, 1995), 910–11.

2 *intuitive* or *anschauliche Vorstellunge*, W*1* 6, 35/H. 2, 7, 41: Payne's translation for *anschauliche Vorstellung* is 'representation of perception'.

3 'Essence' or 'being' are perhaps the most obvious translations of *Wesen*. Payne favours 'inner nature' for *inneres Wesen* and sometimes translates the word *Wesen* on its own as 'inner nature': see, e.g., W*1* 99/H. 2, 118–19, quoted later in the text.

4 John Atwell, *Schopenhauer on the Character of the World: The Metaphysics of Will* (Berkeley: University of California Press, 1995), chs. 3 and 4.

5 Ibid., 80, 81, 91.

6 W*1* 99/H. 2, 118: *geflügelte Engelskopf ohne Leib*. Payne's translation has 'cherub' for *Engelskopf*.

7 W*1* 99/H. 2, 118–19.

8 *MR* 1, 466/Hn. 1, 421 (sect. 621), quoted by Atwell, *Schopenhauer on the Character of the World*, 98.

9 W*1* 100–1/H. 2, 119–20.

10 As Brian O'Shaughnessy has made clear in *The Will* (Cambridge: Cambridge University Press, 1980), ii, 349–51. See also Atwell, *Schopenhauer on the Character of the World*, 82.

11 If a motor nerve is severed in my arm, Schopenhauer says, 'my will can no longer move it' (W*2* 250/H. 3, 283). This would be an act of will that does not 'at once and inevitably' become a movement of the body. But this does not show that there is willing which is mental and not bodily. All it shows, he states, is that the agent's motive cannot causally influence the part of the body it is directed at. On his behalf, we might urge the idea that the act of will of a paralysed or physically damaged person is

a conscious state and also a bodily event that in a normal physiological environment would have been, or become, his or her acting a certain way.

12 *FW* 18/H. 4, 18.

13 *FW* 11/H. 4, 11, my translation (Kolenda is misleading here).

14 *FW* 17/H. 4, 17 (my translation).

15 *W1* 100/H. 2, 119.

16 See O'Shaughnessy, *The Will*, op. cit.

17 *FW* 18/H. 4, 18.

18 The three-fold account of cause, stimulus, and motive is well explained at *FW* 30–7/H. 4, 29–32. See also *WN* 37–8; *W1* 114–17; *W2* 248–50 /H. 4, 21–3; H. 2, 135–40; H. 3, 280–3.

19 See especially 'Objective View of the Intellect', *W2* 272–92/H. 3, 307–31.

20 *W1* 118/H. 2, 141.

21 Ibid.

22 *W1* 124–6/H. 2, 147–50.

23 *W2* 642–3/H. 3, 739 (my translation).

24 *W1* 117. I translate *Erscheinung* as 'appearance', where Payne has 'phenomenon'.

25 *W1* 105/H. 2, 126.

26 See *W1* 490–1/H. 2, 581–3.

27 *W2* 13/H. 3, 15.

28 Thomas Nagel, 'Panpsychism', in *Mortal Questions* (Cambridge: Cambridge University Press, 1979), 180.

29 *W1* 105/H. 2, 126.

30 *W1* 111/H. 2, 133.

31 In a vivid passage Schopenhauer implies that the process of willing in a human agent is the same as that of any natural process, but with the mere addition of consciousness: 'Spinoza . . . says that if a stone projected through the air had consciousness, it would imagine it was flying of its own will. I add merely that the stone would be right' (*W1* 126/H. 2, 150).

32 *W1* 327/H. 2, 385.

33 *W2* 606/H. 3, 695.

34 See *BM* 109–13; *W1* 289–90; *FW* 96–7/H. 4, 174–8; H. 2, 341–2; H. 4, 95–6.

35 *BM* 110–12/H. 4, 175–6.

36 See especially his chapter 'The Metaphysics of Sexual Love', *W2* 531–67/H. 3, 607–51.

37 *Geschlechtstrieb*, which Payne translates as 'sexual impulse'.

38 As Nietzsche realized; see the well-known passage in *On the Genealogy of Morals* (New York: Random House, 1967), III, §6.

39 Schopenhauer considers 'pederasty' in a late appendix to 'The Metaphysics of Sexual Love', *W2* 560–7/H. 3, 643–51. This practice is so

universal that it must in some way be 'natural', he concludes. His solution is once again based on a eugenic premise. In some men the 'pro-
creative force' is either too immature or in a state of deterioration, and
apparently, nature directs such men away from reproductive sex, whose
'product' would have an impoverishing effect on the quality of the species.

40 *W2* 537/H. 3, 615.

41 *W2* 543 /H. 3, 623.

42 *W2* 559/H. 3, 642.

43 See *W2* 536/H. 3, 613.

44 *W1* 294–5/H. 2, 347. Incidentally, this is an aspect of Schopenhauer's
thinking that Nietzsche appears to be perpetuating when he writes: 'I
have learned to distinguish the cause of acting from the cause of acting in
a particular way, in a particular direction, with a particular goal. The first
kind of cause is a quantum of dammed-up energy [*Kraft*] that is waiting
to be used up somehow, for something, while the second is, compared
to this energy, something quite insignificant, for the most part a little
accident in accordance with which this quantum "discharges" itself in
one particular way – a match versus a ton of powder. Among these little
accidents and matches I include so-called purposes [or ends, *Zwecke*].
... The usual view is different: People are accustomed to consider the
goal (purposes, vocations, etc.) as the *driving force* [treibende Kraft], in
keeping with a very ancient error; but it is merely the *directing force*
[dirigirende Kraft] – one has mistaken the helmsman for the steam' (*The
Gay Science* [New York: Random House, 1974], 360). Nietzsche prefixes
these remarks with the statement 'This seems to me to be one of my
most essential steps and advances.' It may have been an advance in his
own understanding, but Schopenhauer had trodden there already.

45 *FW* 43/H. 4, 41–2.

46 Georg Simmel, *Schopenhauer and Nietzsche*, trans. Helmut Loiskandl,
Deena Weinstein, and Michael Weinstein (Amherst: University of Massachusetts Press, 1986), 30.

47 See *W1* 286–307/H. 2, 337–62.

48 *On the Freedom of the Will* (or, more strictly, '... of the human will', in
German *Über die Freiheit des menschlichen Willens*) was written in 1839
and published in 1841 together with the essay *On the Basis of Morality* in
a volume entitled *The Two Fundamental Problems of Ethics* (*Die beiden
Grundprobleme der Ethik*).

49 See *FW* 24/H. 4, 24.

50 *FW* 11/H. 4, 11. Kolenda's translation, 'his own volitions', is questionable, given the immediately following passage in which Schopenhauer
extends the concept *wollen* to embrace states such as rejoicing, fearing, and mourning, which can scarcely be called volitions. Even when

Schopenhauer is discussing 'acts of will' proper (*Willensakte*, e.g., *FW* 14/H. 4, 14), it is unhelpful to use the translation 'volition', given that a *Willensakt* is supposed to be identical with an 'action of the body': see *W1* 100–1/H. 2,119–20, discussed in Section II of this chapter.

51 *FW* 11–12/H. 4, 11–12. Here again, Kolenda's 'bodily emotions' for *körperlichen ... Empfindungen* seems an unhappy and misleading translation.

52 See *W1* 101/H. 2, 120.

53 See *FW* 11, 16, 18/H. 4, 11, 16, 18.

54 See esp. *W2* 248–50/H. 3, 280–3.

55 See Nietzsche, *Human, All Too Human* (Cambridge: Cambridge University Press, 1986), I, sect. 39.

56 *FW* 94/H. 4, 93.

57 *FW* 97/H. 4, 97.

58 *W1* 422/H. 2, 499–500.

59 *FW* 97–8/H. 4, 97.

60 See esp. *W1* 287–8; *W2* 318–21/H. 2, 338–9; H. 3, 361–5.

61 For a presentation of this view see Christopher Janaway, *Self and World in Schopenhauer's Philosophy* (Oxford: Clarendon Press, 1989), 188–97; also Atwell, *Schopenhauer on the Character of the World*, 106–19.

62 See *W2* 197–8/H. 3, 220–2.

63 *FR* 166/H. 1, 112. See Young, *Willing and Unwilling: A Study in the Philosophy of Arthur Schopenhauer* (Dordrecht: Martinus Nijhoff, 1987), 29.

64 Young, *Willing and Unwilling*, 31–2.

65 *W1* 444/H. 2, 526. This occurs in a passage where Schopenhauer is alleging that Kant interposes an 'object of representation' between representation and thing in itself: the point is that there is no such logical space for anything to occupy.

66 *W1* 105/H. 2, 125–6.

67 Atwell, *Schopenhauer on the Character of the World*, 126–7.

68 *W1* 417/H. 2, 494 (Payne translates *Erscheinung*, 'appearance', as 'phenomenon' here).

69 *W1* 421/H. 2, 499.

70 See the account by Dale Snow and James Snow, 'Was Schopenhauer an Idealist?', *Journal of the History of Philosophy* 29 (1991), esp. 636–44.

71 For Schopenhauer as an 'essentialist', see Snow and Snow, op. cit., 644.

72 *W2* 182, 184–5/H. 3, 202–3, 204–6.

73 See *W1* 422–5/H. 2, 500–3.

6 The Influences of Eastern Thought on Schopenhauer's Doctrine of the Thing-in-Itself

Many commentators accept Schopenhauer's claim that there are no significant changes in his thinking after 1818.[1] I, however, argue that there are good reasons for maintaining that there are significant developments in his thought after that date and that these concern his doctrine of the thing-in-itself. Furthermore, I contend that it is Schopenhauer's increasing knowledge of and admiration for Eastern thought which provided the impetus for the changes in doctrine that occurred. I begin by outlining three significant shifts that occurred in Schopenhauer's doctrine of the thing-in-itself after 1818. I then discuss his degree of acquaintance with Eastern thought, and I suggest various similarities to and differences between Eastern teaching and Schopenhauer's doctrine. Finally, I argue that the identified shifts in Schopenhauer's doctrine of the thing-in-itself can be plausibly explained, at least in part, by his increasing familiarity with and appreciation of Eastern thought.

I SHIFTS IN DOCTRINE

Three identifiable shifts in Schopenhauer's doctrine of the thing-in-itself occur between the publication of the first volume of *The World as Will and Representation* in 1818 and his later works. The first shift concerns what he says about the knowability of the thing-in-itself; the second concerns what he says about the nature of the thing-in-itself; and the third concerns his explicit attempt to assimilate his own doctrines about what can be said of the thing-in-itself with Eastern doctrines.

The most important of these shifts is the first.[2] Schopenhauer asserts numerous times throughout his works that the thing-in-itself

171

is will or 'will to life',[3] and he claims that we know this through direct intuition in self-consciousness. For example:

The *thing-in-itself*, this substratum of all phenomena, and therefore of the whole of Nature, is nothing but what we know directly and intimately as *the will*.[4]

However, there are also passages in his later works in which he seems to withdraw the claim that in self-consciousness we are aware of the will as thing-in-itself, suggesting instead that in self-consciousness we are aware of no more than our phenomenal willings. For example:

But this knowledge of the thing-in-itself is not wholly adequate. In the first place, such knowledge is tied to the form of the representation; it is perception or observation, and as such falls apart into subject and object.[5]

If we accept this latter suggestion, Schopenhauer's claim that the thing-in-itself is will seems either to be without foundation or to be a misleading way of making the much weaker claim that the thing-in-itself is called will because in introspective awareness we are closest to the thing-in-itself, and in introspection the object of our awareness is will. While some commentators endorse this interpretation of Schopenhauer's seminal claim that the thing-in-itself is will,[6] I believe that it is implausible for the following reasons. First, it is inconsistent with Schopenhauer's many assertions that the thing-in-itself *is* will and with his claim that metaphysics concerns the thing-in-itself.[7] Second, since these assertions are the principal ways in which Schopenhauer sees his own philosophy as an advance upon that of Kant's, their inconsistency with this interpretation is a major difficulty for it. Third, if Schopenhauer's claim that the thing-in-itself is will rests on the supposition that in introspective awareness of will there are fewer phenomenal forms standing between the thing-in-itself and the knowing subject, his argument is an extremely weak one. For, as both Janaway and Young point out, there are no grounds for believing that a smaller number of phenomenal forms will more truly reveal the nature of underlying reality than a larger number.[8] In light of the preceding considerations, it is more plausible to suggest that the passages in the later works, in which Schopenhauer apparently withdraws his claim of direct acquaintance with the thing-in-itself as will, indicate a shift in his thinking. While in the later works he continues to assert both that the thing-in-itself is will and that we are directly aware of it in self-consciousness, I suggest that the presence of the previously mentioned passages indicates that in the years following the publication of the first volume of *The World as Will and Representation* he became increasingly aware of the difficulties attending this claim.

Schopenhauer's use of the veil metaphor illustrates his uneasiness. For example:

And though no one can recognise the thing-in-itself through the veil of the forms of perception, on the other hand everyone carries this within himself, in fact he himself is it; hence in self-consciousness it must be in some way accessible to him, although still only conditionally.[9]

Schopenhauer wants to claim that just as we both do and do not know an object that is concealed by a veil, so in introspective awareness we both do and do not know the thing-in-itself that is concealed behind the temporal form. Our *not* being able to know the thing-in-itself is consistent with Kant's teaching that introspection yields only knowledge of inner phenomena, and it may be the strong influence of Kant on Schopenhauer's thinking that prompts him to qualify his oft-repeated claim of direct awareness. However, as Schopenhauer holds that the Kantian influence on his thinking is strongest in his youth,[10] it may well be that other factors were also at work. Another explanation is put by Höffding, namely, that Schopenhauer modified his views in the later work after reflecting upon the critical reviews of his earlier work.[11] However, since Schopenhauer was generally disdainful of critics and their comments, it seems that this can be at best a partial explanation. While the influence of both Kant's epistemology and critical reviews may partly explain the previously mentioned passages, a more enduring influence is also called for in order to explain this change in his doctrine after 1818.

The second shift in Schopenhauer's doctrine of the thing-in-itself concerns what he asserts about its nature. The traditional interpretation of Schopenhauer's metaphysics is that the thing-in-itself is will or will to life. He makes this claim many times throughout his writings, and furthermore, as the title of his main work suggests, he also asserts that reality comprises just two aspects, will and representation. For example:

This will alone constitutes the other aspect of the world, for this world is, on the one side, entirely *representation*, just as, on the other, it is entirely *will*.[12]

However, in his later works Schopenhauer introduces the idea that the thing-in-itself has multiple aspects, only one of which is will. Its other aspects are the objects of awareness of such persons as mystics, saints, and ascetics, who have denied the will.

Accordingly, even after this last and extreme step, the question may still be raised what that will, which manifests itself in the world and as the world, is ultimately and absolutely in itself; in other words, what it is quite apart from the fact that it manifests itself as *will*, or in general *appears*, that is to say, is *known* in general.[13]

The third shift in Schopenhauer's doctrine of the thing-in-itself concerns his explicit attempt to assimilate his own views on what can be said about the thing-in-itself with Eastern doctrines. I have identified six passages in which Schopenhauer asserts that the thing-in-itself can be described as will, but only in a metaphorical sense. Of these, three are in his earlier and three in his later works.[14] However, in two of the later passages he explicitly assimilates his own views with what he sees as similar views expressed in Eastern thought, and this assimilation is in keeping with his increasing knowledge of and admiration for the East.

The will as thing-in-itself is entire and undivided in every being; just as the centre is an integral part of every radius; whereas the peripheral end of this radius is in the most rapid revolution with the surface that represents time and its content, the other end at the centre where eternity lies, remains in profoundest peace, because the centre is the point whose rising half is no different from the sinking half. Therefore, it is also said in the Bhagavad-Gita: 'Undivided it dwells in beings, and yet as it were divided; it is to be known as the sustainer, annihilator, and producer of beings.' Here of course we fall into mystical and metaphorical language, but it is the only language in which anything can be said about this wholly transcendent theme.[15]

A further passage is worth mentioning. In the first edition of the first volume of *The World as Will and Representation* (1818), when discussing the state of denial of the will, Schopenhauer draws attention to the ways in which his doctrine and those of the East differ.

We must not evade it, as the Indians do, by myths and meaningless words, such as reabsorption in *Brahman*, or the Nirvana of the Buddhists. On the contrary, we freely acknowledge that what remains after the complete abolition of the will is for all who are still full of the will, assuredly nothing. But also conversely, to those in whom the will has turned and denied itself, this very real world of ours with all its suns and galaxies, is – nothing.[16]

However, in the second edition of the first volume (1844), he adds the following footnote to the preceding passage:

This is also the Prajna-Paramita of the Buddhists, the 'beyond all knowledge', in other words, the point where subject and object no longer exist. See I. J. Schmidt, *Über das Mahajana und Pradschna-Paramita*.

Since the work by Schmidt to which Schopenhauer refers was not published until 1836, it seems that between the publication of the first and second volumes of *The World as Will and Representation*, Schopenhauer's understanding of the Buddhist concept of Nirvana changes, and he sees parallels between his later understanding of that notion and his own doctrine of denial of the will. He suggests that what the two views have in common is the recognition that our ordinary ways of knowing and describing the phenomenal world are inapplicable to knowing and describing reality as it is experienced by saints and mystics.

The previously mentioned passages support the view that in the years following the publication of the first edition of the first volume of *The World as Will and Representation*, Schopenhauer increasingly sought to find parallels between his own and Eastern ideas on what can be said about the thing-in-itself. And this practice at least leaves open the possibility that his increasing knowledge of and admiration for Eastern thought actually influenced his thinking, giving rise to changes in his views concerning the knowability, nature, and ways of describing the thing-in-itself.

In summary, there are three identifiable shifts in Schopenhauer's doctrine of the thing-in-itself between the publication of the first volume of *The World as Will and Representation* and of his later works. They concern its knowability, its nature, and Schopenhauer's explicit attempt to assimilate his own doctrines concerning what can be said about the thing-in-itself with Eastern ideas. While the influence of Kant and of critical reviews may partly explain the first of these shifts, a more enduring influence is also called for to explain all three shifts. In support of my claim that it is Schopenhauer's increasing knowledge of and admiration for Eastern thought that fulfils this role, I next consider Schopenhauer's degree of acquaintance with Eastern thought.

II THE EXTENT OF SCHOPENHAUER'S ACQUAINTANCE WITH EASTERN THOUGHT

Schopenhauer's introduction to the ideas of the Hindus and to Eastern ideas more generally is thought to have occurred in late 1813. He had moved to Weimar after submitting his doctoral thesis, *On the Fourfold Root of the Principle of Sufficient Reason*, and it was in his mother's Weimar salon that he met the orientalist Friedrich Majer. That he was unacquainted with Eastern thought prior to this time seems probable for several reasons. First, he makes no reference to Eastern thought in the 1813 version of his doctoral thesis;[17] second, in his *Manuscript Remains* all but one reference to it date from 1814 on (the one occurring in the period 1809 to 1813); and third, there were relatively few scholarly sources of information about Eastern thought available to Europeans in the early part of the nineteenth century.[18]

A study of Schopenhauer's *Manuscript Remains* suggests that he first becomes acquainted with Hindu thought around 1813–14 but that he did not acquire much knowledge of Buddhism until after 1818. The two earliest volumes of *Manuscript Remains*, dating from 1804 to 1818 and from 1809 to 1818, respectively, contain very few references to Buddhism (I counted two),[19] while there are at least twenty references to Hindu thought in these volumes after 1813, and only one of these was obviously added to the notes at a later date.[20] However, in the third volume of the *Manuscript Remains*, dating from 1818 to 1830, there are at least fifteen references to Buddhist thought and about thirty to Hinduism. In the final *Manuscript Remains*, covering the period 1830 to 1860, there are at least seven references to Buddhism and fifteen to Hindu thought. This means that in the period 1813 to 1818 the *Manuscript Remains* contain approximately two references to Buddhist thought compared to at least twenty references in the period 1818 to 1860, and that for the same periods there are at least twenty and forty-five references, respectively, to Hindu thought. The first volume of *The World as Will and Representation* contains about eight references to Buddhist thought, five of which are added in the later editions (1844 and 1859) of that volume.[21] By comparison, in the second volume, first published in 1844 with a second edition in 1859, there are at least thirty references to Buddhism. References to Hindu thought in the first volume number over fifty, seven of which are added in the later editions,[22] and in the second volume there are over forty-five references to Hinduism.[23] While these figures are only approximate, they indicate a marked rise in Schopenhauer's knowledge of and interest in Buddhist thought from 1818 on, and a strong and consistent interest in Hindu thought from 1813 until his death in 1860. That Schopenhauer was in the habit of adding references to his earlier works is clear from the following footnoted comment in the 1859 edition of the first volume:

In the last forty years Indian literature has grown so much in Europe that if I now wished to complete this note to the first edition, it would fill several pages.[24]

Such comments indicate that Schopenhauer had an abiding interest in Eastern philosophy, and that he was keen to demonstrate parallels between his own doctrines and those of the East.

III   SOURCES OF ACQUAINTANCE OF EASTERN THOUGHT

As well as considering the number of references to Hindu and Buddhist thought in *The Manuscript Remains* and *The World as Will and Representation*, it is instructive to look at Schopenhauer's sources for these references.[25] It seems clear that his early sources of knowledge of Hinduism are the *Oupnek'hat*[26] and the Asiatic journals.[27] While throughout his works he also frequently refers to the *Vedas*, the *Puranas*,[28] and the *Bhagavadgita*, praising the ideas expressed in them and drawing parallels with his own doctrines, it seems that his early references to these primary texts originated from articles in the Asiatic journals rather than from an acquaintance with the texts themselves. It was not until 1838 that a translation of part of the *Vedas* first became available,[29] and the translation of the

Bhagavadgita to which Schopenhauer makes reference in the second volume of *The World as Will and Representation* is that by A. G. Schlegel, which was not published until 1823.[30] Schopenhauer first acquired a copy of the *Oupnek'hat* from the orientalist Friedrich Majer in late 1813,[31] and its subsequent value to him is evident from his statement in *Parerga and Paralipomena* that 'it [the *Oupnek'hat*] is the most profitable and sublime reading that is possible in the world; it has been the consolation of my life and will be that of my death'.[32] He goes on to assert: 'I am firmly convinced that a real knowledge of the *Upanishads* and thus of the true and esoteric dogmas of the *Vedas* can at present be obtained only from the *Oupnek'hat*'.[33] However, in addition to the *Oupnek'hat*, it is clear that Schopenhauer read any available secondary sources that he could find.[34] In the *Manuscript Remains*, in addition to the frequent references to the journals *Asiatic Researches*,[35] *Asiatisches Magazin*,[36] *Asiatick Researches*,[37] and *Asiatic Journal*,[38] Schopenhauer refers to books and articles by oriental scholars of the time. In *Parerga and Paralipomena*, under the title 'Some Remarks on Sanskrit Literature', Schopenhauer discusses the merits of various translations of sacred Hindu texts, and in the course of a discussion of Hindu ideas and the possibility that Indian mythology is remotely related to that of the Greeks, Romans, and Egyptians, he mentions additional texts on Hinduism. In both volumes of *The World as Will and Representation* and scattered throughout his other works, there are many further references to both primary and secondary sources. However, it is noteworthy that all but ten references (seven of which concern either the *Asiatic Researches* or *Asiatisches Magazin*) are to publications after 1818, confirming the view that until that date Schopenhauer's main sources of knowledge of Hindu thought were the *Oupnek'hat* and articles in the Asiatic journals.

Turning now to Schopenhauer's sources of Buddhist teaching, the entries in the first two volumes of the *Manuscript Remains* indicate that Schopenhauer's primary source prior to 1818 is the *Asiatic Researches*; there are only two references to Buddhism in these volumes, and they both refer to that journal as their source.[39] However, from 1818 on, Schopenhauer's sources become more diversified, a fact that he himself alludes to in the second volume of *The World as Will and Representation* when he states that 'up till 1818, when my work appeared, there were to be found in Europe only a very few accounts of Buddhism, and those extremely incomplete and inadequate, confined almost entirely to a few essays in the earlier volumes of the *Asiatic Researches*, and principally concerned with the Buddhism of the Burmese'.[40] The increased availability of information after 1818 is reflected in the *Manuscript Remains* for the later periods, 1818 to 1830, and 1830 to 1860, where he refers to journals and other secondary texts. Also, in the chapter entitled 'Sinology' in his essay *On the Will in Nature*, Schopenhauer recommends to his readers a list of twenty-six works on Buddhism of which he says, 'I can really recommend [them] for I possess them and know them well.' In both volumes of *The World as Will and Representation* and scattered throughout his other works there are many further references to both primary and secondary sources. Only two of these works were published prior to 1818. Finally, in both Grisebach's and Hübscher's listings of titles in Schopenhauer's posthumous library, only three of those that specifically refer to Buddhist thought have publication dates before 1818.

At his death, Schopenhauer had accumulated a library of at least 130 items of orientalia. Given this evidence, as well as the many references to Eastern thought that appear in his works, it seems reasonable to conclude that Schopenhauer had an abiding interest in Hindu and Buddhist ideas throughout his life. In the next section I consider the extent to which these ideas may have exerted an influence on Schopenhauer's own doctrine of the thing-in-itself.

IV   LIKELY INFLUENCE OF EASTERN THOUGHT ON SCHOPENHAUER'S DOCTRINE OF THE THING-IN-ITSELF

Schopenhauer states: 'I owe what is best in my own development to the impression made by Kant's works, the sacred writings of the Hindus, and Plato'.[41] Writing in 1818 in the Preface to the first edition of *The World as Will and Representation*, he says that while Kant's philosophy is the only one with which a thorough acquaintance is positively assumed, a knowledge of Plato is also desirable. And regarding the Hindus, he states:

But if he [the reader] has shared in the benefits of the *Vedas*, access to which, opened to us by the *Upanishads*, is in my view the greatest advantage which

this still young century has to show over previous centuries, since I surmise
that the influence of Sanskrit literature will penetrate no less deeply than
did the revival of Greek literature in the fifteenth century; if, I say, the
reader has also already received and assimilated the divine inspiration of
ancient Indian wisdom, then he is best of all prepared to hear what I have
to say to him. It will not speak to him, as to many others, in a strange
and even hostile tongue; for, did it not sound too conceited, I might assert
that each of the individual and disconnected utterances that make up the
Upanishads could be derived as a consequence from the thought I am to
impart, *although conversely my thought is by no means to be found in the
Upanishads.*[42]

From the last sentence of this passage, it is clear that while
Schopenhauer readily sees parallels between his own philosophy and
that of Hindu thought, he does not believe that the development and
expression of his own ideas is in any way dependent on the ideas
expressed in the sacred Hindu texts. In the second volume of *The
World as Will and Representation* he also disclaims direct influence
of Buddhist ideas, maintaining that

[in] any case, it must be a pleasure to me to see my doctrine in such close
agreement with a religion that the majority of men on earth hold as their
own, for this numbers far more followers than any other. And this agreement
must be yet the more pleasing to me, *inasmuch as in my philosophising I
have certainly not been under its influence.*[43]

However, this disavowal of influence needs to be balanced against
both the developments in Schopenhauer's thought which I discussed
earlier and other remarks that he makes.[44] With regard to the latter,
the following passage written in 1816 is relevant.

Moreover, I confess that I do not believe my doctrine could have come about
before the Upanishads, Plato and Kant could cast their rays simultaneously
into the mind of one man.[45]

While in this passage he does not speak of direct influence, Schopenhauer nevertheless strongly suggests that his reading of the *Upanishads* is essential to the formulation of his own ideas. Also relevant
here are his somewhat ambiguous comments regarding what he sees
as the unchanging character of his philosophy. In the *Manuscript
Remains* he states in a footnote dated 1849:

These sheets, written at Dresden in the years 1814–1818, show the fermentative process of my thinking, from which at that time my whole philosophy emerged, rising gradually like a beautiful landscape from the morning mist. *Here it is worth noting that even in 1814 (in my 27th year) all the dogmas of my system, even the unimportant ones, were established.*[46]

It seems that Schopenhauer became acquainted with oriental thought only in late 1813. Given the preceding two passages, it seems we must assume either that his reading of the *Upanishads* made such a dramatic and sudden impression on him that he could maintain that by 1814 all his ideas were settled, or that in this passage he means that while certain central ideas were formed by 1814, they subsequently developed over the next four years. The latter view is more plausible, particularly since in the immediately preceding passage he himself speaks of the 'fermentative process of my thinking' between 1814 and 1818, and since the previous passage was not written until 1816. Furthermore, given the numerous and varied references to the ideas of the Hindus in the first two volumes of *Manuscript Remains* (at least twenty) and in the first volume of *The World as Will and Representation* (at least fifty), it seems plausible to suppose that the degree of familiarity thus presupposed was acquired over a number of years, rather than all at once in late 1813 to 1814. The preceding passages and argument support the conclusion that Schopenhauer's acquaintance with Hinduism had a significant input into the formation of his own doctrines as they appeared in the first volume of *The World as Will and Representation*.

V SCHOPENHAUER'S LIKELY UNDERSTANDING OF HINDUISM

To make clearer how Eastern ideas may account in part for the presence of passages in Schopenhauer's later works in which he seems to withdraw from his earlier claims concerning the thing-in-itself, it is worth looking at Schopenhauer's likely understanding of both Hindu and Buddhist teaching.

Orthodox Hindu religion recognises the validity of the *Vedas* as the authoritative scriptural texts. Of these texts, the *Upanishads* are the most metaphysical and systematic in style, although there are often seemingly conflicting strands of thought expressed in them, and these have given rise to a range of interpretations. The *Upanishads* represent the final stage in the tradition of the *Vedas*, and for this reason the teaching that is based on them is known as the Vedanta (Sanskrit: 'conclusion of the *Veda*'). Within the Vedanta there exist different sub-schools of thought, the most important of which are the school of Nondualism (Advaita, whose main exponent is the eighth-century philosopher Sankara), qualified Nondualism (Visistadvaita, which develops in the twelfth century), and Dualism (Dvaita, which develops in the thirteenth century). Frederick Copleston notes that Schopenhauer's philosophy bears some resemblance to the most prominent form of Vedanta, Advaita.[47] Although Schopenhauer writes only of the Vedanta and does not mention its various subschools, some of his most important doctrines are mirrored in those of the Advaita school. That he is acquainted with Advaita teaching seems clear from his reference in the *Manuscript Remains* to Windischmann's *Sancara sive de Theologia Vedanticorum*,[48] a book also listed by Grisebach in his catalogue of titles in Schopenhauer's posthumous library.

According to Advaita teaching as articulated by Sankara, Brahman, the Holy Power spoken of in the *Upanishads* and elsewhere referred to as the sustainer of the cosmos, is identical with Atman, the self. Consequently, since they are identical, there is only one Absolute, and similarly, there is only one Self, which is not to be identified with the empirical Ego which undergoes reincarnation. Further, given that Brahman alone is real, the world (together with empirical egos) considered as distinct from Brahman, is an illusion (maya). Sankara's monism not only claims to give a correct interpretation of central scriptural texts, but also claims to preserve simultaneously both the chief insights of the *Veda* and the common-sense attitudes that appear to be in conflict with this illusionist doctrine. He achieves this by introducing the notion of two levels of truth; the higher levels are expressed in the mystical experience of release and identification with Brahman, while the lower ones are expressed in both religious and common-sense descriptions of the world. For the person who has not attained the higher insight, spatio-temporal objects such as trees and rivers are real, but for the person who has attained the higher viewpoint, these objects are illusory, and reality is the undifferentiated 'one' of which the mystics speak.[49]

It is not difficult to see parallels between Advaita philosophy, as just outlined, and the following of Schopenhauer's own doctrines: his

doctrine that the will as thing-in-itself is the sustainer of the world;
his doctrine that the will as thing-in-itself is identical with the will
that is objectified in individual phenomena, a view that he expresses
by asserting the identity of the macrocosm and the microcosm;[50] his
doctrine that there is only one will and only one knowing subject,
in the sense that both lie outside the forms of differentiation, space
and time;[51] his doctrine that our essential nature, the will as thing-
in-itself, is not to be identified with empirical consciousness, since
the former is a timeless One, while the latter is distinct and transient; his doctrine that the will as thing-in-itself alone is real, while
the world (together with consciousness) considered as distinct from
the will as thing-in-itself is an illusion; and his doctrine that there
are two kinds of awareness of reality: perceptual awareness, which
is the foundation of egoism, and mystical awareness, which is the
foundation of moral goodness.[52]

Without dwelling on the closeness of these parallels, there are two
striking instances in which Schopenhauer's doctrines do not find any
agreement with the preceding outline of Advaita philosophy. The
first is his doctrine that the thing-in-itself, or ultimate reality, is a
will that is the source of immense suffering in the world. Such a view
seems incompatible with the Advaita conception of Brahman as the
Holy Power,[53] although it might be thought to have some similarity
with the other conception of it as the sustainer of the cosmos.[54] Of
Schopenhauer's references to Brahman or Brahm or Brahma in the
first volume of *The World as Will and Representation*, all refer to it
in its role as sustainer, creator, and originator. For example:

Each day of the creator Brahma has a thousand such periods of four ages, and
his night again has a thousand such periods. His year has 365 days and as
many nights. He lives a hundred of his years, always creating; and when he
dies a new Brahma is at once born, and so on from eternity to eternity.[55]

In Brahma's role of sustainer, one can see some parallel to Schopenhauer's thing-in-itself in its role as an endlessly striving will to life,
the essence and explanation of all phenomenal reality. For example:

Thus everywhere in nature we see contest, struggle, and the fluctuation of
victory, and later on we shall recognise in this more distinctly that vari-
ance with itself essential to the will. Every grade of the will's objectification
fights for the matter, the space, and the time of another. Persistent matter

must constantly change the form, since, under the guidance of causality, mechanical, physical, chemical, and organic phenomena, eagerly striving to appear, snatch the matter from one another, for each wishes to reveal its own Idea. This contest can be followed through the whole of nature; indeed only through it does nature exist.[56]

That Schopenhauer himself interprets the Hindu conception of Brahma as parallel to his own conception of will is evident from the following passages:

Brahma means originally force, will, wish, and the propulsive power of creation.[57]

The origin of the world (this Samsara of the Buddhists) is itself based on evil; that is to say, it is a sinful act of Brahma, for Indian mythology is everywhere transparent.[58]

The Vedas also teach no God creator, but a world-soul Brahm (in the neuter). Brahma, sprung from the navel of Vishnu with the four faces and as part of the Trimurti, is merely a popular personification of Brahm in the extremely transparent Indian mythology. He obviously represents the generation, the origin, of beings just as Vishnu does their acme, and Shiva their destruction and extinction. Moreover, his production of the world is a sinful act, just as is the world incarnation of Brahm.[59]

The importance of these passages cannot be over-emphasised. For they illustrate Schopenhauer's desire to interpret the doctrine of the *Vedas* so that it accords with his own conception of the thing-in-itself as will. It is also worth emphasising that in the second of the preceding passages he acknowledges that his characterisation of Brahma as evil is an interpretation of Indian mythology rather than an actual statement of accepted Hindu doctrine. This is important since it is doubtful that the similarity between Brahma and the will is nearly as strong as Schopenhauer thinks. While Hindu doctrine asserts that Brahman is the sustainer of the world, it also maintains that Brahman is the ground of all value, the core of the true, the good, and the beautiful.[60] That Schopenhauer recognises that Brahma also has this role is suggested by the following passages:

Just as when Vishnu, according to a beautiful Indian myth, incarnates himself as a hero, Brahma at the same time comes into the world as the minstrel of his deeds.[61]

Therefore, what is moral is to be found between these two; it accompanies man as a light on his path from the affirmation to the denial of the will, or, mythically, from the entrance of original sin to salvation through faith in the mediation of the incarnate God (Avatar): or, according to the teaching of the *Veda*, through all the rebirths that are the consequences of the works in each case, until right knowledge appears, and with it salvation (final emancipation), *Moksha*, i.e., reunion with *Brahma*. But the Buddhists with complete frankness describe the matter only negatively as *Nirvana*, which is the negation of the world or of *Samsara*. If *Nirvana* is defined as nothing, this means only that *Samsara* contains no single element that could serve to define or construct *Nirvana*. For this reason the Jains, who differ from the Buddhists only in name, call the Brahmans who believe in the *Vedas*, Sabdapramans, a nickname supposed to signify that they believe on hearsay what cannot be known or proved.[62]

Such passages suggest that Schopenhauer sees Brahma as the source of good deeds and as the ultimate goal for those seeking salvation.

What then are we to make of Schopenhauer's interpretation of Brahma as something that is evil, and whose sinful act creates this world of suffering? I suggest that Schopenhauer is attempting to interpret Brahman's role as sustainer of the cosmos in a way which accords with his own doctrine of will. But such an interpretation seems forced and artificial, since it is clearly incompatible with the Advaita conception of Brahman that Schopenhauer endorses elsewhere. I suggest that the tension created by these opposing conceptions of the nature of ultimate reality provides a plausible explanation that in part may account for one of the identified shifts that occurred in his thinking between the publication of the first volume of *The World as Will and Representation* and of his later works. As I discussed earlier, whereas in the first volume Schopenhauer is emphatic that the thing-in-itself is exclusively will or will to life, in his later writings there are passages which suggest that the thing-in-itself is will in only one of its aspects, and that it has other aspects that are the focus of mystical awareness. Speculatively, this shift from a strict identity of the will with the thing-in-itself to the view that the will is just one aspect of the thing-in-itself suggests that had Schopenhauer lived longer, he may well have shifted his views even further so as to embrace the idea that the thing-in-itself is not will at all, but instead is solely the object of awareness of those who have achieved salvation. The will, on this view, becomes the esoteric but non-noumenal essence of the world.[63]

I stated earlier that there are two striking instances in which Schopenhauer's doctrines do not find any agreement with the Advaita teaching. The first is his doctrine that the thing-in-itself, or ultimate reality, is a will that is the source of immense suffering in the world, a doctrine that seems incompatible with the Advaita conception of Brahman as the Holy Power. The second point of difference is that for Schopenhauer the thing-in-itself is knowable to normal consciousness, whereas in Advaita teaching, awareness of the higher truth that concerns ultimate reality comes only to those who achieve the special consciousness or pattern of life that comes with the practice of yoga.[64] As I discussed in Section I, Schopenhauer claims numerous times throughout his works that the thing-in-itself is will or will to life and that we are directly aware of it in self-consciousness. Yet, in his later works there are passages in which he withdraws from this claim of direct acquaintance. Instead, he contends that introspective awareness is always temporal and that it conforms to the subject–object divide of phenomenal appearance. Accordingly, it seems that awareness of the thing-in-itself is limited to those who have denied the will and who attain mystical awareness. For example:

Accordingly, at the end of my philosophy I have indicated the sphere of illuminism as something that exists but have guarded against setting even one foot thereon. For I have not undertaken to give an ultimate explanation of the world's existence, but have only gone as far as is possible on the objective path of rationalism. I have left the ground free for illuminism where, in its own way, it may arrive at a solution to all problems without obstructing my path or having to engage in polemic against me.[65]

Such passages are consistent with the Advaita teaching that only those who have attained a higher consciousness can be acquainted with ultimate reality, but they contrast sharply with passages such as the following one, in which Schopenhauer claims that we have a direct acquaintance with the thing-in-itself (or ultimate reality) in self-conscious awareness.

By looking inwards, every individual recognises in his inner being, which is his will, the thing-in-itself, and hence that which alone is everywhere real.[66]

A plausible explanation that may account in part for this shift in Schopenhauer's ideas in the years following the publication of the first volume of *The World as Will and Representation* is the increasing influence of Hindu ideas on his own doctrine concerning the knowability of the thing-in-itself. Hence, in Schopenhauer's later works his views have changed to reflect a greater alignment with Hindu doctrine. Nevertheless, since he never gives up his doctrine that the thing-in-itself, in at least one of its aspects, is will, he also continues to assert in these later works that this claim is grounded in a direct awareness in self-consciousness of the will as thing-in-itself.

VI   SCHOPENHAUER'S LIKELY UNDERSTANDING OF BUDDHISM

To clarify how Eastern ideas might explain the shifts in Schopenhauer's doctrine of the thing-in-itself between the first and second volumes of *The World as Will and Representation*, it is useful to consider his understanding of both Hindu and Buddhist teaching. Having looked briefly at one school of Hindu thought with which it seems likely that Schopenhauer was acquainted, and having examined the similarities and differences that exist between it and Schopenhauer's doctrines, I now propose to consider Schopenhauer's understanding of Buddhist teaching.

It seems likely that with the increasing availability of literature on Buddhist teaching after 1818, Schopenhauer would have been aware of the distinction between the two principal branches of Buddhism, Theravada and Mahayana.[67] That he is acquainted with Mahayana seems clear from his reference to *The Foe Koue Ki*,[68] translated by A. Rémusat and published in 1836. Dauer states that this book, one of the earliest reliable documents on Buddhism known in Germany, is Mahayanist,[69] and she stresses the parallels between Schopenhauer's own doctrines and Mahayana teaching.[70] Copleston, however, restricts comparisons between Schopenhauer and Buddhism to themes common to all Buddhist thinking, such as compassion, the transitory nature of all phenomena, and atheism.[71] Kishan adopts a similar approach, asserting that 'Schopenhauer has no particular predilection for any school of Buddhism.'[72] Nanajivako, however, thinks that Schopenhauer is first acquainted with and influenced by the Theravada teaching of the Burmese, then in middle life becomes influenced by the Mahayana doctrine mainly through the writings on Tibetan Buddhism that were promoted by the Russian St. Petersburg Academy, and finally that in the later phase of his life he is influenced by the Theravada Pali Buddhism of Ceylon.[73] Nanajivako bases this last claim on Schopenhauer's comment concerning two books on Buddhism written by Spence Hardy after his twenty-year stay in Ceylon. Schopenhauer says of these books that they 'have given me a deeper insight into the essence of the Buddhist dogma than any other work'.[74] However, as they were not published until 1850 and 1853, respectively, it is difficult to agree with Nanajivako's claim that Schopenhauer's comment is evidence of the stronger Theravada influence at the time of his preparation of the second volume of *The World as Will and Representation*. While Schopenhauer refers to these books three times in the second volume, and also once in the first volume, these references must have been added only in the 1859 third editions of those volumes. Finally, Abelsen argues that Schopenhauer's conviction of being an original European Buddhist kept him from making a detailed philosophical comparison between his own system and those of the Buddhist schools with which he is acquainted. Consequently, contends Abelsen, the connections which Schopenhauer thinks are obvious remain a matter of atmosphere rather than content.[75] Given this diversity of opinion, my strategy in discussing the likely influence of Buddhism on Schopenhauer is to consider the general comparison between Schopenhauer's philosophy and what is commonly taken to be the essential teaching of Buddhism.[76]

The basic doctrine taught by the Buddha is summed up in the Four Noble Truths. That Schopenhauer is aware of this doctrine is clear from a passage in the second volume of *The World as Will and Representation* in which he lists the four truths.[77]

They affirm the following:

1. Life is permeated by suffering and dissatisfaction.
2. The origin of suffering lies in craving or thirst.
3. The cessation of suffering is possible through the cessation of craving.
4. The way to this cessation of suffering is through the Eightfold Path. This path is an ascending series of practices; the first two concern the right frame of mind of the aspirant,

the next three concern ethical requirements, and the last
three concern meditation techniques that bring serenity and
release. The attainment of peace and insight is called *nirvana*,
and upon its attainment the saint, at death, is not reborn.[78]

It is not difficult to find parallels between these truths and
Schopenhauer's own doctrines. Corresponding to the first truth is
Schopenhauer's pessimistic world-view, which derives from his conviction that the world is a wretched place, permeated by terrible, in-
escapable, and endless suffering.[79] Corresponding to the second truth
is his doctrine that suffering results from the endless and ultimately
aimless striving of all beings, a striving that is inevitable because all
beings are manifestations of the metaphysical will, whose essence is
to strive endlessly.[80] The Buddhist *samsara*, the empirical world permeated by thirst and craving, corresponds to Schopenhauer's world of
representation, the phenomenal world. Furthermore, just as *samsara*
is said to be governed by the causal nexus, so Schopenhauer's world
of representation is governed by the four roots of the Principle of
Sufficient Reason, one of which is the law of causality. Corresponding to the Buddhist doctrine of the impermanence of *samsara* is the
conditioned nature of the world of representation in Schopenhauer's
philosophy, that is, his doctrine that the formal features of the world
of our everyday experience, such as its temporality, spatiality, and
causal connectedness, are contributed by our minds, thereby making
that world (the world of representation) one which is conditioned by
us.

Corresponding to the third truth, namely, that cessation of suffering is possible by cessation of craving, is Schopenhauer's doctrine
that salvation is possible by denial of the will.[81] Associated with this
third truth is another doctrine that finds a parallel in Schopenhauer's
philosophy. It is the Buddhist teaching of re-birth without continuation of individuality. The essential idea of the 'wheel of life' is that
attachment to life (thirst) causes actions (karma), and karma conditions the next life. It is thus thirst that is the energy that drives the
chain of re-births and karma that determines the conditions of the
reborn. Consciousness and hence individuality spring from the karma
of the previous life and are therefore derivative and fleeting. This
idea is also expressed in the Buddhist doctrine of non-self (anatta),
according to which there is no enduring self. Parallel to these ideas

is Schopenhauer's doctrine that it is the will which endures through endless rounds of birth and death; consciousness, by contrast, is but a fleeting manifestation of will, and it perishes with the physical death of beings who possess it. Hence, corresponding to the Buddhist idea of thirst is Schopenhauer's idea that all forms of life are essentially will; corresponding to the Buddhist doctrine of non-self is Schopenhauer's doctrine that consciousness is fleeting; and corresponding to the Buddhist idea that with cessation of thirst release from suffering is possible is Schopenhauer's doctrine that with denial of all willing salvation is attainable.

The next comparison concerns the Buddhist concept of Nirvana and Schopenhauer's doctrine of denial of the will. What is Nirvana? Sri Rahula asserts:

Volumes have been written in reply to this quite natural and simple question; they have, more and more, only confused the issue rather than clarified it. The only reasonable reply to give to the question is that it can never be answered completely and satisfactorily in words, because human language is too poor to express the real nature of the Absolute Truth or Ultimate Reality which is Nirvana.[82]

Despite this disclaimer, Sri Rahula is prepared to make the following remarks about Nirvana. He asserts that if Nirvana is expressed and explained in positive terms, this will inevitably create a false understanding since any positive terms will be tied in meaning to objects and ideas that pertain to experiences of the sense organs. Since a supramundane experience like that of the Absolute Truth is not of such a category, any literal application of ordinary language is bound to be misleading. He goes on to state that it is because of these difficulties that Nirvana is generally expressed in negative terms, such as 'Extinction of Thirst', 'Uncompounded', 'Unconditioned', 'Absence of desire', 'Cessation', 'Blowing out', or 'Extinction'.[83] However, Sri Rahula points out that the use of such negative terms has given rise to the flawed idea that Nirvana itself is negative, expressing self-annihilation. He stresses that Nirvana is definitely no annihilation of self because there is no self to annihilate. Rather, if anything is annihilated, it is the illusion that such a self exists. Furthermore, the notions of 'positive' and 'negative' are themselves misleading. For they belong to the realm of relativity, whereas Nirvana, or Absolute Truth, is beyond such relational categories.[84]

What then is Absolute Truth? It is the truth that there is nothing absolute in the world; that everything is relative, conditioned, and impermanent; and that there is no unchanging, everlasting, absolute substance like Self, Soul, or Atman within or without. To realise this truth is to see things as they are without illusion or ignorance, and this brings about extinction of craving 'thirst' and the cessation of suffering; this is Nirvana. Sri Rahula notes that according to Mahayana doctrine we should understand Nirvana as being no different from Samsara. The same thing is Samsara or Nirvana according to the way you look at it.[85]

Sri Rahula stresses that we must not understand Nirvana to be the natural result of the extinction of craving, since this would be to understand it as an effect produced by a cause. Nirvana cannot be described as 'produced' and 'conditioned', since it is beyond cause and effect; it is simply realised. It is also a mistake to reify Nirvana, as occurs when it is understood as a state or realm or position in which there is some sort of existence, imagined in terms of our ordinary understanding of sensory existence. This mistake is evident in the popular expression 'entering into Nirvana', an expression which, as Sri Rahula makes clear, has no equivalent in the original texts. A similar lack of understanding is evident in the question 'What happens to a Buddha after his death?' The question is ill-formed since Nirvana is realisable in this world and is not a state which one hopes to enter upon death.[86] Huntington elucidates this point in the following passage:

Paradoxically, by stripping away the tendency to reify the screen of everyday affairs, this same recognition simultaneously lays bare the intrinsic nature of all things, which is their 'suchness' (tathata), their quality of being just as they are in reciprocal dependence. What is immediately given in everyday experience is indeed all that there is, for the inherently interdependent nature of the components of this experience is the truth of the highest meaning: both the means to the goal (marga; upaya) and the goal itself, (nirvana).[87]

In other words, the realisation of the highest truth, Nirvana, occurs with the recognition of the inherently interdependent nature of all phenomena in our world of everyday affairs.

In summary, the notion of Nirvana is not easy to explicate adequately. The limitations of language mean that any positive ascriptions may lead to the mistaken view that Nirvana is a state, realm, or position in which there is some kind of existence, imagined in terms of our ordinary sensory existence of subject–object duality. On the other hand, recourse to negative ascriptions may create the equally erroneous impression that Nirvana is an annihilation of Self, a doctrine that is inconsistent with the central Buddhist doctrine of non-self (anatta). Nirvana is often characterised as Absolute Truth, the truth that there is nothing absolute in the world, no substances such as Selves or Souls; instead, all is relative, conditioned, and impermanent. The realisation of this truth is accompanied by the extinction of craving and the cessation of suffering, though these must not be understood as the effects of a cause; rather, they are simply realised as both the means to the goal and the goal itself.

Having briefly outlined core elements of the Buddhist conception of Nirvana, I turn to its counterpart in Schopenhauer's philosophy, denial of the will. Schopenhauer likens denial of the will to the experiences had by mystics.[88] For both denial of the will and mystical experience are accompanied by the disappearance of the phenomenal forms of space, time, and subject–object duality.[89] Some critics argue that Schopenhauer's doctrine of denial of the will implies a 'dismal' nihilism – dismal because if the thing-in-itself is will, the will's destruction leaves only nothingness, and with it the denial of all possibility of value in existence.[90] However, such a conclusion overlooks the passages in Schopenhauer's writings where he talks of the *relative* nature of nothingness and refers to aspects of the thing-in-itself other than will. In the following passage, he draws parallels between his own doctrine of relative nothingness and Buddhist teaching.

As a rule, the death of every good person is peaceful and gentle; but to die willingly, to die gladly, to die cheerfully, is the prerogative of the resigned, of him who gives up and denies the 'will to life'. . . . He willingly gives up the existence that we know; what comes to him instead of it is in our eyes nothing, because our existence in reference to that one is nothing. The Buddhist faith calls that existence Nirvana, that is to say, extinction.[91]

The relative nature of the nothingness as it pertains to denial of the will is again stressed by Schopenhauer in the following passage.

Contrary to silly objections, I observe that the denial of the 'will to life' does not in any way assert the annihilation of a substance, but the mere act of not-willing; that which hitherto willed no longer wills. As we know this being, this essence, the will, as thing-in-itself merely in and through the act of willing, we are incapable of saying or comprehending what it still is or does after it has given up that act. And so for us who are the phenomenon of willing, this denial is a passing over into nothing.[92]

In the next passage the point is made yet again.

That which in us *affirms itself as 'will to life'* is also that which *denies this will* and thereby becomes free from existence and the sufferings thereof. Now if we consider it in this latter capacity as different and separate from us who are the self-affirming 'will to life'; and if from this point of view we wish to call *'God'* that which is opposed to the world (this being the affirmation of the 'will to life'), then this could be done for the benefit of those who do not want to drop the expression. Yet it would stand merely for an unknown x of which only the negation is known to us, namely that it denies the 'will to life' as we affirm it, and hence in so far as it is different from us and the world, but again is identical with both through its ability to be the affirmer as well as the denier, as soon as it *wants* to.[93]

The preceding passages reveal a number of similarities between the Buddhist doctrine of Nirvana, as outlined earlier, and Schopenhauer's doctrine of denial of the will. First, neither Nirvana nor denial of the will is amenable to adequate description in ordinary language. Second, neither Nirvana nor denial of the will entails nihilism; that is, neither entails the denial of all possibility of value in existence. Finally, both Nirvana and denial of the will signify the end of craving or willing and the cessation of suffering. However, alongside these similarities, it is arguable that there is also a significant difference. It is that whereas the Buddhists refuse to discuss Nirvana in terms of a substance ontology – that is, in terms of an enduring independent state or thing, which has identifiable properties that are at least conceptually distinct from the thing which owns them – Schopenhauer's discussion of denial of the will can be interpreted as assuming just such an ontology; that is, of assuming that the thing-in-itself is an enduring propertied thing. For example, he asserts that 'that which hitherto willed no longer wills' and 'what comes to him instead of it is in our eyes nothing, because our existence in reference to that one is nothing'. Arguably, both claims suggest that the thing-in-itself is an enduring independent thing-like entity which reveals other aspects or properties of its nature once it gives up the activity of willing. While the non-temporal and non-spatial character of the thing-in-itself necessarily make it unlike the things of our everyday physical world, it is nevertheless arguable, though not conclusive, that Schopenhauer thinks of the thing-in-itself as a substance-like thing, capable of possessing properties of various kinds.

What are we to make of this alleged difference between Buddhism and Schopenhauer's philosophy? Perhaps Schopenhauer did not grasp that Buddhism rejects substance ontology or perhaps the literature on Buddhism with which he was acquainted was ambivalent on this point. Given that contemporary Buddhist scholars recognise that within Buddhism itself there exists a rival school, the Yogacara, which, its critics argue, resurrects the Vedantic concept of a metaphysical substrate (substance) of all phenomenal appearance, clothing it in the guise of 'dependent nature',[94] each of the previously discussed alternatives has some plausibility. Furthermore, given that Schopenhauer's formative philosophical education was grounded in the Western tradition, a tradition which almost universally assumes a substance ontology,[95] it would hardly be surprising if he interpreted the available Buddhist literature in terms of the ontological assumptions with which he was familiar.

The alleged difference between Schopenhauer and Buddhism over their respective ontological presuppositions is, I believe, important in its own right. However, it is also important as background to the following point. Schopenhauer claims that denial of the will yields only a relative nothing; yet this claim seems to make sense only on the assumption that the thing-in-itself has aspects other than will. As I argued earlier, it is only in Schopenhauer's later work that he introduces a multiple-aspect notion of the thing-in-itself, and only in his later works that he sees parallels between the Buddhist notion of Nirvana and his own doctrine of denial of the will. My contention is that it is his increasing knowledge of and admiration for Buddhism, and in particular his realisation that Nirvana does not mean the end of all possibility of value in existence, that in part may explain this shift in his thinking concerning the nature of the thing-in-itself. This shift from a strict identity between the thing-in-itself and will to a multiple-aspect notion of the thing-in-itself allowed Schopenhauer to assimilate the Buddhist notion of Nirvana with his doctrine that denial of the will is the path to salvation. For just as Nirvana is not simply a negation of everything, but rather represents a way of experiencing the world such that it has positive rather than negative value, so denial of the will is a denial of that which is the source of negative value, making possible the experience of that which is of positive value. This assimilation may appear ill-judged if my earlier suggestion of fundamental ontological differences between Buddhism and Schopenhauer's philosophy is warranted. However, it is unlikely that it would have appeared ill-judged to Schopenhauer. For, as I discussed earlier, there are good reasons for believing that if such differences existed, Schopenhauer would not have been in a position to fully appreciate them.

Finally, there is the fourth truth of Buddha's teaching, which outlines the eight-fold way of attaining enlightenment through the adoption of the right view, the correct ethical practices, and the recommended ascetic and contemplative practices. Corresponding to these steps is Schopenhauer's view that denial of the will requires first of all that a person sees through the *principium individuationis* constituted by space and time. This insight is reflected in a shift from egoistic to altruistic behaviour, and finally to the practice of meditation and a complete withdrawal from the world.[96] However, alongside these similarities, a sharp contrast is also evident. Schopenhauer maintains that denial of the will is an exceptional human experience. However, as I mentioned in Section I, he also contends that awareness of the will as thing-in-itself comes about in ordinary introspective consciousness.[97] If it is the thing-in-itself, albeit in its other aspects, that for Schopenhauer is the object of awareness for those who have denied the will, then it would seem to follow that the thing-in-itself is the object not only of enlightened consciousness, but also of ordinary consciousness. This contention, however, finds no parallel in Buddhism. For in Buddhism, ordinary and enlightened consciousness are radically different from each other. I mentioned in both Sections I and V that there are passages in Schopenhauer's later works in which he appears to withdraw from his claim of direct awareness in ordinary consciousness of the will as thing-in-itself.[98] My hypothesis is that as Schopenhauer became increasingly aware of the epistemological differences between his philosophy and Buddhist teaching, he shifted his views to accord more readily with what he understood of theirs. Hence, in passages from his later works, a clear distinction is made between the objects of ordinary and enlightened consciousness.

VII   CONCLUSION

I have argued that a plausible case can be made for explaining shifts in Schopenhauer's doctrine of the thing-in-itself by suggesting that these changes occurred in response to his increasing knowledge of and admiration for the teachings of the Hindus and Buddhists. I have identified three such shifts; the first concerns the knowability of the thing-in-itself; the second concerns its nature; and the third concerns Schopenhauer's explicit attempt to assimilate his own views on what can be said about the thing-in-itself with Eastern teaching.

The influence of Hindu and Buddhist doctrines, according to which the possibility of enlightenment is restricted to persons who have achieved a refined state of consciousness, offers a plausible explanation that in part may account for the first shift. For in Schopenhauer's later works, while he still asserts that in ordinary introspective consciousness we have direct awareness of the will as thing-in-itself, there are also passages in which he withdraws from this claim. Instead he maintains that ordinary introspective consciousness yields knowledge of phenomena alone, and only mystics and those who have denied the will are aware of reality stripped of its phenomenal forms.

The impact on Schopenhauer of both the Hindu idea of ultimate reality as a Holy Power which is the source of value, and of the Buddhist notion of Nirvana, which can be described negatively as the extinction of suffering, suggests a way of at least partly explaining the second shift. For, in his later works, while he continues to maintain that the thing-in-itself is will or 'will to life' and the source of suffering, he also introduces the idea that the thing-in-itself has other aspects. Speculatively, this shift from a strict identity of the thing-in-itself with will to the view that the thing-in-itself has multiple aspects only one of which is will suggests that had Schopenhauer lived longer, he may well have embraced the view that the thing-in-itself is not will at all; rather it is the object of awareness of saints, mystics and those who have denied the will. The will, by contrast, is the esoteric but non-noumenal essence of the world.[99]

Schopenhauer's familiarity with the Buddhist doctrine which insists that no words can be used to describe Nirvana, offers a persuasive way of accounting in part for the third shift. For it is only in his later works and in later additions to his earlier works that he explicitly attempts to assimilate his own views on the limitations of language in describing the thing-in-itself with Eastern ideas.

In short, it is plausible that the influence of Eastern thought accounts for Schopenhauer's shift from an initial post-Kantian position concerning the thing-in-itself to one more philosophically aligned with what he takes to be the essential tenets of Buddhism and Hinduism.

APPENDIX: SCHOPENHAUER'S ORIENTAL SOURCES

Listed here are references from Schopenhauer's works to literature on Hinduism and Buddhism. As he does not consistently provide full details in noting his references, I have made additions and standardised titles and spelling in accordance with the list of titles in Schopenhauer's posthumous library (see E. Grisebach, *Edita und Inedita Schopenhaueriana* [Leipzig: Brockhaus, 1888], 141–84, and A. Hübscher (ed.), *Der handschriftliche Nachlass*, Fünfter Band [Frankfurt a. M.: Verlag waldemar Kramer, 1968], 319–52).

Grisebach's list of titles was compiled from the auction catalogues of 1869 and 1871, and from the warehouse catalogue of 1880, which had been prepared for the auction of the library that Schopenhauer had bequeathed to his executor, Wilhelm von Gwinner. While Grisebach's list is extensive, he states that it is incomplete, noting that some books were disposed of by Gwinner in other ways. Grisebach also states that it is only in the case of those books that he personally acquired that he can be certain of the bibliographic exactness of the entries on his list. For the sake of consistency, I have chosen to standardise titles in accordance with the details that he provides. However, in cases where these details differ from those provided by Hübscher, I have used the latter since it is the more recent work.

Grisebach lists about 130 items of orientalia in Schopenhauer's posthumous library, while Hübscher lists approximately 150. Whichever figure is more accurate, it represents a considerable collection,

and suggests that Schopenhauer has a strong and abiding interest in
Eastern ideas.

HINDUISM

Manuscript Remains

Polier, *Mythologie des Indous*, Roudolstadt, 1809 (*MR* 1 515/Hn.
1, 465 [1817]); Rhode's *On Religion and Philosophy of the Hindus*,
Leipzig, 1827 (*MR* 2 459 n/Hn. 2, 395 n. [1815–16], which must be a
footnote added to the 1815–16 notes after the 1827 publication date of
the book, *MR* 4 149/Hn. 4/i, 125 [1832]); *Desatir* of unknown author
(*MR* 3 64/Hn. 3, 58 [1820]); Wilson, *Iswara Krishna Sankhya-Karica*,
Oxford, 1837 (*MR* 3 137 n./Hn. 3, 126 n. [1820]); F. Schlegel, *Ueber die
Sprache und Weisheit der Indier, nebst metrischen Uebersetzgungen
indischer Gedichte*, Heidelberg, 1808 (*MR* 3 442/Hn. 3, 403 [1828–
30]); Colebrooke, *On the Philosophy of the Hindous*, Transactions of
the Asiatic London Society, vol. 1 (*MR* 3 682/Hn. 3, 627 [1828–30]);
Max Müller, *Rig Veda, Text and Notes* Sanskrit, London, 1854 (*MR*
4 376/Hn. 4/ii, 17–18 [1852–60]); Max Müller, 'On the Veda and the
Zend Avesta', in Bunsen, *Hippolytus and his age*, London, 1852 (*MR*
4 376/Hn. 4/ii, 18 [1852–60]).

Parerga and Paralipomena, Vol. 2

'Some Remarks on Sanskrit Literature', *P2* 395–402/Z. 10, 435–43.
Obry, *Du Nirvana indien, ou de l'affranchissement de l'âme après
la mort, selon les Brahmans et les Bouddhistes*, Amiens, 1856; the
Edinburgh Review, 1858; Langlès, *Monuments anciens et modernes
de l'Hindoustan*, Paris, 1821; Hardy, *Eastern Monachism*, London,
1850; the *Asiatic Researches*; and Schlegel's translation of the
Bhagavadgita, Bonnae, 1823. Schopenhauer also refers the reader to
his essay *On the Basis of Morality*, Section 22, where in a footnote
discussion of the genuineness of the *Oupnek'hat* he mentions the
secondary texts, F. Windischmann, ed., *Sancara, sive de theologumenis Vedanticorum*, Bonn, 1833; J. J. Bochinger, *Sur la connexion
de la vie contemplative ascétic et monastique chez les Indous et
chez les peuples boudhistes*, Strasbourg, 1831, and the recent (in
his day) translations of the *Upanishads* by Rammohun Roy, Poley,
Colebrooke, and Röer.

Other literature on Hinduism that Schopenhauer refers to in *P2* includes the following: *A Bengal officer, Vindication of the Hindoos from the aspersions of the Reverend Claudius Buchanan, with a refutation of his arguments in favour of an ecclesiastical establishment in British India: the whole tending to evince the excellence of the moral system of the Hindoos*, 1808 (*P2* 223/Z. 9, 243); *The Times*, 1849 (*P2* 223 n./Z. 9, 243 n.); *The Times*, 1858 (*P2* 226/Z. 9, 246); *Edinburgh Review*, 1858 (*P2* 401/Z. 10, 442).

The World as Will and Representation, Vol. 1

Asiatic Researches (see *W1* 4, 48, 381, 388 n./Z. 1, 30, 82; Z. 2, 471, 480 n.); *Oupnek'hat* (see *W1* 181, 283 n., 388 n./Z. 1, 235; Z. 2, 356 n., 480 n.); *Upanishads* (see *W1* xv, xvi, 181, 205, 355 n., 381/Z. 1, 11, 235, 264; Z. 2, 442 n., 471); *Bhagavad-Gita*, trans. A. Schlegel, Bonnae, 1823 (see *W1* 284, 388 n./Z. 2, 358, 480 n.); *Veda* (see *W1* xv, 8, 17, 86, 181, 205, 283 n., 355-7, 374, 380, 388, 419, 495 n./Z. 1, 11, 34, 45, 128, 235, 264; Z. 2, 356, 442, 464, 471, 480, 516, 604 n.); Wilson, *Iswara Krishna Sánkhya Karika*, Oxford, 1837 (see *W1* 382 n./473 n.); Colebrooke, 'On the philosophy of the Hindus': *Miscellaneous Essays*, London, 1837 (see *W1* 382 n./Z. 2, 473 n.); Polier, *Mythologie des Indous*, Roudolstadt, 1809 (see *W1* 384, 388 n., 495 n./Z. 2, 475, 480 n., 604 n.); *Asiatisches Magazin* (see *W1* 388 n./Z. 2, 480 n.); *Puranas* (see *W1* 8, 17, 388, 419, 495 n./Z. 1, 34, 45; Z. 2, 480, 516, 473 n.

The World as Will and Representation, Vol. 2

Asiatic Researches (*W2* 169-70, 505, 608/Z. 3, 197-8; Z. 4, 592, 712); *Bhagavad-Gita*, trans. A. Schlegel, Bonnae, 1823 (see *W2* 326, 473/Z. 3, 381; Z 4, 555); *Oupnek'hat* (see *W2* 457, 607 n., 613/Z. 4, 538, 711 n., 718); *Veda* (see *W2* 162, 457, 475, 506, 508, 608, 613/Z. 3, 89; Z. 4, 538, 557, 592, 596, 712, 718); *Upanishads* (see *W2* 162, 457, 475, 609, 611 n./Z. 3, 189: Z. 4, 538, 557, 713, 715 n.); Colebooke, 'History of Indian Philosophy', in the *Transactions of the Asiatic London Society* (see *W2* 488/Z. 4, 572); F. Windischmann, ed., *Sankara, sive de theologumenis Vedanticorum*, Bonn, 1833 (see *W2* 508 n, 607 n./Z. 4, 596 n., 711 n.); Colebrooke, *Miscellaneous Essays*, London, 1837 (see *W2* 508 n./Z. 4, 596 n.).

On the Will in Nature

Colebrooke, 'Report on the Vedas', in the *Asiatic Researches*, vol. 8 (undated) (*WN* 45/Z. 5, 230); Bopp, 'Sundas and Upasunda', in *Ardschuna's Reise zu Indra's Himmel*, 1824 (*WN* 48/Z. 5, 234).

On the Basis of Morality

Bhagavadgita (*BM*, 213/Z. 6, 314–15).

Excluding the *Asiatiches Magazin* and *Asiatic Researches*, which are dated 1802 and 1806–12, respectively, Grisebach and Hübscher each list approximately forty other titles that specifically refer to Hinduism. While up to eighteen of these have publication dates earlier than 1818, only two (the works by Polier and F. Schlegel) are mentioned in the *Manuscript Remains* in the period before 1818. It therefore seems likely that it was not until after 1818 that Schopenhauer acquired the other works.

BUDDHISM

As Schopenhauer does not consistently provide full details in noting his references, I have, where appropriate, made amendments in accordance with the details provided in Grisebach's list. In cases where Schopenhauer refers to works which do not appear on this list, but which do appear in the bibliography that Schopenhauer himself provides in his chapter 'Sinology' in *On the Will in Nature*, I use the fuller details noted there.

Manuscript Remains, Vols. 3 and 4

Journal Asiatique (*MR* 3 66/Hn. 3, 60 [1820]; 336/Hn. 3, 305 [1825]); *Asiatic Journal* (*MR* 3 349/Hn. 3, 317 [1826]; 424/Hn. 3, 389 [1828]; 658/Hn. 3, 605 [1828–30]); Morrison, *Chinese Dictionary*, 1815 (*MR* 3 60/Hn. 3, 55 [1820]); *San-tsung fa sou*, the principal document of the Buddhist religion (*MR* 3 372/Hn. 3, 339 [1826]); Abel Rémusat, *Mélanges asiatiques*, 1825 (*MR* 3 372/Hn. 3, 339 [1826]; 37 n. /Hn. 3, 306 n. [1826]); Upham, *The History and the Doctrine of Buddhism*, London, 1829 (*MR* 3 675/Hn. 3, 621 [1828–30]); I. J. Schmidt, *Geschichte der Ost-Mongolen und ihres Fürstenhauses*, St. Petersburg, 1829 (*MR* 4 47/Hn. 4/i, 33 [1830–31]); B. Hodgson, descriptions of Buddhism in Nepal as recorded in the *Transactions of the Royal Asiatic Society of Great Britain and Ireland*, London, 1828, and as elucidated by I. J. Schmidt in his essay in *Mémoirs de l'Académie de St. Petersbourg* (*MR* 4 455/Hn. 4/ii, 91 [1852–60]).

On the Will in Nature

'Sinology', *WN* 130–1 n./Z. 6, 327 n. Schopenhauer lists the following works, whose details I amend according to Grisebach's list in cases where the works appear on both lists, but with slightly different details on each: 1. I. J. Schmidt, *Dsanglun oder der Weise und der Thor*, St. Petersburg, 1843; 2. I. J. Schmidt, Several lectures delivered to the Academy of St. Petersburg in 1829–32; Schopenhauer is probably referring to the following lectures listed by Grisebach: *Ueber einige Grundlehren des Buddhaismus*, 1929, *Ueber einige Grundlehren des Buddhaismus*, 1830, *Ueber die sogenannte dritte Welt der Buddhaisten als Forsetzung der Abhandlungen über die ihren des Buddhaismus*, 1831, *Ueber die tausend Buddhas einer Weltperiode der Einwohnung oder gleichmässigen Dauer*, 1832; 3. *I. J. Schmidt, Forschungen im Gebiete der älteren religiösen, politischen und litterarischen Bildungsgeschichte der Völker Mittelasiens, vorzüglich der Mongolen und Tibeter*, St. Petersburg, 1824; 4. I. J. Schmidt, *Ueber die Verwandtschaft der gnostisch-theosophischen Lehren mit den Religionssystemen des Orients, vorzüglich dem Buddhaismus*, Leipzig, 1828; 5. I. J. Schmidt, *Ssanang Ssetsen Chung-Taidschi, Geschichte der Mongolen und ihres Fürsthauses*, St. Petersburg, 1829; 6. Schniefer, two treatises in German in the 'Mélanges Asiatiques tirés du Bulletin Historico-Philol. de l'Acad. d. St. Petersburg', Tome 1, 1851; 7. Samuel Turner, *Gesandtschaftsreise an den Hof des Teshoo Lama. Aus dem Englischen*, 1801; 8. J. Bochinger, *Sur la connexion de la vie contemplative, ascétique et monastique chez les Indous et chez les peuples bouddhistes*, Strasbourg, 1831; 9. *Journal Asiatique*, vol. 7, 1825; 10. E. Burnouf, *Introduction à l'histoire du Buddhisme indien*, Paris, 1844; 11. *Rgya Tch'er Rol Pa*, trans. from Tibetan by Foucaux, 1848; 12. Chi Fa Hian, *Foe Koue Ki*, trans. from Chinese by Abel Rémusat, Paris, 1836; 13. *Description du Tibet*, trans. by Bitchourin and Klaproth, 1831; 14. Klaproth, *Fragments Bouddhiques*, 1831; 15. Spiegel, *Liber de officiis Sacerdotum Buddhicorum*, Bonnae, 1841; 16. Spiegel,

Anecdota Palica, 1845; 17. Fausböll, *Dhammapadam*, Hovniae, 1855; 18. Buchanan, 'On the Religion of the Burmas', and C. Körösa, three articles, including 'Analyses of the Books of the Kandshur', *Asiatic Researches*; 1839; 19. Sangermano, *The Burmese Empire*, Rome, 1833; 20. Turnour, *The Mahawanzo; and a prefatory essay on Pali Buddhistical literature*, Ceylon, 1836; 21. Upham, *The Mahávansi: the Rájá Ratnácari and the Ráyá-vali*, London, 1833; 22. Upham, *The History and doctrine of Buddhism*, London, 1829; 23. Hardy, *Eastern Monachism*, London, 1850; 24. Hardy, *Manual of Buddhism in its modern development*, London, 1853; 25. C. F. Koeppen, *Die Religion des Buddha*, 1857; 26. 'The Life of Buddha' from the Chinese of Palladji in the *Archiv für wissenschaftliche Kunde von Russland*, ed. Erman, vol. xv, Heft 1, 1856.

Other works on Buddhism that Schopenhauer also refers to in 'Sinology' are: *Asiatic Journal*, 1826; Morrison, *Chinese Dictionary*, Macao, 1815; Neumann, 'Die Natur- und Religions-Philosophie der Chinesen, nach den Werken des Tchu-hi', an article in Illgen, *Periodical for Historical Theology*, vol. vii, 1837 (Grisebach lists only *Asiatische Studien*, Leipzig, 1837, against Neumann's name. However, given that the dates of the two titles are the same, they may refer to the same article).

The World as Will and Representation, Vol. 1

Chi Fa Hian, *Foe Koue Ki*, trans. from Chinese by Abel Rémusat, Paris, 1836 (see *W1* 381/Z. 2, 472); Upham, *The History and Doctrine of Buddhism*, London, 1829 (see *W1* 484/Z. 2, 592).

The World as Will and Representation, Vol. 2

I. J. Schmidt, *Uber das Mahâjâna and Pradchnâ-Pâramita der Bauddhen*, 1836 (see *W2* 275/Z. 3, 321–2); *Rgya Tch'er Rol Pa*, trans. from Tibetan by Foucaux, Paris, 1848 (see *W2* 400 n./Z. 4, 473 n.); Upham, *The History and Doctrine of Buddhism*, London, 1829 (see *W2* 488/Z. 4, 572); Hardy, *Manual of Buddhism in its modern development*, London, 1853; Taylor, *Prabodha Chadro Daya*, London, 1812; Sangermano, *The Burmese Empire*, Rome, 1833; *Asiatic Researches*, Köppen, *Die Religion des Buddha*, 1857; Obry, *Du Nirvana indien*, Amiens, 1856; and T. Burnet, *Histoire du Manichéisme* (see *W2* 503–4/Z. 4, 592); Hardy, *Eastern Monachism*, London, 1850;

I. J. Schmidt, *Geschichte der Mongolen und ihres Fürstenhauses*, St. Petersburg, 1829; Colebrooke in *Transactions of the Royal Asiatic Society* (see W2 508 n./Z. 4, 596 n.); *Asiatic Researches* (see W2 608/Z. 4, 712); E. Burnouf, *Introduction à l'histoire du Buddhism Indien*, Paris, 1844 (see W2 623/Z. 4, 730); I. J. Schmidt, *Ueber die Verwandtschaft der gnostisch-theosophischen Lehren mit den Religionssystemen des Orients, vorzüglich dem Buddhaismus*, Leipzig, 1828 (see W2 624/Z. 4, 731).

On the Basis of Morality

Journal Asiatique; vol. ix, *Meng-Tseu*, ed. Stan. Julian, 1824; *Livres sacrés de l'orient*, undated (*BM* 186 n./Z. 6, 132 n.).

Parerga and Paralipomena, Vols. 1 and 2

F. Buchanan, 'On the Religion of the Burmese', *Asiatic Researches*, vol. vi, 1839 (*P1* 116 n./Z. 7, 132 n.); I. J. Schmidt, *Forschungen im Gebiete der älteren religiösen, politischen und litterarischen Bildungsgeschichte der Völker Mittelasiens, vorzüglich der Mongolen und Tibeter*, St. Petersburg, 1824 (*P1* 116 n.; *P2* 153/Z. 7, 132 n.; Z. 9, 168); Sir G. Stanton, *An Enquiry into the proper mode of rendering the word of God in translating the Sacred Scriptures into the Chinese Language*, London, 1848 (*P1* 116 n./Z. 7, 132 n.); S. Hardy, *Eastern Monachism*, London, 1850 (*P2* 84 n., 358/Z. 9, 95 n.; Z. 10, 395); S. Hardy, *Manual of Buddhism*, London, 1853 (*P2* 84 n., 276/Z. 9, 95 n.; Z. 10, 300); Klaproth, *Fragmens Bouddhiques* in the *Nouveau Journal asiatique*, 1831; Koeppen, *Die Lamaische Hierarchie*, undated (*P2* 153/Z. 9, 168); I. J. Schmidt, *Sanang Ssetsen Chung-Taidschi. Geschichte der Mongolen und ihres Fürstenhauses*, St. Petersburg, 1839; *Lettrés édifiantes et curieuses*, 1819 (*P2* 203/Z. 9, 221); Sangermano, *The Burmese Empire*, Rome, 1833; *Asiatic Researches*, vol. vi, ix (*P2* 276/Z. 9, 300); Obry, *Du Nirvana indien, ou de l'affranchissement de l'âme après la mort, selon les Brahmans et les Bouddhistes*, Amiens, 1856 (*P2* 401/Z. 10, 441).

Only two of these works were published prior to 1818. These are: Morrison, *Chinese Dictionary*, Macao, 1815; and Samuel Turner, *Gesandtschaftsreise an den Hof des Teshoo Lama*. Aus dem Englischen, 1801.

Of the works listed in Schopenhauer's posthumous library which specifically refer to Buddhist thought, only three have publication dates earlier than 1818. These are: M. Ozeray, *Recherches sur Bouddhou*, Paris, 1817; Abel Rémusat; *Le livre des récompenses et des peines, traduit du chinois avec des notes et des éclaircissements*, Paris, 1816; and Samuel Turner, *Gesandtschaftsreise an den Hof des Teshoo Lama*, Aus dem Englischen, 1801. The total number of titles specifically referring to Buddhist thought is thirty-eight in Grisebach's list and forty-four in Hübscher's.

NOTES

1 See *W1* xiii–xiv, xxi–xxiii/Z. 1, 9–10; 18–20 for Schopenhauer's claim that there are no significant changes in his thinking after the publication in 1818 of *W1¹*.
2 See H. Höffding, *History of Modern Philosophy* (London: Macmillan and Co., 1915), 226; F. Copleston, *Arthur Schopenhauer: Philosopher of Pessimism* (London: Burns Oates & Washbourne, 1946), 65; P. Gardiner, *Schopenhauer* (Middlesex: Penguin Books, 1967), 173; D. Hamlyn, *Schopenhauer* (London: Routledge & Kegan Paul, 1980), 84–5; C. Janaway, *Self and World in Schopenhauer's Philosophy* (Oxford: Clarendon Press, 1989), 196.
3 See *W1* 110, 112, 113, 119, 120, 128, 181, 184, 275, 280, 282, 286, 287, 288, 289, 290, 292, 301, 328, 354, 366, 402, 421, 436, 474, 501, 503, 504–5, 506, 534; *W2* 14, 16, 18, 136, 174, 201, 206, 214, 239, 245, 259, 299, 307, 308, 309, 313, 320, 322, 335, 348, 443, 472, 484, 497, 501, 530, 579, 589, 600, 601; *WN* 20, 36, 47, 116; *P1* 20, 78, 229, 267, 299, 303, 305; *P2* 46, 48, 90, 94, 95, 176, 312, 313, 383, 599; *FW* 34, 97; *MR 1* 184, 205, 206, 319, 488, 491; *MR 2* 463, 485, 486; *MR 3* 84, 121, 164, 197, 227, 245, 247–8, 365, 572; *MR 4* 110, 139, 211, 217, 223/Z. 1, 155, 157, 158, 165, 166, 228, 235, 238, 347; Z. 2, 353, 356, 361, 363, 364, 365, 367, 378, 410, 441, 455, 497, 519, 536, 580, 612, 614, 615, 616, 618, 650; Z. 3, 23, 24, 27, 158–9, 203, 234, 240, 249, 280, 286, 302, 349, 359, 360, 361, 367, 374, 377, 393, 408; Z. 4, 521, 553, 568, 583, 587, 620, 678–90, 703, 705; Z. 5, 202, 220; Z. 6, 233, 310; Z. 7, 29, 92, 251, 290, 325, 328, 331; Z. 9, 55, 56, 102, 107, 192, 339, 340; Z. 10, 423, 651; Z. 6, 72, 137; Hn. 1, 169, 187, 188, 291, 440, 444; Hn. 2, 399, 419; Hn. 3, 75, 110, 149, 180, 207, 224, 226, 333, 525; Hn. 4/1, 88, 116, 184, 189, 194.
4 *WN*, trans. Hillebrand, 216/Z. 5, 202. Also see *W2* 600; *W1* 162, 436, 503, 504, 345/Z. 4, 703 ; Z. 1, 215; Z. 2, 536, 614, 615, 310. For less explicit

references see *W2* 179, 195, 313, 364; *W2* 288, 290; *FR* 119–20/Z. 3, 209, 228, 367; Z. 4, 433; Z. 3, 363, 365; Z. 5, 99.

5 *W2* 196–7/Z. 3, 229–30. Also see *W2* 182, 185, 197–8, 318, 496, 612: *P1* 42; *MR* 3 40, 114, 171, 353, 472, 595, 713, 716; *MR* 4 296–7/Z. 3, 213, 216–17, 230, 231, 372; Z. 4, 581, 716; Z. 7, 54; Hn. 3, 36–7, 103, 155, 321–2, 432, 546, 657, 600; Hn. 4/i, 261.

6 See G. Simmel, *Schopenhauer and Nietzsche*, trans. Helmut Loiskandl, Deena Weinstein, and Michael Weinstein (Amherst: University of Massachusetts Press, 1986), 33–4; R. Tsanoff, *Schopenhauer's Criticism of Kant's Theory of Experience* (New York: Longman, Green & Company, 1911), 66–70; T. Whittaker, *Reason, A Philosophical Essay with Historical Illustrations* (Cambridge: Cambridge University Press, 1934), 98; A. Hübscher, *The Philosophy of Schopenhauer in Its Intellectual Context, Thinker Against the Tide*, trans. Joachim T. Baer and David Cartwright (Lewiston, N.Y.: Edwin Mellen Press, 1989), 20.

7 *W1* 445/Z. 6, 546.

8 See J. Young, *Willing and Unwilling: A Study in the Philosophy of Arthur Schopenhauer* (Dordrecht: Martinus Nijhoff, 1987), 30; Janaway, *Self and World*, 197.

9 *W2* 182/Z. 3, 213. Also see *W2* 197, 318/Z. 3, 230, 372.

10 See *W1* xiv/Z. 1, 9.

11 See Höffding, *History of Modern Philosophy*, 226 (n. 51).

12 *W1* 4/Z. 1, 31. Also see *W1* 125, 141, 153, 162, 502/Z. 1, 172–3, 191 204–5, 215, 613.

13 *W2* 198/Z. 3, 231. Also see *W2* 560, 644; *P2* 312; *W2* 288, 294, 642; *MR* 3 79; *W1* 405, 411/Z. 4, 656, 754; Z. 9, 339; Z. 3, 338, 343; Z. 4, 753; Hn. 3, 70; Z. 2, 500, 507.

14 *W2* 325, 325–6; *MR* 1 36–7; *MR* 4 35; *W1* 110–12, 410/Z. 3, 380, 381; Hn. 1, 34–5; Hn. 4/i, 23; Z. 1, 155; Z. 2, 506.

15 *W2* 325–6/Z. 3, 381; relevant also to *W2* 325/Z. 3, 380.

16 *W1* 411–12/Z. 2, 508.

17 However, several references to both Hindu and Buddhist thought are added by Schopenhauer in the revised 1847 edition of *FR*. See *FR* 50, 184–8, 208/Z. 5, 47, 141–5, 158. In the third edition, published in 1864, the editor, Julius Frauenstädt, amends the 1847 text to include corrections and additions jotted down by Schopenhauer in an interleaved copy of the 1847 edition. In Frauenstädt's preface to the third edition he lists the principal passages that are new. Of the twenty-four listed, three concern references to Eastern thought and literature. (See *FR*, trans. Mme Karl. Hillebrand [London: G. Bell, 1889], xxvi–xxviii. The three passages in question are in section 34.)

18 See H. G. Rawlinson, 'India in European Literature and Thought', in *The Legacy of India*, ed. G. T. Garratt (Oxford: Clarendon Press, 1937), 35–6; H. G. Rawlinson, 'Indian Influence on the West', in *Modern India and the West*, ed. L. S. S. O'Malley (London: Oxford University Press, 1941), 546–7; L. S. S. O'Malley, 'General Survey', in *Modern India and the West*, 801–2; P. J. Marshall and G. Williams, *The Great Map of Mankind* (London: Dent, London, 1982), 111–12. See also Janaway, *Self and World*, 29.

19 See *MR* 1 456/Hn. 1, 412, and *MR* 2 477/Hn. 2, 412, where Schopenhauer refers to undated editions of the *Asiatic Researches* and *Asiatick Researches*, respectively. Because he does not give publication dates, it is possible that these references are added to his notes after 1818. However, since elsewhere he makes it clear that he has access to these journals prior to 1818 (see *W2* 169/Z. 3, 197, and *MR* 2 459–61/Hn. 2, 395–7), it seems probable that these references are not later additions.

20 I refer to Rhode's *On the Religion and Philosophy of the Hindus*, 1827, which Schopenhauer refers to in a footnote at *MR* 2 459/Hn. 2, 395. He also refers to undated editions of the *Asiatic Researches*, *MR* 1 286, 515/Hn. 1, 260, 465; the *Asiatick Researches*, *MR* 2 477/Hn. 2, 412; and the *Asiatic Magazine*, *MR* 2 262/Hn. 2, 245 (Grisebach notes the correct spelling as *Asiatisches Magazin*). However, for the reasons outlined in note 19, these references are probably not later additions to Schopenhauer's notes.

21 I determined this figure by comparing all references to Buddhism in Payne's translation of the 1859 edition of *W1* to the 1819 first edition of that volume, *W1¹*, edited by R. Malter. The relevant page numbers in Payne's translation of *W1* are as follows: 381, 383, 384, 424, 484/Z. 2, 472, 474, 75, 521–2, 592. The corresponding page numbers in Malter's edition of *W1¹* are as follows: 548–9, 550, 552, 602, 665.

22 The relevant page numbers in Payne's translation of *W1* are as follows: 4, 181, 330, 382 n., 424, 436, 484/Z. 1, 30, 235, 412, 473 n., 521, 522, 592. The corresponding page numbers in Malter's edition of *W1¹* are as follows: 4, 260, 475, 549–50, 602, 617, 665.

23 To determine these approximate numbers, I noted and cross-checked all references in the index of Payne's translation of *The World as Will and Representation* that pertained to Buddhist and Hindu thought. For the *Manuscript Remains*, since there is no index, I scanned the text for similarly relevant references.

24 *W1* 388 n/Z. 2, 480 n.

25 See my appendix, 'Schopenhauer's Oriental Sources', for a listing of the literature on Hinduism and Buddhism referred to by Schopenhauer in his various works.

26 Schopenhauer's *Oupnek'hat* is an 1801 Latin version translated by Anquetil-Duperron of a Persian version translated by Sultan Mohammed Dara Shikoh (brother of Aurangzeb) of the Sanskrit original (see *P2* 396/Z. 10, 436).

27 In 1784 Sir William Jones established the Asiatic Society in Calcutta, the prototype of similar societies in Europe. The society published volumes of proceedings called *Asiatic Researches*, which attracted wide European readership and which were re-issued and translated into French and German. Marshall says that the translations of Sir Charles Wilkins, who made the first English translation of the *Bhagavadgita* in 1785, and who is said to be the first European to really understand Sanskrit, and the essays by Jones in the *Asiatic Researches* set standards that were not to be matched for a generation (Marshall, *The Great Map of Mankind*, 76). Furthermore, Rawlinson notes that in 1805 in the *Asiatic Researches*, H. T. Colebrooke, the greatest of the early orientalists, gave the world the first account of the *Vedas*, which hitherto had been jealously concealed from European eyes (Rawlinson, 'Indian Influence on the West', 546).

28 The *Puranas* consist of a collection of legends that are sometimes said to be part of the fifth *Veda* (*The New Encyclopaedia Britannica*, 15th ed., s.v. 'South Asian Arts', by Pramod Chandra).

29 Rosen published the first edition of some of the hymns of the *Rig-Veda* in 1838 (Rawlinson, 'India in European Thought', 36). At *MR* 4 376/Hn. 4/ii, 17–18, Schopenhauer also mentions the 1854 publication *Rig-Veda, Text and Notes Sanskrit*, by Max Müller. See also Rawlinson, 'Indian Influence on the West', 547–9, for a discussion of the outstanding pioneering achievements of Max Müller from 1845 on. In Rawlinson, 'India in European Literature and Thoughts', 36, the author says that 'the publication, in 1875, of the first of the great series of the *Sacred Books of the East*, under the editorship of Max Müller, made the Hindu scriptures available for the first time to the ordinary reader'.

30 In the two volumes of the *Manuscript Remains* up to 1818, there are three references to the *Bhagavadgita* (*MR* 1 452, 515; *MR* 2 262/Hn. 1, 409, 465; Hn. 2, 245). No details are given for the first two references, but the *Asiatiches Magazin* is given as the source of the third. In *W1* there are two references, one of which refers to the 1802 edition of the *Asiatisches Magazine* (*W1* 388 n./Z. 2, 480 n.). The other is not referenced (*W1* 284/Z. 2, 358). In *W1*, of the two references to the *Bhagavadgita*, one is not referenced (*W1* 473/Z. 2, 555), but the other gives as its source the translation by Schlegel (*W2* 326/Z. 3, 381).

31 See Hübscher, *The Philosophy of Schopenhauer in Its Intellectual Context*, 65–6.

32 *P2* 397/Z. 10, 437.

33 *P2* 398/Z. 10, 438.

34 See also R. K. Das Gupta, 'Schopenhauer and Indian Thought', *East and West* 13, 1 (1962), 32–40, who lists books on Hindu teaching with which Schopenhauer is likely to have been acquainted.

35 See *MR* 1 286, 456, 515; *MR* 2 459–61, 477/Hn. 1, 260 (1814), 412 (1816), 465–6 (1817); Hn. 2, 395–7 (1815–16), 412 (1816–18).

36 See *MR* 1 515/Hn. 1, 465 (1817).

37 See *MR* 2 262/Hn. 2, 245 (1809–13).

38 See *MR* 3 351, 658, 672, 691/Hn. 3, 319 (1826), 605 (1828–30), 618 (1828–30), 36 (1828–30).

39 *MR* 1 456; *MR* 2 477/Hn. 1, 412; Hn. 2, 12.

40 *W2* 169/Z. 3, 197.

41 *W1* 417/Z. 2, 513.

42 *W1* xv–xvi/Z. 1, 11 (italics mine).

43 *W2* 169/Z. 3, 197 (italics mine). See also *W2* 508–9 n., *MR* 3 336/Z. 4, 96 n.; Hn. 3, 305.

44 See Dorothea W. Dauer, *Schopenhauer as Transmitter of Buddhist Ideas*, European University Papers, Series 1, vol. 15 (Berne: Herbert Lang, 1969), 6–9, who notes that while Schopenhauer claims that his own doctrines are independent of the influence of Hindu and Buddhist thought, he is probably much more indebted to them than he realises.

45 *MR* 1 467/Hn. 1, 422.

46 *MR* 1 122 n./Hn. 1, 113 n. (italics mine).

47 F. Copleston, 'Schopenhauer', in *The Great Philosophers* by Bryan Magee (Oxford: Oxford University Press, 1987), 215. While Schopenhauer does not mention the three sub-schools of the Vedanta system, it is clear that he is aware that the Vedanta is only one of several systems of Orthodox Hindu thought (see *MR* 3 442/Hn. 3, 403, where he refers to Schlegel's discussion of the six sects of the Hindus, and *MR* 3 701–4/Hn. 3, 646–8, where he goes on to discuss the merits of these various systems).

48 *MR* 3 701/Hn. 3, 646.

49 Ninian Smart, 'Indian Philosophy', in P. Edwards (ed.), *Encyclopedia of Philosophy* (New York: Macmillan and Free Press, 1967).

50 See *W1* 162, 332; *W2* 486, 591/Z. 1, 216; Z. 2, 414; Z. 4, 570, 692.

51 However, Schopenhauer's knowing self does not seem analogous to the Hindu Self that is identical with Brahman, since Schopenhauer says of the knowing self that it is a tertiary phenomenon. It is metaphysically dependent upon the presence of consciousness, and the latter is in turn an objectification of will (*W2* 278/Z. 3, 325). He also takes the 'I' to be a composite of the knowing and willing subjects, with the willing subject being the more fundamental. On this view, the 'I', or self, is the

intelligible character. However, since Schopenhauer describes the latter as 'an act of will outside time' (*W1* 289/Z. 2, 364), it seems that it too is not identical with the will as thing-in-itself, but is instead a manifestation of it. See Janaway, *Self and World*, for a comprehensive discussion of the inherent tensions in Schopenhauer's philosophy that result from this twofold conception of the self. See also Richard E. Aquila, 'On the "Subjects" of Knowing and Willing and the "I" in Schopenhauer', *History of Philosophy Quarterly* 10, 3 (1993), 241–60. Aquila attempts to overcome the alleged difficulties in Schopenhauer's dual account of the self by interpreting the knowing self as 'the pure form of the directedness of consciousness itself'. As such, it is neither the material that constitutes the body nor the will that is manifest in it, but is rather an irreducible phenomenal 'projection' through those ingredients (248). However, since such a knowing self is clearly not identical with the will as thing-in-itself, there is no parallel with the Atman–Brahman identity of Hindu philosophy.

52 It is also possible to see resemblances between some of Schopenhauer's doctrines and those of the Samkyha school, another of the six main systems of Hindu thought. Resemblances between that school and Schopenhauer's doctrines include its atheism and its explanation of the perceptible world in terms of a single unitary substance, evolving according to rudimentary dynamics. However, there are distinct differences too in that it posits a plurality of eternal selves and a correspondence theory of perception. (See 'Indian Philosophy' in Edwards (ed.), *Encyclopedia of Philosophy*, 156–7.) That Schopenhauer is aware of both the resemblances and differences is clear from his discussion in the chapter 'Remarks on Sanskrit Literature' in *P2* 399/Z. 10, 439–40. There he makes it clear that he values the older Vedic formulation more highly than the Samkhya system.

53 See Helmuth von Glasenapp, 'The Influence of Indian Thought on German Philosophy and Literature', *Calcutta Review* 29 (1928), 203, who also notes this incompatibility. He says 'Whilst, however, for the Vedanta what exists is our eternally blessed spirituality, the Brahma, that is characterised by the attributes Sat, Cit, and Ananda, it is for Schopenhauer a blind and therefore unblessed will'.

54 Kaplan asserts that Brahman refers to the ultimate reality that transcends all differentiation and of which all else is only a manifestation. However, he also notes that the word has a number of other meanings. In its most literal sense it refers to certain rituals in the Vedas, but later it becomes the name of one of the deities, the king or ruler of all the gods, who still remains as the chief of the great trinity of Brahma, Vishnu, and Siva. In another usage it refers to the name of the priestly caste in the

service of the deities (see Abraham Kaplan, *The New World of Philosophy* [London: Collins, 1962], 241). While Schopenhauer writes of Brahman as being 'the original being himself' (*W2* 463/Z. 4, 543), he also says of salvation that it is the 'reunion with Brahma' (*W2* 608/Z. 4, 712). It is clear that he knows that Brahma is one of the three deities and that these are popular personifications of the world-soul Brahm (*P1* 127/Z. 7, 144–5). Consequently, in the following discussion I include his references to all three terms: 'Brahma', 'Brahman', and 'Brahm'. While he refers to a belief in the Vedas as both Brahmanism and Hinduism, I use only the latter term. He also uses the term 'Brahmans' and 'Hindus' to refer to those who teach and practice the doctrine of the Vedas, but again I use only the latter term.

55 *W1* 495 n./Z. 2, 604–5 n. See also *W1* 276, 399/Z. 2, 348, 493, and in the second volume see *W2* 463, 489/Z. 4, 543, 574.

56 *W1* 146–7/Z. 1, 197.

57 *MR* 4 377/Hn. 4/ii, 18. Schopenhauer attributes this derivation of the word 'Brahma' to Max Müller, and he believes that it appears in an essay that Müller contributed to *Hyppolytus*.

58 *P1* 62/Z. 7, 75. See also *FR* (1847), 184/Z. 5, 141–2, where Schopenhauer states, 'Brahma who is born and dies to make way for other Brahmas, and whose production of the world is regarded as sin and guilt'.

59 *P1* 127/Z. 7, 144–5.

60 Kaplan, *The New World of Philosophy*, 242. See also S. Radhakrishnan, 'Hinduism', in Garratt (ed.), *The Legacy of India*, 271, who says, 'The Beyond is Within. Brahman is Atman. He is the *antaryamin*, the inner controller. He is not only the incommunicable mystery standing for ever in his own perfect light, bliss, and peace but also is here in us, upholding, sustaining us.'

61 *P2* 472/Z. 10, 517.

62 *W2* 608/Z. 4, 712.

63 This is the interpretation of Schopenhauer's metaphysics favoured by Julian Young; see Young, *Willing and Unwilling*, ix; see also all of ch. 3. For a very useful discussion of Young's interpretation, see J. Atwell, *Schopenhauer on the Character of the World: The Metaphysics of Will* (Berkeley: University of California Press, 1995), 122–8.

64 See Kaplan, *The New World of Philosophy*, 327–49.

65 *P2* 10/Z. 9, 17.

66 *W2* 600/Z. 4, 703.

67 See Heinrich Dumoulin, 'Buddhism and Nineteenth-Century German Philosophy', *Journal of the History of Ideas* 42 (1981), 458, who says that all of the German philosophers, Kant, Hegel, Schopenhauer, and Nietzsche, knew, though not too clearly, that Buddhism was divided into

two principal branches. That Schopenhauer had acquaintance with the teachings of both branches is evident from the bibliography he provides in his chapter 'Sinology' in *On The Will in Nature* and from his posthumous library. Included are books that refer to the Buddhism of the Ceylonese (Theravada) and to that of the Chinese (Mahayana).

68 *W1* 381/Z. 2, 472.
69 Dauer, *Schopenhauer as Transmitter of Buddhist Ideas*, 32.
70 Ibid., 21.
71 Copleston, *Arthur Schopenhauer*, 227.
72 B. V. Kishan, 'Schopenhauer and Buddhism', in Michael Fox (ed.), *Schopenhauer: His Philosophical Achievement* (Sussex: Harvester Press, 1980), 255.
73 Bhikkhu Nanajivako, *Schopenhauer and Buddhism* (Sri Lanka: Buddhist Publication Society, 1970), 18–20.
74 See *WN*, trans. Hillebrand, 362 n/Z. 5, 327 n.
75 Peter Abelsen, 'Schopenhauer and Buddhism', *Philosophy East & West* 43, 2 (1993), 255.
76 Abelsen argues that any worthwhile comparison must involve the four basic forms of Buddhist philosophy in their own right rather than merely looking at Buddhism *as such* (see Abelsen, 'Schopenhauer and Buddhism', 256). I agree that this approach is desirable if we wish to determine actual correspondences between Schopenhauer's philosophy and Buddhism as currently understood. However, since I wish to look at the possible influence of Buddhist ideas on Schopenhauer's thought, and since we are not in a position to know with any certainty the extent and nature of his knowledge of Buddhism, it is legitimate in this case to restrict the comparison to those more general tenets of Buddhism with which Schopenhauer is likely to have been acquainted.
77 *W2* 623/Z. 4, 730. Schopenhauer refers to E. Burnouf, *Introduction à l'histoire du Buddhisme indien* (Paris, 1844), for an explanation of these truths.
78 Ninian Smart, 'Buddhism' in Edwards (ed.), *Encyclopedia of Philosophy*.
79 *W2* 309–10, 311–12, 322–23; *W2* 581–4; *P2* 293/Z. 3, 388, 390, 403–4; Z. 4, 680–4; Z. 9, 318.
80 *W1* 164, 196, 342–3, 351, 352–3, 363–4; *W2* 204, 580, 599; *P1* 303/Z. 1, 217, 52; Z. 2, 427, 438, 439, 451–2; Z. 3, 237–8; Z. 4, 679, 702 –3; Z. 7, 328.
81 *W1* 379, 397, 405, 412; *W2* 609, 634–7/Z. 2, 469, 491, 500, 508; Z. 4, 713, 743–7.
82 W. Sri Rahula, *What the Buddha Taught* (New York: Grove Weidenfeld, 1959), 35.
83 Ibid., 36.

84 Ibid., 36–7.

85 Ibid., 39–40.

86 Ibid., 40–3.

87 C. W. Huntington, *The Emptiness of Emptiness: An Introduction to the Early Indian Madhyamika* (Honolulu: University of Hawaii Press, 1989), 40.

88 *W1* 410/Z. 2: 506 and *W2* 612/Z. 4, 716.

89 W. T. Stace, 'The Nature of Mysticism', in *Philosophy of Religion: Selected Readings*, ed. W. L. Rowe and W. J. Wainwright (New York: Harcourt Brace Jovanovich, 1973), 268–9.

90 As it is notoriously difficult to be precise in elucidating Schopenhauer's conception of 'denial of the will', my paraphrase 'the denial of all possibility of value in existence' can at best be an educated guess as to the meaning which Schopenhauer would have attached to the phrase. For commentary on the way in which one might interpret 'denial of the will', see L. Navia, 'Reflections on Schopenhauer's Pessimism', in Fox (ed.), *Schopenhauer: His Philosophical Achievement*, 178–81; E. Heller, *Thomas Mann: The Ironic German* (Cambridge: Cambridge University Press, 1958), 50–1; Bertrand Russell, *History of Western Philosophy* (London: Allen & Unwin, 1961), 726.

91 *W2* 508/Z. 4, 596. See also *W2* 608; *W1* 412 n./Z. 4, 712; Z. 2, 508 n.

92 *P2* 312/Z. 9, 339.

93 *MR* 3 376/Hn. 3, 343.

94 Huntington, *The Emptiness of Emptiness*, 63.

95 Consider, for example, the pervasive influence of the notion of 'substance' elaborated in Aristotle's *Metaphysics*. Not only did this notion perdure into the Middle Ages and the writings of St. Thomas Aquinas, but it is also assumed in the *Meditations* of Descartes, often taken to be the founding figure of modern philosophy in the West.

96 *W1* 390, 391–3; *W2* 606/Z. 2, 483, 484–6; Z. 4, 709–10.

97 *WN* 20/Z. 5, 202. Also see *W2* 600; *W1* 162, 436, 503, 504, 345/Z. 4, 703; Z. 1, 215; Z. 2, 536, 614, 615, 310. For less explicit references, see *W2* 179, 195, 313, 364; *W1* 288 290; *FR* 119–20/Z. 3, 209, 228, 367; Z. 4, 433; Z. 2, 363, 365; Z. 5, 99.

98 *W2* 196–7/Z. 3, 299–30. Also see *W2* 182, 185, 197–8, 318, 496, 612; *P1* 42; *MR* 3 40, 114, 171, 353, 472, 595, 713, 716; *MR* 4 296–7/Z. 3, 213, 216–17, 230, 231, 372; Z. 4, 581, 716; Z. 7, 54; Hn. 3, 36–7, 103, 155, 321–2, 432, 546, 657, 660; Hn. 4/i, 261.

99 See n. 63.

7 Ideas and Imagination

Schopenhauer on the Proper Foundation of Art

> The reader who, instead of being keen to learn, is intent only on finding fault, will simply not learn anything. He likes to criticize.
>
> Arthur Schopenhauer[1]

I AESTHETIC CONTEMPLATION: A PRELUDE

Schopenhauer devoted more than one-quarter of his principal work, *The World as Will and Representation*, to aesthetics. The chapters on aesthetics occupy the third section in both volumes of that work and depend for their clarity as much on the metaphysical theory that precedes them as on an acquaintance with the particular arts discussed. For Schopenhauer, genuine aesthetic experience, though rare, leads directly to an apprehension of metaphysical truth, to the core of genuine knowledge. This emphasis on aesthetic experience in obtaining knowledge is unusual, however, for by the middle of the nineteenth century the epistemological authority of the scientific method was pervasively secure throughout Europe.

No stranger to the empirical scientific disciplines, Schopenhauer began higher studies in a faculty of medicine and made progress for more than two years before switching to philosophy, which would become his life's work. Although he insisted on separate emphases for science on the one hand and philosophy on the other, Schopenhauer nevertheless felt it prudent to corroborate his metaphysical claims by attempting to show their appearance in phenomena validated through scientific observation.[2] He kept pace with the sciences throughout his life, eventually concluding that studies of animal behavior and the functional connections of organisms lent support to the core of his philosophical views.[3] Yet despite this respect for and strong grasp of scientific practice, Schopenhauer ultimately insisted on the reliability not of science but of aesthetics as a means by which to recognize metaphysical truth.

From Schopenhauer's metaphysical point of view, the world just is will, 'the innermost essence, the kernel, of every particular thing and also of the whole. It appears in every blindly acting force of nature, and also in the deliberate conduct of man, and the great difference between the two concerns only the degree of the manifestation, not the inner nature of what is manifested.'[4] Aesthetic contemplation reveals the forms of will most objectively, without in the process being subject to the exertions of willing. Thus, aesthetic contemplation as a means of achieving objective, intuitive cognition serves as a source for meaning in life. Rudiger Safranski emphasizes this fact in his philosophical biography.

In Schopenhauer's philosophy, as in no one else's before him, the aesthetic element is accorded the highest philosophical rank. A philosophy which does not explain the world but offers information on what the world actually is and means, such a philosophy, according to Schopenhauer, derives from an aesthetic experience of the world. In his manuscript journals Schopenhauer expressed this even more clearly than in his principal work. 'Philosophy,' he observed in a note of 1814, 'has so long been sought in vain because it was sought by way of the sciences instead of by way of the arts.'[5]

This essay seeks to demonstrate art's centrality within Schopenhauer's metaphysical view of the world. As Bryan Magee observes in a review article of *Schopenhauer, Philosophy and the Arts*, 'His aesthetics are a special application of his metaphysics ... and this means that only if the metaphysics have been accurately grasped are the aesthetics even so much as intelligible.'[6] Schopenhauer's aesthetic theory locates the proper foundation of art in the perceptual apprehension of natural forms. Only on the basis of *fidelity to* this foundation can good art be distinguished from bad art in carrying out its function – a function which is primarily cognitive or illuminative, though it partakes of a palliative dimension.

Because Schopenhauer defers his consideration of particular arts until after a lengthy consideration of their foundation, this essay pays tribute to his line of reasoning through an extensive examination of the conditions for art's foundation. In Section II a discussion of Schopenhauer's metaphysical world view contrasts the scientific approach to knowledge through conceptual abstractions with the aesthetic approach to metaphysical realization through Ideas (objective representations of will as species-types).[7] Section III examines the significance and limitations of the ordinary intellect as it discovers will in itself, a felt experience filtered through the body. This fundamental discovery of will in the self shares with aesthetic contemplation the quality of being *reflective*. Reflection, as the unique capacity of the artistic or philosophical genius, finds expression for the artist in the creative works embodying the Ideas, a topic developed in Section IV. In Section V particular art forms are considered, including the special case of music, which bypasses cognition of Ideas altogether. Discussion concludes in Section VI with a brief review of Schopenhauer's observations on bad art. By highlighting the deviation of bad art from the perceptual character of aesthetic apprehension, the examination reveals the full extent of Schopenhauer's commitment to a metaphysics of artistic viewing.[8]

II   KERNELS AND HUSKS

Schopenhauer agrees with Aristotle that philosophy begins in astonishment and wonder, that the human being is an *animal metaphysicum* (W2 160/H. 3, 176). Metaphysics takes shape as an individual marvels at her own works and then asks, What am I? For great minds, however, reflection does not remain with the self but strives for something beyond individuation. 'Whoever is *great* recognizes himself in all and on the whole, and is therefore concerned about the totality of all things. He tries to understand and to act on that totality ...' (MR 3 29/Hn. 3, 26)

   In approaching an understanding of the totality of existence, Schopenhauer rejects science as the method whereby we might achieve enlightenment; it is different in degree but not in kind from everyday common sense. Like commonsense reasoning, science orients itself toward goal fulfillment, striving, attainment, cause. It remains trapped in covetous motivations which distort perception of the universal. 'What distinguishes science from ordinary knowledge is merely its form, the systematic, the facilitating of knowledge by summarizing everything particular in the universal by means of the subordination of concepts . . .' (*W1* 177/H. 2, 208).

So what is the totality of existence such that science is not in a position to reveal it? The totality of world as will, the persistent and unitary force governing all phenomena. In thrall to the permutations of this totality, human individuals oscillate between extremes of deprivation and ennui, one replacing the other like the steady swing of a metronome.

If we attempt to take in at a glance the whole world of humanity, we see everywhere a restless struggle, a vast contest for life and existence, with the fullest exertion of bodily and mental powers, in face of dangers and evils of every kind which threaten and strike at any moment. If we then consider the reward for all this, namely existence and life itself, we find some intervals of painless existence which are at once attacked by boredom and rapidly brought to an end by a new affliction.

Behind *need and want* is to be found at once *boredom*, which attacks even the more intelligent animals. This is a consequence of the fact that life has no *genuine intrinsic worth*, but is kept in *motion* merely by want and illusion. But as soon as this comes to a standstill, the utter barrenness and emptiness of existence become apparent.[9]

With regard to will as the metaphysical basis of the world, Schopenhauer exudes a thoroughly Sumerian pessimism.[10] Safranski calls Schopenhauer the philosopher of 'metaphysical homelessness,' a philosopher who 'tried to think the "Whole" of the world and of human life, without expecting salvation from that Whole.'[11] Science through its methods cannot even broach the question of this whole.

In all abstract employment of the mind, the will is also the ruler. According to its intentions, the will imparts direction to the employment of the mind, and also fixes the attention; therefore this is always associated with some exertion; but such exertion presupposes activity of the will. Therefore complete objectivity of consciousness does not occur with this kind of mental activity in the same way as it accompanies, as its condition, aesthetic contemplation. . . . (*W2* 369/H. 3, 421–2)

Schopenhauer cites aesthetic contemplation as the condition for objective consciousness. Objective consciousness, in turn, evades will. Escape from will *can occur* in two non-abstract forms. Both involve *separation* of consciousness from individual willing. Aesthetic perception forms the more temporary but accessible path away from the world; mystical abatement of willing through ascetic denial of one's corporeal longings forms the other. Schopenhauer's aesthetic 'salvation' is not moral or theistic in tone but instead has shades of what might be called 'epistemological enlightenment': realizing the way the world is but not through ordinary consciousness. The contemplation of beauty liberates one to understand the hidden, holistic character of the world.

Aesthetic perception, in the apprehension of beauty, serves for Schopenhauer a purpose both affective and effective. In one sense, aesthetic contemplation of the world affects the individual's sense of himself or herself: a peaceful, if temporary, quieting of the will overtakes the ordinary permutations of willing, and in this state the mind is receptive to seeing for its own sake rather than for the demands of will through the principle of sufficient reason, that is, the demand for reasoned explanation as to causes, motivations, behaviors. In a second sense, aesthetic contemplation of the world effects the transition from ordinary consciousness governed by will to a superior state of awareness within what Schopenhauer terms the 'pure subject of knowing.' As the pure subject, the individual can apprehend what Schopenhauer thinks of as timeless Ideas, which distill away the essences of species-types (W2 364/H. 3, 416–17).[12]

Ideas, supervenient on nature itself, present the most adequate objectifications of will to the subject devoid of willing.[13] Will manifests itself at different 'grades' or levels of objectivity – gravitational forces sit at the lowest rung of complexity, plants emerge about half-way up, and human animals occupy the highest rung, where each individual expresses a unique Idea (idealized, essential species-type) in relation to will. Ideas are multi-sided, and even at the lower grades of will there are always new aspects of natural kinds to be apprehended and communicated (W1 224, 230/H. 2, 265, 271–2). In an ice storm or a Siberian tiger, an aloe plant or one's grandfather Joe, will moves in the world through its infinite, myriad forms. Ideas provide the most potent means by which to recognize will's pervasive presence.[14]

The Idea not only governs the content of perception for the pure subject of knowing but also grounds the creation of products – art works – designed to capture such perception. 'The apprehended Idea ... is the true and only source of every genuine work of art. In its powerful originality it is drawn only from life itself, from nature, from the world, and only by the genuine genius, or by him whose momentary inspiration reaches the point of genius' (*W1* 235/H. 2, 227). The genius apprehends the Idea and, through the power of productive imagination, completes, amplifies, fixes, retains, and repeats at pleasure 'all the significant pictures of life, according as the aims of a profoundly penetrating knowledge and of the significant work by which it is to be communicated may require' (*W2* 379/H. 3, 433).

Insofar as will has entered forms and phenomena foreign to its own nature (for will is not itself an object-form or phenomenon, but mere striving), it remains inscrutable, 'an abyss of incomprehensibilities and mysteries for our searching consideration and investigation' (*W2* 195/H. 3, 218). Science grasps phenomenal pluralities and attempts to piece together a whole from various parts. But the world itself is not an aggregate of parts, but rather One. For Schopenhauer, only art can reveal this unity through the productive, imaginative embodiment of Ideas drawn directly from their clear apprehension in nature. Thus, art's value in the philosophy of Schopenhauer emerges from its power to unveil metaphysical truth. It has palliative consequences in its reprieve from willing but functions primarily in service to non-conceptual enlightenment.

The characterization of art as an unveiling, a de-masking, a disrobing of truth from its costume in plurality, presupposes that reality is veiled, masked, clothed in illusion. Metaphors representing this state of affairs find extensive expression throughout Schopenhauer's works. Humanity's true nature is 'veiled by the capacity for dissimulation' (*W1* 156/H. 2, 186); the natures of other things exhibit themselves 'in a manner quite different from their own inner nature, and . . . therefore they appear as through a mask' (*W2* 195/H. 3, 218). The world as will is likened to a stage where objects appear clearly only on another self-conscious stage (art), which allows us to 'survey and comprehend them better. It is the play within the play, the stage on the stage in *Hamlet*' (*W1* 267/H. 2, 315). Human beings, too, act as objects on such a stage, much like puppets: 'those puppets are not pulled from the outside, but each of them bears in itself the clockwork from which its movements result' (*W2* 358/H. 3, 408–9). This vital internal energy is pervasive: it 'can be compared to a rope, stretched above the puppet-show of the world of men, on which the puppets hang by means of invisible threads ...' (*W2* 359/H. 3, 409). Veils, masks, stages – art allows one to peek behind the illusion of plurality and purpose to get nearer the heart of reality itself.

Schopenhauer's commitment to art (and philosophy) as a mode of clarification appears perhaps nowhere so vividly as in his repeated invocation of a metaphor involving kernels and husks. Will, for example, is that One of which all representation is only the visibility, the objectivity: 'It is the innermost essence, the kernel, of every particular thing and also of the whole' (*W1* 110/H. 2, 131). On many occasions Schopenhauer extends the bond between the reality of the world, will, and our perceptual grasp of that reality by noting that inasmuch as we discover will in ourselves, we discover 'the kernel of our true being' (*W2* 293/H. 3, 332). Will 'alone is the real and essential, the kernel of man, and the intellect merely its tool ...' (*W2* 229/H. 3, 258). Will does not proceed from knowledge but the other way around. As such, will 'is the *prius* of knowledge, the kernel of our being' (*W2* 293/H. 3, 332).

Just as art, therefore, aims to illuminate the world as it is, a world of will giving rise to the practical tool of cognitive representation, so does science investigate only the form of that representation, objects floating on the surface of space and time.

Therefore at the present day we see the *husk of nature* most accurately and exhaustively investigated, the intestines of intestinal worms and the vermin of vermin known to a nicety. But if anyone, such as myself for instance, comes along and speaks of the *kernel of nature*, they do not listen; they just think that this has nothing to do with the matter, and go on sifting their husks. (*W2* 178/H. 3, 197–8)

Schopenhauer's entire metaphysics, expressed here in the metaphor of kernels obscured by husks, underpins art's role in revealing the world, a role as valuable to wisdom (*Weisheit*) as that of science. Science as etiology and morphology deals with the 'husks' of objects and processes, with the forms given to us by the principle of individuation and governed by the principle of sufficient reason. Philosophy[15] and art focus on the 'kernel' of being, on will in its objective manifestations. Polarizing what is nominal and what is real, what is etiological and philosophical, what is outer and inner, what is husk and kernel (*W1* 140/H. 2, 166–7), Schopenhauer commits himself to an aesthetic of metaphysical apprehension, one whose purpose aims at the greatest possible acquaintance with the totality of being rather than with abstractly surfacing concepts.[16]

For thousands of years, claims Schopenhauer, philosophers before him made the error of presenting man as 'differing as widely as possible from the animal. Yet they felt vaguely that the difference between the two was to be found in the intellect and not in the will. From this arose in them unconsciously the tendency to make the intellect the essential and principal thing, in fact to describe willing as a mere function of the intellect' (W2 199/H. 3, 223). In Schopenhauer's view, will is primary and intellect emerges as a late-stage developmental necessity in the human species. As a result, epistemological enterprises based on systems of abstract intellect do not retain the singular metaphysical superiority they achieve in other contexts; Schopenhauer equally prizes the perceptual elucidation of the force *behind* intellect.

It is reasonable to wonder whether Schopenhauer sees art as being in tension or in competition with science. Israel Knox, for example, associated Schopenhauer's conception of genius with madness, seeing this as 'the tragic and inevitable result of a philosophy that considers art as antagonistic and superior to science.'[17] Such an assertion misrepresents Schopenhauer, who does not see science as being in opposition to art. For Schopenhauer, art confronts the same question as philosophy – the question of existence – using different techniques. Furthermore, '[t]he etiology and philosophy of nature never interfere with each other; on the contrary, they go hand in hand, considering the same objects from different points of view' (W1 140/H. 2, 167). Since art is kindred to philosophy and philosophy is not in competition with science, then art is not in competition with science either. Rather, Schopenhauer intends art to stand alongside science as a separate but equally potent method for grasping the world. Art gets at a different aspect of reality than does science; art uncovers the kernel of the world, that which *grounds* history, concept, and practical affairs.

III   THE BOUNDARIES OF ORDINARY INTELLECT

If will as the kernel of the world appears most clearly through Ideas in art (or through the experience of music), to what extent can the ordinary intellect be expected to encounter that kernel? Recall that the ordinary human experience of the world, according to Schopenhauer, alternates between restless, frustrated, painful striving against obstacles internal and external, and boredom in the face of satiation, however seldom it comes. People are 'delusively individualized throbs of craving,'[18] seen by Schopenhauer as 'human bipeds' brought together only by 'their vulgarity, pettiness, shallowness, feeblemindedness and wretchedness' (*MR* 4 513/Hn. 4/ii, 125). Given to stylized and exuberant fits of misanthropy, Schopenhauer seems to hold out little hope for human disengagement from the universal cycle of pain and passivity. '[E]very animal obviously has its intellect merely for the purpose of being able to discover and obtain its food. ... Matters are no different with man, only that the greater difficulty of his maintenance and the infinite variety of his needs have here rendered necessary a much greater measure of intellect' (*P2* 97/H. 6, 103).

This greater measure of intellect manifests itself as a sophisticated system of representation, a perceptual and conceptual matrix of space and time that allows the human animal to navigate other forms of will standing in the way of its fulfillment. Will is, after all, Schopenhauer's version of Kant's 'thing-in-itself,' the metaphysical substratum that remains inaccessible to any direct or pure form of consciousness and perception. As Timothy Sprigge notes in his commentary on Schopenhauer's theory of existence, 'Schopenhauer thinks that there must be something of which we somehow register the existence in our perceptual experience, which is what the perceived thing really is.'[19] Still, in its unreflective, non-aesthetic, non-ascetic state,[20] intellect serves will as a vassal might serve a master in search of his ends.

In fact, Schopenhauer finds disengagement from egoistic willing to be rare and intermittent among most human beings, despite their highly developed cognition. In those rare instances when it does occur, disengagement from willing emerges as aesthetic recognition of kinship among all phenomena first through nature and then through the medium of Ideas in art (or, if one chooses the ascetic path, through annihilation of will in self altogether). For the artistic genius, who displays productive as well as perceptual imagination (the result of a surplus of intellect), the process of disengagement is complex, for the Ideas must not only be apprehended but also transferred to a new context. Art, as the product of genius, is the primary catalyst in moving the ordinary intellect out of *engagement with* will and into metaphysical *contemplation of* will. In other words, contemplation of the Ideas effects an oblique but soothing knowledge of will, the kernel beneath all illusory, representational husks.

Awareness of will is not, however, limited to contemplation of Ideas in nature or art, though there is no doubt that for Schopenhauer will is grasped most purely through Ideas or through the unmediated tones of music, of which more will be said in Section V. No; while will in the particular things of the world can be *known* externally in representation through Ideas, will can be *experienced* in the immediacy of one's own body, even for the ordinary intellect still engaged in willing.

> Only in so far as every knowing being is at the same time an individual and thus a part of nature, does the approach to the interior of nature stand open to him, namely in his own self-consciousness. Here it manifests itself most immediately, and then, as we found, as *will*.
>
> Now what the Platonic *Idea* is, considered as merely objective image, mere form, and thereby lifted out of time as well as out of all relations, is the *species* or kind taken empirically and in time; this, then, is the empirical correlative of the Idea. (W2 364–5/H. 3, 417)

What the individual perceives, representationally, through the Idea in art, she also experiences, immediately, as pain, pleasure, force, joy through her body. In this spirit Schopenhauer appears to link his epistemological aesthetic of Ideas with the immediacy of will as experienced and recognized in the individual body. Recognition of will in the ordinary self is ostensibly related to will appearing under the aspect of the Idea through art.[21]

It is important to remember that Schopenhauer takes the posited unity between self and world very literally. In speculating on the possibility of the philosophy of history, for example, Schopenhauer insists that it should 'therefore recognize the identical in all events, of ancient as of modern times, of the East as of the West, and should see everywhere the same humanity, in spite of all difference in the special circumstances, in costume and customs' (W2 444/H. 3, 508). Historical record often differentiates rather than collapses events across the course of time, so it is likely that Schopenhauer's insistence on unity among diverse cultures and traditions owes its allegiance to the ontological singularity of will as an unbroken whole beneath all particular phenomena, including observation of the self. Sprigge observes that 'the yearning which is the core of me and that which is the core of you are really one single yearning which is in a state of estrangement from itself.'[22]

Upon closer inspection, however, this implied unity of will in all its manifestations – the relationship between the discovery of will in the self and the apprehension of will in the world through Ideas in art – is never a clear or comfortable one in Schopenhauer's metaphysical aesthetics. Its ambiguity undermines Schopenhauer's assertion that the interior of nature stands open to the individual through an observation of will in oneself.

Consider: we are never directly acquainted with the thing in itself, with will, but know it only in its individualized or Idealized manifestations.[23] But in Section 18 of Volume 1 Schopenhauer reveals the process of self-awareness in acts of willing, where the apprehension of one's own will is 'far more immediate than is any other. It is the point where the thing-in-itself enters the phenomenon most immediately, and is most closely examined by the knowing subject; therefore the event thus intimately known is simply and solely calculated to become the interpreter of every other' (W2 197/H. 3, 221). The ordinary intellect draws an analogy between its own experience of will and will as it governs other empirical phenomena, whose essences appear most clearly through Ideas.

Against Schopenhauer here it might be argued that, since qualitative purity of access to will as thing-in-itself never gets any more intimate than it does in immediate self-awareness, there is no *necessity* for the ordinary intellect to search for knowledge of the will through Ideas in artistic representation; no metaphysical *imperative* to unify will as manifested in other phenomena with will as examined 'most closely' in one's individual body. And if there is no real need to seek will outside the self, or to draw an analogy between will in the self and will in the world, this calls into question the epistemological role given to art in Schopenhauer's metaphysical system – for art ignites the consciousness whereby Ideas in nature are apprehended.

Furthermore, the implied singularity of will beneath all things is logically problematic within the terms of Schopenhauer's own definitions. He asserts that will discovered in oneself stands as will's most immediate phenomenon and becomes the 'interpreter of every other' phenomenon of will as encountered representationally.

But how can Schopenhauer move from the immediacy of individuated will, which is discovered non-representationally through ordinary, will-driven consciousness, to the conclusion that this same will
underlies the *whole* world, a world conveyed most purely through
Ideas, which are by contrast discovered representationally through
will-less, non-pragmatic consciousness?[24]

Perhaps it could be claimed that Schopenhauer's metaphysics requires an extension from will as immediacy in oneself to will as
portrayed through Ideas in works of art in order to overcome a perceived but illusory plurality of forms in ordinary knowledge. Art, in
this instance, galvanizes awareness of the world's essential Oneness.
Or, it might be suggested that discovery of will in oneself would remain solipsistic and unredeeming, and hence not crucial to Schopenhauer's metaphysical theory, if not extended by analogy to the apprehension of Ideas in art. Being drawn originally from nature, the
Ideas point toward the existence of a world related to but not limited
to the self. In both claims, the ordinary intellect enjoys enlargement
through the dissolution of superficial barriers between will in the
self and will in the world.

However, qualitative differences between ordinary consciousness
and the will-lessness required for aesthetic knowledge of Ideas foil
attempts at unification of will in all the world. Explicitly seeking
links between will in the self and will as represented through Ideas
just is, in itself, a performative exercise in willing, an intellectual
endeavor. Even if there is a desire or an inclination to link one's immediate apprehension of will in the body with other forms of will in
the world, these are themselves *desires* or *inclinations* – movements
of will. Will as perceived through Ideas in art stands in exact contrast
to the willing involved in any conscious attempt to meet a goal, even
the goal of will's unification.

Ideas are after all required to *induce the transition from* ordinary,
goal-governed intellect to the pure subject of knowing, from hectic
immersion in willing to an entirely different state of consciousness
in the absence of willing. There seems no consistent way to unite
such opposed modes of apprehension. Because of this, the posited
oneness of will discovered by the ordinary intellect in the self and
will as perceived by the pure subject of knowing through the Ideas
is an analogous unity only, intellectual in character. Assertions of
oneness do not *unify* will observed in the self and will objectified

through Ideas in any metaphysically substantial way whatsoever, but at most can be said to represent our understanding of will as it appears to us under radically different aspects of the world.

Here we have a troubling inability to reconcile, at the most basic level of Schopenhauer's metaphysics, his two avenues of acquaintance with will – through immediate awareness of the individual body, on the one hand, and through representational awareness of the Ideas in art, on the other (or through the direct evocation of will in music). This lack of reconciliation underscores a mild paradox that is not resolved by Schopenhauer himself. Either there is no qualitative necessity to forge a link between the awareness of will in oneself and perception of will through Ideas in art (one already has intense access to will through one's own body), thus upsetting Schopenhauer's metaphysical ideal of unity; or there is a necessity to forge such a link, but one that defeats aesthetic salvation from will due to its very basis in inclination, that is, egoistic willing.

Yet, Schopenhauer insists on the possibility of genuine if fleeting salvation from willing for even the ordinary intellect. Such salvation, however, emerges neither from the immediate awareness of will in the self nor from an intellectual inference of will in all things, but rather from immersion in the will-less subject of knowing, a state of consciousness fostered by art. Only with the help of genius can the ordinary intellect hope to enter a realm of awareness beyond an illusory self and grasp the world as will without actually willing.

IV THE REFLECTIVE PRODUCTIVITY OF GENIUS

Despite logical problems with reconciling self and world in Schopenhauer's metaphysics, it is nevertheless possible to discern a striking relationship between the way Schopenhauer characterizes the discovery of will in the self and the apprehension through Ideas of will at work in the world. The larger significance of immediate awareness of will in the self emerges in the activity of *reflection*.

He will recognize that same will not only in those phenomena that are quite similar to his own, in men and animals, as their innermost nature, but continued reflection will lead him to recognize the force that shoots and vegetates in the plant, indeed the force by which the crystal is formed, the force that turns the magnet to the North Pole ... all these he will recognize as different only in the phenomenon, but the same according to their inner nature. (*W1* 109–10/H. 2, 131)

By 'reflection' Schopenhauer clearly indicates both a movement in consciousness towards something beyond what initially appears as empirical phenomenon and a capacity to break through ordinary thinking in its application. This emphasis on reflection occurs not only here, in discussion of one's own will through the body, but also in examination of the genius as he contemplates beauty through art.

Schopenhauer contrasts the ordinary intellect immersed in the 'whirl and tumult of life' with the genius, who does not get absorbed by life's tumult but instead becomes objectively conscious of it.

> ... in this sense he is *reflective*.
> It is this *reflectiveness* that enables the painter to reproduce faithfully on canvas the nature he has before his eyes, and the poet accurately to call up again by means of abstract concepts the perceptive present by expressing it, and thus bringing it to distinct consciousness; likewise to express in words everything that others merely feel. The animal lives without any reflective-ness. Its knowledge ... remains subjective; it never becomes objective. (*W2* 382/H. 3, 437)

Soon after this, Schopenhauer declares that poets and artists express distinct curiosity about how the world is constituted. Their 'high calling' to art has 'its root in the reflectiveness which springs primarily from the distinctness with which they are conscious of the world and of themselves, and thus come to reflect on these' (*W2* 382/H. 3, 437). 'By virtue of his objectivity, the genius with *reflectiveness* perceives all that others do not see' (*P2* 418/H. 6, 446).

An intriguing pattern of connection begins to assert itself in otherwise divergent manifestations of will. First, anyone can gain immediate apprehension of will through one's own body, but the transition to a connection between that awareness and the inner life of other entities depends on the activity of a reflective consciousness. Second, since Schopenhauer has on several occasions remarked on the inadequacy of ordinary human intelligence when it comes to disengagement from willing, the odds of grasping the world as will through reflective consciousness must be quite low for ordinary persons, flung as they are into the 'whirl and tumult' of life.

Third, the genius, by contrast, applies reflective consciousness not only to knowledge of the will in himself but to the world as well. This excess of intellect expresses itself reflectively in art, which faithfully reproduces the Idea as it appeared to the genius in nature. Fourth, works of art distill and intensify the experience of the Idea to the degree that even ordinary persons are by virtue of them given a temporary respite from will. This respite allows the ordinary intellect to become the subject of knowing and engage the Ideas on an intimate level, albeit temporarily and through the artist's rendering of his own experience with them.

The contagion of reflectiveness through Ideas in art finds a firm foundation in Schopenhauer. In Chapter xxxiv of Volume 2 of *The World as Will and Representation*, he maintains that 'everyone who reads the poem or contemplates the work of art must of course contribute from his own resources towards bringing that wisdom to light' (W2 407/H. 3, 464). The condition of aesthetic affect is the employment of imagination. Coupled with reflection, imagination links the inner world of the individual to the inner world of entities beyond the self: the will discovered in the self appears, distilled and represented, in the imaginative forms of art. In the apprehension of Ideas the intellect outpaces its own purpose to perceive the kinship between its own body-experience and other forms in the world. In order to achieve this apprehension, however, the ordinary intellect requires an impetus from without, lest it remain in the striving of will through the projects of an individuated mind. That impetus, that catalyst prompting a state of pure knowing, Schopenhauer calls art.

In *On the Will in Nature* Schopenhauer acknowledges that he sees intuitive perception (*Anschauung*) as the basis of all cognition. As art is inherently perceptual, good or effective art catapults the ordinary intellect into a new realm of awareness. While most persons remain caught in 'dull seriousness' in service to will, the artistic genius indulges in 'constant play', beset as he is by an excess of intellect.[25] The genius does not need an impetus from *without* to experience realization of will through the Ideas (whereas the ordinary intellect does require such an impetus) because the genius already has that impetus *within* himself. This makes him susceptible to apprehension of the Ideas in nature *and* makes him capable of productive imagination in the creation of art to embody the Idea apprehended. The genius then tutors the rest of the world in enlightenment.

For Schopenhauer, the genius, by deed of nature, has too much intellect for the job of living at hand. Quite understandably, that intellect turns its energies to other things. It is the job of the intellect to know (*Wissen*), and the intellect of genius continues to 'know' (*Erkennen*), but in a non-discursive form and with an object that detaches itself from ordinary representations. The genius finds himself drawn to and then encountering the beautiful forms of nature. In his contemplation of natural forms, he experiences a transition to a different level of consciousness, one unfettered by the usual pushing and pulling of everyday will. Schopenhauer describes the transition in detail in Section 34 of Volume I of *The World as Will and Representation*. In a peaceful state, the genius as the pure subject of knowing apprehends what is essential to each natural form contemplated, each species-type: its Idea.[26] In recognizing the Idea as a particular grade of will's objectification, the genius encounters will not internally through the body but externally through perception devoid of time, space and sufficient reason (*W2* 364/H. 3, 417).

What is more, in this realization, the felt experience of the genius differs markedly from that of ordinary felt experience through the body. In the apprehension of the Idea, the genius grasps the essential form of a species-type in a holistic way. In such moments, object and subject feel as if they blend into one; the world as encountered (Idea) and the self as encountering (pure subject) meld into an *experientially undifferentiated* phenomenon, even as the general form of subject–object distinction must remain to support the act of conscious encounter itself.

We *lose* ourselves entirely in this object ... we forget our individuality, our will, and continue to exist only as pure subject, as clear mirror of the object, so that it is as though the object alone existed without anyone to perceive it, and thus we are no longer able to separate the perceiver from the perception, but the two have become one. ... (*W1* 178–9/H. 2, 210)

Schopenhauer's identification of this phenomenon – the 'as if' suspension of boundaries in fascinated contemplation – has long been made by artists themselves or by anyone so completely absorbed in something that time evaporates. W. H. Auden termed this phenomenon the 'eye on the object look' and saw in its occurrence the germ of civilization.

How beautiful it is,
that eye on the object look.
To ignore the appetitive goddesses,
to desert the formidable shrines ...
what a prodigious step to have taken.
There should be monuments, there should be odes,
to the nameless heroes who took it first,
to the first flaker of flints
who forgot his dinner,
the first collector of sea-shells
to remain celibate.
Where should we be but for them?
Feral still, un-housetrained, still
wandering through forests without
a consonant to our names ...[27]

   Compare Auden's celebration of contemplative immersion, and the legacy of it in civilization, to Schopenhauer's own portrait of philosophical genius.

The joy of *conceiving directly* and intuitively, correctly and sharply, the *universal and essential aspect of the world* from some angle is so great, that the man to whom it comes forgets all other aims and leaves everything where it is, in order to preserve first for himself and occasionally for others in case there should be those capable of appreciating it, at any rate a dried and colourless mummy of such knowledge, or even a crude and coarse impression of it by sketching its result in abstract concepts. (*MR* 3 23/Hn. 3, 19)

   Although Schopenhauer invokes concepts here, he speaks of philosophical perception as opposed to mere inductive reasoning – in the following paragraph he emphasizes the difference between one who aspires to 'grasp things in their totality' and one who merely 'seeks to ferret out the causal connexion of some particular phenomenon in nature'. Art, Schopenhauer asserts, seeks the totality or the whole behind the apparent plurality of forms. Also, since philosophy and art depend on genius and since they spring from asking the same question, 'What is existence?', it is reasonable to read Schopenhauer's account of contemplative immersion as applying to the intuition of Ideas as well as philosophical epiphany.
   How one *preserves* the intuition of totality is what differentiates philosophy from art. Philosophers encode their impressions in

inadequate concepts (how like music this is: encoding something sublime in notation that captures the mere skeleton of its form!). Artists create a legacy through productive imagination. 'When poets sing of a bright morning, of a beautiful evening ... the real object of their glorification is, unknown to them, the pure subject of knowing, called forth by those beauties of nature' (W2 370/H. 3, 423). When the artistic genius emerges from the state of pure contemplation, he employs his technical skills imaginatively to embody the Idea in an object which, when apprehended, will allow the ordinary intellect to have an aesthetic experience known originally to him.

The path of temporary, individual enlightenment for the ordinary intellect proceeds like this. The genius reflects on a beautiful natural object. This elicits the pure subject of knowing, which raises the perceived object to the level of Idea, whereby consciousness loses itself in contemplation. In this calm consciousness, the genius allows the object of contemplation, the Idea, to fill his apprehension; the Idea stands out of connection with any other entity, including events before it in time or the relational space around the object giving rise to it. Egoistic willing subsides and, whereas the individual knows only particulars, the pure subject of knowing grasps only Ideas (W1 178–9/H. 2, 209–11).

Once experienced, however, the Idea can be resituated by productive imagination in a new spatial location – a work of art (in music the Idea does not engender the work, nor is the product's location spatial). The art work, in turn, calls forth the pure subject of knowing from the ordinary intellect. Art has this power because the efforts of genius have abstracted the Idea from its context in nature, and hence from its relation to matters of concern to will. The removal to a context devoid of practical relations allows the Idea to make its presence felt with more potency.

Schopenhauer derives his intuition of enduring Ideas directly from Plato, and the two share a belief in the superiority of philosophical apprehension over both logical deduction and ordinary sense perception. Yet Schopenhauer never feels compelled to adopt Plato's exact ontology when it comes to the relationship between art and Ideas. On the contrary, the young Schopenhauer confidently takes note of Plato's *great error on art* in his student notebooks on the *Republic* (MR 2 436/Hn. 2, 375), an error Schopenhauer later seems to believe grows out of Plato's confusion between concepts and Ideas (W1 233/H. 2, 275–6). For Schopenhauer a concept is abstract and built

up into unity out of pluralities, while an Idea is 'absolutely perceptive' and falls into plurality through the illusion of the principle of
individuation.

It is this emphasis on perception which ultimately differentiates
Schopenhauer's approach to Ideas from that of Plato. In Plato's *Republic*, the trajectory towards the Ideas follows a distinct line of
progression, beginning at the lowest level of *images*, where copies of
physical reality are taken to be the actual world. This is the realm not
only of imitative art but of childhood, of intellectual immaturity, and
it is followed eventually by the realization that images are merely
shadows of the *visible world*, where ordinary perception yields the
presence of concrete existence. These stages of cognition remain in
the realm of belief or opinion rather than in the realm of truth, however, and only when one progresses from perception to intellection
can one begin to grasp more stable levels of reality.

Within intellection, *logical deduction and mathematics* represent activity on the lower of two levels, deriving conclusions from
facts and propositions as provided. Plato's philosopher may proceed
to the final level of enlightenment in apprehension of the *Forms* or
Ideas, where a grasp of truth comes not from deduction but out of
dialectical conversation directed toward resolution of particulars in
more stable wholes. At the level of Plato's Idea we have nothing like
representation or perception but rather a mental sense of conceptual
purity.

Schopenhauer confesses that he deviates from Plato's distinctive
path, 'pursuing not his footsteps, but our own aim' (*W1* 233/H. 2,
276). He indicates the precise location where his own understanding
of the Ideas leaves off from his predecessor's.

We may take this opportunity to mention yet another point in which our
theory of Ideas differs widely from that of Plato. Thus he teaches (*Republic*,
X [601], p. 288) that the object which art aims at expressing, the prototype
of painting and poetry, is not the Idea, but the individual thing. The whole
of our discussion so far maintains the very opposite, and Plato's opinion is
the less likely to lead us astray, as it is the source of one of the greatest and
best known errors of that great man, namely of his disdain and rejection of
art, especially of poetry. (*W1* 212/H. 2, 250)

Thus, for Schopenhauer, Ideas have nothing to do with abstract intellection, nor is their revelation entirely limited to the province of
philosophical genius. Ideas are grasped even by the ordinary intellect,

not through perception of particular entities in the physical world but through images rendered on the basis of them, rendered by the hand of real genius.

Schopenhauer turns the hierarchy of Plato topsy-turvy: the Idea is glimpsed in nature by the genius, at the level of what Plato terms the 'visible world,' and is filtered 'downward' into images, which subsequently direct the ordinary intellect 'upward' to apprehension of the Idea. Schopenhauer's apprehension remains perceptual, while Plato reserves a grasp of the Ideas for intellection, a grasp that must pass through logical and mathematical reasoning before reaching enlightenment (Schopenhauer rejects the necessity of such a passage outright, as is made clear by his distinction between aesthetics and science). Most obviously, Schopenhauer extols the virtue of images for the ordinary intellect's apprehension of Ideas; Plato undermines artistic images by placing them at several removes from reality and linking their power to appetite.

Unlike the detached, non-perceptual, rational Ideas of Plato, Schopenhauer's Ideas manage to avoid the claws of appetite without losing organic vitality. Their very capacity to alleviate pain (by removing the subject from everyday concerns and effecting her contemplative absorption in art) suggests a living and also contagious phenomenon, one brought into being by the power of genius to direct technical creativity in service to an essential apprehension (W2 420/H. 3, 479). In Schopenhauer, the ordinary intellect has the imaginative and material interventions of genius to bolster enlightenment.

Despite their differences, Plato and Schopenhauer stress the importance of metaphysics, of attending to truths which endure, rather than to the exigencies of everyday life. And they are not so very opposed on art as one might infer when comparing the status of images in their theories. While Schopenhauer embraces perception as a source of enlightenment, whereas Plato rejects it, they nevertheless agree on the inferiority of artistic literal-mindedness and simple copying within their respective systems. Plato's disparagement of mere imitation is well established, encountered not only in the *Republic* but also in the *Ion*. Schopenhauer affirms a similar line of thought when he cautions the artist against too literal a transcription of reality. '[T]he very best in art is too spiritual to be given directly to the senses; it must be born in the beholder's imagination, though it must be begotten by the work of art' (W2 408/H. 3, 465).

With the exception of music, each of the particular arts examined by Schopenhauer depends for its power on the contagion of Ideas, the capacity of the art work to transfer, via material or poetic presentation, the genius' apprehension of what is essential to any given species or natural process. And yet, that contagion relies for its efficacy on avoidance of direct imitation. Something must be left to the imagination of even the ordinary intellect for the art work to ignite perception of the Idea.

Schopenhauer sometimes equivocates over whether ordinary viewers can be moved by Ideas in nature as well as in art.[28] However, he clearly intends art to function as a catalyst toward recognizing the objectifications of will in the world, and he insists that efficacious art must be grounded in natural forms. In his discussion of several arts – architecture, hydraulics, horticulture, landscape painting, sculpture, historical painting, poetry, and music – Schopenhauer intends to demonstrate will's appearance through Ideas. Ideas become perceptually multi-sided as their objects increase in complexity. Complexity culminates in the art of music, which transcends Ideas altogether to trace out the intimate contours of time.

V ART: ITS PARTICULAR FUNCTIONS

By now we have differentiated the cognitive emphasis of art from the strictly epistemological emphasis of science; considered the boundaries of ordinary intellect in its discovery of will through immediate awareness of the body; and investigated the reflective intuition of genius in apprehending will through the Ideas in nature. Determining Schopenhauer's account of art's function in light of these foundations now becomes relatively straightforward. The foundations discussed clarify the *role* Schopenhauer *intends* for the Ideas within his aesthetic metaphysics. All arts serve the same function in proffering a gateway to recalcitrant reality. Particular elements of Schopenhauer's discussion of the arts, however, bring together his overarching concerns in aesthetics.

Schopenhauer was well positioned to consider the function of aesthetics within his larger metaphysical system, for far more than Kant, Hegel, and even Schelling, Schopenhauer cultivated an active and informed appreciation for the arts and thus avoided the remote theoretical distance more characteristic of his predecessors' works. His genuine interest in the arts manifests itself in the detail and expressiveness of his treatment of particular artistic practices, arguably most masterfully in his discussion of music.[29] Schopenhauer listened seriously to music and was himself a flutist, practising his instrument with daily enthusiasm until the last months before his death. Music was not the only art known to him, nonetheless, and throughout his extensive *Manuscript Remains* one can glean the extent to which Schopenhauer studied, thought about, and extemporized on an impressive range of art works.[30]

Some of this acquaintance with the arts no doubt came to Schopenhauer through encounters with artists of all varieties, including the great Goethe, who frequented the fashionable salons hosted by Schopenhauer's mother, Johanna. Johanna Schopenhauer enjoyed considerable fame as a writer of essays and fictions, a 24-volume set of her collected works having been published by 1831. Yet by the middle of the 1830s Johanna's fame and prestige as a writer had begun to fade, an occasion that might well have reinforced Schopenhauer's own earlier disparagement of 'mediocre poets' and their public, which 'always seizes on what is new' (*W1* 246 n./H. 2, 290n.).[31]

Schopenhauer greatly objects to any art that relies upon current fashions or personal knowledge of its context for appreciation, much as he dismisses approaches to art appreciation that stress a factual, historical, or allegorical background over what appears directly to perception (*W1* 245–8/H. 2, 288–93). Art depends directly on nature and the natural patterns of will for its power. Deviations from those patterns distract critical attention from its proper object of consideration.[32] Rather than following fashion in art or seeking the historical roots of a work's context, the 'human mind should select for its consideration that which is destined never to pass away' (*W2* 442/H. 3, 505). Within the limits of human cognition – of representation – 'The Ideas alone are permanent ...' (*W2* 443/H. 3, 506).

Schopenhauer begins his meditation on particular arts by focusing on those Ideas that evoke the character of space. *Architecture* embodies Ideas that represent the lowest grades of will's objectivity – that is, the least full expression of will as a constant striving. Representing will's discord at the lowest level, 'the conflict between gravity and rigidity is the sole aesthetic material of architecture; its problem is to make this conflict appear with perfect distinctness in many different ways' (*W1* 214/H. 2, 252). Architecture also reveals the nature of light (*W1* 216/H. 2, 255) and, when done well, has a wholesome effect on the mind. This effect is not the result of direct imitation of proportions found in flowers, trees, or the human form, which Schopenhauer considers an absurd supposition, but rather of attentive dedication to efficiency in form, which creates in the functional spirit of nature. 'The great merit of the architect consists in his achieving and attaining purely aesthetic ends, in spite of their subordination to other ends foreign to them' (*W1* 217/H. 2, 256).

Schopenhauer's passing remarks on *hydraulics* and *horticulture* reveal his admiration for the forms of the natural world. Hydraulics, in the artistic arrangement of water, seeks to balance fluidity and gravity. Like architecture, it inculcates the lowest grades of will's objectification, that is, phenomena owing their character not to movements in consciousness, behavior, or growth but to the more basic permutations of physical processes. Landscape modification has less practical application than architecture and it also utilizes vegetation, that is, material at a slightly higher grade of will's objectification. Horticulture is nevertheless a less accomplished art than architecture, in Schopenhauer's view, and presents ample possibility for excessive artistic interference, which bungles an otherwise pleasing effect. 'The beauty displayed by it belongs almost entirely to nature; the art itself does little for it. On the other hand, this art can also do very little against the inclemency of nature, and where nature works not for but against it, its achievements are insignificant' (*W1* 218/ H. 2, 257).

Although Schopenhauer believes that the plant world offers itself everywhere for enjoyment without interpretation or mediation by art, he still determines the proper art form for the representation of the Ideas plants offer. Under the rubric of *landscape painting* Schopenhauer groups three different sorts of depictions: still life, ruins, and church interiors; landscape painting proper (living plants in their environments); and paintings with animals. The division is an important one, for Schopenhauer demonstrates within it that point of transition between the emphasis on the pure subject of knowing in aesthetic experience and emphasis instead on the Ideas in apprehension.

Representation as a cognitive possibility can take place because it assumes the form of being-object-for-a-subject. When the ordinary intellect experiences the shift from domination by will into will-lessness, representation is no longer structured by the conventional dichotomies of egoistic subject and necessary object but rather occurs between the pure subject of knowing and the Ideas. Although Schopenhauer has asserted that aesthetic experience effects a sense of melding between subject and object, he nevertheless admits that within such experience one side or the other of the pairing will usually be dominant. Both the pure subject of knowing and the Idea must always be present in aesthetic experience, but the relation between them may tilt to one side or the other in response to the grade of objectification at issue.[33] The grade of will's objectification determines where the stress will fall, with depiction or expression of the lower grades promoting the subjective side through a peaceful frame of mind and depiction or expression of the higher grades emphasizing the objective side through facets of an Idea.

Thus, in architecture, hydraulics, and landscape architecture, peaceful pleasure in the pure subject of knowing predominates over apprehension of the Idea, and the value of encountering these arts resides in their effect on the mind. In the contemplation of paintings depicting still life, ruins, or church interiors, Schopenhauer stresses the transfer of the artist's state of mind through the painting. Benefit accrues to the viewer's subjective side through sympathy with the 'reflected feeling of the profound spiritual peace and the complete silence of the will, which [are] necessary for plunging knowledge so deeply into those inanimate objects, and for comprehending them with such affection, in other words with such a degree of objectivity' (*WI* 219/H. 2, 258).

In what Schopenhauer calls 'landscape painting proper', there is a striking balance between the pure subject of knowing and the Ideas. Although the will-lessness of the artist's consciousness continues to exude its power through paint, the subject matter of plants in their habitats balances the subjective side of contemplation with more objective considerations. Plants, growing and changing in response to environmental stimuli, represent a higher grade of will's objectification than gravity, ruins, or fruit.

When Schopenhauer turns to depictions of animals in both paint and sculpture, he concedes an even higher grade of will's objectification, a grade that swings the balance of emphasis towards representation through Ideas. 'The peace of the subject who knows these Ideas, who has silenced his own will, is present, as indeed it is in any aesthetic contemplation, but its effect is not felt, for we are occupied with the restlessness and impetuosity of the depicted will' (*W1* 219/H. 2, 258). While paintings stress only plant or animal forms, *sculpture* depicts the action, position, and deportment of an animal species. The stress falls firmly on the objective side of representation – on the power of Ideas to reveal nature's truth.

Strangely enough, while animal sculpture best reveals the character of any given species by portraying an animal in three dimensions and in motion, sculpture is less able to evoke the expressive character of human individuals than is painting. The reasons for this arise from a distinction between the grades of objectification obtained by animals and humans.

[I]t is one of the distinguishing features of mankind that therein the character of the species and that of the individual are separated so that ... each person exhibits to a certain extent an Idea that is wholly characteristic of him. Therefore the arts, aiming at a presentation of the Idea of mankind, have as their problem both beauty as the character of the species, and the character of the individual, which is called *character par excellence*. Again, they have this only in so far as this character is to be regarded not as something accidental and quite peculiar to the man as a single individual, but as a side of the Idea of mankind, specially appearing in this particular individual; and thus the presentation of this individual serves to reveal this Idea. (*W1* 224/H. 2, 265)

As individual humans are more complex than individual animals, having obtained self-consciousness as well as knowledge about the world, they express a higher degree of will's objectification than do particular animals. For Schopenhauer, beauty is attributed to the shape or form of a species in general, while expression is linked with the character of the particular human individual. When the aim is to portray the grace and beauty of the human form, the artist is best served by depicting the human being through sculpture, since sculpture conveys both the spatial (beauty) and the temporal (grace) dimensions of the species at rest or in motion. '[B]eauty unfolds itself more completely to contemplation from several points of view; on the other hand, the expression, the character, can be completely apprehended from a single viewpoint' (*W1* 226/H. 2, 266).

When the goal is to depict the Idea of humanity in self-conscious individuality, *historical painting* provides the superior medium for expression. Schopenhauer stresses yet again that the artist does not merely copy the beauty of a particular countenance but rather anticipates and modifies it in depiction. The beauty as anticipated is partly present a priori, before particular experience, for both the artist and the connoisseur 'are themselves the "in-itself" of nature, the will objectifying itself. For, as Empedocles said, like can be recognized only by like; only nature can understand herself; only nature will fathom herself; but also only by the mind is the mind comprehended' (WI 222–3/H. 2, 262–3). Yet, the artist must also have experience of beauty in the world to 'obtain life, precision and range' in its modification (W2 420/H. 3, 479). The depiction of human individuals through historical painting thus integrates beauty, grace, *and* character in a timeless moment, raising the individual depicted to the Idea of its species and bringing to light sides of the Idea that rarely appear.

Only the inward significance of action in historical paintings has merit within Schopenhauer's aesthetics. The outward significance of events depicted is of no metaphysical consequence to him, for history is an exercise in sufficient reason, functioning much like science in unearthing facts for understanding.

History shows us mankind just as a view from a high mountain shows us nature. We see a great deal at a time, wide stretches, great masses, but nothing is distinct or recognizable according to the whole of its real nature. On the other hand, the depicted life of an individual shows us the person, just as we know nature when we walk about among her trees, plants, rocks, and stretches of water. (WI 248/H. 2, 292–3)

Indeed, for Schopenhauer there is more 'inner truth' in *poetry* than there is in history. In painting, he prefers us to understand the Idea of humanity by contemplating the universal struggles of individuals, rather than by unraveling the factual context of a painting's creation or by estimating the historical accuracy of events as portrayed in the frame. Similarly, Schopenhauer encourages us to turn to poetry or autobiography rather than to history if we wish to discover the inner nature not only of humanity but of the world.

If the form of human character can be conveyed in paint, the inner recesses of that character are more fully realized through the medium of words, for 'the presentation of man in the connected series of his efforts and actions, is thus the great subject of poetry' (WI 244/H. 2, 288). Paintings normally depict a particular action or effort. Because human cognition encompasses self-conscious memory, however, the highest degree of will's objectification is obtained in the representation of a series of actions as they occurred through time (W1 245/H. 2, 288–9). Human consciousness has both spatial and temporal aspects, so will is revealed in more of its facets through poetic reflection on these aspects, a reflection itself temporarily devoid of spatial and temporal practicalities. Furthermore, 'all that has ever moved a human heart, and all that human nature produces from itself in any situation, all that dwells and broods in any human breast – all these are his theme and material, and with these all the rest of nature as well' (W1 249/H. 2, 294).

Perhaps its seems odd that Schopenhauer elevates poetry to the highest level of those arts which inculcate Ideas: poems consist of words, which in turn relay abstract conceptions. How can Schopenhauer privilege poetry when poems are impossible without concepts? While he admits that concepts are necessary for poetic understanding and also for poetic expression itself, Schopenhauer notes that poems begin with concepts but do not remain cloistered within abstract universality. 'Just as the chemist obtains solid precipitates by combining perfectly clear and transparent fluids, so does the poet know how to precipitate, as it were, the concrete, the individual, the representation of perception, out of the abstract, transparent universality of the concepts by the way in which he combines them' (W1 243/H. 2, 286–7). Rhythm and rhyme provide aesthetically secondary but useful catalysts in precipitating poetry for the listener or reader by engaging the play of imagination in the conversion of concepts to images.

Repeating a division he used in the division of landscape painting, Schopenhauer divides poetic art into three classes: lyric, epic, and dramatic. Lyrical poetry remains the most subjective of the three, its style as well as its subject matter dwelling upon the tumult of embodied, emotive consciousness (for this reason, Schopenhauer notes that lyrical poetry is best suited to the young, who often seem trapped within just such a subjectivity but for whom subjectivity takes up the whole world!). Epic poetry partakes of subjectivity insofar as its style remains couched in playful meter and convivial tone. Yet, in both romance narratives and spiritual quests, epics involve more outward and serious portrayals of individuals who struggle to live, meet challenges, or obtain goals. In this sense, epics tend more to objectivity than lyrical efforts do.

Finally, the very highest and most objective form of poetry occurs in tragic drama, where both the prose and the subject matter – the sublime attempt of the individual to deny will altogether – invoke a level of *gravitas* unwitnessed in lyrics and epics. '[T]he summons to turn away the will from life remains the true tendency of tragedy, the ultimate purpose of the intentional presentation of the sufferings of mankind' (W2 435/H. 3, 497). Tragedy finds its opposing form in comedy, where the will to life is not only affirmed but often laughed at and made benign. Schopenhauer does not appear to object to comedy per se but rather cautions his reader against too ready an acceptance of its metaphysical message – that existence on the whole is quite good and generally amusing.[34]

Although Schopenhauer indicates tragedy as the highest of all arts in its capacity to depict will at the highest level of objectification – will's own self-denial – he nonetheless proclaims *music* as the most powerful of all the arts (W1 256; W2 448/H. 2, 302–3; H. 3, 512). 'Music . . . gives the innermost kernel preceding all form, or the heart of things' (W1 263/H. 2, 311). Other arts are phenomenal by nature, copying the Idea first apprehended in nature and thus attaining only adequate objectivity. Music, by contrast, is the immediate evocation of will, an objective and direct copy not of Ideas but of will itself (W1 257; W2 447/H. 2, 304; H. 3, 511). Music unveils the inner life of emotion and thought without the accompaniment of actual pain or emotion, and so opens up the full spectrum of will found in nature (W2 451/H. 3, 515–616).

Like the other arts, music can and does have what Schopenhauer considers an 'outer significance,' in this case music's technical dimensions such as mathematical proportions in harmony or the symmetrical form of a symphony. He dismisses these as secondary to music's value. He also disparages program music and other naive attempts to shape music as a representational art (W1 263/H. 2, 310–11). Music is an exceedingly universal language, and so only the inner significance of music matters metaphysically for Schopenhauer: its appeal, he tells us, must remain visceral and not overtly symbolic in order to be effective. Yet, he reserves some aspect of symbol in lauding music's particular power. While rejecting the 'simple realism' of program music, Schopenhauer nevertheless sees the structure of music itself as paralleling the forms of will in the world (W1 259; W2 449/H. 2, 305–6; H. 3, 513–14).

Bass notes ground harmony but do not move themselves as a melody. Their anchoring, low-tonal notes correspond to gravity and the very lowest grades of will's objectification. Ripienos, the middle to high range notes, do indeed move but only in response to necessary stimuli around them. They enter into harmony as well, and so, like the animal kingdom, are positioned between human beings and earthly forces. Finally, musical melody, the highest and principal voice, travels its course to a goal. It sets the tone and structure for the other levels and thus corresponds to human intentionality. The voice of melody mirrors the path of self-conscious will in the world.

In this analogy as in other places, Schopenhauer makes evident the special relationship obtaining between mental life, on the one hand, and the aesthetic way human beings experience their environments, on the other. Music more than any other art unifies self and other. It provides Schopenhauer's most compelling evidence for a metaphysical connection between immediate awareness of will in the self and will in the external world. 'This close relation that music has to the true nature of all things can also explain the fact that, when music suitable to any scene, action, event, or environment is played, it seems to disclose to us its most secret meaning, and appears to be the most accurate and distinct commentary on it' (W1 262/H. 2, 310). Music, along with but slightly more so than the other arts, brings will to its own self-awareness in moments of human reflection.

VI ART: FIDELITY TO FOUNDATIONS

Schopenhauer thus intends art to have a function as well as a foundation; art can be judged as good or bad with reference to these. Art, for Schopenhauer, exists as salvation from will because of the palliative form of its apprehension. Contemplation of Ideas or reflection on music occurs in the peaceful space of objective, will-less knowing. In essence, art affects the pure subject of knowing where enlightenment would otherwise fail to occur among will-governed, human-type bipeds.

Whether speaking of the low-grade architectural arts or the high-grade form of tragedy, Schopenhauer is unequivocal about the basis for genuine achievement in the non-musical arts: 'the apprehension of the objective essence of things which constitutes their (Platonic) Idea ... must be the basis of every achievement in the fine arts' (P2

418/H. 6, 445).[35] 'Apprehension of an Idea, its entry into our consciousness, comes about only by means of a change in us. ... For only thus does knowledge become the pure mirror of the objective inner nature of things. A knowledge so conditioned must be the basis of every genuine work of art as its origin' (W2 367/H. 3, 419). 'Every good painting, every genuine poem, bears the stamp of the frame of mind it depicts. For only what has sprung from perception, indeed from purely objective perception, or is directly stimulated by it, contains the living germ from which genuine and original achievements can result' (W2 371/H. 3, 424).

Art must bring significant individuals, drawn from nature, before our eyes in a way that erases the contingency of accident to reveal what is essential to the species. '[T]he inward significance is the depth of insight into the Idea of mankind which it discloses, in that it brings to light sides of that Idea which rarely appear' (W1 230/H. 2, 272). Here Schopenhauer alludes again to the kernel beneath mere representation – will – which we know directly through bodily experience but apprehend differently and objectively through its portrayal in the art of genius. The emphasis once again falls not on concepts but on apprehension, on what appears.

In contrast to apprehension of the Idea, one might seek in the arts conceptual activity; this, for Schopenhauer, would constitute an abuse of art's function. 'What is merely thought in connexion with the picture becomes of the greatest importance, and interferes with what is perceived. If, even on stage, it is not right for the main incident to take place behind the scenes ... it is obviously a far greater fault in the picture' (W1 232/H. 2, 273–4). The rejection of art on the basis of its allegiance to concepts shows up throughout Schopenhauer's discussion of individual arts.

In architecture, good art focuses on the conflict between gravity and stone, given as this is to promoting calm contemplation. Bad architecture, by contrast, features imitative whimsy through decorative forms. For Schopenhauer, imitation is a conceptual activity, and whimsical play diverts attention away from the force of gravity's impact on stone and toward superficial and unnecessary appellations. Associations called up by architecture must not allude to signs, myths, or symbols but only to the pull of earth's force on those objects standing on it, the magnet of will.

For the visual arts, especially painting, features such as color and harmony of grouping are secondary to perception of Ideas of plant

forms or individuals within the frame or on the plinth. More crucially, because Ideas must reveal aspects of species types and because they are necessary to achieve (non-musical) aesthetic escape
from willing, any painting that indulges in or derives its significance from allusion, historical representation, or allegory neglects
its true function. Since allegory is a form of linking symbols with
concepts through convention alone and not through any natural association, it not only detracts from the mission of art by turning
away from perception; allegory symbolizes something it does not
show (*W1* 237/H. 2, 279–80). In doing so, it deviates from art's roots
in experienced *nature* as the seed of its conception.

'Hence through the allegory a concept is always to be signified,
and consequently the mind of the beholder has to be turned aside
from the depicted representation of perception to one that is quite
different, abstract, and not perceptive, and lies entirely outside the
work of art' (*W1* 237/H. 2, 280). For Schopenhauer, the semiotic of
will is indexical in ourselves and iconic in execution through art.
It is never purely symbolic, never dependent entirely on conceptual
association. 'Now, if there is absolutely no connexion between what
is depicted and the concept indicated by it … but the sign and the
thing signified are connected quite conventionally by positive fixed
rule casually introduced, I call this degenerate kind of allegory *symbolism [Symbol]*' (*W1* 239/H. 2, 282).

In opposition to symbol, Schopenhauer underscores the non-conceptual genesis not only of art but also of its logical predecessor,
original apprehension.

All concepts, all things that are thought, are indeed only abstractions, and
consequently partial representations from perception, and have arisen merely through our thinking something away. All profound knowledge, even wisdom proper, is rooted in the *perceptive* apprehension of things. … A *perceptive* apprehension has always been the process of generation in which every
genuine work of art, every immortal idea, received the spark of life. All
original and primary thinking takes place figuratively. On the other hand,
from *concepts* arise the works of mere talent, merely rational ideas, imita-
tions, and generally everything calculated only for the present need and for
contemporary events. (*W2* 378/H. 3, 432–3)[36]

Note the stress here and elsewhere on perceptive apprehension as
generative, as isolating the living germ, as getting at the essence.
This recalls Schopenhauer's pervasive allusions to kernels and husks

in differentiating metaphysical or artistic apprehension from conceptual or scientific knowing. Kernels are also seeds, embryonic life forms. In straightforward statements as well as in metaphors, Schopenhauer pays tribute to the capacity of genuine art to jumpstart metaphysical awareness.

What matters in poetic drama, for example, is neither accordance with history and fact nor sweeping panoramas for action, but rather 'the truly depicted life of the individual in a narrow sphere [that] shows the conduct of men in all its nuances and forms . . .' (*W1* 247/ H. 2, 291). In other words, good narrative needs strong characters and pregnant situations (*W1* 251/H. 2, 296). The manner of depiction – its fidelity to truth – reminds one of Schopenhauer's commitment to aesthetic realization: 'If only the true is beautiful, and the most cherished adornment of truth is nakedness, then an Idea which appears great and beautiful in prose will have even more true worth than one that has the same effect in verse' (*W2* 429/H. 3, 489–90). Just as color and harmony are secondary characteristics of painting, rhyme and meter are secondary characteristics of speech. Even as he proclaims the power of the Idea, Schopenhauer moves his theory of the arts toward the condition of his other pathway to salvation: the pure, the clear, the ascetic.

In tragedy, the hero struggles against pain, defeat, boredom; in short, against will. His eventual, sublime transcendence over will vitiates will's stranglehold, and the observer, in witnessing the tragic hero's turn away from will through its denial in himself, apprehends for herself the side of an Idea both ennobling and self-denying (*W1* 253; *W2* 433/H. 2, 298–9; H. 3, 495). Schopenhauer admires the great Greek tragedies, as well as much of Shakespeare, for their stress on the timeless struggle of individuals in the face of life's repeated challenges. By contrast, he dismisses drama that is too 'timely' or concerned (as is the way of youth) with 'outward' appearances instead of with will as it is discovered through the Ideas. As mentioned in Section V, fashionable drama depends too heavily on encoded signs whose potential for clear interpretation fades with the context that bore them.

Finally, Schopenhauer returns discussion to matters of immediate apprehension with a consideration of aberrations in music. Music requires *no* words to make itself known, and so Schopenhauer considers opera an inferior hybrid of drama and music, where both would be best left alone (*P2* 433/H. 6, 461–2). In his own theory he merges the referential aspect of art (music as heard refers directly to will without spatial representation) with the formal aspect (just as one feels will in the self, so one feels music in the rhythm of one's heart),[37] thus separating music from the other arts in bypassing cognition through Ideas. As Lydia Goehr notes, 'Music is pure temporal process, the dynamics of which directly correspond to the flow of Will's emotional life.'[38] 'Instrumental music is the perfect language that speaks temporally from within itself; it is unsullied by empirical content.'[39]

Bryan Magee agrees that there is something special about time in Schopenhauer's philosophy.[40] Certainly Schopenhauer isolates music as the most supreme of all arts due to its immediate evocation of will, much like immediate access of one's intellect to will through the body. Will in the body has a palpable dimension, a felt experiential quality that does not always retreat to a particular location; its effect can be diffuse. In other words, will in the self is experienced as something *felt while* intellect considers it, rather than as something *located* representationally in the world. It approximates to musical rhythm, a tactile occurrence that also manifests itself aurally. Will's texture as experienced by individuals is thus understood temporally, as a phenomenon moving through time, almost entirely without spatial representation in the aural experience of it (its notational representation cannot be heard and so symbolizes, rather than functions as, music).

The musical genius, therefore, does not need to turn to the imaginative production of representations or materials to express an essential aspect of a species-type through the Idea. Rather, in noting the form of music, the genius allows the dynamic of will to possess him. Its patterns flow through his ears to the hands, to the instrument, the pen, and not through concepts (*W1* 258/H. 2, 304–5). 'Thus music is as *immediate* an objectification and copy of the whole *will* as the world itself is, indeed as the Ideas are, the multiplied phenomenon of which constitutes the world of individual things' (*W1* 257/H. 2, 304). 'As a result of all this, we can regard the phenomenal world, or nature, and music as two different expressions of the same thing; and this thing itself is therefore the only medium of their analogy, a knowledge of which is required if we are to understand that analogy' (*W1* 262/H. 2, 309).

The analogy of music and nature cannot be understood conceptually; it is not a comparison of concepts, for music resists all content and thus linguistic definition. How then are they to be understood? Through the oblique prism of imaginative reflection. The discovery of will in the self and the experience of hearing music involve immediacy. Just as discovery of will in the self relies upon the potential for imaginative reflection to move beyond the illusion of isolated individuality, so too does music bypass the borders of concrete form to evoke the form of the will most directly. Music, while taking shape through genius in notation outside the self, can also be accompanied within the self. Schopenhauer sees music as the most abstractly universal and yet the most intimately individual form of art. In its apprehension the individual apprehends herself and the whole of nature as well. A heart beats: one hears it, one feels it. Such is it with music: sound and felt time merge through the body of humanity.

Music needs no Idea to mediate its presence, for it is always already among us. The texture of its apprehension is woven of time as felt through the body, of reflection turned back as an echo in singing. In the other great arts, the pure subject of knowing melds with the Idea in an *experientially undifferentiated* whole of contemplative absorption. In great music, the will meets with itself in profound rhythms of embodied sound. If non-musical art remains faithful to its function by standing naked on its foundation of apprehension through Ideas, Ideas emerging from species types in nature, then music needs no faith, for it *is* the foundation and the human heart its species – a self-apprehensive mode of expression of will in succession through time.[41]

NOTES

1   *MR* 4 304/Hn. 4/i, 269.
2   *On the Will in Nature,* subtitled *A Discussion of the Corroborations from the Empirical Sciences that the Author's Philosophy Has Received Since Its First Appearance.*
3   Rudiger Safranski, *Schopenhauer and the Wild Years of Philosophy,* trans. Ewald Osers (Cambridge, Mass.: Harvard University Press, 1989), 293.
4   *WI* 110/H. 2, 131.
5   Safranski, *Schopenhauer and the Wild Years of Philosophy,* 217–18.

6 Byran Magee, review of Dale, Jacquette, *Schopenhauer, Philosophy and the Arts* (Cambridge: Cambridge Unviersity Press, 1996) in *Times Literary Supplement* 4864 (1997), 8.

7 Christopher Janaway discusses Schopenhauer's distinction between *Erkenntniß*, meaning cognition or realization, and *Wissen*, meaning knowledge of a propositional or conceptual sort. He concludes that only conceptual, transferable propositions can be called 'knowledge' in a traditional epistemological sense, whereas empirically based apprehensions or intuitions are more properly called 'cognition.' Although it is the case that *Erkenntniß* means 'cognition' in a philosophically technical sense, it is also possible to translate Schopenhauer's use of the word as 'realization' in some contexts, especially those where he stresses the ideas of vision, apprehension, and unveiling. Payne amalgamates *Erkenntniß* and *Wissen* without making any distinction between them whatsoever. I shall attempt to make the relevant distinctions where needed but shall also refrain from avoiding too distracting an emphasis on cognition when the point at hand calls for realization as apprehension. See Christopher Janaway, *Self and World in Schopenhauer's Philosophy* (Oxford: Clarendon Press, 1989), 51, 161–2.

8 Safranski, *Schopenhauer and the Wild Years of Philosophy*, 287.

9 *P2* 287/H. 6, 305.

10 The ancient Sumerians were a deeply pessimistic people, reacting in part to the extreme environmental conditions in Mesopotamia, a land of dramatic contrasts. Schopenhauer is not unlike them in predicating a metaphysical system on the natural patterns revealed around him. Notes historian Warren Hollister, 'Weeks of blistering heat might be followed by torrential rains that turned fields into marshlands and immobilized the population ... the price of civilization in Mesopotamia was constant insecurity. The Sumerians projected this ever-present dread into their conceptions of humanity and its gods.' See C. Warren Hollister, *Roots of the Western Tradition: A Short History of the Ancient World* (New York: McGraw-Hill, 1991), 17.

11 Safranski, *Schopenhauer and the Wild Years of Philosophy*, 345.

12 The conceptualization of the aesthetic as 'effective' is used cautiously here, as consciousness outside ordinary willing is not causal at all. Still, aesthetic contemplation is a condition for the enlightenment of the pure subject of knowing and, as some transition must take place between ordinary consciousness and the pure subject, that transition is here aligned with aesthetic contemplation.

13 Schopenhauer borrows the concept and terminology of the 'Idea' from Plato, though the extent of consistency between the two thinkers remains in scholarly dispute. Schopenhauer considers his own Ideas to be

direct descendants of their Platonic forebears (P_I 46 /H. 5, 50–1) but nevertheless feels free to modify Plato's ontological hierarchy to suit his own metaphysical purposes. This will be taken up in the final section, but for a thorough examination of Schopenhauer's debt to Plato, consult Christopher Janaway, 'Knowledge and Tranquility: Schopenhauer on the Value of Art,' in Jacquette, *Schopenhauer, Philosophy and the Arts*, 39–61. Other relatively recent examinations of Plato's philosophy and Schopenhauer include William Desmond, 'Schopenhauer and the Dark Origin of Art,' in Eric von der Luft (ed.), *Schopenhauer: Essays in Honor of His 200th Birthday* (Lewiston, Maine: The Edwin Mellen Press, 1988), 101–22; and James Chansky, 'Schopenhauer and Platonic Ideas: A Groundwork for an Aesthetic Metaphysics' in von der Luft, op. cit., 67–81.

14 John Atwell notes correctly that the purity of vision attained in aesthetic contemplation cannot be entirely devoid of will, for knowledge itself, even that of the Ideas, depends upon our capacity for representation, which is an outgrowth of intellect and thus of will. Nevertheless, in aesthetic contemplation we are able to renounce egoistic or subjective willing, thus clearing a path for more adequately objective perceptions of Ideas in the world. See Atwell, *Schopenhauer on the Character of the World* (Berkeley: University of California Press, 1995), 155.

15 See W2 407/H. 3, 464–5: philosophy and art aim at the same ends by different methods, function as two sides of the same coin or as wine to grapes.

16 For a clear exposition of the different functions of ideas as 'contemplative intuitions' and of concepts as 'rational abstractions,' see Bernard Bykhovsky, *Schopenhauer and the Ground of Existence*, trans. Philip Moran (Amsterdam: B. R. Grüner Publishing Co., 1984), 147–8.

17 Israel Knox, 'Schopenhauer's Aesthetic Theory,' in Michael Fox, ed., *Schopenhauer: His Philosophical Achievement* (Brighton: Harvester Press, 1980), 137.

18 T. L. S. Sprigge, *Theories of Existence* (Middlesex: Penguin Books Ltd., 1984), 90.

19 Ibid., 79.

20 Meditative withdrawal from all types of willing provides human beings with the most enduring form of escape and salvation from will. As this is the subject of another chapter, however, and as we are here concerned with the more temporary escape of aesthetic salvation, ascetic practices will not be discussed.

21 Safranski, *Schopenhauer and the Wild Years of Philosophy*, 263.

22 Sprigge, *Theories of Existence*, 86.

23 See Atwell, *Schopenhauer on the Character of the World*, 126, and Bryan Magee, *The Philosophy of Schopenhauer*, 2nd edition (Oxford: Clarendon

Press, 1997). This new edition of Magee's classic work includes an extensive discussion of several misconceptions of Schopenhauer's thought, one of which is the belief that individual human beings have direct, unmediated access to the thing-in-itself.

24 Janaway, *Self and World in Schopenhauer's Philosophy*, 195-9. This account provides a very detailed analysis of the problematic nature of the subject–object configuration of consciousness and establishes the necessary futility of any explanatory account holding between the thing-in-itself and the apprehension of will through immediacy or other forms of cognition.

25 *WN* 83/H. 4, 77.

26 Atwell believes that the genius not only apprehends but actually effects Ideas, thus relegating Ideas to a subsidiary ontological status caused by or brought into being by pure knowing. Schopenhauer does admit that the pure subject 'raises the contemplated object to the Idea' (*W1* 179/H. 2, 211), though the exact power of such 'raising' is not entirely clear.

27 W. H. Auden, 'Horae Canonicae,' in *Selected Poems*, ed. Edward Mendelson (New York: Vintage Books, 1979), 220-1.

28 I have discussed these tensions in Schopenhauer previously. See Cheryl Foster, 'Schopenhauer's Subtext on Natural Beauty,' *British Journal of Aesthetics* 32 (1992), 21-32; and Cheryl Foster, 'Schopenhauer and Aesthetic Recognition,' in Jacquette, ed., *Schopenhauer, Philosophy and the Arts*, 133-49.

29 Several detailed accounts of Schopenhauer's review of the arts themselves have been offered in other contexts. Schopenhauer writes fluidly and well, but, as was the fashion in 19th-century German philosophy, he explores his artistic preferences and prejudices ad nauseam while sometimes neglecting to cultivate a critical distance. For strong synopses of Schopenhauer's catalogue of the arts, see Patrick Gardiner, *Schopenhauer* (Middlesex: Penguin Books, 1967); David Hamlyn, *Schopenhauer* (London: Routledge & Kegan Paul, 1980); Georg Simmel, *Schopenhauer and Nietzsche* trans. Helmut Loiskandl, Deena Weinstein, and Michael Weinstein (Amherst: University of Massachusetts Press, 1986); Bryan Magee, *The Philosophy of Schopenhauer*, 2nd edition. Schopenhauer's lasting contribution to aesthetic theory might not in fact be his criticism of the arts themselves (perhaps with the exception of music), but rather the manner in which he conceives their value.

30 See, for example, *MR* 1 337-9/Hn. 1, 306-8, where even at a young age Schopenhauer is confident about his views on allegory in the arts.

31 Schopenhauer neither respected nor got on well with his mother, and she could not embrace his curmudgeonly personality or self-absorbed devotion to philosophy. Although she attained more immediate fame than

her son during her years of productivity, his would prove to be the more enduring, for today her works are rarely if ever read. On an unusually symbolic note, she began her memoirs under straitened financial conditions during late 1837 but died when she reached the point of Arthur's birth in April 1838.

32 When Schopenhauer was seeking a new home for himself in 1814, he sought a place which, first among many things, was 'a place of residence which would offer me the beauties of nature.' His commitment to the aesthetics of nature is unwavering throughout his main philosophical works, though often this commitment is obscured by his overarching attentions to art. See Safranski, *Schopenhauer and the Wild Years of Philosophy*, 191.

33 For a compact and accurate table depicting the ontological relationship among the grades of objectification, see Atwell, *Schopenhauer on the Character of the World*, 137.

34 In W1 225–6/H. 2, 265–6 Schopenhauer suggests that sculpture conveys the will to live, while painting expresses will's denial. An intriguing connection can be drawn between this observation and his comments on comedy: comic depiction, especially the 'burlesque' identified by Schopenhauer, often depends upon physical exaggeration and slapstick convention for its effect. These devices are much more physical in character than the subtle and muted tones mastered by the truly accomplished dramatic actor. Too much physicality reduces serious drama to caricature or pastiche and thus robs it of any grave impression it may wish to leave. Comedy, by contrast, often benefits from exuberant excess of action and gesture and leaves everyone feeling merry.

35 For critical discussions on the ontology of the Idea, see Atwell, *Schopenhauer on the Character of the World*, 133–7.

36 Payne's translation of one particular sentence in this quotation runs counter to something of great importance to Schopenhauer. Schopenhauer asserts, 'Alles Urdenken geschieht in Bildern,' which Payne translates as 'All original and primary thinking takes place figuratively.' This is problematic for two reasons. First, the word 'figurative' in English means to use a concept metaphorically or non-literally: because it involves substituting one set of properties for another, this raises the question of whether 'figurative' connotes the conventional, symbolic mental activity scorned by Schopenhauer. While he allows for metaphors in poetry, he does so only because they lead *away* from concepts towards images. Now, a figurative utterance, even a silent one, is just that – an utterance – and logically prior to that utterance comes the *perception* of properties shared by two different entities. Therefore, it seems unlikely that Schopenhauer intends original thinking to take place linguistically rather than

imagistically. This leads to the second problem in the translation: *Bildern* means, quite literally, 'pictures'; I can find no archaic use of 'Bildern' for 'figürlich.' *Urdenken* also has no English equivalent. A literal translation would read, 'All proto-thinking takes place in pictures.' I believe that Schopenhauer wishes to make a claim like this: 'All foundational thinking occurs imagistically' or, more awkwardly, 'All true thinking occurs pictorially.' Payne also translates *Erkenntniß* as 'knowledge' in this passage but, given Schopenhauer's distinction between *Erkenntniß* (cognition, realization) and *Wissen* (knowledge in a propositional sense), this detracts from the emphasis here on the apprehensive quality of this insight. True insight comes to us through perception in the form of realization. The overall tone is one of spontaneous seeing rather than deliberate inference.

37 This point is discussed in a similar fashion by Lawrence Ferrarra, 'Music as the Embodiment of the Will,' in Jacquette, op. cit., 195–6.

38 Lydia Goehr, 'Schopenhauer and the Musicians: an Inquiry into the Sounds of Silence and the Limits of Philosophizing about Music,' in Jacquette, *Schopenhauer, Philosophy and the Arts*, 206.

39 Ibid., 217.

40 Magee, *The Philosophy of Schopenhauer*, 130.

41 I am grateful to Christopher Janaway for making insightful suggestions which led to the improvement of this essay; to Ronald Hepburn, with whom many of the ideas explored here were first discussed; and to my students and colleagues at the University of Rhode Island, whose patience allowed me to test earlier versions of the essay for general inscrutability.

8   Schopenhauer's Narrower Sense of Morality

Arthur Schopenhauer's philosophizing was motivated by ethical questions and concerns from its dawn to its twilight. In 1813, as he initiated his labour on his main work, *The World as Will and Representation* (1819), Schopenhauer envisioned a philosophy that would be metaphysics and ethics in one.[1] Seventeen years later, with the vain hope of drawing an audience sufficient to justify a second edition of his unsuccessful main work, he published his additional reflections on the philosophy of nature as *On the Will in Nature*, in which Schopenhauer claimed more entitlement than Spinoza to call his metaphysics 'ethics.'[2] And in his final book, *Parerga and Paralipomena* (1851), which provided Schopenhauer with his first taste of the fame he desired so desperately, he wrote that his 'real philosophy' culminated in a 'higher metaphysical-ethical standpoint' (*P1* 313/H. 5, 333), something he self-consciously suspended to produce the eudemonology articulated in the essay 'Aphorisms on the Wisdom of Life'. As the great Schopenhauerian scholar Arthur Hübscher has noted, Schopenhauer 'placed the ethical attitude at the centre and conclusion of his thinking.'[3] The ethical attitude, however, was also at the beginning of his philosophical thought.

Yet Schopenhauer is not known for his moral philosophy. If it makes sense to write about his 'philosophical fame,' it is based on his metaphysics of the will, and if it makes sense to talk about the 'notoriety' of his philosophy, it is grounded in the deep pessimism of his thought. This is not to say that Schopenhauer's commentators have ignored his moral philosophy. Rather, key elements of Schopenhauer's metaphysical-ethical standpoint have received considerable attention. In particular, Schopenhauer's theory of salvation as denial of the will has received extensive commentary. There are good reasons for this, moreover, since it is the concluding discussion of the final book, the 'ethical book' (W1 272/H. 2, 320), of *The World as Will and Representation*, and Schopenhauer's theory of salvation provides the locus at which his metaphysics and pessimism coalesce. By arguing that salvation follows from denying the will, Schopenhauer claimed that this, 'the *worst* of all possible worlds' (W2 583/H. 3, 669), is overcome by denying that which gives the world its horrid tone, the will. In addition, since the denial of the will entails the denial of everything that constitutes human existence, Schopenhauer's theory of salvation enabled him to illustrate his most important of all truths, 'it would be better for us not to exist' (W2 605/H. 3, 695).

Although Schopenhauer gave pride of place to his higher metaphysical-ethical standpoint by making his theory of salvation the concluding discussion of *The World as Will and Representation* and by calling it that 'to which my real philosophy leads' (P1 313/H. 5, 333), it is only one aspect of his ethics. The themes of his higher metaphysical-ethical standpoint, such as the moral significance and value of the world, death, eternal justice, the metaphysics of sexual love, asceticism, and salvation, show that Schopenhauer employed a considerably broad conception of ethics, one that does not square with the majority of contemporary work in ethics. Schopenhauer's work on these topics, however, contains some of the most problematic and unconvincing dimensions of his philosophy. By concentrating on Schopenhauer's higher metaphysical-ethical standpoint, it is difficult to understand how Schopenhauer has contributed and could contribute to contemporary moral thought.

To appreciate how Schopenhauer has contributed and could contribute to moral thought, one has to turn to his writings concerning 'morality in the narrower sense' (W2 589/H. 3, 676),[4] whose most extensive discussion is found in *On the Basis of Morality* (1839), a work which, as Iris Murdoch has said, 'contains much humane wisdom on the subject of morals.'[5] *On the Basis of Morality* provides a framework to organize Schopenhauer's reflections on 'morality in the narrower sense,' one that begins to show the significance of his moral thought. [6] It provides a provocative critique of Kant's ethics, one that both anticipates and motivates contemporary criticisms of Kantian-style deontological ethics; it presents a descriptive virtue ethics, concentrating on moral character and moral psychology; it offers a unified theory of the virtues and vices; it draws on affinities to Eastern thought; and it grounds Schopenhauer's ethics in a metaphysics that accords moral status to non-human animals.

I SCHOPENHAUER'S CRITIQUE OF KANT'S ETHICS

Schopenhauer saw himself as Kant's true philosophical heir, and he took great pride in calling himself a Kantian. Yet Schopenhauer's allegiance to his Kantian heritage did not extend to Kant's ethics. Unlike Kant's theoretical philosophy, which Schopenhauer viewed as expressing some of the grandest insights ever produced by the human mind, he regarded Kant's practical philosophy as an intellectual catastrophe, the unfortunate product of Kant's love for architectonic symmetry, a rashness gained by Kant's increasing philosophical reputation and the debilitating effects of old age. Certainly, Schopenhauer criticized Kant's metaphysics and epistemology, but he did so in a way that he perceived as maintaining some fidelity to Kant. But instead of criticizing Kant's ethics to correct it, to parley Kantian perspectives into a more adequate philosophical view, as he thought he did with Kant's theoretical philosophy, Schopenhauer aimed to demolish Kant's ethics to clear the ground for the erection of his own moral foundations. So in *On the Basis of Morality*, Schopenhauer spent over one-third of his work harshly criticizing Kant's ethics, doing this because 'opposites illustrate each other, and my foundation (for ethics) is, in essentials, diametrically opposed to Kant's' (*BM* 47/H. 4, 115). Nowhere else and never again would Schopenhauer express such an extreme opposition to the views of his philosophical ancestor.[7]

Although there is something of an overstatement to John Atwell's claim that 'Schopenhauer enumerates most of the criticisms urged against [the ethics of] Kant over the past two centuries,'[8] it is not far from the mark. Schopenhauer's critique of Kant's ethics is grand in scope and covers numerous dimensions of Kant's practical philosophy. It is also uneven in quality. Sometimes it suffers from questionable interpretations of Kant and selective readings, and sometimes Schopenhauer seems simply to contrast his views with Kant's to illustrate Kant's flaws. Rather than summarizing Schopenhauer's many challenges to Kant and assessing his interpretations and criticisms of Kant, I will highlight elements of his Kant critique that either anticipate or motivate important lines of criticism of Kant helping to prompt the current renewal of interest in virtue ethics. I will contend that Schopenhauer, a virtue ethicist himself, should be recognized as one of the philosophical ancestors of the present reassessment of 'modern moral philosophy.' I will also emphasize those elements of his Kant critique that aid our understanding of Schopenhauer's narrower sense of morality.

Schopenhauer argues that Kant's ethics begins with a false step, namely, that he assumes a controversial conception of ethics: 'In a practical philosophy we are not concerned with stating reasons for what happens, but with giving laws as regards what *ought to happen, even though it may never happen*' (BM 52/H. 4, 120).[9] Since Kant fails to justify this claim, Schopenhauer charges that his theory rests on a *petitio principii*; that Kant needed to show that there are non-empirical moral laws governing human behaviour. Why, Schopenhauer asks, should we assume that there are moral laws prescribing human conduct, especially if it is possible that what these laws prescribe might never have happened? While this assumption allows Kant to develop a system of ethics in a legislative, imperative form, Schopenhauer contends that Kant employs a concept of moral law divorced from a meaningful context. The original meaning of 'law,' he argues, is civil law, a human institution founded by convention and agreement. By rejecting any empirical grounds for his conception of moral law, Schopenhauer asserts that Kant separates his idea of moral law from 'human ordinance, State institution, or religious doctrine' (BM 53/H. 4, 121), frameworks that would provide significance to the idea of law. The novelty of Kant's assumption, that there are non-empirical prescriptive moral laws that are categorically binding, requires a justification.

Schopenhauer does not consider, however, whether Kant's non-empirical law conception of ethics receives a justification in works other than the *Groundwork* at this point. Instead Schopenhauer moves to detect the source of Kant's conception of ethics. Schopenhauer senses the spurs of the ancestor of Kant's view in his discussion of the absolute necessity of moral laws in the Preface to the *Groundwork*, where Kant uses the command 'Thou shalt not lie (*Du sollt nicht lügen*)' as an example of a moral law. Schopenhauer notes that Kant took his lead from theological ethics, since his

256 DAVID E. CARTWRIGHT

example of a moral law is one of the Ten Commandments, something that is easily seen by Kant's following an archaic German practice of translating the Decalogue using *'Du sollt'* and not the standard *'Du sollst.'* Thus Schopenhauer views Kant as following an unfortunate philosophical trend; 'In the centuries of Christianity, philosophical ethics has generally taken its form unconsciously from the theological' (*BM* 54/H. 4, 122). The problem is that theological ethics is essentially dictatorial and its commands are categorical because they represent the will of God. Philosophical ethics must, Schopenhauer thinks, prove its claims. Unfortunately, Kant's failure to justify his conception of ethics, Schopenhauer believes, shows his unwitting allegiance to theological ethics.

Schopenhauer argues, moreover, that Kant's law conception of ethics places him in a precarious position, since he rejected theology as the basis of morality. While he agrees with the Kantian claim that ethics is distinct from and independent of theology, Schopenhauer also believes that this stance implies that philosophical ethics is also distinct from theological moral concepts. The problem is that Kant's use of moral concepts like 'moral law,' 'command,' 'duty,' and 'obligation,' each used in a categorical sense, each viewed as binding on agents regardless of their interests, requires a theological context to make sense.[10] For example, the command 'Thou shalt not lie' presupposes a commander, and for the command to be conatively effective, the commander must be imagined as having the power to enforce commands by either promised rewards or threatened punishments. Within a theological context, God serves as this commander. Kant's rejection of this theological context undermines the significance of his basic moral concepts, according to Schopenhauer, since 'separated from the theological hypotheses from which they came, these concepts lose all meaning' (*BM* 54–5/H. 4, 122–3).

Schopenhauer sees Kant's moral theology as confirming his analysis of the theological roots of Kantian ethics. So he reads Kant's doctrine of the highest good, the synthesis of happiness and virtue, and his postulates of practical reason, freedom, the immortality of the soul, and the existence of God, as an after-the-fact introduction of the theological context necessary for the meaning of Kant's basic moral concepts: 'Thus that *ought*, said to be so *unconditioned*, nevertheless in the background postulates a condition, and indeed more than one, namely, a reward, plus the immortality of the person to be rewarded, and a rewarder' (*BM* 55/H. 4, 123–4). Kant's moral theology is not based on his ethics, as Kant argues; rather, Schopenhauer claims that Kant confused the context presupposed by the logic of his moral language with what he regarded as its result. So we see, Schopenhauer avers, 'He [Kant] needed only to bring out expressly the concepts that lay hidden at the basis of his morals, implicitly put there by the *ought (Soll)* or *obligation*, and state them explicitly as postulates of practical reason' (*BM* 57/H. 4, 125). It is as if the logic of Kant's moral concepts forced him to articulate their presumptions in his moral theology. The problem is, however, that Kant has a theological morality instead of a moral theology.

Schopenhauer's attempt to show the theological basis of Kant's law conception of ethics begins to mount his challenge to Kantian 'internalism,' the view that the recognition of a moral law implies that an agent has a motive or reason for acting according to the law. Schopenhauer rejects internalism, arguing that the recognition of a moral law does not motivate or present a reason for acting unless the moral law is contingently related to an agent's interest in, or desire for, an end enjoined by the law. Schopenhauer suggests that Kant's doctrine of the highest good and his postulates of practical reason ultimately provide reasons for an agent to follow a moral law by appealing to an agent's desires. For example, the moral law 'Thou shalt not lie' will motivate if it is understood as stating 'If you desire to realize the supreme good, then you should not lie' or 'If you desire God's rewards or desire not to suffer God's punishments, then you should not lie,' provided that the agent desires the end mentioned in the antecedent clause of the hypothetical statement. In this regard, Schopenhauer claims that Kant's moral laws are 'essentially and inevitably *hypothetical*, and never *categorical*, as he asserts' (*BM* 55/H. 4, 123). To use Kant's terminology, Schopenhauer holds that Kant's moral laws, if they motivate, are hypothetical imperatives of prudence.[11] Moreover, if an agent were to obey these hypothetical imperatives, Schopenhauer claims that the agent's action would not possess moral worth because these actions would be egoistic, having as the end of the agent happiness either by being rewarded or by avoiding punishment, that is, 'it will always be selfish, and consequently without moral value' (*BM* 55/H. 4, 123).

Schopenhauer continues his argument by analysing several examples of Kant's application of the categorical imperative, which

Schopenhauer states as 'Act only in accordance with that maxim which you can at the same time *will* to become a universal law for all rational beings' (*BM* 88/H. 4, 155).[12] Schopenhauer's analysis of an example from the *Groundwork* illustrates his line of reasoning. Here Kant considers a person who is flourishing and who is considering adopting an attitude of indifference toward the fate of others, recommending that we neither help nor harm others. Kant claims that there is nothing self-contradictory about this attitude, but that indifference could not be willed to become a universal law, since 'A will that decided on this would contradict itself, because *cases can occur* in which a man *needs* the love and sympathy of others, and in which, through such a natural law that is evolved from his own will, he would deprive himself of all *hope of the help he desires for himself*' (*BM* 90/H. 4, 156).[13] Schopenhauer's emphases make it clear why he regards Kant's application of the categorical imperative as explicitly appealing to an agent's self-interest. That is, the reason an agent would not will indifference as a universal moral law is that the agent would thereby recommend that others not help him or her in a time of need. The hypothetical nature of the categorical imperative is apparent, Schopenhauer thinks, since the command 'You ought to help others' is cognitively effective only if the agent desires the help of others. So the alleged categorical form of the moral law is hypothetical, namely, 'If you desire that others help you, then you ought to help others.' If the agent lacked the desire to receive aid from others, the agent could 'very well will injustice and uncharitableness as a universal maxim' (*BM* 91/H. 4, 157).

Thus Schopenhauer finds a dilemma inherent in Kantian theory. For an agent to do what the categorical imperative renders as a moral law, the agent must have some desire independent of the moral law. This desire is either self-interested, in which case the action would lack moral worth on Kantian grounds, or the desire is 'moral' and the categorical imperative only recommends the means to realize the end of the agent's already moral desire. In both cases, moral laws are hypothetical. To return to the last example of the flourishing individual, Schopenhauer suggests that the proper form of the moral law is either 'If you desire that others help you, then you ought not be indifferent to their fate' or 'If you desire the well-being of others, then you ought not be indifferent to their fate.' In both cases, motivation is external to moral laws, and the moral law only recommends the means for satisfying a pre-existing desire.

One might claim that Schopenhauer is not being fair to Kant, since his point concerning the categorical imperative is that the universality of a person's maxims is the criterion for determining moral laws. So what Kant's examples are designed to show is not the motivation for following moral laws, but how one determines whether a person's maxim could become a universal law valid for all rational beings. In the case of the flourishing individual, Kant shows that rational agents could not will indifference as a universal law and, consequently, that they have a duty not to be indifferent to others. Thus it appears that Schopenhauer confuses a line of reasoning, showing that a maxim of indifference cannot become a universal law, with what would motivate an agent to act from the categorical statement 'You ought not be indifferent to the fate of others.' To handle the issue of motivation, Kant posits a unique type of motivation for obeying moral laws – that a consciousness of the dutifulness of an action can serve as a motive sufficient for an action, and that this motive operates independently of and, if necessary, contrary to an agent's natural inclinations. So Kant claims that humans can act for the sake of duty or from duty (*aus Pflicht*), and that actions possess moral worth only if they are done from duty. 'Duty,' Kant claims, 'is the necessity to act out of respect (*Achtung*) for the law,'[14] and it is the moral incentive of respect that moves an agent to act for the sake of duty.

Schopenhauer is aware of Kant's account of moral motivation but finds his account untenable for a number of reasons. He illustrates some of these problems by tracing them to Kant's non-empirical ethics, noting that 'Even Kant himself confesses . . . that we have *no absolutely certain instances* of an inclination to act out of duty' (*BM* 67/H. 4, 135). Kant's agnosticism concerning the existence of purely moral actions, Schopenhauer contends, is problematic when taken against his claim that moral laws are knowable a priori 'independent of all *inner and outer experience*, "resting simply on *concepts of pure reason, a synthetic proposition a priori*"' (*BM* 61/H. 4, 129).[15] Whereas Kant had demonstrated, Schopenhauer believes, that all of our experiences of an objective world *must* conform to the a priori forms of cognition, the alleged a priori moral law is admitted to have no certain instances. This, Schopenhauer remarks, is a strange 'concept of a priority' (*BM* 65/H. 4, 133). Moreover, even if it were the case that the moral law necessarily conditioned experiences in the way that the a priori forms of space, time, and causality do, Kant would contradict one of his deepest insights, since the moral law would be like space, time, and causality in applying only to the phenomenon, and 'everywhere (e.g. *Critique of Practical Reason* [5:37]) it is precisely *what is moral within us* that he describes as being in the closest connection with the true *essence-in-itself* of things, in fact, as directly touching this. Even in the *Critique of Pure Reason*, wherever the mysterious *thing-in-itself* stands out somewhat more clearly, it proclaims itself as that which is *moral* in us, as will' (*BM* 65/H. 4, 133).

When it comes to Kant's moral incentive of respect, Schopenhauer finds it a thinly veiled paraphrase of commitments associated with a theological form of ethics. Again, Schopenhauer uses Kantian agnosticism concerning purely moral actions to challenge Kant's *Groundwork* definition of duty as the necessity to act out of respect for the moral law. Schopenhauer complains that, in light of Kantian agnosticism, he is employing an odd concept of necessity, since what is necessary happens and is inevitable, and Kant admits that an action performed out of respect for a law might never have happened. Schopenhauer notes that Kant claims that a dutiful action is objectively necessary but subjectively accidental, thereby implying that human agents may not be determined to act by their consciousness of the dutifulness of an action. But if this is Kant's argument, Schopenhauer contends, the idea of the necessity of an action 'is nothing but a cleverly concealed and very forced paraphrase of the word *ought*' (*BM* 67/H. 4, 135). Moreover, Schopenhauer claims that Kant is merely describing 'obedience [*Gehorsam*]' in ordinary German when Kant states that '*Respect* signifies simply the subordination of my will to a law. The immediate determination by law and the consciousness of this are what is called *respect*' (ibid.).[16] Thus the true meaning of Kant's definition of duty is 'Duty signifies an action which *ought* to be done out of *obedience* to a law' (*BM* 68/H. 4, 136).

Even if it were possible to act from respect for the moral law or from duty, Schopenhauer argues that Kant's perspective would be found repugnant to anyone possessing genuine moral sensitivity. To show this, he considers Kant's example of a man who is 'cold in temperament and indifferent to the suffering of others' and who 'does good, not from inclination, but from duty.'[17] Unlike Kant, who claims that this man begins to manifest a moral worth of character that is the highest beyond all comparison, Schopenhauer argues that

Kant's judgment is counterintuitive, an example of the opposite of a charitable action, which is more adequately characterised by the Christian doctrine of love for others as the basis of charity. Indeed, Schopenhauer even claims that Friedrich Schiller's satire of Kant's moral pedantry in *Scruple of Conscience and Decision* is not far from the mark by citing passages from the *Critique of Practical Reason* where Kant asserts that moral laws are not to be obeyed 'from voluntary inclinations or any endeavour, gladly undertaken of itself,'[18] and that right-thinking persons find compassion and sympathy nuisances, feelings that 'provoke the desire to be released from these, and to be subject only to legislative reason.'[19] Schopenhauer views Kant's rejection of the moral significance of kind-hearted feelings as being 'opposed to the genuine spirit of virtue; not the deed, but the willingness to do it, the love from which it results, and without which it is dead work, this constitutes its meritorious element' (*W1* 526/H. 2, 624). To advocate that virtuous deeds be performed out of regard to abstract maxims of law, Schopenhauer thinks, is comparable to the demand 'that every genuine work of art must result from a well-thought-out application of aesthetic rules' (*W1* 527/ H.2, 624). The absurdity of this is that, at best, pale images of the good are produced and not the genuine article.

Schopenhauer's rejection of the central role Kant assigns reason in ethics undergirds almost every dimension of his Kant critique. In addition to Schopenhauer's dismissal of Kant's non-empirical ethics, in which Kant claims that pure reason is the source for discovering moral laws, he also decries what he perceives as a basic presumption of Kant's view, that 'the inner and eternal essence of humans consist in reason' (*BM* 64/H. 4, 132). For Schopenhauer, reason (*Vernunft*) is simply the faculty of concepts, the ability to form general and non-imagistic representations that are symbolized and fixed by words. Reason, like the understanding (*Verstand*), the faculty of perception, is secondary and phenomenal, 'whereas the real kernel in man, that which alone is metaphysical and therefore indestructible, is *his will*' (*BM* 64/H. 4, 132). Since Schopenhauer shares what he regards as a Kantian commitment, believing 'the undeniable moral significance of human conduct to be quite different from, and not dependent on, the laws of the phenomenon, to be not even capable of explanation according to them, but to be something directly touching the thing-in-itself' (*W1* 422/H. 2, 499–500), Schopenhauer concludes

that reason and rational conduct do not 'touch' that which is significant in ethics, which is the will, and that Kant's ethics fails to satisfy
one of Kant's own commitments.[20]

The secondary status of reason also figures centrally in
Schopenhauer's rejection of the Kantian account of moral behaviour
as rational behaviour. Schopenhauer views reason instrumentally,
as functioning to determine possible means to fulfil a person's ends,
with these ends being a function of a person's will. Since it is the
will that both determines a person's ends and provides the conative impetus for action, the will is responsible for a person's conduct
and the moral quality of this conduct. Because Schopenhauer identifies a person's will with a person's character, he claims that his
view shows that we are the true doers of our deeds. Reason itself is
morally ambivalent, Schopenhauer argues; a person with a good will
employs reason to realize his or her ends, just like a person with an
evil will. Reason, then, is simply contingently connected to morality. Thus Schopenhauer claims that it is surprising that Kant would
identify virtue with reason, and he believes that his own view of
reason's relationship to morality comports with traditional religious
and philosophical views, where 'it never occurred to anyone *prior* to
Kant to identify just, virtuous, and noble conduct with *reasonable*
or *rational*, but the two have been clearly distinguished and kept
apart. . . . Only after Kant, for then virtue was supposed to spring from
pure reason, did the virtuous and the reasonable become one and the
same; this despite the usage of all languages, which is not accidental,
but the work of universal human, and therefore coherent and consistent knowledge' (*BM* 83/H. 4, 150). Indeed, Schopenhauer notes
that 'reasonable' and 'vicious' are consistent descriptions of a person's conduct and character; that great wickedness is possible only
through reason. Conversely, he asserts that great noble-mindedness
can coexist with great unreasonableness.

The voluntaristic Schopenhauer, then, rejects the Kantian vision
of rational agency, the view that reason is practical; that reason has
causal efficacy over the will. He contends, moreover, that Kant himself recognized that he could not justify his view, citing a passage
from the *Groundwork* where Kant reflects, 'But how can *pure reason* by itself be *practical* without other motives that may be taken
from somewhere else; that is, how can the *mere principle of the universal validity of all its maxims* as laws, without any object of the

will in which any interest could previously be taken, provide by itself a motive and produce an interest that would be called purely moral; or, in other words, how can pure reason be practical? To explain this, all human reason is inadequate and all effort and work are spent in vain' (*BM* 102/H. 4, 167).[21] Schopenhauer reads Kant's confession as committing him to the absurd view that there is an actuality that is not conceivable as possible: 'We must therefore stick to the conviction that what cannot be either conceived *as possible* or proven *as actual* has no credentials for its existence' (*BM* 102/H. 4, 168). Thus Schopenhauer does not find it surprising that Kant posits the moral law and practical reason as a 'fact of reason' in the *Critique of Practical Reason*, which reverses his work in the *Groundwork*. Instead of reading this move as providing a new direction for grounding morality, Schopenhauer sees this as a movement to a pre-critical stance, an admission of the inadequacy of his reasoning in the *Groundwork*, and the source by which Reinhold, Fichte, Schelling, and Jacobi made mischief with Kant's views: 'Thus in the Kantian school practical reason with its categorical imperative appears more and more as a hyperphysical fact, as a Delphic temple in the human soul. From its dark sanctuary oracular sentences infallibly proclaim, alas! not what *will*, but what *ought* to happen' (*BM* 79/H. 4, 146).[22]

II   THE METHOD OF ETHICS AND MORAL SCEPTICISM

Schopenhauer's critique of Kantian ethics prepares the grounds for his basis of morality. Schopenhauer believes that he has demonstrated that 'Kant's practical reason and categorical imperative are wholly unjustified, groundless, and fictitious assumptions, and... Kant's ethics lacks a solid foundation' (*BM* 48/H. 4, 116). In place of Kant's non-empirical, rationalistic, and prescriptive ethics, Schopenhauer develops an empirical, voluntaristic, descriptive virtue ethics, one that concentrates on moral psychology and character, includes a sketch for a unified theory of both the virtues and vices, and concludes with a metaphysics of morals that explains the basic or primary phenomena (*Urphänomene*) of his ethics. Throughout his assessment of Kant's ethics, Schopenhauer articulates the general requirements for any adequate account of the basis of morality: it must locate morality empirically in the conduct of human beings without employing mystical interpretations, religious dogma, or transcendent hypotheses (cf. *BM* 138/H. 4, 202); it must clearly distinguish between the 'what' of a system of ethics, the principle that summarizes the line of conduct to which it attributes moral worth, and the 'why' of ethics, the explanation or justification of that principle (cf. *BM* 68/H. 4, 136); it must explain how humans are capable of overcoming their deeply egoistic tendencies (cf. *BM* 75/H. 4, 143); and it must show that the ethical significance of human conduct is metaphysical, that it 'reaches beyond this phenomenal existence [*dieses erscheinende Daseyn*] and touches eternity' (*BM* 54/H. 4, 122). Schopenhauer believes that Kant tried to meet these requirements but that he failed.

Schopenhauer's empirical method of ethics is a specific instance of his general philosophical methodology. Just as the task of the philosopher is to provide a comprehensive explanation of the totality of human experiences, that of the moral philosopher is to provide a unified explanation of moral experience. So Schopenhauer claims that

the purpose of ethics is to indicate, explain, and trace to its ultimate ground the extremely varied behaviour of humans from a moral point of view. Therefore there is no other way for discovering the foundation of ethics than the empirical, namely, to investigate whether there are generally any actions to which we must attribute *genuine moral worth*. Such will be actions of voluntary justice, pure philanthropy, and real magnanimity. These are then to be regarded as a given phenomenon that we have to explain correctly, that is, trace to its true grounds. Consequently, we have to indicate the peculiar motive that moves a human to actions of this kind, a kind specifically different from any other. This motive together with the susceptibility to it will be the ultimate ground of morality, and a knowledge of it will be the foundation of morals. This is the humble path to which I direct ethics; it contains no construction a priori, no absolute legislation for all rational beings *in abstracto*. (*BM* 130/H. 4, 195)

Schopenhauer describes his method of ethics by discussing 'voluntary justice,' 'pure philanthropy,' and 'real magnanimity,' actions that possess moral worth or positive moral value. His statement, however, makes it clear that he conceives of the purpose of ethics as explaining human behaviour from a moral point of view. Consequently, Schopenhauer employs the same method to explain actions that are either morally reprehensible (*moralisch verwerfliche*) or morally indifferent (moralisch indifferente), neither reprehensible nor worthwhile. By explaining what moves humans to perform actions with a particular moral value, and by indicating why humans are susceptible or receptive to the motives for these actions, Schopenhauer believes that morality is grounded by locating it in human psychology.[23] This is also true of Schopenhauer's account of a moral point of view. The moral point of view becomes a function of both agents' affective responses to their deeds and those of impartial witnesses. Actions possessing moral worth draw agents' feelings of self-satisfaction, the approbation of conscience, and 'call forth the approbation and respect of impartial witnesses' (BM 140/H. 4, 204); those that are morally reprehensible evoke a form of inner self-censure in agents, the sting of conscience or a feeling of disapprobation, and the disapprobation of impartial witnesses; and actions that are neither morally reprehensible nor worthwhile are those for which agents' consciences remain silent and which evoke no affective response from impartial witnesses. Thus the basis of judgements of moral values becomes a function of an agent's feelings or will.

Schopenhauer believes that knowledge of the foundation of morals (Fundament der Moral), or philosophical understanding of ethics, is obtained by correctly explaining human behaviour from a moral point of view. Instead of using the idea of a moral point of view to establish the existence of moral phenomena, Schopenhauer attempts this by refuting moral scepticism. He ignores some of the epistemological challenges presented by moral scepticism, such as the sceptical theses that moral claims are neither true nor false and that moral claims cannot be justified, to consider moral scepticism as the charge that 'there is no natural morality at all that is independent of human institutions' (BM 121/H. 4, 186); that morality cannot be founded on an appeal to either the natures of things or human nature. Schopenhauer reads the moral sceptic as a psychological egoist, someone who would claim that egoism, the desire for one's own well-being, is the motive for all human behaviour. So Schopenhauer understands the moral sceptic as claiming that there are no instances of 'voluntary justice,' 'pure philanthropy,' and 'real magnanimity'; that these types of actions are impure and apparent; and that people are moved to perform these allegedly altruistic actions due to the coercive power of the state, the quest for civic honour, or religious beliefs that promise rewards or threaten punishment.

Schopenhauer argues that the moral sceptic fails to prove conclusively that there is no genuine morality. He believes that the arguments of the moral sceptic show only that we should 'moderate our expectations of the moral tendency in humans and consequently of the natural foundation of ethics' (BM 128/H. 4, 193) because much that passes as moral behaviour is egoistic. There are, Schopenhauer contends, instances in which individuals who lack religious faith act justly and kindly even when a misdeed would not have been detected and when they would have benefited by performing a misdeed. Consequently, the moral sceptic cannot explain these actions, Schopenhauer concludes, and there must be non-egoistic motives for these actions.

Schopenhauer is aware, however, that his own reply to the moral sceptic is inconclusive. Like Kant, Schopenhauer recognizes that motives are epistemically opaque; that for all we know, the 'dear self' may underlie all of our actions. So when Schopenhauer presents his paradigm case of an action possessing moral worth, the heroic sacrifice of the Swiss folk hero Arnold von Winkelried, who in 1386 at the battle of Sempach gave his life to save his comrades, he recognizes that someone could imagine a selfish intent behind von Winkelried's action. If this were true, Schopenhauer concedes, ethics would be a science without an object, like astrology and alchemy. He dismisses this sceptic, however, by claiming that he will only 'address myself to those who admit the reality of the matter' (BM 139/H. 4, 204).

Schopenhauer's treatment of moral scepticism signifies his general attitude toward any form of scepticism. He never takes any form of scepticism as a viable philosophical stance, although he concedes that it cannot be conclusively refuted. Subsequently, Schopenhauer uses scepticism as a foil for developing his own anti-sceptical posture. In the case of moral scepticism, Schopenhauer articulates directly one of the fundamental assumptions of his ethics – that there are altruistic actions. It is curious, moreover, that Schopenhauer is not sensitive to the challenge moral scepticism also mounts to his belief that there are morally reprehensible actions. For just as the moral sceptic attempts to show that allegedly morally worthwhile actions are egoistic and not 'moral,' the moral sceptic also reduces morally reprehensible actions to egoism and thereby implies that there are no *natural* moral values, either positive or negative. Seen in this context, the other assumption of Schopenhauer's ethics must be that there are purely malicious actions.[24]

Yet, if Schopenhauer's commitment to the existence of non-egoistic actions signifies a bedrock assumption of his ethics, it also stands at the same level as his acceptance of the Kantian rejection of egoism as the basis of moral value. Just as his acceptance of this Kantian claim is not simply a relic of his Kantian heritage, his commitment to the existence of non-egoistic actions is not simply the product of Schopenhauer's own moral intuitions. Rather, Schopenhauer sees these commitments as consistent with mainstream themes in both Eastern and Western moral traditions. While he recognizes dissenters within these traditions, as well as some of the ways these traditions embody developments that obscure some of their fundamental insights, he employs these traditions to provide support for his views. When, for example, he presents his moral principle within the course of his critique of Kant, a principle that articulates the line of conduct to which moral worth is attributed, *Neminem laede, imo omnes, quantum potes juva* (Injure no one; on the contrary, help everyone as much as you can), he claims that its purport is something concerning which 'all teachers of ethics are really in agreement' (*BM* 69/H. 4, 137). Schopenhauer's strategy of invoking his commonalities with religious and philosophical traditions functions in a secondary way in his empirical method of ethics, providing data that both support some of his guiding assumptions and confirm the adequacy of his views. Put in these terms, it seems as if Schopenhauer's appeal to traditions locks him into a vicious circle. However, it serves to show that his moral intuitions are not idiosyncratic and that the results of his philosophy are not as odd as they might seem. Yet what serves as the confirmation of his views is not that mainstream intellectual traditions share his insights, but that he can produce a philosophical system that has an explanatory force greater than that of rival theories; one that preserves insights from other traditions within a context in which the totality of human experiences receives a unified explanation, something these traditions could not accomplish.

Schopenhauer develops a topology of motives to explain human behaviour from a moral point of view. Like Thomas Nagel, Schopenhauer views ethics as part of psychology, and he attributes a metaphysics to the moral quality of a person's behaviour. Unlike Nagel, whose aims are broadly Kantian, Schopenhauer resolves the psychology of ethics into a matter of will rather than reason, and he sees a metaphysics expressed in a person's behaviour instead of a metaphysical conception of oneself that leads to a person's behaviour.[25] So Schopenhauer's conception of a moral point of view emphasizes an agent's and an impartial spectator's feelings of approbation or disapprobation toward the intent or willed end of an action and not toward its consequences. This move leads Schopenhauer to interiorize morality, to look at a deed from the inside, as it were, and not to its exterior, its outer phenomenal shell. Since Schopenhauer reads the types of motives to which a person is receptive or susceptible as a function of a person's will or character, he connects the moral evaluation of an action to that of a person's will or character. Because he regards a person's will or character as a metaphysical dimension of personality, moral assessment becomes metaphysically significant.

Schopenhauer details four fundamental incentives for human actions. He understands human action as intentional, having as an ultimate end something that is either 'in agreement with or contrary to a will' (BM 141/H. 4, 205). By identifying weal or well-being (Wohl) with ends in agreement with a will, and woe or misfortune (Wehe) with ends contrary to a will, Schopenhauer views all actions as aiming at someone's well-being or misfortune. Since Schopenhauer claims that actions can aim at either an agent's own or another's well-being or misfortune, he concludes that there are four basic incentives for human action. They are: egoism (Egoismus), which is the desire for an agent's own well-being; compassion (Mitleid), which is the desire for another's well-being; malice (Bosheit), which is the desire for another's misfortune; and an unnamed incentive, which is the desire for an agent's own misfortune. Schopenhauer does not discuss this unnamed incentive in On the Basis of Morality, and he only mentions it in a footnote in the second volume of The World as Will and Representation, 'in the interest of systematic consistency' (W2 607n./H. 3, 697n.). He claims elsewhere, however, that it possesses ascetic rather than moral value.[26] Schopenhauer argues that egoism is the motive for morally indifferent actions; malice is the motive for morally reprehensible actions; and compassion is the motive for actions possessing moral worth. Schopenhauer believes, moreover, that everyone is susceptible to each of these motives to various degrees, and for each of these fundamental incentives, there are degrees of their expression; that is, some malicious actions express a greater desire for another's woe than others, and some compassionate actions express a greater concern for another's well-being than do other compassionate actions. Schopenhauer claims that the moral value of a person's character is a function of the kind and degree of the motives that dominate his or her behaviour.

III EGOISM AND MALICE: THE 'ANTIMORAL' INCENTIVES

Schopenhauer considers the 'antimoral' incentives of egoism and malice prior to the 'moral' incentive of compassion. Like Dante, who exposes us to the inferno before showing us paradise, Schopenhauer considers the darker side of human conduct prior to its brighter side. This approach, he brags, shows that his 'path [to ethics] differs from that of all other moralists' (BM 136/H. 4, 201). Although Schopenhauer's approach may seem to be a general expression of his pessimism, it is his metaphysics of the will that commits him to the recognition that egoism is the most basic and general motive for human behaviour. Because of his perception of the centrality of egoism in human conduct, and because of the moral and logical connections he draws between egoism and malice, it is only natural that Schopenhauer would consider these motives before the motive of compassion.

Schopenhauer's exploration of the antimoral incentives leads him to sketch a unified theory of the vices, something that has been relatively neglected by both classical and contemporary advocates of virtue ethics. As Christine McKinnon notes, proponents of virtue ethics have maintained 'an almost total silence on the subject of vice.'[27] Although Schopenhauer's analyses of egoism and malice tend to be as theory laden as any of his work, so that if one does not share his metaphysical commitments, his accounts of egoism and malice appear artificial and ad hoc at crucial points, he manages to tease out some significant moral and explanatory connections between character traits, dispositions, attitudes, feelings, and beliefs of individuals inclined to act egoistically or maliciously.

Schopenhauer views egoism as expressing 'the natural standpoint' (W1 332/H. 2, 392), claiming that 'the chief and fundamental incentive in humans as in the animal is *egoism*, that is, the craving

for existence and well-being' (*BM* 131/H. 4, 196). He accounts for
the centrality of egoism as a motive for human behaviour through
both his metaphysics of the will and a phenomenological description
of consciousness. Every member of the phenomenal world, or the
world as representation, is an expression of the metaphysical will,
which Schopenhauer conceives of as a constantly striving, goal-less
force that imprints its nature on each and every one of its manifestations. Schopenhauer subscribes to a hierarchical ontology that ranges
from the will's most universal and general expressions, the forces of
nature, to the will's most particular and specific expressions, the
human character. He argues that 'every grade of the will's objectification fights for the matter, the space, and the time of another' (*W1*
146–7/H. 2, 174), so conflict and strife become central features in
Schopenhauer's animistic world view. In this regard, a central claim
of Schopenhauer's explanation of the world as representation is that
everything strives to be, strives to be a spatio-temporal material object, and that this striving to be breeds conflict. With conscious entities, both humans and non-human animals, this striving to be is a
drive for self-preservation and general well-being, a striving for existence, pleasure, and freedom from pain. Since Schopenhauer believes
that only humans possess reason, only humans have the ability to
deliberately and systematically plan the means to secure their own
well-being and freedom from misfortune. He contends, therefore,
that both humans and non-human animals behave egoistically insofar as both are innately inclined to strive for their own well-being,
but that only human behaviour can be self-interested (*eigennützig*),
as only humans have reason.

Schopenhauer views egoists, those disposed simply to pursue their
own interests without considering the interests of others, as expressing a subjective form of consciousness. For egoists, Schopenhauer
claims:

Everyone is himself the whole world, for everything objective exists only indirectly, as mere representation of the subject, so that everything is always
closely associated with self-consciousness. The only world everyone is actually acquainted with and knows, is carried about by him in his head as his
representation, and is thus the center of the world. Accordingly, everyone
is all in all to himself; he finds himself to be the holder and possessor of all
reality, and nothing can be more important to him than his own self. ... [I]n

his subjective view a man's own self assumes these colossal proportions.
...(BM 132–3/H. 4, 197)

The subjective perspective embodied in the behaviour of the egoist
can assume such 'colossal proportions' that given the choice between
the destruction of the world or their own destruction, the egoist
would choose the former, according to Schopenhauer. There is even
something sadly comic about the attitude of the egoist, Schopenhauer
claims, since the world is peopled by egoists, each one of whom lives
as if he or she is the only real being, believing that only his or her
well-being is significant, when in reality, from an objective point of
view, he or she is one among many, whose interests are viewed by
others with the same indifference that he or she regards the interests
of others.

Schopenhauer's phenomenological description of the subjective
consciousness associated with egoists implies that the behaviour of
egoists fails to recognize others by failing to recognize the interests others have in not suffering and obtaining their own well-being.
Schopenhauer does not mean that egoists are solipsists, but rather
that they act as if they were by not restraining their behaviour based
on its effects on others. This failure to consider the well-being of
others shows why egoism is a motive for neither morally reprehensible nor morally worthwhile behaviour, since the ultimate aim of
egoism is simply an agent's own well-being. Egoism reflects 'the natural standpoint,' according to Schopenhauer, because it is a disposition central to living beings, one that entails inevitable conflicts
generated in a world populated with numerous individuals pursuing their own well-being, affirming their wills, and this naturally
leads to intrusions on the wilful behaviour of others, which constitutes wrongful behaviour; 'This breaking through the boundary of
another's affirmation of will has at all times been directly recognized,
and its concept has been denoted by the word *wrong* [*Unrecht*]' (W1
334/H. 2, 394). Schopenhauer sees egoism as leading to theft, slavery,
injury, mutilation of others, murder, and even cannibalism (he does
say that the will is a hungry will!).

The connections Schopenhauer draws between egoism and wrongful conduct appear to suggest that egoism is not simply a motive
for morally indifferent or morally neutral behaviour, but that it is

necessarily connected to wrongful conduct. Schopenhauer does not draw this conclusion, however, because of his 'morality of disposition [*Moralität der Gesinnung*]' (*BM* 137/H. 4, 202), which focuses on agents' intents or ultimate ends rather than simply on the consequences of their actions. Thus he claims that 'Egoism can lead to all kinds of crimes and misdeeds, but the pain and injury thus caused to others are merely the means, not the end, and therefore appear here only as an accident' (*BM* 135–6/H. 4, 200). Like Kant, Schopenhauer views egoism as morally ambivalent; there is nothing that logically ties it to wrongful or rightful conduct. Sometimes people are harmed or wronged by egoists, and sometimes they are helped or aided. It all depends on how others stand in relationship to egoists' interests. In either case, egoists are indifferent to the effects of their behaviour on others. Yet, because of the inevitable conflicts bred by individuals pursuing their own self-interests, the harmful conduct engendered by egoism serves as the basis for Schopenhauer's Hobbesian view of the state, whose laws are geared to repress the negative effects of egoism by meting out penalties sufficient to make it in most people's interests not to pursue ends that result in theft, murder, and cannibalism. As Rudolf Malter aptly notes, 'the prevention of the suffering of wrong is the theme of Schopenhauerian political theory.'[28]

Schopenhauer does, however, distinguish between egoism and extreme egoism (*äusserster Egoismus*), between agents for whom the desire for their own well-being is relatively mild and agents for whom the desire for their own well-being is intense and becomes the leitmotif of their behaviour. Schopenhauer summarizes the line of conduct of extreme egoists by the maxim '*Neminem juva, imo omnes, si forte conducit, laede* [Help no one; on the contrary, injure all people if it brings you any advantage]' (*BM* 136/H. 4, 200). Schopenhauer regards extreme egoism as a motive that precludes the development of the virtue of justice because extreme egoists knowingly engage in a form of life in which harming others is systematically tied to the pursuit of their own well-being, and the virtue of justice is expressed by the disposition not to harm others.

Schopenhauer also associates a set of specific vices with extreme egoism, that is, 'intemperance, lust, selfishness, avarice, covetousness, injustice, hardness of heart, pride, arrogance, and so on' (*BM* 136/H. 4, 201). Each of these vices represents character flaws associated with varying degrees of wilful self-affirmation, which range from self-indulgences like intemperance and lust, to an inflated sense of self-worth like pride and arrogance, to injustice itself, the tendency to knowingly harm others in pursuit of one's own ends. Schopenhauer calls these vices brutal (*thierisch*), suggesting that people who possess them are animalistic. Whereas egoists manifest selfishly thoughtless behaviour, extreme egoists manifest such an excessive occupation with their own self-interests that their behaviours reflect vicious dispositions.

Schopenhauer views malice, like egoism, as an antimoral incentive. Whereas Schopenhauer characterizes the wills of egoists, even extreme egoists, as expressing indifference to the effects of their behaviour on others and, for that reason, conceives of egoism as an antimoral incentive, Schopenhauer views characters disposed to malice as morally depraved. While Schopenhauer considers both extreme egoists and malicious characters as possessing evil characters, he claims that malicious characters, instead of being simply brutal, express 'devilish [*teuflisch*]' (BM 136/H. 4, 201) attitudes toward others.[29] The devilish character of individuals disposed to malice reveals a profoundly different attitude toward others than that of the egoist: the malicious personality expresses the desire for another's misery. Like compassion, malice is non-egoistic; its ultimate object is not the agent's own well-being. Thus malice reflects another of Schopenhauer's ethical commitments, namely, the moral value of an action is a function of a person's willing about the well-being of others; 'the moral significance of an action can lie only in its reference to others. Only in respect to these can it have moral worth or reprehensibility [*Verwerflichkeit*]' (BM 142/H. 4, 206). Malice, Schopenhauer contends, is the motive for morally reprehensible actions. The vices he associates with malice include 'envy, disaffection, ill will ... malicious joy at another's misfortune [*Schadenfreude*] ... perfidy, thirst for revenge, cruelty, and so on' (BM 136/H. 4, 201). Each of these vices denotes a smaller or greater measure of the desire to harm another, ranging from prying curiosity, the intrusive attempt to discover something about others to diminish their status, to treating others with contempt (petulance), to hatred, and to overt cruelty.

Schopenhauer frames his evaluations of malice on the intuition that it is worse to recognize that others have interests and to act intentionally against them than it is to act against them while not recognizing their interests. Egoists, who lack the virtue of justice, which is a disposition not to harm others, also lack a desire to help others, and subsequently they lack the virtue of philanthropy. Whereas egoists act as if they were the only real beings by not recognizing the interests of others, malicious characters act directly against the interests others have in not suffering. Since the ultimate end of malice is another's misfortune, the malicious personality does not act as if others do not exist. Indeed, malicious persons must recognize the suffering of others to find significance in life. While Schopenhauer claims that both egoists and malicious characters act as if others are non-egos, as if others are radically and fundamentally different from themselves, they do so in profoundly different ways. The egoist treats others as non-egos by not counting or recognizing their interests, the malicious character by intentionally acting against others' interest in not suffering. Thus, malicious characters also lack the virtues of justice and philanthropy, since they harm others and fail to render aid to the suffering of others.

Schopenhauer analyses malice as a form of ill will toward others, one that is expressed most frequently in its mildest forms, such as 'backbiting,' and he claims that it 'becomes quite obvious in outbursts of anger that are often out of all proportion to their cause, and could not prove to be so violent if they had not been compressed, like powder in a gun, as a long borne and inwardly brooding hatred' (BM 134/H. 4, 199). The desire to harm others can also result, he claims, from a recognition of the ubiquitous distribution of faults, vices, weaknesses, and imperfections among humanity; so that for the malicious character, 'the world may appear to be from the aesthetic standpoint a cabinet of caricatures, from the intellectual, a madhouse, and from the moral, a den of sharks and swindlers' (BM 135/H. 4, 199).[30] When ill will becomes a dominant mode of a person's life, Schopenhauer claims, you have a misanthrope.

The ill will Schopenhauer associates with malice is conceptually and behaviourally linked to envy for another's good fortune and to *Schadenfreude*, a feeling of delight arising from the perception of another's misfortune. Schopenhauer believes that all humans are susceptible to these forms of ill will to some degree, but he sees envy as the more pervasive feeling; one that is more human and, for that reason, somewhat excusable. Schopenhauer distinguishes between different expressions of envy based on its object. Envy may be felt toward another's 'gifts of fortune,' such as reputation, wealth, and social status, or toward another's 'gifts of nature,' such as beauty or intelligence. In both cases, envy reveals to its agents their lack of these gifts in either kind or extent. Envy for another's gifts of fortune is relatively easy to overcome, Schopenhauer argues, because the envious person can take consolation for his or her lack of these traits by either hoping for 'help, pleasure, and assistance, protection, advancement, and so on from one who excites his envy' (*P2* 216/H. 6, 231) or by imagining that he or she will someday have the same gifts. It is difficult to overcome envy based on gifts of nature, Schopenhauer holds, because gifts of nature are innate, and this means that the envier has no hope of gaining these traits. Because of this hopelessness, the envious person may desire to take revenge against the person who is envied. However, the envier is frequently restrained from taking direct revenge against the other because of either fear of social sanctions or inability. So, Schopenhauer contends, envy becomes 'a Proteus of stratagems in order to wound without showing itself' (*P2* 217/H. 6, 231). Enviers may take revenge by deliberately ignoring the qualities they envy, by praising the mediocre and inferior as a means of putting down the envied, and/or by ridiculing and treating with contempt the envied person.

Schopenhauer claims that envy is reprehensible, but he argues that *Schadenfreude* is worse. While he believes that both envy and *Schadenfreude* are opposites of his moral incentive, compassion, the ways in which they 'oppose' compassion are significantly different. Envy opposes compassion because it is felt towards another's good fortune, whereas compassion is felt towards another's misfortune. The reprehensibility of envy is due to the desire to see the other lose that for which he or she is envied, and this amounts to a desire to see the other harmed by the loss of his or her good fortune. Compassion, however, manifests a contrary desire, since compassion desires another's well-being. *Schadenfreude* opposes compassion from another direction. Like compassion, *Schadenfreude* is a response to another's misfortune, but unlike compassion, which includes a feeling of sorrow for another's woe, *Schadenfreude* delights in another's woe. Consequently, Schopenhauer views *Schadenfreude* as appearing when compassion 'should find a place' (*P2* 215/H. 6, 229), and he claims that a disposition to *Schadenfreude* is fiendish and diabolical: 'There is no more infallible sign of a thoroughly bad heart and profound moral worthlessness than an inclination to a sheer and undisguised malignant joy of this kind' (*BM* 135/H. 4, 200). It is, Schopenhauer claims, 'the worst trait in human nature' (*P2* 215/H. 6, 229).[31]

One might have expected Schopenhauer to reserve his strongest condemnation for cruelty proper, for those who actively cause the suffering they so readily crave. Indeed, Schopenhauer calls *Schadenfreude* 'impotent cruelty' (*BM* 162/H. 4, 225), emphasizing its passive nature, since a person inclined to *Schadenfreude* simply enjoys another's misfortune. This expectation overlooks, however, what Schopenhauer means by a morality of disposition, where it is not the act but the inclination to act that is significant. Just as he argues that both extreme egoists and envious people may never fully act according to their inclinations, because they are restrained by social sanctions, their inability, or both, the same is true of those disposed to *Schadenfreude*. What is important is that each of these types of individual are disposed to act, and would act, out of this devilish desire in the absence of restraint. Thus the reprehensibility of *Schadenfreude* is that it desires another's misfortune, even though a *schadenfreudig* individual may never act to cause another pain.

The desire for another's woe, the disposition to harm others, which is expressed by envious or *schadenfreudig* individuals, is the leitmotif of truly malicious or wicked individuals, those who are actively cruel. In *The World as Will and Representation* Schopenhauer explains wicked personalities by attributing to them an excessive and vehement will to life. Since Schopenhauer holds that willing is equivalent to suffering, individuals with an excessive will suffer excessively. These individuals discover that all of their strategies to pursue their own well-being are doomed to failure; that nothing will ultimately sate their will; that fulfilment of their desires only shifts their willings to new objects; and that the securing of one of their ends never delivers its promise of satisfaction. So Schopenhauer argues:

He [the wicked character] sees that, with fulfilment, the wish changes only its form, and now torments under another form; indeed, when at last all wishes are exhausted, the pressure of will itself remains, even without any recognized motive, and makes itself known with terrible pain as a feeling of the most frightful desolation and emptiness. If from all this, which with ordinary degrees of willing is felt only in a smaller measure, and produces only the ordinary degree of dejection, there necessarily arise an excessive inner torment, an eternal unrest, an incurable pain in the case of a person who is the appearance of the will reaching to extreme wickedness, he then seeks indirectly the alleviation of which he is incapable directly, in other words, he tries to mitigate his own suffering by the sight of another's, and at the same time recognizes this as an expression of his power. The suffering of another becomes for him an end in itself; it is a spectacle over which he gloats; and so arises the phenomenon of cruelty proper, of bloodthirstiness, so often revealed by history in the Neros and Domitians, in the African Deys, in Robespierre and others. (*W1* 364/H. 2, 430)

Schopenhauer's explanation of extreme wickedness may suggest that this form of malice is egoistic, even though Schopenhauer stresses that a wicked person 'will often not shrink from great harm to himself in order to injure others' (*BM* 192/H. 4, 253). It seems that if the wicked person bears this harm, it could be to realize the delight associated with exercising the power to cause another pain and, thereby, of having another's misery over which he or she 'gloats' (*W1* 364/H. 2, 430).[32] So it appears that the malicious character is motivated by egoism. While Schopenhauer's analysis of extreme wickedness mentions that individuals consumed by this passion take pleasure in another's misery, Schopenhauer does not believe that taking pleasure in an action is sufficient to show that an action aims at the agent's own well-being. Schopenhauer is committed to a theory of motivation in which any satisfied desire is, in some sense, pleasant. So it is not unusual for him to mention some sort of pleasure experienced by anyone who satisfies a desire. Yet it is the intended end of an action that marks it as non-egoistic or signifies whether or not it is egoistic. As S. I. Benn notes, 'He [a malicious character] is no less disinterested in rejoicing in it [another's misfortune] than a benevolent person who rejoiced in someone else's good fortune'.[33] In either case, the pleasure associated with these actions is an unintended result of successfully accomplishing the end one desires.

IV COMPASSION: THE MORAL INCENTIVE

Schopenhauer claims that 'only insofar as an action has sprung from compassion does it have moral worth; and every action resulting for any other motives has none' (*BM* 144/H. 4, 208–9).[34] Schopenhauer's reduction of actions possessing moral worth to actions motivated by compassion, the desire for another's well-being, takes the form, at first, of an argument by elimination. Schopenhauer attempts to

explain actions possessing moral worth, actions like voluntary justice, pure philanthropy, and real magnanimity, by uncovering the
motive for these types of actions. Since Schopenhauer conceives of
actions of pure justice as actions in which agents restrain their behaviour to keep from harming others, and actions of pure philanthropy
as actions in which agents seek another's well-being, he argues that
neither egoism nor malice is a motive for these types of actions. In
both cases, he contends, the ultimate end of agents' actions is to advance others' well-being either by refraining from harming them or
by relieving their misfortune. Because the ultimate end of egoistic
actions is an agent's own well-being, and that of malicious actions is
another's misfortune, he concludes that neither egoism nor malice is
the motive for actions possessing moral worth. Thus Schopenhauer
concludes that these actions must be motivated by compassion because he has eliminated two of his three fundamental incentives.
Since Schopenhauer realizes, however, that arguments from elimination are not fully satisfying because of their negative nature, his
second strategy is to show that the virtues of justice (*Gerechtigkeit*)
and philanthropy (*Menschenliebe*) follow from compassion. These,
he believes, are the cardinal virtues, the virtues from which 'all the
virtues flow' (*BM* 167/H. 4, 230).[35] Thus Schopenhauer believes that
he will demonstrate that all virtues follow from compassion by showing how these cardinal virtues are derived from compassion.

Before he attempts to derive justice and philanthropy from compassion, Schopenhauer confronts a significant problem for his ethics
of compassion. In light of the centrality of egoism in human conduct, how is it possible for agents to desire another's well-being?
Schopenhauer argues that this is possible only through a form of
identification with another that moves a person to treat another's
woe like his or her own. This identification occurs, he states, when
'I suffer directly with him [*Ich . . . geradezu mit leide*], I feel *his* woe
as I ordinarily feel only my own; and, likewise, I directly desire his
weal in the same way I otherwise desire only my own. But this requires that I am in some way *identified with him*, in other words,
that this entire *difference* between me and everyone else, which is
the very basis of my egoism, is eliminated, to a certain extent at
least' (*BM* 143–4/H. 4, 208).

Schopenhauer's understanding of compassion is literal, that is, he
means that agents literally experience another's suffering through

compassion. Schopenhauer emphasizes this when he rejects the Italian philosopher Ubaldo Cassina's attempt in *Saggio analitico sulla compassione* (*Analytical Essay on Compassion*) (1788) to explain compassion as a function of imagining another's suffering as one's own. Schopenhauer argues:

> This is by no means the case; on the contrary, at every moment we remain clearly conscious that *he* is the sufferer, not *we*; and it is precisely in *his* person, not in ours, that we feel the suffering, to our grief and sorrow. We suffer *with* him [*Wir leiden*, mit *ihm*] and hence *in* him; we feel his pain as *his*, and do not imagine that it is ours. In fact, the happier our state, and hence the more the consciousness of it is contrasted with the other man's fate, the more susceptible we are to compassion. (*BM* 147/H. 4, 211–12)

It is easy to understand why Schopenhauer regards compassion as the great mystery of ethics, since he believes that compassion involves immediate participation in another's suffering, a participation that involves the experience of another's suffering in the other's body. To explain the possibility of this extraordinary experience, Schopenhauer will ultimately appeal to his metaphysics of the will. At this point in his argument, however, Schopenhauer believes that he has provided a plausible explanation of how the experience of compassion overcomes the deeply egoistic tendencies of humans. Compassionate agents are moved to pursue the well-being of others because they experience others' suffering as their own. Since suffering typically presents a motive for agents to seek to relieve or eliminate it, and since compassionate agents recognize that it is another's suffering that they experience, they desire the other's well-being, just as the experience of their own suffering excites the desire for their own well-being. Schopenhauer's account of the motivational force of compassion shows, he thinks, that his moral motive overcomes egoism and that it has little to do with an agent's reason or intelligence – that it announces itself spontaneously. In this way, Schopenhauer sees his explanation of the moral motive as answering one of the defects of Kant's; it shows how the moral motive overcomes egoism.

Schopenhauer's moral principle, *Neminem laede, imo omnes, quantum potes, juva*, contains two commands that summarize lines of conduct to which moral worth is attributed.[36] *Neminen laede*, the injunction to 'Hurt no one,' signifies the virtue of justice, and *omnes*, *quantum potes, juva*, the injunction to 'Help everyone as much as you can,' denotes the virtue of philanthropy. Schopenhauer views justice and philanthropy as expressing different degrees of compassion, and he argues that compassion is a response to any sentient being, human and non-human alike. He associates compassion for animals so intimately with goodness of character that he asserts 'that whoever is cruel to animals cannot be a good human' (*BM* 179/H. 4, 242). Although Schopenhauer's analyses of compassion tend to focus on compassion as the response of one person to another, he suggests that animals, while lacking a 'conscious morality' because they lack reason, are susceptible to compassion. Thus it is meaningful to talk about 'goodness and badness' (*BM* 151/H. 4, 215) of the characters of different species of animals and of the individual characters of the highest genera of animals. Schopenhauer also believes that compassion can be a unifying motive of groups of people, motivating large-scale actions to relieve the sufferings of groups: '[A]fter long deliberation and difficult debates, the magnanimous British nation gave twenty million pounds to purchase the freedom of the Negro slaves in its colonies' (*BM* 166/H. 4, 230). It is likely that Schopenhauer's claims about non-humans having compassion and jointly compassionate actions towards the generalized suffering of a group of persons are unique within the Western moral tradition.

Schopenhauer's derivation of the virtue of justice from compassion is straightforward. He considers justice the first degree of compassion, since it is negative. Schopenhauer believes that we are originally inclined to harm others because of our needs and desires or our feelings of hatred and anger, which may arise from the inevitable conflicts inherent in living in a peopled world. Our own experiences are directly and immediately given, compared to the sufferings of others, which are indirect and mediated. So our own experiences possess, Schopenhauer claims, the *jus primi occupantis*, the right of first occupancy, and have a conative impetus which inclines us to act in ways that harm others. The first degree of compassion, he claims, 'opposes and impedes those sufferings which I intend to cause to others by my inherent antimoral forces' (*BM* 149/H. 4, 213). The negative nature of this expression of compassion is that it inclines agents not to do as they planned; it leads them to refrain from doing that which they originally intended. Thus the prospect of the other's suffering moves them not to cause this harm. So Schopenhauer claims, 'If my disposition is susceptible to compassion up to that degree, it will restrain me, wherever and whenever I feel inclined to use another's suffering as a means to the attainment of my ends; it is immaterial whether that suffering is instantaneous or comes later, whether it is direct or indirect, or effected through intermediate links' (*BM* 149/H. 4, 214).[37]

Whereas compassion as the source of justice acts as a restraining motive for either an egoistic or a malicious action, compassion as the basis of philanthropy assumes a positive character: 'This second degree is clearly distinguished from the first by the *positive character* of the action resulting from it, since compassion now not only restrains me from injuring another, but even impels me to help him' (*BM* 163/H. 4, 227). Schopenhauer explains this greater degree of compassion as being founded on a more deeply felt participation in another's distress, a participation that senses the suffering of the other as more urgent and greater. Depending on the urgency or greatness of the other's suffering, compassion can move agents, Schopenhauer believes, to perform lesser or greater sacrifices for the patient of compassion, with such sacrifices consisting in 'expenditure of my bodily and mental powers on his behalf, in the loss of property, health, freedom, and even life itself' (ibid.). Since philanthropy consists in helping others, Schopenhauer believes that it is clear how compassion is the basis of philanthropy. In being compassionate towards the suffering of another, compassionate characters are led to treat the other's suffering as their own – they desire to secure the other's well-being by relieving the other's suffering.

Schopenhauer's description of compassion highlights both its cognitive and conative functions in moral behaviour. In a sense, Schopenhauer blends these functions by emphasizing that compassion involves a recognition of another's suffering as an evil not to be caused (justice) or as an evil to be relieved (philanthropy). This is contrasted with the indifference to another's suffering found in egoism, which is not so much a cognitive as a conative defect. The egoist is not moved by the suffering engendered by the pursuit of the agent's well-being. It is not that the egoist does not recognize another's suffering; rather, the egoist is not moved to refrain from acting because another will suffer. When egoism rises to a dominant form of life for an individual having self-interests whose realization systematically entails that others must suffer, Schopenhauer regards individuals of this type as possessing an evil character, one that is systematically unjust. Malice, like compassion, has both a cognitive and a conative function. It involves the recognition that others suffer, but instead of simply failing to recognize this as an evil not to be produced, the prospect of the other's misery moves the malicious character to bring about this suffering. This is not to say that Schopenhauer believes that a malicious person recognizes the other's suffering as a 'good,' but that despite the recognition that suffering is an evil, the malicious personality is moved to act to produce this suffering. In this way, malicious persons have more evil characters than extreme egoists, and they engage in behaviours more reprehensible than those of extreme egoists. The very worst malicious characters personify pure evil for Schopenhauer, the devil, in contrast to the very best characters, who personify the saint.

V   METAPHYSICAL GROUNDING OF THE
URPHÄNOMENE OF ETHICS

'Virtues,' Schopenhauer claims, 'must be qualities of the will' (*P2* 203/H. 6, 217), as are vices. As qualities of the will, both virtues and vices are deep-seated dispositions of character. Since Schopenhauer identifies a person's character as a person's essence, virtues and vices become markers of the moral quality of a person. Moreover, because Schopenhauer finds that the moral quality of a person's conduct follows from a person's character, and because it is a person's character that ultimately bears responsibility for a person's conduct, he conceives of virtues and vices as intimately connected to individual agency for which the person bears the responsibility. Virtuous and vicious persons are the doers of their deeds, according to Schopenhauer, even though neither virtuous nor vicious persons chose their character.[38] The ethical difference is 'innate and ineradicable' (*BM* 187/H. 4, 249), according to Schopenhauer: 'The wicked man is born with his wickedness as much as the serpent is with its poisonous fangs and glands; and he is as little able to change his character as the serpent its fangs' (ibid.). There is no such thing as moral education, Schopenhauer argues, if by moral education one means a form of abstract knowledge that changes a person's ultimate moral ends. In this sense, Schopenhauer claims that morality cannot be taught. At best, instruction can only alter the choice of means a person employs to realize his or her ultimate ends, that is, 'can point out to the egoist that by giving up small advantages, he will obtain the greater . . .' (*BM* 194/H. 4, 255) or 'through instruction concerning the circumstances of life, and thus by enlightening the mind, even goodness of character can be brought to a more logical and complete expression of its true nature' (ibid.). Yet, in these cases, a person's character is not transformed, Schopenhauer believes; 'The head becomes clear; the heart remains unreformed' (*BM* 195/H. 4, 255). The 'heart,' a person's character or will, moreover, is that which is metaphysical, so that the moral quality of a person's behaviour is metaphysically significant.

Schopenhauer's axiology of character stresses the complexity of types of moral characters. Some evil characters are worse than others and some are 'better,' that is, less evil. The same is true of good characters. Yet Schopenhauer details a basis for a unified theory of the virtues and vices grounded in a person's character. Evil characters, those who express the vices of injustice, malice, or both, pursue ends in such a way that they treat others as non-egos; their behaviour shows that they assume a distinction between themselves and others. Extreme egoists act as if others have no interests; the interests of others are ignored even when others are harmed. Malicious characters do not simply and thoughtlessly harm others due to an increasingly inflated form of self-concern; rather, their ends are directly the woe of others. Good characters, conversely, engage in a form of behaviour in which a lesser degree of distinction between self and other is manifest. Just characters restrain their behaviour when there is the prospect that they will harm others. Philanthropic characters do not simply refrain from harming others; rather, they are disposed to directly aid suffering others. Good characters, Schopenhauer claims, act as if others are 'I once more' (*BM* 211/H. 4, 272), using the Vedic formula '*Tat tvam asi* [This art thou]' (*W1* 374/H. 2, 443) to express the keynote of their dispositions. The behaviour of a good character shows that '*he makes less of a distinction than do the rest between himself and others*' (*BM* 204/H. 4, 265). The magnitude of willing, its kinds, degrees, and strength, towards the well-being of others underlies Schopenhauer's classification of moral character types. This notion also undergirds particularized dispositions of character that receive specific names as virtues and vices. Thus the vice of intemperance, a vice of injustice, is a disposition to over-consume goods even when it harms others. Thus it is a disposition that ignores the needs of others. The vice of *Schadenfreude*, a vice of malice, is a disposition to delight in another's misery. Conversely, the virtue of honesty, a virtue of justice, is a disposition not to deceive another to secure one's own interests at the other's expense, while the virtue of charity, a virtue of philanthropy, is a disposition to make some sacrifice to relieve another's misery or misfortune.

Wittgenstein, writing in a quasi-Schopenhauerian mood, claims that 'The world of the happy man is different from that of the unhappy man.'[39] The same is true, according to Schopenhauer, of the worlds of good and evil characters. Evil characters express the standpoint that the world and others are non-egos, and good characters express the standpoint that everything is an 'I once more.' Schopenhauer identifies these attitudes as expressions of a mode of knowledge that shows itself 'not only in individual actions, but in the whole nature of consciousness and disposition [*Stimmung*], which is, therefore, so essentially different in the *good* character from that which it is in the *bad*' (*BM* 211/H. 4, 272). Because the evil character perceives the world as non-ego, Schopenhauer attributes to it an attitude of hostility to the world: 'Thus the keynote of his disposition is hatred, spitefulness, suspicion, envy, and *Schadenfreude*' (ibid.). Evil characters have no confidence that others would ever help them in time of need, and if they were ever to receive help, evil persons would regard this as an act of stupidity and would not show gratitude. Thus Schopenhauer sees evil characters as suffering a form of moral isolation, radical separateness from others, one that easily leads to a general mood of despair. The good character, however, 'lives in an external world that is homogeneous with his own true being' (ibid.). The keynote of a good person's disposition is friendliness, Schopenhauer writes, and good characters assume that others take the reciprocal interest in their well-being that they take in others' well-being. Thus good characters enjoy a sense of moral solidarity with others, a solidarity that enables them to ask for the assistance of others with assurance of their aid.

Although Schopenhauer argues that good and evil characters seem to live in different worlds, there is only one world against which Schopenhauer measures their desires, attitudes, and behaviours. Good persons express a form of life that is metaphysically warranted, whereas evil persons live entangled in a 'delusion' (*W2* 606/H. 3,

695–6). By treating others as non-ego, the evil person posits a wide gulf, an absolute distinction, between self and others. While Schopenhauer believes that the perspective of the evil character seems justified from an empirical point of view, this point of view is itself unjustified. Schopenhauer appeals to the truth of transcendental idealism to justify his position. Space and time, the *principium individuationis*, which makes plurality possible, is simply a function of human cognition and, as such, applies only to appearances of things, to representations, and not to things in themselves. Behind appearances stands the metaphysical will, something Schopenhauer believes that he demonstrates in *The World as Will and Representation* and in *On the Will in Nature*. By living as if others are 'I once more,' good people express practically that which is expressed theoretically by Schopenhauer's metaphysics – everything is an expression of the single metaphysical will. Because good persons act as if everything is one, he calls their behaviour 'practical mysticism insofar as it ultimately springs from the same knowledge that constitutes the essence of all mysticism proper' (*BM* 212/H. 4, 273). The 'great mystery' of compassion, the motive of good characters' conduct, is solved by attributing to compassion an intuition that glances through the *principium individuationis* to recognize that their 'inner being exists' (ibid.) in others. In this way, Schopenhauer's narrower sense of morality ends, grounded in his metaphysics of the will.[40]

NOTES

1 See *MR* 1 59/Hn. 1, 55 (sect. 92).
2 See *WN* 140/H. 4, 141.
3 Arthur Hübscher, *The Philosophy of Schopenhauer in Its Intellectual Context*, trans. Joachim T. Baer and David E. Cartwright (Lewiston, N.Y.: Edwin Mellen Press, 1989), 91. I have argued for the centrality of ethics in Schopenhauer's philosophy in 'Schopenhauer as Moral Philosopher – Towards the Actuality of his Ethics,' *Schopenhauer-Jahrbuch* 70 (1989), 54–65.
4 Schopenhauer refers to his *The Two Fundamental Problems of Ethics* (*Die beiden Grundprobleme der Ethik*, 1841) as dealing with morality in the narrower sense. This book is composed of two essays originally written for prize essay contests. The first, *On the Freedom of the Human Will* (*FW; Ueber die Freiheit des menschlichen Willens*, 1839), received the prize offered by the Norwegian Scientific Society, while the second, *On*

the Basis of Morality (*BM*; *Ueber die Grundlage der Moral*, 1840), whose original title was 'On the Foundation of Morality' (*Ueber das Fundament der Moral*), failed to receive the prize from the Royal Danish Society of Scientific Studies despite being the only entry. In the Preface to the first edition of this book, Schopenhauer claims that these essays 'mutually contribute to the completion of a system of the fundamental truths of ethics' (*BM* 3/H. 4, v), and, in 1847, with his characteristic lack of modesty, he claims that it was 'the most important ethical work that has appeared in the last sixty years' (*FR* 74/H. 1, 50). Since Schopenhauer's essay on the freedom of the will concentrates primarily on his views on freedom and determinism, it deals with issues outside the scope of this essay.

5 Iris Murdoch, *Metaphysics as a Guide to Morals* (New York: Allen Lane/ Penguin Press, 1992), 63.

6 The core of writings that constitute Schopenhauer's direct work on ethics are *W1*, Book 4; *W2*, chapters XL–XLIX; *WN*, 'Reference to Ethics'; *FW*; *BM*; and *P2*, chs. 8 and 9. Schopenhauer's work in the narrower sense of morality receives two different presentations. In his main work, it is presented presuming his metaphysics of the will. In *BM* he develops it and then grounds it in his metaphysics. Schopenhauer folds his analysis of morally worthwhile behaviour into his theory of salvation by arguing that 'from the same source from which all goodness, affection, virtue, and nobility of character spring, there ultimately arises also what I call denial of the will to life' (*W1* 378/H. 2, 447). This 'source' is a form of recognition of the metaphysical unity of being – that everything is an expression of the will. For a concise description of the transition from virtue to asceticism, see John E. Atwell's *Schopenhauer on the Character of the World: The Metaphysics of the Will* (Los Angeles: University of California Press, 1995), 155–6.

7 There are points of contact and shared perspectives between Kant and Schopenhauer. The idea of a good will functions centrally in their ethics, although they have different concepts of the will and what constitutes its goodness. Both Kant and Schopenhauer reject consequentialist theories of moral value, propose a morality of disposition (*Moralität der Gesinnung*), view self-interested actions as lacking moral value, and attribute a transcended character to moral behaviour. Yet, as D. W. Hamlyn notes in his fine general study of Schopenhauer, 'His rejection of Kant is not simply a rejection of Kantian ethical questions; it is also a rejection of Kantian questions in this field' (*Schopenhauer* [London: Routledge & Kegan Paul, 1980], 136).

8 John E. Atwell, *Schopenhauer: The Human Character* (Philadelphia: Temple University Press, 1990), 91. Lawrence A. Blum contends that

On the Basis of Morality has 'several powerful insights and perspectives on moral philosophy,' and he draws on some elements of Schopenhauer's critique of Kant's ethics and his views on compassion, but he also finds that Schopenhauer's Kant critique is 'mostly unsympathetic, and often grossly distorted'; see his *Friendship, Altruism and Morality* (London: Routledge & Kegan Paul, 1980), 211, n. 35.

9 References to Kant's works cite the volume and page number of the *Akademie* edition, *Kants gesammelte Schriften*, edited by the Royal Prussian Academy of Sciences (Berlin: Georg Reimer, later Walter de Gruyter, 1900 –). Schopenhauer is quoting *Groundwork of the Metaphysic of Morals (Grundlegung der Metaphysik der Sitten*, 1785), 4:426. The emphases are Schopenhauer's.

10 Schopenhauer anticipated one of the central theses G. E. M. Anscombe advances in 'Modern Moral Philosophy,' *Philosophy*, 33 (1958), 1–19, a paper frequently cited as reviving the interest of Anglo-American philosophers in virtue ethics. Like Schopenhauer before her, Anscombe argues that the central concepts of a law conception of ethics, such as 'moral duty,' 'moral obligation,' and the 'moral sense of ought,' are legalistic concepts derived from Judaeo-Christian moral thought, and that these concepts do not make sense without the existence of a law giver, God. She then diagnoses one of the ills of modern moral philosophy as the retention of these concepts and the rejection of their theological framework, and she states that the central concepts of a law conception of ethics 'ought to be jettisoned' (1). Like Anscombe, Richard Taylor advocates a return to an ethics of virtue, but unlike Anscombe, Taylor's views are informed by Schopenhauer. In his *Good and Evil* (New York: Macmillan, 1970), concerning *BM*, Taylor writes that 'the effect of this work on my own philosophy has probably been more profound than anything that I have ever read' (xii). Schopenhauer's influence on *Good and Evil* can be detected in Taylor's critique of Kantian ethics, his moral psychology, his voluntaristic account of good and evil, and some of his methodological commitments. Schopenhauer's influence on Taylor can also be detected in *Reason Faith and Ethics* (Englewood Cliffs, N.J.: Prentice-Hall, 1985; reprinted as *Virtue Ethics: An Introduction*, Interlaken, N.Y.: Linden Books, 1991), in his critique of Kant's ethics, and in his criticisms of modern moral philosophy: 'The Modern age, more or less, repudiating the idea of a divine law giver, has nevertheless tried to retain the ideas of moral right and wrong, not noticing that, in casting God aside, they have also abolished the conditions of meaningfulness for moral right and wrong as well' (2f.). For replies to Schopenhauer-like claims concerning the meaninglessness of terms like 'moral duty' and 'ought' in the absence of a moral legislator, see John Atwell, *Ends and Principles in Kant's Moral Thought*

(Dordrecht: Martinus Nijhoff, 1986), 218–20; Alan Donagan, *The Theory of Morality* (Chicago: University of Chicago Press, 1977), 2–3; Kurt Baier, 'Radical Virtue Ethics,' *Midwest Studies in Philosophy* 13 (1988), 126–9.

11 The charge that Kant's moral laws are hypothetical rather than categorical imperatives prefigures Philippa Foot's well-known 'Morality as a System of Hypothetical Imperatives,' *The Philosophical Review* 81 (1972), 305–16, where she argues that morality has been conceived mistakenly as possessing a categorical force that binds agents regardless of their interests. Foot argues that morality is a system of hypothetical imperatives whose binding force lies precisely in the interests and desires people happen to possess. In regard to the Kantian claim that acting rationally is acting morally, Foot holds a position much like that of Schopenhauer; 'The fact is that the man who rejects morality because he sees no reason to obey its rules can be convicted of villainy but not inconsistency. Nor will his actions necessarily be irrational. Irrational actions are those in which a man in some way defeats his own purposes, doing what is calculated to be disadvantageous or to frustrate his ends. Immorality does not *necessarily* involve any such thing' (311).

12 Although Schopenhauer placed this passage in quotation marks, as far as I can determine, Kant never used this as a formula of the categorical imperative. It is close, however, to the formula of universal law given in *Groundwork* 4:421.

13 *Groundwork* 4:402 (Schopenhauer's emphases).

14 *Groundwork* 4:400.

15 Kant, *Critique of Practical Reason* 5:31 (Schopenhauer's emphases).

16 Kant, *Groundwork* 4:401 n. Schopenhauer ignores Kant's phenomenological description of respect found in this footnote.

17 See Kant, *Groundwork* 4:398. Also see Schopenhauer's analysis of this example at *W1* 525–6/H. 2, 623.

18 *Critique of Practical Reason* 5:84.

19 *Critique of Practical Reason* 5:118.

20 While Schopenhauer agrees with Kant, despite their different conceptions of reason, that humans are distinct from other animals because they possess reason, he rejects the consequent Kantian claim that non-human animals are not morally considerable. Schopenhauer condemns the view that 'beings devoid of reason (hence animals) are *things* and therefore should be treated merely as *means* that are not at the same time an *end*' (*BM* 95/H. 4, 161). Schopenhauer views Kant's exclusion of non-human animals from the moral sphere as another indication of how theology intrudes into Kant's morality: 'Thus, because Christian morality leaves animals out of account ..., they are at once outlawed in philosophical

morals; they are mere "things", mere *means* to any ends whatsoever' (*BM* 96/H. 4, 162). For Schopenhauer, non-human animals are morally considerable because they, like humans, are essentially will, and they too suffer. Because of the unenlightened view towards non-human animals found in mainstream Western theology and philosophy, Schopenhauer recognizes a superiority in Eastern intellectual traditions and prides himself on sharing their moral insights. For an excellent discussion of Schopenhauer's views concerning the moral status of non-humans, see G. E. Varner's 'The Schopenhauerian Challenge in Environmental Ethics,' *Environmental Ethics* 7 (1985), 209–29.

21 *Groundwork* 4:461 (Schopenhauer's emphases).

22 Henry E. Allison quotes this passage in *Kant's Theory of Freedom* (Cambridge: Cambridge University Press, 1993), 230, and he argues, contrary to Schopenhauer, that Kant's appeal to the 'fact of reason' marks an advance in Kant's thought. Allison's sophisticated treatment of Kant's moral philosophy and his moral psychology aptly show that Schopenhauer's criticisms are often based on a rather superficial reading of Kant. Allison agrees, however, with Schopenhauer's judgment that Kant's treatment of the moral law as a 'fact of reason' shows that Kant's deduction in *Groundwork* failed; see 201.

23 Moritz Schlick applauded Schopenhauer on this point: 'Thus the central problem of ethics concerns the causal explanation of moral behaviour; all others in relationship to it sink to the level of preliminary or subordinate questions. The moral problem was clearly formulated in this way by Schopenhauer, whose sound sense of reality led him to the correct path here (if not the solution) and guarded him from the Kantian formulation of the problem and from the post-Kantian philosophy of value'; see his 'What Is the Aim of Ethics?' in *Logical Positivism*, ed. A. J. Ayer (New York: Free Press, 1959), 263.

24 Nietzsche adopts the gown of the moral sceptic against Schopenhauer in *Human, All Too Human*, and he attempts to reduce both malice and compassion to egoism; see my 'Nietzsche's Use and Abuse of Schopenhauer's Moral Philosophy for Life' in Christopher Janaway (ed.), *Willing and Nothingness: Schopenhauer as Nietzsche's Educator* (Oxford: Oxford University Press, 1998).

25 See Nagel's *The Possibility of Altruism* (Princeton, N.J.: Princeton University Press, 1970), 1, 14.

26 In a letter to Johann August Becker, which is perhaps Schopenhauer's most significant letter about his ethics, he claims that the desire for one's own woe has ascetic rather than moral value; see Arthur Schopenhauer, *Gesammelte Briefe*, ed. Arthur Hübscher (Bonn: Bouvier, 1987), Dec. 10, 1844, 221.

27 See her 'Ways of Wrongdoing: A Theory of Vices,' *The Journal of Value Inquiry* 23 (1989), 319.

28 See his *Arthur Schopenhauer: Transzendentalphilosophie und Metaphysik des Willens* (Stuttgart/Bad Cannstatt: Frommann-Holzboog, 1991), 357. For a concise description of Schopenhauer's political philosophy, see Bryan Magee's fine study, *The Philosophy of Schopenhauer* (Oxford: Clarendon Press, 1987), 202–5.

29 An evil (*böse*) character is disposed to harm others, whereas a good (*gut*) character is disposed to help them; see *W1* 362–3/H. 2, 428–9 and *BM* 204/H. 4, 264–5. I discuss Schopenhauer's views on moral character in 'Schopenhauer's Axiological Analysis of Character,' *Revue Internationale de Philosophie* 42 (1988), 18–36.

30 At *P2* 202/H. 6, 215–16, Schopenhauer recommends that we consider the misery, unhappiness, anxiety, and pain others suffer so that we avoid misanthropy. His point is that these considerations should awaken our compassion.

31 Although Nietzsche criticizes Schopenhauer's condemnation of *Schadenfreude*, it is likely that Schopenhauer's analysis of the ill will expressed in malice informed Nietzsche's concept of *ressentiment*. See section 103 of the first volume of Nietzsche's *Human, All Too Human*.

32 In *Schopenhauer: The Human Character*, Atwell argues that 'cruelty appears to be a form, albeit perhaps an extreme form, of egoism, and not a unique "moral incentive" ' (105).

33 See his 'Wickedness,' *Ethics* 95 (1985), 805. Benn quotes Schopenhauer's description of extreme wickedness from *W1* 364/H. 2, 430, to motivate his analysis of 'malignity,' which Benn views as a form of wickedness in which a person rejoices in contemplating another's suffering as an evil.

34 I present an analytical model of Schopenhauer's conception of compassion, and I criticize it and his derivations of the virtues of justice and philanthropy in 'Compassion,' in *Zeit der Ernte: Festschrift für Arthur Hübscher zum 85. Geburtstag* (Stuttgart/Bad Cannstatt: Frommann-Holzboog, 1982), 60–9. One of the most counterintuitive theses Schopenhauer maintains is the negative nature of happiness, pleasure, and well-being, where these states are the absence of unhappiness, pain, and misfortune; see, for example, *BM* 146/H. 4, 210.

35 William K. Frankena cites Schopenhauer and agrees with his claim that philanthropy and justice are the cardinal moral virtues; 'It seems to me that all of the usual virtues (such as love, courage, temperance, honesty, gratitude, and considerateness), at least insofar as they are *moral* virtues, can be derived from these two. Insofar as a disposition cannot be derived from benevolence and justice, I should try to argue either that it is not a

moral virtue . . . or that it is not a virtue at all,' *Ethics* (Englewood Cliffs, N.J.: Prentice-Hall, 1973), 65.

36 It is odd that Schopenhauer does not provide a set of specific virtues for each of his moral maxims, something he did for the maxims he attributed to extreme egoism and malice. He does claim, however, that the virtues of justice and philanthropy cover the same moral terrain, respectively, as Kant's 'duties of law and duties of virtue' (*BM* 148/H. 4, 212). From his discussion of the cardinal virtues in *BM*, sections 17 and 18, fairness, conscientiousness, and honesty would be particular virtues of justice, and benevolence, charity, and love would be particular virtues of philanthropy.

37 Schopenhauer views principles as 'indispensable to a moral course of life' (*BM* 150/H. 4, 214). Principles, he argues, summarize the habits of mind associated with moral conduct. The just individual shows steadfast adherence to principles, according to Schopenhauer. Since principles of justice are derived from compassion, he calls this resolve 'indirect compassion.' When one's resolve to follow principles of justice is challenged by other motives – suppose, for example, that the agent is tempted to keep something of value he or she found instead of following the rule 'Return property to its rightful owner' – Schopenhauer claims that one can enliven one's resolve by reawakening one's compassion through a consideration of 'the trouble, grief, or lamentation of the loser' (*BM* 152/ H. 4, 216). In this way, by following principles, Schopenhauer claims, compassion operates in just individuals 'not so much *actu* as *potentiâ*' (*BM* 151/H. 2, 215).

38 For a good discussion of Schopenhauer's 'actualism,' his belief that whatever a person has done is the only thing he or she could have done, see Atwell's *Schopenhauer: The Human Character*, 67–74. Atwell attempts to show that there are 'many types of ethical judgments compatible with both actualism regarding action and the unchangeability of the moral character' (74).

39 Ludwig Wittgenstein, *Tractatus Logico-Philosophicus*, 6. 43. For an insightful discussion of Schopenhauer's influence on Wittgenstein's view of the self, see Christopher Janaway, *Self and World in Schopenhauer's Philosophy* (Oxford: Clarendon Press, 1989), 317–42.

40 For criticisms of Schopenhauer's morality of compassion, see Atwell, *Schopenhauer: The Human Character*, 98–23; Bernard Bykhovsky, *Schopenhauer and the Ground of Existence*, trans. Phillip Moran (Amsterdam: Grüner, 1984), 121–45; Hamlyn, *Schopenhauer*, 133–46; Max Scheler, *The Nature of Sympathy*, trans. Peter Heath (Hamden, Conn.: Shoe String Press, 1973), 51–5; Georg Simmel, *Schopenhauer and Nietzsche*, trans.

Helmut Loiskandl, Deena Weinstein, and Michael Weinstein (Amherst: University of Massachusetts Press, 1986), 118–25; and Julian Young, *Willing and Unwilling: A Study in the Philosophy of Arthur Schopenhauer* (Dordrecht: Martinus Nijhoff, 1987), 103–22. Nietzsche opposed Schopenhauer's morality of compassion throughout most of his philosophical career; see my 'Kant, Schopenhauer, and Nietzsche on the Morality of Pity,' *Journal of the History of Ideas* 45 (1984), 83–98, and 'The Last Temptation of Zarathustra,' *Journal of the History of Philosophy* 31 (1993), 49–69. I defend Schopenhauer against some of Nietzsche's criticisms of his *Mitleids-Moral* in 'Schopenhauer's Compassion and Nietzsche's Pity,' *Schopenhauer-Jahrbuch* 69 (1988), 557–67.

9 Schopenhauer on Death

> We abhor *death*, and as nature does not lie and the fear of
> death is the voice of nature, there must yet be some reason
> for this.
>
> Schopenhauer [1]

I ON DEATH AND LIFE AS DYING

The concept of death is a fundamental adjunct of Schopenhauer's
metaphysics of appearance and Will. Schopenhauer interprets death
as the aim and purpose of life. He maintains that to live is to suffer,
that the triumph of death is inevitable, and that existence is a constant dying. Yet Schopenhauer also insists that death is the denial
of the individual will or will-to-live; that birth and death as events
in the phenomenal world are alike unreal; that death is not complete annihilation; and that suicide, though not morally objectionable, is philosophically pointless because it affirms the will-to-live.
The paradoxes in Schopenhauer's reflections on the nature of death
must be understood in order to appreciate what he means by the
empirical will in its relation to Will as thing-in-itself in his unique
brand of post-Kantian idealism. [2]

What is death? How should philosophy explain the significance
of the extinction of individual consciousness? Schopenhauer's frequently misunderstood pessimism consists in his affirmation of all
phenomena as manifestations of Will as thing-in-itself in essential
self-conflict. Schopenhauer regards the hopeful expectancy that embraces life as a deluded involvement with the most superficial aspects
of the world as appearance. He eulogizes death as a welcome release

from the individual will's condemnation to a life of ineffectual suffering. In his masterwork, *The World as Will and Representation*, Schopenhauer asserts:

At bottom, optimism is the unwarranted self-praise of the real author of the world, namely of the will-to-live which complacently mirrors itself in its work. Accordingly optimism is not only a false but also a pernicious doctrine, for it presents life as a desirable state and man's happiness as its aim and object. Starting from this, everyone then believes he has the most legitimate claim to happiness and enjoyment. If, as usually happens, these do not fall to his lot, he believes that he suffers an injustice, in fact that he misses the whole point of his existence; whereas it is far more correct to regard work, privation, misery, and suffering, crowned by death, as the aim and object of our life (as is done by Brahmanism and Buddhism, and also by genuine Christianity), since it is these that lead to the denial of the will-to-live. (W2 584/H. 3, 671)

As a consequence of his metaphysics of time, Schopenhauer argues that existence is a constant dying, a process of the individual empirical will moving inexorably toward death as its aim and purpose. By virtue of dwelling in the world of appearance, individual existence is caught up in the flow of time whereby the present is continually streaming into the past. Schopenhauer seems to conceive of the past as a kind of repository of death, of no longer existent events, from which he concludes that life, like sand through an hourglass, trickles through the narrow bottleneck of the present moment into the dead past, and that existence is therefore both a constant process of dying and a momentary postponement of ongoing death.

[The individual's] real existence is only in the present, whose unimpeded flight into the past is a constant transition into death, a constant dying. For his past life, ... from the testimony regarding his will that is impressed in it, is entirely finished and done with, dead, and no longer anything. Therefore, as a matter of reason, it must be indifferent to him whether the contents of that past were pains or pleasures. But the present in his hands is constantly becoming the past; the future is quite uncertain and always short. Thus his existence, even considered from the formal side alone, is a continual rushing of the present into the dead past, a constant dying. And if we look at it also from the physical side, it is evident that, just as we know our walking to be only a constantly prevented falling, so is the life of our body only a constantly prevented dying, an ever-deferred death. (W1 311/H. 2, 366–7)

Thus, in the second volume of his major treatise, Schopenhauer quotes Lord Byron's *Euthanasia* with approval, and regards the sentiment it expresses as congenial to his own outlook on the nature of death when Byron proclaims:

> Count o'er the joys thine hours have seen,
> Count o'er thy days from anguish free
> And know, whatever thou hast been,
> 'Tis something better not to be.[3]

At its best, according to Schopenhauer, life is a delayed dying. The pessimism that characterizes Schopenhauer's philosophy implies that life is nothing positive, but rather a temporary reprieve from death, toward which life is implacably directed. Considered in itself, there is no value to life. We can take heart only in the mercifully brief time we may be required to live, which Schopenhauer regards as punishment for the sin of existence. Suffering is unavoidable because the will-to-live reflects the internal self-conflict of Will as thing-in-itself. There is nothing to look forward to as the meaning or final reward or consummation of life except its termination in death. Schopenhauer considers only a dismal prospect of life leading finally to death, of the fleeting duration of life as its one redeeming virtue in eventually ending the suffering of the individual will-to-live.[4]

II AWARENESS OF DEATH

We learn about death by analogy. We see others die and draw the inference that death must also finally visit each of us. The further conclusion that death is the cessation of consciousness and irreversible destruction of the self, or the hopeful expectation of an afterlife in which consciousness in the persistence of the soul survives bodily death, are the two predominant reactions to the awareness of death in reason and religious faith. The awareness and anticipation of death distinguishes human beings from nonhuman animals in Schopenhauer's epistemology and philosophy of mind. He explains:

The animal learns to know death only when he dies, but man consciously draws every hour nearer his death; and at times this makes life a precarious business, even to the man who has not already recognized this character of constant annihilation in the whole of life itself. Mainly on this account, man has philosophies and religions. ... (*W1* 37/H. 2, 44)

It is tempting to criticize Schopenhauer as lacking a sufficient understanding of animal psychology. The closer observation of animal behavior may suggest a recognition of potential death in the way that some higher nonhuman animals deliberately act to preserve their safety, as though they comprehended the mortal danger and the possibility of dying. Similar interpretations in field studies by naturalists indicate that the way in which some higher nonhuman animals react to the death of other animals, especially when it strikes parents, offspring, and siblings, also evinces a primitive awareness of death.

Awareness of death appears to be neither a necessary nor a sufficient condition for self-consciousness, let alone more particularly for human self-consciousness. Schopenhauer nevertheless strikes a resonant chord when he assimilates philosophy and religion as distinctively human pursuits motivated at least indirectly and in part by human awareness of and preoccupation with death. We might agree with Schopenhauer that even if nonhuman animals have some limited prior awareness of death, including the possibility or inevitability of their own deaths, animals do not know about or live in expectation and anticipation of their own deaths in the same way or to the same extent as human beings. Schopenhauer is right to infer that human self-consciousness stands in a special epistemic relation to the fact of death, with far-ranging implications for many aspects of human culture for which there are no obvious parallels in nonhuman animal behavior. The innocence of nonhuman animals in the face of death is in stark contrast with human understanding of the inevitability of death.

Schopenhauer explains the awareness of death as an outcome of the emergence of reason and self-consciousness. The awareness of death is made the origin not only of philosophy and religious belief, but more specifically of what Schopenhauer defines as the characteristic need for metaphysics. Schopenhauer remarks:

Only after the inner being of nature (the will-to-live in its objectification) has ascended vigorously and cheerfully through the two spheres of unconscious beings, and then through the long and broad series of animals, does it finally attain to reflection for the first time with the appearance of reason (*Vernunft*), that is, in man. It then marvels at its own works, and asks itself what it itself is. And its wonder is the more serious, as here for the first time it stands consciously face to face with *death*, and besides the finiteness of all existence, the vanity and fruitlessness of all effort force themselves on it more or less. Therefore with this reflection and astonishment arises the *need for metaphysics* that is peculiar to man alone; accordingly, he is an *animal metaphysicum*. (W2 160/H. 3, 175–6)

Schopenhauer goes so far as to say that death is the decisive pre-condition without which there could be no philosophy. It is unclear whether Schopenhauer is thinking of the awareness of death as a requirement for the philosophical attitude, or of an imaginable race of immortal but otherwise indistinguishably human beings as inca-pable or entirely without need of philosophy. Schopenhauer, in his valuable supplement to the fourth book of *The World as Will and Representation*, 'On Death and Its Relation to the Indestructibility of Our Inner Nature,' appeals to Socrates's pronouncements about death as the source of philosophy:

Death is the real inspiring genius or Musagetes of philosophy, and for this rea-son Socrates defined philosophy as θανάτου μελέτη [preparation for death]. Indeed, without death there would hardly have been any philosophizing. (W2 463/H. 3, 528–9)

The awareness of death is a strange kind of knowledge. The mind cannot express its apprehension of death, according to Schopenhauer, because all of its concepts derive from the objectification of Will in appearance as the individual will-to-live, of which death is the antithesis. Schopenhauer describes the knowledge of death dialecti-cally as an imagined interrogation of the will-to-live in which the will is hypothetically questioned concerning its desire to continue suf-fering. The conflict experienced by individual will can be conceived as ending only when the empirical self is destroyed. The mind tries unsuccessfully to represent death as the negation of its knowledge and experience of life, as an oblivion of consciousness in which the individual will altogether ceases to exist. Schopenhauer writes:

In the hour of death, the decision is made whether man falls back into the womb of nature, or else no longer belongs to her, but –: we lack image, con-cept, and word for this opposite, just because all these are taken from the objectification of the will, and therefore belong to that objectification; consequently, they cannot in any way express its absolute opposite; accordingly, this remains for us a mere negation. However, the death of the individual is in each case the unweariedly repeated question of nature to the will-to-live: 'Have you had enough? Do you wish to escape from me?' (W2 609/H. 3, 699)

The suggestion is that although we can have no representational knowledge of death beyond its negation of the experience of individual willing, nature itself presents a concept of death in its beckoning toward a release from the sufferings of will. Even the desire to sustain life according to Schopenhauer is confused and discordant. The idea of death confronts each person not as the positive representation of an event or a state of being, but more abstractly as the possibility of a definitive end of the individual will's suffering. There is a conflict in the mind's imperfect effort to represent death when the suffering of the individual will induces it to improve its condition by willing its destruction.

III   INEVITABILITY AND UNREALITY OF DEATH

Schopenhauer dwells morbidly on the inevitability of death. He repeats the commonplace that every moment of life brings us one step closer to the abyss. Yet we cannot avoid taking an avid interest in life when death is not immediately at our door, knowing all the while that in the end death must prevail.

Every breath we draw wards off the death that constantly impinges on us. In this way, we struggle with it every second, and again at longer intervals through every meal we eat, every sleep we take, every time we warm ourselves, and so on. Ultimately death must triumph, for by birth it has already become our lot, and it plays with its prey only for a while before swallowing it up. However, we continue our life with great interest and much solicitude as long as possible, just as we blow out a soap-bubble as long and as large as possible, although with the perfect certainty that it will burst. (W1 311/H. 2, 367)

Although Schopenhauer regards death as the purpose of life, he insists that death is only phenomenal. Schopenhauer's distinction between the world as Will or thing-in-itself and as appearance, together with his view of the individual empirical will as belonging to the phenomenal world as representation, implies that the life and

death of the individual will or will-to-live are alike unreal. Schopenhauer states:

As the [W]ill is the thing-in-itself, the inner content, the essence of the world,
but life, the visible world, the phenomenon, is only the mirror of the [W]ill,
this world will accompany the will as inseparably as a body is accompanied
by its shadow; and if will exists, then life, the world, will exist. Therefore
life is certain to the will-to-live, and as long as we are filled with the will-
to-live we need not be apprehensive for our existence, even at the sight of
death. It is true that we see the individual come into being and pass away;
but the individual is only phenomenon, exists only for knowledge involved
in the principle of sufficient reason, in the *principium individuationis*. Naturally, for this knowledge, the individual receives his life as a gift, rises out
of nothing, and then suffers the loss of this gift through death, and returns
to nothing. We, however, wish to consider life philosophically, that is to
say, according to its Ideas, and then we shall find that neither the [W]ill, the
thing-in-itself in all phenomena, nor the subject of knowing, the spectator
of all phenomena, is in any way affected by birth and death. Birth and death
belong only to the phenomenon of the will, and hence to life. . . . (*WI* 275/H.
2, 324)

Nor again according to Schopenhauer is death absolute. The individual will, by virtue of being a manifestation of the world as Will,
has a dual nature. It is at once the ephemeral subject of life and death
and the expression in the world as representation of the real world or
thing-in-itself, the world as Will, blind urging or aimless, undirected
desire. 'There is something in us, however,' Schopenhauer relates,
'which tells us that this is not so, that this is not the end of things,
that death is not an absolute annihilation' (*WI* 324/H. 2, 383).

Schopenhauer's thought at first makes it seem as though he is
holding out the possibility for survival after death. If death is not
absolute annihilation, then some part of a living person must persist
after the event of death. This Schopenhauer admits, but only in a
highly attenuated sense that precludes the possibility of an afterlife
for the empirical self.[5] The Will as thing-in-itself, of which each individual will is an expression in the world as representation, cannot
be destroyed. This is not the comforting sense of survival by which a
particular person with specific memories and expectations continues
after the body's death, as projected by popular religions and mind–
body dualisms in the tradition of Plato and Descartes. Schopenhauer offers no more than the metaphysical indestructibility of any

nonpersonal phenomenal entity in the world of appearance. I may not be totally annihilated at the moment of my death, but this is true at most only in the same diluted sense that trees and rocks cannot be totally annihilated. All material things are manifestations of Will as thing-in-itself, and as such contain an immortal, indestructible part that persists even after they have physically disintegrated, leaving no empirically identifiable trace. The nonfinality of death is no more than the persistence of Will as thing-in-itself that endures regardless of the state of the empirical world as representation, with or without its accidental habitation by living persons or intelligent subjects of individual will. That death is not total annihilation for Schopenhauer is true enough, yet death remains the total annihilation of the self, soul, or subject in the sense of individual will or particular empirical personality.[6]

IV   DEATH, SUFFERING, AND THE WILL-TO-LIVE

Schopenhauer paints a *vanitas* still life, like a Dutch canvas with a grimacing skull, a pocket watch, and an overturned wine glass, to put death in perspective and remind us that it awaits every individual at the end of even the happiest life. He holds, as have other thinkers of pessimistic conviction, that few persons would voluntarily choose to live their lives over again, but gratefully look forward to death as a release. Schopenhauer conjectures:

> But perhaps at the end of his life, no man, if he be sincere and at the same time in possession of his faculties, will ever wish to go through it again. Rather than this, he will much prefer to choose complete non-existence.... Similarly, what has been said by the father of history (Herodotus, vii, 46) has not since been refuted, namely that no person has existed who has not wished more than once that he had not to live through the following day. Accordingly, the shortness of life, so often lamented, may perhaps be the very best thing about it. (*W1* 324–5/H. 2, 382–3)

Schopenhauer's position is in part an extrapolation from the ability of suffering to 'sanctify' the individual by withdrawing him or her from false attachment to the phenomenal will-to-live. If this is true of suffering, then the effect can be achieved to an even greater degree by the contemplation of death. Schopenhauer's conclusion is in part an extrapolation from the ability of suffering to confer salvation

and 'sanctify' the individual by quieting desire and the will-to-live.
A similar concept of separation from the will-to-live is described
by William James as *anhedonia*, a symptom of what he calls 'the
sick soul' in *The Varieties of Religious Experience*.[7] Prolonged suffering eventually makes the will lose interest in life, an effect that
Schopenhauer believes is even more enhanced by a full awareness of
the necessity of death.

[I]f suffering has such a sanctifying force, this will belong in an even higher
degree to death, which is more feared than any suffering. Accordingly, in the
presence of every person who has died, we feel something akin to the awe
that is forced from us by great suffering; in fact, every case of death presents
itself to a certain extent as a kind of apotheosis or canonization. Therefore
we do not contemplate the corpse of even the most insignificant person
without awe, and indeed, strange as the remark may sound in this place, the
guard gets under arms in the presence of every corpse. Dying is certainly to be
regarded as the real aim of life; at the moment of dying, everything is decided
which through the whole course of life was only prepared and introduced.
Death is the result, the *résumé*, of life, or the total sum expressing at one
stroke all the instruction given by life in detail and piecemeal, namely that
the whole striving, the phenomenon of which is life, was a vain, fruitless,
and self-contradictory effort, to have returned from which is a deliverance.
(*W2* 636–7/H. 3, 732)

There is thus a kind of reciprocity between life and death in Schopenhauer's pessimistic philosophy. All life tends toward death, and
could not be otherwise in light of being swept along in the phenomenal flux of time. Schopenhauer maintains that suffering makes life
so miserable that only the fear of death restrains the individual will
from self-destruction, while if life as a whole were enjoyable, the idea
of death as the culmination of life would be intolerable. In his zero-
sum philosophical bookkeeping, Schopenhauer accordingly observes
that nonphilosophical spirits find comfort in the fact that death can
be anticipated as a deliverance from suffering, knowing that eventually the anguish must come to an end, and that the malaise experienced during life, no matter how extreme, at least falls short of
annihilation and the unknown.

If life in itself were a precious blessing, and decidedly preferable to non-
existence, the exit from it would not need to be guarded by such fearful
watchmen as death and its terrors. But who would go on living life as it is,

if death were less terrible? And who could bear even the mere thought of death, if life were a pleasure? But the former still always has the good point of being the end of life, and we console ourselves with death in regard to the sufferings of life, and with the sufferings of life in regard to death. (W2 578–9/H. 3, 664)

Yet, because death and life are merely phenomenal episodes in the world of appearance, they are unreal. Therefore, the philosopher or mystic who understands the unreality of death has no reason to fear it, while knowledge of the unreality of life equally removes the reluctance of most ordinary persons to accept death as a release from suffering.

However, he will be least afraid of becoming nothing in death who has rec-ognized that he is already nothing now, and who consequently no longer takes any interest in his individual phenomenon, since in him knowledge has, so to speak, burnt up and consumed the will, so that there is no longer any will, any keen desire for individual existence, left in him. (W2 609/H. 3, 699–700)

V ETHICS AND METAPHYSICS OF SUICIDE

It would appear, then, that Schopenhauer positions himself for an enthusiastic philosophical defense of suicide.[8] If to live is to suffer, and if life and death are unreal anyway, why permit oneself to suffer needlessly? If life has death as its aim and purpose, if life is only an ephemeral headlong descent toward death swept along in the torrents of time, and if death is nothing to be feared, then why should not every enlightened consciousness destroy itself in order to escape the sufferings of individual will and achieve life's purpose more quickly and deliberately? Death is good, according to Schopenhauer; it is a blessing to those who have come to see existence as ineluctable suffering in the world of appearance, and the brevity of life, contrary to conventional will-dominated opinion, is its best feature.[9] So, once we get the picture, why not make life even briefer?

Schopenhauer, on the contrary, vehemently denies any universal philosophical recommendation to suicide. He regards self-murder as it is usually practiced as an unworthy affirmation of the will-to-live by those who wish to escape pain rather than seek nondiscursive awareness of Will in suffering. There is no salvation from individual will to be found in individually willed annihilation; we should rather endure suffering until death arrives on its own to free us. But why? Is Schopenhauer's position necessitated by or even logically consistent with the concept of death he has elaborated? Or is Schopenhauer, having offered a powerful motivation for self-destruction, merely trying awkwardly now, within his pessimistic and arguably nihilistic philosophical system, to accommodate the squeamishness of traditional morality about the problem of suicide?

The first hint of Schopenhauer's efforts to distance himself from advocating suicide does not emphasize the wrongness of the act itself, but rather questions the legitimacy of the motives one might have for such violence. He describes suicide as a 'vain and therefore foolish action,' but he does not immediately condemn it as a moral transgression:

Conversely, whoever is oppressed by the burdens of life, whoever loves life and affirms it, but abhors its torments, and in particular can no longer endure the hard lot that has fallen to just him, cannot hope for deliverance from death, and cannot save himself through suicide. Only by a false illusion does the cool shade of Orcus allure him as a haven of rest. The earth rolls on from day into night; the individual dies; but the sun itself burns without intermission, an eternal noon. Life is certain to the will-to-live; the form of life is the endless present; it matters not how individuals, the phenomena of the Idea, arise and pass away in time, like fleeting dreams. Therefore suicide already appears to us to be a vain and therefore foolish action; when we have gone farther in our discussion, it will appear to us in an even less favourable light. (*W1* 280–1/H. 2, 331)

Schopenhauer falls far short of Kant's repudiation of suicide as a violation of the categorical imperative when, in a famous passage of the *Foundations of the Metaphysics of Morals*, Kant explains:

A man who is reduced to despair by a series of evils feels a weariness with life but is still in possession of his reason sufficiently to ask whether it would not be contrary to his duty to himself to take his own life. Now he asks whether the maxim of his action could become a universal law of nature. His maxim, however, is: For love of myself, I make it my principle to shorten my life when by a longer duration it threatens more evil than satisfaction. But it is questionable whether this principle of self-love could become a universal law of nature. One immediately sees a contradiction in a system of nature whose law would be to destroy life by the feeling whose special office is to impel the improvement of life. In this case it would not exist as nature; hence that maxim cannot obtain as a law of nature, and thus it wholly contradicts the supreme principle of all duty.[10]

Kant decides that suicide for the sake of self-love is self-contradictory. The categorical imperative in its main formulation requires that we ought always to act in such a way that we can will the maxim of our action to be universal for every rational being. Here the 'can' that enforces moral reasoning appears to be logical possibility. We test the morality of an action by asking whether it is logically possible for the maxim that justifies the act to be accepted by every rational being. If our willing such universal acceptance is logically possible, then the categorical imperative entails that we are obligated by duty to follow the maxim; if as reasoning moral agents our willing universal acceptance of the maxim is not logically possible, if and only if willing the universal acceptance of the maxim implies a contradiction (however loosely construed by Kant), then the categorical imperative entails that we are forbidden to follow the maxim in any of its consequences. Self-love, according to Kant, runs into a contradiction when it tries to will that all rational beings should commit suicide when 'by a longer duration [life] threatens more evil than satisfaction,' for it simultaneously seeks to improve and destroy.

This is not the place to enter into a dispute about whether Kant's categorical imperative forbids suicide. Arguably, the maxim Kant considers, to choose death merely when life offers more pain than pleasure, as opposed, say, in order to avoid excruciating, incurable, chronic pain, is too weak to represent the kind of reasoning a person actually contemplating suicide is likely to entertain. Schopenhauer makes explicit both his intellectual debt to and his disagreements with Kant in *On the Basis of Morality*. Here he states, concerning Kant's moral philosophy, that 'the ... criticism of Kant's foundation of morals will be in particular the best preparation and guide – in fact the direct path – to my own foundation of morals, for opposites illustrate each other, and my foundation is, in essentials, diametrically opposed to Kant's.'[11] With respect to Kant's formalist moral injunctions against suicide as an implication of the categorical imperative, Schopenhauer is unimpressed with the claim that moral reason cannot consistently will the suicide's maxim to be universal law. He argues:

Moreover, in the examples given by him as an introduction to that classification, Kant supports the duties of law first ... by the so-called duty to oneself, that of not ending one's life voluntarily when the evils outweigh the pleasures. Therefore this maxim is said to be not even *conceivable* as a universal law of nature. I say that, as the power of the State cannot intervene here, this very maxim shows itself unchecked as an *actually existing law of nature*. For it is quite certainly a universal rule that man actually resorts to suicide as soon as the immensely strong, inborn urge to the preservation of life is definitely overpowered by great suffering; daily experience shows us this. ... At any rate, arguments against suicide of the kind put forward by Kant ... certainly have never yet restrained, even for one moment, anyone who is weary of life. Thus a natural law incontestably existing as a fact and daily operating is declared to be *simply unthinkable* without contradiction, in favor of the classification of duties from Kant's moral principle![12]

Schopenhauer offers a remarkably similar argument against suicide in which he also describes the reasoning of the potential suicide as contradictory. By contrast with Kant, however, Schopenhauer locates the contradiction in the suicide's simultaneous denial and affirmation of the will-to-live. More important, unlike Kant, Schopenhauer, especially in his essay 'On Suicide' in the second volume of *Parerga and Paralipomena*, finds nothing morally objectionable in principle to suicide.[13] The first reference to such a contradiction appears in the first volume of *The World as Will and Representation*, where Schopenhauer detects an inconsistency in the Stoic concept of the 'blessed life' in including a counsel of suicide for those in dire straits. Schopenhauer now states that:

we find a complete contradiction in our wishing to live without suffering, a contradiction that is therefore implied by the frequently used phrase 'blessed life.' This will certainly be clear to the person who has fully grasped my discussion that follows. This contradiction is revealed in this ethic of pure reason itself by the fact that the Stoic is compelled to insert a recommendation of suicide in his guide to the blissful life (for this is what his ethics always remains). This is like the costly phiol of poison to be found among the magnificent ornaments and apparel of oriental despots, and is for the case where the sufferings of the body, incapable of being philosophized away by any principles and syllogisms, are paramount and incurable. Thus its sole purpose, namely blessedness, is frustrated, and nothing remains as a means of escape from pain except death. But then death must be taken with unconcern, just as is any other medicine. Here a marked contrast is evident between the Stoic ethics and all those other ethical systems mentioned above. These ethical systems make virtue directly and in itself the aim and object, even with the most grievous sufferings, and will not allow a man to end his life in order to escape from suffering. But not one of them knew how to express the true reason for rejecting suicide, but they laboriously collected fictitious arguments of every kind. This true reason will appear in the fourth book in connexion with our discussion. (*WI* 90–1/H. 2, 108)

Schopenhauer identifies a different kind of contradiction than Kant in criticizing the rationale for suicide. In the essay 'On Suicide' Schopenhauer argues that 'We then of necessity hear [from "monotheistic" religious teachers] that suicide is the greatest cowardice, that it is possible only in madness, and such like absurdities; or else the wholly meaningless phrase that suicide is "wrong," whereas there is obviously nothing in the world over which every man has such an indisputable *right* as his own person and life.'[14] Schopenhauer's objection to suicide, as commentators have frequently observed, is metaphysical rather than moral. Schopenhauer holds that

[S]uicide, the arbitrary doing away with the individual phenomenon, differs most widely from the denial of the will-to-live, which is the only act of its freedom to appear in the phenomenon, and hence, as Asmus calls it, the transcendental change. ... Far from being denial of the will, suicide is a phenomenon of the will's strong affirmation. For denial has its essential nature in the fact that the pleasures of life, not its sorrows, are shunned. The suicide wills life, and is dissatisfied merely with the conditions on which it has come to him. Therefore he gives up by no means the will-to-live, but merely life, since he destroys the individual phenomenon. (*WI* 398/H. 2, 471)

If we reach the level of Schopenhauer's insight into the world as Will and representation, and if we see individual willing as inherently a life of suffering, then we cannot be satisfied with suicide as a philosophical solution to the predicament of life. The objection is that there is a kind of contradiction, different in force and content than the inconsistency that Kant recognizes in applying the categorical imperative to the question of suicide, in the individual will's willfully seeking to exterminate itself as a way of escaping the wretchedness of willing.[15] Suicide ends life, but as the result of a willful decision in the service of the individual will-to-live, it cannot by its very nature altogether transcend willing.[16] The only logically coherent freedom to be sought from the sufferings of the will is not to will death and willfully destroy the self, but to continue to live while quieting the will, in an ultra-ascetic submissive attitude of sublime indifference to both life and death.[17]

VI SUICIDE NO SOLUTION TO THE PROBLEM OF WILLING

In confronting desperately incurable pain or unbearable humiliation or ruin, the person contemplating suicide in ignorance of Schopenhauer's ontology of Will as thing-in-itself is caught up in the contradiction of trying to annihilate the individual will-to-live, but on analysis is actually affirming the will-to-live by removing all physical or emotional pain along with the total elimination of consciousness.

Death (the repetition of the comparison must be excused) is like the setting of the sun, which is only apparently engulfed by the night, but actually, itself the source of all light, burns without intermission, brings new days to new worlds, and is always rising and always setting. Beginning and end concern only the individual by means of time, of the form of this phenomenon for the representation. Outside time lie only the will, Kant's thing-in-itself, and its adequate objectivity, namely Plato's Idea. Suicide, therefore, affords no escape; what everyone *wills* in his innermost being, that must he *be*; and what everyone *is*, is just what he *wills*. (*W1* 366/H. 2, 433)

Schopenhauer is sometimes interpreted as holding that suicide is metaphysically futile because there can be no escape from Will as thing-in-itself. Frederick Copleston, for example, in *Arthur Schopenhauer: Philosopher of Pessimism*, states that 'Individual consciousness is indeed destroyed [in the act of suicide], i.e. phenomenal existence, but man's inner nature, identical with Will, persists and can never be destroyed.'[18]

Against such a view, the obvious objection is that if Schopenhauer is right that Will is thing-in-itself, and that the individual empirical will or will-to-live is a representation of Will, then nothing anyone does or fails to do, chooses or chooses not to do, can make any difference to the individual's essential nature before or after death. In that case, there can be no sound Schopenhauerian objection to philosophical suicide, provided that the agent is not deluded about what self-induced death can accomplish. The preceding passage, however, contains a more subtle line of reasoning.

It is true that Schopenhauer believes that there can be no real annihilation of the true as opposed to the apparent phenomenal nature of the individual will-to-live. He develops this position eloquently in *The World as Will and Representation* and again in his *Parerga and Paralipomena* essay 'On the Doctrine of the Indestructibility of Our True Nature by Death.'[19] But more should be said about the contradiction entailed by the act of suicide. Suicide affords no escape from willing because the concept of escape implies survival or persistence from a worse to a better state – while for Schopenhauer, the soul or psychological subject of individual willing perishes along with the death of the body. Yet something more philosophically interesting is contained in Schopenhauer's enigmatic remark that 'what everyone *wills* in his innermost being, that must he *be*; and what everyone *is*, is just what he *wills*.' What can this mean? Schopenhauer seems to accept the proposition that the content of individual willing defines each individual will as a unique entity. We are what we desire and what we choose for ourselves, that toward which we are impelled as the objectification of our innermost character. Schopenhauer reemphasizes his earlier position that consciousness of death affirms the will-to-live:

On this inexpressible *horror mortis* rests also the favourite principle of all ordinary minds that whoever takes his own life must be insane; yet no less is the astonishment, mingled with a certain admiration, which this action always provokes even in thinking minds, since such action is so much opposed to the nature of every living thing that in a certain sense we are forced to admire the man who is able to perform it. Indeed, we even find a certain consolation in the fact that, in the worst cases, this way out is actually open to us, and we might doubt it if it were not confirmed by experience. For suicide comes from a resolve of the intellect, but our willing of life is a *prius* of the intellect. Therefore this consideration ... also confirms the primacy of the *will* in self-consciousness. (W2 240/H. 3, 271)

This is part of the remarkable anticipation of existentialist philosophy that many commentators have attributed to Schopenhauer.

In this connection, it is no accident that Albert Camus begins his essay 'An Absurd Reasoning' in the collection *The Myth of Sisyphus* with the pronouncement that 'There is but one truly serious philosophical problem, and that is suicide. Judging whether life is or is not worth living amounts to answering the fundamental question of philosophy.'[20]

Suppose that in contemplating suicide I simply will to end my life. As a disciple of Schopenhauer's metaphysics of Will as thing-in-itself and of the individual will or will-to-live as phenomenal representation of Will, I will to end my life not as part of a witless plan to benefit myself, or with the idea of destroying even the Will as thing-in-itself that I manifest in my individual will-to-live, but merely as a way of fulfilling my purpose by terminating my empirical consciousness and returning to Will as thing-in-itself. This desire 'in my innermost being,' by hypothesis, according to Schopenhauer, partially constitutes who and what I am. This is something I cannot change or escape by ending my life, but is something that I shall have become as long as my will is active. I am (in a certain sense eternally and indestructably) what I will, even if I will to cease willing.

Conversely, whoever is oppressed by the burdens of life, whoever loves life and affirms it, but abhors its torments, and in particular can no longer endure the hard lot that has fallen to just him, cannot hope for deliverance from death, and cannot save himself through suicide. Only by a false illusion does the cool shade of Orcus allure him as a haven of rest. The earth rolls on from day into night; the individual dies; but the sun itself burns without intermission, an eternal noon. Life is certain to the will-to-live; the form of life is the endless present; it matters not how individuals, the phenomena of the Idea, arise and pass away in time, like fleeting dreams. Therefore suicide already appears to us to be a vain and therefore foolish action. . . . (W1 280–1)

Yet the point of a philosophically enlightened suicide for a Schopenhauerian would nevertheless be the rationally justifiable desire to bring about an end to the suffering of further continued willing and to eliminate personal consciousness and the individual empirical will-to-live that through empirical circumstances no longer wills to live. This is a Kantian-type contradiction only if Schopenhauer stubbornly requires that we continue to designate whatever the individual will wills as will-to-live when the content of what the individual will has come to will is rather the will-not-to-live. It appears more

plausible in such a case to speak of the will-to-live having been gradually or dramatically replaced by a reluctant but possibly equally
determined will-to-die. That such a decision might be reached, at
some point in a Schopenhauerian's existence, moral questions aside,
may not be as hopelessly metaphysically confused as Schopenhauer
tries to portray.[21]

VII   RENUNCIATION OF INDIVIDUAL WILL IN
ASCETIC SUICIDE BY STARVATION

Schopenhauer makes a curious exception for a particular kind of suicide. He finds philosophically praiseworthy the suicide of an ascetic
who in renunciation of the will-to-live chooses the extraordinary
course of slow death by starvation. In *The World as Will and Representation*, Schopenhauer writes:

Thus [the saint] resorts to fasting, and even to self-castigation and self-
torture, in order that, by constant privation and suffering, he may more
and more break down and kill the will that he recognizes and abhors as the
source of his own suffering existence and of the world's. Finally, if death
comes, which breaks up the phenomenon of this will, the essence of such
will having long since expired through free denial of itself except for the
feeble residue which appears as the vitality of this body, then it is most welcome, and is cheerfully accepted as a longed-for deliverance. It is not merely
the phenomenon, as in the case of others, that comes to an end with death,
but the inner being itself that is abolished; this had a feeble existence merely
in the phenomenon. This last slender bond is now severed; for him who ends
thus, the world has at the same time ended. (*W1* 382/H. 2, 451–2)

There appears to be a special kind of suicide, quite different from the ordinary, which has perhaps not yet been adequately verified. This is voluntarily
chosen death by starvation at the highest degree of asceticism. Its manifestation, however, has always been accompanied, and thus rendered vague and
obscure, by much religious fanaticism and even superstition. Yet it seems
that the complete denial of the will can reach that degree where even the
necessary will to maintain the vegetative life of the body, by the assimilation of nourishment, ceases to exist. This kind of suicide is so far from being
the result of the will-to-live, that such a completely resigned ascetic ceases
to live merely because he has completely ceased to will. No other death
than that by starvation is here conceivable (unless it resulted from a special
superstition), since the intention to cut short the agony would actually be
a degree of affirmation of the will. The dogmas that satisfy the faculty of

reason of such a penitent delude him with the idea that a being of a higher nature has ordered for him the fasting to which his inner tendency urges him. (W1 400–1/H. 2, 474)

The theme is first explored in Schopenhauer's early *Manuscript Remains* (Hoyerswerda 1813), where he declares that 'The highest degree of asceticism, the total denial of the temporal conscious-ness, is the *voluntary death through starvation*; of this only two instances have so far come to my knowledge.' Then he continues: 'From absolutely pure asceticism we cannot think of any other death than that through starvation, since the intention to avoid a long agony and affliction is already an affirmation of the world of the senses.'[22]

Schopenhauer's sanction of the ascetic's suicide by starvation may appear unpersuasive. If we try to imagine ourselves in that situation, we naturally think of the overwhelming desire for nourishment that would undoubtedly accompany a prolonged death fast. This is hardly the kind of occurrence that is likely to help anyone overcome the suf-fering of individual will. But what Schopenhauer seems to have in mind, and what in this kind of case could only excite his admiration about the ascetic's decision, is a scenario in which the ascetic has so completely renounced the will-to-live that starvation is accepted without further stirrings of will in the form of physical cravings. What is supposed to be noble about this special method of suicide for Schopenhauer is not the death that it occasions, but the subject's radical separation from all objects of the individual will-to-live, as opposed to and including what Schopenhauer rightly or wrongly re-gards as the further manifestation of the will-to-live even in the self-love-motivated will-to-die. The ascetic who embarks on a course of death by starvation presumably does so as a manifestation of neither the will-to-live nor the will-to-die, but with an absolute indifference to any type of individual willing whatsoever.

Still, there is another condition that the starving ascetic must sat-isfy in order to meet Schopenhauer's moral requirement. Schopen-hauer contends that persons as self-conscious beings have a supreme duty to place knowing over willing.[23] The starving ascetic must first attain the highest degree of philosophical wisdom, for there can be no justified exception from such an epistemic obligation even for the saintly suicide. Schopenhauer suggests a solution to the difficulty when he indicates that the pinnacle of knowledge required is achieved precisely in the event and as a result of this cruel death. The knowledge that every subject is supposed to seek is facilitated by the ascetic's suppression of will. The denial of will in turn constitutes the profound indifference to life and death that makes suicide by starvation possible. So concludes Schopenhauer:

> Suffering approaches and, as such, offers the possibility of a denial of the will; but he rejects it by destroying the will's phenomenon, the body, so that the will may remain unbroken. This is the reason why almost all ethical systems, philosophical as well as religious, condemn suicide, though they themselves cannot state anything but strange and sophistical arguments for so doing. But if ever a man was kept from suicide by purely moral incentive, the innermost meaning of this self-conquest (whatever the concepts in which his faculty of reason may have clothed it) was as follows: 'I do not want to avoid suffering, because it can help to put an end to the will-to-live, whose phenomenon is so full of misery, by so strengthening the knowledge of the real nature of the world now already dawning on me, that such knowledge may become the final quieter of the will, and release me for ever.' (W1 399–400/H. 2, 473)

It is unacceptable, from Schopenhauer's standpoint, for the ascetic deliberately to choose death by any method, including starvation, as a philosophical answer to the problem of willing or as a philosophically justifiable way of ending the struggles and suffering of individual willing. The ascetic's philosophically acceptable suicide by starvation occurs as an unwilled but equally unresisted outcome of the unqualified indifference of will to the superficial phenomena of life and death.[24]

The trouble with Schopenhauer's philosophy of death is also revealed in these extreme conclusions. If the philosophically appropriate response to the transgression of individual willing is to withdraw from the will-to-live by assuming an ascetic attitude of indifference to both life and death, then why should death be preferred? If suffering sanctifies, then why should the philosopher look with approval at the saint's unwillful and will-denying suicide by starvation? If we admire the starving ascetic at all, it is probably because we suppose that starving oneself to death requires an extraordinary act of will, rather than for Schopenhauer's reason involving the total suppression of will. The separation from the will-to-live to the extent needed in order to starve to death, according to Schopenhauer, cannot occur as

the result of a willful decision. But if the act is not so deliberately
chosen, then in what sense can it be meaningfully attributed to the
character of the saint? In what way does the unwillful suicide by
starvation through a supposedly exalted indifference to the will-to-
live redound to the ascetic's credit if the event is not the result of a
conscious decision? The best that Schopenhauer can say is that the
denial of will and the obliteration of will resulting from the ascetic's
unwillful death through starvation is a good thing. But such a death is
good not because it results from starvation, but only on the grounds
that it is generally better, according to Schopenhauer's pessimism,
for the world to contain less willing and therefore less suffering; the
same might equally be said of any death through accident, disease,
or even murder.[25]

Here the deeper contradictions underlying Schopenhauer's concept of death begin to surface. If the goal of philosophy is to reconcile individual will to the misery of existence and the elimination
of consciousness in unreal death as the end and purpose of unreal
life, then it appears impossible to explain why anyone should prefer
death to a life of even the most acute turmoil, suffering, and pain. If
the aim of life is death, and if death is unreal, then why should the
philosopher not hasten to it? The moral obligation of the individual
will that has attained to an understanding of the world as Will and
representation would seem to be to eliminate individual willing by
any means at its disposal in order, by the destruction of consciousness, to return from its state of phenomenal misery to Will as reality.
The philosopher is not to choose suicide as a bad-faith affirmation
of the will-to-live in an abject effort to avoid suffering. But why,
according to Schopenhauer, should a person not do so while enjoying good health, the love of family and friends, productive activity,
and all of life's pleasures, precisely in order to fulfill life's purpose
by ending it for philosophical reasons immediately upon achieving
realization of the appearance–reality distinction? If suffering sanctifies, and if sanctification is a good thing, then it must be wrong to
avoid, let alone willfully avoid, the vicissitudes of the will-to-live,
no matter how unpleasant. Indeed, despite himself, Schopenhauer
appears to rely on the repugnance an individual will-to-live might
naturally feel for life construed as unmitigated suffering in order to
uphold death as preferable to the willful continuation of life. Yet
any sort of preference is already a sublimated expression of the will-
to-live, even, paradoxically, when it embraces the idea of an ideal

death. The main problem in Schopenhauer's philosophy is not the internal conflict of will which it deprecates, but the inconsistencies in Schopenhauer's pessimism as he tries in a more positive light to demystify the meaning of death.[26]

NOTES

1 *MR* 3 623/Hn. 3, 574 (sect. 175).
2 See *W1* 275–284/H. 2, 323–35, and passim.
3 Quoted in *W2* 588/H. 3, 675.
4 *W2* 507/H. 3, 581: 'Death is the great reprimand that the will-to-live, and more particularly the egoism essential thereto, receive through the course of nature; and it can be conceived as a punishment for our existence.' In the asterisked footnote, Schopenhauer adds: 'Death says: You are the product of an act that ought not to have taken place; therefore, to wipe it out, you must die.' *MR* 1 74 (Hoyerswerda 1813): 'For with the empirical consciousness we necessarily have not only sinfulness, but also all the evils that follow from this kingdom of error, chance, wickedness and folly, and finally death. Death is, so to speak, a debt contracted through life, as are also the other evils that are determined with less certainty (*haec est conditio vivendi*). The Bible and Christianity through the fall of man rightly introduce into the world death and the troubles and miseries of life. ... ' But see John E. Atwell, *Schopenhauer: The Human Character* (Philadelphia: Temple University Press, 1990), 202–4: 'Since being born is not an action on the part of the person who is born – for it is not done in virtue of a motive – being born is not a criminal action. It follows that death is not a punishment for an "action" of being born. ... For the person who has abandoned egoism, who has ceased to affirm the will-to-live, there is no guilt of existence. It is only natural existence, that is, existence devoted to affirmation of the will-to-live, that generates guilt and makes one deserving of suffering. And only for such a person is death a dreadful prospect. For the person who has denied the will-to-live, death poses no terror, no dread, nothing to fear; in fact, he or she has come to conquer death, which is to say he or she has achieved freedom.'
5 Schopenhauer, 'On the Doctrine of the Indestructibility of Our True Nature by Death,' *P2* 272/H. 6, 290: 'life ... may certainly be regarded as a dream and death as an awakening. But then the personality, the individual, belongs to the dreaming and not to the waking consciousness; and so death presents itself to the former as annihilation.'
6 *MR* 1 370/Hn. 1, 336 (Dresden 1815): 'And now ... as man is nature herself and indeed at the highest degree of her consciousness; moreover, as nature is only the will-to-live together with the phenomenon of this,

it is appropriate for man, as long as he is the [W]ill (or nature), to console himself about his own death and the death of his friends by looking back at the immortal life of nature, which he himself is, – the will-to-live objectified.'

7 William James, *The Varieties of Religious Experience: A Study in Human Nature* (The Gifford Lectures on Natural Religion 1901–2) (London: Longmans, Greene and Co., 1935), 145–7. James refers to Theodule Armand Ribot's original sense of *anhedonia* as an indifference to life resulting from liver disorders in his *Psychologie des sentiments* (1897), 54.

8 Frederick Copleston, *Arthur Schopenhauer: Philosopher of Pessimism* (New York: Barnes & Noble Books, 1975), 91: 'It might be thought that in view of this grim picture of human life, Schopenhauer would recommend suicide; but, though he refused to recognise any valid moral reason for condemning suicide, he considered that it is no real solution to life's tragedy.'

9 See *W1* 324–5/H. 2, 382–3. Also 'On Suicide', *P2* 310/H. 6, 329: 'On the whole, we shall find that, as soon as a point is reached where the terrors of life outweigh those of death, man puts an end to his life. The resistance of the latter is nevertheless considerable; they stand, so to speak, as guardians at the gate of exit. Perhaps there is no one alive who would not already have made an end of his life if such an end were something purely negative, a sudden cessation of existence. But it is something positive, namely the destruction of the body, and this frightens people back just because the body is the phenomenon of the will-to-live.'

10 Immanuel Kant, *Foundations of the Metaphysics of Morals*, translated by Lewis White Beck (New York: Macmillan Publishing Company, 1959), 39–40.

11 *BM* 47/H. 4, 115.

12 *BM* 93–4/H. 4, 159–60.

13 'On Suicide,' *P2* 306–11/H. 6, 325–9.

14 *P2* 306/H. 6, 325. Also 307/H. 6, 326: 'If criminal law condemns suicide, that is not an ecclesiastically valid reason and is, moreover, definitely ridiculous; for what punishment can frighten the man who seeks death? If we punish the *attempt* to commit suicide, then we are simply punishing the want of skill whereby it failed.'

15 *P2* 309/H. 6, 328: 'I have expounded in my chief work, volume one, §69, the only valid moral reason against suicide. It lies in the fact that suicide is opposed to the attainment of the highest moral goal since it substitutes for the real salvation from this world of woe and misery one that is merely apparent. But it is still a very long way from this aberration to a crime, such as the Christian clergy would like to stamp it.' See Georg Simmel, *Schopenhauer and Nietzsche*, translated by Helmut Loiskandl,

Deena Weinstein, and Michael Weinstein (Amherst: University of Massachusetts Press, 1986), 131–2.

16 Christopher Janaway, *Schopenhauer* (New York: Oxford University Press, 1996), 89: 'The question whether Schopenhauer's higher view of death could be consoling is a difficult one. He tries to inculcate the thought that one's own death has no great significance in the order of things. But if one accepted his reasons for taking this attitude, ought one not to think that one's life has just as little significance? And is that a consoling thought? Schopenhauer appears to think so....'

17 *W1* 399–400/H. 2, 472–3: 'Just because the suicide cannot cease willing, he ceases to live; and the will affirms itself here even through the cessation of its own phenomenon, because it can no longer affirm itself otherwise. But as it was just the suffering it thus shunned which, as mortification of the will, could have led it to the denial of itself and to salvation, so in this respect the suicide is like a sick man who, after the beginning of a painful operation that could completely cure him, will not allow it to be completed, but prefers to retain his illness.'

18 Copleston, *Arthur Schopenhauer: Philosopher of Pessimism*, 91. See Simmel, *Schopenhauer and Nietzsche*, 132–3: 'The annihilation of will does, indeed, remove the possibility of suffering, but this procedure is unnecessary if the annihilation of the phenomenon completely cuts off the reality of will. ... The weakness of Schopenhauer's argumentation in this case is obvious, especially as it pertains to life's suffering, because in the instance of suicide alone, the treatment of the symptoms is as radically potent as is the internal annihilation of the will to live. ... Though it might seem paradoxical, suicide might seem to be justified in less radical cases, whereas it would not be a proper remedy for a profound and total distaste with life. In the case of radical ennui Schopenhauer is correct and shows profound perception, though weak argumentation, in claiming that an external annihilation of life would be a totally useless and contradictory expression of an inner separation of life from itself.'

19 *P2* 267–82/H. 6, 284–300.

20 Albert Camus, *The Myth of Sisyphus and Other Essays*, translated by Justin O'Brien (New York: Vintage Books, 1955), 3.

21 Schopenhauer further criticizes suicide as a puerile metaphysical experiment in 'On Suicide', *P2* 311/H. 6, 330: 'Suicide can also be regarded as an experiment, a question we put to nature and try to make answer, namely what change the existence and knowledge of man undergo through death. But it is an awkward experiment, for it abolishes the identity of the consciousness that would have to listen to the answer.'

22 *MR* 1 74–5/Hn. 1, 69 (Hoyerswerda 1813). *W1* 402/H. 2, 476: 'Between this voluntary death springing from the extreme of asceticism and that

resulting from despair there may be many different intermediate stages and combinations, which are indeed hard to explain; but human nature has depths, obscurities, and intricacies, whose elucidation and unfolding are of the very greatest difficulty.'

23 I have discussed Schopenhauer's elevation of knowing over willing at length in Dale Jacquette, 'Schopenhauer's Metaphysics of Appearance and Will in the Philosophy of Art,' in Jacquette (ed.), *Schopenhauer, Philosophy, and the Arts* (Cambridge: Cambridge University Press, 1996), 1–36. See also contributions to the same volume with many relevant quotations from Schopenhauer on this topic by Janaway, 'Knowledge and Tranquility: Schopenhauer on the Value of Art,' 39–61; Atwell, 'Art as Liberation: A Central Theme of Schopenhauer's Philosophy,' 81–106; and Paul Guyer, 'Pleasure and Knowledge in Schopenhauer's Aesthetics,' 109–32.

24 *MR* 1 369/Hn. 1, 335 (sect. 499) (Dresden 1815): 'Whoever has perceived the true nature of the world, sees life in death, but also death in life; the two are only different but inseparable aspects of the objectification of the [W]ill.' And 370–1/Hn. 1, 336–7: 'But just as death is essential to life, yet it is the distressing side of life, that in which the inner emptiness and unreality of the will-to-live most frequently expresses itself, the identity of life and suffering. Considered in this way, there is in exchange for death only one consolation, namely that, just as the phenomenon of the will-to-live must come to an end, this will itself can freely come to an end. If the will itself has ended, in other words has turned, then death is no longer a suffering, because a will-to-live no longer exists.'

25 Simmel, *Schopenhauer and Nietzsche*, 133: 'In rejecting suicide while affirming the motivation to negate the will, Schopenhauer must evade the fact that suicide removes the individual organism, which is the only tool for producing suffering, without any trace or potential for further suffering.... The renunciation of life and ascetic resignation from all desire that Schopenhauer proposed as the perfection and sanctification of the soul are too comprehensive and fundamental to be motivated merely by suffering, even if the metaphysical unity of the world translates all suffering into the personal soul. We rarely find that this is the motivation for renouncing the will by the holy penitents and ascetes of all religions, who Schopenhauer deems to be the embodiments of his ideal.'

26 I am grateful to The Institute for the Arts and Humanistic Studies at The Pennsylvania State University for a Term Fellowship during 1997–9 which made possible the completion of this research project, among others. An extract of the essay was presented at the North American Schopenhauer Society, American Philosophical Association, Central Division, Chicago, 6–9 May 1998, under the title 'Schopenhauer on the Ethics of Suicide.'

10 Schopenhauer's Pessimism

I SCHOPENHAUER'S QUESTION

In Book Five of *The Gay Science* Nietzsche writes that 'unconditional and honest atheism' is 'the locus of Schopenhauer's whole
integrity' and 'the *presupposition* of the way he poses his problem'.
If we reject the 'meaning' Christianity assigns to the world, then,
writes Nietzsche, '*Schopenhauer*'s question immediately comes to
us in a terrifying way: *Has existence any meaning at all?*' (*Gay Science* §357). It is true that, for Schopenhauer, everything in ordinary
life is characterized by *Nichtigkeit*,[1] or nothingness, which might
suggest the thought that life is meaningless. (Payne translates the
term as 'vanity', which loses much of its power.) But Schopenhauer
tends to speak more often in the vocabulary of value, asking whether
life is a business which covers its costs, whether the world is bank-
rupt, whether this world is the best, or the worst, possible.[2] Thus,
with regard to pessimism, I shall take Schopenhauer's prime question to be: What value does existence have? and more particularly:
What is the value of my being what I am? For Schopenhauer, as
Nietzsche implies, certain answers that were once thinkable on the
assumption of Christian dogma – that each of us is an immaterial substance or a pure, rational soul or part of some supernatu-
ral design – are not available. These dogmas are false, according
to Schopenhauer. We have to face the question of value as material, biological individuals; and Schopenhauer's response is that the
value in such existence is not – cannot be – greater than the value
non-existence would have had. Paradoxically, as he says, 'nothing
else can be stated as the aim of our existence except the knowledge that it would be better for us not to exist' (*W2*, 605/H. 3, 695).

My guiding question is simply: How does Schopenhauer reach this predicament?

II PESSIMISM AND OPTIMISM

Schopenhauer's philosophy incorporated an extremely negative evaluation of ordinary human life from the start, but he did not initially use the term 'pessimism' to describe it. In the first edition of *The World as Will and Representation* he merely mentions optimism a couple of times in tones of passionate condemnation:

If we were to conduct the most hardened and callous optimist through hospitals, infirmaries, operating theatres, through prisons and slave-hovels, over battlefields and to places of execution; if we were to open to him all the dark abodes of misery, where it shuns the gaze of cold curiosity, he too would certainly see in the end what kind of a world is this *meilleur des mondes possibles* [best of possible worlds].[3]

I cannot here withhold the statement that *optimism*, where it is not merely the thoughtless talk of those who harbour nothing but words under their shallow foreheads, seems to me to be not merely an absurd, but also a really *wicked* [*ruchlose*], way of thinking, a bitter mockery of the unspeakable sufferings of mankind. (*W1* 326/H. 2, 384–5)

Not until the second edition of *The World as Will and Representation* does he begin, occasionally, to refer to 'pessimism' as the preferred view:

I cannot ... put the *fundamental difference* of all religions in the question whether they are monotheistic, polytheistic, pantheistic, or atheistic, but only in the question whether they are optimistic or pessimistic.... The power by virtue of which Christianity was able to overcome first Judaism, and then the paganism of Greece and Rome, is to found solely in its pessimism, in the confession that our condition is both exceedingly sorrowful and sinful, whereas Judaism and paganism were optimistic. (*W2* 170/H. 3, 187–8)

In the ... third book of the *Stromata* of Clement the antagonism between optimism together with theism on the one hand, and pessimism together with asceticism on the other, comes out with surprising distinctness.... But at the same time it becomes apparent that the spirit of the Old Testament stands in this antagonism with that of the New ... the former is optimistic, and the latter pessimistic. (*W2* 620–1/H. 3, 713)

In the revised version of his first volume Schopenhauer also added some striking complaints against optimism:

> The demand for so-called poetic justice rests on an entire misconception of the nature of tragedy, indeed of the nature of the world ... for what wrong have the Ophelias, the Desdemonas, and the Cordelias done? But only a dull, insipid, optimistic, Protestant-rationalistic, or really Jewish view of the world will make the demand for poetic justice. (W1 253–4/H. 2, 299).

> We should interpret Jesus Christ always in the universal, as the symbol or the personification of the denial of the will to life.... That Christianity has recently forgotten its true significance, and has degenerated into shallow optimism, does not concern us here. (W1 405–6/H. 2, 480)

Perhaps surprisingly, given his unwavering atheism and the contrast we saw Nietzsche draw between the Schopenhauerian worldview and the Christian,[4] when Schopenhauer turns his mind to the optimism–pessimism issue in so many words, he consistently takes his own view to coincide with the ethical core of Christianity proper, read as ascetic resignation or self-denial in the face of a world that contains only suffering. He makes similar links in the discussions of optimism and pessimism in *On the Will in Nature* (1836) and *Parerga and Paralipomena* (1851).[5] The pessimistic or 'world-denying' religions are New Testament Christianity (if properly interpreted), Brahmanism, and Buddhism. Schopenhauer assimilates these three so strongly that he is convinced that the New Testament 'must somehow be of Indian origin'.[6] Ranged against such insightful pessimistic systems, and hence on the 'shallow' or 'wicked' optimistic side, are the Old Testament, Judaism, and 'Jewish–Protestant rationalism',[7] which is also manifest in the 'university philosophy' of the nineteenth century. Optimism is a consequence of 'Jewish monotheism'.[8] Pantheism (Spinoza's in particular) is also 'essentially optimism',[9] but Schopenhauer attributes that to the covert influence of monotheism:

> [In pantheism] we have not started dispassionately from the world as the thing to be explained, but from God as that which is given.... For from a first and impartial view, it will never occur to anyone to regard this world as a God. It must obviously be an ill-advised God who could think of no better amusement than to transform himself into a world like the present one. (P2 100/H. 6, 106)

Another way of saying this is that 'Spinoza ... could not get rid of the Jews'.[10] Hence, directly or indirectly, monotheism can be seen as the root of all wicked optimism. If we examined the world with no hint of a thought about God in our minds, we would never reach the idea that the world is good.

In *Parerga* especially there is a demonizing of Jewish thought. Nietzsche's vividly expressed reverse preference for the Old Testament over the Christianity of the New[11] is just one respect in which his view of Judaism is more positive than Schopenhauer's. It is certainly more complex too.[12] For what Schopenhauer objects to here is quite simple. The 'Jewish' doctrine that has been so influential in European philosophy (up to and including Hegel) is 'the doctrine that the world has its existence from a supremely eminent personal being and hence is also a most delightful thing and πάντα καλὰ λίαν.'[13] Schopenhauer is primarily offended by the notion that the world we inhabit (whether created or not) is a fine place, and by the idea that it fulfils some end in itself, indeed by the idea that it, and we, are here for any purpose at all.[14]

Having alluded to Leibniz initially with the expression '*meilleur des mondes possibles*', Schopenhauer confronts this 'founder of systematic optimism' more openly towards the end of the second volume of *The World as Will and Representation*.[15] Despite alleging that Leibniz's attempt to prove that this is the best of all possible worlds is 'sophistical', he does not really explain why. Instead he contrives a counter-argument to the effect that this is the *worst* of all possible worlds. It goes as follows:

[P]ossible means not what we may picture in our imagination, but what can actually exist and last. Now this world is arranged as it has to be if it were to be capable of continuing with great difficulty to exist; if it were a little worse, it would be no longer capable of continuing to exist. Consequently, since a worse world could not continue to exist, it is absolutely impossible; and so this world itself is the worst of all possible worlds. (W2 583/H. 3, 669)

In brief: if things became 'worse' or 'more difficult' for this world, it must cease to exist. Schopenhauer then provides an extraordinary catalogue designed to convince us that everything exists at the utter limit of precariousness: a small change in the orbits of the planets could de-stabilize the solar system, forces beneath the earth's crust could erupt to destroy it, a change in atmospheric conditions could extinguish all life, nine-tenths of the human species are already balanced on the edge of extinction, nature has given each individual barely the means to survive.

Even if all this is true, however, what does it show? Surely not that things could be worse in no possible respect. We can imagine a world exactly like the actual one but assign one additional week of pointless, unremitting pain to the lot of every single sentient being. There is no reason to believe that such a world could not continue to exist and every reason to think it would be worse. Schopenhauer appears to want to avoid any such attack by exploiting the distinction between 'what we may picture in our imagination' and what 'can actually exist and last'. He wants to take 'possible' worlds as meaning something like 'viable' worlds (as opposed to, say, worlds whose description contains no contradiction). But his insertion of 'actually' here threatens confusion. The question should not be how many viable worlds there actually are – presumably the answer is 'one' – but how many non-actual worlds would be viable. Schopenhauer has not shown the impossibility of viable worlds other than this one, yet worse than it. He closes by saying that the world of extinct, now fossilized creatures was another world, which must have been worse – worse than the worst of all viable worlds – because it was not possible for it to continue. However, it is unclear in what sense the world of the dinosaurs was not simply the actual world we inhabit, and unclear why their span of life cannot count as 'continuing to exist' in just the way ours does. Finally, even if we allow that their world was distinct from ours, was worse than it, and in Schopenhauer's sense was 'not possible', it still would not follow that there could be no worse possibilities for us.

This argument is, therefore, very far from convincing.[16] But it matters little because it comes late in the day and does not contain the real reasons for Schopenhauer's all-encompassing pessimism. Nor are these reasons dependent on his extensive researches into Indian religions and the history of Christianity, or simply on his many powerful evocations of the pointless horrors and disappointments of human life. This mass of evidence may be what makes optimism 'cut so strange a figure on this scene of sin, suffering, and death',[17] but it is not sufficient to motivate the extreme view Schopenhauer advocates: that it would be better if you and I and the whole world had never existed. For the real motivations of his pessimism we shall have to look at Schopenhauer's metaphysics of the will, something he invented before using the term 'pessimism' and before undertaking his more extensive forays into comparative religion. For though it has been claimed that Schopenhauer's pessimism has no close link with his central metaphysics,[18] I shall argue that the opposite is true.

III HAPPINESS AS ELUSIVE OR ILLUSORY

An essential element in Schopenhauer's pessimism is his unmasking of a naive set of views humans are prone to hold about the nature and attainability of happiness, whereas in truth, he asserts, 'Everything in life proclaims that earthly happiness is destined to be frustrated, or recognized as an illusion' (W2 573/H. 3, 657). Schopenhauer often equates happiness (Glück) with the satisfaction (Befriedigung) of a state of willing.[19] Willing sometimes is satisfied. So it is not an illusion that happiness happens. Nevertheless, he thinks, it does not have the weight or significance in one's life that one is prone to give it. Firstly, time distorts our interpretation of happiness: 'happiness lies always in the future, or else in the past, and the present may be compared to a small dark cloud driven by the wind over a sunny plain' (W2 573/H. 3, 657–8); we can see it is bright everywhere else, but we are always in the cloud's shadow. It is harder to sustain a rosy view of the present than of the past or future: we look back on former events and realize we were happy without appreciating it when they were present, or we aspire to unparalleled fulfilment if only some set of events will come about somewhere ahead of the present cloud. It is especially concerning future happiness that we are prone to illusion: that it will be somehow radically different from our present state. In truth 'the enchantment of distance shows us paradises that vanish like optical illusions' (W2 573/H. 3, 657). We should reflect that, when the circumstances we want come about, they will be the present; and in that present we shall begin willing anew. Each present will contain a wish or desire that looks ahead to its own resolution. Possession of one's goal takes away its charm[20] – sexual possession included: 'everyone who is in love will experience an extraordinary disillusionment after the pleasure he finally attains' (W2 540/H. 3, 619). A related point is that there is no absolute satisfaction. Human beings are incorrigibly restless – 'every satisfied desire gives birth to a new one'[21] – and so no particular achieved happiness, in

Schopenhauer's sense, can remove all our wants, and none can endure for long. And yet we tend to pursue happiness as if it could be
both permanent and all-resolving.

We tend also to pursue happiness as if it were likely, or even guar-
anteed, that the world should turn out to be in accordance with what
we will.

The careless and thoughtless youth imagines that the world exists in order
to be enjoyed; that it is the abode of a positive happiness . . . his life is a more
or less deliberate pursuit of positive happiness and this, as such, is said to
consist of positive pleasures. . . . This hunt for game that does not exist at
all leads, as a rule, to very real and positive unhappiness that appears as
pain, suffering, sickness, loss, care, poverty, disgrace, and a thousand other
miseries. The undeceiving comes too late. (*P1* 407/H. 5, 434)

The belief that the point or value of one's life consists in the attainment of whatever one wills is a further illusion. So, part of the
wickedness of optimism[22] is that it causes unhappiness by inculcat-
ing these false beliefs about happiness, beliefs whose consequences
are pain and disillusionment. It is better, Schopenhauer argues, to
seek nothing positive from a world which owes one nothing and to
concentrate on minimizing our pain.

If many human beings think that attaining satisfaction of what
they will is what gives their lives positive value, that such satisfaction is more likely than not to come about, and that it can eventually
constitute an enduring state of positive well-being which will forever
dispel the cloud of the present, then Schopenhauer's pessimism can
already have an educative effect if it succeeds in uncovering and challenging this naive outlook. Yet, however false and pernicious such
views are, Schopenhauer also maintains that humanity at large cannot help adopting them. Although 'everything in life' may proclaim
to the philosopher that happiness is not what it seems, everything
in the nature of living beings makes happiness seem to them what
it is not. In one of his finer passages Schopenhauer writes:

There is only one inborn error, and that is the notion that we exist in order
to be happy. It is inborn in us, because it coincides with our existence itself,
and our whole being [*Wesen*] is only its paraphrase, indeed our body is its
monogram. We are nothing more than the will to life, and the successive
satisfaction of all our willing is what we think of through the concept of
happiness. (*W2* 634/H. 3, 729)

It is what we are, our being or essence, which leads us astray. Hence to progress further in understanding Schopenhauer's views on optimism and pessimism, we must engage with his metaphysical account of the human individual.

IV WILL TO LIFE

Now Schopenhauer is clear that each of us is a material thing and an organism. For all organisms, to exist is to strive towards some end or other, to be continually pointed in a direction. The direction or end that governs all others is the perpetuation of life: its maintenance in the material individual one is, and the generation of life in the form of offspring. As particular manifestations of *Wille zum Leben*, will to life, we tend towards survival and reproduction, and this sets the common form of our existence:

The fundamental theme of all the many different acts of will is the satisfaction of the needs inseparable from the body's existence in health; they have their expression in it, and can be reduced to the maintenance of the individual and the propagation of the species. (W1 327/H. 2, 385)

Because we live, we must strive. However the actual content of our striving may be elaborated, its form, set by the will to life, locates us always somewhere on a cycle of willing and attaining. Any determinate episode of willing comes to an end, but not willing itself. Nothing we achieve by willing could ever erase the will itself; as Schopenhauer says,

its desires are unlimited, its claims inexhaustible, and every satisfied desire gives birth to a new one. No possible satisfaction in the world could suffice to still its craving, set a final goal to its demands, and fill the bottomless pit of its heart. (W2 573/H. 3, 657)

Let us note two immediate points about this will which Schopenhauer says constitutes our essence. Firstly, although the will to life operates in conscious and rational life forms, it is not essentially rational or conscious. Will manifests itself 'blindly' – that is, without consciousness or mentality of any kind – in the vast majority of nature, including the human organism. So the will to life within me is not a quasi-mind, not a consciousness, not something working rationally towards purposes. It is the principle that organizes me, this individual human being, just as it organizes a snail or an oak tree, so that I tend towards being alive and propagating the species I belong to.

Secondly, life is an unchosen goal of our striving. Later we rationally choose to live – or perhaps embrace an allegiance to life by some less explicit process – but the will to life already inhabits us prior to any understanding or deliberation. In a sense, the primary will to life 'in' me is not *my* will. Schopenhauer would rather say that the will to life manifests itself as me (among other things). Georg Simmel puts it well in his classic lectures of 1907: 'I do not will by virtue of values and goals that are posited by reason, but I have goals because I will continuously and ceaselessly from the depth of my essence.'[23]

Finally, the will that expresses itself in me, or as me, has no ultimate end or purpose to which it tends:

[T]he will dispenses entirely with an ultimate aim and object. It always strives, because striving is its sole nature, to which no attained goal can put an end. Such striving is therefore incapable of final satisfaction; it can be checked only by hindrance, but in itself it goes on for ever. (W1 308/H. 2, 364)

One consequence, for Schopenhauer, is that there can be no absolute good. What is good is by definition, for Schopenhauer, what satisfies an end for which some part of reality strives or towards which it naturally tends. He inverts the rationalist commonplace that we will what we understand as good. For him, something is good solely in virtue of our willing it; good is defined as 'fitness or suitableness of an object to any definite effort (*Bestrebung*) of the will' (W1 360/ H. 2, 425). In that case, an 'absolute good' or 'highest good, *summum bonum*' would be 'a final satisfaction of the will, after which no fresh willing would occur', but 'such a thing cannot be conceived. The will can just as little through some satisfaction cease to will always afresh, as time can end or begin; for the will there is no permanent fulfilment which completely and forever satisfies its craving' (W1 362/H. 2, 427–8). Willing continues in the world in perpetuity. But since absolute value could be possessed only by a state of affairs in which nothing more was willed, no state of affairs can ever possess absolute value – it would involve a contradiction to think otherwise. There is good only locally, relative to some particular occurrence or state of willing.

V   THE ARGUMENT FROM THE UBIQUITY OF
SUFFERING WITHIN THE STRUCTURE OF WILLING

I want now to reconstruct one of Schopenhauer's arguments for pessimism that relies on an intimate link between the human will and suffering. Suffering is defined by Schopenhauer as the will's 'hindrance through an obstacle placed between it and its temporary goal' (WI 309/H. 2, 365), while, as we have seen, the opposite state, '*satisfaction*, well-being, happiness' consists in the will's attainment of its temporary goal. Suffering, non-attainment of goals, will be a likely occurrence in the life of a being that wills. This very fact might be a reason for questioning optimism, but on its own it is hardly grounds for pronouncing that non-existence should be preferred to the life of a willing being. However, for Schopenhauer, suffering is more than just one ingredient in such a life: it is a permeating and necessary feature of it. To see this, let us consider the structure of willing in a schematic way.

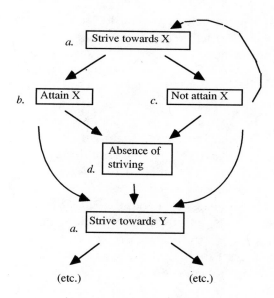

A being will strive towards some goal, X, and will either attain X or not attain X. The latter state, marked as *c* in the diagram, is a state of suffering. It seems that there are just three subsequent possibilities once a goal is not attained. Having not attained a goal, I may continue to strive for it nevertheless. This is the route looping back to the original state of striving, which, repeated endlessly, is the nightmare of Tantalus and other mythical figures whom Schopenhauer is prone to mention:

[S]o long as our consciousness is filled by our will, so long as we are given up to the throng of desires with its constant hopes and fears, so long as we are the subject of willing, we never obtain lasting happiness or peace.... Thus the subject of willing is constantly lying on the revolving wheel of Ixion, is always drawing water in the sieve of the Danaids, and is the eternally thirsting Tantalus. (W1 196/H. 2, 231)

Powerful though the symbolism of this route is for a pessimist, there are, of course, others: I may move on to another goal, or I may cease for a while to strive towards any goals. What we have next to establish is that, for Schopenhauer, both states a and d – both striving itself and the absence of striving – also constitute or presuppose forms of suffering.

On the first point Schopenhauer declares: 'all striving [Streben] springs from want or deficiency, from dissatisfaction with one's own state or condition, and is therefore suffering so long as it is not satisfied' (W1 309/H. 2, 365). The assumption appears to be that a wholly self-sufficient state, a state of lacking nothing (or at least registering no lack), would continue in principle perpetually, without tending towards any change of state brought about by will. Thus any episode which is a being's striving for a goal assumes that the being is, or at least registers itself as, lacking something. Being aware of the lack of something is not sufficient to make me suffer. The awareness of lack must present itself as painful as such. A clear example would be a felt deficiency or incompleteness, such as thirst or a feeling of homesickness, in which the awareness of something's being lacking is inseparable from some degree of suffering. (But I suppose Schopenhauer must include cases where one painfully feels a deficiency or incompleteness because one makes a rational judgement of a situation as detrimental to oneself. Thirst is a form of suffering, but so is recognizing [while not feeling thirst] that one is in a desert without a sufficient water supply.) At any rate, Schopenhauer requires us to suppose that whenever we strive after any goal, we are aware of lacking something in some manner which amounts to pain or suffering. Hence to be in a state of type a in the diagram presupposes that one suffers. But because our ordinary life is, in its essence, a mani-festation of will, there is no end in ordinary life to the occurrence of states of type *a*. So we must always return to some state of suffering. We have, perhaps, come a small step closer to pessimism.

How plausible, though, is the claim that whenever we strive for a goal, the striving presupposes an awareness of lack which amounts to suffering? David Cartwright[24] finds this point unconvincing, say-ing that having a desire does not entail being in misery. That is true, but it mistakes what Schopenhauer alleges in the passage just quoted.[25] The claim is rather that every episode of *striving* entails *some degree* of painful lack or dissatisfaction. Let us look at this more closely. Firstly, does striving always presuppose an aware-ness of lack, or a dissatisfaction, of any kind? Cartwright suggests this is not always true for desiring: I may desire to retain my good health, which I believe I have rather than lack, and with which I am satisfied. However, Schopenhauer's point (at least in the last quoted passage) was one about *Streben*, striving or trying. (i) Striving, I take it, must be episodic rather than dispositional, whereas the desires just mentioned may be construed as dispositions; and (ii) striving must aim at change in a way that desire need not. So the question we must ask is: When an episode of my behaviour is describable as my striving to retain good health – which by hypothesis I do not lack – must I be experiencing some 'dissatisfaction with my own state or condition'? The answer, arguably, is Yes: part of what distinguishes striving from mere wanting is that I regard the prior state of affairs (the state of affairs minus my striving) as deficient in whatever it requires to ensure my goal. If I register the state of affairs minus my striving as involving no such deficiency, arguably it becomes unin-telligible to describe me as striving or trying to retain my health.

Even if we allow that to strive for something presupposes some dissatisfaction, Cartwright makes another objection: such dissatis-faction commonly 'lacks the vital tone which is associated with misery'.[26] This is correct. But it misses the mark as regards Schopen-hauer's argument. Schopenhauer does not hold that each episode of willing involves the subject in misery; rather that, as a presuppo-sition of there occurring an episode of willing, dissatisfaction or a painfully felt lack must be present in some degree. Misery is, let us say, some prolonged frustration of what is willed or massive non-attainment of goals basic to well-being. Most lives contain some

misery and some lives contain mostly misery, facts which Schopenhauer has not forgotten and of which he writes movingly. But his
point here is that all lives, even those free of misery, inevitably contain numerous, if minuscule, dissatisfactions. Each occurrence of
striving presupposes a state with some degree of negative value for
the being that strives. Hence, if we are looking for positive value
within life, we shall not find it in any of the states of type *a*.

But it is time we mentioned other parts of the picture. First, consider state *d* in the diagram. May we not hope that a lack of goals to
strive for will indicate a lack of the feeling that anything is lacking
– an absence of suffering, a respite that counterbalances states *a* and
c? Here is Schopenhauer's answer:

> The basis of all willing ... is need, lack, and hence pain, and by its very
> nature and origin [any animal] is therefore destined to pain. If, on the other
> hand, it lacks objects of willing, because it is at once deprived of them again
> by too easy a satisfaction, a fearful emptiness and boredom come over it; in
> other words, its being and its existence itself become an intolerable burden
> for it. Hence its life swings like a pendulum to and fro between pain and
> boredom, and these two are in fact its ultimate constituents. (*W1* 312/H. 2,
> 367–8)

This is one of Schopenhauer's tragi-comic master strokes. (Elsewhere
he says: 'Suppose the human race were removed to Utopia where everything grew automatically and pigeons flew about ready roasted
... then people would die of boredom or hang themselves' [*P2* 293/
H. 6, 311].) The state of having nothing to strive for readily becomes
one in which we suffer from not having anything whose lack we feel.
We painfully miss the differently painful state of having something
to strive for. The grip of pessimism tightens again. Either of the routes
a–c–a contains only suffering. So now does route *a–c–d*. Routes
a–b–a and *a–b–d* contain satisfaction, but only sandwiched between
two forms of suffering. Satisfaction is thus never anything permanent and always lapses again into painful lack or painful boredom.
Schopenhauer expresses the situation thus:

> [A]bsolutely every human life continues to flow on between willing and
> attainment. Of its nature the wish is pain; attainment quickly begets satiety.
> The goal was only apparent; possession takes away its charm. The wish, the
> need, appears again on the scene under a new form; if it does not, then

dreariness, emptiness, and boredom follow, the struggle against which is just as painful as is that against want. (*W1* 313–14/H. 2, 370)

But why would such an existence be one we should prefer not to have? That attitude might intelligibly be occasioned by the complete shipwreck of all one's aims. But that is not the situation of every human being, as Schopenhauer wisely concedes:

This is the life of almost all men; they will, they know what they will, and they strive after this with enough success to protect them from despair, and enough failure to preserve them from boredom and its consequences. (*W1* 327/H. 2, 386)

If most lives are spiced with a sufficiently varied set of goals, and if, as human beings shuffle between the different forms of suffering, they come round to the state 'Attain X' sufficiently often, then it is still unclear why that is a kind of existence not to be chosen above non-existence.

But now we must go back and examine a central part of Schopenhauer's claim that happiness is illusory:

All satisfaction, or what is commonly called happiness, is really and essentially always *negative* only, and never positive. . . . [T]he satisfaction or gratification can never be more than deliverance from a pain, from a want. . . . [N]othing can ever be gained but deliverance from some suffering or desire; consequently, we are only in the same position as we were before this suffering or desire appeared. (*W1* 319)

We feel pain, but not painlessness; care, but not freedom from care; fear, but not safety and security. We feel the desire as we feel hunger and thirst; but as soon as it has been satisfied, it is like the mouthful of food that has been taken, and which ceases to exist for our feelings the moment it is swallowed. (*W2* 575/H. 3, 659)

The thesis here – call it 'the negativity of satisfaction' – is that attainment of what one strives for is not accompanied by any positive feeling. Satisfaction is not only dependent upon one's having suffered, but is itself merely the temporary absence of suffering, which soon yields again to suffering. If this is true, then state *b* in my diagram can do little to counterbalance the sufferings which are presupposed at every other point. The conclusion that non-existence would have been preferable at least comes within sight: 'all life is suffering', as

Schopenhauer helpfully puts it (*W1* 310/H. 2, 366). Life is suffering of different kinds, plus some neutral stretches where suffering is briefly absent before new suffering arrives.

Before looking at some objections to this desperate game of pinball, I shall note that Schopenhauer uses this last point – the negativity of satisfaction – to advance another extremely brief argument for his pessimistic conclusion, an argument which we may call 'the argument from the sheer existence of suffering':

> it is quite superfluous to dispute whether there is more good or evil in the world; for the mere existence of evil decides the matter, since evil can never be wiped off, and consequently can never be balanced, by the good that exists along with or after it.
>
> *Mille piacer' non vagliono un tormento.*[27]
>
> For that thousands had lived in happiness and joy would never do away with the anguish and death-agony of one individual; and just as little does my present well-being undo my previous sufferings. Therefore, were the evil in the world even a hundred times less than it is, its mere existence would still be sufficient to establish a truth that may be expressed in various ways ... namely that we have not to be pleased but rather sorry about the existence of the world; that its non-existence would be preferable to its existence; that it is something which at bottom ought not to be. (*W2* 576/H. 3, 661)

This is the most extreme statement of pessimism: any suffering at all invalidates the whole world. But it is difficult to see why I should reject or think badly of existence simply on the grounds of its containing some suffering. It is true that no happiness I can attain expunges my sufferings or those of anyone else. But then equally, no suffering I undergo can remove, in one sense, whatever happiness there has been and might be once again. Admittedly, present distress can obliterate any experiential access to past happiness and make it seem to count for nothing. But is not the reverse also true? On your happiest day, your worst torments might be forgotten and so seem to lack any significance. Schopenhauer's conviction that any suffering tips the balance against life depends crucially on the thesis of the negativity of satisfaction. With this as a premise, it becomes conceivable how one could conclude that no satisfaction or happiness can compensate for a single suffering. Yet the resultant discounting of happiness still seems perversely one-sided.

VI OBJECTIONS

There are some clear objections to Schopenhauer's use of willing and suffering in these arguments. Firstly, he seems guilty of ignoring or stipulating away positive feelings that occur within the pattern of willing and attainment. As Simmel puts it, 'he should not ... have overlooked the positive moment of happiness which differentiates it as a psychological fact from sleep and death, the two other states that end suffering'.[28] Sleep and death stop my striving; but satisfaction, which Schopenhauer defines as the cessation of striving, is at least a different kind of cessation from that in sleep or death. The difference is not simply that in satisfaction I am conscious when my striving ceases, and in the other cases not – at least sometimes there are positive feelings of satisfaction, and these cannot be argued away on any of the grounds Schopenhauer adduces: (i) that satisfaction or happiness is always relative to prior dissatisfaction; (ii) that satisfaction is temporary and yields to further dissatisfactions; or (iii) that the sum of feelings of dissatisfaction is likely to be greater than the sum of satisfactions. None of these points entails that there are no positively felt satisfactions. So Schopenhauer can no longer claim that felt satisfaction must count for nothing in the balance against suffering. Life might still be worth living, at least for what feelings of satisfaction it does contain, if that is where we should look for its worth.

A subtler point, also made by Simmel, is that Schopenhauer fails to recognize that there is felt happiness along the route from striving to attainment but before its terminus. 'Expected happiness is truly experienced', notes Simmel, and the will's progress towards attainment is 'attended more by a pleasurable sensation than a painful one'.[29] There is wisdom in these thoughts: we often feel positive enjoyment at the prospect of attaining what we actually lack, and the actions through which, while lacking it, we strive towards it, may also be pleasurable. Many human practices consist of arrangements designed to prolong a struggle: for instance, mountaineering, where to be lifted without effort to the summit would remove not just striving and pain, but the very pleasure which gives the activity its point. So Schopenhauer's model of willing as movement from a wholly painful lack to its mere obliteration is unrealistic. Even states of unfulfilled striving cannot always be set down on the side of suffering pure and simple.

A final objection is to Schopenhauer's implicit notion of positive and negative value in general. An undefended assumption in his argument is a stark form of hedonism: something adds positive value to life if and only if it involves a felt pleasure, while something contributes negative value if and only if it involves a felt pain. So if a sequence of states from felt lack through striving to satisfaction contains no feelings of pleasure, but only feelings of suffering yielding to a neutral state in which those feelings are erased, then there could be no positive value in that sequence of states for the subject. But this is questionable in a number of obvious and familiar ways. Are felt pleasures and pains the sole bearers or contributors of value? Why do outcomes of our actions other than pleasures and pains count for nothing? Is there not a self-sufficient value, irreducible to amounts of pleasure and pain, in certain activities which are fundamental to our nature and well-being? So we can certainly question whether Schopenhauer is right to use any form of hedonic calculus at all. And when we combine this with our criticism of the negativity of satisfaction thesis, we see that Schopenhauer has done something quite bizarre: he has used as the test of value a hedonic calculus in which each felt pain accumulates points on the down side of life, but where the total figure for satisfaction is permanently set at zero. From here it seems too short a distance to pessimism, or no distance at all. If the good can be solely the felt satisfaction of attaining what is willed, but if no positive satisfaction is ever felt, then the good is nothing but a satisfaction we could never feel. And is that not to say that whatever could be good must always be valueless? To start from here would be an absurdity.

Still, we are left with a relatively pessimistic description of things. A basic state of ours as living creatures, and one to which we must constantly return, is one of dissatisfaction or painful lack. The attainment of a goal never stops us from slipping back into further states of dissatisfaction. And there is constantly the likelihood of prolonged or many-sided failure of attainment, turning dissatisfaction into misery, or over-attainment leading to wretched aimlessness. Because of our nature, which none of our strivings has the power to alter, some suffering is inevitable and great suffering is perfectly possible for any of us. I suppose this is somewhere near the truth. But what attitude should we adopt towards life if it is thus correctly described? Schopenhauer's view is that each suffering drains away some (or even all) of the potential value from life, which nothing can restore. But Nietzsche's attitude to the same description, which he arguably accepts,[30] is diametrically opposed. In clear allusion to his 'teacher' Schopenhauer (as he calls him), Nietzsche asks whether suffering is an objection to life and firmly answers No: it is a sign of strength and greatness of character to affirm one's sufferings as an integral and in some sense desirable element in one's life. We know that people who have endured pain far more than the average may utter the sub-Nietzschean (if prosaic) thought 'I wouldn't change anything if I had my life over again' (to which Nietzsche adds '...an infinite number of times'[31]). In a rough and ready way this suggests that people's lives can make sense to them partly because of their sufferings, not in spite of them. A pessimistic description of life is compatible with an affirmation of it.

VII AFFIRMATION, DENIAL, AND THE SELF

Schopenhauer's pessimism has, I believe, deep foundations in his metaphysics, in particular in his conception of the self. Consider the following two questions: (1) Would not suicide be the appropriate solution to the predicament Schopenhauer alleges we are in? (2) If we could live but in some sense become detached from willing, would that be another solution? Schopenhauer answers No to question 1: suicide is not a solution – surprisingly perhaps. And he answers Yes to question 2, which might also seem odd if we recall the pain attaching to boredom. Should not permanent detachment from all willing be a *longueur* in every sense? Schopenhauer's answers to these two questions rest on his conception of an extraordinary state, possible for at least some individuals, which he calls 'denial of the will', a state that altogether alters the significance of striving and suffering for them. On the one hand, this altered state is wholly different from boredom. On the other hand, someone who commits suicide fails to reach the altered state and instead continues to affirm the will. Some explanations are required.

'[The] will to life ... must be denied if salvation is to be attained from an existence like ours', Schopenhauer writes (*W1* 405/H. 2, 479). He remarks ironically that denial of the will is the only state we might consider as a candidate for the 'highest good': there is no such thing, but if we wish to give that expression an emeritus position, then figuratively the *summum bonum* is

the complete self-effacement and denial of the will, true will-lessness, which alone stills and silences for ever the craving of the will; which alone gives that contentment that cannot again be disturbed; which alone is world-redeeming. (*W1* 362/H. 2, 428)

This would be, he acknowledges, 'self-denial or self-renunciation, *abnegatio sui ipsius*; for the real self is the will to life' (*W2* 606/H. 3, 695), or, as he often says, our 'being' or 'essence'. So Schopenhauer advocates a radical and difficult cure: denial of, or loss of identification with, our essence. If the solution to pessimism lies in abnegating *one's real self*, then the justification for this must be that *being what one is* is not worthwhile. It is this rejection of all value in the essence of humanity that roots Schopenhauer's pessimism deep in his metaphysics.

Schopenhauer writes with impressive intensity about the temporary state of will-lessness to be found in aesthetic experience. And he recalls this experience in an attempt to convey the blessedness of prolonged will-lessness in 'denial of the will':

aesthetic pleasure in the beautiful consists, to a large extent, in the fact that, when we enter the state of pure contemplation, we are raised for the moment above all willing, above all desires and cares; we are, so to speak, rid of ourselves. We are no longer the individual that knows in the interest of its constant willing... but the eternal subject of knowing purified of the will.... From this we can infer how blessed must be the life of a man whose will is silenced not for a few moments, as in the enjoyment of the beautiful, but for ever, indeed completely extinguished, except for the last glimmering spark that maintains the body and is extinguished with it. Such a man who, after many bitter struggles with his own nature, has at last completely conquered, is then left only as pure knowing being.... Nothing can distress or alarm him any more; nothing can any longer move him; for he has cut all the thousand threads of willing which hold us bound to the world, and which as craving, fear, envy, and anger drag us here and there in constant pain. (*W1* 390/H. 2, 461–2)

As I see it, a contrasting pair of higher-order evaluative attitudes has now entered the picture. One takes – explicitly or implicitly – some attitude of acquiescence or refusal towards one's existence as an organic embodiment of the will to life, caught in the cycle of willing and suffering. The ordinary person who registers wants and strives to satisfy them adopts an implicit second-order attitude of 'affirmation' towards the body in which they arise. I say 'implicit' because this attitude is the natural, more or less unreflective state of human beings. Schopenhauer says: '*The affirmation of the will* is the persistent willing itself, undisturbed by any knowledge, as it fills the life of man in general. . . . [I]nstead of affirmation of the will, we can also say affirmation of the body' (*W1* 326–7/H. 2, 385). The will to life is also what Christianity calls the 'natural man' (*W1* 404–5/H. 2, 479). In addition to pursuing goals dependent on the needs of the bodily individual, human beings also do something which other animals do not: *they regard this pursuit as the point of their existence.* Denial of the will is a release from identification with the embodied individual one is, a way of not seeing this point in its existence, and in this sense one way of being 'rid of oneself'.

Back to suicide. Schopenhauer's discussion of suicide is often found puzzling. For not only does he disapprove of it – why, if existence is never worth more than non-existence? – but his disapproval rests on the grounds that 'suicide is a phenomenon of the will's strong affirmation' and that the suicide 'gives up by no means the will to life' (*W1* 398/H. 2, 471). The explanation is that the suicide is the ordinary person whose attitude concerning the point of life is unrevised, but whose actual life has not delivered enough of the outcomes which are considered, wrongly, to give it its point.

The suicide wills life, and is dissatisfied merely with the conditions on which it has come to him. . . . He wills life, wills the unchecked existence and affirmation of the body, but the combination of circumstances does not allow of these, and the result for him is great suffering. (*W1* 398/H. 2, 471)

The assessment that leads to suicide faults the circumstances of the individual's actual life for failing to permit a sufficiently smooth transition from felt deficiency to its removal or from striving to satisfaction. But Schopenhauer's point is that the subject who makes this assessment still does so from a standpoint of identification with the individual: this subject's attitude is that of 'willing the unchecked existence and affirmation of the body'. Because of this self-identification the suicide remains caught within the cycle of lacks and replenishments. But once suffering overwhelmingly gains the upper hand, this cycle seems to have let the individual down. 'Just because the suicide cannot cease willing, he ceases to live'. The suicide, then, is no different in principle from any ordinary individual in affirming the will to life. On the other hand, the hopelessness of the suicide, who has not 'conquered his own nature', is quite opposed to the state of denial of the will to life. And for a similar reason, the will-lessness attained in denial of the will to life cannot be equated with the aimlessness of boredom. The bored person, like the suicide, like the ordinary human being, still wrongly acquiesces in his or her bodily, striving existence and thinks that existence can gain value from goals pursued and needs satisfied. He or she suffers from the lack of goals because he or she continues – in what I have called a 'higher-order' evaluative attitude – to affirm the pursuing and attaining of such goals as the locus of value.

Thus 'denial of the will' stands opposed to ordinary affirmation, to boredom, and to the view of the suicide. It does so by virtue of a re-orientation of one's self-identification. The self for Schopenhauer has unusual complexity. Each human individual is an organism that is part of the world of objects, but he or she is also subject of knowledge: 'That which knows all things and is known by none is the *subject*.... Everyone finds himself as this subject, yet only insofar as he knows, not in so far as he is object of knowledge. But his body is already object' (*W1* 5/H. 2, 5). What is this subject? It is not part of the spatio-temporal world, but the extensionless point from which experience of a spatio-temporal world is had, and which that experience presupposes, in the manner of Kant's transcendental unity of apperception. 'Subject' is not a kind of thing that occurs within the world. This subject which I am (or find myself as) is not the individual, which by definition is a spatio-temporal entity for Schopenhauer (space and time providing the principle of individuation). Elsewhere Schopenhauer discusses the relationship between this subject or 'I' and the organic individual, saying that the 'I' is the 'focus of brain activity': objectively, states of the brain occur, but the 'I' is what the human organism 'finds itself as' *from the point of view of its own experience*. Since the organism is in turn a manifestation of the will to life, he is able to say this:

This *knowing* and conscious 'I' is related to the will ... as the image in the focus of the concave mirror is to that mirror itself; and, like that image, it has only a conditioned, in fact, properly speaking, a merely apparent reality. Far from being the absolutely first thing (as Fichte taught, for example), it is at bottom tertiary, since it presupposes the organism, and the organism presupposes the will. (W2 278/H. 3, 314–15)

We are accustomed to regarding this knowing 'I' as our real self, but in so doing we are in error: the real self is the will (W2 239/H. 3, 270).

While rational thought and the subject's self-consciousness are instruments of the will to life and of the organism, they also give rise to a curious split in our self-conception. For this will to life can confront consciousness as something distinct from the thinking, knowing subject that consciousness presupposes. It is as if the motor which propels me, the primum mobile from which I am inseparable, and which indeed is me, must present itself to me, the thinking, rational subject, as an agency alien to myself. Schopenhauer portrays the knowing subject as lacking autonomy vis-à-vis the will. That I am a being that wills life and must strive for other mediate goals, and hence must suffer, does not issue from *my* choices. Furthermore, no contrivance of rationality, no episode of conscious willing, no steps I take, even when successful, can make it the case that the willing in me ceases. This means that it is not within our power whether or not we strive and are open to suffering. The self-conscious subject is a kind of victim of its underlying real self, the will to life. The life of willing in non–self-conscious animals has the same pattern as in human life (though it lacks some kinds of suffering for which conceptual thought is necessary: for instance, anxiety about the future, remorse about the past). But since they do not have this 'I' as a competing locus of selfhood, other animals cannot see themselves as victims of the will to life, as humans can.

Schopenhauer says that our own nature leads us to commit the 'inborn error' of thinking we exist in order to be happy: 'our whole being is only the paraphrase' of this error, 'indeed our body is its monogram' (W2 634/H. 3, 729). It is what we are that is the problem. The solution, then, is to reach a state in which one becomes indifferent to happiness and unhappiness, unattached to the body, not wedded to the furtherance of any goals which an individual willing being might pursue. The threat of suffering is neutralized if one stands in an attitude of renunciation towards the whole round of willing and attainment. One must still exist in order to take this attitude, and

Schopenhauer's thought is that one can do so while identifying one-self wholly with the pure subject of knowledge, that fiction cast up by the organism, which yet we 'find ourselves to be'. Thus free from our allegiance to the individual, the body, we can have a kind of pure knowledge, which is had from the perspective of no place within the world, and stands no closer to the needs and goals of any one indi-vidual as opposed to others. Elsewhere Schopenhauer allies himself with Plato's view in the *Phaedo*, saying that the notion of liberating the soul from the body is better expressed as liberating oneself from the will (see *W2* 608–9/H. 3, 699–70).

But the subject lacks autonomy even here: one cannot achieve this liberated state of will-lessness by an act of will. Just as the presence of the will to life in me does not result from my conscious choice or intention, so too the will to life – once more conceived as a sep-arate agency within me – must turn and abolish itself. There are two routes by which this may occur. The inferior or second route (δεύτερος πλοῦς[32]) is that of overwhelming individual suffering. An individual may suffer so much that his or her will to life gives out spontaneously. The individual continues to exist, but in a state of detachment from living as an end, indifferent to the prospering or ruin of the individual he or she happens to be, 'purified ... by the deepest grief and sorrow'.[33] The superior and rarer route is that of knowledge, or an exceptionally anti-egoistic vision attained by those whom Schopenhauer calls saints.[34] The saint reaches an understand-ing that he or she is not fundamentally distinct from the world as a whole, that individuality itself is an illusion:

[S]uch a human being,[35] recognizing in all beings his own true and innermost self, must also regard the endless sufferings of all that lives as his own, and thus take upon himself the pain of the whole world....He knows the whole, comprehends its inner nature, and finds it involved in a constant passing away, a vain striving [*nichtigen Streben*], an inward conflict, and a continual suffering....Now how could he, with such knowledge of the world, affirm this very life through constant acts of will, and precisely in this way bind himself more and more firmly to it, press himself to it more and more closely? ... [T]hat knowledge of the whole ... becomes the *quieter* of all and every willing. The will now turns away from life; it shudders at the pleasures in which it recognizes the affirmation of life. The human being attains to the state of voluntary renunciation, resignation, true composure, and complete will-lessness. (*W1* 379/H. 2, 447–8)

Descriptions of such saintly insight and serenity are found, Schopenhauer reminds us, in a number of world religions, whence they can be salvaged from among the various theistic dogmas.

Schopenhauer thus provides the paradigm of the stance Nietzsche calls resignationism, or no-saying or life denial[36] – while handing Nietzsche on a plate the claim that this is the uniting feature of Hinduism, Buddhism, Platonism, and Christianity. For Nietzsche this is the controlling, degenerate, sick ideal against which we must make war. We might say: the pathos of Schopenhauer is that, revealing to us our 'true nature' in the will to life, he sees precisely this as what we must disown before our existence can claim to have value. We might also find pathological in Schopenhauer that which Nietzsche diagnosed and felt revulsion for: the view that my only hope lies in the withering away of my sense of individuality or in my suffering so severely that the will to life within me is broken. At least to the unconverted, that these can be *hopes* at all is grotesque. That *only* such outcomes could give positive value to our existence, and to that of the whole world, is surely Schopenhauer's most pessimistic thought.

NOTES

1 See *W2* ch. 46 : 'Von der Nichtigkeit und dem Leiden des Lebens', literally 'On the Nothingness and the Suffering of Life'.

2 See esp.*W2* 574–84/H. 3, 658–71.

3 *W1* 325/H. 2, 383, adapted from Payne's translation by omitting material not present in the 1819 *W1¹* edition. When Schopenhauer revised this passage for re-publication, he threw in 'torture-chambers' for good measure, and finished his tour for the optimist by 'allowing him to glance into the dungeons of Ugolino where prisoners starved to death'.

4 In other places Nietzsche criticizes Schopenhauer severely for remaining stuck with Christian values, especially in his account of morality. See *Human, All Too Human* I, preface, §1; *Beyond Good and Evil*, §§65, 186; *On the Genealogy of Morals*, Preface, §5; *Twilight of the Idols*, 'Skirmishes of an Untimely Man', §§35, 37; *Ecce Homo*, 'The Birth of Tragedy', §2.

5 See *WN* 132–3, 139–42; *P1* 35, 61–2, 73, 76, 183, 192; *P2* 100, 258, 300–10, 378–94/H.4, 131–4, 140–4; H. 5, 39–40, 65–7, 78–9, 81, 195, 204–5; H. 6, 106–7, 275, 318–29, 402–19.

6 *P2* 380–1/H. 6, 404–5.

7 *P1* 35/H. 5, 39–40.

8 *P1* 61/H. 5, 65–6.

9 *W2* 643–4/H. 3, 739–40.

10 *W2* 645/H. 3, 741–2. Schopenhauer adds a Latin quote to the effect that '[a smelling bottle] long retains the smell of that which filled it'.

11 See Nietzsche, *On the Genealogy of Morals* III, §22.

12 See Yirmiyahu Yovel, 'Nietzsche, the Jews, and *Ressentiment*', in Richard Schacht (ed.), *Nietzsche, Genealogy, Morality* (Berkeley: University of California Press, 1994), 214–36; and Jacob Golomb (ed.), *Nietzsche and Jewish Culture* (London: Routledge, 1997).

13 *P1* 192/H. 5, 205; *Panta kala lian*, 'everything [was] very good'. See also *W2* 623–5/H. 3, 716–18 and *P2* 301/H. 6, 319–20.

14 On the latter idea, see *P2* 258–9/H. 6, 275–6.

15 *W2* 582–4/H. 3, 668–70.

16 Even more curious is a lengthy footnote to the final edition of *The World as Will and Representation* printed in Schopenhauer's lifetime (1859), where he records a traveller's description of a squirrel being mesmerized and devoured by a snake in Java, and is prepared to pronounce this mere anecdote 'important... as an argument for *pessimism*': '[T]hat such a poor innocent squirrel... is compelled, step by step, reluctantly, struggling with itself and lamenting, to approach the snake's wide, open jaws and hurl itself consciously into these, is so revolting and atrocious, that we feel how right Aristotle is in saying ἡ φύσις δαιμονία μέν ἐστι, οὐ δὲ θεία. How frightful is this nature to which we belong!' (*W2* 356/H. 3, 406).

17 *W2* 583/H. 3, 669–70.

18 See Bryan Magee, *The Philosophy of Schopenhauer* (Oxford: Oxford University Press, 1983), 13–14.

19 E.g., *W1* 309/H. 2, 365. Sometimes he specifies that the *rapid transition* from willing to satisfaction is happiness. See *W1* 260/H. 2, 307–8, in his discussion of musical expression: 'as rapid transition from wish to satisfaction and from this to a new wish are happiness and well-being, so rapid melodies without great deviations are cheerful'.

20 *W1* 314/H. 2, 370: Schopenhauer is misleading when he says in the same breath that the goal was 'only apparent'. The goal was genuinely one's goal, but it was only apparent that attaining it would be finally satisfying.

21 *W2* 573/H. 3, 657.

22 See *P1* 406/H. 5, 433–4.

23 Georg Simmel, *Schopenhauer and Nietzsche*, trans. Helmut Loiskandl, Deena Weinstein, and Michael Weinstein (Amherst: University of Massachusetts Press, 1986), 30.

24 David E. Cartwright, 'Schopenhauer on Suffering, Death, Guilt, and the Consolation of Metaphysics', in E. von der Luft (ed.), *Schopenhauer: New Essays in Honor of his 200th Birthday* (Lewiston, N.Y.: Edwin Mellen Press, 1988), 51–66.

25 My case is weakened, and Cartwright's strengthened, by a prominent parallel passage, *W1* 196/H. 2, 230–1, in which Schopenhauer says, 'All *willing* springs from lack, from deficiency, and thus from suffering'. In this passage, willing (*Wollen*) explicitly includes 'wish' (*Wunsch*) and 'desiring' (*Begehren*).

26 'Schopenhauer on Suffering', 59.

27 'A thousand pleasures do not compensate for one pain' (Petrarch).

28 *Schopenhauer and Nietzsche*, 64.

29 Ibid., 55–6.

30 See Ivan Soll, 'Pessimism and the Tragic View of Life: Reconsiderations of Nietzsche's *Birth of Tragedy*', in Robert C. Solomon and Kathleen Higgins (eds.), *Reading Nietzsche* (New York and Oxford: Oxford University Press, 1988), 104–31.

31 For this use of the doctrine of the eternal recurrence of one's life, see Nietzsche, *The Gay Science*, §341. In *Beyond Good and Evil*, §56, Nietzsche treats the willing of eternal recurrence as the 'opposite ideal' to that of Schopenhauer and as a consequence of 'thinking pessimism through to its depths'.

32 'Second sailing': *W1* 392/H. 2, 463.

33 *W1* 393/H. 2, 464.

34 See esp. *W1* 378–9/H. 2, 446–8.

35 Payne translates *Mensch* as 'man' here. But although Schopenhauer is not noted for his fairness towards women (see the notorious 'On Women', *P2* 614–26/H. 6, 650–63), we should not make him more sexist than is necessary. One of his prominent examples of denial of the will is that of Madame de Guyon, 'that great and beautiful soul, whose remembrance always fills me with reverence' (*W1* 385/H. 2, 455; see also *W1* 391/H. 2, 462, which gives extracts from Guyon's *Autobiography*).

36 See *On the Genealogy of Morals*, Preface, §5; *The Birth of Tragedy*, 'Attempt at a Self-criticism', §6; *The Gay Science*, §370; *Twilight of the Idols*, 'Morality as Anti-Nature', §5; ibid., 'Skirmishes of an Untimely Man', §§35–7; ibid., 'What I Owe to the Ancients', §5; *Ecce Homo*, 'The Birth of Tragedy', §2; *Nietzsche contra Wagner*, 'We Antipodes'.

11 Nietzsche, Schopenhauer, and Dionysus[1]

> If Schopenhauer ... posited a general depression as the
> tragic condition, if he suggested to the Greeks (– who to
> his annoyance did not 'resign themselves' –) that they had
> not attained the highest view of the world – that is *parti
> pris*, logic of a system, counterfeit of a systematizer: one
> of those dreadful counterfeits that ruined Schopenhauer's
> whole psychology, step by step (– arbitrarily and violently,
> he misunderstood genius, art itself, morality, pagan
> religion, beauty, knowledge, and more or less everything).
>
> Nietzsche, *The Will to Power*, §851

> Do you desire the most astonishing proof of how far the
> transfiguring power of intoxication can go? – 'Love' is this
> proof: that which is called love in all languages and
> silences of the world.
>
> Nietzsche, *The Will to Power*, §808[2]

I READING NIETZSCHE'S SCHOPENHAUER

It would not be misleading to say that at the time he wrote *The Birth of Tragedy*, Nietzsche was so steeped in Schopenhauer that he perceived whatever he perceived through the lens of Schopenhauerian distinctions and categories. Certainly it is hard to make sense of the concepts of the Apollonian and Dionysian, and many other insufficiently explained aspects of Nietzsche's argument in that cryptic work, without relating them to Schopenhauer's more explicit and extensive arguments.

This close relationship has frequently been mentioned. But its implications for the interpretation of *The Birth of Tragedy* and related

344

texts have not been described, I believe, with sufficient complexity. For although Nietzsche often simply appropriates Schopenhauer's concepts and categories without much explanation, in such a way that the reader who is unacquainted with Schopenhauer will be at a loss to understand why a certain connection is made, or how one step follows on from the previous one, Nietzsche is also, by this time already, profoundly critical of much of Schopenhauer's account of both cognition and desire and profoundly hostile to his normative 'pessimism.' Most of the basis for the explicit denunciation of Schopenhauer in later works such as *The Case of Wagner* and our epigraph (from 1888) is already firmly in place. But Nietzsche's strategy, in *The Birth*, is not, as later, to use direct argument or explicit polemic against his revered predecessor. Instead, he proceeds by stealth, using Schopenhauer's very terms to undermine his distinctions and arguments, borrowing the surface of his language to subvert the core of this thought. The reader must, in this situation, proceed with the utmost deftness and care, becoming what Nietzsche none too modestly said any good reader of his text must be: 'a monster of courage and curiosity; moreover supple, cunning, cautious; a born adventurer and discoverer.'[3]

Far too few accounts of Nietzsche's thought pause to give any exegesis of Schopenhauer's central notions and arguments – with the result that even the most attentive reader is not put in a position to grasp the origins of a term, the significance of a reference. This is especially unfortunate since Schopenhauer writes with a directness and simplicity none too common in the German philosophical tradition, so that it is quite feasible to attempt to supply a clear and economical summary of the elements of his thought that most influenced Nietzsche's picture of Dionysus. The result, I think, will be a more adequate understanding not only of the language of *The Birth*, but also of Nietzsche's philosophical motivations for saying what he did about desire and for defending love, sexual desire, and the body in the way in which he defended them.

II THINKING AS DREAMING: THE ROLE OF THE BODY

Like Kant, Schopenhauer argues that our faculties of perception and thought do not and cannot grasp an intrinsic structure of the world as it is in itself, apart from the operations of the mind. What we grasp we grasp under certain categories of mind, without the use of which nothing could be grasped. Kant repudiates the idealistic way of understanding his arguments, arguing, apparently, that it is not a mental entity, a fabrication of our own minds, that we grasp when we grasp a thing: it is the external world, *as demarcated by* the categories of mind that are necessary for the possibility of experience. He takes it, furthermore, that by showing these categories to be necessary for the possibility of experience, he has validated them and shown their objective reality. There is, for Kant, no stronger argument for the reality and objectivity of something than a transcendental argument showing that it is necessary for the possibility of experience and thought.

Schopenhauer, by contrast, took Kant's line of reasoning in an idealistic direction (at times interpreting Kant his way, at times explicitly criticizing him). What we experience in perception and thought is not, he argues, a world of things out there, things in themselves – even as shaped by the categories of mind. Instead, we grasp our own representations of things in perception and thought. Instead of looking out at the world through eyeglasses that structure it in a particular way, we are looking, so to speak, into mirror glasses that simply give us back what we ourselves are and have made up.[4]

From his readings in Indian philosophy, Schopenhauer borrows the metaphor of thinking as dreaming, and of its contents as a 'web of *maya*' or illusion (W1 17, 365/H. 2, 20, 431). Our whole cognizing of the world, he insists, is like looking at a dream that we ourselves have made (W1 365; cf. 98/H. 2, 431–2; cf. 117–18). We are dimly aware that we are dreaming, and we dream on. Citing Shakespeare, Plato, Sophocles, Pindar, and Calderón, as well as 'the *Vedas* and *Puranas*,' he concludes: 'Life and dreams are leaves of one and the same book ... we find no distinct difference in their nature, and are forced to concede to the poets that life is a long dream' (W1 17–18/ H. 2, 20–1).

The special role of one's own body in the scheme of representation must now be mentioned. The body seems to be known to the agent directly and immediately. And indeed, Schopenhauer concedes that it is 'for us immediate object, in other words, that representation which forms the starting-point of the subject's knowledge, since it itself with its immediately known changes precedes the application of the law of causality, and thus furnishes this with the first data' (W1

19/H. 2, 22–3). But it is most important to emphasize that representation, however immediate, is what a person's body is. Our especially intimate perceptual connection with it does not suffice to place it outside the veil of *maya*. 'For the purely knowing subject as such, this body is a representation like any other.... Its movements and actions are so far known to him in just the same way as the changes of all other objects of perception' (*W1* 99/H. 2, 118–19).

But our experience of the world contains something else, something different. And here we arrive at the more obscure and tantalizing, but also more profoundly original, aspect of Schopenhauer's thought. We have, says Schopenhauer, the feeling that this story of dreaming cannot be the entire story about our lives. '[W]e ask whether this world is nothing more than representation. In that case, it would inevitably pass by us like an empty dream, or a ghostly vision, not worth our consideration' (*W1* 98–9/H. 2, 118). We cannot get at this something more by looking at the world from without, so to speak: for this approach, characteristic of all conventional inquiry, confines us to representations. We get a hint about the further element, however, if we consider further our relation to our own bodies.

Our bodies are for us objects of sense perception and thought. But there is another relation we have to them: for we move and act. There is a striving, desiring, straining something about us that does not coolly contemplate and represent, but surges and pushes. This kinetic and desiderative aspect of the person Schopenhauer calls will. (And indeed, like Nietzsche much later, he argues that will is present not only in human beings, but in all of nature.[5]) Will is inseparable from body: 'Every true, genuine, immediate act of the will is also at once and directly a manifest act of the body' (*W1* 101/H. 2, 120). The notion of will subsumes, and somehow connects, movement from place to place, all forms of desire, and the experience of pleasure and pain. It appears that will is a kinetic reaching out or striving that explains all movement; the experience of willing is painful, and Schopenhauer seems to believe that its goal is some sort of pleasure or satisfaction (*W1* 101/H. 2, 120–1). A being can relate to its own body either through will or in representation, depending on whether cognitive awareness or some need to act is dominant; and Schopenhauer depicts these two relations as revealing two aspects of a single entity: 'What as representation of perception I call my body, I call my will in so far as I am conscious of it in an entirely different way comparable with no other' (*W1* 102–3/H. 2, 122). (The difficulty of describing will seems to be connected, for Schopenhauer, with its complete lack of cognitive intelligence.)

Schopenhauer seems to intend will to be closely connected with erotic needs and aims – though we must remember that willing as such involves no representation of any object, and thus erotic willing, found 'in every blindly acting force of nature, and also in the deliberate conduct of man' (*W1*, 110/H. 2, 131), is erotic impulse or appetite more than object-directed desire. This erotic urge, he claims, propels all beings ceaselessly forward into movement and action, into the various forms of change and becoming that characterize the world of nature. It is, he insists, not a mysterious form of force that needs to be inferred from experience by a complex argument, but rather something 'known absolutely and immediately, and that so well that we know and understand what will is better than anything else' (*W1* 111/H. 2, 133). (Indeed, he uses the concept of will to explain the concept of force, which he takes to be more elusive.) The claim that will is more familiar than anything else suggests that willing is not confined to erotic desire or appetite narrowly understood, but is a very general notion of striving and longing. Schopenhauer, however, does insist on its close connection with sexuality and reproduction – and, in his misogynistic writings, with woman as the source of unrest and disorder. (And indeed, when Schopenhauer speaks of what is most familiar, we must always bear in mind the obsessive and sexually tormented personality that is doing the asserting.)

It is important to notice that the will, in and of itself, is not an individual or a plurality of individuals. It contains in itself no principle of individuation (called by Schopenhauer by the Latin term *principium individuationis* [*W1* 112–13/H. 2, 134 and elsewhere]). It attains individuation only insofar as it is linked, in experience, with the representation of the body whose moving force it is. This is so, Schopenhauer explains, because in and of itself the striving that is will is not situated in time and space (which, for him, are forms of representation). But orientation in time and space is necessary for the demarcation of a thing as an individual. Therefore the body qua distinct individual is but 'phenomenon.' On the other hand, Schopenhauer believes that the body's shape and form, as it bounds itself off in space and time, shows forth clearly the nature of the will that inhabits and moves it, and gives its outside a form that one could predict by simply experiencing this will. In a remarkable passage (reminiscent of the passage in Aristotle's *De Caelo* II. 12, in which the projecting shapes of animal bodies are connected with their lower-than-godlike forms of life),[6] Schopenhauer asserts: 'Teeth, gullet, and intestinal canal are objectified hunger; the genitals are objectified sexual impulse; grasping hands and nimble feet correspond to the more indirect strivings of the will which they represent' (*W1* 108/H. 2, 129). Thus, though one cannot exactly perceive the will in itself, it would be correct to think that watching a body in motion, especially rapid nimble motion, is a way of understanding something about the nature of the will; so we might say that the keenest insight into willing that we could gain through our representing senses might be gained by watching a chorus of intertwining dancing limbs, of grasping hands and nimble feet, overlapping in unclearly individuated groupings. And when we understand further that Schopenhauer holds music to be a representation of the kinetic aspects of willing, and, in effect, a mimesis of will in general, in all its forms (*W1* §52), we understand that this group of dancing limbs should dance to music and blend its own motion with the motion of the music. If, further, we wished to include and stress the connection of will with sexuality, we could, following Schopenhauer's indications, make our dancing chorus a chorus of satyrs. This conclusion is drawn not by Schopenhauer, but by Nietzsche. Though in one way it is a brilliant application of Schopenhauerian thinking, we shall see to what un-Schopenhauerian ends he puts it.

To begin to make clearer Schopenhauer's relationship to Dionysus, we should now attempt to ask what the experience of will, of life lived as will, is like, as he conceives it. First of all, we must insist that, qua will, the human being is not intelligent. It exercises neither perception nor thought. In fact, it is no different, qua will, from the other animals and from inanimate objects in nature. The urge or desire that moves the willing body is not itself a form of perceptual awareness, though, of course, it may be accompanied by such awareness. Second, the willing being is not artistic: it neither makes things up nor transforms itself. All that is on the side of representation. (And later we shall see that will does not even inspire creation, but serves always as a drain on the energies and attention of the creator.) Willing is brutish, unformed, undisciplined. Third, the willing being is not, as such, aware of itself as a being at all, or of other beings as the distinct beings they are. Again, as we have already said, all this belongs on the side of representation. In other words, the erotic urge itself does not represent to itself an object or understand itself to be a distinct subject or seat of desire. It is a generalized urge to merge with what it cannot itself conceive or see. Finally, willing is closely connected with the experience of pain and deficiency. This connection we shall shortly investigate.

III PESSIMISM AND TRAGIC SPECTATORSHIP

But Schopenhauer does not introduce the dichotomy between will and representation simply as an analysis of cognition and action. The analysis is accompanied by, and grounds, a normative view of life that is famously known as Schopenhauer's 'pessimism.' According to this view, willing is, for higher creatures at least, the source of endless suffering. We escape suffering only to the extent that we escape the bondage of willing; and it is good to cultivate those elements in human life that deliver us from that bondage insofar as this is possible. Since it is here that Nietzsche will break most decisively with Schopenhauer, we need to pause to understand, as best we can, Schopenhauer's arguments for this extreme view concerning desire and striving, and the view of art that is inseparable from it.

Schopenhauer's denunciation of willing is eloquent and moving. But the arguments go by very quickly, and considerations of several different sorts are introduced in sequence, in such a way that it is left to the reader to figure out how they are related to one another. Our analysis can focus on this central paragraph – which, as we shall see, both articulates the normative view and prepares the way for the related analysis of art:

All *willing* springs from lack, from deficiency, and thus from suffering. Fulfilment brings this to an end; yet for one wish that is fulfilled there remain at least ten that are denied. Further, desiring lasts a long time, demands and requests go on to infinity; fulfilment is short and meted out sparingly. But even the final satisfaction itself is only apparent; the wish fulfilled at once makes way for a new one; the former is a known delusion, the latter a delusion not as yet known. No attained object of willing can give a satisfaction that lasts and no longer declines; but it is always like the alms thrown to a beggar, which reprieves him today so that his misery may be prolonged till tomorrow. Therefore, so long as our consciousness is filled by our will, so long as we are given up to the throng of desires with its constant hopes and fears, so long as we are the subject of willing, we never obtain lasting happiness or peace. Essentially, it is all the same whether we pursue or flee, fear harm or aspire to enjoyment; care for the constantly demanding will, no matter in what form, continually fills and moves consciousness; but without peace and calm, true well-being is absolutely impossible. Thus the subject of willing is constantly lying on the revolving wheel of Ixion, is always drawing water in the sieve of the Danaids, and is the eternally thirsting Tantalus. (W1 196/H. 2, 230–1)

In this paragraph (whose ideas and examples show how deeply Schopenhauer was steeped in both Platonic and Hellenistic, as well as Eastern, thought),[7] we seem to have at least four distinct arguments against the life of willing. First, willing seems inferior as a mode of existence (and later will be seen to be inferior to contemplation in particular) because its source is always in some felt lack or pain. (This is an argument repeatedly used by Plato in several dialogues to establish the inferiority of bodily appetite to the desires associated with thinking and contemplating.[8]) The idea seems to be that our desire for food and drink, for sexual gratification, and for the other related objects of will is not a pure positive desire brought into being by the beauty and value of the goal by itself: a being who had no painful hunger would have no reason to do something so odd as putting food into its mouth, and a being who did not experience sexual need and tension would never conceive the project of engaging in such an intrinsically peculiar activity. (And Schopenhauer's writings on women and sexuality suggest just how peculiar, and indeed profoundly disgusting, he took the activity to be.[9]) But this makes the activity, as Plato would put it, 'impure' – contingent on a bad state of affairs, and not choice-worthy in itself. Second, the satisfaction of desire is never total or completely effective: desires are always gratified piecemeal, so that the subject is always in a state of longing, even at the point of satisfying one of his many longings. Third, satisfaction is brief, desire long: the moment of fulfillment is 'short and meted out sparingly,' while 'demands and requests go on to infinity.' Again, we can understand this point most vividly if we think of the bodily desires, and especially sexual desire, as the central cases that Schopenhauer has in mind. (The reference to 'demands and requests,' especially, suggests that he is thinking of the effort one must go through to gain sexual satisfaction.) Fourth and finally, Schopenhauer argues that satisfaction is so unstable that it is an illusion to suppose that one has ever in fact actually been satisfied. The reference to the Danaids (used by both Plato in the *Gorgias* and Lucretius in Book III of his poem to make related points)[10] suggests that there is no stable resting point in desire, even though we may delude ourselves into thinking that there is. For our longing is renewing itself even as we satisfy it.

From all of this, Schopenhauer draws the conclusion that true happiness, which he understands, in a manner influenced by both Epicurus and Indian thought, to mean a condition of freedom from pain and disturbance, is impossible so long as we go through life under the sway of the will. And an avenue of escape is open to us: through the abstract and contemplative mode of attention characteristic (he believes) of our relationship to art.

Before we can understand this, however, we must add one further piece to the picture. For Schopenhauer seems to hold that if we were not aware of pains and desires that are ours as opposed to someone else's, and in general aware of the practical relation in which our body stands to a world of objects that may or may not fulfill its needs, we would not become aware of ourselves as distinct individuals marked off from other individuals. It is, apparently, only the disturbance occasioned by the greedy will that makes us focus on our distinct selves, rather than on the abstract and formal properties of that which surrounds us. And much the same is true of our awareness of other objects. When we are moving through the world as desiring agents, we are aware of the objects that surround us as (a) particulars and (b) related in one or another way to our interests, helping or thwarting our desires. Although Schopenhauer is not fully explicit about how interest relativity and particularity are related, it would appear that, as in the case of our own self-awareness, it is interest relativity that prompts us to focus on objects in our context as particulars. For example, the reason I might attend to a certain dog before me as a particular dog, rather than as exemplifying some abstract properties of doghood – or, even more abstractly, certain properties of form and color – would be that I am worrying about whether it is going to bite me. If I am liberated from that practical worry, I am free to contemplate the dog's abstract form. Again, to use what is always for Schopenhauer the central case, if I should get enmeshed in all the difficulties that follow from attending to a certain human being as irreducibly particular, not exactly the same as any other – rather than having the more stable satisfactions yielded by contemplating him or her as an abstract form – the reason for this is likely to be desire. It is clear that for Schopenhauer particularity of attention also heightens and complicates desire; but I think what he means to say is that if I did not in the beginning have sexual impulses that have the problematic character he has described, I would never initiate the spiral of need and attention that is characteristic of erotic love in the first place. Nothing would call my attention down from its lofty contemplative heights to the concrete realities of my context. It is the pressure of need for an actual sexual object that drives attention downward, although, once it is there, attention also creates further difficulties, binding me to the frustrating 'demands and requests' characteristic of the life of particular love, as Schopenhauer knows it.

Now what art does, as Schopenhauer sees it, is to step in as a doctor for the attention, calling perception and thought back from the world of particulars to the contemplation of abstract and general forms. When we look at a painting or a statue, he argues, our attention to it has two properties: it is focused on the abstract, and it is without awareness of any relation the object may have to our own needs and interests.

Raised up by the power of the mind, we relinquish the ordinary way of considering things, and cease to follow under the guidance of the forms of the principle of sufficient reason merely their relations to one another, whose final goal is always the relation to our own will. Thus we no longer consider the where, the when, the why, and the whither in things, but simply and solely the *what*. (*W1* 178; cf. 198/H. 2, 210; cf. 233–4)

Schopenhauer has in mind, it seems, the enormous difference between the way in which one attends to a painting or statue of a beautiful person and the way in which one attends to such a person in the context of desire and action. In the latter case, one is filled with painful yearning and longing, with 'demands and requests,' with anxious questions about when and how our satisfaction will be achieved. In the process, the 'what' of the object (as Proust so brilliantly and repeatedly demonstrates) more or less disappears, in the sense that its formal and structural properties come into focus only in relation to our own greedy desires. When, on the other hand, one contemplates a painting or statue of a beautiful person, one is 'raised up' above all this, and encouraged to attend to pure general qualities of form and shape, quite apart from their relation to the will. It is only in this contemplative mode that we can be said to understand the object. Furthermore, Schopenhauer continues, we lose in the process the painful awareness of our own individuality and subjectivity that characterizes daily life. We forget about our selfish needs and are able to 'lose ourselves' in the object, becoming 'a clear mirror of the object' (WI 178/H. 2, 210), a bare subject of cognition without any properties but those of receptive attention. This forgetfulness of self Schopenhauer finds extremely valuable, not only because it liberates the individual subject from its pain and suffering, but also because, by diminishing selfishness, it promotes sympathy and other desirable social attitudes.

Thus the aesthetic attitude liberates, so long as we are caught up in it; when aesthetic experiences cease, we are again at the mercy of our greed:

The storm of passions, the pressure of desire and fear, and all the miseries of willing are then at once calmed and appeased in a marvellous way. For at the moment when, torn from the will, we have given ourselves up to pure, will-less knowing, we have stepped into another world, so to speak, where everything that moves our will, and thus violently agitates us, no longer exists. This liberation of knowledge lifts us as wholly and completely above all this as do sleep and dreams. Happiness and unhappiness have vanished; we are no longer the individual; that is forgotten; we are only pure subject of knowledge. We are only that *one* eye of the world which looks out from all knowing creatures, but which in man alone can be wholly free from serving the will. In this way, all difference of individuality disappears so completely that it is all the same whether the perceiving eye belongs to a mighty monarch or to a stricken beggar; for beyond that boundary neither happiness nor misery is taken with us. There always lies so near to us a realm in which we have escaped entirely from all our affliction; but who has the strength to remain in it for long? As soon as any relation to our will, to our person, even of those objects of pure contemplation, again enters consciousness, the magic is at an end. We fall back into knowledge governed by the principle of sufficient reason; we now no longer know the Idea, but the individual thing, the link of a chain to which we also belong, and we are again abandoned to all our woe. (WI 197–8/H. 2, 233)

The aesthetic attitude, in short, is unstable. Our attention to the aesthetic object is rarely pure and complete for long. (And this is all the more so since Schopenhauer's examples are usually examples of contemplation of nature, to which we bear, as well, many practical relations.) But in its rare moments of success we understand the true function of the aesthetic in human life: 'namely the deliverance of knowledge from the service of the will, the forgetting of oneself as individual, and the enhancement of consciousness to the pure, will-less, timeless subject of knowing that is independent of all relations' (W1 199/H. 2, 234).

Tragedy, in Schopenhauer's view, is an especially valuable art form because, in addition to nourishing the aesthetic attitude, as do all forms of art, it reminds us, by its content, of the many motives we have for turning toward art and away from the will. It is thus peculiarly self-reinforcing. For tragedy represents (in a general form, fit for contemplation) all the sufferings to which human beings are prone if they live the life of will and desire. Agreeing closely with the picture of tragedy's function that we get in a Stoic such as Epictetus (who defines tragedy as 'what happens when chance events befall fools'), Schopenhauer holds that the sufferings of tragedy are the sufferings of humanity, insofar as it lives the life of desire. And, like Epictetus again, who urged a detached and contemplative spectatorship that would discover in tragedy further motives for living a life of Stoic detachment,[11] Schopenhauer argues that good tragic spectatorship leads, very effectively, to a renunciation of will and desire:[12]

For the whole of our discussion, it is very significant and worth noting that the purpose of this highest poetical achievement is the description of the terrible side of life. The unspeakable pain, the wretchedness and misery of mankind, the triumph of wickedness, the scornful mastery of chance, and the irretrievable fall of the just and the innocent are all here presented to us; and here is to be found a significant hint as to the nature of the world and of existence.... The *motives* that were previously so powerful now lose their force, and instead of them, the complete knowledge of the real nature of the world, acting as a *quieter* of the will, produces resignation, the giving up not merely of life, but of the whole will to life itself.... Only a dull, insipid, optimistic, Protestant-rationalistic, or really Jewish view of the world will make the demand for poetic justice, and find its own satisfaction in that of the demand. The true sense of the tragedy is the deeper insight that what the hero atones for is not his own particular sins, but original sin, in other words, the guilt of existence itself:

> Pues el delito mayor
> Del hombre es haber nacido.
> ('For man's greatest offence
> Is that he has been born.')

as Calderón (*La Vida es Sueño*) frankly expresses it (*W1* 252–4/H. 2, 298–300).

I have quoted this passage at length not only to establish Schopenhauer's account of the function of tragedy; and not only to illustrate the extreme vehemence, and even violence, with which he denounces his more optimistic opponents; but also in order to give evidence of the Christian and even Catholic origins of Schopenhauer's loathing for the will, and of the account of tragedy that expresses it. Here, more clearly than elsewhere, he frankly concedes that a view of original guilt or sin, connected with our bodily existence and its sexual origins and strivings, underlies his account of what tragedy teaches. And it is no surprise to find him turning to Calderón, whose tragedy is steeped in these Catholic views, for expression of the fundamental 'guilt' that, as he sees it, all beings bear. Tragedy shows not only suffering, but also *atonement*. And the atonement is for an offence, *delito*, connected with birth itself.

Schopenhauerian pessimism is an odd amalgam of Hellenistic, Christian, and Eastern influences, but its conclusion here is clear: the body and its urges are bad, are both guilty and delusive; and nature as a whole, becoming as a whole, is infected with that guilt and those delusions. Through art, and especially tragic art, we comprehend these facts in a general way. The experience of spectatorship, which already, in its cognitive structure, exemplifies detachment from will, gives us, through this comprehension, new motives to reject and blame life as both evil and false.

Schopenhauer's relationship to Euripides' Dionysus in the *Bacchae* now begins to look very complex. On the one hand, his account of experience captures very well the fluidity of identity that is central not only to Euripides' play but, very likely, to the experience of the participant in Dionysian religion as well.[13] The desiring subject is not a stable substance, but a part of nature in continual motion; individuation and boundaries are temporary, factitious. Using this view, with its emphasis on the dreamlike qualities of representation, one can well start to explain the transformations of the Dionysus of the *Bacchae*, as he appears to his followers, as they now flow toward unity with the burgeoning erotic life of nature, now become aware of their bodies, and the bodies of others, as distinct individuals. (We could, for example, usefully think of Agave's recognition of Pentheus as a transition from will accompanied by only minimal representation to the clarity of distinct representation, detached to some extent[14] from will.)

On the other hand, there is much in Schopenhauer that does not fit well with Euripides' play or, indeed, with anything in ancient Greek tragedy. His emphasis on the lack of intelligence and artistry in appetite fits badly with the *Bacchae*'s depiction of Dionysus, and the sexual and natural forces he embodies, as powerfully artistic, as authors of sudden, subtle transformations closely related to the transformations involved in theater itself. If Dionysus, god of intoxication and sexual energy, is (in Schopenhauer's terms) will, he is also a playwright, a stage director, a most subtle and versatile actor.[15] The desires he arouses are neither unintelligent nor lacking in their own sort of order. Nor is the pessimistic condemnation of all sexuality and all becoming – especially insofar as it rests on a notion of original sin – at all at home in the world of the *Bacchae* or in the ancient world generally. Dionysus is cruel, excessive, amoral. And the play shows human Dionysian energies to be both glorious and terrible, transfiguring and pitiless, fertile and fatal. It does not, however, in any way condemn the body as evil or conception and birth as filthy. The cruelty and arbitrariness of life are seen as inseparable from its mysterious richness.[16] In general – although usually I shrink from such generalizations – I think we can say confidently that the notion of original sin, as it figures (for example) in the tragedies of Calderón, is altogether foreign to Greek tragedy and to ancient Greek thought.

Finally, Schopenhauer's account of tragic spectatorship, closely tied to the recognition of guilt and emphasizing detachment and resignation as goals, is very hard indeed to link with anything that could have gone on in the ancient theater. The Dionysian festivals, whatever they were, were not celebrations of renunciation of the will to life.[17] As I have suggested, if Schopenhauer's view of the spectator is close to anything in the ancient world, it is to the radical reconstruction of the spectatorship that we see in Stoic accounts of the function and meaning of tragedy, which had considerable influence on the Christian tragedians dear to Schopenhauer's heart.

We shall now see that Nietzsche, while availing himself of Schopenhauer's terms of analysis, develops in a positive way exactly those aspects of Schopenhauer's thought that I have said to be genuinely promising avenues of approach to ancient tragedy in general and to the *Bacchae*'s Dionysus in particular. He uses them, however, to construct a complex subversion of the core of Schopenhauer's normative view, and to produce an account of the tragic universe and tragic spectatorship that might with real justice be called (as he calls them) Dionysian.

IV   NIETZSCHE'S DIONYSUS: ARTISTIC PASSION

Nietzsche's Apollo and Dionysus are, up to a point, simply Representation and Will in Greek costume. The reader of *The Birth of Tragedy* who has not read Schopenhauer is likely to be puzzled by Nietzsche's rapid introduction of these two fundamental 'drives' or 'tendencies' in human nature, and by the hasty manner in which one of these is linked with cognitive activity, but also with dreaming, with visual art, and with the awareness of general forms, the other with movement and sexuality, with intoxication, with the awareness of particularity, with the absence of a clear individuation of the self. All this is far easier to understand if we see the opening section as a précis of familiar Schopenhauerian notions, accepted as accurate accounts of universal tendencies and therefore transposed back into antiquity. And Nietzsche's failure to give arguments connecting the different features of his gods becomes comprehensible when we realize that these connections, as argued for by Schopenhauer, would have seemed second nature to most of his audience, given the enormous popularity of Schopenhauer's work; and they would easily have been able to supply the missing arguments for linking intoxication with loss of the *principium individuationis*, dreaming with awareness of the abstract and the general. (We can also begin to understand the irritation that the classical scholar Wilamowitz experienced when seeing controversial modern categories taken as an unquestioned starting point for the interpretation of classical antiquity.[18]) Even the veil of *maya* makes its appearance in Nietzsche's portrait of Apollo, though it is clear that at this date Schopenhauer would have been Nietzsche's only source for Indian thought. Up to a point, then, Nietzsche presents himself as an uncritical acolyte of Schopenhauerian metaphysics.

But a fundamental difference also makes itself felt very close to the beginning. Nietzsche later criticizes Schopenhauer far more explicitly than he does in this work (see, for example, *The Case of Wagner*; *Twilight of the Idols* IX, 'Skirmishes of an Untimely Man'; *The Will to Power*, §851, cited as the first epigraph here). And in his 'Attempt at a Self-Criticism,' added to *The Birth of Tragedy* in 1886, he criticizes himself for the obscurity introduced by his uncritical use, in the original text, of certain Schopenhauerian terms that did not really fit his argument. But – as he also states in that remarkably insightful brief discussion – his fundamental opposition to Schopenhauer was already present in this work, though not in a polemical or an especially obvious form.

That opposition emerges almost immediately, as Nietzsche presents both the Dionysian and the Apollonian as both 'tendencies' and 'drives' (*Tendenzen*; *Triebe*) in human nature; also as 'impulses', as 'energies that are satisfied.'[19] In other words – a point Nietzsche was to make and remake throughout his career – cognitive activity is itself thoroughly practical, and can only be explained as answering a practical need. Apollonian activity is not detached and coolly contemplative, but a response to an urgent human need, namely, the need to demarcate an intrinsically unordered world, making it intelligible for ourselves. What Nietzsche was to argue in detail against traditional epistemology, in works ranging from 'On Truth and Lying in the Extra-Moral Sense' (1873) to *Beyond Good and Evil* and the fragments of his last years, is here already in essence: all of our cognitive activities, including logical reasoning, including the abstracting and generalizing tendencies, are profoundly practical – ways in which we try to master the world and to make ourselves secure in it.[20] The metaphor of Apollonian activity as dreaming now takes on a subtly un-Schopenhauerian sense. For instead of simply expressing the idealism inherent in Schopenhauer's account of representation, it now makes (without explicit commitment to idealism and in a way perfectly compatible with Nietzsche's later, more Kantian view)[21] the further point that this activity often succeeds only through self-deception: having effected an ordering, we convince ourselves that it is really the way the world is.

On the other side, the Dionysian, while itself a drive demanding satisfaction, is not unintelligent, not devoid of cognitive activity. The Dionysian experience, as described in §1, is an experience of 'enchantment' or 'charm' or 'ecstasy' – of a heightened awareness of freedom, harmony, and unity. Finally, it is the experience of being made, oneself, 'a work of art' by the subtly crafting power of desire. Both drives equally are now, at the opening of §2, called 'art impulses' and 'artistic energies which burst forth from nature herself.' For Schopenhauer, art could make (in music) a representation of will, but this was a far cry from the will itself, which could never be or make art. Nietzsche's view of sensuality is more complex. His satyrs are themselves most subtle artists, his sexual energy is disciplined as well as joyful; and we are not far from the exuberant playful reference to Ovid: ' "Nitimur in vetitum," under this sign my philosophy will conquer one day.' Toward his era's own 'forbidden,' in defiance of both Christian and Schopenhauerian views of the badness of the sensual and the erotic, he strives, in 1872 already, in the name of the artistry of Dionysus.

If both Apollo and Dionysus are need-inspired, worldly, and practical, and if these are nature's two art impulses, it is not difficult to see that Nietzsche is also giving a picture of *art* very different from the one familiar in the Kantian tradition and developed in his own way by Schopenhauer. In the Kantian tradition, our interest in and response to the beautiful is altogether separate from our practical interests. Aesthetic attention to an item in nature, or to a made work of art, is distinct from practical attention, since aesthetic attention simply contemplates the object for its beauty (or its other aesthetic properties) and refuses to ask what role the object might play in the agent's particular life. To return to our earlier example, aesthetic attention to a dog that stands before me is attention to its formal properties of shape and color, combined, perhaps, with the kinetic formal properties that it exhibits in movement. If I am attending to the dog as a creature that may or may not bite me, that is interested practical attention, and is altogether distinct from, and even subversive of, the aesthetic. Schopenhauer, as we have seen, develops this idea, though in his own particular way. On the one hand, he insists on the detachment of aesthetic contemplation from practical need and interest, and, indeed, sees the main purpose of art in its ability to free the spectator from practical interest. On the other hand, as that description betrays, he finds a function for art in the spectator's life – and, indeed, is even willing to say that its 'purpose' is something that it does for human lives, namely, to encourage in every spectator the denial and renunciation of life.

From *The Birth of Tragedy* on through his latest works, Nietzsche consistently opposed this picture of the arts, denying that we can understand the role that works of art play in human lives, or even adequately explain particular judgments of beauty and ugliness, without connecting these to human practical needs – and needs that are directed toward living and affirming life, rather than toward resignation and denial. This direction of thought is evident enough in *The Birth of Tragedy*, from the moment when, introducing Apollo, Nietzsche speaks of 'the arts generally, which make life possible and worth living' (§1). As we shall shortly see, his account of the tragic spectator develops this picture further. And the 'Self-Criticism' of 1886 asserts that the purpose of the book as a whole, 'this audacious book,' was 'to look at science in the perspective of the artist, but at art in that of life' ('Attempt at a Self-Criticism,' §2) – a purpose that surely does make the book 'audacious' in terms of contemporary German views of art and the aesthetic. This audacious purpose was developed without an explicit assault on Kant or Schopenhauer. And indeed, Nietzsche in 1886 criticizes himself for having 'tried laboriously to express by means of Schopenhauerian and Kantian formulas strange and new valuations which were basically at odds with Kant's and Schopenhauer's spirit and taste' (§6). But we cannot mistake the sharpness of the break with Kant and Schopenhauer signaled by a passage in §5 of the work, where Nietzsche mentions as a dogma of his era the idea that art should be contemplative and detached, dedicated to the silencing of desire:

… we know the subjective artist only as the poor artist, and throughout the entire range of art we demand first of all the conquest of the subjective, redemption from the 'ego', and the silencing of individual will and desire; indeed, we find it impossible to believe in any truly artistic production, however insignificant, if it is without objectivity, without pure contemplation devoid of interest.

Nietzsche here refers to the central aesthetic notions of both Schopenhauer and Kant as cultural dogmas. Although he neither endorses nor criticizes these dogmas here, his reference to them will later function as prelude to Nietzsche's own very different account of things, according to which art, and the artist, are deeply involved in the exploration of, and the response to, human need.

In *The Birth of Tragedy*, then, in connection with his portrayal of both Apollo and Dionysus as passionate, interested, and needy elements of the personality, Nietzsche begins to develop what will become a major theme in his work: the idea that art does not exist apart from life, in detachment from or even in opposition to its concerns. Art, indeed, is not for art's sake, but for life's sake. As he puts the point in *Twilight of the Idols*, in a context in which he also speaks of Dionysus and the Dionysian:

Nothing is more conditional – or, let us say, narrower – than our feeling for beauty. Whoever would think of it apart from man's joy in man would immediately lose any foothold.... Art for art's sake – a worm chasing its own tail.... A psychologist, on the other hand, asks: what does all art *do*? does it not praise? glorify? choose? prefer? (IX, 'Skirmishes of an Untimely Man,' §§20, 24)

In the early sections of *The Birth of Tragedy*, Nietzsche has, then, while relying on Schopenhauer, subverted his views in three crucial ways: by insisting on seeing representation as a response to need; by portraying desire and the erotic as intelligent, artistic forces; and by portraying art as having a practical function. And with our references to a repudiation of resignation, and to humanity's joy in humanity, we now arrive at the fourth and most fundamental break with Schopenhauer: Nietzsche's complete rejection of the normative ethics of pessimism in favor of a view that urges us to take joy in life, in the body, in becoming – even, and especially, in face of the recognition that the world is chaotic and cruel. But at this point we must turn to Nietzsche's account of tragedy itself, and of the tragic spectator. For it is in this connection that he breaks with pessimism – in the name of Dionysus.

V LIFE IN THE PERSPECTIVE OF ART

'How differently Dionysus spoke to me! How far removed I was from all this resignationism!' ('Attempt at a Self-Criticism,' §6). So Nietzsche retrospectively describes his early work's rejection of Schopenhauer's analysis of tragedy. Since he here apologizes, and rightly so, for the obscurity of the way in which this goal was pursued in *The Birth of Tragedy* itself, charging himself with having 'spoiled Dionysian premonitions with Schopenhauerian formulations' (§6), it seems prudent for us to begin our own analysis with two later and clearer passages in which he describes the function of art in terms that make clear the very un-Schopenhauerian nature of his normative view. In a fragment that probably dates from either 1886 or 1887-8,[22] and is a draft for a new preface to *The Birth of Tragedy*, Nietzsche explains that that work portrays the world of nature as 'false, cruel, contradictory, seductive, without meaning' (*The Will to Power*, §853). This being the case, life is made worth living, made joyful and made human, only by art – that is to say, in the largest sense, by the human being's power to create an order in the midst of disorder, to make up a meaning where nature itself does not supply one. In creative activity (associated by Nietzsche not only with the arts narrowly understood, but also with love, religion, ethics, science – all seen as forms of creative story making), we find the source of what is in truth wonderful and joyful in life. And if we can learn to value that activity and find our own meaning in it, rather than looking for an external meaning in God or in nature, we can love ourselves and love life. Art is thus the great anti-pessimistic form of life, the great alternative to denial and resignation:

Art and nothing but art! It is the great means of making life possible, the great seduction to life, the great stimulant of life.

Art as the only superior counterforce to all will to denial of life, as that which is anti-Christian, anti-Buddhist, anti-nihilist *par excellence*....

Art as the *redemption of the man of action* – of those who not only see the terrifying and questionable character of existence but live it, want to live it, the tragic-warlike man, the hero....

Art as the *redemption of the sufferer* – as the way to states in which suffering is willed, transfigured, deified, where suffering is a form of great delight.... A highest state of affirmation of existence is conceived from which the highest degree of pain cannot be excluded: the *tragic-Dionysian* state. (*The Will to Power*, §853)

In this passage, the 'tragic-Dionysian state' is a state in which one takes delight in *oneself* and one's own activity, rather than, as so frequently happens in a religious or postreligious age, searching for a meaning from without. Dionysus gives us our example, so to speak: following him, we delight in the play of appearance, the gestures of theater; we delight in making it all up, as we do, as we must.

Although this passage is from a preface to *The Birth of Tragedy*, and although it makes reference to Dionysus, it tells us little about the role of the arts narrowly understood, and of tragic art in particular, in Nietzsche's view of human affirmation. It uses the notion of art in a broad sense; and though we suspect that the affirmation of creation that is problematic in the case of science, religion, and love may well be easier to achieve in the fine arts, thus making the fine arts a kind of paradigm of a stance toward the world that one could then try to achieve in the rest of one's life, Nietzsche does not make that connection explicit. He does so elsewhere, however, nowhere more plainly than in a passage from *The Gay Science* (1882) entitled 'Our Ultimate Gratitude to Art':

If we had not welcomed the arts and invented this kind of cult of the untrue, then the realization of general untruth and mendaciousness that now comes to us through science – the realization that delusion and error are conditions of human knowledge and sensation – would be utterly unbearable. *Honesty* would lead to nausea and suicide. But now there is a counterforce against our honesty that helps us to avoid such consequences: art as the *good* will to appearance.... As an aesthetic phenomenon existence is still *bearable* for us, and art furnishes us with eyes and hands and above all good conscience to be *able* to turn ourselves into such a phenomenon. (*The Gay Science*, §107)

Nietzsche's view is, then, not the simple inversion of Schopenhauer's. For he agrees with Schopenhauer that what an honest gaze discovers in the world is arbitrariness and the absence of any intrinsic meaning.[23] But he disagrees about the consequences of this discovery for humanity's view of itself. Schopenhauer's human being, noticing that his positing of an order in things is negated by the experience of life, becomes nauseated with life, and with himself for having lived a delusion. Nietzsche's human being, noticing these same things about the world, is filled with Dionysian joy and pride in his own artistry. For if there is no intrinsic order in things, how wonderful, then – and indeed, how much more wonderful – that one should have managed to invent so many beautiful stories, to forge so many daring conceptual schemes, to dance so many daring and improbable dances. The absence of a designing god leads to a heightened joy in the artistic possibilities of humanity.

But this response, as *The Gay Science* argues, requires the arts. For Nietzsche believes that if we had an example of a human activity in which fiction-making is loved for its own sake, and correspondence to an antecedently existing external order is not the chief value, we would be able to respond affirmatively to the collapse of our search for external religious and metaphysical meanings. The arts show us that we can have order and discipline and meaning and logic from within ourselves: we do not have to choose between belief in God and empty chaos.[24] Centuries of Christian teaching have left us with so little self-respect for our bodies and their desires that we are convinced that anything we ourselves make up must be disorderly and perhaps even evil. The arts tell us that this is not so; they enable us to take pride in ourselves and the work of our bodies.[25] And this means that art can be, for its spectators, a guide and a paradigm, showing something far more general about how all of life can be confronted.

And it is in this context that we must understand the significance of the claim that 'as an aesthetic phenomenon existence is still *bearable* for us' – Nietzsche's version of *The Birth of Tragedy*'s famous dictum that 'it is only as an *aesthetic phenomenon* that existence and the world are eternally justified' (§5, §24). Usually, this remark is taken to imply some sort of amoral aestheticizing of existence, a playful overturning of all moral and political categories in the name of detached aesthetic values. We have already seen that Nietzsche actively scorns the detachment of the aesthetic from the practical and ridicules the notion of art for art's sake: so it is in the context of his own view of the aesthetic, which is deeply practical, that we ought to interpret these remarks – though this has too seldom been observed. *The Gay Science* tells us plainly what, in context, they mean. Existence is bearable for us in the face of the collapse of otherworldly faith only if we can get ourselves to regard our lives, with pride, as our own creations: to regard them, that is, as we now regard works of fine art. *The Birth of Tragedy* adds a further twist:[26] in this way and in no other, we find life *justified*: that is, having abandoned all attempts to find extrahuman justification for existence, we can find the only justification we ever shall find in our very own selves and our own creative activity. But Nietzsche insists that this is a kind of justification, and even *eternal* justification (looking far ahead, perhaps, to the idea of eternal recurrence, which involves asking whether one wills one's actions to be the way the world will be for all eternity). None of this involves restricting the evaluation of life to the aesthetic sphere, as distinct from the ethical or social: as we have seen, Nietzsche repudiates that separation as offering a reductive view of the aesthetic. Nor does it involve any preference for free, undisciplined play over order and structure: for it is Nietzsche's view, repeatedly asserted, that art teaches us, perhaps above all, a love for order and discipline, the hatred of '*laisser aller*' (especially in *Beyond Good and Evil*, §188). It does mean that we have criteria enough for the justification of our lives in the praising, glorifying, and choosing that are characteristic of great art, as Nietzsche describes it. And it means too, of course, that art will play in human life exactly the opposite role from the role it plays for Schopenhauer. For instead of giving the human being a clue to a way in which life might be despised and the body repudiated, it gives the human being a clue to a way (or, indeed, many different ways) in which life might be embraced and the body seen as a sphere of joy.

If we now return to *The Birth of Tragedy* equipped with this general picture, we can see that – beneath its obscuring use of Schopenhauer's language of 'metaphysical comfort' – it is actually telling this very story, portraying 'Dionysian tragedy' as a source, for its spectator, of an affirmation of human life in the face of the recognition that existence is not intrinsically meaningful or good. Tragedy, Nietzsche announces (agreeing, so far, with Schopenhauer), shows its spectator 'the terrible destructiveness of so-called world history as well as the cruelty of nature,' so that he is 'in danger of longing for a Buddhistic negation of the will' (§7). The energies that Nietzsche associates with Dionysus reveal to the spectator – apparently, as he later states, through a process of sympathetic identification with the hero – the 'horror and absurdity of existence' (§7). For the hero embodies in his person the inexorable clash between human aspirations and their natural/divine limits (§9): his demand for justice in an unjust universe entails terrible suffering. The spectator witnesses this suffering: and this produces a temporary suspension of the motives for continued action. The spectator now resembles Hamlet:[27]

... both have once looked truly into the essence of things, they have gained knowledge, and nausea inhibits action; further action could not change anything in the eternal nature of things; they feel it to be ridiculous or humiliating that they should be asked to set right a world that is out of joint. (§7)

In other words, the spectator has reached the state of the Schopenhauerian spectator or is on the verge of it. But it is not in this condition that tragedy leaves him.

What now takes place, according to Nietzsche's account (as best I can make out), is that the elements of the drama that Nietzsche has associated with Dionysus – the sheer exuberant energy of the choral music and dance – give the spectator an example of order asserted in the face of disorder, of an artistic making that does not depend on any external order in nature, and (through the idea that the chorus was originally composed of satyrs) of the joy and fertility of the body, asserted in the face of its vulnerability to suffering. Seeing how Dionysus and the energies he represents transform the world, the spectator is seduced back into life, brought to affirm life, and his own cognitive order-making activity, by the very erotic and bodily energies that were, for Schopenhauer, the best reasons to get away from life. 'Art saves him – and through art – life.' Art is 'a saving sorceress, expert at healing. She alone knows how to turn these nauseous thoughts about the horror or absurdity of existence into notions with which one can live.'

This artistic process requires, Nietzsche stresses, a highly complex interweaving of the Apollonian and Dionysian capacities – both in the drama itself and in the spectator's reactions to it. At the end of §7, the satyr chorus is called 'the saving deed of Greek art,' and the satyrs are made the 'Dionysian companions' of the audience, who are now said to 'permit themselves to be represented by such satyrs' (§8) and are themselves called 'Dionysian men' (§8). In the chorus, Nietzsche insists, and by their vicarious identification with the chorus, the spectators see something true of themselves as natural bodily beings. To the 'painfully broken vision of Dionysian man' these satyrs appear – not as the civilized, dressed-up shepherds of an effete pastoral (§8), but as 'a symbol of the sexual omnipotence of nature.' This is not, however, he stresses, the sexuality 'of a mere ape' (§8) – but something 'sublime and divine ... unconcealed and vigorously magnificent.' The spectator can view this image of his own sexual being with 'sublime satisfaction.' Thus, as a Dionysian, the spectator views the Dionysian image of himself, seeing his own body as something sophisticated, orderly, and splendid, partaking itself of the human capabilities for artistry that have been associated with Apollo.

And shortly we are told that the Dionysian chorus – and the spectators through the chorus – create themselves, without ever ceasing to be satyrs and hence Dionysian, the Apollonian vision of the tragic hero. The 'Dionysian reveler sees himself as a satyr, *and as a satyr, in turn, he sees the god*, which means that in his metamorphosis he beholds another vision outside himself, as the Apollonian complement of his own state' (§8). Thus the Dionysian dancers, far from being noncognitive Schopenhauerian animals, are actually dreamers. They become the cognitive avenue through which the entire order of the dramatic action is dreamed or viewed. And who is the central object of this dream? The suffering hero, as we have said. But we have now been told that this hero is none other than Dionysus the god: 'the real stage hero and center of the vision' (§8), Dionysus, appearing 'in a variety of forms, in the mask of a fighting hero,... an erring, striving, suffering individual' (§10). Thus the spectators' shuddering before the hero's anguish becomes their affirmation of the joyous rebirth and the versatile artistry of the god.

In short, the achievement of Greek tragedy, according to Nietzsche, was, first of all, to confront its spectator directly with the fact that there is just one world, the world we live in, the chancy, arbitrary, but also rich and beautiful world of nature. It is not redeemed by any 'beyond'; nor is it given even the sort of *negative* meaning, in relation to a beyond, that it is given in Christian tragedy. Nietzsche throughout his life finds it amazing that the Greeks should have been able to confront so truthfully the nature of life without taking flight into religion of the world-denigrating, resignationist sort. He finds an explanation for this unique courage of affirmation in the structure of tragic art. Tragedy shows that the world is chancy and arbitrary. But then, by showing how life beautifully asserts itself in the face of a meaningless universe, by showing the joy and splendor of human making in a world of becoming – and by being itself an example of joyful making – it gives its spectator a way of confronting not only the painful events of the drama, but also the pains and uncertainties of life, both personal and communal – a way that involves human self-respect and self-reliance, rather than guilt or resignation. Instead of giving up his will to life, the spectator, intoxicated by Dionysus, becomes a work of art and an artist.

VI   AN ART OF THIS-WORLDLY LOVE

The achievements of *The Birth of Tragedy* are thus both substantial and preparatory. Already Nietzsche breaks with the essence of Schopenhauerian thinking, and he offers the beginning of an account of tragic theater that is radically at odds with Schopenhauer's. But at the same time, much more work clearly remains to be done in developing these anti-Schopenhauerian lines of arguments – as is already clear from the fact that I have had to refer ahead so frequently in order to clarify central ideas, and sometimes even in order to state them fully. Each of the four subversions of Schopenhauer that I have discussed here recurs, in fact, as a central theme in Nietzsche's later philosophical thought. The connection of cognitive activity with human needs – already elaborately developed in the 1873 essay 'On Truth and Lying in the Extra-Moral Sense' – is also a major theme of *The Gay Science, Beyond Good and Evil*, and many later fragments. The intelligence and artistry of the body and bodily desire are discussed in *The Gay Science, Twilight of the* Idols, and, above all, *Zarathustra*. The connection between art and human need, as we have seen, is the subject of frequent later discussion. And finally, the central project of Nietzsche's mature thought is the attempt to work out in detail an alternative to Schopenhauerian pessimism and resignation as a response to the discovery that the universe has no intrinsic purpose. The project begun in *The Birth of Tragedy*, in which the example of Dionysian art 'saves' humanity from nausea, is continued in Zarathustra's attempt to free humanity from disgust with itself, and from the need for a beyond, and to return humans to a love of themselves and of the world of becoming, now seen as 'innocent' rather than as flawed by original guilt. In the 1886 'Self-Criticism,' Nietzsche announces that the real message of his early work is not one that we should associate with the 'metaphysical comfort' delivered by the otherworldly longings of the Christian romanticism of *Faust*. Instead, his work teaches 'the art of *this-worldly* comfort,' pointing directly ahead to 'that Dionysian monster who bears the name of Zarathustra' (§7).

But instead of trying to follow these further elaborations of Nietzsche's Dionysian view of life, which would clearly require a book, I want instead to conclude this essay by examining closely just one later passage, in which Nietzsche's mature account of Dionysian intoxication is developed with particular clarity and beauty, bringing together succinctly all the criticisms of Schopenhauerian pessimism that we have described. Written in the spring of 1888, it is an account of the Dionysian power of intoxication and the relation of this power to artistic creation:

Do you desire the most astonishing proof of how far the transfiguring power of intoxication can go? – 'Love' is this proof: that which is called love in all the languages and silences of the world. In this case, intoxication has done with reality to such a degree that in the consciousness of the lover the cause of it is extinguished and something else seems to have taken its place – a vibration and glittering of all the magic mirrors of Circe –

Here it makes no difference whether one is man or animal; even less whether one has spirit, goodness, integrity. If one is subtle, one is fooled subtly; if one is coarse, one is fooled coarsely; but love, and even the love of God, the saintly love of 'redeemed souls', remains the same in its roots: a fever that has good reason to transfigure itself – And in any case, one lies well when one loves, about oneself and to oneself: one seems to oneself transfigured, stronger, richer, more perfect, one *is* more perfect – Here we discover *art* as an organic function: we discover it in the most angelic instinct, 'love'; we discover it as the greatest stimulus of life – art thus sublimely expedient even when it lies –

But we should do wrong if we stopped with its power to lie: it does more than merely imagine; it even transposes values. And it is not only that it transposes the *feeling* of values: the lover *is* more valuable, is stronger. In animals this condition produces new weapons, pigments, colors, and forms; above all, new movements, new rhythms, new love calls and seductions. It is no different with man. His whole economy is richer than before, more powerful, more *complete* than in those who do not love. The lover becomes a squanderer: he is rich enough for it. Now he dares, becomes an adventurer, becomes an ass in magnanimity and innocence; he believes in God again, he believes in virtue, because he believes in love; and on the other hand, this happy idiot grows wings and new capabilities, and even the door of art is opened to him. If we subtracted all traces of this intestinal fever from lyricism in sound and word, what would be left of lyrical poetry and music? – *L' art pour l'art* perhaps: the virtuoso croaking of shivering frogs, despairing in their swamp – All the rest was created by love – (*The Will to Power*, §808)

In this highly complex passage we see what we could well call Nietzsche's final praise of Dionysus, and of the energies of *eros*[28] and intoxication with which Nietzsche has associated his name. It is Nietzsche's version of Plato's praise of madness in the *Phaedrus* – and it clearly alludes to the *Phaedrus*, both in its references to the lover's growing wings and in its insistence on love's magnanimity. We see, splendidly expressed, Nietzsche's counterview to the Schopenhauerian view of erotic desire. Instead of being an unintelligent force of bondage and constraint, dooming its subject to a life of delusion, Nietzsche's *eros* is a clever and subtle artist (or rather, as he appropriately qualifies the claim, it is as subtle as the lover is); it transforms its subject into a being who seems stronger, richer, deeper. But these semblances are also realities: for the artistry of human desire makes the human being into a work of art. Love's magic is illusion in the sense that it corresponds to no preexisting reality in the order of things. And yet it is its own this-worldly reality, and its fiction-making makes fictions that are gloriously there. Nietzsche adds, as elsewhere, that this intoxication of the erotic is a great motive to the affirmation of life in general.

Finally, in what is surely the passage's most shocking claim – from the point of view of traditional German aesthetics – art is not only not pure of practical interest, it is actually the outgrowth of a profoundly erotic interest. And, furthermore, it is well that this should be so, Nietzsche insists. For (echoing here the argument of the *Phaedrus*) he argues that art without this transfiguring power would be something mean and bare, something cold, stingy, and cramped. All in art that is magical, that is vibration and glitter, that is intoxication and adventure, that is lyrical and generous – all this is created by love. Nietzsche here completes his attack on Schopenhauerian pessimism, praising the madness of erotic love.[29]

NOTES

1 This essay began as the second part of a two-part account of Nietzsche's relationship to Dionysus and to Euripides' *Bacchae*. For in a general introduction to *The Bacchae of Euripides*, trans. C. K. Williams (New York: Farrar, Straus, and Giroux, 1990), I discuss the relationship between Nietzsche's approach to ancient tragedy and Aristotle's, arguing that Aristotle's insistence on a firm distinction between character and

fortune, and his insistence that the tragic emotions of pity and fear must take as their object a hero who remains good in character throughout misfortune, may not allow us to do justice to the portrait of human personality in a play such as the *Bacchae*, which depicts in a remarkable way the fluidity of the self, its susceptibility to mysterious transforming influences and inspirations. I argue that Nietzsche's conception of the Dionysian provides a better avenue of approach to these elements in the play.

2 All translations of Nietzsche are from versions by Walter Kaufmann.

3 *Ecce Homo*, 'Why I Write Such Good Books,' § 3.

4 This analogy, however, is not perfect, for it suggests that there is some way the world is outside of our cognitive ordering, and that it would in principle be possible to have access to that intrinsic ordering.

5 Schopenhauer dramatically states: 'Spinoza says that if a stone projected through the air had consciousness, it would imagine it was flying of its own will. I add merely that the stone would be right' (*W1* 126/H. 2, 150).

6 See the discussion of this and related passages in Nussbaum, *The Fragility of Goodness* (Cambridge: Cambridge University Press, 1986), 373–4.

7 On the Hellenistic views in question, see Nussbaum, 'The Stoics on the Extirpation of the Passions,' *Apeiron* 20 (1987), 129–75; on Plato, see Nussbaum, *Fragility*, ch. 5. Schopenhauer refers frequently to the Hellenistic philosophers, both Epicurean and Stoic, citing the texts in both Greek and Latin. (It is not necessary to list citations because Payne's good index provides a reliable enumeration of passages.) He knows the views of the Greek Stoics well, citing fragments of Chrysippus from sources such as Diogenes Laertius, Stobaeus, and Plutarch. He also knows the Roman Stoic authors, frequently citing Epictetus, Marcus Aurelius, and especially Seneca, who provides the epigraph to volume 2 and is cited fourteen times in the text. These citations are drawn from many different texts and show that Schopenhauer has a wide-ranging knowledge of Seneca's work. Epicurus is another favorite: he is cited thirteen times, with a similar breadth of knowledge.

8 See Nussbaum, *Fragility*, ch. 5.

9 See *P2* 316/H. 6, 335–6; 'On Women,' *P2* 614–26; *W2* 555–7; *MR* 3, 260/H. 6, 650–63; H. 3, 636–40; Hn. 3, 238.

10 Plato, *Gorgias*, 493a; Lucretius, *De Rerum Natura*, III, 1003–10.

11 See Nussbaum, 'Poetry and the Passions: Two Stoic Views,' in *Passions and Perceptions*, ed. J. Brunschwig and M. Nussbaum (Cambridge: Cambridge University Press, 1992).

12 See Nussbaum, *Fragility*, ch. 3.

13 See my 'Introduction' to the Williams translation of the *Bacchae* for an interpretive argument and references to the literature.

14 Only to some extent, however, for it is most important that she sees Pentheus as a particular individual and becomes aware of the dead body's relation to her own interests.

15 See Helene Foley, *Ritual Irony: Poetry and Sacrifice in Euripides* (Ithaca and London: Cornell University Press, 1985), and Charles Segal, *Dionysiac Poetics and Euripides' Bacchae* (Princeton: Princeton University Press, 1982).

16 See my 'Introduction' for an argument to this conclusion.

17 On the difficulties this poses for the Stoics in defending the tragic poets as sources of wisdom, see Nussbaum, 'Poetry and the Passions.'

18 For an account of the controversy involving Wilamowitz's critique of *The Birth of Tragedy*, see M. S. Silk and J. P. Stern, *Nietzsche on Tragedy* (Cambridge: Cambridge University Press, 1981), ch. 5.

19 *The Birth of Tragedy*, §1. On the interpretation of *BT*, see the detailed commentary by Silk and Stern, *Nietzsche on Tragedy*.

20 Schopenhauer writes that 'Logic is ... without practical use' (*W1* 46/H.2, 54). Contrast Nietzsche's treatment of logic in 'On Truth and Lying,' *The Gay Science* §111 ('Origins of the Logical'), *Beyond Good and Evil*, Part I, etc.

21 See here John T. Wilcox, *Truth and Value in Nietzsche* (Ann Arbor: University of Michigan Press, 1974). There appear to be three stages in Nietzsche's thinking with respect to the Kantian thing in itself. In the first stage he speaks of 'the unknowable X of the Thing in itself' ('On Truth and Lying'), strongly suggesting that there is some way reality is beyond our perceiving and conceiving, and that we can refer to it, at least to say that we can't know it. In the second stage, he concludes that since we have no access to any such independent reality, we are not entitled to say anything about it, and it has nothing to do with our investigations of the world. In the final stage, represented by the late fragments, he concludes that if we really lack all access to a mind-independent reality, we are not even entitled to speak, as Kant does, of 'things in themselves': for the only meaning 'thing' could possibly have in any human language is a thoroughly human meaning. He concludes that the notion of 'thing in itself' is a contradiction in terms. (Here his position seems close to the antiskeptical internal realism of Hilary Putnam.) For a more recent discussion, see also Maudemarie Clark, *Nietzsche on Truth and Philosophy* (Cambridge: Cambridge University Press, 1990).

22 See Kaufmann's discussion of dating in a footnote to his translation. His argument for dating the fragment to 1886, rather than 1887–8, seems to me unconvincing.

23 Strictly speaking, a consistent Nietzschean is not entitled to say anything, one way or another, about how the world is outside of experience:

so if we take these remarks (and related remarks in later works) to be about 'things in themselves,' they will be incompatible with Nietzsche's mature position. It seems best to take many such statements as referring to the world as we interpret it in our perceptual experience; and many of Nietzsche's contrasts between the order we make and the chaos we experience are best understood as contrasts between perception and concepts. This is especially clear in 'On Truth and Lying,' but if we follow its lead, we can give a consistent reading to many otherwise puzzling passages.

24 It is very important to understand how many constraints Nietzsche thinks there are on such artistic making: see, for example, 'On Truth and Lying,' *The Gay Science* §110–11, etc. Compare Nelson Goodman, 'Worlds, Works, Words,' in *Ways of Worldmaking* (Indianapolis: Hackett Publishing Company, 1979).

25 This belief in the strong potential of art for human affirmation leads Nietzsche to be especially contemptuous of distinguished artists who submit to the authority of convention and/or religion on these matters. His scathing treatment of the otherworldliness of the ending of *Faust* (*Zarathustra*, 'On the Poets') is closely connected to his denunciation of the poets as valets of the reigning morality in *Genealogy of Morals* III. And in *The Case of Wagner* he explains Wagner's development as the capitulation of an originally free spirit to the combined pressure of Christianity and Schopenhauer; he tells the reader that the *Ring* was originally supposed to end with Brünnhilde singing a song 'in honor of free love, putting off the world with the hope for a socialist utopia in which "all turns out well" – but now gets something else to do. She has to study Schopenhauer first; she has to transpose the fourth book of *The World as Will and Representation* into verse. *Wagner was redeemed*' (§4).

26 Kaufmann, in a footnote, says that 'bearable' is different from 'justified' – and one could hardly deny that this is so. But I think he is wrong to draw from this difference the conclusion that Nietzsche intends a strong contrast between the two ideas and has actually changed his attitude between the two works. The general point made by the two remarks seems very much the same: for in Nietzsche's view, the search for a justification for existence is motivated by the need to make life bearable.

27 Again, this suggests some sort of identification with the hero.

28 'Love' throughout is *eros* – except when Nietzsche mentions the 'angelic' variety of love, only to point out that its real roots are erotic.

29 I am grateful to Tom Carpenter, Chris Faraone, and Stephen Halliwell for valuable discussion of the issues, and to Chris Janaway for his editorial good judgment and patience.

12 Schopenhauer, Will, and the Unconscious

It is a commonplace of the history of ideas that there is an extremely close relationship between Schopenhauer and Freud. Nietzsche too is often cited as a philosophical precursor of Freud, but the proto-Freudian elements in his thought are naturally regarded as derived from his Schopenhauerian legacy.

The question of influence, or at any rate continuity, between Schopenhauer and Freud is of interest and importance on its own account, but it has further dimensions. Freud's life and writings are subject to continued interrogation, and his claims for the originality of psychoanalysis are regularly disputed. Whether or not enquiry into the origins of psychoanalysis can do anything to resolve the abiding controversy surrounding the discipline, they at least promise to increase our understanding by helping us to see what makes a conception of the unconscious specifically psychoanalytic.[1]

On Schopenhauer's side, the interest is this. Indisputably, Freud's ideas have sunk deep into the natural consciousness of twentieth-century Western culture. If Freud's central theoretical concept does descend ultimately from Schopenhauer, then this is a reason, or a further reason, for regarding Schopenhauer's philosophy as having a special importance for our self-understanding.

In this essay, I attempt to give some substance to this claim for Schopenhauer's contemporary significance. The first section surveys the main parallels of Schopenhauer with Freud, and the second pursues a question concerning Schopenhauer's concept of will which the comparison with Freud forces us to address. The sections that follow aim to bring out Schopenhauer's distinctiveness by setting him in a historical context. By comparing Schopenhauer's conception of the unconscious with that of the absolute idealists, I will try

375

to indicate how his remarkable anticipation of Freud is bound up with the feature which distinguishes his philosophical project most fundamentally from that of his rival post-Kantians.

I   SCHOPENHAUER'S PSYCHOANALYTIC INSIGHTS

Schopenhauer did not formulate an integrated set of theoretical concepts to describe and explain the workings of the unconscious, and important specific Freudian hypotheses – such as the Oedipus complex and everything that goes with the developmental theory – are absent from his writings.[2] Nevertheless, Schopenhauer formulated the key concepts of Freud's metapsychology. Most of the relevant material is found in volume two of *The World as Will and Representation*.[3]

Schopenhauer returns time and again to the theme of the superficiality of consciousness, which he compares to the surface of a globe or a sheet of water, the depths of which are largely unknown to us, but are where our thinking and resolving take place truly. Ideas are regarded by Schopenhauer as unconscious in themselves: for an idea to be rendered conscious, an extra operation is required, turning (as in Freud's account of the method of free association) on the laws of association. Hence the fragmentary character of the stream of consciousness, our inability to 'give any account of the origin of our deepest thoughts', and the possibility of astonishment at one's own mental life. Consciousness, like a magic lantern, can display only one image at a time, and is related to the mind as a whole as a traveller in an intermittently illuminated labyrinth. The thread of personal identity is preserved, not by memory or any other function pertaining to representation, but by will, which is what determines an idea to become conscious.[4]

Underlying this model of mental life is Schopenhauer's idea that will 'brings forth consciousness for its own ends'.[5] Consciousness and the knowing ego, on his account, are ontologically dependent on the will because they are its instrument: in so far as we take an objective view of cognition, we find its complete explanation as a tool of the will, a 'brain-function' evolved in response to the increased discriminatory needs of complex organisms.[6] Cognition is thus by its nature 'already something secondary, a mere product'.[7] The will itself is entirely without consciousness and is independent of cognition.[8]

Because the primacy of the will is a metaphysically grounded, hence necessary aspect of our psychological structure, the intellect is inherently susceptible to disturbance from the will.[9] When not actually falsifying our knowledge, will (in the shape of desire and emotion) colours the representation of all objects in which it is interested.[10] Ordinary mental life involves a constant process of unconscious redirection of focal consciousness in accordance with our interests, emotions, and wishes.[11] Our own desires and emotions are partially unknown to us, due to their unwelcome character, with the result that we sometimes get to know about the 'real resolutions and secret decisions' of our own will only by spying them out, 'like those of a stranger': the intellect may need to 'surprise the will in the act of expressing itself, in order merely to discover its real intentions', for it may be 'such a stranger to the will that occasionally it is even mystified thereby'.[12]

Schopenhauer's description of the operation whereby self-ignorance is achieved could not be closer to Freud's account of repression:

[The will] makes its supremacy felt in the last resort. This it does by prohibiting the intellect from having certain representations, by absolutely preventing certain trains of thought from arising, because it knows, or in other words experiences from the self-same intellect, that they would arouse in it any one of the emotions previously described [anger, resentment, humiliation, shame, etc.]. It then curbs and restrains the intellect, and forces it to turn to other things. However difficult this often is, it is bound to succeed the moment the will is in earnest about it; for the resistance then comes not from the intellect, which always remains indifferent, but from the will itself; and the will has an inclination in one respect for a representation it abhors in another. Thus the representation is in itself interesting to the will, just because it excites it. At the same time, however, abstract knowledge tells the will that this representation will cause it a shock of painful and unworthy emotion to no purpose. The will then decides in accordance with this last knowledge, and forces the intellect to obey.[13]

Similarly, Schopenhauer sketches the Freudian notion of wish fulfilment: 'the will, when its servant, the *intellect*, is unable to produce the thing desired, compels this servant at any rate to picture this thing to it, and generally to undertake the role of comforter, to pacify its lord and master, as a nurse does a child, with fairy-tales'.[14]

This conception of the intellect's subordinacy is put to work in Schopenhauer's theory of madness.[15] Madness consists – Schopenhauer explains, in an arresting anticipation of Freud's early theories of hysteria and neurosis – in a failure in the function of memory due to an intensification of the normal process of the will's opposition to antipathetic psychological material. Normally, the resistance of the will to uncongenial ideas occurs in a way that preserves the coherence of mental life, adverse events undergoing a process of intellectual assimilation. Madness results when the operation is bungled due to the intolerable emotional charge of (in Freudian language) the traumatic idea and the arbitrariness of the fictitious ideas employed in defence. The intellect has then 'given up its nature to please the will; the person then imagines what does not exist';[16] 'the immediate present is ... falsified through a fictitious connexion with an imaginary past'.[17] The function to be served by madness remains, all the same, intelligible: it is a search for refuge. Schopenhauer evinces in this context a clear notion of the mechanisms of projection and introjection which are of major importance in post-Freudian Kleinian theory: 'we can regard the origin of madness as a violent "casting out of one's mind" of something; yet this is possible only by a "putting into the head" of something else'.[18]

As regards the general nature of the ends to which the will is directed – the content of human motivation – Schopenhauer unequivocally assigns supreme importance to sexuality. Sexuality is 'the invisible central point of all action and conduct', 'the cause of war and object of peace, the basis of the serious and the aim of the joke', 'the key to all hints and allusions, and the meaning of all secret signs and suggestions'. Its pre-eminence and permeation of conscious motivation follow from the metaphysics of book 2 of *The World as Will and Representation*: the essence of man is will, will to life, the concentrated expression of which is sexuality.[19] Though not apprehended as such by the individual, sexuality carries forward the will to life of the species, with the result that each individual is immediately subject to two distinct imperatives: to advance his or her own interest and that of the human species. These interact in the rationally unmediated manner of physical forces, whence all of the irrationality familiarly displayed in human relations wherever sexual love is present; sexual love being, on Schopenhauer's analysis, the delusion whereby the will of the species is experienced, in the mute form of anticipation of pleasure, as the good of the individual.[20] Schopenhauer thus employs a form of psychological explanation which rests on instinct, and introduces the crucial Freudian idea that the actions of individuals can exhibit a purposiveness which transcends their own conception while nevertheless deriving from their inner constitution.

This does not exhaust the points of contact between Schopenhauer and Freud. A full inventory would include, among other topics, their shared view of the negative nature of pleasure;[21]

Schopenhauer's grasp of the close connection between moral conscience and irrationality, the superego's potential for savagery, as Freud would formulate it;[22] and Schopenhauer's theory of dreaming, which regards it as a function distinct from imagination and memory, related to brain activity, inwardly directed, and (like wish fulfilment, on Freud's theory) constituted by a reversal of the usual relation between action and perception.[23]

The similarity of the two thinkers also extends to matters of culture and world-view. It has been suggested, for example, that Schopenhauer's *Dialogue on Religion* lies behind Freud's views on religion in *The Future of an Illusion*;[24] and Thomas Mann observes that Schopenhauer's account of the role of fate closely parallels Freud's discussion of character.[25] Schopenhauer and Freud also share a political conservatism, founded on the application of broadly utilitarian principles of reasoning, together with a conviction that the best of which people are capable collectively is very little.

The depth and range of Schopenhauer's anticipation of psychoanalytic ideas makes it appropriate to regard him, from the point of view of intellectual originality, as the true philosophical father of psychoanalysis.[26] Freud did not, however, cite Schopenhauer as an influence. Indeed, he repudiated the suggestion that Schopenhauer had provided a source of psychoanalytic concepts while acknowledging the main points of their agreement.[27] Given the wide dissemination of Schopenhauer's ideas in late-nineteenth-century Europe – with Eduard von Hartmann's massively influential *Philosophy of the Unconscious* standing as a connecting link[28] – Freud's disavowal of an early inspirational reading of *The World as Will and Representation* may be taken at face value. Freud was exposed to a variety of philosophical influences, including Schopenhauerian ways of thinking, but he certainly never embraced, or set about giving application to, Schopenhauer's (or anybody else's) metaphysics.[29] The true route of historical influence, I will suggest in the final section, is both deeper and less direct.

II WILL IN SCHOPENHAUER

The key point in the convergence of Freud and Schopenhauer concerns, as the previous section has indicated, the concept of the unconscious and its character as will. Closer examination reveals, however, that the correspondence of concepts here is not entirely straightforward, reflecting a difficulty, or at any rate a complication, in Schopenhauer's doctrine of will.

As we have seen, Schopenhauer holds, like Freud, that the mind of the human individual is in part unconscious. Further, Schopenhauer thinks of the unconscious parts of the mind not exclusively as merely unattended to, like Leibniz's *petites perceptions*, or as merely latent mental contents which have been put out of play or deactivated, but as including elements which are active and efficacious independently of consciousness, along the lines of the dynamic unconscious in Freud. And Schopenhauer also holds, of course, that the essence of the individual human being is will: 'man's will is his authentic self, the true core of his being'.[30] These ideas are brought together in Schopenhauer's general claim for the priority of will over intellect, which mirrors Freud's hypothesis that the intellectual operations of the mind are determined in ways that we are unaware of and that express our desires rather than any cognitive interest.

It is thus natural to think that the central core of the human personality which Schopenhauer calls will corresponds to Freud's *Ucs.* or id.[31] However, it would be a mistake to identify the Freudian unconscious with the world-will of Schopenhauer: though the absence of the 'I' of self-consciousness from both may foster the impression of such a correspondence, Freud does not conceive id as having the trans-personal status of Schopenhauer's world-will, which stands beyond the possibility of individuation.[32] The Freudian unconscious is individuated in the same way as persons are. Admittedly, the sense in which my unconscious is 'mine' is under some strain – I cannot access its contents, the id is impersonal, repressed material does not cohere with the ego – but it cannot be correct to locate it outside the bounds of the self.[33]

But nor can the will which corresponds to the unconscious of Freud be the will of the individual, in the sense that Schopenhauer affirms when he speaks of human character, since this comprehends the person's conscious agency.[34] In so far as this is so, the parallel with Freud appears to break down: there is on Schopenhauer's picture no one part of the mind which is distinguished by being at once unconscious, individual, and essentially constituted by will in a way that the rest is not.

In itself this would not matter, beyond setting a limit to Schopenhauer's anticipation of Freud, and in a moment I will state more precisely the sense in which there is in Freud a conceptual innovation absent from Schopenhauer. But first we must consider another respect in which they appear to diverge, one which seems to entail that Schopenhauer has, in fact, no room for the Freudian unconscious.

If we compare Freud's *Ucs.* or id with Schopenhauer's will, they appear to be conative in quite different senses. Both pertain to action and contrast with cognition, of course, but not in the same way. Schopenhauer's concept of will is to be grasped, he tells us, by reference to our immediate awareness of voluntary bodily movement: this is 'the nearest and clearest *phenomenon* of the thing-in-itself'.[35] The *Ucs.* or id, by contrast, comprises motivational states: what it is for one's *Ucs.* or id to be a certain way is for one to be motivated to some end, determined by the 'ideas' which provide its content and by the quality and aim of instincts. The intentional directedness of the content of the *Ucs.* or id, however primitive and remote from that of conscious desires, is what distinguishes it from merely somatic states.

So there is a firm contrast between Schopenhauer's paradigm of will and Freud's source of unconscious motivation.[36] Not only do bodily acts of will and motivational states comprise discrete stages in the psychological sequence which comprises human action, acts of will lying at the end of a chain that begins with motivational states (desires, wants, 'pro-attitudes'),[37] but they have exclusive characters: bodily willing is essentially non-representational, whereas motivational states involve essentially the representation of an end.

One thing that might be said here, by way of restoring parallelism between the two thinkers, is that even if the Freudian *Ucs.* or id is not in itself constituted of will in Schopenhauer's sense, it is nevertheless altogether of a piece with psychoanalytic thinking to suppose that it is *experienced*, unconsciously, in just such terms. That is, *Ucs.* or id contents are subjectively represented as having the quality of bodily strivings – as thrusting, pushing, impelling, and so on. The notion that in the unconscious the mental is characteristically represented as corporeal makes this a natural thing to say, and the idea can be shown to be implicit in many specific psychoanalytic hypotheses.[38]

Whatever the value of this suggestion, a general difficulty has emerged in understanding Schopenhauer's concept of will. The observation that will, as exemplified in bodily striving, differs in nature from Freudian motivational states invites the suspicion that Schopenhauer's concept of will runs together two quite different things: on the one hand, acts of volition identical with movings of one's body ('raising one's arm'), and on the other, intentional actions ('signalling'). The first can be called a 'feeling',[39] but the second, which involves conceptually structured, reflexive consciousness, cannot. There can be little doubt that Schopenhauer consistently uses the term 'will' to refer to both,[40] but since they are such different things, it must be asked which he has in mind when he speaks of will as 'the nearest and clearest phenomenon of the thing-in-itself'. Does will in its primary use – that is, prior to the reflective, philosophically motivated extension involved in its application to nature as a whole[41] – refer to intentional action or to voluntary bodily movement? And if he means both, how can this double reference be defended as coherent?[42]

Some have interpreted Schopenhauer as returning the first answer or have offered this as the best reconstruction of his account.[43] If this reading is accepted, then will in Schopenhauer ceases to be heterogeneous with the Freudian unconscious. But there are, I think, conclusive reasons for pinning will in its primary application to bodily willing. The first is exegetical. If Schopenhauer meant by will intentional action, then its 'nearest and clearest phenomenon' would be not bodily action, but rather resolving, deciding, intention-forming, and so forth – determining oneself and *meaning* to do such and such.[44] If Schopenhauer really meant by will something so close to what Kant means by practical reason, then we would have to conclude that he misled himself entirely by so emphasising the role of the body in action.

Second, and most important, to identify the will with intentional action is to lose the only genuine opportunity to make sense of Schopenhauer's insistence on the inherent blindness of will (and thus also, it may be argued, of his pessimism). Schopenhauer's insight, I suggest, is that at the core of every intentional action there is something which can be isolated from any representation of an end, and which we can grasp as subsisting independently of the framework of rationality which is constitutive of intentional action and of any other teleological structure.[45] Because bodily willing contains in itself no representation of whatever end the agent has it in view to realise by moving his or her body, it is to that extent independent of practical reason and its objects.[46] Teleology constitutes the form of intentional action, but not of the acts of bodily will enclosed within it. It is this which permits and encourages Schopenhauer to reverse, at a metaphysical level, the usual order of understanding: beneath the truth that we perform individual bodily movements in order to realise the ends we set ourselves in intentional action lies, he holds, the truth that we perform intentional actions at all, only and solely because we are will. Thus, at the deepest level of explanation, we act because we will, rather than will in order to act – rational action is a mere occasion for will.[47] End-directedness is thus a creation of, and explained by, will: purposiveness can exist only as supervening on the manifestation of will, which is in itself beyond the possibility of purpose, just as it is beyond the possibility of individuation. Schopenhauer's description of will as 'will to life' follows from his assertion of its blindness: the suffix 'to life' simply reminds us of the fact that will's highest phenomenal objectification is in life; it does not designate life as the end of will, and it no more imports purposiveness than does the description of a body as having impetus.[48]

If, by contrast, will is identified with intentional action, then the claim that it is blind reduces to the innocuous point that purposiveness is independent of consciousness. Schopenhauer must then be accused of a gross confusion of this point with the much stronger claim that being is inherently non-rational or arational,[49] and his whole notion of the inherent non-rationality of existence is jeopardised: if the essence of existence is will, and if will is by its nature end-directed, then there is every reason to think that the world exists to serve an ultimate, if unknown, rational purpose.

If will in its primary use refers to bodily willing, not intentional action, these difficulties disappear. However, we then face a problem. For it seems to follow that all of the elements in our psychology which have representational content – wants, desires, emotions, and so on – are not, after all, primary instances of will. Schopenhauer, it would then seem, must assimilate everything that common sense considers conative (apart from bodily willing) to cognition, and cannot accommodate the ordinary sense in which a want or desire has an intrinsic relation to agency lacked by belief.[50]

The solution, I suggest, is in the first place to see how Schopenhauer may extend the notion of will up from bodily willing to the motivational part of the mind without simply confusing two different senses of will. What he may say is that when we abstract from our immediate awareness of bodily willing everything that pertains to its psychological role, something remains, which cannot, ex hypothesi, be characterised in psychological terms, and to that extent must remain indefinable, beyond being described as 'pure awareness of striving' (Brian O'Shaughnessy suggests 'spirit in motion'[51]). And this something, he may then say, we grasp as also manifest in intentional action and in motivational states: though a desire is not a doing, to desire something is to be in a state which is of the same nature as a doing.[52] This is what in general distinguishes a desire from a belief and makes wanting X different from believing that it would be good for me to have X; it accords with our ordinary conception of desire as something that *moves* one to act. Similar points apply to the differential extension of will through the psychological domain to encompass affective and hedonic phenomena and to exclude perception and belief.[53]

What may be added next to Schopenhauer's account is the claim that, while the motivational parts of the mind are related to will in the way that is true of all psychological phenomena – they objectify it – they are so related to a different *degree*: they comprise an especially *intense* expression of will, just as, on the bodily plane, the sexual organs comprise an especially concentrated expression of will.[54] That is, Schopenhauer needs a sense in which will is *in* phenomena, and more so in some than others, in addition to being *behind* all of them.[55] He needs this notion in order for his metaphysic of will to have any connection with (and to receive corroboration from) his observations on the influence of the will on the intellect in human psychology, and in order for the general account that he gives in *On the Will in Nature* of the corroboration of his metaphysics by empirical research to be intelligible:[56] unless will is evidenced in 'horizontal' relations between phenomena (such as elements of human psychology), in addition to the general 'vertical' relation of the phenomenal to the extra-phenomenal, Schopenhauer's claim that the will can be seen at work in the phenomenal world, in a sense which connects with his claim that the world is will, must be rejected as misguided.

The interpretation I have suggested makes it intelligible that will is manifest in motivation in a way that it is not in cognition, and it also restores agreement between Schopenhauer and Freud: Schopenhauer himself may not say that the dynamically unconscious parts of the mind are a more intense expression of the will than the conscious parts, but his philosophy at least does not preclude the idea. The idea of a differential expression of will by different species of phenomena – for example, different psychological functions – marks the distance between Schopenhauer's conception of the relation of the phenomenal to the trans-phenomenal and that of Kant, a point that I will come back to later.

Let us return to the respect in which Schopenhauer does not anticipate Freud's thinking about the unconscious. What makes Freud's theory of the unconscious more than a mere regimentation, or terminological recasting of notions implicit in ordinary psychology, is its account of the mind as composed of distinct systems, containing different sorts of content, governed by different laws, serving different functions, associated with different developmental stages, and exhibiting a degree of mutual independence. In other words, Freudian theory is bound up with a partitive conception of human personality.[57] We find only a trace of this in Schopenhauer: to the extent that Schopenhauer is willing to speak of parts of the mind, what he envisages is only parts in the familiar, weak sense of aspects of personality found in ordinary psychological talk.[58] Hence the absence from Schopenhauer, noted earlier, of any single concept doing duty for Freud's unconscious or id.

There is, therefore, a sense in which we speak misleadingly when we say that Schopenhauer and Freud share a concept of the unconscious. Another related way of making the point (and explaining why it should have seemed to Freud that his claim to theoretical originality was sound) is in terms of the criteria of identity for concepts. The more loosely a concept is defined, the easier it is to push back its intellectual ancestry; granted a certain level of abstraction, we could say that the unconscious was first discovered by Plotinus. Clearly, intellectual history requires a more stringent view of the identity of concepts. One way of supplying this is to draw a sharp distinction between theoretical concepts which are *empirically determinate* – ones whose content is fixed by a theory comprehending an integrated set of concepts, at the lowest level of which are concepts with systematic criteria of application – and those which are not. In these terms, Schopenhauer and Freud do not share a concept of the unconscious: Schopenhauer's is of the second type, and Freud's is of the first.

III   THE UNCONSCIOUS IN KANT

Given that it is not due to any commitment on Freud's part to Schopenhauer's philosophy, what explains the extraordinary proximity of Schopenhauer to Freud?

At one level, it may be said that the convergence derives from a common fund of evidence. While the material which psychoanalysis takes as data for its conjectures is in part dependent on the transference created by the clinical situation, it is also substantially available in ordinary psychological existence – in the dreams, lapses, parapraxes, failures of self-knowledge, unbidden thoughts, alien impulses, and more extended patterns of irrationality observable in one's own and others' mental lives. In addition, Schopenhauer's frequent asylum tours in Berlin provided him with the opportunity to study more florid and overt forms of mental disturbance.[59] To some extent, therefore, it may be said that Schopenhauer formed his proto-psychoanalytic conjectures on the same empirical basis as Freud. But this is obviously a shallow explanation, since the same body of empirical data is available to all and sundry, and Schopenhauer evidently cannot be supposed to have incipiently anticipated Freud's theoretical development. Schopenhauer was engaged in applying *metaphysical* ideas to human observation, not in attempting to construct a theory around a clinical practice.

So the interesting question is what made it possible for Schopenhauer to arrive, by metaphysical means, at an early crystallisation of Freud's concept of the unconscious – what in the general nature of Schopenhauer's philosophical project allowed it to give rise to claims of a psychoanalytic sort. The other post-Kantian idealists also put the accent on man as a practical rather than a theoretical being, but none of them (so I will argue) can correctly be interpreted as having anticipated Freud's discovery of the unconscious. And Kant's own philosophical position can hardly be thought to contain the seeds of any Freudian ideas. An explanation is therefore wanted for why, of all the philosophical developments which issued from Kant's Copernican revolution, Schopenhauer's should reach up to psychoanalysis in a way that the others do not.

As with so many aspects of Schopenhauer's philosophy, the answer must begin with a consideration of Kant. Although, as just said, there is nothing in Kant's philosophy that tends remotely in the direction of Freud, there are two respects in which Kant may be said to have laid the conditions for the notion of the unconscious to be introduced into philosophical discourse in a novel way: first, directly through his notion of transcendental synthesis, and second, indirectly through his account of the conditions under which representations become cognitions.[60] The chief locus of both themes is the Transcendental Deduction of the *Critique of Pure Reason*, the core of Kant's transcendental theory of experience.

Interpretations vary greatly, but all concur that Kant meant in the Deduction to forge some extremely tight connections between self-consciousness and the capacity for objective judgement, and that the key to his argument is meant to lie in the notion that our representations must be such that the 'I think' can accompany them, that is, such that I can judge them to be mine. On one common reading of the Deduction, Kant means to show that all of my mental states, in order to belong to me and to qualify as mental states at all, must be ones that I can *ascribe* to myself. If so, Kant's philosophy is committed to a strong equivalence of the mental not just with consciousness, but also with self-consciousness.

Whether the conclusion of the Deduction is really to be expressed in this strong form is questionable, but even if it does not quite follow from it that mentality and consciousness, or representation and self-consciousness, are equivalent, it would seem, thus far, that transcendental philosophy cannot provide grounds for introducing the notion of the unconscious.

There is, however, another side to the matter. On Kant's account, the link between self-consciousness and judgement lies in their common dependence on a priori concepts, called by Kant the 'categories'; more precisely, in the employment of the categories, or rules corresponding to them, in what Kant calls 'synthesis'. Synthesis in general means unification, and the specific synthesis adduced in the Deduction is a priori synthesis according to the categories – spontaneous, subjective, rule-governed activity whereby the data supplied by sense are given conceptual form, and judgeable objects are constituted. Kant thus offers a transcendental explanation of self-consciousness: its condition of possibility lies in the subject's employment of a priori concepts in synthetic activity, apart from which there could be no 'I'.

Now the operations of transcendental synthesis are evidently not conscious in any ordinary sense because they are neither presented to consciousness as such nor capable of being so presented. Introspection, whether on the part of pre-philosophical consciousness or that of the transcendental philosopher, does not and could not disclose any mental content under the description 'application to the sensory manifold of a priori rules yielded by the categories'. We are conscious of the *products* of transcendental synthesis, not of the activity of synthesis itself.[61] Thus, we have the option of saying that transcendental synthesis – the acts themselves and the subject who performs them – is unconscious.[62]

Whether this option should, in Kant's own terms, be taken is uncertain.[63] There are several reasons why it may be thought appropriate to conceptualise the subject of the Transcendental Deduction in this way, and while some of them may reflect confusions or bad practice in Kant interpretation, others do not.

It would be a mistake to think of Kant's account of transcendental synthesis – which he expresses in terms of a multi-tiered order of syntheses attached to different faculties[64] – as a matter of venturing hypotheses about the structure of an otherwise unknown 'transcendental mind'. Kant's breakdown of synthesis, and his division of the subject into powers, is not psychological speculation, but is directly extrapolated from the objects of representation: the subject is specified exclusively in terms of functions corresponding to different respects in which the objects of our cognition are conditioned. In this sense, it is inappropriate to describe Kant as engaging in 'transcendental psychology', for he makes no claim about how the self is constituted in itself, and the subject to which synthetic operations are referred is not to be identified with the noumenal or intelligible self.

Nevertheless, it should be acknowledged that transcendental synthesis in Kant is not 'something merely logical'. The whole programme of transcendental explanation demands that transcendental synthesis be, in however qualified a sense, something real: if the Copernican revolution consists in explaining the objects of cognition idealistically, in terms of our mode of cognition, then talk of subjective activity as the source of the constitution of appearances must be more than a mere *façon de parler*. Transcendental synthesis has a 'mental' character, in the way that Hume's 'propensities' – being mechanistic in character, unrelated to rationality, and off the edge of the bundle of perceptions which comprises the self – arguably do not. So it cannot be said that the notion of (un)consciousness is categorically inapplicable to transcendental synthesis in the sense that it is to a purely logical reconstruction of the conditions of human knowledge.

To this it should be added that the delicate balance which Kant seeks to maintain in his theoretical philosophy between his positive claims about transcendental subjectivity, and his denial that we have knowledge of the self as a thing in itself, comes under particular pressure when we ask how the subject of theoretical knowledge is related to the subject of practical reason; at this point, the impetus to postulate an underlying ground of unity of the subject may become irresistible.[65] If for this (or any other) reason it should seem mandatory to construe Kant as committed to the reality of the self qua underlying ground of the 'I think', then a place is immediately made for a distinctively transcendental notion of the unconscious. Transcendental subjectivity will not be unconscious in any ordinary, empirical sense, but the concept will nevertheless have intelligible application to it.

The other way in which Kant's philosophy makes room for the notion of the unconscious derives from the idea of representations that do not admit of being accompanied by the 'I think'. As indicated earlier, it is open to interpretation whether the Deduction is really meant to deny the possibility of mental states that cannot be taken up into self-consciousness. Kant's theoretical philosophy is, after all, not directly engaged with the topic of the nature and extent of the mental, as opposed to the epistemological, role of representations: it is concerned exclusively with the conditions under which representations can function cognitively, that is, relate to objects. Thus it might be held that, though it does follow from the Deduction that representations which cannot be brought to self-consciousness are extraneous to the analysis of cognition and objectivity, it does not follow that they are per se impossible.

In any case, Kant himself makes a number of remarks suggesting that representations outside the scope of judgement and self-consciousness are indeed possible; most clearly in a letter, where he says that sensory representations which could not 'reach that unity of consciousness that is necessary for knowledge of myself' could nevertheless 'carry on their play in an orderly fashion' and 'even have an influence on my feeling and desire, without my being aware of them'.[66] This would leave it open that subjective elements properly classifiable as mental states but incapable of being accompanied by the 'I think', possessing causal efficacy in place of rationality, may be postulated if the demands of empirical explanation require it, consistent with the teachings of the Deduction.

Hence, a second avenue to the existence of the unconscious is created by Kant's theory of experience: the necessary connection argued by Kant between consciousness and rationality suggests indirectly the possibility of a counterposed sphere of subjectivity characterised by unconsciousness and non-rationality. In this way Kant's philosophy allows the unconscious to be formulated as a topic for (empirical) psychology, though it does not give any reason for pursuing research into it.

It is evident that, of the two ways in which a notion of the unconscious might be developed from a basis in Kant's philosophy – through the concept of transcendental synthesis and through the possibility of representations outside self-consciousness – it is the second which has affinity with the dynamic unconscious of Freud. But those of Kant's successors who accepted his system as the proper starting point for future philosophical developments – with the exception of Schopenhauer – introduced a conception of the unconscious by the first route, as will now be seen.[67]

IV THE UNCONSCIOUS IN FICHTE, SCHELLING, AND HEGEL

The post-Kantian who did most to make the notion of the unconscious central to transcendental philosophy is Schelling, whose early philosophy supplied the bridge from Fichte to Hegel. The relevant writing of Schelling's is his *System of Transcendental Idealism* (1801). In this work Schelling proceeds from a form of explanation developed by Fichte, in whose transformation of Kant's transcendental idealism the subject – now under the title of the absolute 'I' – has the function of providing a total explanation of the objects and structure of experience. The transcendental subjectivity whose operations Kant had confined to synthesising, that is, giving form to an independently given content, becomes in Fichte a subjectivity that *posits*, that is, has responsibility for content as well as form. In Fichte's case, as in that of Kant, this region of subjectivity may be described as unconscious. The distinction of conscious and unconscious was not in fact part of Fichte's philosophical terminology, but it is naturally employed in elucidating his distinction between the determinate consciousness of the empirical self and the positing operations of the absolute self.[68]

In Schelling's *System*, sustained and explicit reference is made to the unconscious.[69] Nature is conceived as the product of the self's unconscious activity, more specifically, of the 'productive imagination', a faculty introduced by Kant and accorded by Fichte the role of generating empirical reality. It follows that what the conscious self apprehends as empirical objectivity is the absolute self qua unconscious of itself. In this system art finds a place: works of art have a privileged position as exemplifications of the unity of conscious and unconscious factors which constitutes reality, a unity which philosophy can only outline in the barest fashion.

What differentiates Schelling's explicit use of the notion of the unconscious from Fichte's implicit use of it – and gives it a further dimension lacked by transcendental subjectivity in Kant and Fichte – is a change in the overall structure of absolute idealism introduced by Schelling. It became clear to Schelling that Fichte's notion of the absolute self's 'positing' of the objective empirical world, the 'non-I', is deeply non-explanatory: Fichte could not say why, whenever I think 'I am', the objective world is necessarily apprehended as *already* there, as independent and external; Fichte's subjectively biased idealism failed to acknowledge the truth in realism.[70] The task consequently set for philosophy, in Schelling's view, was to grasp reality as a whole from two sides, objectively as well as subjectively. Schelling's philosophy of nature (*Naturphilosophie*) was meant to do this by showing how finite, conscious intelligence necessarily arises out of nature, conceived as a self-subsistent, teleological totality.[71] What Schelling designates as the unconscious is thus not simply subjective: it has equally an objective aspect, which can be grasped in the philosophy of nature. The transcendental unconscious in Schelling therefore belongs not just to the subject, but to the whole which comprises the subject's unity with the object.[72]

In Hegel's philosophy, the same transcendental unconscious is present as in Schelling.[73] Though Hegel departs from Schelling with regard to terminology, the phenomenological part of Hegel's philosophy – his *Phenomenology of Spirit* – describes the process by which consciousness attains realisation of the identity of subject and object, which involves on its part a movement of ever-deepening self-explication, in which what initially appears to consciousness to be other than itself is grasped as its own, the scope of subjectivity thereby being constantly expanded. The transcendental unconscious figures in Hegel in the form of what he calls the *an sich* of consciousness, which refers to whatever is merely implicit, or undeveloped, and awaits transformation into explicitly self-conscious, self-determining subjectivity.[74] Since this conception of a movement of consciousness is indissolubly connected with Hegel's conception of dialectical movement, the transcendental unconscious in his philosophy is a concomitant of his philosophical methodology, as well as being, as it is in Schelling, a metaphysical postulate.

There is one point where Hegel may seem to come close to a Freudian conception of the unconscious. In the third part of his *Encyclopaedia of the Philosophical Sciences*, in the context of a treatment of 'subjective Spirit' – a reconstruction of the individual human mind in terms of Hegel's logic – Hegel introduces the idea of the 'feeling soul', a developmental stage at which mind consists in corporeal sentience, mere passivity.[75] The interest of this, Hegel says, is that it defines a pre-intelligent condition into which the later subject of intelligent consciousness may lapse. Such, according to Hegel, is the nature of mental disease.[76]

Some have seen in Hegel's theory of madness a far-reaching anticipation of psychoanalysis, but this is highly questionable. It is true
that Hegel has a concept of regression, and that he uses freely the language of mental division, thereby approximating to Freud's conception of psychological structure built out of the residues of different
developmental stages. In this respect Hegel is in advance of Schopenhauer. However, Hegel does not formulate the concept of the unconscious as a source of motivation, co-active and intercommunicating
with rational consciousness. His model is rather one of rational consciousness and 'degraded' consciousness as *alternating* conditions.
The mental pathology considered by Hegel includes psychotic breakdown and other, less pronounced aberrations in mental life, such as
somnambulism and catalepsy, but the field of neurosis does not exist for him. As a result, Hegel's theory is conceptually on a par with
the theories of mental dissociation ('second consciousness') to which
Freud opposed the psychoanalytic unconscious. So although Hegel
has a place for representations outside self-consciousness – they figure in a piece of empirical psychology incorporated into Hegel's transcendental analysis of human subjectivity – he does not grant them
anything like the action-determining, intellect-subordinating role
they have in psychoanalysis and in Schopenhauer. To do so would
contradict the conception of rational autonomy which lies at the
centre of Hegel's philosophy.[77]

V   THE UNCONSCIOUS IN SCHOPENHAUER

It can now be explained how the very different manner in which
the notion of the unconscious figures in Schopenhauer's philosophy
reflects the deep difference between his development of Kant's transcendental idealism and that of the absolute idealists.

The unconscious in Schopenhauer is not introduced in the context of an account of the conditions of possibility of objects, framed
in terms of transcendental subjectivity. It is, instead, grounded on
the ambition to explain features of the world, including human personality, by reference to an underlying reality.

For this reason, Schopenhauer's philosophy is not a form of *transcendental* philosophy. Transcendental philosophy may be defined
by the following features.[78] First, it seeks to explain the possibility
of objects in a sense which is continuous with the preoccupations of

pre-Kantian epistemology, and it is meant to resolve the problem of skepticism set by Descartes. For this reason, Kant's 'transcendental turn' is also often referred to as an 'epistemological turn': though it does not merely substitute epistemological for metaphysical questions, it incorporates an epistemological reorientation by virtue of its policy of taking up metaphysical questions with reference to the conditions under which things can become objects for us. Second, the form of philosophical explanation employed in transcendental philosophy is not based on any appeal to how things really are, to the real constitution of either the subject or its objects. Third, it employs self-consciousness – inclusive of its practical form, the power of self-determination – as the fundamental principle of philosophical explanation.[79]

The Analytic of the *Critique of Pure Reason* having provided the model, the absolute idealists discovered new versions and combinations of these three tenets. They differ from Kant in claiming to arrive at knowledge of how things really are – of things in themselves, in Kant's language – but, on their account, this knowledge is a *result* reached on the basis of a philosophical methodology that, like Kant's, rigorously excludes any initial appeal to real constitutions, and by means of which the initial distinction of appearance and underlying reality is qualified or eroded. (The genius of absolute idealism lies in its reconciliation of Kant's apparently restrictive philosophical method with a claim to knowledge of Reality, through an identification of the form of reality with that of self-consciousness.)

Schopenhauer's philosophy, by contrast, lacks all three of the defining features of transcendental philosophy. First, Schopenhauer's account of knowledge is not fundamentally geared towards solving the problem of skepticism.[80] This is indicated by his description of the world of phenomena as an illusion, a veil of *maya*,[81] and by his concession that 'theoretical egoism' – the view 'which regards as phantoms all phenomena outside its own will' – remains an impregnable fortress.[82]

Second, as already observed, the pattern of explanation to which Schopenhauer ties metaphysics, and thus his conception of what makes metaphysics possible after Kant, is firmly realist: his argument for conceiving the world as will on the basis of the character of its phenomena involves referring them for their explanation to the constitution of something real and underlying, a ground which has its constitution (character, quality) independently of the subject and of the phenomena which derive from it.[83] This derivation is expressive rather than causal – causality being restricted by Schopenhauer to the phenomenal realm – but it nevertheless exhibits the essential form of realist explanation. Indeed, the very conception of *the world* as setting a 'riddle', and as offering itself to the philosopher as a 'cryptograph' for 'deciphering' – as compared with Kant's use of the conflicts of reason, an intra-subjective datum, to launch his Copernican revolution – implies a realist conception of philosophical explanation.[84]

This point is unaffected by the qualification that Schopenhauer enters,[85] to the effect that our knowledge of ourselves qua things in themselves is tempered by the temporal form of our consciousness. Whether this means, for example, that the world is therefore will only in a metaphorical sense, or that will is not identical with things in themselves,[86] Schopenhauer must maintain that his 'way from within' yields a true representation of trans-phenomenal reality, a representation of how it is in itself, and not merely how it appears. Otherwise, his explanation of the world in terms of will has no deeply different status from the explanations of the natural sciences, the ultimate contentlessness of which he stresses at length and appeals to as leaving room for explanation which only metaphysics can fill.

From this it follows that Schopenhauer's conception of things in themselves is quite different from that of Kant, contrary to the impression that Schopenhauer gives of conceptual continuity. Things in themselves are not, for Schopenhauer, essentially a corollary of the attempt to construct a transcendental theory of experience. The primary meaning of 'thing in itself' for Schopenhauer is the immediately underlying explanatory ground of phenomena – their 'kernel'[87] – not, as in Kant, an object conceived as something to which our cognition must conform.[88] This explains why, as noted earlier, Schopenhauer conceives the relation of the phenomenal to the trans-phenomenal realms so differently from Kant, such that phenomena can manifest the non-phenomenal to varying degrees: the trans-phenomenal element that Schopenhauer refers to as the thing in itself is *immanent* in the phenomenal – its substratum and inner constitution – in a way that makes no sense for Kant.[89]

And third, self-consciousness, far from enjoying any kind of methodological privilege, is regarded by Schopenhauer as a source of error in metaphysics. Self-consciousness gives rise to the illusions of freedom of will and of the primacy of thinking over willing.[90]

Many other features of Schopenhauer's philosophy can be adduced to make the point that Schopenhauer's philosophical project is independent of transcendental philosophy.

Schopenhauer's use of the principle of sufficient reason, and his view of its status,[91] are entirely remote from the sort of justification which Kant thought it necessary to provide for the principles of the understanding; its application to the phenomenal world is not a case of transcendental proof in Kant's sense.[92]

The principle of idealism espoused by Schopenhauer – the correlativity of subject and object, 'the inseparable and reciprocal dependence of subject and object, together with the antithesis between them which cannot be eliminated'[93] – entails a repudiation of what was for Kant (and through him, in modified forms, for Fichte, Schelling, and Hegel) the deepest problem of theoretical philosophy and the proper successor to the Cartesian problem of skepticism: namely, the problem expressed in the question that Kant put in his famous letter to Herz, 'What is the ground of the relation of that in us which we call "representation" to the object?'[94] By affirming the necessary mutual implication of subject and object without having recourse to the kinds of complex arguments for transcendental idealism that Kant advanced in the Aesthetic, Analytic, and Antinomy of his first *Critique* – that is, by advancing the principle as an apodictic or quasi-analytic truth – Schopenhauer effectively denied the need for and possibility of a philosophical theory of the relation of subject and object in the sense that Kant, and again the absolute idealists, sought to provide.

Finally, Schopenhauer's view of human action as on a continuum with animal behaviour and other organic processes – his analysis of it as an elaboration of stimulus-and-response, and built on the same pattern[95] – means that a fundamental datum of transcendental philosophy, the construal of human freedom as involving irreducible reflexivity and spontaneity, is simply denied by Schopenhauer.

These differences, I suggest, distance Schopenhauer from Kant far more profoundly than the apostasy involved in his claim to have discovered (abruptly, without taking the long route of absolute idealism) the identity of the thing in itself. This now appears as but a symptom of a more radical departure. The carrying forward of Kant that we find in Schopenhauer consists in a detachment of Kant's idealism from the transcendental method on the basis of which Kant developed it. Schopenhauer signals his methodological divergence from Kant in many ways, not least by his repudiation of Kant's attempt to distance himself from Berkeley[96] – a Berkeleyan construal of Kant's talk of appearances being the natural way of understanding his idealism once the transcendental methodology has been stripped away.

Schopenhauer thus dismantled the Kantian structure in an opposite way from Fichte, Schelling, and Hegel. Whereas the absolute idealists stuck to Kant's transcendental programme and either modified or abandoned the subjective character of his idealism, Schopenhauer held fast to the subjectivity of the idealism and disposed of Kant's transcendental method.[97] In Kant's terms, Schopenhauer's idealism thus reverts to 'dogmatism' and counts, like Berkeley's idealism, as a form of transcendental realism. Kant passed the same verdict on absolute idealism, but for quite different reasons.[98]

We are now able to explain how it was possible for Schopenhauer to arrive, on the basis of Kantian resources, at a conception of the unconscious so close to Freud's. Schopenhauer was able to use the conceptual space in Kant's picture in ways that the absolute idealists could not. Because the absolute idealists provided new accounts of the conditions of possibility of objects by pursuing Kant's conception of transcendental subjectivity, their resulting transcendental conception of the unconscious could have no relation to Freud's. And because of their commitment to self-consciousness as the fundamental principle of philosophical explanation, they could not exploit the second route to the unconscious derivable from Kant, the existence of representations unaccompanied by the 'I think'.

Schopenhauer, by contrast, broke with the programme of transcendental philosophy, at bottom by rejecting the problem of the subject–object relation. The world could thus present itself to Schopenhauer as a 'cryptograph', and natural phenomena, including human psychology, could be interpreted as directly manifesting the constitution of an underlying reality. Because Schopenhauer's idealism was not transcendental, natural phenomena could be taken as displaying reality, and the reality displayed in them did not need to be invested with the form of self-consciousness; it could, on the contrary, be regarded as foreign and inimical to self-consciousness and its attendant rationality.[99] Transcendental philosophy makes this move impossible because it requires that all general, structural features of nature be treated as functions of transcendental subjectivity, and regards the form of self-consciousness as ineliminable from reality.

At the same time, Schopenhauer's break with transcendental philosophy allowed him to exploit the second route to the unconscious admitted by Kant: mental phenomena unaccompanied by the 'I think' become, in Schopenhauer, philosophically significant, simply by virtue of their status as natural phenomena, hence as clues to the solution of the human cryptograph. And because the metaphysical core of the human being was no longer, for Schopenhauer, occupied by the apparatus of transcendental subjectivity, it could be filled with an underlying reality, and Schopenhauer, reading the book of nature in the same disenchanted way as Freud, filled it with a very similar content.

The deep common ground of Schopenhauer and Freud is, therefore, their acceptance of the reality of nature. Strange though it may seem to attribute such a belief to the Berkeleyan Schopenhauer, it is clearly present in the form of his conviction, inseparable from the method of his metaphysics, that nature expresses ultimate truth. So, by a metaphysical route that rejects the transcendental demand that nature be subordinated to rational subjectivity, Schopenhauer arrives at the same unencumbered view of the human psyche as Freud's scientific naturalism.[100]

VI   THE UNCONSCIOUS IN NIETZSCHE

As noted at the beginning of this essay, Nietzsche is standardly paired with Schopenhauer as a philosophical precursor of Freud's, and in the case of Nietzsche it may be thought, on account of his repudiation of metaphysics, that the relation of philosophy to psychoanalysis is even closer.[101] Though this is not the place for a detailed study of Nietzsche, it is appropriate to ask if this view is correct: Can it be maintained that Nietzsche stands in the history of ideas as a kind of mediating term between Schopenhauer and Freud? If so, we could tell the story of the concept of the unconscious in terms of its evolution from a metaphysical origin in Schopenhauer, through its naturalistic purification of metaphysical elements in Nietzsche, to the fully scientific, naturalistic version that we find in Freud. Appearances to the contrary, I will suggest that the lines of historical

Schopenhauer, Will, and the Unconscious   399

continuity should not be drawn in this way, and that the concurrence of Schopenhauer with Freud runs much deeper than that of Nietzsche with Freud.

The key issue concerns what is to be made of Nietzsche's declared naturalism, because this is the chief element which makes it seem as if Nietzsche's thought runs smoothly into Freud's. Nietzsche's intention of raising up the idea of nature in opposition to other-worldly metaphysics, and of referring his interpretations of beliefs, values, and practices to a bodily, biological, evolutionary, or instinctual conception of human personality, is one of the foremost themes in his writings after *The Birth of Tragedy* and one of the least surrounded with exegetical controversy.[102] Indeed, a case can be made for saying that the idea of nature as an overarching principle, and the correlative animalisation of man, is more fundamental to Nietzsche's philosophy than are his doctrines of will to power or perspectivism. The idea of life, which for Nietzsche is straightforwardly tied to nature, provides the most constantly recurring and solid term of reference in his attempts to articulate a new mode of valuation. Nietzsche's dissolution of belief in the essential unity of the self and the will – an important respect in which he may be held to come much closer to Freud than Schopenhauer, who appears, by contrast, to adhere to a conception of the metaphysical integrity of the individual not remote from Kant's – is carried out in terms of a reduction to natural drives.[103] Even Nietzsche's concepts of will to power and perspective implicate the notion of nature, in so far as the notion of force through which the former is explained is a natural one, and the latter is standardly explicated by Nietzsche in functional terms, on the model of a natural organism with an interest in adaptation and survival.

In spite of all this, I suggest that there is reason for not pressing the commitment to nature in Nietzsche. If Nietzsche's philosophy is construed as a thoroughgoing naturalism, then it is staked on the truth of certain motivational claims about human psychology. Difficulties then immediately present themselves concerning the consistency of Nietzsche's claims to psychological knowledge with his generally skeptical outlook. Even if the question of consistency is waived, it is extremely hard to see whence the authority of Nietzsche's motivational interpretations of beliefs and values, understood naturalistically, could derive – and it is absolutely essential that they should be well grounded, for, on the naturalistic interpretation, it is only to the extent that they have demonstrable support that we have reason for taking seriously Nietzsche's attack on our moral and other convictions.

More specifically, the strategy of attempting to vindicate Nietzsche by construing him as an anticipator of Freud confronts a problem. If Nietzsche formed his views without employing the systematic clinical methods on which Freud relied, then either Freud's methods are inessential to his conclusions, in which case Freud's views are on no firmer ground than Nietzsche's, and his authority cannot be appealed to in order to vindicate Nietzsche; or Freud's methods are what render his results epistemically reliable, in which case Nietzsche's 'anticipations' of Freud amount to nothing more than inspired guesses – correct guesses, perhaps, but not ones for which Nietzsche had sufficient justification to warrant the enormous philosophical weight he put on them.[104]

Moreover, even if Nietzsche is granted the psychological knowledge which the naturalistic reconstruction requires him to have, it remains extremely unclear how this alone could allow him to achieve his philosophical aims. Psychoanalytic interpretations which ascribe motives for beliefs and values do not imply directly anything whatsoever regarding their truth value or rationality, and indeed need not weaken our confidence in them at all, since the determinants of belief and action that Freud identifies at the level of the dynamic unconscious never preclude their having other, rational determinants. In standard psychoanalytic interpretations of conscious rational phenomena – of judgements and intentional actions, as opposed to dreams and symptoms – a multiplicity of determinants is revealed, unconscious motives at most explaining the selection of one particular rational ground rather than another.[105] Thus, even if we suppose Nietzsche to have achieved a level of proto-psychoanalytic insight into the psychological hinterland of metaphysical and moral belief, it remains unexplained how this is to be converted into philosophical critique: such insight might suffice to occasion doubt, but it would not deliver the categorical negative claims which Nietzsche is generally taken to be making.

For these reasons, the naturalistic reading of Nietzsche appears to make his critique of traditional philosophy much less powerful than it is widely regarded as being. In Kant's terms, it leaves him in the position of a dogmatic naturalist – one who poses no more of a threat to reason than Hume, whose challenge the Kantian system has already successfully assimilated. Similarly, it is hard to see how a Nietzsche grounded in naturalistic psychology could be thought to have much leverage against Schopenhauer.

But if the basis of Nietzsche's critique of metaphysics and morality is not provided by naturalism, what then does it consist of? One suggestion is to see it as involving a partial return to the tradition of transcendental philosophy. Nietzsche may be viewed as pursuing the programme which begins with Kant's *Critique of Practical Reason*, and is taken much further by Fichte, whereby theoretical knowledge is evaluated from the perspective of practical consciousness. Nietzsche adds the crucial and decisive twist that practical, value-demanding consciousness is dissociated from moral consciousness. For the consciousness of duty which comprises the 'sole fact of reason' for Kant, and provides the fulcrum of Fichte's system, Nietzsche substitutes a negative fact, namely, consciousness of decadence and impending nihilism. What Kant and Fichte call the 'perspective of practical reason' thus becomes in Nietzsche a perspective from which motivational disquisitions are to be mounted, and what they call the 'interest of practical reason' is retitled by him life, in the name of which morality is criticised.

The concept of the unconscious as it figures in Nietzsche may then be understood as a kind of repository for the motives that his critique discovers in our values and beliefs – his interpretation of these being grounded in, and guided by, the unconditional demand that value be recovered. So conceived, the unconscious becomes once again fundamentally independent of naturalism, since its content is now supplied by hermeneutically extrapolated conditions of possibility of values rather than putative psychological facts. At the same time, Nietzsche's espousal of naturalism is intelligibly related to his philosophical goals: the announcement of a return to nature serves to express the discovery that the non-natural metaphysics of Kant and Fichte serve a value which is inimical to our true practical interest. Naturalism in Nietzsche may thus be regarded as in part a rhetorical matter[106] and in part a methodological principle, a maxim adopted in a regulative spirit to direct the interpretation of moral and metaphysical ideas.

There is no guarantee that Nietzsche's philosophy will, on this transcendental interpretation, prove ultimately persuasive, but it at least avoids stumbling at the first hurdle: it allows Nietzsche to appeal to the general case for taking the transcendental turn in philosophy in launching his project, and to ground it not on any claim about psychological reality but on the demands for value which appear in the self-reflection of the subject.[107] On this interpretation, Nietzsche appropriates the central idea of Schopenhauer's metaphysics, the doctrine of will in its many aspects, but relocates it in a transcendental context – as it were, doing to Schopenhauer, in reverse, exactly what Schopenhauer did to Kant.

If this is right, then there is a difference in philosophical status between Nietzsche's and Freud's concepts of the unconscious.[108] This does not, of itself, imply that there is no agreement between them regarding the *content* of human motivation, and at this level there are numerous analogies to be found – between Nietzschean bad conscience and Freudian repression, and so on. But even here, agreement ultimately gives way to disagreement in just the way that the transcendental account of Nietzsche would predict. To take a key example, the motive that is ultimately revealed to lie at the bottom of what Nietzsche calls the 'ascetic ideal' is the demand for suffering to have a *meaning*[109] – a motive of a non-naturalistic kind that has no analogue or place in psychoanalytic theory but is firmly attached to the concerns of transcendental philosophy. It is worth adding that although Nietzsche talks in general terms of tracing ideas back to the body, the explanations which are important for him, and which impress us, tend not to be couched in naturalistic terms at all.[110]

This bears out the conclusion of the previous section: that the concurrence of Schopenhauer with Freud has the depth that it does, not despite but *because of* Schopenhauer's metaphysics: in Schopenhauer's naturalistic metaphysics, as in Freud's scientific naturalism, the concept of the unconscious has a realistic justification, in comparison with the transcendental role which it plays in absolute idealism and in Nietzsche.[111]

VII   SCHOPENHAUER'S IRRATIONALISATION OF EXISTENCE

Underlying the similarity between Schopenhauer's and the psychoanalytic conception of the mind is another, more diffuse but no less important respect in which a path runs from Schopenhauer to Freud.

This concerns the background conditions of psychoanalysis, the general outlook that makes its conception of human beings possible.

Freud holds that the motivating forces of human action at the bottom level do not consist in and cannot be translated into rational purposes, ends which an agent qua rational could set himself; psychoanalytic interpretations are grounded on the notion that desire – conceptualised as *Trieb*: wish, phantasy and so on – enjoys a fundamental autonomy, in terms of its content and efficacy, in relation to our cognitive powers. The forces motivating human agents, according to Freud, cannot be represented by the agents whose projects they determine *as* reasons for action, and so do not allow themselves to be incorporated into the reflexive, internal representation of subjects as self-determining (the self-representation analysed and defended by Kant). Our agency cannot therefore be fully expressed in the language of rational purposes.

Now we tend to think of this as a *result* of psychoanalysis because it was Freud who made the idea empirically determinate in a way that it had not previously been. But it is highly plausible to hold that the true relation, both historically and conceptually, is the reverse. In order for psychoanalytic interpretations to so much as make sense, a good deal must already be in place. Specifically, it is necessary to have abandoned the expectation – encouraged, if not engendered, by the Enlightenment – of discovering uniquely rational structures in the mind. And in order for this change in psychological outlook to take place, a broader shift of perspective is needed: a change in the psychological domain of this radical sort presupposes a new image of reality as a whole, a reconception of the world to which psychological processes belong.

This transformation is the product of several trends in post-Enlightenment culture, but Schopenhauer provided it with its clearest and most trenchant articulation. Georg Simmel captures the point by talking of the 'demotion of the rational character of life [*Vernichtung des Vernunftcharakters des Lebens*]' effected by Schopenhauer.[112] Freud never acknowledged this broad shift of perspective as a presupposition of psychoanalysis, and it is so deeply embedded in the mood of late modernity as not to appear as such. It is nevertheless indispensable for anything like Freud's view of human beings. The importance of Schopenhauer in the pre-history of psychoanalysis consists not so much, or not only, in his having fashioned a prototype of the Freudian unconscious, but in his having, through a metaphysical redescription of existence as such, cast human beings in a light which allows the sorts of explanation offered by psychoanalysis to enter human self-reflection.

In conclusion, the following observations on the historical and contemporary significance of Schopenhauer may be made. Schopenhauer's philosophy occupies a singular, Janus-like position in the history of thought. It stands at the junction of two originally united strands of the Enlightenment at the point of their final separation: rationalist humanism and scientific naturalism.[113] In addition, it communicates the one to the other and provides each with an inverted image of itself. The spirit of rationalist humanism which received expression in Kant's philosophy, and which the transcendental tradition took radical measures to attempt to preserve, is confronted by Schopenhauer with the naturalistic image of the world but expressed in its own language, the language of metaphysics – in such a way that rationalist humanism is forced to view itself as (to borrow Schopenhauer's description of Hegel) bad Christianity.[114] On the other side, scientific naturalism beholds itself in Schopenhauer recast in the metaphysical terms that it repudiates, as if in caricature.

At the centre of Schopenhauer's philosophy, viewed in this light, stands his conception of the unconscious. It provides, on account of its double, natural–metaphysical character, the primary point at which Enlightenment rationalism registers the impact of naturalism.[115] The recognition that the ultimate ground of our motivation has a surd, non-rational character is the reflective equivalent of the immediate awareness, to which Schopenhauer drew attention, of ourselves as bodily will: in both cases, we overstep the bounds of Kantian subjectivity.

Schopenhauer attempted to lead us, by means of a philosophical argument, from immediate self-awareness as bodily will to a metaphysical theory, and thence to a reconception of our psychology. At the present time, however, it is perhaps fair to say, we subscribe so unhesitatingly (whether or not consistently) to naturalism that Schopenhauer's metaphysical detour is no longer needed to convince us of the fundamentally non-rational character of our motivation. Schopenhauer's argumentative route from immediate self-relation as bodily will to a reflective self-relation which incorporates the unconscious – the self-relation theorised in psychoanalysis – has become unnecessary because the disposition to conceive ourselves explicitly in Kantian terms has grown weaker. The conversion of our culture to naturalism is the reason why Freud, when he offered justifications for the hypothesis of the unconscious, saw the need to dispute the identification of the mental with consciousness, but not to engage with Kantian conceptions of the human subject. Schopenhauer thus contributed to a development which resulted in his own metaphysics being left behind.

Contemporary naturalism understands itself as independent of any metaphysics, and is bound to regard the vision of the world in Schopenhauer's metaphysics as, at best, a mythological expression of the truth contained in the naturalistic conception of the world. Should it transpire, however, that there is a dimension of our self-representation which cannot be reconstructed in naturalistic terms, then naturalism would have to acknowledge that there is, after all, an angle from which the world does indeed appear to be just as Schopenhauer describes it. According to the tradition of thought represented by Kant, the dimension in which naturalistic self-representation is impossible is that of value. And this view is accepted by Schopenhauer and Nietzsche, for both regard the question of the meaning of existence as one that transcends all natural conception.[116] If so, then naturalism, while denying that Schopenhauer's metaphysics offers a true description of reality, is obliged to grant it a kind of relative truth: it must allow that Schopenhauer's philosophy gives a true description of how the world looks when viewed from the perspective of value. As it might be put, from the point of view of value, naturalism is equivalent to the doctrine that the world is Will; even if naturalism, as a theoretical philosophy, is not metaphysical, it brings with it a metaphysical representation. This, it would seem, is how Nietzsche, in accepting the task of transcendental philosophy but rejecting its defence of value, experienced his Schopenhauerian legacy. Unless contemporary naturalism can do better with the problem of value than Nietzsche believed it could, Schopenhauer's metaphysics are as much a problem for it as they were for Nietzsche.[117]

NOTES

1 Two classic studies of this sort are L. L. Whyte, *The Unconscious Before Freud* (London: Friedman, 1979), and Henri Ellenberger, *The Discovery of the Unconscious: The History and Evolution of Dynamic Psychiatry*

(New York: Basic Books, 1970). A more recent work that offers, in place of historical study, a highly original philosophical account of the development of the concept of the unconscious in the modern period is Michel Henry, *The Genealogy of Psychoanalysis*, trans. Douglas Brick (Stanford, Calif.: Stanford University Press, 1993); chapters 5 and 6 are devoted to Schopenhauer. I attempt to summarise the distinguishing features of the Freudian unconscious in 'The unconscious', in *The Cambridge Companion to Freud*, ed. Jerome Neu (Cambridge: Cambridge University Press, 1991), 136–60.

2 Schopenhauer's doctrine of the fixity of character precludes an account of formative development; see *W2* 233–7/H. 3, 263–7.

3 In *W2* chapters 14, 15, 19, 22, 32, 42, and 44. The similarities between Schopenhauer and Freud are surveyed in R. K. Gupta, 'Freud and Schopenhauer', in *Schopenhauer: His Philosophical Achievement*, ed. Michael Fox (Sussex: Harvester, 1980), 226–35, and are more comprehensively documented in Christopher Young and Andrew Brook, 'Schopenhauer and Freud', *International Journal of Psychoanalysis* 75 (1994), 101–18, and Paul-Laurent Assoun, *Freud: la philosophie et les philosophes* (Paris: Presses Universitaires de France, 1976), pt. II, whose account is the most penetrating. See also W. Bischler, 'Schopenhauer and Freud: a comparison', *Psychoanalytic Quarterly* 8 (1939), 88–97; Nancy Proctor-Gregg, 'Schopenhauer and Freud', *Psychoanalytic Quarterly* 25 (1956), 197–214, an imaginary encounter between Schopenhauer and Freud in the Hereafter; Ernst Cassirer, *The Myth of the State* (Oxford: Oxford University Press, 1946), 31–2; and Thomas Mann, 'Freud and the future', in *Essays of Three Decades*, trans. H. T. Lowe-Porter (London: Secker & Warburg, 1947), 411–28.

4 *W1* 135–40, 238–9/H. 3, 148–53; 269–70. *FW* 22/H. 4, 22: 'the self-consciousness is a very limited part of our entire consciousness. While inwardly obscure, our consciousness is oriented, with all its objective powers, entirely outward. ... Thus it is there, on the *outside*: great clarity and illumination spread themselves before the gaze of consciousness. But on the inside it is dark like a thoroughly blackened telescope.' Schopenhauer's imagery strongly recalls Freud's discussion of the 'gaps' in consciousness which force us to adduce an underlying psychic reality: *Standard Edition of the Complete Works of Sigmund Freud*, trans. under the general editorship of James Strachey, in collaboration with Anna Freud, assisted by Alix Strachey and Alan Tyson (London: Hogarth Press, 1953–74), vol. 14, 166–7.

5 *W2* 140 /H. 3, 153.

6 *W2*, ch. 22. 'Knowledge is, so to speak, the sounding-board of the will, and consciousness is the tone produced thereby' (*WN* 75/H. 4, 68).

7 *W2* 287/H. 3, 326.

8 *W2* 201–2, 277/H. 3, 224–6, 313. This allows Schopenhauer to give a highly Freudian picture of neonatal mental life (*W2* 234–5/H. 3, 264–5). The conceptual possibility of unconscious purposiveness is affirmed by Schopenhauer in the context of his general discussion of organic nature: 'the final cause is a motive that acts on a being by whom it is not known', (*W2* 332/H. 3, 378); see also *W1* 114–17; *W2* 203–7; *WN*, 26–46/H. 2, 135–40; H. 3, 227–32; H. 4, 9–33.

9 On the primacy of the will and its ramifications, see *W1* 150, 292–3;*W2*, 201–44, 273–4; *WN* 78–81; *P2* 67–70/H. 2, 178–9, 344–6; H. 3, 224–76, 308–10; H. 4, 71–5; H. 6, 70–4. Maurice Mandelbaum, in *History, Man and Reason: A Study in Nineteenth-Century Thought* (Baltimore: Johns Hopkins University Press, 1971), 320ff., observes that Schopenhauer's view of the relation of the will to the intellect nevertheless grants a high degree of autonomy to the latter. In this respect, too, he and Freud are in agreement. The notion that the intellect is subject to the will (in a manner distinct from the purely rational sense affirmed by Descartes in his Fourth Meditation) goes back to the Counter-Enlightenment: see Frederick Beiser, *The Fate of Reason: German Philosophy from Kant to Fichte* (Cambridge, Mass.: Harvard University Press, 1987), 9–10, 85–9, with respect to Hamann, Herder, and Jacobi; and James O'Flaherty, *The Quarrel of Reason with Itself: Essays on Hamann, Michaelis, Lessing, Nietzsche* (Columbia, S.C.: Camden House, 1988), ch. 2, on Hamann. O'Flaherty attributes to Hamann (104–5) aconception of the dynamic unconscious, but with heavy qualification.

10 *W2* 141, 215, 373/H. 3, 151, 241, 426–7.

11 *W2* 400/H. 3, 457–8.

12 *W2* 209–10/H. 3, 233–6, where several examples are given. See also *W1* 296; *FW* 50/H. 2, 349–50; H. 4, 48–9. In *BM*, §§13–14, Schopenhauer accepts skepticism about self-attributed moral motivation and the ubiquity of egoistic motivation; at *BM* 137–8/H. 4, 202 he writes, 'we are sometimes just as much in error about the true motives of our own actions as we are over those of others'.

13 *W2* 208/H. 3, 233. The need for self-esteem is attributed with a capacity for strategic rationality (*W2* 210/H. 3, 235), paralleling Freud's account of the protective operations of the preconscious.

14 *W2* 216/H. 3, 243. See also *W1* 187/H. 2, 220 on imaginationas wish fulfilling.

15 *W1* 192–3 /H. 2, 226–8; and *W2* , ch. 32.

16 *W2* 401/H. 3, 458.

17 *W1* 192/H. 2, 226–7.

18 *W2* 401/H. 3, 458.

19 *W2* 513–14/H. 3, 588–9.

20 *W2* ch. 44.

21 See *BM* 146/H. 4 , 210–11 and Freud, op. cit., vol. 18, 7–9.

22 See *BM* 127/H. 4, 192 and Freud, op. cit., vol. 19, 51–6.

23 *P1* 229–51/H. 5, 244–67.

24 Philip Rieff, *The Mind of the Moralist* (Chicago: University of Chicago Press, 1979), 3rd edn., 295–9.

25 op. cit., 418.

26 Assoun identifies Schopenhauer as the 'centre idéologique' of Freud's thought, op. cit., 137. David Hamlyn – in *Schopenhauer* (London: Routledge, 1980), 87–8 and in 'Schopenhauer on action and the will,' in *Idealism Past and Present*, ed. Godfrey Vesey (Cambridge: Cambridge University Press, 1982), 132 – suggests that Schopenhauer does not anticipate Freud's theory of the unconcious because, for Schopenhauer, consciousness and motives are 'essentially interwined'. But even if Schopenhauer is bound to endorse a necessary connection between consciousness and motives of the sort that agents can take as reasons for action, it does not follow that he must hold the same of motives which do not fit that description; and these, it may be argued, are the very sorts of motives which comprise the Freudian unconscious. Assuming motives to be representations, a commitment to the existence of unconscious representations would then follow. The following section defends this construal of Schopenhauer.

27 See Freud, op. cit., vol. 14, 15 (regarding insanity and repression); vol. 17, 143–4 (regarding the instinctual unconscious); vol. 18, 49–50, and vol. 22, 107 (regarding the death instinct); and vol. 20, 59–60 (regarding the emotions, sexuality and repression). In vol. 7, 134, and vol. 19, 218, Freud appeals to Schopenhauer for corroboration of his views on sexuality; similarly in vol. 13, 87, regarding the importance of death in neurotic-obsessive thought.

28 Hartmann's *Philosophy of the Unconscious: Speculative Results According to the Inductive Method of Physical Science*, trans. William Coupland (London: Kegan Paul, 1931), first published in 1869, was known to Freud, who refers to it in *The Interpretation of Dreams* (op. cit., vol. 4, 134, and vol. 5, 528). It is fair to say that Hartmann's contribution consisted in the scale and systematicity of his presentation of the topic; his attempts to fuse Schopenhauer with other metaphysical systems, and his endeavour to relate the unconscious to epistemology, wherein his claim to originality lies (as he stresses in his preface to the eighth edition), are without lasting philosophical import. The predictable effect of Hartmann's extraordinary syncretism is to render the concept of the unconscious nebulous and elusive in a way that it is not in Schopenhauer himself.

29 If Freud is to be assigned a formative philosophical hero, the evidence points to Feuerbach, whom he refers to in a letter of 7 March 1875 as 'one

whom I revere and admire above all other philosophers' (*The Letters of Sigmund Freud to Eduard Silberstein 1871–1881*, ed. Walter Boehlich, trans. Arnold Pomerans [Cambridge, Mass.: Harvard University Press, 1990], 96).

30 *FW* 21/H. 4, 21.

31 *Ucs.* and id are not the same, but in the present context the difference is unimportant.

32 Furthermore, the identification would generate an absurdity on Schopenhauer's side, for we would then need to credit world-will with representations in order to explain repression, as noted by Henry, op. cit., 188: 'how can will want to repress the importunate representation when will doesn't represent anything, when it doesn't know anything about representation?'

33 Freud denies, for example, that one can disavow moral responsibility for the contents of one's dreams: op. cit., vol. 5, 620, and vol. 19, 133. The comparison of the unconscious with Schopenhauer's world-will makes rather more sense in the case of Jung, who advocates a picture of human individuality as shading off into an impersonal reality. There is also a similarity between Jung's theory of archetypes and Schopenhauer's theory of Platonic ideas. References to Schopenhauer are frequent in Jung's writings, and Jung records him in his autobiography as a major influence: see *Memories, Dreams, Reflections*, trans. Richard and Clara Winston (London: Collins, 1961), 88–9, 309. See James Jarrett, 'Schopenhauer and Jung', *Spring: An Annual of Archetypal Psychology and Jungian Thought* (1981), 193–204, and Marilyn Nagy, *Philosophical Issues in the Psychology of C. G. Jung* (Albany: State University of New York Press, 1991), 64, 73–4, 79, 129, 144, 161–5, 231–4.

34 Thomas Mann's claim that 'Schopenhauer's sinister domain of will is entirely identical with what Freud calls the unconscious, the "id" – as, on the other hand, Schopenhauer's intellect entirely corresponds to the Freudian ego' (op. cit., 408; see also 417), is therefore incorrect. Nor does Freud's ego correspond to the intellect in Schopenhauer, since the ego encompasses both conscious and pre-conscious motivation. Freud's own statement that Schopenhauer's 'unconscious "Will"' is equivalent to the mental instincts of psychoanalysis' (op. cit., vol. 17, 143–4) is also inaccurate, since unconscious will in Schopenhauer would include the non-instinctual, merely pre-conscious.

35 *W2* 197/H. 3, 221.

36 Which is not undone by recalling that Freud characterises *Ucs.* or id in 'economic' terms – as a store of energy for the 'psychic apparatus' – because on his account all species of psychological phenomena can be so characterised.

37 For an analysis of this sort, see Brian O'Shaughnessy, *The Will: A Double Aspect Theory* (Cambridge: Cambridge University Press, 1980), vol. 2, ch. 17. O'Shaughnessy's account of the will supplies a superlative elucidation of Schopenhauer's thought; see Christopher Janaway, *Self and World in Schopenhauer's Philosophy* (Oxford: Oxford University Press, 1989), 221–9.

38 At least this is so in the context of the Kleinian development of Freud's theories, where the unconscious is understood in terms of the concept of phantasy. See Richard Wollheim, 'The bodily ego', in *Philosophical Essays on Freud*, ed. Richard Wollheim and James Hopkins (Cambridge: Cambridge University Press, 1982), 124–38.

39 *W1* 109/H. 2, 130.

40 E.g., *FW* 17/H. 4, 16–17.

41 *W1*, §21.

42 The ambiguity is noted by John Atwell in *Schopenhauer on the Character of the World: The Metaphysics of Will* (Berkeley: University of California Press, 1995), 104–5. A cognate problem, concerning whether our knowledge of ourselves as subjects of agency is for Schopenhauer direct or indirect, is raised by David Hamlyn in 'Schopenhauer on action and the will', 133. Hamlyn's solution – in terms of a distinction between knowledge *that* I am a subject of doing and knowledge of *what* I do – allows itself to be developed in the terms that I suggest later.

43 Hamlyn, op. cit., ch. 5; Young, *Willing and Unwilling: A Study in the Philosophy of Arthur Schopenhauer* (Dordrecht: Martinus Nijhoff, 1987), ch. 6.

44 See *W1* 100/H. 2 ,119, where it is denied that resolves are 'real acts of will'. Janaway, op. cit., 202, observes that in *W2* 248–9/H. 3, 280–2, Schopenhauer marks the distinction between will and intentional action terminologically by referring to the latter as *Willkür*; see also *WN* 36–8/H. 4, 21–3.

45 Nietzsche, it is noteworthy, reads Schopenhauer in just this way, accusing him of a 'basic misunderstanding' of the will, 'as if craving, instinct, drive were the *essence* of will', and contrasting this with his own conception of will in terms of command, which belongs to the sphere of intentional agency. See *The Will to Power*, trans. Walter Kaufmann and R. J. Hollingdale (New York: Vintage Books, 1968), §84.

46 To be sure, bodily willing is object directed in the sense that any voluntary bodily movement is a moving *of* some particular part of one's body in some manner, but (on an identity theory of the will like Schopenhauer's) the 'of' relation in question is at a vanishing point, for the will simply *is*, or becomes, the movement which is its 'object'. Bodily willing is thus a limiting case of object-directedness.

47 As Schopenhauer puts it, motives – reasons for action – 'set in motion' the 'individual manifestations' of will (*WN* 20/H. 4, 2–3); 'being accompanied by knowledge' is a mere 'circumstance' of the will (*W1* 105/ H. 2, 126); motives can do no more than 'alter the direction of the will's effort' (*W1* 294/H. 2, 347); 'all teleological facts can be explained from the will' (*WN* 51/H. 4, 39).

48 An excellent statement of this interpretation is in Georg Simmel, *Schopenhauer and Nietzsche*, trans. Helmut Loiskandl et. al. (Cambridge, Mass.: MIT Press, 1986), 23ff.: 'In order to understand the meaning of this will, which is reputed to be our metaphysical reality, one should not seek it in singular psychological facts of volition oriented to certain goals, but in what remains after we have separated volition from all the contents, images, and motives that make up its raiment, its phenomenal form' (23); 'Schopenhauer finds a general act of will in every act of will that is singular on account of its separate content' (26); 'I do not will by virtue of values and goals that are posited by reason, but I have goals because I will continuously and ceaselessly from the depths of my essence. Purpose is but the expression or logical organization of willed events' (30). See also Henry, op. cit., 170ff.

49 Young, for example, who does make the identification, consistently draws the conclusion that what Schopenhauer 'extends throughout nature is not just will but the rationalising mode of explanation' (op. cit., 71) – which obliges him to attribute to Schopenhauer an obvious confusion regarding the sense in which the will can be blind (72). Atwell, op. cit., 105, comments on the absurdity of holding that my own involuntary movements and those of all non-rational beings are in virtue of the exercise of practical reason. He sees, however, no alternative to the view that will consists in intentional action on the grounds that 'it is the only thing of which I am immediately conscious' and literally know – which is where my view departs from his.

50 Raising the question of which side of the will–representation divide motives fall on, see Janaway, op. cit., 213ff.

51 Op. cit., vol. 1, l–lii. Simmel speaks of the 'transpsychological being' of will, op. cit., 34.

52 Some will object that they find nothing remaining after the initial abstraction. To this Schopenhauer may simply reply that *something* must be left over, for if there is not, then the concept of will just is the concept *of* a psychological role, and while this (functionalist) position may be consistent, Schopenhauer, given his broadly Cartesian orientation, has no reason for paying it any attention.

53 *W1* 18, 100, 101; *W2* 202; *FW* 11/H. 2, 21–2, 119–20, 120–1; H. 3, 255–6; H. 4, 11.

54 *W1* 108, 330; *W2* 514, 571/H. 2, 129–30, 389–90; H. 3, 588–9, 655.

55 The immanence of will in a phenomenon is to be distinguished from its 'visibility', which is an epistemological matter, and from its (degree of) objectification, which is what determines the phenomenon's kind.

56 E.g., *WN* 87/H. 4, 83: 'let us carefully observe the violent fall of a stream over masses of rock, and ask ourselves whether so decided an effort, such raging, can occur without an exertion of strength, and whether any exertion is conceivable without will'. For further good examples, see the chapter 'Physiology of plants'.

57 I discuss the nature and extent of this conceptual feature in *Irrationality and the Philosophy of Psychoanalysis* (Cambridge: Cambridge University Press, 1993).

58 E.g., *W2* 196–7/H. 3, 219–20, where Schopenhauer qualifies the simplicity of the self, but only in terms of the distinction of intellect and will. Schopenhauer's sustained contrast of 'the will' with 'the intellect' in *W2*, ch. 19, comes closer to the idea of psychological partition, but there is no sign of its being intended to amount to more than a contrast.

59 Claimed in Gupta, op. cit., 231. Schopenhauer's descriptions of his own mental life recall strongly Freud's descriptions of obsessional neurosis: see the extract from his journal quoted in Rüdiger Safranski, *Schopenhauer and the Wild Years of Philosophy*, trans. Ewald Osers (London: Weidenfeld, 1989), 286.

60 The earliest explicit appearances of the concept of the unconscious in Western philosophy belong mainly to mystical and theological contexts, such as Plotinus. In the modern period, Leibniz makes important use of the concept in his account of *petites perceptions*: see *New Essays on Human Understanding*, trans. Peter Remnant and Jonathan Bennett (Cambridge: Cambridge University Press, 1981), 53–6, 164–7. In *Philosophy and the Good Life: Reason, the Passions and Human Happiness in Greek, Cartesian and Psychoanalytic Ethics* (Cambridge: Cambridge University Press, 1998), ch. 2, sect. 5, John Cottingham shows that Descartes admitted a kind of unconscious, contrary to what is universally believed, in the context of the passions, but it is not a supporting element of his epistemology and metaphysics. On the unconscious before 1800, see the references in Whyte, op. cit., chs. 5 and 6.

61 It is necessarily the case, on Kant's account, that transcendental synthesis cannot be accompanied by the 'I think' because transcendental synthesis is precisely what is supposed to make the I-thinkability of representations possible. This is essential for the argument of the Deduction. If we could have consciousness of our transcendental syntheses, then we would have consciousness of our selves independently of and prior to our synthetic activity, contrary to the order of explanation

affirmed in the Deduction. Furthermore, we would then also have consciousness of the material which is subjected to synthesis, raw sensory data, and Kant would then be committed to the axiom of empiricism which it is the Deduction's aim to destroy.

62 For a clear reconstruction of such a line of thought, whereby one arrives at a 'théorie de l' *inconscience de la conscience transcendentale'*, see Pierre Lachièze-Rey, *L'idéalisme kantien* (Paris: Vrin, 1950), 432–50. Lachièze-Rey argues that this position is incoherent, but that it can be avoided by grasping that the empirical self is a phenomenal construction, a mere reference point. Hartmann, op. cit., pt. I, 21–2, 325, affirms the unconscious status of the Kantian a priori in general, speaking of the 'unconscious category' and 'the unconscious production of Space'.

63 Affirming the unconsciousness of transcendental synthesis, see Norman Kemp Smith, *A Commentary to Kant's 'Critique of Pure Reason'*, 2nd edn. (London: Macmillan, 1923), xliii–v, 263–7, 272–9, 295–7; compare H. J. Paton, *Kant's Metaphysics of Experience: A Commentary on the First Half of the 'Kritik der reinen Vernunft'*, 2 vols. (London: Allen & Unwin, 1936), vol. 1, 572–9, and vol. 2, 393–4, 422.

64 *Critique of Pure Reason*, trans. Norman Kemp Smith (2nd edn., London: Macmillan, 1933), A 98–104, B 151–2.

65 See Dieter Henrich, 'The unity of the subject', in *The Unity of Reason: Essays on Kant's Philosophy* (Cambridge, Mass.: Harvard University Press, 1994), 17–54.

66 Letter to Marcus Herz, 26 May 1789, in Kant, *Philosophical Correspondence, 1759–99*, ed. and trans. Arnold Zweig (Chicago: University of Chicago Press, 1967), 153–4. See also *Critique of Pure Reason*, A 89–91/B 122–3, A 112/B 131–2, A 320/B 376. In pt. I, §5 of his *Anthropology from a Pragmatic Point of View*, trans. Mary Gregor (The Hague: Nijhoff, 1974), entitled 'Of the ideas which we have without being conscious of them', Kant sounds much like Leibniz, tending to treat the unconsciousness of an idea as a function of its lack of clarity; he writes, 'the field of *obscure* ideas is the largest in man. But ... this field shows us only the passive side of man, as the plaything of sensations' (17), whence its philosophical unimportance for Kant.

67 It is an issue distinct from anything discussed here, whether other sorts of parallels between Kant and Freud may be drawn; for some interesting suggestions as to how the method of psychoanalysis may be understood in Kantian terms, see Theodor W. Adorno, 'Der Begriff des Unbewußten in der transzendentalen Seelenlehre', in *Gesammelte Schriften*, Bd. I, *Philosophische Frühschriften*, ed. Rolf Tiedemann (Frankfurt: Suhrkamp, 1973), 224–302.

68 See, e.g., Dieter Henrich, 'Self-consciousness, a critical introduction to a theory', *Man and World: An International Philosophical Review* 4 (1971), 3–28, 24. And Fichte himself: 'The highest within me, independently of consciousness and the immediate object of consciousness, is the impulse. The impulse is the highest representation of the intelligence in nature. Hence, the impulse is the immediate *feelable* (substance or element of feeling,) but on no account feeling itself, since feeling is already a consciousness', in *The Science of Rights*, trans. A. E. Kroeger (Philadelphia: Lippincott, 1869), 497. The earliest instance of the tendency of post-Kantian idealism towards a conception of the unconscious is provided by Solomon Maimon, a contemporary of Kant. Maimon's criticisms of transcendental idealism led him to introduce the notion of an infinite reason or infinite mind, of which human minds are but schemata, and on which their power of cognition depends; and to postulate 'infinitesimals of sensation', differential elements of perceptual cognition (akin to Leibniz's *petites perceptions*) which belong to the subject qua passive, prior to the synthetic activity which delivers consciousness of objects. Maimon's *Versuch über die Transcendentalphilosophie, mit einem Anhang über die symbolische Erkenntnis und Anmerkungen* (Berlin: Voß & Sohn, 1790), *Gesammelte Werke*, ed. Valerio Verra, vol. II (Hildesheim: George Olms, 1965), may be regarded as having made the first moves in transforming Kantian into absolute idealism. See Samuel Atlas, *From Critical to Speculative Idealism: The Philosophy of Solomon Maimon* (The Hague: Martinus Nijhoff, 1964), chs. 5, 6.

69 *System of Transcendental Idealism*, trans. Peter Heath, intro. Michael Vater (Charlottesville: University Press of Virginia, 1993), 58–9, 75–9, 203–36.

70 See Schelling, *On the History of Modern Philosophy*, trans. Andrew Bowie (Cambridge: Cambridge University Press, 1994), 109–10.

71 See Schelling, *Ideas for a Philosophy of Nature*, trans. Errol E. Harris and Peter Heath (Cambridge: Cambridge University Press, 1988), Introduction and Supplement.

72 On the unconscious in Schelling, see Michael Vater's introduction to Schelling's *System*, xxvii–xxxii, Andrew Bowie, *Schelling and Modern European Philosophy* (London: Routledge, 1993), ch. 3, and Dale Snow, *Schelling and the End of Idealism* (Albany: State University of New York Press), 110–40. Bowie (96) and Snow (121, 129) refer to Schelling as a precursor of Freud. This may be contested, however, since Schelling's admission of 'irrational' unconscious elements has to do with there being ultimately surd or brute factors in philosophical analysis, and has no relation to the content or character of human motivation. In

his essay on freedom of 1809, Schelling reconceives the unconscious in relation to 'will' and makes statements that recall Schopenhauer: 'In the final and highest instance there is no other Being than Will. Will is primordial Being', *Philosophical Inquiries into the Nature of Human Freedom*, trans. James Guttman (La Salle, Illinois: Open Court Press, 1986), 24. Christopher Janaway has drawn my attention to the evidence of Schopenhauer's acquaintance with this work in his Student Notebooks, *MR* 2, 353–5/Hn. 2, 314–15. But Schelling's will retains a much closer connection with the will of practical reason in Kant and Fichte than with Schopenhauer's will: it is 'a will of the understanding', the origin of 'primal reason' (34–7). Recognising the rationalism of the absolute idealists' concept of will, Hannah Arendt excludes them from the history she gives of the ascent of volitionism in modern philosophy: see *The Life of the Mind*, vol. 2, *Willing* (London: Secker & Warburg, 1978), ch. 13.

73 See Hegel's early *Faith and Knowledge*, trans. Walter Cerf and H. S. Harris (Albany: State University of New York Press, 1977), 71–2.

74 On occasion, Hegel uses the term 'unconscious' to describe areas of subjectivity, e.g., in the chapter of the *Phenomenology* dealing with the development of ethical consciousness: 'In this way there arises in consciousness the antithesis of the known and the unknown, just as in [ethical] substance there was an antithesis of the conscious and the unconscious', *Phenomenology of Spirit*, trans. A. V. Miller (Oxford: Oxford University Press, 1977), §467.

75 *Philosophy of Mind*, trans. A. V. Miller (Oxford: Clarendon Press, 1971), §§403–8. I am grateful to David Snelling for drawing my attention to this material.

76 Ibid., 122–4.

77 On Hegel's theory of mental disorder and its similarities with Freud, see Darrel Christensen, 'Hegel's phenomenological analysis and Freud's psychoanalysis', *International Philosophical Quarterly* 8 (1968), 356–78, and 'The theory of mental derangement and the role and function of subjectivity in Hegel', *Personalist* 49 (1968), 433–52. Jean Hyppolite, 'Hegel's phenomenology and psychoanalysis', in *New Studies in Hegel's Philosophy*, ed. Warren Steinkraus (New York: Holt, 1971), 57–70, takes a psychoanalytic approach to Hegel, mediated by Lacan, which, in my view, wrongly assimilates the transcendental to the Freudian unconscious. Daniel Berthold-Bond, in *Hegel's Theory of Madness* (Albany: State University of New York Press, 1995), ch. 5, also regards Hegel as very close to Freud. A much more cautious relating of Freud to Hegel is presented in Paul Ricœur, *Freud and Philosophy: An Essay on Interpretation*, trans. Denis Savage (New Haven: Yale University Press,

1970), 459–83; Ricœur stops with the claim that there are 'relations of homology' (461) between them.

78 The definition that follows is by intention a narrow one. The reasons for this, which concern the more specific topic of this essay, will become clear.

79 Characterisations of transcendental philosophy may be found in Henry Allison, *Kant's Transcendental Idealism: An Interpretation and Defense* (New Haven: Yale University Press, 1983), chs. 1, 2; Robert Pippin, *Kant's Theory of Form: An Essay on the 'Critique of Pure Reason'* (New Haven: Yale University Press, 1982), chs. 1, 8, and Pippin, *Hegel's Idealism: The Satisfactions of Self-Consciousness* (Cambridge: Cambridge University Press, 1989), pts. I, II; Klaus Hartmann, 'On taking the transcendental turn', *Review of Metaphysics* 20 (1966), 223–49; and Dieter Henrich's writings, e.g., *Selbstverhältnisse: Gedanken und Auslegungen zu den Grundlagen der klassischen deutschen Philosophie* (Stuttgart: Reklam, 1982) and 'The identity of the subject in the transcendental deduction', in Eva Schaper and Wilhelm Vossenkuhl, eds., *Reading Kant: New Perspectives on Transcendental Arguments and Critical Philosophy* (Oxford: Blackwell, 1989), 250–80.

80 As Hamlyn observes, op. cit., 51; see Schopenhauer's comments on skepticism in *W1* §5, and Janaway, op. cit., 167–9.

81 E.g., *W1* 8, 17–18/H. 2, 9, 20–2, which refers to 'the *long* dream (life)'.

82 *W1* 104/H. 2, 124. Also relevant is the sympathy that Schopenhauer occasionally shows for mysticism: see *P2* 9–10 and *W2* 184–6/H. 3, 204–8. For Kant – who regards things in themselves as having at least conceptual form – any admission of the possibility of mystical knowledge implies a profound skepticism, destroying the value of the controlled restrictions on knowledge imposed by Critical philosophy.

83 See *W2*, chs. 20, 23–4, 26, and 28 and *WN* passim. Realism is flagged in Schopenhauer's very definition of metaphysics (*W2* 164/H. 3, 180): immediately after describing metaphysics as 'so-called knowledge that goes beyond the possibility of experience . . . information about that by which . . . experience or nature is conditioned' – which allows itself to be read as consistent with the Kantian conception of metaphysics – Schopenhauer adds: 'that which is hidden behind nature, and renders nature possible'. This realist conception is essential for the possibility of a posteriori metaphysics that Schopenhauer upholds against Kant.

84 See *W2* 170–1, *W2* 182–5, *W1* 427–8/H. 3, 187–90, 202–6; H. 2, 505–6 and Kant, *Critique of Pure Reason*, A vii–xiii, B xiv–vi. In *WN* 77–9/ H. 4, 70–3, Schopenhauer affirms that his standpoint is 'essentially foreign' to that of the *Critique of Pure Reason* because he considers our cognition 'not, as is usual, from within, but realistically from a standpoint outside itself, as something foreign'; his own path he describes as

'realistic-objective, viz., starting from the objective world as that which is given'; Schopenhauer claims to gain for Kant's discoveries 'the objective point of view', making 'its whole meaning plain'. See also *W2*, ch. 22, on the 'objective view of the intellect', a notion precluded by Kant's transcendental programme.

85 *W2*, ch. 18.

86 An interpretation defended by Young, op. cit, ch. 3. His and other interpretations are examined in Moira Nicholls, 'The Kantian inheritance and Schopenhauer's doctrine of will', *Kant-Studien* 85 (1994), 257–79, and in Atwell, op. cit., ch. 5.

87 *W2* 183/H. 3, 203–4.

88 See *Critique of Pure Reason*, B xvi.

89 See Dale Snow and James Snow, 'Was Schopenhauer an idealist?', *Journal of the History of Philosophy* 29 (1991), 633–55, esp. 642–5. Recognising that the concept of the thing in itself changes between Kant and Schopenhauer, consequent upon the change of philosophical method, throws light on other issues. First, it dissolves the worry that Schopenhauer fails to give a basic justification for supposing that things in themselves exist at all (see Hamlyn, op. cit., ch. 5): this may be answered by saying that their existence is implied by his conception of philosophical explanation. Second, it accounts for the uncertainty (referred to in note 86) as to whether Schopenhauer genuinely intends an outright identification of things in themselves with will: the identification is intended, but only in so far as 'things in themselves' carries a new, non-Kantian meaning.

90 *FW*, ch. 2 and 42–3; *W2* 205–6/H. 4, 41–2; H. 3, 228–30. It is important not to be misled by the fact that Schopenhauer moves from knowledge of oneself as will to knowledge of the world as will: self-consciousness is, trivially, a condition of first-person knowledge of will, but it is not part of the intrinsic nature of will; what Schopenhauer appeals to in his explanation of the world is something given *in* the first-person perspective, and not the perspective itself.

91 He regards it as not in need of, and as incapable of, receiving proof: see *FR* §14, §16. See Hamlyn, op. cit., 12, 24–5, 50–1.

92 *Critique of Pure Reason*, A 782–94/B 810–22.

93 *W1* 31/H. 2, 37.

94 Letter to Marcus Herz, 21 February 1772, in Kant, *Philosophical Correspondence*.

95 *FW* 30–3; *WN* 36–8, 76ff/H. 4, 29–32; H. 4, 21–3, 70. At *WN* 88ff. H. 4, 84 it is denied that the contrast between self-determination and heteronomy is fundamental. '[M]otivation is causality seen from within' (*FR* 214/H. 1, 145).

96 *W1* 434–5/H. 2, 514–15.

97 The same conclusion – that Schopenhauer breaks with the driving concerns of transcendental philosophy – is expressed from a different angle by Henry, who attributes to Schopenhauer 'the explicit and crucial rejection of the interpretation of being as representivity', a 'devalorization of the concept of representation . . . that is not relative but absolute' (op. cit., 130–1). Young, op. cit., 12–13, acknowledges that Schopenhauer's idealism, and his theoretical philosophy in general, are not transcendental; see also Janaway, op. cit., 141. On Schopenhauer's epistemological departure from Kant, see Mandelbaum, op. cit., 314ff. Rudolf Malter provides, in 'Schopenhauers Transzendentalismus', *Schopenhauer-Jahrbuch* 66 (1985), 29–51, an extremely sophisticated defence of the transcendental character of Schopenhauer's philosophy. However, the viability of Malter's interpretation rests ultimately, as he makes plain, on his reconstruction of Schopenhauer's doctrine of salvation. An explicit reply to his position is beyond the bounds of this essay.

98 Kant's *Open Letter on Fichte's Wissenschaftslehre*, 7 August 1799, in *Philosophical Correspondence*, 253–4, refers to Fichte's vain 'attempt to cull a real object out of logic'; Kant's criticism of Schopenhauer would presumably have been the symmetrically opposite one: that he attempts to cull a reality out of blind intuition. To claim that Schopenhauer is set apart from the current that runs from Fichte to Hegel in the way that I have suggested is not, of course, to deny that there are striking similarities between them (especially between Schopenhauer and Schelling, as regards the turn to nature and their monism; see Janaway, op. cit., 203–6). It does mean, however, that these can be misleading in so far as they disguise more fundamental differences.

99 Will 'wills itself', according to Schopenhauer, but the echo of self-consciousness in this reflexivity is as faint as possible: to put it in the characteristic language of absolute idealism, will does not *relate itself to itself* as will in the sense that the self 'relates itself to itself as a self'. Will's 'willing itself' reduces to simple will to life.

100 Later developments in the history of philosophy bear on the theme of transcendental versus realist conceptions of the unconscious. One such is Hans Vaihinger's 'positivist idealism', better known as the 'philosophy of *as if*' (*Philosophy of 'As If': A System of the Theoretical, Practical and Religious Fictions of Mankind*, trans. C. Ogden [London: Routledge, 1924], first published in 1911). Vaihinger regards intellectual constructions, including the metaphysics defended by Kant in the *Critique of Pure Reason* and his postulate of freedom, as developed in response to our practical interest qua physical, striving creatures, and as having value but wholly lacking objective reference. The organic function of

thought is described by Vaihinger as primarily unconscious (op. cit., 7, 9). The unconscious in Vaihinger is therefore, in the terms I have employed, conceived realistically, Kant being effectively subsumed in a Schopenhauerian perspective. Hartmann's philosophy of the unconscious, where Kant's philosophy is also filtered through Schopenhauer's (see note 28), again construes the unconscious realistically. The relatively slight non-historical philosophical value that we now attach to Vaihinger's and Hartmann's syncretic endeavours reflects, arguably, their failure to appreciate the depth of the separation of Schopenhauer from Kant. In *The Unconscious and Eduard von Hartmann: A Historico-Critical Monograph* (The Hague: Nijhoff, 1967), Dennis Darnoi concludes that Hartmann's attempt to reconcile idealism and materialism is 'misconceived' (167).

101 One of the earliest English-language commentators to draw attention to the connection is Walter Kaufmann: see his *Nietzsche: Philosopher, Psychologist, Antichrist* (New York: Meridian, 1956), 79, 188–9, 214. For a recent example, see Henry Staten, *Nietzsche's Voice* (Ithaca: Cornell University Press, 1990), ch. 5. Freud himself described Nietzsche, along with Schopenhauer, as 'another philosopher whose guesses and intuitions often agree in the most astonishing way with the laborious findings of psychoanalysis' (op. cit., vol. 20, 60). Lorin Anderson documents the evidence of actual influence in 'Freud, Nietzsche', *Salmagundi* 47–8 (Winter–Spring 1980), 3–29. Paul-Laurent Assoun, *Freud et Nietzsche* (Paris: Presses Universitaires de France, 1980), pt. II, provides an exhaustive comparison of the two; 169–86 focus on the concept of the unconscious.

102 See, e.g., *Beyond Good and Evil*, §230; *The Gay Science*, §§109, 294; *Twilight of the Idols*, 'Morality as anti-nature', §4; and 'Expeditions of an untimely man', §48. See Richard Schacht, *Nietzsche* (London: Routledge, 1983), ch. 5, and Schacht, *Making Sense of Nietzsche: Reflections Timely and Untimely* (Urbana: University of Illinois Press, 1995), ch. 10, on *The Gay Science* as the principal text in which Nietzsche set forth his programme of naturalisation.

103 See, e.g., *On the Genealogy of Morals*, First Essay, §13, and *Beyond Good and Evil*, §19, where Nietzsche provides an analysis, pitched against Schopenhauer, of human agency in terms of a manifold of sub-agencies. On their respective views, see Christopher Janaway, 'Nietzsche, the self, and Schopenhauer', in *Nietzsche and Modern German Thought*, ed. Keith Ansell-Pearson (London: Routledge, 1991), 119–42.

104 Excellent criticisms of Nietzsche's naturalism appear in Daniel W. Conway, 'Returning to nature: Nietzsche's *Götterdämmerung*', in *Nietzsche: A Critical Reader*, ed. Peter R. Sedgwick (Oxford: Polity

Press, 1995), 31–52. See Peter Poellner, *Nietzsche and Metaphysics* (Oxford: Clarendon Press, 1995), sect. 4.1, on the weakness of Nietzsche's naturalistic 'utility argument' against claims to knowledge, and in the same connection Maudemarie Clark, *Nietzsche on Truth and Philosophy* (Cambridge: Cambridge University Press, 1990), 121–3. Bernard Williams, in 'Nietzsche's minimalist moral psychology', *European Journal of Philosophy* 1 (1993), 4–14, acknowledges the difficulty described here, and suggests that Nietzsche may rely on an appeal to what it is realistic to suppose about human psychology, in place of a far-reaching or contentful naturalism; but it may be doubted that much of Nietzsche can be reconstructed on such a basis.

105 For an example of a psychoanalytic interpretation of a philosophical position which is advanced independently of its philosophical criticism, see Richard Wollheim, *F. H. Bradley* (Harmondsworth: Penguin Books, 1959), Epilogue.

106 Conway, op. cit., suggests, for independent reasons, that Nietzsche's naturalism ultimately falls under the description of myth-making.

107 See Gilles Deleuze, *Nietzsche and Philosophy*, trans. Hugh Tomlinson (New York: Columbia University Press, 1983), ch. 3, on the continuity of Nietzsche's conception of critique with that of Kant. Elements of a transcendental, non-naturalistic reconstruction of Nietzsche also emerge in the context of Critical Theory; see Peter Pütz, 'Nietzsche im Lichte der kritischen Theorie', *Nietzsche-Studien* 3 (1974), 175–91, and William Outhwaite, 'Nietzsche and critical theory', in Sedgwick ed., op. cit., 203–21. Jürgen Habermas, in *Knowledge and Human Interests*, trans. Jeremy Shapiro (Boston: Beacon Press, 1971), ch. 12, reads Nietzsche as proceeding from a transcendental starting point, though as ultimately led astray by naturalistic misconceptions. Paul Ricœur famously groups together Nietzsche and Freud (with Marx) as 'masters' of the 'school of suspicion' (op. cit., 32) on the basis of a Critical, non-naturalistic reading of both thinkers; see op. cit., bk. I.

108 As Assoun puts it, in Nietzsche the unconscious is a 'fonction de principe', and there is no tendency to hypostatise it (*Freud et Nietzsche*, 170–1).

109 *The Genealogy of Morals*, Third Essay, §28.

110 Schacht, *Nietzsche*, 270–2, notes how Nietzsche's talk of reduction to the bodily can only be taken as 'provisional'.

111 The conclusion that Nietzsche is less closely aligned than Schopenhauer with Freud might be challenged from the angle of Nietzsche's devaluation of consciousness: while it is true that Schopenhauer too insists on the relative inefficacy of consciousness, Nietzsche has an explanation of this fact, which Schopenhauer does not, in terms of the essential

non-unity of the self. It does not follow, however, that Freud's conception of personhood is Nietzschean, for while it is true that Nietzsche has the idea of psychological partition that, I said earlier, is missing from Schopenhauer, Nietzsche also goes much further in the direction of a quasi-Humean conception of the self, and on my account (op. cit., 201–6) Freudian psychoanalysis employs a non-Humean conception of the self. Assoun contrasts the different ways in which Nietzsche and Freud effect a 'décentrement' of the subject in *Freud et Nietzsche*, 289.

112 Op. cit., p. 30; see 27–31, 46–52.

113 See Assoun's account of Schopenhauer's role in mediating naturalism and metaphysics in the late nineteenth century, and of how this is relevant to Freud (op. cit., 206–30).

114 *W2* 444/H. 3, 507–8.

115 Michel Foucault suggests a parallel, brief but arresting account of the appearance of the concept of the unconscious in Western thought, citing Schopenhauer among others, in *The Order of Things: An Archaeology of the Human Sciences* (London: Tavistock, 1974), 326–7. His full suggestion in the chapter is that the unconscious is a necessary product of the attempt to make man an object of knowledge; also, he alleges a paradox in transcendental discourse. The paradox is doubtful, but Foucault's thesis that a notion of the unconscious is an inevitable function of the Enlightenment project of self-knowledge is independent of it.

116 Nietzsche may deny the moral meaning of the world, as Schopenhauer puts it, and believe that we must cease asking after it, but he recognises that man's need for metaphysics has still to be overcome: this need is precisely our problem, for Nietzsche, and it cannot be eliminated by a simple exercise of the will to truth which underlies our pursuit of knowledge of nature.

117 Max Horkheimer states Schopenhauer's key philosophical insight as follows: 'The highest, the most real, the metaphysical being to which philosophers had directed their view . . . . is *not* at the same time the good. Degrees of reality are not degrees of perfection' ('Schopenhauer today', in Fox ed., op. cit., 26). Clearly, this is a thought which contemporary naturalism regards as virtually a conceptual truth. According to Horkheimer, this insight makes Schopenhauer's thought 'infinitely modern' and something that we now believe 'by instinct' (op. cit., 31).

I wish to thank Christopher Janaway for extremely helpful comments on this essay.

13 Schopenhauer and Wittgenstein

Language as Representation and Will

It is common to complain that Schopenhauer has not received the recognition he deserves. At first sight, this complaint may seem unfounded. Over the past 150 years, Schopenhauer has reached a wider general public than most great philosophers. He has also influenced leading artists such as Wagner, Thomas Mann, and Proust. Finally, he has had a tremendous, if often indirect, influence on continental philosophy. His emphasis on the will and his anti-intellectualism were the driving forces behind life philosophy (*Lebensphilosophie*),[1] a movement which, through Nietzsche, influenced existentialism and post-modernism. His pessimism was appreciated by unorthodox Marxists like Horkheimer. And his discussion of the unconscious has obvious parallels with psychoanalysis, which itself has exerted a significant collateral influence on continental philosophy.

Nevertheless, the worry that Schopenhauer may be unduly neglected is not without foundation. In the current climate, professional philosophy, as opposed to cultural studies or literary theory, is increasingly dominated by analytic philosophy, even on the Continent. And Schopenhauer's influence on analytic philosophy in general has been even smaller than that of other nineteenth-century German philosophers like Hegel and Nietzsche. This is unjust, since his work features at least as many analytic arguments as theirs. Here are a few prominent examples:

1. Schopenhauer anticipated both Mill's celebrated critique of Hume, according to which invariable temporal succession does not suffice for a causal relation, and Bennett's critique of Kant's Second Analogy (*FR*, §23).[2]

422

2. Like contemporary analytic ethicists, he contends that Kant's Categorical Imperative does not provide a rational foundation for altruism (*BM*, §7).[3] It does not apply to someone who can be reasonably confident that, because of her physical and mental strength, she will never require the assistance of others.

3. Schopenhauer tackles the libertarian idea that the experience of free volition refutes determinism through the same distinction between *freedom to act* and *freedom to will* invoked by analytic philosophers of action: that I did what I wanted would only entail that I could have done otherwise if I could have *willed* to act other than I in fact did (*FW*, ch. 2).[4]

Schopenhauer's attacks on others display the combination of intelligence, aggression, and irony that analytic philosophers are so fond of. At the same time, analytic philosophers are liable to be less impressed by the constructive part of his work, since his own metaphysical system 'seems to collapse under even the gentlest analytic probing'.[5] Nor have many of them tried to separate the wheat from the chaff by extracting the important insights which are hidden within that system.

There is an important exception, however. Wittgenstein, the most influential force behind the rise of analytic philosophy, was steeped in Schopenhauer's work when he was young. According to the testimony of his pupils, Wittgenstein read Schopenhauer as a sixteen-year-old. Schopenhauer's version of transcendental idealism provided the basis for his first philosophical position, which he abandoned only under the influence of Frege's conceptual realism.[6] Wittgenstein's first philosophical writings show no trace of this influence; they are exclusively concerned with problems in the philosophy of logic and mathematics inherited from Frege and Russell. But to some extent he returned to Schopenhauer during World War I. It is probable that Wittgenstein reread Schopenhauer sometime during the war, presumably as a result of his experiences as a front-line soldier. In any event, the *Notebooks 1914–1916*, which contain preparatory material for the *Tractatus*, increasingly combine purely logical reflections with direct allusions to Schopenhauer.[7] In the *Tractatus* the allusions are less frequent and direct, but topics such as God, ethics, aesthetics, solipsism, the will, and mysticism are discussed in a Schopenhauerian spirit.

Wittgenstein explicitly refers to Schopenhauer only on occasion. And those references are not always flattering.

Schopenhauer is quite a *crude* mind, one might say. I.e. though he has refinement, this suddenly becomes exhausted at a certain level and then he is as crude as the crudest. Where real depth starts, his comes to an end. One could say of Schopenhauer: he never searches his conscience. (CV, 36)

I think I see quite clearly what Schopenhauer got out of his philosophy – but when I read Schopenhauer I seem to see to the bottom very easily. He is not deep in the sense that Kant and Berkeley are deep.[8]

On the other hand, even in the later Wittgenstein there are important allusions to Schopenhauer. Furthermore, in 1931 Wittgenstein drew up a list of influences on his thinking which comprised 'Boltzmann, Hertz, Schopenhauer, Frege, Russell, Kraus, Loos, Weininger, Spengler, Sraffa' (CV, 19).

The fact that Schopenhauer influenced Wittgenstein has been widely recognized. However, it has been glossed in conflicting ways. Most Wittgenstein scholars either maintain or imply that Schopenhauer influenced the early Wittgenstein, but – for better rather than worse – not the later work.[9] Similarly, a majority of Schopenhauer scholars are content to concentrate on the early Wittgenstein as an example of Schopenhauer's influence in philosophy. By contrast, Brian Magee has written of 'Schopenhauer's all-pervasive influence on Wittgenstein' and that '[I]f one were to remove from the *Tractatus* everything that derives from Schopenhauer, Frege and Russell, I doubt if much would remain, though it has to be said that the mix itself is highly original, and the thought-processes vertiginously intelligent. And to do Wittgenstein justice, he knew that as a thinker he lacked fundamental creativity'.[10]

Magee supports this second magnanimous concession by reference to a passage mentioned earlier, in which Wittgenstein writes 'I think that there is some truth in the idea that I really only think reproductively. I don't believe I have ever *invented* a line of thinking, I have always taken one over from someone else' (CV, 18–19). What Magee fails to mention is that this remark is part of a longer discussion in which Wittgenstein expresses general doubts about the creative powers of Jews (CV, 16–22). So, one conclusion to draw is that, by his own admission, Wittgenstein was no more creative than Spinoza, Heine, Marx, Freud, Mahler, or Einstein!

A second conclusion is that on this occasion Wittgenstein succumbed to a Jewish self-hatred which is neither original nor respectable. Ironically, like his misogyny, Wittgenstein's anti-Semitism was probably influenced by Schopenhauer, directly or indirectly. Schopenhauer accused Judaism of being crude, superficial, and lacking in 'metaphysical tendency' because of its realism, optimism, and omission of immortality ($P1$, §13 n.; $P2$, §179). To be sure, Schopenhauer's anti-Semitism was not a patch on the psychopathological self-hatred of Otto Weininger. But Schopenhauer influenced the latter, especially in that the negative significance he attaches to Judaism is metaphysical rather than, for example, social or racial. Weininger expanded this into the more general charge of an intellectual deficiency; according to his notorious Sex and Character, Jews lack creativity and genius. This idea much impressed young Ludwig, and it resurfaced briefly during 1931 in the passage quoted by Magee.[11]

Instead of taking Wittgenstein's anti-Semitic remarks at face value, we need to have another look at the actual impact of Schopenhauerian ideas on his work. One obstacle which needs to be negotiated here is that this impact is often inextricably linked to a more general Kantian influence on Wittgenstein. Some Schopenhauerians have simply assumed that Wittgenstein assimilated Kantian ideas solely through reading Schopenhauer. But this is mistaken. Although he professed to get 'only occasional glimpses of understanding' from Kant, we know that he read the Critique of Pure Reason as a prisoner of war in 1918.[12] Furthermore, the remarks quoted earlier show that he rated Kant above Schopenhauer. Wittgenstein was also familiar with the work of the philosopher-scientist Heinrich Hertz, which had strong Kantian affinities. Finally, Kantian problems like the status of mathematics formed an important part of the questions he inherited from Frege and Russell.[13]

Consequently, Wittgenstein's relation to Schopenhauer cannot be discussed without some side glances at the overall Kantian tradition. In some cases, it is clear that he was influenced by Kantian ideas independently of Schopenhauer, for example, in his Hertzian reflections on the non-empirical framework of empirical science. In other cases, notably his anti-intellectualism, it is clear that some of the impetus came *either* from Schopenhauer *or* from thinkers influenced by him, such as Weininger, Mauthner, Spengler, and perhaps Nietzsche. In yet other cases, it is not possible to pin down the precise source, but nor is it essential to a fruitful historical comparison.

With these caveats in mind, I shall argue that both of the extreme views regarding Schopenhauer's influence on Wittgenstein are mistaken. Even Wittgenstein's early work consists no more of footnotes to Schopenhauer than it consists of footnotes to Frege and Russell.[14] Moreover, like Frege and Russell, Schopenhauer influenced Wittgenstein by way of inspiration *and* opposition alike. On the other hand, that influence did not cease after the *Tractatus*. It became more transient and remote, yet also, in some areas, more important to current debates.

To substantiate this verdict, I shall discuss the most important areas of influence.[15] Section I concerns the nature of philosophy, logic, and mathematics. It argues that Wittgenstein's conception of mathematics and logic owes less to Schopenhauer than has been claimed, that his conception of philosophy is closer to Kant than to Schopenhauer, but that Schopenhauer's stress on representation paved the way for Wittgenstein's linguistic transformation of Kant, from a philosophy reflecting on preconditions of experience to a philosophy reflecting on preconditions of symbolic representation. Section II discusses Schopenhauer's intensive influence, partly mediated through Weininger, on the discussion of ethics and aesthetics in the *Tractatus*. Section III turns to the vexed question of solipsism in the *Tractatus*. Against many Wittgenstein commentators I shall argue that Wittgenstein did condone a type of transcendental solipsism, and against many Schopenhauer commentators that his position is influenced by Schopenhauer. Section IV deals with that part of Schopenhauer's influence on Wittgenstein which has been least explored, namely, the will and its relation to intentionality. The later Wittgenstein elaborated Schopenhauer's insight that the special relation we have to our voluntary actions shows that willing is not simply something that 'happens to us'. He also realized, however, that language is not an autonomous system but presupposes the volitional powers of human agents. In this respect, therefore, he moved from the idea of language as representation to the idea of language as will. I end by venturing a brief explanation of why Schopenhauer's influence on Wittgenstein has not carried over to analytic philosophy as a whole.

I PHILOSOPHY, LOGIC, AND MATHEMATICS

Both Schopenhauer and Wittgenstein stand in the tradition of critical philosophy inaugurated by Kant. Kant distinguishes between traditional metaphysics, which he labels 'dogmatic' or 'transcendent' and his own 'critical' or 'transcendental' metaphysics. Transcendent metaphysics is futile speculation because it seeks knowledge of things that lie beyond all possible experience (God, the soul, freedom of the will). But transcendental metaphysics is legitimate. It is based on a prior investigation of the possibility of metaphysics and therefore confines itself to what is accessible to human knowledge, namely, the realm of possible experience. Like all metaphysical claims, those of transcendental metaphysics are 'synthetic a priori': they are substantial claims about reality – hence synthetic – but are not based on experience – hence a priori. Yet they have this special status not because they are about objects beyond experience, but because they express necessary preconditions for the possibility of experiencing ordinary objects. For example, we experience objects as located in space and time and as centres of qualitative changes which are subject to causal laws. According to Kant, these are not empirical facts about human nature, but necessary or structural features of experience. They hold true of all 'appearances', the empirical world which alone can ever be an object of human knowledge. They do not hold true of 'things as they are in themselves', reality when conceived independently of the possibility of human experience, but this 'noumenal' reality lies inevitably beyond the bounds of our knowledge.

Schopenhauer accepts not just Kant's distinction between a phenomenal world of appearances and a world of the thing in itself, but also his critique of 'dogmatic metaphysics', which includes 'speculative theology' and 'rational psychology' (*W*1, Appendix, esp. 417–28/H.2, 494–507). He is hostile to the speculations of the pre-Kantian rationalists and scathing about the even grander speculations of the German idealists. Any attempt to derive substantive truths about the universe and our place within it from self-evident a priori premises is futile, since such derivations can amount to no more than vacuous

transformations of definitions or tacitly presupposed factual claims
(*W1* 76; *W2* 186/H.2, 90–1; H.3, 207).

Throughout his career, Wittgenstein regarded philosophy as a
critical enterprise. Like Kant, the *Tractatus* sets philosophy the task
of drawing the bounds between legitimate forms of discourse – notably the 'contestable sphere of science' (TLP, 4.113) – and illegiti-
mate philosophical speculation – what Kant and Schopenhauer call
'dogmatic metaphysics' and Wittgenstein simply 'metaphysics'.
Once more in line with Kant, he claims that philosophy is not so
much a doctrine which extends knowledge as a critical activity which
curbs the excesses of metaphysics and clarifies non-philosophical
thoughts – their epistemic status in Kant, their logical structure in
Wittgenstein (4.112, 6.53; A 11–12/B 25–6, A 735/B 763, A 850–1/B
878–9). Indeed, Kant anticipated many of the subversive methodological ideas that have put Wittgenstein in the bad books of contemporary analytic philosophers, including his contention that there are no
discoveries in philosophy, only the dissolution of conceptual confusions (PI, §119).

It is crucial to note that Schopenhauer and Wittgenstein develop
the idea of critical philosophy in strikingly different ways. Whereas
Schopenhauer seeks to circumvent Kant's anti-metaphysical restrictions, Wittgenstein radicalizes them. Both, however, react to a familiar tension in Kant's position. Right from the start, Kant's successors
claimed that he himself had transgressed the bounds of knowledge
he was trying to set. For example, he was committed to the idea that
things in themselves *cause* sensations in us and thereby give rise to
the material aspects of the phenomenal world. But according to Kant,
causal relations are structural features imposed on the world by the
human mind; hence they can only obtain between appearances, not
between things in themselves and our sensations.

The German Idealists reacted to this predicament by claiming that
metaphysics is possible if one abandons the distinction between appearances and things in themselves, and by claiming knowledge of a
metaphysical reality such as Hegel's Absolute. Schopenhauer shared
the desire to rehabilitate metaphysics beyond the strict limits set
by Kant's critique. But he does so by building on a Kantian distinction between the world as it is in itself and the world as it appears.
'The world is my representation' (*W1* 3/H.2,3), namely, what appears

to the knowing subject. It is governed by structural features (space, time, causation) which are imposed on it by that subject. But the world as representation is an objectification of an underlying reality. Unlike the world of experience, this ultimate reality contains no individuals, whether material objects or agents, because it lies beyond the principle of individuation, which is provided by space and time. The thing in itself is an undifferentiated unity, a world will of which all individual things, including human beings, are mere manifestations. In organic nature this will appears as a 'will to life' (*Wille zum Leben*), a kind of blind striving directed towards the preservation and propagation of life (*W1* §§18–22). My actions are determined not just by my individual character and experiences, but also by this will to life which I share with all others.

Schopenhauer insists against Kant that we can know not only that there is a world in itself which appears to us, but also what its nature is. Without such knowledge, we could have no solution to the dual problem of metaphysics, 'the riddle of the world' and the 'riddle of the self' (*W1* 427–8/H.2, 505–6). Furthermore, since the principle of individuation is provided by space and time, it is impossible to use the plural 'things in themselves' as Kant does; there is just one undifferentiated thing in itself. Finally, to avoid the problem of positing a causal relation between thing in itself and phenomena, Schopenhauer speaks of their relation as one of 'manifestation' or 'objectification' (*W2* 245/H.3, 277).

According to Schopenhauer, Kant shares with traditional metaphysics the following assumptions (*W1* 426/H.2, 505):

1. Metaphysics is a science of that which transcends experience.
2. As such it has to be a priori, independent of all experience.
3. We have knowledge of a priori principles of this kind, for example, the law of causation.

Kant parts company with them in claiming that these principles are not ontological truths, but 'mere forms of our intellect'. Consequently, they hold only of appearances, not of the thing in itself, as required by (1). 'Accordingly, metaphysics is impossible, and its place is taken over by the critique of pure reason'.

This summary is inaccurate since it fails to distinguish between the transcendent metaphysics Kant repudiates and the transcendental metaphysics through which he seeks to rehabilitate the subject. But the inaccuracy might help to explain why Schopenhauer was so keen to circumvent Kant's prohibition of knowledge of the thing in itself.

Like Kant, Schopenhauer holds that metaphysics is an inevitable tendency of the human intellect (B xx, 362ff.; W2, ch. 17). On that assumption, it is tempting to think that there *must* be a third way 'between the doctrine of omniscience of the earlier dogmatism and the despair of the Kantian Critique' – provided one holds that the latter prohibits all metaphysics, that is. As a matter of fact, however, Kant repudiates (1); it holds only for transcendent metaphysics, not for transcendental metaphysics, which describes the preconditions for the possibility of experience. But in this passage Schopenhauer appears to equate 'metaphysics' with 'transcendent metaphysics'.

In order to preserve the possibility of metaphysics, Schopenhauer takes issue with (2) on empiricist grounds. He accuses Kant of committing a *petitio principii* in assuming that 'only what we know prior to all experience can extend possible experience'. Rather, 'perception is throughout the source of knowledge' (W2 180–1, 41/H.3, 199–200, 47–8), metaphysical knowledge included.

> Therefore, I say that the solution to the [metaphysical] riddle of the world must come from an understanding of the world itself; and hence that the task of metaphysics is not to pass over experience in which the world exists, but to understand it thoroughly, since inner and outer experience are certainly the principal source of all knowledge. (W1 428/H.2, 507)

We can achieve knowledge of the world beyond experience by extrapolating from the world of experience. The simplest and most coherent way to account for the empirical data is to view them as an expression of something beyond all empirical data, an underlying thing in itself which turns out to be will.[16] Accordingly, what Schopenhauer objects to in dogmatic metaphysics is not the fact that it purports to extend knowledge beyond experience, but two other features: its optimism and its rationalism. The picture of the world as the harmonious emanation of a rational principle is nothing but wishful thinking, worthy of theology but not of philosophy.

And instead of putting its speculations on the sound basis of experience, dogmatic metaphysics invokes reason, distorting it into a
'wholly imaginary, false and fictitious' 'faculty of the supersensuous'
(FR §34, esp. 166, 181/H.1, 112, 123).

Schopenhauer's verdict is harsh but, in my view, just. Alas, it is
unclear whether his own empirical metaphysics fares much better.
He justifies the move from empirical data to claims about the thing
in itself by an inference to the best explanation. It is clear that such
inferences can lead from empirical observations to scientific theories. But it is unclear how they could lead from scientific claims
about experiences to metaphysical claims about the thing in itself,
which, as Schopenhauer himself seems to recognize on occasion (W2
197/H. 3, 221) is unknowable in principle.

Wittgenstein rejects Schopenhauer's specific doctrine that we
know the thing in itself through awareness of our own willing (see
Section IV). More important, he tries to reformulate critical philosophy in a way which prevents it from violating its own restrictions,
namely, by switching from Kant's attempt to draw the limits of *human knowledge* to a more radical attempt to draw the limits of *meaningful discourse*.

Like Kant but unlike Schopenhauer, Wittgenstein accepts (2), the
idea that metaphysics is a priori. This is not just a facile 'etymolog-
ical argument concerning the word metaphysics', as Schopenhauer
alleges (W1 427/H.2, 505–6). Rather, it serves to avoid the pitfall of
either reducing metaphysics to empirical science or bringing it into
conflict with science and the causal explanations science alone can
provide.

Philosophy is not one of the natural sciences. (The word 'philosophy' must
mean something whose place is above or below the natural sciences, not
beside them.) (TLP, 4.111)

It was true to say [in the *Tractatus*] that our considerations could not be
scientific ones.... We must do away with all [causal] *explanation*, and description alone must take its place. And this description gets its light, that is
to say its purpose, from the philosophical problems. These are, of course, not
empirical problems; they are solved, rather, by looking into the workings of
our language. (PI, §109)

Wittgenstein also agrees with Kant on how to explain this a priori
status of philosophy. Ever since its inception, philosophy has been

regarded as akin to science in being a cognitive discipline which aspires to provide knowledge about some kind of reality, whether it be Platonic ideas, Aristotelian essences, or the sensory stimuli of the British empiricists. Kant's 'Copernican Revolution' (B xvii) challenged this consensus by taking what I call a 'reflective turn'. In its most general form, which is shared by Wittgenstein, the idea is this. Philosophy differs from the sciences not just quantitatively, by describing different kinds of objects or more general features of reality, but qualitatively. Unlike science and common sense, it is concerned not with reality and its objects, but with the way we experience, represent, or depict reality in non-philosophical discourse. Philosophy does not describe objects of any kind, not even the abstract entities postulated by Platonism. Instead, it is a second-order activity which reflects on the necessary preconditions of our knowing, experiencing, or depicting the objects of the material world in common sense and science. Philosophical problems or propositions are a priori not because they concern a peculiar, non-empirical reality, but because they concern the formal or structural features of experiencing or depicting empirical reality (A 56/B 81; PI, §90).

Although Schopenhauer accepts the Copernican revolution in so far as the formal features of appearances are concerned, he rejects its metaphilosophical implications. He occasionally maintains that philosophy investigates the basis and limits of the empirical knowledge provided by the sciences (*W1*, §15). But this is only a propaedeutic task. Regarding the positive task of achieving metaphysical insights into the thing in itself, he insists that we should ignore the formal features of the way we experience the world, the conceptual framework of experience, and go back to the *experienced world itself.*

But does it not rather seem positively wrong-headed that, in order to solve the riddle of experience ... we should close our eyes to it, ignore its contents, and take and use for our material merely the empty forms of which we are *a priori* conscious? Is it not rather in keeping with the matter that the *science of experience in general* and as such should draw also from experience? ... Is it not inconsistent and absurd that he who speaks of the nature of things should not look at the things themselves, but stick only to certain abstract concepts? It is true that the task of metaphysics is not the observation of particular experiences; but yet it is the correct explanation of experience as a whole. Its foundation, therefore, must certainly be of an empirical nature. (*W2* 180–1/H.3, 200–1)

The picture of metaphysics which emerges here is Aristotelian rather than Kantian. Just as for Aristotle metaphysics describes the most general, not specific, features of particular objects but 'being qua being' (*Metaphysics* IV.1), the most general features of objects, for Schopenhauer, metaphysics describes not particular experiences but the general nature of experience as a whole.

Whereas Schopenhauer goes back on Kant's reflective turn, Wittgenstein gives it a linguistic twist. Kant tried to demarcate what we can know (phenomena or possible objects of experience) from what we cannot know (things in themselves that transcend all possible experience). From Jacobi to Bradley this has provoked the complaint that one cannot draw the distinction between the knowable realm of appearances and the unknowable realm of things in themselves without tacitly presupposing some knowledge of the latter. Wittgenstein diagnosed the same problem. 'In so far as people believe that they can see the "limits of human understanding", they naturally also believe that they can see beyond these' (CV, 15).

He avoids this problem by switching from the limits of knowledge to the limits of thought and by conceiving of the latter as limits of meaningful discourse. Philosophy can establish the limits of thought by drawing limits to the *linguistic expression of thought*. Indeed, these limits *must* be drawn in language:

> [F]or in order to be able to draw the limits of thought, we should have to find both sides of the limit thinkable (i.e. we should have to be able to think what cannot be thought). It will therefore only be in language that the limit can be drawn, and what lies on the other side of the limit will simply be nonsense. (TLP, Preface)

By definition, what lies beyond the limits of thought cannot be thought, and hence cannot be meaningfully talked about. Accordingly, the limits of thought cannot be drawn by propositions talking about both sides, but only *from the inside* (4.113–15). Instead of issuing doctrines about where the limits of thought lie, philosophy delineates the linguistic rules which determine whether a combination of signs makes sense, that is, capable of representing the world. Beyond these bounds lie not unknowable noumena or things in themselves, but only nonsensical combinations of signs. Metaphysical propositions are not just false or unfounded, they are literally nonsensical.

And this verdict applies not just to dogmatic metaphysics but equally to any attempt to state the bounds of sense, including the pronouncements of the *Tractatus*.

> My propositions serve as elucidations in the following way: anyone who understands me eventually recognizes them as nonsensical.... (He must, so to speak, throw away the ladder after he has climbed up it.) He must transcend these propositions, and then he will see the world aright. (6.54)

The ladder-image occurs in Mauthner[17] and Schopenhauer (*W2* 80/ H.3, 87). In Wittgenstein, it turns philosophy from a doctrine about the limits of knowledge into an activity, namely, of showing, by means of logical analysis, which sign combinations make sense – these are confined to the empirical propositions of science – and which signs amount to metaphysical nonsense (TLP, 6.53–7).

The early Wittgenstein's solution to the predicament of critical philosophy is heroic but ultimately self-refuting. Wittgenstein later avoided self-refutation by granting that the rules of language can be expressed in meaningful propositions, provided that these 'grammatical propositions' are not mistaken for scientific or metaphysical descriptions of reality. Whether this position is tenable cannot be discussed here,[18] but it is an ingenious attempt to avoid the predicament of critical philosophy. In any event, Wittgenstein's belief that in drawing limits to knowledge critical philosophers inevitably transgress these limits is borne out by both Kant and Schopenhauer. The former does so willy-nilly, the latter in a spirit of defiance. Neither of them manages to avoid metaphysical claims of a highly problematic nature.

It is sometimes claimed that Schopenhauer inspired Wittgenstein's linguistic turn, and in particular his conception of philosophy as a kind of linguistic therapy.[19] Like Schopenhauer, Wittgenstein held that the source of philosophy lies in puzzlement and perplexity.[20] But as regards the philosophical role of language, the analogies do not reach very far. It is true and important that Schopenhauer pointed out that linguistic understanding cannot depend on appropriate mental images crossing the hearer's mind (*W1*, §9). Like Frege, he thereby anticipated the later Wittgenstein's anti-mentalist conception of understanding, although neither Schopenhauer nor Frege match the detail and acuity of Wittgenstein's arguments.

It is also true that Schopenhauer suggested that the categories, the essential features of thought or experience detected by Kant, correspond to grammatical types (*W1* 477–8/H.2, 566–7). But at the same time he insisted that 'grammar is related to logic as are the clothes to the body'. He stands in the tradition of modern philosophy – exemplified by the logic of Port-Royal and by Locke – which regards language both as a source of philosophical mistakes and as a potential source of philosophical insights, because it is a partly distorting and partly revealing mirror of thought or experience (see, e.g., *W2* 40, 66–7/H.3, 46–7, 70–2). By contrast, Wittgenstein broke with that tradition in maintaining that language and thought are internally related: philosophical confusion arises not from ignoring the mental or experiential reality behind language – the body concealed by the clothes – but from distorting language itself.

At the same time, Schopenhauer may have contributed indirectly to the way in which the *Tractatus* transformed Kant's reflective turn. He made representation rather than experience or consciousness the focus of transcendental philosophy, for example, by claiming that 'the concept of consciousness coincides with that of representation' or that 'all knowing is a making of representations' (*W1*, §10; and *W2* 194/H.3, 216–17). This may have paved the way for Wittgenstein's interest in the general idea of the relation between thought and reality rather than in the more specific notion of experience. Wittgenstein then interpreted this relation as symbolic or linguistic rather than mental, as depiction (*Abbildung, Darstellung*) rather than *Vorstellung*. In this he was perhaps inspired by Hertz, who characterized science as making models of reality, models which he described sometimes in the traditional mentalist vein, sometimes neutrally in terms of *Darstellung*.

It has also been claimed that Schopenhauer is a significant inspiration behind Wittgenstein's account of logic and mathematics. Thus Magee states that 'Wittgenstein got what was probably his most important idea from Schopenhauer, namely the idea that analytically true propositions are tautologies'. But this is far from obvious. The claim that some logical truths are tautologous goes back at least to Kant (*Logik*, §§36–7). Kant characterized formal logic as analytic but distinguished between two types of analytic propositions: those in which the containment of the predicate in the subject concept is *implicit* as in 'All bodies are extended', and those in which it is *explicit*, as in 'All extended things are extended'. The latter he labels 'tautological', and he insists that unlike the former they are 'virtually empty or devoid of consequences', since they do not even explicate the subject. In the nineteenth century 'tautological' was used widely to indicate that formal logic, in particular the law of identity 'A = A', is trivial and pointless, since it does not extend our knowledge. In this capacity, Wittgenstein would have encountered the term in Coffey's *The Science of Logic*, which he reviewed in 1913. And although Russell passionately denied that logical truths are tautological, he labelled '(p v p) ⊃ p' the 'principle of tautology'. Even Frege admitted that a logical truth like 'p ⊃ p' seems 'almost without content'.[21]

Schopenhauer goes beyond these authors by claiming that *all* analytic propositions are tautological (*P2*, §23; see also *W2* 610/H.3, 700–1). But this is the only noteworthy use of the term in his whole oeuvre. Mauthner gave it much greater emphasis, and went even beyond Schopenhauer in claiming that not just logical and mathematical truths but even empirical truths are tautological once known.[22] Equally, in maintaining that 'nothing more can follow from a proposition than what in reality it already states itself' (*W2* 186/H.3, 207), Schopenhauer merely repeated current orthodoxy. Indeed, it was precisely this idea which led both Descartes and the British empiricists to take such a dim view of the value of deductive argument.

Most important, although Wittgenstein was not the first to characterize logic as tautological, he was the first to *explain* logic's tautological nature in a way which is *both precise and general*, that is, not confined to either the principle of identity or propositions involving literal repetitions or propositions of subject–predicate form, as in Schopenhauer. Moreover, he uses this explanation to make out a good case for the claim that logical propositions do not describe reality but reflect linguistic rules. Logical truths are tautologies because they combine (according to rules of truth–functional combination) empirical propositions in such a way that all factual information cancels out. This has nothing to do with Schopenhauer, who toed the traditional line of defining logic as a substantive science, namely, of the 'laws of thought' governing our mental operations (*FR*, §9), precisely the view Wittgenstein sought to undermine.

Schopenhauer's real influence on Wittgenstein's philosophy of logic and mathematics concerns a more general but equally important point. He treated the intellect 'as a mere tool in the service of the will' (W2 205/H.3, 228–9) and thought as a biological function. He thereby founded an anti-intellectualist tradition. The members of that tradition are not necessarily irrationalist, in the sense of forsaking the practice of rational argument. However, like Hume, they contend that reason and intellect do not have the exalted autonomous position traditionally accorded to them, but are rooted in human life and social practice. This anti-intellectualist tradition was continued, with respect to mathematics, by Brouwer and Spengler. Spengler was (understandably) critical of Schopenhauer's contempt for history. But he commended Schopenhauer for having recognized that the will is superior to the intellect.[23] Wittgenstein, in turn, acknowledged Spengler's influence on his philosophy of mathematics.[24] He was presumably alluding to the discussion of the cultural diversity and relativity of mathematics in chapter II of *The Decline of the West*. But there is a more general debt to Schopenhauer and Spengler. Wittgenstein's philosophy of logic and mathematics is constructivist in the general sense of detecting the roots of even these seemingly abstract and autonomous subjects in the requirements of human behaviour. At the same time, Wittgenstein replaces Schopenhauer's vitalist emphasis on the requirements of life understood as an organic force by an emphasis on the requirements of social human practice, which brings him closer to Marxism and American pragmatism.

II ETHICS AND AESTHETICS

The oeuvres of Schopenhauer and Wittgenstein are among the few literary highlights of German philosophical prose. Moreover, both of them were highly self-conscious about their manner of writing, and both saw a close connection between questions of style and questions of content. Schopenhauer self-consciously modelled his style on Hume's and declared literary style to be the 'physiognomy of the spirit', a faithful image of the movement of thought (W1 446; W2 73/H.2, 528–9; H.3, 78–9). Wittgenstein had self-professed aesthetic ambitions and regarded 'correct style' as integral to good philosophizing (CV, 39, 87; Z, §712).

On the other hand, Wittgenstein's style was not notably influenced by Schopenhauer.[25] Schopenhauer's great strength lies in his ability to tell a gripping philosophical yarn, aided by his ability to construct a dynamic interplay between different themes – an ability which has frequently been compared to that of a great composer. By contrast, Wittgenstein deplored his own failure at reining in his thought for the purposes of a coherent philosophical narrative, and with some justification (PI, Preface). Furthermore, neither the marmoreal remarks of the *Tractatus* nor the often ironic dialogue of the *Philosophical Investigations* resemble Schopenhauer's writings. Like the title, the style of the *Tractatus* is reminiscent of Spinoza, while the *Investigations* displays light touches closer to Lichtenberg than to Schopenhauer's aphorisms, which tend to be more robust and, on occasion, heavy-handed.

Passing from literary practice to philosophical theory, Schopenhauer and the early Wittgenstein are united in linking ethics and aesthetics. This is alien to the analytic debate but unremarkable in the cultural tradition they shared. In a seminal passage of the *Critique of Judgement* (§59), Kant suggested that beauty is a 'symbol of morality', and this idea had been developed by Friedrich Schiller in his *Letters on the Aesthetic Education of Humankind*. What is distinctive about our protagonists is

1. the proximity of the link;
2. the fact that ethics no less than aesthetics evolves around an attitude of contemplation;
3. that the link is forged by a kind of mysticism, a supreme but ineffable insight into the nature of the world.

In Schopenhauer, aesthetics and ethics are closely linked because both are dimensions of human life in which we can achieve a kind of release or redemption. Unfortunately, following the dictates of the will can never afford us humans genuine satisfaction. 'Salvation' can come only through self-denial and self-renunciation, through rejecting the real self, the will to life as it is embodied in each individual (*W1* 405; *W2* 605–6/H. 2, 479–80; H. 3, 694–6). Both in artistic appreciation and in acts of compassion we escape, however temporarily, from the dictates of the will to life and transcend our own individual standpoint (the *principium individuationis*) by realizing that we are merely the phenomenal manifestations of a single world-will. The most sustained form this denial of the will can take is in the life of saints or through the experience of suffering. But the tranquil experience of the beautiful is a more common and more precarious phenomenon of the same kind (*W1*, §§68–71).

We are capable of perceiving beautiful objects for their own sake without having the practical designs we otherwise do. Schopenhauer elaborates this into the claim that aesthetic appreciation is the 'will-less contemplation of Ideas'. It involves both a subjective suspension of willing and the most objective kind of knowledge, an insight into the thing in itself beyond the veil of appearances. In experiencing a work of art, we transcend the structural features peculiar to appearances, that is, time, space, and causation.

> [W]e no longer consider the where, the when, the why, and the whither of things, but simply and solely the *what*. Further, we do not let abstract thought, the concepts of reason, take possession of our consciousness, but, instead of all this, devote the whole power of our mind to perception, sink ourselves completely therein, and let our whole consciousness be filled by the calm of contemplation of the natural object actually present, whether it be a landscape, a tree, a rock, a crag, a building, or anything else. We *lose* ourselves entirely in this object. ... What is thus known is no longer the individual thing as such, but the *Idea* ... at the same time, the person who is involved in the perception is no longer an individual, for in such perception the individual has lost himself; he is *pure* will-less, painless, timeless *subject of knowledge*....It was this that was in Spinoza's mind when he wrote '*mens aeterna est, quatenus res sub aeternitatis specie concipit*' (*Ethics*, V, prop. 31, schol.) (*W1* 178–9/H.2, 210–11)

The content of the work ceases to be particular because it comes to embody a universal Idea. At the same time, we momentarily lose consciousness of ourselves as individuals distinct from the contemplated object. Aesthetic experience transcends the empirical knowledge and abstract thought of science. It acquaints us with the 'inner nature of the world' by asking not about the 'whence, whither and why' but 'about the *what* alone'. 'From such knowledge we get philosophy as well as art', and also 'that disposition of mind which alone leads to true holiness and to salvation from the world' (*W1* 274/H.2, 323).

Like Schopenhauer, the early Wittgenstein regards ethical and aesthetic value as ineffable, places it outside the world – what is represented – and links it with a metaphysical will. We also find a contrast between scientific knowledge, on the one hand, and the insights of aesthetics, ethics, and philosophy, on the other. However, there is an

immediate difference in that Wittgenstein characterizes the sphere
of science not by reference to the Kantian ideas of space, time, and
causation, but more generally as the sphere of *contingent facts*, of
states of affairs which may or may not obtain (TLP, 1–2.0141).

Wittgenstein brings ethics and aesthetics even closer together
than Schopenhauer. 'Ethics and aesthetics are one' (TLP, 6.421; NB,
24.7.16). This sibylline pronouncement was not a promising start for
someone who later vowed to teach us differences. It perhaps displays
the influence of Weininger, who proclaimed that 'logic and ethics
are fundamentally the same, they are no more than duty to oneself'
(*Sex and Character*, 159).[26] One has a moral obligation to strive for
logical clarity and ultimately for genius. In the *Tractatus*, Wittgenstein tries to give philosophical substance to Weininger's identification of logic – which for him is equivalent with philosophy – and
ethics. Only the empirical propositions of science are meaningful,
since they picture contingent states of affairs (truly or falsely). What
Wittgenstein calls the 'higher' (6.42, 6.432), all areas of *value*, share
with the logical structures of language the fate of being *ineffable*;
they cannot be said, that is, expressed in meaningful propositions,
but only shown. Logic, ethics, and aesthetics are united by virtue
of being 'transcendental'. They are concerned not with what is 'accidental' – contingent matters of fact – but with what could not be
otherwise – the 'preconditions of the world' (NB, 24.7.16; TLP, 6.13,
6.421). Hence they cannot be expressed in meaningful propositions
(which must be 'bipolar' – capable of being true but equally capable
of being false), but only shown.

However, unlike the logical structure of language, which is shown
by empirical propositions properly analysed, ethical and aesthetic
values are not even *shown* by any meaningful propositions, although
they may be shown in actions, attitudes, or works of art.[27] If this is
indeed Wittgenstein's view, it coincides with that of Schopenhauer,
who claimed that the knowledge which underlies virtue 'cannot be
communicated, but must dawn in each of us. It therefore finds its
real and adequate expression not in words, but simply and solely in
deeds, in conduct, in the course of a person's life' (*W1*, §66).

Unlike logic, ethics and aesthetics are not just transcendental,
linked to the preconditions of symbolic representation, but transcendent. 'The problem of life' remains untouched even if all scientific
problems have been solved (NB, 7.10.16; TLP, 6.43, 6.45, 6.521). The

answer to the problem of life, namely, 'the meaning of life' and of the world, is *God* (NB, 11.6./8.7.16; TLP, 6.521). But God *transcends* the world, since HE 'does not reveal himself *in* the world'. More generally, values 'cannot lie *within* the world', which 'itself is neither good nor evil'. Instead, their 'bearer' is a Schopenhauerian metaphysical will outside the world. 'One could say (à la Schopenhauer): it is not the world of representation that is either good or evil, but the willing subject' (TLP, 6.41–6.431; NB, 2.8.16).

Ethics and aesthetics are based on a mystical experience. In line with tradition, both Schopenhauer and Wittgenstein characterize mysticism by reference to two features.[28]

1. It not only lies beyond all possible knowledge, but is also incommunicable or ineffable, something 'which cannot be put into words' but 'shows itself' (W2 611/H.3, 701–2; TLP, 6.522).

2. It is a feeling of union with God or the universe, 'a consciousness of the identity of one's own inner being with that of all things, or with the kernel of the world' (W2 613/H.3, 704).

Both points are central to Schopenhauer's treatment of ethics and aesthetics. Against Kant he insists that conceptual thought is 'as unfruitful for genuine virtue as it is for genuine art' (W1, §67). '[M]oral excellence stands higher than all theoretical wisdom' (BM, §22). For the denial of the will ultimately requires the mystical insight into one's identity with an impersonal world-will in which Schopenhauer seeks refuge (W2 610–13/H.3, 700–4).

In the early Wittgenstein, ethics and aesthetics are based on a similar mystical attitude, a 'contemplation' or 'feeling' of the world *sub specie aeternitatis*, that is, from the outside, as a 'limited whole' (TLP, 6.45).

The work of art is the object seen *sub specie aeternitatis*; and the good life is the world seen *sub specie aeternitatis*. This is the connection between art and ethics. The usual way of looking at things sees objects as it were from the midst of them, the view *sub specie aeternitatis* from the outside. (NB, 7.10.16)

Wittgenstein not only duplicates Schopenhauer's allusion to Spinoza, he also provides his own version of Schopenhauer's contrast between the *why* of scientific investigation and the *what* of the mystical contemplation. In looking at the world from outside, I marvel not at *how* the world is but *that it is* (TLP, 5.552f.; NB, 20.10.16). Finally, both ethics and aesthetics involve 'looking at the world with a happy eye', a stoic acceptance of the facts (NB, 20.10.16; TLP, 6.43).

The connections between these mystical pronouncements in Schopenhauer and Wittgenstein are reasonably clear. But the pronouncements themselves suffer from 'complete unclarity' (NB, 2.8.16), over and above the mystic's call of duty. In the case of aesthetics, content can be given to Wittgenstein's remarks by reference to Schopenhauer's discussion. Like Schopenhauer, he seems to think that in aesthetic experience we achieve a profound insight because of two features:

1. The subject's consciousness is completely taken up by the object he contemplates, with the result that during the aesthetic experience this object becomes the subject's entire world.
2. The experience transcends space and time; its object is seen 'together with space and time instead of in space and time' (NB, 7.–8.10.16).

Nevertheless, Wittgenstein's gnomic remarks add nothing significant to Schopenhauer's much more detailed discussion of aesthetics.

The comparison is more fruitful in the case of ethics. Here Wittgenstein can be seen as resolving an inconsistency in Schopenhauer.[29] What is more, he does so in a way which preserves Schopenhauer's premium on contemplation in ethics. For both Schopenhauer and Wittgenstein, the good life does not involve any imposition of my will on the course of events, but an attitude – 'seeing the world aright'. However, it has been remarked that there is an incompatibility between two Schopenhauerian ideas: on the one hand, the most desirable condition is one in which the will is denied and hence nothing is wanted; on the other, compassion – an exercise of the will – is essential to morality (W2, chs. 47–9). Indeed, the very idea of the 'will turning against itself' (W1 412/H.2, 487 and §68) is problematic, since such a denial of the will would itself have to be an act of the will. Underlying these two inconsistencies is an even larger tension. Since the cosmic will which constitutes the thing in itself is so quintessentially undesirable, it is difficult to see how the mystical experience of feeling at one with this will should provide a kind of moral salvation.

Wittgenstein avoids these difficulties by adopting a Kantian distinction between *good* and *bad* willing (NB, 21./24./29.7.16; TLP, 6.43). Equally Kantian (but, unlike this distinction, also in line with Schopenhauer) is the view that the consequences of an action are ethically irrelevant, unlike the spirit in which it is performed. But Wittgenstein's rationale is Spinozistic rather than Kantian. He identifies being good with being happy and being bad with being unhappy (8./29./30.7.16). Reward and punishment are crucial to ethics but 'reside within the action itself' (6.422). Good willing alters not facts in the world, but only the 'limits of the world', namely, the 'attitude of the subject to the world'. A good will is its own reward because it looks at the world with 'a happy eye'; it accepts the brute facts – whatever is the case and whatever happens – with equanimity rather than rejection (6.43; NB, 20.10.16). This stoic attitude is the ethical result of the mystical view of the world *sub specie aeternitatis* (NB, 4.11.16; TLP, 6.45).

In the area of values (aesthetics, ethics, mysticism), Schopenhauer's influence on the early Wittgenstein is least diluted. Yet it is often mediated by Weininger and all but disappears in Wittgenstein's later reflections on life and art.[30]

III TRANSCENDENTAL SOLIPSISM

While the idea that nothing exists apart from oneself and the contents of one's mind has rarely been endorsed explicitly, idealists or phenomenalists have been tempted by or even implicitly committed to it. The discussion of solipsism (5.6–5.641) marks the intersection of the logical and mystical parts of the *Tractatus*. The 'key to the problem [of] how much truth there is in solipsism' is that '*the limits of my language* mean the limits of my world'. *What* the solipsist means is that 'the world is *my* world'. This inexpressible truth manifests itself in 'the fact that the limits of *language* (of the only language which I understand) mean the limit of *my* world' (5.62).

In *Insight and Illusion*, Peter Hacker undertook the first thorough investigation of Schopenhauerian themes in the *Tractatus* and the *Notebooks*. His main conclusions were that the early Wittgenstein's remarks on the topic condone a position which Hacker characterizes

as transcendental solipsism, and that this position was heavily influenced by Schopenhauer's transcendental idealism. These claims
have been greeted by conflicting protests from Wittgenstein and
Schopenhauer scholars. Thus Ernst-Micheel Lange grants that
Schopenhauer was a solipsist *malgré lui*, but he insists that the early
Wittgenstein rejects this position of Schopenhauer. By contrast,
Christopher Janaway holds that *if* Wittgenstein condoned solipsism,
he could have been inspired by Schopenhauer only by way of mis-
interpretation.[31] I shall argue that both are half right. The early
Wittgenstein condoned a highly complex form of solipsism which
he regarded as an inevitable consequence of Schopenhauer's transcendental idealism, and rightly so, given his perspective.

Three separate questions are before us: Does the early Wittgenstein condone a form of solipsism? Does Schopenhauer's transcendental idealism point in the direction of solipsism? Was Wittgenstein's treatment of solipsism influenced by Schopenhauer?

As regards the last, two points are certain. One is that Schopenhauer was not the only source for Wittgenstein's discussion of solipsism. According to Russell's principle of acquaintance, every meaningful word must stand for something within the individual's immediate present experience. This suggests a semantic 'solipsism of the
present moment' according to which only the sense data I am presently aware of are real. Russell escapes this conclusion by an inductive inference to the conclusion that there probably are other
minds.[32] The early Wittgenstein was hostile to this kind of response
to scepticism, but he followed Russell in regarding solipsism not just
as an ontological or epistemological problem, but also as a semantic
one.

It is equally certain, however, that the way Wittgenstein discusses
solipsism is shaped mainly by Schopenhauerian themes, terms, and
analogies, which he may have picked up either from Schopenhauer
himself or from Weininger.[33] This is no coincidence, since his discussion of solipsism is part of a general Kantian approach to the self.
According to Cartesianism, the self is a soul substance attached to
the body; according to Humean reductionism, it is only a bundle of
mental episodes, since no such unitary substance is encountered in
introspection. Kant rejected both positions. There are no criteria of
identity for Cartesian souls, yet the idea of mental episodes without a subject is incoherent. In place of the Cartesian soul substance

he introduced two other notions: the 'transcendental unity of apperception', a formal feature of judgements, namely, that they can be prefixed by 'I think'; and a 'noumenal self' which is the locus of free will and the moral law.

Both notions have their counterparts in Schopenhauer's distinction between the phenomenal world and the world as it is in itself. As regards the former, he espouses a radical idealism. 'The world is my representation'; it is nothing but the totality of representations that appear to the subject. But the 'subject of knowledge' to which the world as representation appears is merely an 'indivisible point'. It cannot be encountered in experience, just as the eye 'sees everything except itself'. Nevertheless, it is a 'centre of all existence' and determines the limits of the world. For the world is my representation, and the idea of a world without a representing subject is a contradiction in terms (W1 3–5, 15, 332; W2 277–8, 486, 491/H.2, 3–6, 17–18, 391–2; H.3, 313–15, 556–7, 562–3). Schopenhauer replaced the noumenal self by a superindividual will which underlies both the subject and the object that make up the world as representation. As regards both cognition and volition, however, the individual – 'the microcosm' – is identical with the world – 'the macrocosm' (W1 162; W2 486/H.2, 193; H.3, 556–7).

Weininger combined this idea with themes from Schopenhauer's aesthetics. In a real genius, the world and the I become one: 'The great philosopher like the great artist possesses the whole world in himself; they are the conscious microcosms'.[34]Like Schopenhauer, he expresses the identity of individual and world sometimes as an 'identity of microcosm and macrocosm', sometimes as the individual soul being 'a microcosm' which encompasses the world (an idea which goes back to Paracelsus).

'The I, the I is what is deeply mysterious', writes Wittgenstein (NB, 5.8.16; see FR 211–12/H.1, 143). Like Kant and Schopenhauer, he rejects the Cartesian idea of the 'thinking, presenting subject'. In a book entitled The World as I Found It, no self would (Hume) or could (Kant, Schopenhauer) be mentioned. Like the eye of the visual field, the self is not a possible object of experience; and it cannot be inferred from the content of experience either. There is a 'human soul' which is the legitimate subject matter of psychology, yet it is not a unitary self but only an array of mental episodes (5.631–4; NB, 7.8./11.8.16).

Again, in line with Kant and Schopenhauer, Wittgenstein combines this rejection of the Cartesian soul with acceptance of a 'metaphysical subject' or 'philosophical I' which enters philosophy through the fact that *the world is my world*. This metaphysical subject is not a part of the world but nevertheless its 'centre', being both 'a presupposition of its existence' and its 'limit'. The relation of *what we experience*, our field of consciousness, to the *subject of experience*, is analogous to that of the *visual field* to the *eye*, not the sense organ, but what he later called the 'geometrical eye'. This self is not part of the world we can experience, but an 'extensionless point', and the human individual is a 'microcosm' (NB, 11.6./4.8./12.8./2.9./12.10.16; TLP, 5.633–5.64).

The prima facie case for detecting *some* version of solipsism in the *Tractatus* is overwhelming. Wittgenstein concedes not only that solipsism contains a kernel of truth, as anti-solipsist interpreters have it, but that 'what the solipsist *means* is quite correct' – namely, that the world is my world. His only explicit criticism is that the solipsist tries to say what can only be shown. But, as we have seen, this is equally the predicament of the whole *Tractatus*. In so far as the book condones, for example, a picture theory of the proposition, it also condones a kind of solipsism. Both of these are ineffable truths which can be shown but cannot be said. Wittgenstein does not just put words in the mouth of 'the solipsist', but writes *in propria persona* (TLP, 5.621–5.63, 6.43–6.431):

World and life are one. I am my world. (The microcosm.)

The world of the happy man is different from the world of the unhappy man. So too at death, the world does not alter but comes to an end.

These are paradigmatic expressions of solipsism. Moreover, the *Notebooks* are full of purple passages which identify the world with *life*, life with *consciousness in general*, and consciousness with the *metaphysical self*. At one point, Wittgenstein even judges other philosophical positions by their compatibility with the 'strictly solipsistic point of view'.[35]

Lange recognizes this problem for the anti-solipsistic interpretation. He tries to overcome it by claiming that in the *Notebooks* Wittgenstein originally adopted a Schopenhauerian solipsism, but then, by his own accounts, travelled from 'idealism' through 'solipsism' to 'pure realism' because 'I too belong with the rest of the

world' (15.10.16; see Section IV). However, the evidence for an abandonment of solipsism is at best inconclusive. Throughout the *Notebooks*, Wittgenstein links the 'ethical will' firmly to an individual,
namely, himself; and in the very next entry he claims that 'in a higher
sense' the Schopenhauerian 'world-will' is '*my* will', just as my representations are the world (2.9./12.–7.10./4.11.16; TLP, 5.64f).

The weightiest argument against the solipsistic interpretation is
independent of developmental hypotheses. For Wittgenstein solipsism collapses into 'pure realism' (TLP, 5.64). But this realism is the
other side of an austere transcendental solipsism in which Schopenhauer's analogy of the eye and the visual field takes the place of the
transcendental unity of apperception. Although the subject of experience cannot be part of experience, it is a logical feature of any
experiences *I* could have that they belong to me. In his own later
words: 'The subject – we want to say – does not drop out of the experience but is so much involved in it that it cannot be described' (PG,
156; see PR, §47). Any representation of the world occurs from a perspective which is *uniquely mine*. But since it is logically impossible
that it should occur from any other perspective, this fact cannot be
expressed in a meaningful bipolar proposition.

Because representation is linguistic, transcendental solipsism
takes a linguistic turn.[36] The 'connection between solipsism' and
'the way a sentence signifies' is that 'the I is replaced by the sentence and the relation between the I and reality is replaced by the
relation between the sentence and reality'.[37] The relation between
sentence and reality depends on the metaphysical subject, a linguistic soul which breathes life into mere signs. Language is *my* language
because mere signs (noises or inscriptions) turn into symbols through
my 'thinking the sense of the proposition' (TLP, 3.11). This, in turn, is
possible only by linking the elements of the propositional sign – the
names – with the elements of the situation depicted, which is done
through acts of meaning. '*By* my correlating the components of the
picture with objects, it comes to represent a situation and to be right
or wrong'. 'I know what I mean; I mean just THIS' (22.6.15; 26.11.14;
see 31.5./20.6.15; TLP, 2.1511). Such acts cannot be performed by the
empirical self, which is merely a complex of psychic elements, and
must hence be acts of the *metaphysical* or *willing subject*. 'Things
acquire "meaning" only in relation to my will' (NB, 15.10.16; PG,
144–56). I can correlate with names only objects I experience, and
what I cannot project is not language. '*I* have to judge the world,

to measure things' (NB, 2.9.16). The need for acts of meaning may explain why some passages suggest that the metaphysical subject of representation is identical with the 'willing subject', which is the bearer of good and evil (5.633, 5.641; NB, 21./24./29.7./2.8./2.9.16; see Section IV).

This transcendental solipsism is compatible with empirical realism: it does not assert that 'I am the only person that exists' or reject empirical propositions about the external world or 'other minds'. The truth of solipsism manifests itself in the very possibility of representation and in the logical form of all empirical propositions: fully analysed 'A is in pain' refers only to pain behaviour of which I am aware, while 'I am in pain' refers directly to my experience. The methodological solipsism which Wittgenstein adopted in the early 1930s makes explicit these commitments of the early work. It analyses all propositions, including those about other minds, into propositions referring to the immediate experience of a 'centre'. Although Wittgenstein recognizes that such a mono-centred language can have anyone at its centre, he also insists that a language with *him* at the centre is particularly suitable (PR, ch. VI).

The kernel of truth in the anti-solipsistic interpretation is that by giving up the idea of an individual ego, and by treating the subject of representation as merely a formal point of reference (analogous to Kant's transcendental unity of apperception and Schopenhauer's eye of the visual field), Wittgenstein stretched the notion of solipsism, perhaps beyond the breaking point.

This peculiar position derives from Schopenhauer, not because the latter condoned solipsism, or because Wittgenstein misinterpreted him as doing so, but because Wittgenstein remained unconvinced by the way in which he sought to avoid solipsism. Schopenhauer was aware of the danger that his transcendental idealism, based on the claim that the world is my representation and on the identification of microcosm and macrocosm, might slide into 'theoretical egoism', as he called it. He sought to block this slide. But he was forced to concede that solipsism is irrefutable; and he departed from it only through insisting that the subject of experience is not a mental substance and that everything is a manifestation of a superindividual will (W1 103–6; W2 193/H.2, 123–6; H.3, 215–16).

The crucial point is that this manoeuvre combines two moves Wittgenstein rejected – the 'Russellian' ploy of regarding solipsism as irrefutable yet barren, and the claim that the world is a manifestation of a will which is not just impersonal but even non-individual. The former falls foul of Wittgenstein's injunction 'scepticism is not irrefutable but obviously nonsensical, when it tries to raise doubts where no questions can be asked' (TLP, 6.51). The latter relies on Schopenhauer's theory of the objectification of the will which the young Wittgenstein rejected (see Section IV).

Nevertheless, one might protest, whether or not Wittgenstein liked that theory, it does set Schopenhauer apart from any solipsism or absolute idealism. According to Schopenhauer, the world is not the representation of a single individual, but of a subject which cannot be empirically individuated – an abstract I.[38] But note that this defence is belied by the very first sentence of Schopenhauer's masterpiece. Although everyone can say 'The world is my representation', everyone must use the first-person possessive pronoun. This is no coincidence, but is connected to a general problem commentators have detected in Schopenhauer's description of moral salvation.[39] How can I overcome egoism by realizing my ultimate identity with the universe? For either the world in itself is totally deprived of individuality, in which case I cannot find myself in it; or I can find myself in it, in which case I somehow extend my concept of self to the world as a whole, which would turn altruism into a gigantic form of egoism.

Wittgenstein's transcendental solipsism is based on the recognition of this difficulty. Unless the will is simply an extrinsic force, it must be 'my will' that permeates the world (NB, 11.6.16). Although 'I can speak of a will that is common to the whole world', it must be 'in a higher sense *my* will' (NB, 17.10.16). Neither the I of representation nor the I of willing can be deprived of its personal and individual nature the way Schopenhauer does. The alternative to preserving these features through a kind of solipsism is to regard the I no longer as a manifestation of the thing in itself, but as an individual person. This is the option developed in the later Wittgenstein's account of intentionality and the will.

IV THE WILL AND INTENTIONALITY

In attesting to Schopenhauer's influence, Anscombe and Geach also mention that even as a youngster Wittgenstein repudiated Schopenhauer's metaphysics of the will (see n. 5). For Schopenhauer, the world as it appears to us is a manifestation of an underlying reality, an impersonal will. We can know this reality, since our bodies are direct manifestations of it and since, in our voluntary actions, we have access to our own *willing*, the only event we understand 'from within', not merely as a phenomenon that happens to us (*W1*, §19; *W2*, ch. 17; *FR* 214/H.1, 145).

Wittgenstein's hostility to this idea is borne out by his early discussion of the will. He distinguishes between 'the will as a phenomenon ... of interest only to psychology' and 'the will as the subject of ethical attributes'. The former is part of the mental episodes which constitute the 'soul' studied by psychology; the latter is housed in the metaphysical self and hence is ineffable (TLP, 6.423; NB, 21.7.16). By contrast to Schopenhauer, for Wittgenstein the metaphysical will is not a primordial force operating in the world, but an ethical 'attitude of the subject to the world'. It does not alter the facts but rather 'the limits of the world' (NB, 4.11.16), namely, the metaphysical self's attitude towards the facts which constitute the world.

Underlying this position is the view that 'the world is independent of my will', that I am 'completely powerless' to bend events to my will (TLP, 6.373; NB, 11.6., 5.7, and 8.7.16). The idea that my bodily movements are subject to my will 'makes it look as if one part of the world [my body] were closer to me than another'. This is precisely Schopenhauer's position. But Wittgenstein regards it as 'intolerable', partly because, for him, the only relation I can have to the world is that of depicting it (NB, 4.11.16; see TLP, 5.62ff.). Another rationale is Wittgenstein's Humean conception of causation, according to which the relation between any two empirical events is always contingent rather than necessary (TLP, 5.135ff.).[40] This holds equally for my volitions, which are mental events, and my bodily movements. If what we 'wish' happens, this is only a contingent 'physical connection' between 'will and world', a connection which *itself* is *not* under my control (TLP, 6.374).

From this perspective, Schopenhauer is doubly wrong. I cannot be intuitively certain of my future intentional actions; and my body does not occupy a special place. Granted, some parts of my body are under my control, while others are not. But this only means that in the former case there is a contingent connection between a mental event and the movement of the part. Even '*my* body' is 'a part of the world among others', on a par with stones, animals, or the bodies of others (NB, 2.9./12.10.16; see TLP, 5.631, 5.641).

Thus the *Tractatus* presents a purely *contemplative* conception of the will: my metaphysical will is merely an ethical attitude to the world, and my phenomenal will is an empirical process beyond my control. Certain passages in the *Notebooks* put pressure on this paradoxical position. For one thing, they distinguish between mere *wishing* and *willing*. The former is indeed merely a mental phenomenon that may or may not be followed by a bodily movement. The latter, however, is not contingently related to action; it 'is acting'. Hence it can involve certainty and a feeling of responsibility. I can state authoritatively not only which of my movements are voluntary but also, for example, that I shall raise my arm in five minutes. Furthermore, the relationship between volition and act is not that of cause and effect; the volition is 'the action itself'. This is precisely Schopenhauer's position, as is the claim that 'the act of will is not an experience' (8.–9.11.16). 'By no means do we recognize the real, immediate act of the will as something different from the action of the body, and the two as connected by the law of causality; both are one and indivisible' (W2 36/H.3, 41–2; see W1, §§18, 55).

These passages follow Schopenhauer's seminal insight that willing is not a hidden causal antecedent of observable behaviour, but without necessarily condoning the idea that through my awareness of my bodily movements I have a more immediate access to a thing in itself. For Wittgenstein it also seems that thinking itself involves an exercise of the will, and may be impossible without our controlling at least certain mental events (NB, 21.7.16). This intimates a major difficulty in the *Tractatus*, which insists on the impotence of the will while tacitly relying on acts of the metaphysical will for connecting language with reality (see Section III).

On his return to philosophy, Wittgenstein developed these glimmerings of the *Notebooks*.[41] He undermined both sides of the *Tractatus*, the empiricist view of the will as a mental episode and the transcendental view of the will as an 'extensionless point' beyond experience. According to the empiricist, '"willing too is merely an experience" (the "will" too only "representation"). It comes when it comes, and I cannot bring it about' (PI, §611). But it is precisely the hallmark of intentional action that we do not say of it that 'it comes when it comes'. The relation between willing and bodily movement is *not* merely contingent, as the *Tractatus* had it: 'when "I raise my arm", my arm goes up' (PI, §§612–21).

Schopenhauer is on Wittgenstein's side here in so far as he denies that the ultimate agent is merely an experience. But as regards normal human agency (short of the mysteries of the thing in itself and the 'intelligible character'), his transcendental idealism, and especially his determinism concerning the phenomenal world, places him firmly in the empiricist camp. He portrays us as utterly detached from our own actions. Our uncertainty in practical deliberation is not about *what we should do*, but about *what will happen* as a matter of fact. Once the intellect has presented all the motives involved, 'it awaits the real decision just as passively and with the same excited curiosity as it would that of a foreign will' (*W1*, §55). But this picture makes a nonsense of agency because it ignores the crucial lesson of what Wittgenstein regards as the 'Schopenhauerian conception' of the will:

The will can't be a phenomenon, for whatever phenomenon you take is something that *simply happens*, something we undergo, not something we *do*. The will isn't *something* I see happen, it's more like my being involved in my actions, my *being* my actions. (PG, 144)

Wittgenstein divests this insight into the active nature of voluntary action from Schopenhauer's transcendental idealism. When we try to 'distinguish between *all the experiences* of acting plus the doing (which is not an experience) and *all* those experiences without the element of doing', the element of doing appears 'redundant'. Nothing is left over in experience when we subtract the experience of one's arm rising from the experience of raising one's arm. But this does not show that there is a real doing left over which is *not* in experience. Willing, unlike wishing, is not a mental event prior to or accompanying the bodily action. It is the action, as the *Notebooks* suggested, yet not in a mysterious Schopenhauerian sense but in 'the ordinary sense' (PG, 145; PI, §§614–21).[42] The difference between voluntary and non-voluntary movement does not lie in anything phenomenal or noumenal, any event within experience or beyond it, but in the context, and in what the agent is capable of doing in a given situation.

The later Wittgenstein diverges from Schopenhauer in a second crucial respect. His account of intentionality undermines the dichotomy of will and representation. Representation itself *presupposes* the will, namely, the voluntary powers of human beings. Like

willing, thinking, intending, or meaning something are not 'phenomena' or 'appearances'. That is to say, they are not acts, activities,
events, processes, or states, whether in the mind or in the brain,
which accompany our words and actions. Against passages in the
earlier work which suggest that a proposition can represent reality
'off its own bat', Wittgenstein points out that pictures are not intrinsically representational: 'it is not the picture which intends, but we
must intend something by it'. He adds, however, that if this intending, in turn, is a mere 'process', 'phenomenon', or 'fact', it is no less
'dead' than the picture on its own. Phenomena cannot constitute a
'living thought' capable of depicting reality, for they are something
that 'simply *happens*' to us and that we observe 'from outside'. By
contrast, willing, thinking, or meaning something are not. They require that we are 'in the action' or thought, as its true 'agent' or
subject (PG, 143–4, 148; Z, §§236–8).

For example, if I utter the words 'Napoleon was impetuous', any
mental images or words that cross my mind will be irrelevant to
whether I meant Napoleon I or Napoleon III, unless I can *recognize*
them as a genuine expression of my thoughts (which will not be the
case, e.g., with compulsive images or a tune running through my
head).

If God had looked into our minds he would not have been able to see there
whom we were speaking of. . . . Meaning is not a process which accompanies
a word. For no process could have the consequences of meaning. (PI, 217–8;
see §641)

That I mean Napoleon I has the consequence that my utterance is
to be taken, or *counts as*, one about Napoleon I rather than someone
else. It commits me to a certain claim, which in turn makes intelligible certain subsequent moves in the language game and precludes
others as nonsensical. No such normative consequences could follow from a description of some mental or physiological process that
went on while I made the utterance. Wittgenstein draws a similar
lesson from *Moore's paradox*, the fact that it is 'absurd' to say, for
example, 'It's raining, but I don't believe it'. If 'I think/believe that
it's raining' reported a mental or neurophysiological state or process
of mine, this utterance would not be paradoxical. For there could be
no inconsistency between describing how things are with me and
describing the weather (PI, 190–2).

The (implicit) conclusion is that only those creatures can think, intend, or mean something which are capable of authoritatively avowing, explaining, and elaborating what they think (etc.), and which can be *responsible* for what they think (etc.). Intentionality cannot rest on mere phenomena, since it requires the capacity for voluntary and responsible action which is the prerogative of rational agents. Wittgenstein explicitly links this position to the aforementioned 'Schopenhauerian conception' of the will as something which does not merely happen to us (PG, 144). But Wittgenstein's unification of representation and will introduces important differences.

Schopenhauer acknowledged that we think of the subject of knowledge and the subject of willing as one and the same. Yet he regards this as 'a miracle *par excellence*': 'the identity of the subject of willing with that of knowing by virtue of which ... the word "I" includes and indicates both, is the knot of the world, and hence inexplicable' (FR 211–2/H. 1, 143). Matters are exacerbated by the tension between his idealism and his materialist account of the intellect as a brain function. Objectively speaking, the subject of representation reduces to the brain and the subject of willing to the body. At the same time, however, he insists that a pure materialism cannot account for the subject which experiences and comprehends the world (W2 245 vs. W2 13/H.3, 277 vs. 15–16). Finally, both the knowing subject and the body are mere manifestations of the cosmic will. 'Far from being the absolutely first thing (as Fichte taught, for example), it [the knowing and conscious *ego*] is at bottom tertiary, since it presupposes the organism, and the organism presupposes the will' (W2 278/H.3, 315).

According to Schopenhauer's idealism, material objects depend for their existence on a subject of representation. According to his materialism, the subject is merely a feature of a material object – the brain. And according to his vitalism, both are epiphenomena of a will to life. Wittgenstein cuts through these complexities and thereby explains the alleged miracle. Both the subject of representation and the subject of willing are simply the flesh-and-blood person. Both Schopenhauer and the later Wittgenstein repudiate Cartesian dualism and agree that we are essentially embodied. Schopenhauer's claim that 'the whole body is nothing but the objectified will' (W1 100/H. 2, 119–20) is echoed in Wittgenstein's claim that 'the human body is the best picture of the human soul' (PI, 178). But Wittgenstein holds that we are individual speakers and agents rather than mere manifestations of an ultimate reality bereft of individuality. As a result, he accounts for intentionality by employing Schopenhauerian themes and insights against Schopenhauer's metaphysics.

This also helps to explain why Schopenhauer has not influenced analytic philosophy in general, in spite of undeniable affinities. Writing in 1963, Patrick Gardiner (*Schopenhauer*, 1–3) explained the neglect of Schopenhauer within contemporary Anglophone philosophy partly by reference to the general decrease of interest in metaphysical speculation. In the meantime, metaphysical speculation has staged a remarkable comeback. Of course, there has also been a revival of interest in Schopenhauer. But the content and style of Schopenhauer's metaphysics still militate against its reception. Analytic philosophers with a reductionist frame of mind, although close in spirit to much of his naturalistic and deterministic anthropology, tend to be hostile to his 'literary' style and his 'existentialist' themes. At the same time, their Wittgensteinian (loosely so-called) adversaries, in spite of sympathies for these aspects of his work, tend to be sceptical about his grand metaphysics, and especially about the idea that everything, including human actions, is ultimately the manifestation of a single cosmic force.[43]

NOTES

1 See H. Schnädelbach, *Philosophy in Germany* (Cambridge: Cambridge University Press, 1984), ch. 5.

2 Jonathan Bennett, *Kant's Analytic* (Cambridge: Cambridge University Press, 1966), 222.

3 E.g., T. Nagel, *Equality and Partiality* (Oxford: Oxford University Press, 1991), ch. 5.

4 For the analytic discussion, see the references in G. Watson, ed., *Free Will* (Oxford: Oxford University Press, 1982), 2–4. For Schopenhauer, see C. Janaway, *Schopenhauer* (Oxford: Oxford University Press, 1994), 76–9.

5 Janaway, *Schopenhauer*, Preface.

6 See G. H. von Wright, 'Biographical Sketch', in N. Malcolm, *Ludwig Wittgenstein. A Memoir*, rev. 2nd ed. (Oxford: Oxford University Press, 1984), 6; P. T. Geach, 'Review of Colombo's Italian Translation of Tractatus', *Philosophical Review* 66 (1957), 558; G. E. M. Anscombe, *An Introduction to Wittgenstein's Tractatus* (London: Hutchinson 1959), 11–12.

7 I use the following abbreviations for Wittgenstein's work: NB, *Notebooks 1914–16* (Oxford: Blackwell, rev. ed., 1979); TLP, *Tractatus Logico–*

Philosophicus (London: Routledge and Kegan Paul, 1961); PR, *Philosoph-ical Remarks* (Oxford: Blackwell, 1975); PG, *Philosophical Grammar* (Oxford: Blackwell, 1974); PI, *Philosophical Investigations* (Oxford: Blackwell, 1958; first edn. 1953); Z, *Zettel* (Oxford: Blackwell, 1967); CV, *Culture and Value* (Oxford: Blackwell, 1980). With respect to both Schopenhauer and Wittgenstein, I have occasionally modified the trans-lations.

8 *Recollections of Wittgenstein*, ed. R. Rhees (Oxford: Oxford University Press, 1984), 158; see also 105.

9 E.g., M. Tanner, *Times Literary Supplement*, 28 October 1983, 1189; P. M. S. Hacker, *Insight and Illusion* (Oxford: Oxford University Press, 1986; 1st edn. 1972), ch. IV.

10 *Times Literary Supplement*, 14 October 1983, 1126; *The Philosophy of Schopenhauer* (Oxford: Clarendon Press, 1983), 290.

11 For Weininger's baneful influence on Wittgenstein and the anti-Semitic background of the remarks in CV, see R. Monk, *Ludwig Wittgenstein: The Duty of Genius* (London: Jonathan Cape, 1990), 19–25, 279–80.

12 Cf. von Wright, 'Biographical Sketch', 19, and Monk, *Ludwig Wittgen-stein*, 158. There is also a passage (CV, 11) which suggests that he was familiar with the 'diallelus' argument in the Introduction of the Jäsche *Logik*. See my 'Kant and Wittgenstein: Philosophy, Necessity and Repre-sentation', *International Journal of Philosophical Studies* 5 (1997), 285–305.

13 Indeed, Frege is a much more Kantian thinker than is commonly realized. See my 'Vorsprung durch Logik: The German Tradition in Analytic Phi-losophy' in A. O'Hear (ed.), *German Philosophy since Kant* (Cambridge: Cambridge University Press, 1999).

14 For the way in which the *Tractatus* incorporates Frege's and Russell's technical apparatus in a philosophical conception of logic that differs radically from theirs, see Hacker, *Insight and Illusion*, ch. II, and H. J. Glock, 'Cambridge, Jena or Vienna: The Roots of the Tractatus', *Ratio* 5 (1992), 1–23.

15 In addition to these general areas of influence, it has been contended that Wittgenstein directly borrowed key terms from Schopenhauer. Morris Engel has pointed out that 'family resemblance' (*Familienähnlichkeit*) occurs in *W* 1, §§17, 28 and *W*2, ch. 31 ('Schopenhauer's Impact on Wittgenstein', in M. Fox [ed.], *Schopenhauer: His Philosophical Achieve-ment* [Sussex: Harvester, 1980], n. 7). But he does not use the term for Wittgenstein's specific purposes. Magee adds 'forms of life' (*Philosophy of Schopenhauer*, 302), but without providing specific references. One pas-sage he may have in mind is *W*1, §54: 'the form of all life is the present'. But the term Schopenhauer uses is *Form des Lebens* or *Form alles Lebens*.

In any event, as a German compound noun, *Lebensformen* is too unremarkable to require explanation. As regards the idea, Wittgenstein could not have been influenced by this passage, since it refers to a feature of our individual lives rather than to a culture or social formation. A term which Wittgenstein probably did borrow from Schopenhauer is *metalogisch* (*FR*, §33; *W1*, §9). But unlike Schopenhauer, he rejects the idea that there are truths which are more fundamental than those of logic (Glock, *A Wittgenstein Dictionary*, 'metalogic').

16 See Janaway, *Self and World in Schopenhauer's Philosophy*, 198–9.

17 *Beiträge zu einer Kritik der Sprache* (Stuttgart: Cotta, 1901–3), vol. 1, 2.

18 See my *A Wittgenstein Dictionary*, 'philosophy' and 'nonsense'.

19 E.g., M. Engel, 'Schopenhauer's Impact on Wittgenstein,' in M. Fox (ed.), *Schopenhauer: His Philosophical Achievement*.

20 W 2 170/H. 3, 187–8; TLP, 3.324; PG, 193; *Wittgenstein's Lectures, Cambridge 1930–32* (Oxford: Blackwell, 1980), 1.

21 See Coffey, *The Science of Logic* (London: William and Norgate, 1912), 23; B. Russell and A. N. Whitehead, *Principia Mathematica* (Cambridge: Cambridge University Press, 1927; 1st edn. 1910), *1.2; Frege, 'Compound Thoughts', in B. McGuinness (ed.), *Collected Papers* (Oxford: Blackwell, 1984), 50.

22 *Beiträge zu einer Kritik der Sprache*, vol. 3, 301, 324–5.

23 *The Decline of the West*, vol. I, ch. 5.1.2 and 5.2.10.

24 See Hacker, *Insight and Illusion*, 120–1.

25 E. M. Lange, *Wittgenstein and Schopenhauer* (Cuxhaven: Junghans, 1989), ch. I, maintains that Schopenhauerian ideas about the 'form of philosophy' hold the key to the structure of the *Tractatus*, and in particular to its numbering system. He takes his cue from the passage 'There is a truth in Schopenhauer's view that philosophy is an organism, and that a book on philosophy, with a beginning and an end, is a sort of contradiction' (*Wittgenstein's Lectures 1932–5*, ed. A. Ambrose (Oxford: Blackwell, 1984), 43), a reference to the contrast between 'systematic' and 'organic philosophy' (*W1*, Preface to 1st edn.). For a discussion of these claims, see my review in *Philosophical Investigations* 16 (1993).

26 *Sex and Character* (London: Heinemann, 1906). Weininger's position may, in turn, be influenced by a (contentious) reading of Schopenhauer according to which charitable acts require an intellectual insight into the fact that individuality matters only at the level of appearances.

27 Letter to Engelmann, 9.4.17; in Paul Engelmann, *Letters from Ludwig Wittgenstein, with a Memoir*, ed. B. F. McGuinness, trans. L. Furtmüller (Oxford: Blackwell, 1967).

28 It should be noted that Schopenhauer is not the only possible source for Wittgenstein's position. A similar account of mysticism is provided by

Russell's 'Mysticism and Logic' of 1914, reprinted in his *Mysticism and Logic* (London: Longmans, 1918), ch. X.

29 Magee, *Schopenhauer*, 242, 287.

30 One exception is the 'Lecture on Ethics' of 1929, which still presents a *Tractarian* position. But an area where the later Wittgenstein may have been influenced by Schopenhauer is religion. Both adopt a fideistic position according to which religious doctrines are untenable when understood literally, as cognitive claims about the world, but can be interpreted charitably as expressions of feelings or attitudes.

31 Hacker, *Insight and Illusion*, 1st edn., ch. III; 2nd edn., ch. IV; Lange, *Wittgenstein und Schopenhauer*, ch. V; Janaway, *Self and World in Schopenhauer's Philosophy*, 324–6.

32 *The Problems of Philosophy* (Oxford: Oxford University Press, 1980; 1st edn., 1912), 8–9.

33 The second possibility is raised and defended by R. Haller, *Questions on Wittgenstein* (London: Routledge, 1988), 95–6.

34 *Über die Letzten Dinge* (Vienna and Leipzig: Braumüller, 1918), 169.

35 *Geheime Tagebücher* (Vienna: Turia & Kant, 1991), 8.2.14.; see NB, 11.6./1.–2.8.16.

36 As Hacker showed in *Insight and Illusion*, ch. 3.

37 'The Big Typescript' (TS 213), 499.

38 Janaway, *Self and World in Schopenhauer's Philosophy*, 324–5.

39 Gardiner, *Schopenhauer*, 276–7; Janaway, *Schopenhauer*, 82–3, 88–9.

40 A. P. Griffiths, 'Wittgenstein and the Four-Fold Root of the Principle of Sufficient Reason', *Proceedings of the Aristotelian Society* 50 (1976), 1–20, detects the roots of this position in Schopenhauer. In my view, however, the similarities are not close enough to warrant such a specific attribution.

41 See Hacker, *Mind and Will* (Oxford: Blackwell, 1996), ch. V.

42 And in cases in which I want to ϕ but fail, it is the trying to ϕ.

43 For helpful comments on previous drafts of this essay, I am grateful to Peter Hacker and especially Chris Janaway. I should also like to thank the Alexander von Humboldt Foundation for awarding me a research fellowship at the University of Bielefeld during which the work on this essay was completed.

BIBLIOGRAPHY

WORKS BY SCHOPENHAUER

German Texts

Schopenhauer: Sämtliche Werke, ed. Arthur Hübscher, 7 vols. (3rd edn.;
Wiesbaden: F. A. Brockhaus, 1972; 4th edn.; 1988).
Werke in zehn Bänden (Zürcher Ausgabe), ed. Arthur Hübscher, 10 vols.
(Zurich: Diogenes, 1977).
Sämtliche Werke, ed. Wolfgang Frhr. von Löhneysen, 5 vols. (2nd edn.; Darm-
stadt: Wissenschaftliche Buchgesellschaft, 1968).
Werke in fünf Bänden: Nach den Ausgaben letzter Hand, ed. Ludger
Lütkehaus, 5 vols. (Zurich: Haffmans Verlag, 1988).
Die Welt als Wille und Vorstellung, 2 vols., ed. H.-G. Ingenkamp (Stuttgart:
Reclam, 1987).
Faksimilenachdruck der 1. Auflage der Welt als Wille und Vorstellung, ed.
Rudolf Malter (Frankfurt am Main: Insel, 1987).
Der handschriftlicher Nachlass, ed. Arthur Hübscher, 5 vols. (Frankfurt am
Main: Kramer, 1970).
Gesammelte Briefe, ed. Arthur Hübscher (Bonn: Bouvier, 1987).
Philosophische Vorlesungen, aus dem handschriftlichen Nachlass, ed.
Volker Spierling, 4 vols. (Munich: R. Piper, 1984–6).

English Translations

Essays and Aphorisms, trans. R. J. Hollingdale (Middlesex: Penguin Books,
1970).
Essay on the Freedom of the Will, trans. Konstantin Kolenda (Indianapolis:
Bobbs-Merrill, 1960).
Manuscript Remains, trans. E. F. J. Payne, 4 vols. (Oxford: Berg, 1988).
On the Basis of Morality, trans. E. F. J. Payne (Oxford: Berghahn Books, 1995).

On the Fourfold Root of the Principle of Sufficient Reason, trans. Mme. K. Hillebrand (London: G. Bell, 1889).

On the Fourfold Root of the Principle of Sufficient Reason, trans. E. F. J. Payne (La Salle, Ill.: Open Court Press, 1974).

On the Will in Nature, trans. Mme. K. Hillebrand (London: G. Bell, 1903).

On the Will in Nature, trans. E. F. J. Payne (New York: Berg, 1992).

On Vision and Colors, trans. E. F. J. Payne (Oxford: Berg, 1994).

Parerga and Paralipomena, trans. E. F. J. Payne, 2 vols. (Oxford: Clarendon Press, 1974).

Prize Essay on the Freedom of the Will, ed. Günter Zöller, trans. E. F. J. Payne (Cambridge: Cambridge University Press, 1999).

Schopenhauer's Early Fourfold Root, trans. F. C. White (Aldershot: Avebury, 1997).

The World as Will and Idea, trans. R. B. Haldane and J. Kemp, 3 vols. (London: Kegan Paul, Trench, Trubner, 1883–6).

The World as Will and Idea: abridged in one volume, trans. J. Berman, ed. D. Berman (London: Everyman, 1995).

The World as Will and Representation, trans. E. F. J. Payne, 2 vols. (New York: Dover Books, 1969).

WORKS ON SCHOPENHAUER

Abelsen, Peter, 'Schopenhauer and Buddhism', *Philosophy East and West* 43 (1993), 255–78.

Alperson, Philip, 'Schopenhauer and Musical Revelation', *The Journal of Aesthetics and Art Criticism* 40 (1982), 155–66.

Aquila, Richard E., 'On the "Subjects" of Knowing and Willing and the "I" in Schopenhauer', *History of Philosophy Quarterly* 10 (1993), 241–60.

Atwell, John E., 'Art as Liberation: A Central Theme of Schopenhauer's Philosophy', in Jacquette (ed.), *Schopenhauer, Philosophy, and the Arts*, 81–106.

Atwell, John E., 'Nietzsche's Perspectivism', *Southern Journal of Philosophy* 19 (1981), 157–70.

Atwell, John E., *Schopenhauer: The Human Character* (Philadelphia: Temple University Press, 1990).

Atwell, John E., *Schopenhauer on the Character of the World: The Metaphysics of Will* (Berkeley: University of California Press, 1995).

Atwell, John E., 'Schopenhauer on Women, Men, and Sexual Love', *The Midwest Quarterly* 38 (1997), 143–57.

Atwell, John E., 'Schopenhauer's Account of Moral Responsibility', *Pacific Philosophical Quarterly* 61 (1980), 396–404.

Berman, David, 'Schopenhauer and Nietzsche: Honest Atheism, Dishonest Pessimism', in Janaway (ed.), *Willing and Nothingness: Schopenhauer as Nietzsche's Educator*, 178–95.

Bilsker, Richard, 'Freud and Schopenhauer: Consciousness, the Unconscious, and the Drive Towards Death', *Idealistic Studies* 27 (1997), 79–90.

Bischler, W., 'Schopenhauer and Freud: A comparison', *Psychoanalytic Quarterly* 8 (1939), 88–97.

Boullart, Karel, 'Schopenhauer et le problème de l'immanence ou l'impertinence du pessimisme intégrale', *Revue Internationale de Philosophie* 42 (1988), 82–100.

Bozickovic, Vojislav, 'Schopenhauer on Kant and Objectivity', *International Studies in Philosophy* 28 (1996), 35–42.

Bridgwater, Patrick, *Arthur Schopenhauer's English Schooling* (London and New York: Routledge, 1988).

Budd, Malcolm, *Music and the Emotions* (London: Routledge, 1985), ch. V.

Bykhovsky, Bernard, *Schopenhauer and the Ground of Existence*, trans. Philip Moran (Amsterdam: Grüner, 1984).

Caldwell, William, *Schopenhauer's System in Its Philosophical Significance* (1896; repr. Bristol: Thoemmes Press, 1993).

Cartwright, David E., 'Compassion', in *Zeit der Ernte: Festschrift für Arthur Hübscher zum 85. Geburtstag* (Stuttgart and Bad Cannstatt: Frommann-Holzboog, 1982).

Cartwright, David E., 'Kant, Schopenhauer, and Nietzsche on the Morality of Pity', *Journal of the History of Ideas* 45 (1984), 83–98.

Cartwright, David E., 'Nietzsche's Use and Abuse of Schopenhauer's Moral Philosophy for Life', in Janaway (ed.), *Willing and Nothingness: Schopenhauer as Nietzsche's Educator*, 116–50.

Cartwright, David E., 'Schopenhauer as Moral Philosopher – Towards the Actuality of his Ethics', *Schopenhauer-Jahrbuch* 70 (1989), 54–65.

Cartwright, David E., 'Schopenhauer on Suffering, Death, Guilt, and the Consolation of Metaphysics', in E. von der Luft (ed.), *Schopenhauer: News Essays in Honor of His 200th Birthday*, 51–66.

Cartwright, David E., 'Schopenhauerian Optimism and an Alternative to Resignation?', *Schopenhauer-Jahrbuch* 66 (1985), 153–64.

Cartwright, David E., 'Schopenhauer's Axiological Analysis of Character', *Revue Internationale de Philosophie* 42 (1988), 18–36.

Cartwright, David E., 'Schopenhauer's Compassion and Nietzsche's Pity,' *Schopenhauer-Jahrbuch* 69 (1988), 557–67.

Cartwright, David E., 'The Last Temptation of Zarathustra,' *Journal of the History of Philosophy* 31 (1993), 49–69.

Chansky, James, 'Schopenhauer and Platonic Ideas: A Groundwork for an Aesthetic Metaphysics', in E. von der Luft (ed.), *Schopenhauer, New Essays in Honor of His 200th Birthday*, 67–81.

Chansky, James, 'The Conscious Body: Schopenhauer's Difference from Fichte in Relation to Kant', *International Studies in Philosophy* 24 (1992), 25–44.

Ci, Jiwei, 'Schopenhauer on Voluntary Justice', *History of Philosophy Quarterly* 15 (1998), 227–44.

Clark, Maudemarie, 'On Knowledge, Truth, and Value: Nietzsche's Debt to Schopenhauer and the Development of his Empiricism', in Janaway (ed.), *Willing and Nothingness: Schopenhauer as Nietzsche's Educator*, 37–78.

Clark, Maudemarie, and Leiter, Brian, 'Introduction', in Friedrich Nietzsche, *Daybreak*, trans. R. J. Hollingdale (Cambridge: Cambridge University Press, 1997), vii–xxxiv.

Colvin, Stephen Sheldon, *Schopenhauer's Doctrine of the Thing-in-itself and His Attempt to Relate It to the World of Phenomena* (Providence: Franklin Press, 1987).

Cooper, David E., 'Self and Morality in Schopenhauer and Nietzsche', in Janaway (ed.), *Willing and Nothingness: Schopenhauer as Nietzsche's Educator*, 196–216.

Copleston, Frederick, *A History of Philosophy, Vol. 7/ii: Schopenhauer to Nietzsche* (New York: Image/Doubleday, 1963).

Copleston, Frederick, *Arthur Schopenhauer: Philosopher of Pessimism* (London: Barnes and Noble, 1975).

Copleston, Frederick, 'Schopenhauer', in Bryan Magee (ed.), *The Great Philosophers* (Oxford: Clarendon Press, 1987), 210–30.

Cyzyk, Mark, 'Conscience, Sympathy, and Love: Ethical Strategies toward Confirmation of Metaphysical Assertions in Schopenhauer', *Dialogue* 32 (1989), 24–31.

Dauer, Dorethea, *Schopenhauer as Transmitter of Buddhist Ideas* (European University Papers, Series I, vol. 15; Berne: Herbert Lang, 1969).

Decher, Friedhelm, 'Nietzsche: Metaphysik in der "Geburt der Tragödie" im Verhältnis zur Philosophie Schopenhauers', *Nietzsche-Studien* 14 (1985), 110–25.

Decher, Friedhelm, *Wille zum Leben – Wille zur Macht: Eine Untersuchung zu Schopenhauer und Nietzsche* (Würzburg: Königshausen und Neumann, 1984).

Desmond, William, 'Schopenhauer and the Dark Origin of Art', in von der Luft (ed.), *Schopenhauer: Essays in Honor of His 200th Birthday*, 101–22.

Deussen, Paul, *The Elements of Metaphysics*, trans. C. M. Duff (London: Macmillan, 1984).

Dickie, George, 'Taste and Attitude: The Origin of the Aesthetic', *Theoria* 39 (1973), 153–70.

Diffey, T. J., 'Schopenhauer's Account of Aesthetic Experience', *The British Journal of Aesthetics* 30 (1990), 132–42.

Dumoulin, Heinrich, 'Buddhism and Nineteenth-Century German Philosophy', *Journal of the History of Ideas* 42 (1981), 457–70.

Durer, Christopher S., 'Moby Dick's Ishmael, Burke, and Schopenhauer', *The Midwest Quarterly* 30 (1989), 161–78.

Ebeling, Hans, and Lütkehaus, Ludger (eds.), *Schopenhauer und Marx: Philosophie des Elends – Elend der Philosophie?* (Königstein in Taunus: Hain, 1980).

Engel, S. Morris, 'Schopenhauer's Impact on Wittgenstein', in Fox (ed.), *Schopenhauer: His Philosophical Achievement*, 236–54.

Engelmann, Jörg, 'Schönheit und Zweckmäßigkeit in der Architektur', *Schopenhauer-Jahrbuch* 65 (1984), 157–69.

Ferrarra, Lawrence, 'Music as the Embodiment of the Will', in Jacquette (ed.), *Schopenhauer, Philosophy, and the Arts*, 195–6.

Figl, Johann, 'Nietzsche's Begegnung mit Schopenhauers Hauptwerk. Unter Heranziehung eines frühen unveröffentlichen Exzerptes', in Schirmacher (ed.), *Schopenhauer, Nietzsche und die Kunst*, 89–100.

Foster, Cheryl, 'Schopenhauer and Aesthetic Recognition', in Jacquette (ed.), *Schopenhauer, Philosophy, and the Arts*, 133–49.

Foster, Cheryl, 'Schopenhauer's Subtext on Natural Beauty', *British Journal of Aesthetics* 32 (1992), 21–32.

Fox, Michael (ed.), *Schopenhauer: His Philosophical Achievement* (Brighton: Harvester Press, 1980).

Gabriel, G., *Grundprobleme der Erkenntnistheorie. Von Descartes Zu Wittgenstein* (Paderborn: Schöningh, 1993), 117–28.

Gabriel, G., 'Conservatismus aus Pessimismus: Schopenhauer, die Soziale Frage und das Glück', *Neue Deutsche Hefte* 183 (1994), 476–97.

Gardiner, Patrick, *Schopenhauer* (Middlesex: Penguin Books, 1967; repr. Bristol: Thoemmes Press, 1997).

Goedert, Georges, 'Schopenhauer – Ethik als Weltüberwindung', *Schopenhauer Jahrbuch* 77 (1996), 113–31.

Goehr, Lydia, 'Schopenhauer and the Musicians: An Inquiry into the Sounds of Silence and the Limits of Philosophizing about Music', in Jacquette (ed.), *Schopenhauer, Philosophy, and the Arts*, 200–28.

Gonzalez, Robert, 'Schopenhauer's Demythologization of Christian Asceticism', *Auslegung* 9 (1982), 5–49.

Goodman, Russell B., 'Schopenhauer and Wittgenstein on Ethics', *Journal of the History of Philosophy* 17 (1979), 437–47.

Gorevan, Patrick, 'Scheler's Response to Schopenhauer', *Schopenhauer Jahrbuch* 77 (1996), 167–79.

Gray, Ronald, 'The German Intellectual Background', in Peter Burridge and Richard Sutton (eds.), *The Wagner Companion* (London: Faber and Faber, 1979), 34–59.

Griffiths, A. Phillips, 'Wittgenstein on the Fourfold Root of the Principle of Sufficient Reason', *Proceedings of the Aristotelian Society*, suppl. vol. 50 (1976), 1–20.

Griffiths, A. Phillips, 'Wittgenstein, Schopenhauer, and Ethics', in *Understanding Wittgenstein* (Royal Institute of Philosophy Lectures, vol. 7; London: Macmillan, 1974), 96–116.

Grisebach, E., *Edita und Inedita Schopenhaueriana* (Leipzig: Brockhaus, 1888).

Gupta, R. K. Das, 'Freud and Schopenhauer', in Fox (ed.), *Schopenhauer: His Philosophical Achievement*, 226–35.

Gupta, R. K. Das, 'Schopenhauer and Indian Thought', *East and West* 13 (1962), 32–40.

Guyer, Paul, 'Pleasure and Knowledge in Schopenhauer's Aesthetics', in Jacquette (ed.), *Schopenhauer, Philosophy, and the Arts*, 109–32.

Haber, Honi, 'Arthur Schopenhauer', *Journal of the History of Ideas* 56 (1995), 483–99.

Haffmans, Gerd, *Über Arthur Schopenhauer* (Zurich: Diogenes, 1978).

Hall, Roland, 'The Nature of the Will and Its Place in Schopenhauer's Philosophy', *Schopenhauer Jahrbuch* 76 (1995), 73–90.

Haller, Rudolf, 'Was Wittgenstein a Neo-Kantian?', *Questions on Wittgenstein* (Lincoln: University of Nebraska Press, 1988), 44–56.

Hamlyn, D. W., *Schopenhauer* (London: Routledge & Kegan Paul, 1980).

Hamlyn, D. W., 'Schopenhauer and Freud', *Revue Internationale de Philosophie* 42 (1988), 5–17.

Hamlyn, D. W., 'Schopenhauer on Action and the Will', in Godfrey Vesey (ed.), *Idealism Past and Present* (Royal Institute of Philosophy Lectures, vol. 13; Cambridge: Cambridge University Press, 1982), 12–40.

Hein, Hilde, 'Schopenhauer and Platonic Ideas', *Journal of the History of Philosophy* 4 (1966), 133–44.

Higgins, Kathleen Marie, 'Schopenhauer and Nietzsche: Temperament and Temporality', in Janaway (ed.), *Willing and Nothingness: Schopenhauer as Nietzsche's Educator*, 151–77.

Hollingdale, R. J., 'The Hero as Outsider', in Bernd Magnus and Kathleen Marie Higgins (eds.), *The Cambridge Companion to Nietzsche* (Cambridge: Cambridge University Press, 1996), 71–89.

Horkheimer, Max, 'Schopenhauer Today', in Fox (ed.), *Schopenhauer: His Philosophical Achievement*, 20–33.

Hübscher, Arthur, *Schopenhauer: Biographie eines Weltbildes* (Stuttgart: Reclam, 1967).

Hübscher, Arthur, *The Philosophy of Schopenhauer in Its Intellectual Context: Thinker Against the Tide*, trans. Joachim T. Baer and David E. Cartwright (Lewiston, N.Y.: Edwin Mellen Press, 1989).

Humphrey, Ted, 'Schopenhauer and the Cartesian Tradition', *Journal of the History of Philosophy* 19 (1981), 191–212.

Jacquette, Dale, 'Schopenhauer on the Antipathy of Aesthetic Genius and the Charming', *History of European Ideas* 18 (1994), 373–85.

Jacquette, Dale (ed.), *Schopenhauer, Philosophy, and the Arts* (Cambridge: Cambridge University Press, 1996).

Jacquette, Dale, 'Schopenhauer's Circle and the Principle of Sufficient Reason', *Metaphilosophy* 23 (1992), 279–87.

Jacquette, Dale, 'Schopenhauer's Metaphysics of Appearance and Will in the Philosophy of Art', in Jacquette (ed.), *Schopenhauer, Philosophy, and the Arts*, 1–36.

Janaway, Christopher, 'Kant's Aesthetics and the Empty Cognitive Stock', *Philosophical Quarterly* 47 (1997), 459–76.

Janaway, Christopher, 'Knowledge and Tranquility: Schopenhauer on the Value of Art', in Jacquette (ed.), *Schopenhauer, Philosophy, and the Arts*, 39–61.

Janaway, Christopher, 'Nietzsche, the Self, and Schopenhauer', in Keith Ansell-Pearson (ed.), *Nietzsche and Modern German Thought* (London: Routledge, 1991), 199–42.

Janaway, Christopher, *Schopenhauer* (Oxford: Oxford University Press, 1994).

Janaway, Christopher, 'Schopenhauer as Nietzsche's Educator', in Janaway (ed.), *Willing and Nothingness: Schopenhauer as Nietzsche's Educator*, 13–36.

Janaway, Christopher, *Self and World in Schopenhauer's Philosophy* (Oxford: Clarendon Press, 1989).

Janaway, Christopher, 'The Subject and the Objective Order', *Proceedings of the Aristotelian Society* 84 (1983–4), 147–65.

Janaway, Christopher (ed.), *Willing and Nothingness: Schopenhauer as Nietzsche's Educator* (Oxford: Clarendon Press, 1998).

Janik, Allan S., 'Schopenhauer and the Early Wittgenstein', *Philosophical Studies (Ireland)* 15 (1966), 76–95.

Jarrett, James, 'Schopenhauer and Jung', *Spring: An Annual of Archetypal Psychology and Jungian Thought* (1981), 193–204.

Kanovitch, Abraham, *The Will to Beauty: Being a Continuation of the Philosophies of Arthur Schopenhauer and Friedrich Nietzsche* (New York: Henry Bee Co., 1923).

Kishan, B. V., 'Schopenhauer and Buddhism', in Fox (ed.), *Schopenhauer: His Philosophical Achievement*, 255–61.

Knox, Israel, 'Schopenhauer's Aesthetic Theory', in Fox, ed., *Schopenhauer: His Philosophical Achievement*, 132–46.

Kossler, Matthias, 'Empirie, Transzendentalismus und Transzendenz: Neue Literatur zu Arthur Schopenhauer', *Philosophischer Rundschau* 43 (1996), 273–96.

Krukowski, Lucian, *Aesthetic Legacies* (Philadelphia: Temple University Press, 1992).

Lange, Ernst Michael, *Wittgenstein und Schopenhauer: Logisch-philosophische Abhandlung und Kritik des Solipsismus* (Cuxhaven: Junghans-Verlag, 1989).

Leiter, Brian, 'The Paradox of Fatalism and Self-Creation in Nietzsche', in Janaway (ed.), *Willing and Nothingness: Schopenhauer as Nietzsche's Educator*, 217–57.

Lovejoy, A. O., 'Schopenhauer as an Evolutionist', *The Monist* 21 (1911), 195–222.

Lukács, Georg, *The Destruction of Reason*, trans. Peter Palmer (London: Merlin Press, 1980), ch. 2, sect. 4.

Magee, Bryan, *Misunderstanding Schopenhauer* (London: University of London Germanic Studies, 1990).

Magee, Byran, Review of Dale Jacquette (ed.), *Schopenhauer, Philosophy and the Arts*, in *Times Literary Supplement* 4864 (1997), 8.

Magee, Bryan, *The Philosophy of Schopenhauer* (Oxford: Clarendon Press, 1983).

Magee, Bryan, *The Philosophy of Schopenhauer* (2nd edn.; Oxford: Clarendon Press, 1997).

Maidan, Michael, 'Max Scheler's Criticism of Schopenhauer's Account of Morality and Compassion', *Journal of the British Society for Phenomenology* 20 (1989), 225–35.

Maidan, Michael, 'Schopenhauer on Altruism and Morality', *Schopenhauer-Jahrbuch* 69 (1988), 265–72.

Malter, Rudolf, *Arthur Schopenhauer: Transzendentalphilosophie und Metaphysik des Willens* (Stuttgart and Bad Cannstatt: Frommann-Holzboog, 1991).

Malter, Rudolf, *Der eine Gedanke: Hinführung zur Philosophie Arthur Schopenhauers* (Darmstadt: Wissenchaftliche Buchgesellschaft, 1988).

Malter, Rudolf, 'Schopenhauer's Transzendentalismus', *Schopenhauer-Jahrbuch* 66 (1985), 29–51.

Mann, Thomas, 'Schopenhauer', *Essays of Three Decades*, trans. H. T. Lowe-Porter (New York: A. A. Knopf, 1947).

McGill, Vivian J., *Schopenhauer: Pessimist and Pagan* (New York: Brentano, 1931; repr. New York: Haskell House, 1977).

McLaughlin, Sigrid, *Schopenhauer in Russland: Zur literarischen Rezeption bei Turgenev* (Wiesbaden: Harrassowitz Verlag, 1984).

Murdoch, Iris, *Metaphysics as a Guide to Morals* (New York: Allen Lane/Penguin Press, 1992), ch. 3.

Nanajivako, Bikkhu, *Schopenhauer and Buddhism* (Kandy, Sri Lanka: Buddhist Publication Society, 1970).

Navia, L., 'Reflections on Schopenhauer's Pessimism', in Fox (ed.), *Schopenhauer: His Philosophical Achievement*, 171–82.

Neeley, Steven G., 'A Re-examination of Schopenhauer's Analysis of Bodily Agency: The Ego as Microcosm', *Idealistic Studies* 22 (1992), 52–67.

Neeley, Steven G., 'The Knowledge and Nature of Schopenhauer's Will', *Schopenhauer Jahrbuch* 77 (1996), 85–112.

Neeley, Steven G., 'Schopenhauer and the Limits of Language', *Idealistic Studies* 27 (1997), 47–67.

Nelson, Byron, 'Wagner, Schopenhauer, and Nietzsche: On the Value of Human Action', *The Opera Quarterly* 6 (1989), 29–32.

Neymeyr, Barbara, *Ästhetische Autonomie als Abnormität: Kritische Analysen zu Schopenhauers Ästhetik im Horizont seiner Willensmetaphysik* (Berlin: Walter de Gruyter, 1996).

Nicholls, Moira, 'Schopenhauer, Young, and the Will', *Schopenhauer-Jahrbuch* 72 (1991), 143–57.

Nicholls, Moira, 'The Kantian Inheritance and Schopenhauer's Doctrine of Will', *Kant-Studien* 85 (1994), 257–79.

Nicholls, Moira, 'Schopenhauer, Feeling and the Noumenon', *Schopenhauer Jahrbuch* 76 (1995), 53–71.

Nietzsche, Friedrich, 'On Schopenhauer (1868)', in Janaway (ed.), *Willing and Nothingness: Schopenhauer as Nietzsche's Educator*, 258–65.

Nietzsche, Friedrich, 'Schopenhauer as Educator', in *Untimely Meditations*, trans. R. J. Hollingdale (Cambridge: Cambridge University Press, 1983), 125–94.

Nussbaum, Martha C., 'The Transfiguration of Intoxication: Nietzsche, Schopenhauer, and Dionysus', *Arion*, Third Series, vol. 1, no. 2 (1991), 75–111.

Oxenford, John, 'Iconoclasm in German Philosophy', *The Westminster Review*, n. s. 3 (1853), 388–407.

Paulsen, Friedrich, *Schopenhauer, Hamlet, Mephistopheles: Drei Aufsätze zur Naturgeschichte des Pessimismus* (Berlin: Cotta Verlag, 1905).

Pfeiffer, Konrad, *Zum höchsten Dasein: Goethes Faust im Lichte der Schopenhauerschen Philosophie* (Berlin: Walter de Gruyter, 1949).

Philonenko, Alexis, *Schopenhauer: Une Philosophie de Tragedie* (Paris: Vrin, 1980).

Philonenko, Alexis, 'Schopenhauer Critique de Kant', *Revue Internationale de Philosophie* 42 (1988), 37–70.

Pothast, Ulrich, *Die eigentliche metaphysische Tätigkeit: Über Schopenhauers Ästhetik und ihre Anwendung durch Samuel Beckett* (Frankfurt: Suhrkamp, 1982).

Proctor-Gregg, Nancy, 'Schopenhauer and Freud', *Psychoanalytic Quarterly* 25 (1956), 197–214.

Rethy, Robert, 'The Tragic Affirmation of the *Birth of Tragedy*', *Nietzsche-Studien* 17 (1988), 1–44.

Roberts, Julian, *German Philosophy: An Introduction* (Atlantic Heights, N.J.: Humanities Press International, 1988), ch. 4.

Safranski, Rüdiger, *Schopenhauer and the Wild Years of Philosophy*, trans. Ewald Osers (London: Weidenfeld and Nicolson, 1989).

Schirmacher, Wolfgang (ed.), *Schopenhauer, Nietzsche und die Kunst* (Vienna: Passagen Verlag, 1991).

Schirmacher, Wolfgang, 'Schopenhauer und die Postmoderne', *Revue Internationale de Philosophie* 42 (1988), 71–81.

Schirmacher, Wolfgang (ed.), 'Schopenhauer und Nietzsche – Wurzeln gegenwärtiger Vernunftkritik', *Schopenhauer-Jahrbuch* 65 (1984), 5–115.

Schirmacher, Wolfgang (ed.), *Zeit der Ernte: Studien zum Stand der Schopenhauer-Forschung: Festschrift für Arthur Hübscher zum 85. Geburtstag* (Stuttgart and Bad Cannstatt: Frommann-Holboog, 1982).

Schlechta, Karl, 'Der junge Nietzsche und Schopenhauer', *Schopenhauer-Jahrbuch* 26 (1939), 289–300.

Schmidt, Alfred, 'Schopenhauer und der Materialismus', in *Drei Studien über Materialismus* (Frankfurt am Main: Ullstein, 1979), 21–79.

Schnädelbach, Herbert, *Philosophy in Germany 1831–1833* (Cambridge: Cambridge University Press, 1984), ch. 5.

Simmel, Georg, *Schopenhauer and Nietzsche*, trans. Helmut Loiskandl, Deena Weinstein, and Michael Weinstein (Amherst: University of Massachusetts Press, 1986).

Snow, Dale, and Snow, James, 'Was Schopenhauer an Idealist?', *Journal of the History of Philosophy* 29 (1991), 633–55.

Snow, James, 'Schopenhauer's Style', *International Philosophical Quarterly* 33 (1993), 401–12.

Soll, Ivan, 'Pessimism and the Tragic View of Life: Reconsiderations of Nietzsche's *Birth of Tragedy*', in Robert C. Solomon and Kathleen Higgins (eds.), *Reading Nietzsche* (New York and Oxford: Oxford University Press, 1988), 104–31.

Soll, Ivan, 'Schopenhauer, Nietzsche, and the Redemption of Life through Art', in Janaway (ed.), *Willing and Nothingness: Schopenhauer as Nietzsche's Educator*, 79–115.

Soll, Ivan, 'The Hopelessness of Hedonism and the Will to Power', *International Studies in Philosophy* 18 (1986), 97–112.

Sorg, Bernhard, *Zur literarischen Schopenhauer-Rezeption im 19. Jahrhundert* (Heidelberg: Winter Verlag, 1975).

Spierling, Volker, 'Die Drehwende der Moderne. Schopenhauer zwischen Skeptizismus und Dogmatismus', in Spierling (ed.), *Materialien zu Schopenhauers 'Die Welt als Wille und Vorstellung,'* 14–83.

Spierling, Volker, *Materialien zu Schopenhauers 'Die Welt als Wille und Vorstellung'* (Frankfurt am Main: Suhrkamp, 1984).

Sprigge, T. L. S., *Theories of Existence* (Middlesex: Penguin Books, 1985), 77–94.

Stenius, Erik, *Wittgenstein's "Tractatus": A Critical Exposition of Its Main Lines of Thought* (Ithaca, N.Y.: Cornell University Press, 1960), ch. xi, 214–26.

Stewart, Jon, 'Schopenhauer's Charge and Modern Academic Philosophy: Some Problems Facing Philosophical Pedagogy', *Metaphilosophy* 26 (1995), 270–8.

Stolnitz, Jerome, ' "The Aesthetic Attitude" in the Rise of Modern Aesthetics', *The Journal of Aesthetics and Art Criticism* 36 (1978), 409–22.

Taminiaux, Jacques, 'Art and Truth in Schopenhauer and Nietzsche', *Man and World* 20 (1987), 85–102.

Taylor, Charles Senn, 'Nietzsche's Schopenhauerianism', *Nietzsche-Studien* 17 (1988), 45–73.

Taylor, Richard, 'Schopenhauer', in D. J. O'Connor (ed.), *A Critical History of Western Philosophy* (London: Free Press of Glencoe, 1964), 365–83.

Taylor, Terri Graves, 'Platonic Ideas, Aesthetic Experience, and the Resolution of Schopenhauer's Great Contradiction', *International Studies in Philosophy* 19 (1987), 43–53.

Tilghman, Benjamin R., *Wittgenstein, Ethics and Aesthetics: The View from Eternity* (Basingstoke: Macmillan, 1991).

Touey, Daniel, 'Schopenhauer and Nietzsche on the Nature and Limits of Philosophy', *Journal of Value of Inquiry* 32 (1998), 243–52.

Tsanoff, R., *Schopenhauer's Criticism of Kant's Theory of Experience* (New York: Longmans, Green & Co., 1911), 66–70.

Varner, G. E., 'The Schopenhauerian Challenge in Environmental Ethics', *Environmental Ethics* 7 (1985), 209–29.

Volkelt, Johannes, *Arthur Schopenhauer: Seine Persönlichkeit, seine Lehre, sein Glaube* (Stuttgart: Fromann, 1st edn. 1900; 4th edn. 1910).

von der Luft, Eric (ed.), *Schopenhauer: New Essays in Honor of His 200th Birthday* (Lewiston, N.Y.: Edwin Mellen Press, 1988).

Wagner, Gustav Friedrich, *Schopenhauer-Register*, 2nd edn., ed. Arthur Hübscher (Stuttgart and Bad Cannstatt: Frommann-Holzboog, 1982).

Welsen, Peter, *Schopenhauers Theorie des Subjekts: Ihre transzendental-philosophischen, anthropologischen und naturmetaphysischen Grundlagen* (Würzburg: Königshausen und Neumann, 1995).

White, F. C., *On Schopenhauer's Fourfold Root of the Principle of Sufficient Reason* (Leiden: E. J. Brill, 1992).

Wicks, Robert, 'Schopenhauer's Naturalization of Kant's a Priori Forms of Empirical Knowledge', *History of Philosophy Quarterly* 10 (1993), 181–96.

Young, Christopher, and Brook, Andrew, 'Schopenhauer and Freud', *International Journal of Psychoanalysis* 75 (1994), 101–18.

Young, Julian, 'A Schopenhauerian Solution to Schopenhauerian Pessimism', *Schopenhauer-Jahrbuch* 68 (1987), 53–69.

Young, Julian, 'Is Schopenhauer an Irrationalist?', *Schopenhauer-Jahrbuch* 69 (1988), 85–100.

Young, Julian, 'Schopenhauer's Critique of Kantian Ethics', *Kant-Studien* 75 (1984), 191–212.

Young, Julian, 'The Standpoint of Eternity: Schopenhauer on Art,' *Kant-Studien* 78 (1987), 424–41.

Young, Julian, *Willing and Unwilling: A Study in the Philosophy of Arthur Schopenhauer* (Dordrecht: Martinus Nijhoff, 1987).

Young, Julian, 'Wittgenstein, Kant, Schopenhauer and Critical Philosophy', *Theoria* 50 (1984), 73–105.

Zimmern, Helen, *Arthur Schopenhauer: His Life and Philosophy* (London: Longmans Green & Co., 1876).

Zöller, Günter, Review of Barbara Neymeyr, *Ästhetische Autonomie als Abnormität: Kritische Analysen zu Schopenhauers Ästhetik im Horizont seiner Willensmetaphysik*, in *Journal of the History of Philosophy* 36 (1998), 458–9.

Zöller, Günter, 'Schopenhauer and the Problem of Metaphysics: Critical Reflections on Rudolf Malter's Interpretation', *Man and World* 28 (1995), 1–10.

INDEX